CONSOLIDATED PBY CATALINA

CONSOLIDATED PBY CATALINA

The Peacetime Record

DAVID LEGG

Naval Institute Press

Annapolis, Maryland

First published in the UK in 2002
by Airlife Publishing Ltd

Published and distributed in the United States of
America and Canada by the Naval Institute Press,
291 Wood Road, Annapolis, MD 21402-5035

Library of Congress Catalog Card No. 2001090591.

ISBN 1-55750-245-5

Printed in Hong Kong

This book is dedicated to my father John Legg who would have liked to see it.

Cat's tail chase – Plane Sailing Air Displays' Cyclone-powered PBY-5A VP-BPS leads Cat Air's R-1830-equipped PH-PBY during the 1997 Flying Legends air display at Duxford, England. *Stephen Dodd*

ACKNOWLEDGEMENTS

This book has been put together over the last five years or so using information and data from many sources. A select bibliography appears at the back of the book, but it is appropriate here to thank the many individuals who have helped me in some way by providing assistance in my research. Their correspondence over the years has been invaluable, both in producing this present volume and in compiling *The Catalina News* magazine for the Catalina Society. Some have provided material that has not been used in this book as their contributions fall outside its scope, and although their names have not been included, thanks are due to them also. Inevitably, I will have unintentionally omitted some names and I apologise to those who feel they should be included and have not been.

Mark Aldrich, Gregory Alegi, Shlomo Aloni, Morten Andersen, Bert Anido, Peter Berry, Alan Bransom, Ted Burnett, John Chapman, Jacques Chillon, Marc Commandeur, J. M. Cooling, Paul Crellin, Carl d'Agnese, Ian Debenham, Bill Devins, Jeanne-Pierre Dubois, Eric Dumigan, Ken Ellis, Chuck Ellsworth, Grétar F. Felixson, Keith Fitton, Santiago A. Flores, Pål Forus, Clarence Fu, Darryl Gibbs, Geoff Goodall, Jennifer Gradidge, Wynnum B. Graham, Marlene Gray, Kay Hagby, Dan Hagedorn, Donald M Hannah, Noam Hartoch, John Havers, Torben Jensen, Petur P. Johnson, Silvano Jung, Bill Kelly, Terry Kelly, Sergio Barriga Kfret, Steve Kinder, Jacques Lauray, Dr J. S. Leake, Bob Livingstone, Peter London, Lars E. Lundin, Al MacNutt, Ron Mak, Peter Marson, Russell Mason, Jack Meaden, Xavier Meal, Ken Measures, José López Mera, Larry Millberry, Ricardo Bonalume Neto, David Nicolle, Bjorn Nordbo, Jorge Félix Núñez, Michael O'Leary, Keith Palmer, Roberto Parragué, John Powell, François Prins, Michael Prophet, Ragnar Ragnarsson, Jon C. B. Ramsay, Andrew C. Robins, Jim Sanders, Antonio Luis Sapienza, José Luis Gonzalez Serrano, Bill Slate, Harry Sluyter, Ted Spencer, Rasmus Svihus, Chris Thornburg, Jerry Vernon, Jirina and Pavel Vincenc, Paul Whelan, Martin Willing, Marilouise P. Wood and Roberto Yáñez. Ragnar Ragnarsson, Mark Aldrich, Keith Palmer and Wynnum Graham provided valuable feedback and suggestions whilst the production list appendix was being compiled.

Thanks also to the late Brian Cooper and to Bill Sewell for their encouragement.

The photographs used in this book have all come from my own collection. Where the original photographer and/or supplier is known, the appropriate credit line has been given. Where no name is quoted, the original supplier is not known or has been forgotten, and I apologise for any omissions. I am very grateful indeed for all those who have supplied me with photographs in the past. I would particularly like to thank Jennifer M. Gradidge and the late Peter Keating for giving me unlimited access to their extensive negative collections some years ago. Ron Mak, Jack Meaden and Bill Larkins have also been most helpful in providing illustrations. Stephen Dodd has for some time supplied excellent prints from negatives when asked to do so and I am very grateful to him. Lastly, the photographic supplier Brian Pickering/MAP of Sleaford, Lincolnshire has been a source of photos for some years, and his monthly photo lists, advertised widely in the British aviation press, are recommended to all aviation enthusiasts, not just Catalina fans.

Grateful thanks are also due to the late John Watts and Arthur Gibson and to Paul Warren Wilson, all of Plane Sailing Air Displays, for the opportunity of some great Catalina flying between 1985 and 1998; also to their other pilots, including Dizzy Addicott, John Alsford, Mike Carter, John Romain, Mike Searle, Martin Sharman, Keith Sissons, Alan Walker and the late Pete Treadaway, all of whom have safely flown me from A to B at one time or another in Catalina G-BLSC/VP-BPS. I am also grateful to Mike Shirley-Beavan and Boo Chrisp of Bushbuck Safaris, Pierre and Antoinette Jaunet of The Catalina Safari Company and to their pilots Dave Evans and Bryan McCook for some wonderful East African Catalina flying in Z-CAT during 1992.

Finally, I wish to thank my wife Julie and children Edward, Susannah and Oliver for their patience and understanding in allowing me to pursue my interest in Catalinas.

David Legg, February 2001

CONTENTS

THE CATALINA SOCIETY

The Catalina Society was formed in 1986 to support the operation of an airworthy Catalina, then registered in the UK as G-BLSC. The Society brought together hundreds of individuals with an interest in the type, whether from operational wartime experience or from a later affection for the aircraft. Whilst the focus for the members was 'their' Cat, regularly displayed at airshows throughout Europe, they also received regular editions of the illustrated Society magazine, *The Catalina News*, bringing varied articles on Catalinas past and present, military and commercial.

Today, the Society continues to acknowledge the great contribution made to aviation history by the Consolidated Catalina and its crews and has members in many countries. At the time of publication, the Society is not linked to a specific operational Catalina, although it is intended that the associated operating company, Plane Sailing Air Displays, will acquire one in the future. Anyone with an interest in the Catalina will find membership of the Catalina Society worthwhile.

Membership details can be obtained by visiting the Catalina Society web site at www.catalina.org.uk or writing to Plane Sailing Air Displays, Duxford Airfield, Duxford, Cambridgeshire, CB2 4QR, England. The web site and *The Catalina News* will, from time to time, feature updates to this book.

ABBREVIATIONS

The following abbreviations have been used throughout this book:

auw	all up weight
BOE CAN	Boeing of Canada
CAN	Canadair
CAN VIC	Canadian Vickers
CDC	Commonwealth Disposals Commission
C/n.	Construction number (see note below)
c/s	colour scheme

CON NO	Consolidated New Orleans
CON SD	Consolidated San Diego
Dbr	Damaged beyond repair
G/I	Ground instructional (airframe)
id	identity
Ntu	Not taken up
pi	previous identity
Soc	Struck off charge
Wfu	Withdrawn from use

Note: During early San Diego production, Consolidated used two types of identity number. The first was the c/n, running from 1 onward. The other number (the manufacturing or Mfg number) was used to identify individual aircraft within contract batches. On occasion, the latter numbers have been quoted as c/ns and where this has been done in the past in other data sources, they are quoted in the tables alongside the genuine c/n. For the late New Orleans-built aircraft, the construction numbers listed are those following on in sequence from San Diego production. However, New Orleans had its own local sequence of identity numbers – see the introductory notes to the Production Tables in the appendices.

INTRODUCTION

The Consolidated Catalina has fascinated me for years. As a child in the 1960s, I recall the type featuring in books about the Second World War and, like many other schoolboys with an interest in such matters, I remembered it particularly because of its unusual 'blister' gun positions on the rear hull and its drop-down wingtip floats. The fact that it was a flying boat added to its character. Whilst opinions might have differed as to whether or not it was an attractive aircraft, the Cat certainly was distinctive! Later, in the 1970s as a vintage aircraft enthusiast, I sought out surviving Catalinas and Cansos in British Columbia during a visit there and this added to my interest in the type. But it was the acquisition in 1984 of an airworthy Catalina by a group of British pilots that really started my obsession with the type!

In February 1985, I was one of a small number of individuals gathered at a rather chilly RAF Manston in Kent to witness the arrival of Plane Sailing Air Displays' newly acquired Catalina at the end of its long delivery flight from South Africa. I had previously volunteered to work on the aircraft as part of a support team helping the owners with their aim of displaying it on the European air display circuit. For the next twelve years it operated successfully at hundreds of shows, and I was lucky enough to fly in it on many occasions. This Catalina received its own 'fan club' with the formation of the Catalina Society by my colleague Russell Mason in early 1986, and I began contributing written material for its magazine, *The Catalina News*, from the outset. After five or six issues, I took over the Editor's role and have maintained it ever since. It was in order to produce articles for *The Catalina News* that I began to research Catalina history more closely.

The origins of this book can be traced back to an envelope full of press cuttings and unsorted data that Russell had received in the post from a correspondent in Canada, Jerry Vernon. He handed me the package one evening when we met for a drink in a pub after work in the City of London, and I can recall eagerly sifting through this accumulation of paper. I quickly realised that here was a small start to my aim of unearthing the history of all the Catalinas built! Later, I produced a list of surviving Catalina airframes for a series of articles in *The Catalina News*, but this only utilised a fraction of the data that I was now gathering from around the world. So, the idea of a Catalina survivors book came about, but even this was to end up being extended to cover wider territory.

This book is not intended to be a complete history of the Consolidated PBY Catalina. Other authors have produced studies that have described world-wide wartime use of the PBY, and therefore a further volume covering that ground would lead to repetition. However, there is a substantial part of the Catalina story that has in the past received only brief mention in other works, and that is its operation in peacetime. This omission is understandable

– it was after all conceived as a military aircraft, and it was mainly its service in the Second World War that ensured its rightful place in the annals of aviation history. Designed for the peacetime United States Navy in the mid-1930s, it was beginning to face obsolescence by the end of that decade. However, the advent of the Second World War brought rejuvenation for the type in the form of design enhancements and huge orders that led to mass production in several locations. More PBYs were built than any other flying boat by some considerable margin – almost 3,300 units manufactured excluding the unknown quantity built in the Soviet Union under licence. The type served with distinction around every part of the globe and with many Allied air arms, and as a result, it is not surprising that most writers have concentrated on the PBY in terms of its military service as a long-range patrol bomber, anti-submarine warfare, convoy escort and air-sea-rescue aircraft.

It was the addition of an undercarriage in particular, and the resultant amphibious capability that this bestowed on the Catalina, that led to a huge increase in the type's flexibility and ensured that its wartime service was to be only part of the overall story. Even so, it is doubtful that its designers could have envisaged that examples of the Catalina would still be flying in the 21st century! The aim of this book is to look in detail at this other, important part of Catalina history, and in so doing, the story is brought right up to date with a survey of the large number of airframes that still survive and in some cases are still airworthy.

The initial development of the type and its pedigree is not ignored, however, as this helps to put the later 'career' of the Catalina in context. Then, the text goes on to briefly cover the pre-war usage of the early PBYs by the US Navy and the interesting stories of the pre-war 'commercials'. With the Second World War over, the Catalina entered the next phase of its operating life, one that to date has lasted some 55 years and looks set to continue for some time yet! The various chapters describe the Catalina's peacetime military usage with air forces and navies the world over, and also studies the widespread roles that it fulfilled with commercial owners – passenger airliner, general transport, luxury air yacht, photographic and geophysical survey platform, forest fire fighter and air display star.

In addition to the survivors, separate chapters study some of the known Catalina wrecks that are scattered around the world and some of the unfortunate losses that have befallen the Catalina population over recent years. There are also detailed appendices and a select bibliography.

A brief note on layout is worth making. Throughout the various tables, the airframes are described under 'type' by the designation they carried at the time they were put into service. Thus, whilst a Catalina may have flown post-war as a commercial *Super Catalina* conversion or a Model 28-5ACF for example, it will be listed as a PBY-5A, OA-10A or Canso A, depending on how it first flew.

In researching for this book, I have come across some anomalies concerning individual aircraft, and it is clear that different researchers have their own opinions as to some details. Errors have cropped up in some previous books, either as the result of unfortunate typographical slips or unsubstantiated research, and these have sometimes been perpetuated – something by no means confined to Catalina history and an ever present peril for the aviation writer! Where doubt exists as to the accuracy of data, I have tried to seek out the most likely version whilst highlighting other theories. I hope that this book does not create any 'new' errors, although the odd slip is probably inevitable. I hope that where data are subject to doubt, this book may act as a catalyst for revealing the truth, and I would invite fellow researchers to submit any comments or additions to me. Additionally, I would welcome the opportunity to acquire photographs of Catalinas, particularly those relevant to the subject matter of this book. Unusually, for a book of this kind, it is my intention to provide an update service through both the Catalina Society magazine *The Catalina News* and the Catalina Society web site to be found at www.catalina.org.uk

One
THE PBY AND ITS PREDECESSORS

As already stated in the introduction, the PBY series of flying boats was originally conceived to meet a requirement for a military aircraft and it built on Consolidated's experience with earlier flying boat designs. These earlier types had included the commercial Model 16 Commodore and the military Model 22 Ranger/P2Y series.

The Commodore was itself a development of the Model 9 Admiral, or XPY-1 to give it its US Navy designation. The XPY-1 was designed as a US Navy flying boat with the capability of linking the United States West Coast with Hawaii. It was a metal twin-engined monoplane – the first US Navy monoplane seaplane – with a crew of five, the two pilots being in an exposed cockpit, the navigator in the bow, the radio operator in the centre section and the engineer aft. Armament consisted of one 0.30 in machine gun forward of the cockpit and two further 0.30 in guns in an open area further back along the upper hull. Power came from two 450 hp Pratt & Whitney R-1340-38 Wasp engines, although, later, a third engine was installed above the wing. The XPY-1 first flew on 10 January 1929, from Anacostia in Washington DC, but it was destined to be a limited edition of one, the

Navy ordering the cheaper Martin XP2M and P3M flying boats instead. The solitary Admiral was given the military serial A-8011.

Although the Admiral was not a success in terms of military orders, it did give rise to interest from the commercial sector, and this led to the Consolidated Model 16, or Commodore. Design changes included more powerful engines in the shape of two Pratt & Whitney R-1860 Hornets Bs of 575 hp each and a hull that could accommodate up to 32 passengers in some luxury. Initially, it had been hoped that the new type would be sold to the Detroit and Cleveland Navigation Company, which had plans to use the Commodore between destinations around Lake Erie, and to Pan American Airways, but in the event no orders materialised. However, orders did come from Tri-Motor Safety Airways, which wanted to use the type to link North and South America. The prototype first flew on 28 September 1929, and in due course fourteen were built at the Consolidated factory at Buffalo, New York. All those built operated with the launch customer, which, by the time of the first delivery, had been renamed New York, Rio & Buenos Aires Line, or NYRBA, only to be merged with Pan American in September 1930. Production of the Commodore ceased in the following November.

Ultimately, the type saw quite wide usage with NYRBA and Pan American and, later, with Panair do

The first of the line – the Model 9 Admiral, or XPY-1, was Consolidated's first flying boat design. It is shown here in original twin-engined layout. The fore and aft gun positions are clearly visible. Even at this early stage, there are similarities to the later Catalina's hull shape.
MAP/Real Photos

Model 16 Commodore NC658M Rio de Janeiro of New York, Rio and Buenos Aires Line on its beaching gear. Up to 32 passengers could be carried in what was Consolidated's first commercial flying boat.
via Barry Dowsett

NYRBA Line's NC659M *Havana* in company with an
unidentified Ford Tri-Motor. The rather complicated wing
strut arrangement is evident.
MAP

Brazil, SANA (Sociedad Argentina de Navegación
Aérea), the Brazilian Air Force, CNAC (China National
Airways Corporation), Chamberlin Airlines and
Bahamas Airways. The eleventh example off the produc-
tion line flew with the latter airline and was only broken
up in 1949 after being damaged in a hurricane.

Although the fact that Consolidated's founder
Reuben Fleet was directly involved in the management
of NYRBA clearly enabled his company to produce and
sell his own design, the Commodore none the less indicated that Consolidated was able to build a successful
flying boat for commercial use. The next flying boat to be
built by the company however, was, another design for
the military.

Again based on the earlier, unsuccessful Model 9
Admiral monoplane flying boat, the Model 22 Ranger
shared the same upper wing but also incorporated a
lower, shorter-span wing supporting the two floats. It too
had a covered cockpit for the flight crew as on the
Commodore, and it was at first powered by three Wright
R-1820E Cyclones of 575 hp, later reduced to two. Given
the US Navy designation XP2Y-1 and serial Bu8939, the
initial example took to the air for the first time on
26 March 1932.

Consolidated went on to produce another 23
twin-engined P2Y-1s for the US Navy, and these were
allocated serials Bu8986 to 9008. The final aircraft was
completed in June 1933, and was modified a few months
later to become the first PY2-2 powered by two 750 hp
R-1820-88s. These engines were mounted upon the wing

The prototype XP2Y-1 Ranger A-8939 in its short-lived
three-engined configuration in early 1932. The addition of a
lower wing mounted shoulder-fashion on the hull made the
type a sesquiplane.
MAP/Real Photos

leading edge rather than between the hull and the upper
wing as on the P2Y-1. Nearly all the latter were subsequently upgraded to P2Y-2 standard. The two unconverted aircraft were exported, one to Colombia for air force
use and the other to Japan. Incredibly, the South
American aircraft remained in service until as late as
1948, by which time it had been supplemented by a
number of Catalinas. The Japanese example was used
commercially during the Second World War.

There followed a further 23 P2Y-3s (Bu9551 to 9571
and 9618 to 9619) of similar configuration to the P2Y-2
but with uprated R-1820-90 engines and greater fuel
capacity. A further six were produced to meet an

This P2Y-2 of VP-15 clearly shows the engines repositioned from between the wings to the wing leading edge.
MAP/Real Photos

Argentine Navy order in mid-1936, and these flew on until 1947 when, like the Colombian P2Y-1, they were replaced by Catalinas. The US Navy aircraft were used by various patrol squadrons, and many ended up at NAS Pensacola in Florida, where they were used to train flying boat crews, including many who were later to become RAF Catalina personnel.

The Commodore and Ranger designs only bore a passing resemblance to the PBY inasmuch as the side profile of the lower hull and step were similar. Both types showed evidence of reliability and the capability of long distance flight for both military and commercial users, and it was whilst the early examples of the P2Y series were being produced that the Consolidated designer, Isaac Laddon, began design work on what was eventually to become the Consolidated Model 28/PBY Catalina series.

This design was known initially by its military designation XP3Y-1, and was prompted by a 1933 United States Navy contest inviting manufacturing companies to submit entries to meet the requirements for a military patrol flying boat with an operational range of 3,000 miles and a cruise of 100 mph. Consolidated submitted its design and the US Navy liked what it saw. Reuben Fleet's company was rewarded with a contract to build one aircraft at the end of October 1933. Rival firm Douglas had previously been given a similar contract to develop its own submission – the XP3D-1; indeed, the Douglas aircraft was the first to fly, beating the

This P2Y-3 on the slipway at San Diego shows the variant's more powerful R-1820-90 engines.

Consolidated aircraft off the water by more than a month.

Isaac Laddon incorporated a number of novel features into his XP3Y-1 layout, in particular the pylon-mounted parasol wing and the retractable floats that changed the flying boat's wingspan in flight. The competing Douglas, on the other hand, was rather more conventional, slightly smaller overall, with the wing mounted shoulder-like high up the hull sides and with engines raised above the wing surface on pylons. The powerplant chosen for both the designs was the 825 hp Pratt & Whitney R-1830-58 Twin Wasp, a good choice that in uprated versions was to see the PBY series through to the end of production in 1945. Performance for both the

The XP3Y-1 was the prototype of what was to become the PBY Catalina series. In this view, Bu9459 shows the broad chord wing and tip-mounted floats that were one of the type's trademarks. The rudder shown in this view was the second design to be tested.

XP3Y-1 and XP3D-1 was broadly similar, although the Consolidated design had the edge. What really clinched the Consolidated aircraft for the Navy, however, was the unit price – the Douglas design at $110,000 was as much as $20,000 dearer than the XP3Y-1. It will never be known whether the Douglas aircraft would have gone on to be such a famous and durable design as the Catalina had it won through and been accepted by the US Navy.

The sole XP3Y-1 was built at Buffalo in New York, construction starting toward the end of 1933. Its first flight was undertaken from the Naval Air Station at Norfolk in Virginia, this decision being taken because of the possibility of icing on Buffalo's Niagara River. The almost complete airframe was taken by rail to Norfolk NAS, where final assembly took place, and the maiden flight was successfully achieved on 21 March 1935. Further test flights were conducted from Norfolk and Anacostia. The flying boat was given the US Navy serial Bu9459.

The US Navy made a few recommendations for modifications, which included a rear hull extension, the installation of a gun position in the lower hull aft of the keel and a revised profile to the bow turret. Generally, though, the clean lines of the hull and wings were to remain virtually unaltered through all the subsequent versions of the PBY. The only major change to the design came during the Second World War, when the Naval Aircraft Factory came up with the rather more aggressive-looking PBN-1 Nomad. However, one particular problem dogged the design from beginning to end – directional stability. The XP3Y-1 alone underwent three changes of rudder profile, and even after these were introduced, problems persisted. In fact, rudder redesign was to be a feature of the subsequent Consolidated

Model 28/PBY series throughout its design life and even on into the post-war period! In all other respects, however, Laddon had got it right. The prototype received uprated engines in the shape of the Pratt & Whitney R-1830-64 of 850 hp, and it became the XPBY-1 prototype.

Prior to being re-engined, Bu9459 proved its ability to make long-distance flights by completing the journey between Norfolk, Virginia and Coco Solo, Panama Canal Zone, and then flying on to San Francisco, California. This occurred in October 1935, and the latter leg created a record for the longest distance flown by a seaplane up to that time.

Satisfied with its choice, the US Navy placed its first order with Consolidated at the end of June 1935, this being for a total of 60 aircraft to be known as the PBY-1, and the company began to plan production at its new facility at Lindbergh Field, San Diego, California. Incidentally, the PBY designation recognised the type's ability to operate not only in the originally intended patrol role but also as a bomber – P=Patrol, B=Bomber, Y=Consolidated. Service deliveries began in September of the following year, with the first examples going to VP-6 and VP-11, both based at the Navy's North Island facility across San Diego Bay from the Consolidated factory. The former squadron soon relocated to Pearl Harbor, Hawaii, and flew its twelve aircraft in a non-stop formation delivery flight, a feat to be copied by various other squadrons as they took on aircraft and left the USA to establish their new overseas bases. Other squadrons to take delivery of PBY-1s included VP-12 at Sands Point, Washington, and VP-3 at the Panama Canal Base of Coco Solo.

The sixty PBY-1s gave good patrol squadron service during the pre-war period, and a number were still based in Hawaii at the time of the Japanese attack on Pearl Harbor in December 1941 though they had all been relegated to second-line service by then. None were to remain in use in post-war peacetime. This first US Navy batch of PBYs was serialled consecutively in the sequence Bu0102 to Bu0161.

Even before the first of the 60 PBY-1s were delivered, the US Navy issued a follow-on order in July 1936 for 50

PBY-1 Bu0134, aircraft 10 of VP-12, on the water, probably at its Lake Washington base. The removable cockpit-roof-mounted loop antenna is just visible behind the nearest propeller. The crewman in the aft hatch appears to be about to stow the canvas drogue used for manoeuvring on the water. Rudder stripes were blue, outlined in black.
MAP

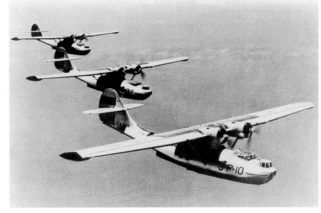

aircraft, to be designated PBY-2 and serialled Bu0454 to Bu0503. The main distinguishing feature between the PBY-1 and PBY-2 was a re-designed horizontal tail and elevator assembly, although some of the PBY-2s also had Curtiss props rather than Hamilton Standards. In addition, the PBY-2 had an increased bomb load capability. Deliveries began in the summer of 1937, and the PBY-2

PBY-1s coded 8, 9 and 10 of VP-3 in close formation shortly after delivery. This squadron had red rudder bands.
MAP/Real Photos

Clearly visible in this group of VP-11 and VP-12 PBY-1s is the type's full-span elevators, later to be reduced in size on subsequent variants.

VP-11 later received PBY-2s, including Bu0484 shown here. Rudder stripes were willow green. The pylon-mounted wing and its supporting struts are clearly shown.

The PBY-3, illustrated here by Bu0842 without squadron markings, had the carburettor intakes relocated to the top of the engine cowlings. The engines themselves were the -66 version of the Pratt & Whitney R-1830.
MAP/Real Photos

Aircraft 12 of VP-13 was a PBY-4, serial Bu1241. In this view, the -4's prop spinners can be seen. Bu1241 was used for trials of the rear hull 'blister' turret that was to become such a familiar feature on the Catalina. It was also used to test the rudder profile that was to be seen on subsequent versions up to the PB2B-1 and PBY-5A.
MAP/Real Photos

flew with VP Squadrons 2, 7, 10, 11 and 17 from bases in the USA, Hawaii and the Canal Zone. By mid-1942, the remaining PBY-2s had been relegated to second-line, training and support roles, and like its predecessor, had been withdrawn from use entirely by the war's end.

The next US Navy order was for 66 PBY-3s, placed in November 1936. Again, only detail differences distinguished the new variant. It shared the PBY-2's tail redesign but was powered by the more powerful P&W R-1830-66 of 900 hp rather than the earlier -64, and this change necessitated a relocation of the carburettor air intake from underneath the lower cowling to above the top cowling close to the exhaust outlet. Prior to the outbreak of hostilities with Japan, the US Navy flew PBY-3s within VP Squadrons 7 and 9 at San Diego; 4, 18, 21 and 22 at Pearl Harbor and VP-5 at Coco Solo. The type also equipped Seattle-based VP-16 and VP-32. A number of PBY-3s were lost in the attack on Pearl Harbor, and subsequently this variant followed the lead of its two earlier versions and was relegated to second-line tasks, with some examples still being on US Navy charge as late as May 1945. The 66 PBY-3s carried the Bu numbers 0842 to 0907.

A further change of powerplant to the 1050 hp R-1830-72 and the addition of prop-spinners distinguished the PBY-4 from the PBY-3. However, the PBY-4 was to be produced in smaller numbers, only 33 being ordered, with serials Bu1213 to 1245, of which 32 were actually built as PBY-4s. They served with VP-1 (later VP-21 for a while) at Pearl Harbor and in the Philippines, where the Squadron was designated VP-101. It also equipped VP-18 at Pearl Harbor. The latter squadron was renumbered VP-26 in July 1939, and went out to the Philippines to become VP-102. It was around this time that the US Navy PBYs began to lose their colourful pre-war liveries and started to adopt a more sober blue-grey. Although the type continued in use after the outbreak of hostilities, it was declared obsolete by the war's end. Like the PBY-1, -2 and -3 before it, none served as either military or commercial aircraft beyond 1945.

Consolidated continued to look at the PBY design and

make modifications to it. Three of the last PBY-4s (serials Bu1241, 1242 and 1243) were used as pattern aircraft for rear hull blister gun emplacements installed in place of the sliding hatches that had been employed up to that point. They also had minor modifications to the rudder trailing edge. Bu1241/13-P-12 of VP-13 was also used for trials of yet another vertical tail/rudder design, and both the blisters and the new rudder were to become standard for the PBY-5 variant to follow.

With all PBYs delivered and no further orders from the US military forthcoming, future prospects for the type were not looking so rosy by the summer of 1939. However, events in Europe were to change all that and lead to production levels that could never have been envisaged when the XP3Y-1 was first on the drawing board! The British ordered Model 28-5s/PBY-5s in some numbers, and this revitalised production. The US Navy

An in-service view of PBY-5, hull code 2 of VP-44. It is shown in the standard US Navy colour scheme of non-specular Blue-Grey over Light Grey with 'meatball'-style roundels, used up to May 1942.
via Barry Dowsett

PBY-4 Bu1245 was modified by the manufacturers and became an amphibian – the prototype XPBY-5A. It still retained the PBY-4 rudder and prop spinners, however. *MAP/Real Photos*

also ordered 200 PBY-5s with 1,050 hp Pratt & Whitney R-1830-72 engines at the end of December 1939, with deliveries beginning in the following September, although the final 33 aircraft were built as PBY-5As. Follow-on orders continued as the war progressed and the USA's involvement in it expanded. The British-inspired name *Catalina* was bestowed on the type, the USA also adopting this sobriquet, and thereafter it became the type's official name, although it continued to be called the PBY by many US servicemen, along with other less polite nicknames!

As mentioned above, the final PBY-4 was not initially delivered to the US Navy for squadron use but was retained by the manufacturers for further design work. In fact, it was used for trials of the amphibious undercarriage system that was to provide future Catalinas with so much flexibility and that was ultimately to ensure the type's longevity. Bu1245 had its weight increased by 2,300 lb through the addition of two main wheel units, a nose wheel assembly and associated wheel well bays and

Another view of Bu1241, showing its amphibious undercarriage in the retracted position. *Convair via Jack Meaden*

doors. Although at first it was not fitted with blisters and it retained the original shape PBY-4 rudder, it became the prototype PBY-5A (XPBY-5A), first flying as such on 2 November 1939. The US Navy, realising the type's potential, decided that its then current order for PBY-5s should be amended to PBY-5As, and thereafter ordered many more. The British remained distinctly cool about the added wheels, however, and stuck to the pure flying boat variant, although one small order for twelve amphibious Catalina IIIs was placed.

As an interesting aside, Bu1245 was later delivered to the US Navy and used as a staff transport in both the Atlantic and Canal Zones. Starting in March 1943, it underwent modifications that saw it lose its amphibious undercarriage but gain a PBY-5 tail and blisters. More radically, it lost its bow turret in favour of a faired-over 'clipper' bow – shades of things to come in the post-war commercial sector – and had an internal fit allowing seating for a number of passengers. In this unarmed guise, it became the PBY-5R *Sea Mare*.

At the start of hostilities between the USA and Japan in December 1941, the disposition of operational PBY squadrons was as shown in the table below. In addition, VP-13 at San Diego had a mixture of PBY-5s and PBY-4s on strength for training.

Table 1. Operational PBY Squadrons as at December, 1941

Patrol Wing	Patrol Squadrons	Location	Types on Inventory
Pat Wing 1	VP-11, VP-12, VP-14	Kaneohe, Hawaii	36 PBY-5s
Pat Wing 2	VP-21, VP-22 VP-23, VP-24	Ford Island, Pearl Harbor	27 PBY-3s 18 PBY-5s
Pat Wing 3	VP-31 VP-32	Coco Solo, Canal Zone	11 PBY-5s 13 PBY-3s
Pat Wing 4	VP-41 VP-42, VP-43, VP-44	Sitka, Alaska Seattle, Wash.	24 PBY-5s
Pat Wing 5	VP-51, VP-52	Norfolk, Va.	28 PBY-5s
Pat Wing 6	In course of formation	Alameda, Calif.	9 older PBYs
Pat Wing 7	VP-71, VP-72, VP-73	Norfolk, Va.	36 PBY-5s
Pat Wing 8	VP-81 VP-83	In course of formation	8 PBY-5s 10 PBY-5As
Pat Wing 10	VP-101, VP-102	Cavite, Philippines	28 PBY-4s

This unidentified US Navy PBY-5A is typical of pre-May 1942 examples with its red-centred meatball roundels and red-and-white-striped rudder.

A later US Navy PBY-5A is Bu08098, probably photographed toward the war's end. It has a radome atop the cockpit and the name *Harriet* on the bow. Bu08098 went on to serve with the US Coast Guard and was struck off charge at the end of January 1946.
MAP/Real Photos

Prior to the USA entering the Second World War, the second production PBY-5, Bu2290, was transferred by the US Navy to the US Coast Guard, with which it adopted the serial V189. Initially flown in a high-visibility livery of overall aluminium but with yellow-orange upper wing surfaces and red and white vertically striped rudder topped with blue, it later adopted a more sober grey scheme when in wartime use up in Alaska. It remained in service until at least 1943, when it was stationed in the

San Francisco area, and it was the predecessor for many more wartime and post-war United States Coast Guard (USCG) Catalinas.

As the war progressed, Catalinas of both flying boat and amphibian varieties continued to be produced at the Consolidated factory in San Diego, production later being switched to the plant at New Orleans. Aircraft were supplied not only to the US forces and the Royal Air Force but also to the Royal Australian Air Force, Royal Canadian Air Force, Netherlands Navy and Royal New Zealand Air Force. Additional production was contracted out to Canadian Vickers, initially at St Hubert and later at Cartierville, Quebec, and to Boeing of Canada at Sea Island, Vancouver, BC.

Typical of a Royal Air Force Catalina is FP229/N, a well-worn Mk IB that served with 302 Ferry Training Unit, 270 and 205 Squadrons before being struck off in September 1944. Clearly visible are the ASV aerials on the forward hull and wings, and the South East Asia Command (SEAC) two-tone blue roundels and fin flash.

In the main, the design of the Catalina remained fairly constant once PBY-5 production commenced, the main

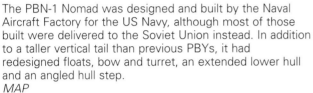

The PBN-1 Nomad was designed and built by the Naval
Aircraft Factory for the US Navy, although most of those
built were delivered to the Soviet Union instead. In addition
to a taller vertical tail than previous PBYs, it had
redesigned floats, bow and turret, an extended lower hull
and an angled hull step.
MAP

The tall tail of the Nomad was also used on the PB2B-2
flying boat and the amphibious PBY-6A. The latter version
is illustrated here by Bu46642, the fourth to be built. It
later became N9553C on the US Civil Aircraft Register, but
its eventual fate is unknown.
MAP/Real Photos

modifications being the addition of an amphibious
undercarriage to some versions, changes to the bow turret and to the vertical and horizontal tail surfaces. The
latter redesign was a feature of the flying boat PB2B-2
and PBY-6A. It also appeared on the somewhat more radical but less successful PBN-1 Nomad developed by the
Naval Aircraft Factory in Philadelphia and supplied to
both the US Navy and the USSR. In addition to the
changed tail, the Nomad also had a revised hull and float

shape and a new bow turret.

Other books about the Catalina provide a greater
degree of detail on the many variants of the Catalina and
their wartime service. Suffice to say that it was to be the
PBY-5A and PBY-6A that, in the main, were to provide
post-war military and commercial operators with
Catalinas, some of which have continued flying in civilian hands into the third millennium! A full production
table for the PBY/Catalina series appears in Appendix 2.

Two
THE PRE-WAR
COMMERCIAL PBYs

At the same time as the early military PBYs were being built, Consolidated produced a number of commercial Model 28s that, but for the outbreak of war, could perhaps have been the forerunners for further airline orders. As things turned out, the war led to mass production of later military variants that, in turn, resulted in large numbers of commercial Catalinas coming from war surplus stocks after the conflict had ended and the type was finally declared 'obsolete'. No further Catalinas were built specifically for commercial use, however, with the exception of licence-produced GSTs in Russia.

The pre-war commercials are summarised in Table 2, and this is followed by a more detailed look at each of the aircraft:

Table 2. Pre-war commercials

Type	C/n	Registration	Notes
Model 28-1	C-1	NC777	*Guba* P&W R-1830-64 850hp. To Russia as URSS L-2
Model 28-2	C-2	?	Wright Cyclone R-1820-G3 840 hp
Model 28-2	–	?	Wright Cyclone R-1820-G3 840 hp
Model 28-2	–	?	Wright Cyclone R-1820-G3 840 hp
Model 28-3	C-3	NC777 (2)	*Guba* (2). P&W R-1830-64 850 hp. To Britain as AM258, G-AGBJ, SM706
Model 28-4	C-4	NC18997	*Transatlantic* P&W R-1830-72 1,050 hp
Model 28-5	C-5	NX21732/ (N)P9630/P9630	P&W R-1830-S1C3G 1,050 hp

Note: Various sources quote differing model numbers for the seven commercial Model 28s. The above list is believed to be the correct version, although John Wegg in *General Dynamics Aircraft and Their Predecessors* by Putnam quotes the three Russian exports as Model 28-1s, NC777(2) as a Model 28-2 and P9630 as a Model 28-4.

Model 28-1 c/n C-1 NC777 *Guba*

This first commercial Model 28 was completed at San Diego in June of 1937 and was equivalent to the United States Navy PBY-1. Indeed, the US Navy gave its permission for the aircraft to be acquired by a civilian but would not allow it to venture outside the USA until its own aircraft had been in operation for twelve months or more. The first customer for a commercial PBY was Dr Richard Archbold, who was researching on behalf of the American Museum of Natural History. He had been to

The first commercial PBY NC777 *Guba* is seen here over the San Jacinto Mountains in Southern California before being released by Richard Archbold to the Russians. *via John Millar*

Seen here in Alaska, URSS L-2 is being refuelled during a break from the search for the missing Russian aircraft URSS N-209. *via Jack Meaden*

Guba is shown here after being dismantled and prior to shipment to Russia. The nationality markings URSS and the Consolidated company crest can be seen on the hull and tail respectively. *M. Kelman via Jack Meaden*

A later view of *Guba* in the Soviet Union, having been
repainted as CCCP L-2.
via Marc Commandeur

New Guinea on two occasions in the previous five years
to study wildlife and plants, and needed a suitable aircraft capable of water operations to support his future
expeditions. Registered NC777, his first Consolidated flying boat was named *Guba*, a Papuan word meaning
squall, and on 24 June 1937, very soon after its first flight,
it was flown non-stop across the USA (from San Diego to
New York), creating a record as the only flying boat
to have done so. Having successfully completed this
flight, Archbold must have felt more than ready to take
his new acquisition to New Guinea for his next project,
due in November of the same year, and he began the necessary fitting-out. However, other events intervened and
Guba was destined not to go with Archbold.

In mid-August 1937, the Russian aviator Sigismund
Levanevsky went missing whilst engaged on a 4,000-mile
trans-Polar flight in his four-engined Bolkhovitinov DB-a
monoplane URSS-H209. Contact with Levanevsky and
his crew was lost after a final message reported engine
problems at a position estimated to be some 300 miles
beyond the North Pole en route to Fairbanks in Alaska.
No trace of aircraft or crew was ever found. During the
extensive search operation, the Russian authorities
approached Consolidated's Reuben Fleet, requesting that
they be allowed to purchase *Guba* with its long-range
capabilities. Fleet acted as intermediary and Archbold
agreed to sell his flying boat, ordering a replacement at
the same time. The Russians had previously expressed an
interest in acquiring and licence-producing PBYs, so the
link with Fleet already existed.

Having obtained the *Guba*, the Russians almost immediately flew it up to the Northwest Territories in Canada,
and once there, it was initially based at Coppermine,
from where search flights were carried out. Flights were
also conducted using the Mackenzie River at Aklavik. In
charge of these flights was the Australian pilot Sir Hubert
Wilkins, himself a respected explorer with experience in
the Polar region. After a month of fruitless searching covering some 19,000 miles, the water landing areas used by
Guba could no longer be utilised because of the increas-
ing risk of icing, and the search was abandoned. During
this period, NC777 was reregistered with the Russian

markings URSS L-2, these being carried prominently on
the rear hull and rudder.

Once its mission was over, the PBY was flown south
to New York and disassembled and shipped across the
Atlantic to Russia, arriving in the summer of 1938. It
was subsequently used by the Soviet Government as
CCCP L-2 for transporting freight, but is also reported to
have been armed with guns and bomb racks. By July
1942, the former *Guba* was still in service, and on the 19th
of that month was provided by the Soviets for the use of
the US Navy in an attempt to save the American ship
Winston Salem that, as part of the PQ17 convoy, had run
aground at Novaya Zemlya. The mission was successful
and the ship was refloated, but on 26 July the PBY was
destroyed at its moorings there when the German submarine U-601 slipped into Moller Bay and shelled both it
and the nearby radio station. Thus ended the career of
the first commercial PBY, although, in a strange twist of
fate, U-601 was itself destroyed on 25 February 1944, by
Catalina JX223/M of the RAF's 210 Squadron.

When *Guba* was first flown, it was identical to the
standard US Navy PBY-1 except for its lack of armament
and an additional window between the wing lift struts
on the starboard side of the hull. Once Archbold took
delivery, but before the sale to the Russians, the wing-
mounted pitot tube was replaced by a unit mounted on a
three-foot-long forward-sloping mast atop the cockpit
roof. This was primarily to aid routine servicing whilst
on the proposed operations in New Guinea. Propeller
spinners were installed after initial test flights and a D/F
loop was fitted to the cabin roof aft of the cockpit and forward of the wing's supporting pylon. A Consolidated
Aircraft Company emblem appeared on either side of the
vertical tail surfaces, whilst the nose bore triangular
insignia representing the expedition the aircraft had been
intended to support. They consisted of the letter A for
Archbold surrounded by three five-pointed stars.

The author has seen one reference to this aircraft
(from a private source) that suggests it may have been
allocated the civilian registration NX21731 before NC777,
but this is not confirmed. What is certain is that NX21731
was later used on the prototype Consolidated Model 31
from mid-1939 until 1942.

Model 28-2 c/n C-2 plus two further aircraft supplied to the Soviet Union

As mentioned above, Russia was already in discussion
with Consolidated about the purchase and subsequent
licence-production of PBYs at the time that they acquired
the original *Guba*. An order was struck between the
manufacturers and Amtorg, the Russian agents, which
initially led to the supply of three Model 28-2s. The first
example, construction number C-2, was built in San
Diego and flown on test flights from there before being
dismantled and shipped to Russia, where it was re-
assembled and put into use. The other two PBYs ordered
by the Russians were produced by Consolidated as kits
of major parts and then shipped to their new owners,
who assembled them and used them as pattern aircraft
for future licence production at Tagonrog on the Sea of
Azov near Rostov. Variously described as either Model
28-1s or 28-2s, they were unlike all the other PBYs produced in North America inasmuch as they were powered

Seen here on a pre-delivery test flight is the first of the
three Model 28-2s delivered to Russia as pattern aircraft
for future local production. It is equipped with Wright
R-1820-G3 engines in place of the usual P&Ws. The
modified bow profile is clearly visible.
Convair via Jack Meaden

by Wright Cyclone R-1820-G3 840 hp engines with closer-
fitting cowlings rather than the more usual Pratt &
Whitneys. The reason for this was that the Russians were
familiar with the Cyclone powerplant as it was already
under licence production by them as the M-62. The other
main difference between these three aircraft and contemporary PBYs was the shape of the bow, which featured a
humped fairing over the turret area.

Further details of subsequent Russian production
may be found under 'Russia', in Chapter Eight.

The second *Guba*, also registered NC777, could be
distinguished from its predecessor by the tear-drop-shaped
DF loop housing on the wing centre section, just visible in
this photograph between the two engines. Also clearly
shown is the cockpit-roof-mounted pitot tube and mast.
John Wegg Collection

Model 28-3 c/n C-3 NC777 (2) *Guba*

Having sold his first *Guba* to the Russian Government, as
related earlier, Dr Richard Archbold immediately
ordered a replacement from Consolidated so that he
could continue with his planned expedition to New
Guinea. The aircraft that was subsequently supplied to
him was a Model 28-3, equivalent to the military PBY-2.
This second aircraft bore exactly the same registration
and name as the first, although it is sometimes incorrectly referred to as *Guba II*. There were various detail differences between it and the original aircraft. These included
reinforced ice shield panels on the hull aft of the cockpit
to prevent damage from propeller ice, and a tear-drop-
type D/F loop on the wing centre section rather than the
earlier circular loop above the cockpit, although the latter
had been tried on the second aircraft initially. In common
with the first *Guba*, *Guba* number 2 had prop spinners
and a cockpit roof-mounted pitot mast. It also shared the
same tail and nose insignia. Once *Guba* number 2 had
been delivered to its new owner, it was flown on a shake-
down trip during December 1937, from San Diego to
Miami and from there to Havana, Cuba. It then returned
to California.

The aerial part of Dr Archbold's third New Guinea expedition commenced on 2 June 1938, when *Guba* left San Diego once more, this time bound for Hollandia. The purpose of the expedition was to explore the Snow Mountains of Dutch New Guinea. Hollandia was reached after seven days in a total flying time of 32 hours, with stopovers at Honolulu and Wake Island.

At first, a number of reconnaissance flights were made around the local area, and on 15 July *Guba* was put down successfully on the 3,225 metre high Lake Habbema for the first time. The lake was to be used as a base for the expedition. Having proved that landings and take-offs from the lake were possible, it was used to ferry in supplies from Hollandia. *Guba* continued to support the needs of the expedition, and ultimately flew nearly 170 flights, lifting a total of 220 tons of equipment and supplies. The expedition was considered to be a great success, due in no small measure to the assistance of *Guba*. The flying boat was flown out of Hollandia for the last time on 12 May 1939, and it left for Port Moresby in Papua New Guinea before continuing on to Sydney, Australia. It was then overhauled at the QANTAS maintenance base at Rose Bay. Whilst there, Dr Archbold agreed to charter *Guba* to Captain P. G. Taylor in order that he could carry out a series of survey flights of the Indian Ocean. The purpose of these flights was to evaluate possible landing sites for flying boats in the vast area of ocean between Australia and East Africa. Such bases were considered important, not only for possible peacetime use, but also as an alternative to the existing land-plane routes that might be disrupted in time of war in the Far East. As it turned out, the work of the survey was put to good use only a few months later when war broke out and it became obvious that Allied flying boat bases would be needed in the area. Captain Taylor's own association with PBYs did not end there, as he went on to deliver early RAAF Catalinas to Australia from the USA and fly long-distance flights in the RAF Catalina JX275, *Frigate Bird*. More famously, he also pioneered the air route from Australia to South America in his PB2B-2 Catalina VH-ASA *Frigate Bird II*.

Taylor acted as the Commonwealth Government representative on the Indian Ocean survey flights in *Guba*, with Russell Rogers as pilot, Gerry Brown as first engineer, Steve Barrinka as second engineer, Captain Lewis Yancey as navigator and Jack Percival as second Government representative and media correspondent. They left Rose Bay on 3 June 1939, bound for Port Hedland, more than 1,000 miles north of Perth on Australia's west coast, where they positioned for the first stage of the crossing of the Indian Ocean. Subsequent legs of the survey took them to the Cocos Islands, Batavia, Christmas Island, the Cocos once more, then on to Diego Garcia, various locations in the Seychelles and finally Mombasa in Kenya, where the flight ended on 21 June. At this point, 'Bill' Taylor left for Australia by ship. The Trans Indian Ocean Survey Flight had ended but *Guba* was still far from home!

Not long after, *Guba* flew on across Africa to Dakar via Kisumu, Coquilhatville and Lagos, then on across the Atlantic Ocean to St Thomas in the West Indies. From there it turned north to Floyd Bennett Field, New York, on 4 July. After arrival in the USA, it was exhibited at the

Guba number 2 and the crew who were involved in the Trans-Indian Ocean Survey Flight of June 1939. From left to right are Gerry Brown, Lewis Yancey, Capt P. G. Taylor, Russell Rogers, Jack Percival and Steve Barrinka. The mast-mounted pitot tube can be seen above the cockpit, whilst the reinforced strip to prevent ice damage is above R. J. Brown's right shoulder.
via Jack Meaden

The exploration of Papua New Guinea by *Guba* and its crew was commemorated in September 1984 by the issue of this postage stamp.
Bill Kelly

New York World's Fair, where it remained on display until the exhibition closed at the end of the year. The *Guba* crew then flew it back to San Diego at the conclusion of the first-ever round-the-world flight by a flying boat. It was also the first aerial circumnavigation of the world at the point of greatest global circumference.

Once its adventures with Dr Archbold and Captain Taylor were over, NC777 number 2 was acquired by the British Purchasing Commission (BPC) under contract A-916 of 1940, and it was intended initially for use as a training aircraft in Canada. This superseded an earlier plan by the Ministry of Aircraft Production to use it to ferry loads of aluminium across the Atlantic Ocean from the USA, this metal being a raw material in short supply at the time. This idea fell through, however. After acquisition by the BPC, NC777 was given the British military serial AM258, incorrectly as it turned out because these

As SM706, the second *Guba* ended its days with Saunders Roe in North Wales, and it is seen here on its beaching gear at the company's base at Beaumaris.
Peter London

marks had already been allocated to the first aircraft in a batch of Consolidated Liberators. The Liberator went on to fly with this serial and was later lost in a fiery crash at Prestwick in Scotland on 13 September 1943.

The duplication of the RAF serial seems to have been of little consequence, as there were alternative plans afoot for the former *Guba*. A signal was received in Canada ordering its delivery to the UK, its export licence having been granted on 21 September 1940. It had already been partly modified to military standards by the manufacturers under Contract A-1127. On 25 October 1940, the aircraft left Botwood, Newfoundland, piloted by Captain I. G. Ross on a flight of extreme cold and discomfort for the crew, the airframe not having the benefit of heating or oxygen. Matters were made even worse when the navigator's hull window was broken by shards of ice being flung from the props and, presumably, missing the hull reinforcement strips designed to prevent such damage. Despite these difficulties, this flight was to be the first successful aerial crossing of the North Atlantic in the winter season. After a flight lasting 16.5 hours, the PBY landed at Stranraer in Scotland, where it briefly remained until delivered to 205 Squadron, Coastal Command, at Pembroke Dock in Wales two days later.

Shortly thereafter, Lord Beaverbrook, who was on the lookout for replacement flying boats for use by BOAC, decided to release AM258 so that it could be used on services between the flying boat base at Poole in Dorset and Lisbon. It was registered as G-AGBJ to the Ministry of Aircraft Production in December 1940, its type Certificate of Airworthiness being awarded on the 13th. Thus, it was the first British civil registered flying boat of the PBY family. On the 23rd, it flew from Pembroke Dock to BOAC's maintenance base at Hythe, Southampton, and on the 30th the airline became the registered owner, although technically it was the property of the Government. At this stage in its career, the flying boat still carried the name *Guba*.

BOAC started using G-AGBJ in March 1941, after initial crew training had been carried out at Pembroke Dock, and it was put into service on the Poole–Lagos route. During its time with BOAC it flew a total of 1,343 hours, and the airline retained the PBY until December 1943. Although it was not to join their other Catalinas on

the famous *Double Sunrise* route between Perth and Ceylon run in conjunction with QANTAS, it was none the less offered to the Australian airline to support that operation. The offer was declined, and on 14 January 1944 the civil registration was cancelled and ownership was taken on by Saunders Roe at Beaumaris, Anglesey. The civil registration appears to have remained in place until later in the year, when the military serial SM706 was allocated for use by the Air Council.

Saunders Roe had already been engaged for some time in the modifying and fitting out of Catalinas and other marine types to RAF specifications following delivery from the USA on Lend-Lease terms. Although *Guba's* flying days were over, Saunders Roe used it for testing experimental flying boat moorings for the Ministry of Aircraft Production at Pwllheli, Caernarvon. It eventually fell victim to a severe gale, during which it capsized and sank. Despite this, it was salvaged and all useful equipment was removed before it was towed out to sea on its final voyage and then scuttled. No record of the dates for the sinking have been unearthed, but the civil registration documents quote under the date of 13/9/44 that the 'aircraft will probably be reduced to salvage unless acquired by Transport Command', which may indicate that it was damaged prior to that date. Saunders Roe records show that SM706 was launched at Beaumaris on 10 August 1945, so this is probably the date that she was towed out for the final 'burial at sea'. Neither have any photographs been found of *Guba* number 2 wearing the identities G-AGBJ or AM258, although they do exist from the time it was painted as SM706. It is sad that this interesting aircraft did not survive the war years to be saved for posterity, particularly as it created several records during its earlier adventures.

Model 28-4 c/n C-4 NC18997 *Transatlantic*

This aircraft was the sole Consolidated Model 28 built specifically to satisfy an airline order despite efforts to interest various other companies in both this type and projected larger machines. Even this particular Consolidated aircraft was only ordered to carry out survey flights for future transatlantic services by another type – the Sikorsky VS-44! In the event, of course, the war intervened and large-scale commercial flights by flying boats across the Atlantic were severely restricted and subsequently replaced by land-based types after the war's end.

But to return to NC18997, this was ordered by American Export Lines, a well-known shipping company

Shown on a pre-delivery test flight, the sole American
Export Airlines Model 28-4 has had its registration
NC18997 modified to NX18997.
via John Millar

operating services across the Atlantic, which was planning to diversify into the airline business. In September,
1938, it placed an order with Consolidated for a commercial Model 28 so that it could carry out initial exploratory
flights to its future intended destinations. By the following April, the aircraft was being air-tested out of San
Diego, and it was then ferried to the Floyd Bennett
seaplane base at Brooklyn via Norfolk, Virginia, during
early June.

It was formally accepted by the new airline in New
York in June 1939, and had the name *Transatlantic*
bestowed upon it. It was painted in American Export
Airlines' full livery of silver and black with the company's red and blue emblem emblazoned on the forward
hull. The bow did not feature a turret but was instead
faired over – shades of the 'clipper' bow common on
many post-war commercial Catalinas. Survey flights
commenced on 30 June, when NC18997 left Floyd
Bennett in the early afternoon bound for Horta in the
Azores, where it arrived the next morning. From Horta,
it flew on to Lisbon, then Biscarosse on France's west
coast before departing for its final destination of
Marseille/Marignane, where it arrived just before 17.00
hours on 3 July. The return flight was made from

Marseille on the 6th and routed direct to Lisbon, then
Horta and Floyd Bennett, where it arrived at 09.50 hours
on the 9th.

The second survey flight started on 14 July, destined
for Marseille via Botwood, Newfoundland; Foynes,

NX18997 on the ground at San Diego. In addition to
American Export Airlines insignia, it wears the
Consolidated company emblem on the lower rudder. The
clipper bow was later to be seen in similar form on many
post-war ex-military PBYs.
via John Millar

Ireland and Biscarosse. The return flight to the USA from Marseille was made via Lisbon and the Azores and ended on 19 July. The final survey trip started on 28 July from Floyd Bennett destined for Marseille, and was made via Botwood and Biscarosse but with no intermediate stop at Foynes. On 1 August, a trip to St Nazaire was undertaken before flying on to Biscarosse, Lisbon and Horta, finally terminating in New York on 4 August. In all, nearly 25,000 miles were covered on the three flights between the US East Coast and Europe.

In the end, despite the sterling service given by the *Transatlantic*, American Export ordered the bigger, four-engined Sikorsky 'boat, with its 32-seat capacity and greater speed. NC18997 went on to serve with the US Navy on transport flights and was given the serial Bu99080, but was eventually retired from service in November of 1944. Some photographs show the letter C in the registration blocked out by an X, indicating that the aircraft was still registered in the Experimental category and not certificated for passenger service.

Model 28-5 c/n C-5 NX21732/NP9630/P9630

The British Air Ministry needed to acquire flying boats during the build-up of air power prior to the Second World War and was looking for types in addition to the indigenous Short Sunderland. Although the Consolidated PBY series seemed suitable, British hopes were initially pinned on the Saro Lerwick, which, in addition to being faster, also sported power-operated turrets. However, the Lerwick eventually proved to be something of a failure, and so official eyes were turned back to the USA and the San Diego headquarters of Consolidated. As a result, the British Purchasing Commission ordered a single PBY-4 for evaluation purposes under contract number B988730/39.

This aircraft was manufacturer's construction number C-5, a modified PBY-4, power being provided by a pair of Pratt & Whitney R-1830-S1C3G engines rated at 1,050 hp. Originally registered in the USA as NX21732, it was allocated the British military serial P9630 and painted silver and black overall, with RAF roundels on the hull and upper and lower wing surfaces, although it does not appear to have carried a fin flash. For the transatlantic delivery flight, the serial was modified by

the addition of the letter N at the beginning, presumably to make it appear to be a US civil registration. Unfortunately, no photographs have been traced showing this aircraft as NX21732. In a document issued by the Civil Aeronautics Authority on 8 July 1939, in which the ferry flight was authorised, the civil registration is referred to as NRP9630. Other contemporary official papers confirm that: 'The owners of the aircraft will not be required to exhibit the letter "R" (for Restricted category) on the aircraft'. These same documents also state that authorisation for the flight was conditional on neither the aircraft nor its equipment involving military secrets.

NP9630 was flown across the Atlantic Ocean to the UK, and in so doing was the first American military aircraft to achieve the flight during the Second World War. The crew for this flight was the same as Dr Richard Archbold had used on his own PBY *Guba*. Various sources differ as to the exact route taken, one quoting San Diego–Botwood–Newfoundland–Felixstowe, whereas another states San Diego–New York–Felixstowe. It is most likely that it routed through both New York and Botwood. The arrival at Felixstowe was on 17 July 1939, where it was taken on by the resident Marine Aircraft Experimental Establishment, or MAEE. Contemporary reports state that the arrival in the Felixstowe area was earlier than planned and coincided with an air exercise going on at the time. As a result, the PBY had to cruise around for some three hours before it could land!

Shortly after being received by the MAEE, it was shown off to the aviation press and was reported in the leading aircraft periodicals of the day. After testing at the MAEE, P9630 was used in further trials with various home-based operational Coastal Command squadrons alongside their usual equipment. These squadrons included 209 operating Supermarine Stranraers at Invergordon and Felixstowe, 210 with Sunderlands at Pembroke Dock and Invergordon, 228 with Sunderlands at Pembroke Dock and 240 who were flying Saunders Roe Londons from Invergordon and Sullom Voe. Whilst with 209 Squadron, P9630 acquired its squadron code WQ, which was painted on the rudder, although it is not known if it adopted an individual aircraft letter as well. After the trials, it returned to the MAEE, which had in the meantime relocated to Helensburgh in Scotland, where the risk of enemy air attack was less than at Felixstowe.

During its evaluation, both with the MAEE and with operational squadrons, P9630 flew quite widely around home waters as well as further afield. During September 1939, it is known to have flown to Iceland from Invergordon on a reconnaissance mission, and during this sortie it was forced to land because of fog. This caused a minor diplomatic incident as Iceland was neutral at the time! Later in the same month it flew twice to Sullom Voe to take secret paperwork there. On a later visit to the same base, on 14 November, P9630 arrived during an enemy air attack and it had the misfortune to be fired on by 'friendly' gunners, even though it had displayed the correct colours of the day! No damage was sustained to plane or crew, the latter including Dennis Briggs flying as 2nd pilot and later to achieve fame as one of the airmen who spotted the German battleship *Bismark* whilst flying in 209 Squadron's Catalina I AH545/WQ-Z.

For its delivery flight to the UK, P9630 was re-marked as NP9630, as seen here in this air-to-air photograph. *Convair via Jack Meaden*

RAF crews who flew P9630 around this time were impressed with its sophisticated instrumentation and communications equipment, the retractable wingtip floats and its flying characteristics generally.

This PBY met its untimely end in a landing accident at Dumbarton on 10 February 1940, whilst on a flight from Rhu. It sank and, although it was salvaged, it never flew again. Although its flying career was short, history was to prove that this particular flying boat, built on a non-military contract, was to pave the way for massive orders for the Royal Air Force, which was to bestow the famous Catalina name on the type.

Despite ongoing and determined efforts by Consolidated's marketing men, no further commercial orders for the Model 28 were forthcoming, and in the end, the need for increased production of the new PBY-5 and subsequent versions meant that any further thought of non-military aircraft was abandoned. This is ironic as one proposed version of the Model 28 aimed at the civil market was an amphibian, the configuration in which the type was to have such a long and successful post-war commercial career, once it was declared surplus by the

P9630, the sole Model 28-5 ordered for evaluation by the British Air Ministry prior to its trans-Atlantic delivery flight. Of note are the prop spinners and removable crew access ladder leading to the rear sliding hatch.
via Jack Meaden

military! The great success of the military PBY-5s also meant that proposed commercial versions of the larger Model 31 Corregidor had to take a back seat and did not proceed beyond the concept stage.

Three
POST-WAR USAGE

With the Second World War over, the various military air arms that were operating the Catalina in all its different marks began a rapid reduction of their fleets. Further details are given under the entries for the individual countries involved. In summary, the USA continued to operate amphibious versions with the United States Army Air Force (United States Air Force from September 1947 onward), the US Navy and the US Coast Guard, but none of these were flying pure flying boat PBY-5s or PBN-1 Nomads post-war. Indeed, only one complete US Navy PBY-5 was to survive for posterity, this being Bu08317, which can be found today lovingly restored at the United States Naval Aviation Museum at Pensacola in Florida. Large numbers of Navy, Army and Coast Guard Catalina amphibians were commercialised throughout the late-1940s and the 1950s, however.

Of the Commonwealth air forces, the Royal Air Force disposed of its entire fleet with almost indecent haste, but the Royal New Zealand Air Force and Royal Australian Air Force continued to use their Catalinas in decreasing numbers for a few more years, small numbers transferring to the commercial sector. The Royal Canadian Air Force did not operate flying boat Cansos post-war,

although they used a good number of their amphibious Canso As well into the 1960s. Many of the Canso As were subsequently disposed of to civil operators as they came up for tender, although no pure flying boat versions were sold for commercial use.

So, having acquitted itself so well during the war, the Catalina found itself suddenly poised to embark on a new career once it had ended. The irony is that, having been conceived as a flying boat, its saving grace as far as its future longevity was concerned was the fact that it had been developed into an amphibian! The addition of a retractable undercarriage gave the PBY so much more flexibility that many post-war commercial and military operators leapt at the chance of buying up surplus military examples. In fact, as time went on, a fair number of the aircraft that continued in use were operated almost entirely from land and rarely if ever ventured onto water! Conversely, as will be seen, the ability to operate from water led to the Catalina flying in commercial roles that were far beyond the original vision of the Consolidated design office! Notwithstanding the above, a small number of pure flying boat examples did fly commercially, although even some of these were originally built as amphibians and had had their undercarriage units removed and the bays plated over.

Once hostilities were over, companies specialising in the purchase of ex-military aircraft, including Catalinas, began to spring up. Whilst some of these were only interested in reducing their acquisitions to spares, others began converting them to commercial aircraft or

Most Royal Air Force Catalinas were disposed of within a very short time of the war ending. Here, several examples are having useful parts removed at Kisumu in Kenya before being towed out into Lake Victoria and scuttled.
via John MacDonald

Throughout the late 1940s and 1950s, surplus US Navy, US Coast Guard and USAAF/USAF Catalinas either found their way to new operators or languished in open storage awaiting an uncertain fate. This unidentified PBY-6A was mouldering away in the north-east USA in the 1950s in company with the Canadian-registered Avro Lancaster X CF-KHH.
via Eric Dumigan

Post-war, a variety of vertical tail shapes was to be seen on surviving Catalinas. These were: (i) the stock PBY-5/PBY-5A shape as seen here on the former RCAF Canso A Z-CAT, photographed at sunset on Lake Tanganyika, Tanzania, in August 1992 *(Author)*; (ii) the horn-balanced version illustrated by C-FNJE, a one-time Newfoundland and Labrador water bomber *(Eric Dumigan, Oshawa, Ontario, May 1996)*; (iii) the taller PBY-6A tail as originally installed on US Navy Bu64017, now N285RA, and seen at North Weald, England in 1999 *(Author)*; and (iv) the squared-off design used on many of the Wright Cyclone-powered Super Catalinas, here shown on G-BLSC during a re-spray at RAF Barkstone Heath, England, in April 1985 *(Author)*.

reconditioning them for use by the military air arms of other countries. This was particularly the case in the USA, where substantial numbers were snapped up during the post-war years by such companies as Southern California Aircraft Corporation of Ontario, California; Charles H. Babb Inc. of Burbank, California; Babb Co. of Linden, New Jersey; Trade Ayer, also of Linden, New Jersey; Aero Corp. of Atlanta, Georgia; and the Aircraft Instrument Corporation of Miami, Florida. Later, companies such as Pan Air Corporation in New Orleans and Steward-Davis of Long Beach, California, engaged in the overhaul and upgrading of Catalina airframes. The work of some of these companies is covered later in this chapter. In Canada, too, a small number of companies carried out post-military work on ex-RCAF Canso As, including de Havilland Aircraft of Canada Ltd, Aircraft Industries of Canada Ltd and Canadian Car and Foundry. De Havilland converted PBYs for use by the Dutch Navy, Royal Danish Air Force, Canadian Pacific Airlines and Rexco among others. Even one-off conversions were carried out by such companies as Noorduyn Norseman Aircraft of Cartierville, Quebec. In addition, specialist firms later became involved in fire-bombing conversions in both Canada and the USA. Catalina Aero Services based at Nanaimo on Vancouver Island still have the ability to carry out luxury conversions for the commercial sector to this day.

Most surplus Catalinas were gathered together at specific storage sites, the US Navy using Litchfield Park, Arizona, in particular. Once sold to new owners, it was usual for a civil identity to be daubed on the hull and the aircraft flown out to be converted for its future use. The Catalina received the US Type Certificate 785 during

1947, the appropriate designation being the Model 28-5ACF. From this point onward, many different conversions were carried out, so that, as years have gone by, very few, if any, of the remaining PBYs are identical in appearance.

Many, but not all, commercial conversions involved the removal of nose and blister turrets, together with all armament. Where nose turrets came off, a 'clipper' bow was put in its place. There were basically three types of clipper bow – a rounded version where the lower and upper hull were curved to meet in a smooth if rather

(i) For passenger convenience, many post-war commercial Catalinas had an air stair incorporated into the rear hull, as shown here on SLAFCO's N31235 at Moses Lake, Washington. This was a more comfortable alternative to climbing in through the blisters or cargo hatch. *(Ray Williams)*; (ii) Nose turrets were often removed and, in their place, a 'clipper' bow installed. These varied in profile, this one belonging to Plane Sailing Air Displays' G-BLSC/JV928, as seen at RAF Mildenhall, England, in May 1985 *(Author)*; (iii) Where blisters were left *in situ*, they were often modified. This photo shows a hinged inner frame on Cat Air's PH-PBY at Duxford, England, in 1997 *(Author)*; whilst photo (iv) shows a one-piece tinted version on the luxuriously appointed N69RF *(Ray Williams)*.

bulbous nose shape of completely new profile, and a more angular version where the bomb-aimer's rectangular panel (or triangular window in the case of the PBY-6A) remained in place but the upper bow was swept down to meet it. The third, less common, variety was a pointed glass fibre nose cone that was installed over the bomb aimer's position and the turret ring, these features remaining in place under the new nose! An example of the latter conversion is to be found on the last PBY-6A to be built, N9825Z. The rounded version of the clipper bow added 5.5 inches to the overall hull length. The hull blisters were usually replaced by hinged or sliding cargo hatches.

As well as the bulk of the former military equipment being removed, the flight engineer's instrument panel was relocated from the pylon between hull and wing to the cockpit. Often, additional windows were cut into the

hull for the convenience of those on board. The PBY rudder, that had seen various changes in its shape over the years in order to improve directional stability, also came in for attention, and many commercial Catalinas received a horn balance projecting forward over the vertical fixed tail surface.

As time went on, some companies specialised in producing their own distinctive brand of Catalina conversions, and these are described below together with one or two 'might-have-been' projects.

The *Landseaire*

The Southern California Aircraft Corporation, headed by Glenn E. Odekirk, was involved in post-war Catalina conversion work at its base in Ontario, California. In addition to refurbishing PBYs for military air arms such as that of the Dominican Republic, it also developed its own brand of commercial Catalina known as the Landseaire, a rather neat play on words that well summarised the aircraft's flexible capabilities. By the early 1950s, it was turning out smartly appointed aircraft for civilian customers, mostly in the USA. Odekirk's vision was to produce a luxury air yacht that could be used just as well on water as on land and would thus give its probably wealthy owner plenty of flexibility in operation.

The *Landseaire* conversion started with the removal of all non-essential military equipment and the relocation of the flight engineer's controls to within the pilot's cockpit. The inside of the hull was then opened up and a comfortable interior was installed, in some cases including seating that doubled as sleeping accommodation for up to eight people. Accessories included individual lighting, radio, curtains, air conditioning and telephone. The rudder was altered so that it included a horn balance. What particularly distinguished the *Landseaire* conversions from others was the work done on the blisters. The port unit was modified so that instead of opening 'eyelid

Illustrating the *Landseaire* conversion is the former US Navy PBY-5A N68756. In this 1952 profile, the various modifications can be seen, including 'clipper' bow, extra hull windows, D/F loops above the cockpit, under-wing dinghies, 'running board' below the blisters and horn-balanced rudder.
MAP

fashion' as on the original, the inner part of the blister framing was hinged and would open wide with support from a strut. The starboard unit was replaced by a one-piece blown transparency made of Lucite that offered exceptional vistas through good-quality optical material. This transparency alone cost around £1,000 at 1953 prices – the entire airframe after conversion was priced at that time at £100,000, or $265,000! A great measure of convenience was afforded by the air-stairs that were built into the rear hull in place of the original hatch for the rear-facing gun. When the Catalina was on terra firma, the air-stair made entering the hull much easier than climbing up ladders and coming in through the blisters. The company also claimed that the stairs could be used as a diving board when the Cat was on water. As an alternative, some versions had a small 'running board' attached to the hull side just underneath the blisters. The air-stair was lowered using electrical switches within the aft hull or located in the main undercarriage well. Internally, the hull was sound-proofed with fibreglass material and the floor of the hull was carpeted. There was also a shower, WC and fully equipped galley.

For water-borne operations, a 14 ft dinghy could be carried under each of the wings just outboard of the lift struts, and these could be lowered to the water surface using integral electrically powered winches. The reverse operation was also possible. In flight, the boats could be used as panniers for luggage or equipment.

The cruising speed of a *Landseaire* was published as being 175 mph, with a maximum range of 3,000 miles. Elements of the *Landseaire* design, such as the air-stairs, found their way into other versions of the Catalina, and even now, in the 21st century, Catalina Aero Services of Nanaimo, British Columbia, will convert an otherwise standard airframe into *Landseaire* format with rear stairs and modified blisters, including the one-piece unit in tinted transparent material.

The Super Catalina

The Super Catalina conversion was conceived by Steward-Davis Inc. of Long Beach, California, and in later years became known by the shorter name *Super Cat*. In order to provide greater power – and flexibility in the event of engine failure – the traditional Pratt & Whitney R-1830s were removed and replaced by 14-cylinder 1,700 hp Wright R-2600 Cyclones as used on the B-25 Mitchell. Indeed, the installation had much in common with that of the B-25. Promotional material suggests that it could also be made available in 1,900 hp format. In addition to interior changes, this variant normally sported a much-enlarged rudder in order to give the greater control authority required by the additional 500 hp on each side. This unit was normally of a somewhat basic, squared-off shape, although some *Super Cats* flew with a standard PBY-6A vertical tail and rudder unit. No records exist to show that any PBY with standard PBY-5-style rudder flew with Cyclones. There were, however, at least two standard P&W-powered Catalinas that had *Super Cat* rudders!

Other refinements on the *Super Cats* included air-stairs, 'clipper' bows, prop-spinners, wheel hub covers and under-wing dinghies. In many cases, the blisters remained in place. Although Steward-Davis marketed the design, it seems that it may also have been carried out by other organisations. Noorduyn Norseman Aircraft in Montreal, Quebec converted the ex-US Navy PBY-5A

CF-MIR to a *Super Cat*, although it bestowed its own designation upon it, christening it rather inaccurately as a *Super Canso S/C 1000*.

Over the years, many of the *Super Cat* conversions were used by American borate and water bombing companies on the West Coast, mainly because of the additional power they offered over the standard version. These companies included Hemet Valley Flying Services of Hemet, California, and SLAFCO of Moses Lake, Washington. Alaska Coastal-Ellis Airlines preferred the type in favour of conventional P&W-powered aircraft, as did Antilles Air Boats, and the *Super Cat* also found favour with the Canadian survey company Geoterrex, which operated four.

The *Skybarge*

Another Steward-Davis design was the *Skybarge*, but, unlike the Super Catalina, this did not go beyond the drawing board. Drawings released in the mid-1960s seem to show standard P&W engines, but the company intended the conversion to have Wright R-2600-20 Cyclones of 1,900 hp. The intention was to remove portions of the upper hull from positions immediately aft of the cockpit and aft of the wing trailing edge in order to create two cargo holds for freight carriage. The holds were to be capable of holding items up to 8 ft long by 7 ft 6 in wide. The general arrangement drawings released by Steward-Davis do not show how the forward hold was to be covered but it seems likely that this would have been achieved using either a removable or a hinged cover. The rear freight area was covered by means of a rearward-sliding hatch that incorporated the blisters. Each freight hold was to be equipped with a hoist capable of lifting individual loads up to 4,000 lb weight. The forward hold was designed to carry up to 4,660 lb, and the rear 7,340 lb.

Performance was quoted as enabling a 50 ft high object to be cleared after take-off within 1,400 ft from land and 2,000 ft from water with an 11,400 lb payload. Improved performance would have been possible by the even more radical addition of up to three Steward-Davis Jet-Packs. These were auxiliary jet engines that could be

The Avalon Aviation Turbo Canso Waterbomber powered by Rolls Royce Dart turbine engines

Avalon Aviation, the well-known Canadian water bombing company, considered converting Catalinas to turboprop power, and this artist's impression shows what a Rolls-Royce Dart-powered Catalina would have looked like if the project had gone ahead.
Avalon Aviation

mounted under or over the wings and atop the hull superstructure, which the company did successfully market for use on such aircraft as the Fairchild Packet.

Ultimately this intriguing idea for a Catalina freighter did not fly, although Steward-Davis must have thought there was a market for it, presumably in places such as Northern Canada, Alaska and South America.

The Turbo Canso

The Canadian forest-fire-fighting company, Avalon Aviation, started design studies that would have resulted in a Catalina with two Rolls-Royce Dart turboprops. Sometime prior to this, a Dart-powered B-17 of all things was used for land-based fire fighting, and, in more recent times, turbo C-47s have been operated on transport duties in some numbers in South Africa and Latin America (in England, the idea had been tried out on Dakotas many years earlier but only on a trial basis). Thus, the installation of modern engines in an old airframe was a proved concept. The Turbo Cat was stillborn, however, with just an artist's impression left to remind us of what it might have looked like in action!

The *Bird Innovator*

The Bird Oxygen and Breathing Equipment Inc. acquired a *Landseaire* Catalina conversion registered N5907 in 1962. Within a year, Bird started to carry out modifications to the airframe, the first noticeable difference being the addition of a *Super Cat*-type rudder. It retained the standard Pratt & Whitney Twin Wasp power-plants, however.

The Bird Corporation, as the owner had now been renamed, was of course very aware that the original Catalinas had been designed for long range and endurance at the expense of power and speed, and that, as a result, single-engine performance could be marginal at high all-up weights. They had also been the victim of two engine failures within a short space of time. So, whilst some post-war commercial Catalina operators chose the 1,700 hp R-2600 Cyclone Super Catalina as the

A Steward-Davis drawing of the proposed Skybarge variant of the mid-1960s.

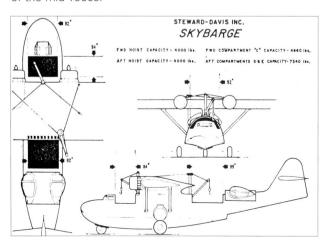

STEWARD-DAVIS INC.
SKYBARGE

FWD HOIST CAPACITY - 4000 lbs.   FWD COMPARTMENT "C" CAPACITY - 4660 lbs.
AFT HOIST CAPACITY - 4000 lbs.   AFT COMPARTMENTS D & E CAPACITY - 7340 lbs.

route to more flexibility, Bird looked for a more radical answer! Its reasons seem to have been based on a desire to avoid any increase in noise and vibration and higher maintenance and operating costs. It also discounted a conversion to turboprop power and the addition of jet packs. The result of its feasibility studies was unconventional, to say the least – the one and only four-engined Catalina! Appropriately, it was christened the *Bird Innovator*.

The decision was taken to install two 340 hp Lycoming GSO-480-B2D6 six-cylinder air-cooled engines, one in each outer wing panel, alongside the existing radial engines. The installations were made with a three-degree outward cant, and the slim cowling profile ensured a very clean appearance with the top of the cowlings flush with the upper wing surface and with minimal frontal area. The full depth of the engine and cowls was only slightly in excess of the maximum aerofoil thickness. Exhausts were fitted to discharge downward. Each power-plant was equipped with its own 375 US gallon fuel supply in three inter-connecting bladder tanks, together with a 15 gallon oil tank and CO_2 fire protection bottle. The P&Ws retained their original propeller units, whilst the new Lycomings drove three-bladed Hartzell 83XF-3A reversible-pitch, fully feathering units. These gave the aircraft the ability to reverse when manoeuvring and made braking and taxiing on water and land much easier. All four engines had spinners fitted to the propellers.

The Bird Innovator progressed to four-engined format in several stages. In this photo, it has a Super Cat-style rudder, clipper bow, wheel covers, air stair and one-piece blister, but still retains two P&W R-1830s.
Jennifer M. Gradidge

In order to accommodate the two extra engines, several structural modifications were necessary. Additional stringers and stress plates were built into the wing to maintain strength, and aileron cables were re-routed. The ailerons themselves were fitted with Flettner tabs to further aid control. Power to the Lycomings was controlled using the cockpit roof levers originally intended for the Pratt & Whitneys, the remaining controls being situated adjacent to the main engine counterparts. Auxiliary engine instruments were placed within a panel on top of the standard instrument array.

A heavy-duty battery pack was installed aft, and this enabled balance of the airframe to be maintained. Inside the aircraft, the fittings included seating for up to sixteen passengers, a galley, shower and air conditioning. The entire conversion added something like 3,500 lb to the standard amphibious Catalina's weight.

So, what of the *Innovator*'s performance? Maximum cruising speed was 200 mph, while the normal cruise at 5,000 ft and a gross weight of 34,000 lb was 158 mph. At 11,000 ft and 64 per cent power, cruise with all engines operating was 152 mph. With one of the Lycomings shut down and prop feathered, cruise was 144 mph, reduced to 120 mph with both Lycomings out. Speed with one main engine out reduced further to 125 mph. Take-off run from dry land at 34,000 lb auw was 1,000 ft with full power or under 2,000 ft with 85 per cent power. Rate of climb on 75 per cent power and all engines running was 750 ft per minute.

These performance figures exceeded the original design specifications set by Bird, and the company subsequently claimed that the *Innovator* was the highest-performance and safest large amphibian then available. In fact, the design was offered as a conversion to other Catalina owners, and a projected version would have featured a cargo door, presumably in place of the rear hull blisters. Unfortunately for Bird, there were no takers and

Later, the P&Ws were joined by two six-cylinder
Lycomings. Dinghies can be seen under the wings, whilst
the starboard blister has been covered with protective
material.
Jennifer M. Gradidge

the *Innovator* was destined to remain a limited edition of
one!

During much of its four-engined phase, two fourteen-
foot boats were carried under the *Innovator*'s wings, one
on each side of the hull in between the radial and in-line
engines. They were modelled on the *Landseaire* modification and could be used to carry equipment and supplies
whilst in flight.

The aircraft went on to serve the Bird Corporation for
many years before being sold and passing through a
number of commercial and private owners. It remained
in its four-engined configuration until Ron Ruble
acquired it in the late 1990s and de-converted it back to a
twin-engined Cat. The history of this aircraft may be
found under the registration N5PY in Chapter Nineteen.

This close-up shows the starboard side Lycoming
installation on the solitary Bird Innovator N5907. This photo
was taken in the late 1980s when the aircraft was in
storage at Tico in Florida.

SPECIALIST ROLES

During its long post-war career as a commercial aircraft,
the Catalina was used in a variety of ways. These included the relatively conventional roles of passenger and
freight transport, executive aircraft and rich man's airborne yacht. As time went on, it also carved out a niche
for itself in a small number of highly specialised roles.
The first – aerial survey – relied on the type's ability to fly
steadily for long periods whilst being equipped with a
variety of external equipment hung around its airframe.
The other – aerial fire fighting and spraying – was to a

great extent based on the Catalina's water-landing capability, although ironically a number of those flown in the
USA against forest fires were land based. It is a fact that
these two activities have contributed greatly to the
Catalina's longevity and have been responsible for
the continued existence of many of the world's remaining
flying specimens. Catalinas have also been involved in
air display and film work and in some notable long-
distance flights.

Fairly typical aerial survey equipment is shown here on the Geoterrex/Terra Surveys Super Catalina C-FMIR when based in South Africa around 1984. The 'stinger' tail contains a magnetometer, whilst the 'bomb' under the rear hull was an electromagnetic receiver that could be paid out behind the aircraft when airborne. The electro-magnetic transmitter cabling that formed a loop around the entire airframe can be partially seen on the right-hand side of the photograph.

Survey Catalinas

During the 1960s and through to the mid-1980s, a number of companies used Catalinas for aerial surveying, mapping and photography. Although these were, in the main, Canadian-based companies, contract work took the aircraft and their crews all over the world, and some of the Canadian-registered Cats spent periods on other registers, including those of Australia and the USA. The Canadian survey firms included Aero Magnetic Surveys, Canadian Aero Services, Geoterrex (who also traded as Terra Surveys), Kentings (part of the Hunting Group), Questor Surveys, Spartan Air Services and Survair. Australian operators included Adastra Hunting Geophysics, Executive Air Services and Selco Exploration, whilst the best-known US company involved in aerial survey with PBYs was Barringer Research. The post-war Royal Canadian Air Force also used a number of their amphibious Canso As for mapping in the very north of the country.

Aerial mapping was fairly straightforward inasmuch as the airframe merely had to have provision for cameras and other recording equipment. Of course, it also required precision flying from the crews involved. Probably the most significant mapping contract carried out by commercial Catalinas was that involving two of

the Kenting Catalinas in the mid-1950s. As briefly mentioned above, Kentings was a Canadian firm in the Hunting Group of companies, and it flew a number of Catalinas, both as survey aircraft and as fire-fighters. The survey planes were used for both photographic/mapping work and geophysical exploration. At the end of 1953, two of Kenting's aircraft were chartered to the Falkland Islands and Dependencies Aerial Survey Expedition. The expedition had contracted Kenting's parent company, Hunting Aerosurveys Limited, to carry out the aviation aspects of the survey that had been planned to photograph and map both the Falkland Islands and Grahamland (now known as the Antarctic Peninsula). The survey was being carried out against a background of disputes between Chile and Argentina over sovereignty of those areas, and it was deemed essential that more accurate maps than those available at the time be drawn up.

The two Catalinas involved – CF-IGJ and CF-IJJ – had been acquired in the USA and were externally in stock condition except that their blisters had been replaced with hatches. Their tail surfaces and outer wings were prominently painted bright red to make them more easily located in case of emergency. Most accounts of the expedition describe the two Catalinas as Cansos, but as neither of them had served with the RCAF this is incorrect, although no doubt the Canadian members of the crews referred to them as such. Thus they were perpetuating the myth that the amphibious Catalina was known as the Canso, regardless of pedigree. The two Cats flew out of Toronto on 26 November 1955, and reached Port Stanley in the Falklands on 31 December, having made intermediate stops in the Caribbean, in Brazil and at Montevideo. The first attempt at surveying the Falklands was not particularly successful because of poor weather conditions and insufficient time available, and both aircraft flew on to Deception Island in the South Shetlands

A variation of the type of survey equipment carried is shown in this picture of C-FJJG when operated by Survair. The magnetometer boom is bigger than that shown in the preceding photograph of C-FMIR, whilst the huge framework of the transmitting coil can just be seen ahead of the nose.
Alan MacNutt

sizes over the years – they placed the transmitting coil in a large nose extension. This nose apparatus took the form of a forward-facing supporting frame onto which was mounted the vertical coil. Various shapes and sizes of coil were used, and at least one of Kenting's aircraft had a set of three circular coils mounted forward of the bow in a large and somewhat elaborate arrangement. Photos exist of a third arrangement in which the so-called *Super Canso* C-FMIR of Survair had large vertical endplates installed on each wingtip.

Regardless of the actual type of installation, the basic mode of operation was the same. The Catalina would be flown at a low level of around 150 ft in a pattern of grids over the area thought likely to yield the sought-after mineral deposits. The electromagnetic equipment searched for conductors in the ground based on what is known as the induction principle. The transmitter coil and its alternating current induced eddy currents in the ground below the aircraft. The on-board equipment could then detect conductive areas of base metals underground for possible future excavation. The survey Cats would normally fly with two pilots and an electronics operator, with further backup on the ground by way of engineers, data analysts and geophysicists. The hull would also be equipped with various other types of equipment, including cameras and recorders.

Catalinas were used for many years in the survey role, and in addition to flying throughout Northern Canada, were also seen in the USA, Ireland, the Channel Islands, Surinam, Guyana, Nigeria, South Africa, Senegal, Sweden, India, the Pacific and Australia. The last Catalinas to be used for surveying were C-FMIR and C-GGDW of Geoterrex Surveys based in Ottawa and C-FJJG of Toronto-based Kenting Earth Sciences.

on 10 January 1956, a distance of some 700 miles from the Falklands. Both in the Falklands and at Deception Island, the two Catalinas were operated from water, although at the latter location, a slipway enabled them to come out onto dry land for maintenance. Again, adverse weather had an effect on the success of the operation, but some thousand square miles of photography was achieved before the Catalinas headed north again to Port Stanley, then on to Canada, arriving in March.

Both aircraft returned to Port Stanley on 15 October 1956, and they managed to complete the Falkland Islands survey before once again heading south to Deception Island in early December to finish off the Antarctic part of the contract. Whilst there, the expedition was visited by HRH Prince Philip. CF-IGJ and CF-IJJ returned home to Canada via Port Stanley and Montevideo in March 1957.

The geophysical survey work carried out by Catalinas involved more radical alterations and additions to the basic airframe than that required for air-to-ground photography and mapping. Basically, the aerial search for mineral deposits and ores depended on the use of an electromagnetic system, and as far as Catalinas are concerned, there were two basic types of configuration. The first, as used by such companies as Geoterrex, Terra Surveys and Barringer Research, consisted of a loop of cable that surrounded the airframe from attachment points on the outer wings, nose and rear hull. This loop acted as a transmitter for the electromagnetic primary field. The electromagnetic receiver equipment was housed in a towed 'bird' that could be paid out behind the Catalina when in flight on a long demagnetised cable. A magnetometer was contained within a 'stinger' tail extension aft of the rudder.

The other main type of geophysical equipment used on the Catalina was seen on aircraft operated by Kenting and Canadian Aero Services. Whilst the magnetometer was still housed in a tail boom – Kenting used various

Fire-Fighting and Aerial Spraying Catalinas

The Catalina was widely used as a water and borate bomber in the fire-suppression role for many years, primarily in North and South America and Canada, although, during the 1960s, a number operated in the South of France. In the 1990s, the type again became popular, this time in Spain and Portugal, despite the availability of more modern, purpose-made amphibious types such as the Canadair CL-215 and CL-415. The Catalina was well suited to operate as a fire fighter because of its ability to scoop water from lakes or calm sea surfaces and then drop it on forest fire sites. The process could then be repeated time and time again without the necessity of landing back at a distant airfield. This saved time provided that there were lakes or sea near to the fire, and it only became necessary to return to a land base for fuel or because of crew fatigue. The Catalinas could, however, also be loaded up at land bases, and some Canadian-based aircraft and most of those used in the USA were frequently replenished at airfields with specially installed tankage, even though this lengthened the time from loading to dropping. The two main reasons for replenishment at land bases were the relative absence of lakes in California compared with, say, Canada, and the use of different additives, some of which required mixing with water prior to loading the aircraft.

The first trials of water bombing equipment on a

The first aerial fire-fighting trials using the Catalina were carried out by Austin Airways on CF-JTL. This design used two under-wing water tanks filled from lakes by extending probes, but it did not go on to see extensive use.
Larry Milberry/CANAV Book Collection

Catalina took place in May 1960 in Canada and involved the development of under-wing tanks. Austin Airways were already operators of the Catalina/Canso in Northern Canada and decided to investigate the idea of using the type to combat forest fires at the suggestion of their senior pilot, Jim Bell. He had observed smaller aircraft types with more modest capacity engaged in fighting fires, and felt that the Catalina would be ideal for the job. Austins broached the idea with the company that carried out most of their maintenance, Aircraft Industries of Canada (AIC). They quickly devised a system based on two 350-gallon circular-section tanks, one being suspended under each wing close to the lift struts. The tanks were filled using a somewhat flimsy-looking, hydraulically operated probe that would lower into the water at the appropriate moment whilst the aircraft skimmed across the water surface 'on the step', thus forcing water up into the tanks. The pointed tail cone on each tank hinged upward, and this allowed the pilot to jettison the contents onto the conflagration below. Any Catalina fitted with such tanks could of course be used for other purposes because the inner hull remained unobstructed and the tanks could be removed quite simply during the 'off seasons'.

The external tank system was tested on CF-JTL, a former US-registered Catalina leased by Austin and AIC. Trials took place on the Richelieu River and from Mississquoi Bay, Lake Champlain, and the concept was proved. Later, it saw some operational use in Quebec and Newfoundland, and AIC produced several sets of tanks. Unfortunately, early interest shown by the Ontario Department of Land and Forests did not convert into orders and so the system cannot be considered a great commercial success. None the less, it no doubt convinced the fire-fighting industry that the Catalina was an aircraft that had potential as a fire-fighting aircraft, and so it was to prove.

Shortly after the Austin Airways trials, Toronto-based Field Aviation became involved in looking at the use of Catalinas against forest fires in Canada. Their chief engineer, J Knox Hawkshaw, received a government request to consider converting a Catalina to hold internal water tanks that could be replenished using a probe system similar to that pioneered by Austin Airways and AIC. Although initially sceptical, Hawkshaw went on to design a system, and this was trialled on Kenting Aviation's CF-NWY during 1961. The system proved effective for many years, and it was used as the basis for other conversions by companies such as Fairey Aviation of Canada, Avalon Aviation and Flying Fireman. Fields themselves carried out numerous conversions. The same idea was also used in the later custom-built water bombers built by Canadair. Some crews disliked the Fairey conversion as the position of the internal tanks made it difficult to reach the main gear emergency lowering devices, use of which involved a crew member climbing into the empty tank, often still smeared with sticky additives!

A few American companies also developed their own Catalina conversions, a number of which were based on Wright Cyclone-powered *Super Cats*. In the main, no Special Type Certificate (STC) was required as the conversion was regarded as an agricultural modification! Later versions used varying-capacity tanks, and some aircraft used at ground bases had their wingtip floats removed to save precious weight. In America, the fire fighters tended to be called 'tankers' rather than 'bombers'. Various different tank capacities have been available to fire-fighting companies, depending on which design was used for the original conversion. Field Aviation's Hawkshaw system offered a total capacity of 800 gallons, whilst Fairey Canada's version enabled a further 100 gallons to be hauled aloft. The added power

Later developments saw Catalinas and Cansos equipped with internal tanks and drop doors in the lower hull, and this configuration became standard on fire-fighting PBYs. This Province of Newfoundland and Labrador aircraft (C-FNJC) is seen at Goose Bay in 1989 with its drop doors in the open position.
Robin Budworth

Replenishing the internal tanks from a lake was achieved by lowering a probe into the water whilst skimming across the surface at 60–65 kt. This probe on PBY-6A N285RA is shown in the retracted position just aft of the hull 'step'. *Author*

of the Cyclone-equipped *Super Cats* meant that as much as 1,200 gallons could be taken on board. One veteran tanker pilot expressed his opinion that the best fire-fighting Catalina variant was the *Super Cat*, although the R-1830-engined PBY-6A was also a great aircraft, its servo tabs offering better handling through lighter control forces.

The Hawkshaw system involved installing two 400-gallon tanks inside the Catalina's hull at a position located on the centre of gravity so that the filling and emptying of the tanks did not affect the aircraft's handling too much. The bottom of the tank floor was the hull itself, and this had two dump doors cut into it that hinged downward, allowing the bomb load to drop. Once skimming the Catalina along the water surface, the pilot lowered the probe and this forced water up into the tanks. The probe itself was similar to a domestic drainpipe with a right-angled joint at the pick-up end, and it was located in the lower hull immediately behind the step. The probe orifice measured some 4.5 inches in diameter. Apertures were cut into the upper hull so that when the tanks were full, any excess water was forced out through the vents to avoid rupturing the tank. The tanks had internal plates to minimise surging of the water within. This Hawkshaw design stood the test of time and is still in use today, as are the original techniques for fighting fires from the air.

Where natural sources of water are available to fill the tanker aircraft, the normal procedure is to depart the land base empty, reconnoitre the drop zone, then proceed to the pick-up point, where the landing area is surveyed for wave patterns, obstacles and floating debris if this has not already been done by ground-based support crews. The pilot then sets up a standard water landing approach, ensuring that the pick-up probe is retracted and the hull bomb doors firmly shut. At this point, the speed and attitude of the Catalina are crucial to a safe pick-up. Normally, pick-ups are conducted with wingtip floats in the up position as this gives the pilots a greater degree of manoeuvrability, although, should something go wrong and it becomes necessary to abort a pick-up

and remain on the water, a rapid response from the pilot is required in order to get the floats lowered and avoid a wing settling in the water.

The speed on the step for a water pick-up should be a steady 60–65 kt. Once the aircraft is on the water at this speed, the pick-up probe can be lowered by the co-pilot, and at this point, the crew need to be prepared for the bow to pitch down and to take corrective action to avoid porpoising. If the probe is lowered too soon, the bow is likely to tuck in, with the possible risk of catastrophic deceleration and sinking. The same is liable to occur if the drop doors or nose wheel doors are not retracted correctly. Once the probe has been lowered and water is being taken on, the throttles need to be opened to maintain the 60–65 kt optimum speed. Once the tanks are full, the probe is retracted and the throttles are opened further to lift the by now heavily laden aircraft from the water surface. In ideal conditions, the pick-up run would take around 15 seconds and cover about 1,600 ft. Clearly, the co-ordination of timing and speed are crucially important when operating on restricted lengths of water. Because the tanks are installed on the PBY's centre of gravity, accurate handling during the pick-up will mean that very little in the way of trim change is required. In the event of a power loss or engine failure at this point, the Catalina flight crew are rather more fortunate than others inasmuch as they can very quickly lose weight by jettisoning their cargo of water within a very short space of time! Indeed, the load can be jettisoned in less than one second!

Once over the target area, the crew open the bomb doors using an electrically operated switch, release the water and then close the doors once more before heading back to the nearest suitable lake to fill up and repeat the exercise. The tanks themselves are lined with corrosion-proofing material to prevent the adverse effect of the additives that are mixed with the water. These additives have included Phos-Check, Tenoguard, Gel-Guard and Firetrol, as well as coloured dyes. The dye enables aerial fire-fighters to see where they have dropped their loads, whilst the other additives thicken up the water to prevent

This Cyclone-powered PBY-6A is still operated as N85U by Flying Fireman Inc in Washington State. Here, it is shown dropping its load of water in anger against a fire in the north-western USA. The twin door system is plainly visible. *via Eric Johnson*

it spreading too thinly and also coat the ground below with fire-retardant material. The latter is used on the ground surrounding fires to prevent the flames spreading. The additives themselves have always been categorised into two varieties – long-term and short-term retardants.

An example of a long-term retardant is Firetrol. This is normally mixed up in a silo at a ground base and pumped into the aircraft by hose immediately prior to departure. It is bright orange in colour and very heavy. Usually, the load would be dropped using one bomb door at a time, after which the pilot would probably fly his Catalina to the nearest lake and load up with water for further drops. Gel-Gard, on the other hand, was a short-term retardant carried in a container behind the main water tanks in the hull. During a water pick-up, the red Gel-Gard dust was forced into the water compartment by compressed air. The mixture was intended to produce a drop that would not turn into a mist, but its success was mixed and this somewhat unpopular product was discontinued in the late 1970s. More recently, a foam retardant has become more common-place, and this is still used by the Catalinas of Buffalo Airways in the North West Territories of Canada. The foam is mixed with water as it is taken on. Apparently, foam is less popular with ground-based fire-fighters as its makes a slippery surface on the forest floor!

It can perhaps be seen from the above that not only is a special kind of aircraft needed for airborne fire fighting, but the crew have to be special, too. The Catalina crews need to be excellent flying boat pilots with the ability to operate out of unfamiliar lakes, sometimes of restricted size, and then fly confidently in hilly, tree-covered terrain often shrouded in smoke and with other aircraft in close proximity. They need to be fit enough to haul the heavily laden Cat around, to anticipate every next move and give the appropriate control input in time to achieve it, and to be meticulous in their cockpit checks to avoid running out of fuel or landing with drop doors open or probe extended. They have to clearly understand the type of fire they are dealing with and the properties of the retardant being used. For example, water on its own will evaporate very quickly in the heat of a major fire, and therefore it needs to be dropped accurately and from the right height if it is to be effective. Drop it from too high and the volume of water will change to a mist that will disperse and do little to quell the flames. If the trees that are being 'bombed' are of a great height and the bombing run is not carried out low enough, the water will not penetrate the foliage cover and reach the ground fire below.

In the past, many fire-fighting aircrew have been paid on the number of drops carried out, and this can lead to fatigue and increased chances of accident. It has not been unknown for Catalinas to carry out in excess of 100 drops in a day, although it would now be rare for this utilisation rate to be reached.

In its hey-day in Canada, the Catalina and Canso was in use with the Provincial Governments of Newfoundland and Labrador, Quebec and Saskatchewan, as well as private sector operators such as Flying Fireman Ltd, Avalon, Kenting and Norcanair. In the States, they were used by Sis-Q Flying Services,

Another view of PBY-6A N85U as it heads down a forested valley with pilot Eric Johnson at the helm to combat a fire raging below.
via Eric Johnson

Hemet Valley Flying Services, SLAFCO, Firefly, B. B. Bursons, Rosenbalms, Cal-Nat and, most recently, by Airborne Fire Attack and Flying Fireman Inc. The French *Protection Civile* used PBY-5As/Cansos and PBY-6As in the South of France and Corsica, and ASPAR have used a mixture of Catalina types both in their native Chile and in Spain and Portugal. The latter two countries have also seen other Catalina operators flying PBYs during the 1990s. By the late 1990s, very few Catalinas were still being used to fight fires, although they were still active in the North West Territories of Canada with Buffalo Airways and with Flying Fireman Inc. in Washington State.

Most Catalina operators in the aerial fire-suppression business have painted their aircraft in garish, high-visibility colours to avoid collisions, and in common with other fire-fighting types, they have normally carried prominent hull or tail codes, sometimes based on the state or region in which the operator was based.

Whilst water bombing has, over the years, taken its toll in terms of wrecked Catalinas and crew losses, it is none the less true to say that nowhere near as many examples of this great aircraft would have survived into the twenty-first century if they had not previously flown in this role.

The Catalina was also used for aerial spraying of forests, usually to eradicate such destructive creatures as the budworm, and for this purpose the wings were fitted with spray bars fed from internal tanks in the hull. The PBY-6A in particular was used in this role in the North West States of the USA in the late 1950s.

Air Display and Film Work
It is perhaps not surprising that such a distinctive and famous aircraft as the Catalina should prove to be a popular air display performer, although, in reality, the type has never performed in great numbers. The Royal Canadian Air Force sometimes flew its Cansos at

The Catalina makes for a distinctive sight at air shows. Here, the Plane Sailing Super Cat G-BLSC performs at a display in the late 1980s before it had its rear hull blisters put back on. The Catalina's ability to drop its floats as part of the display routine always proves popular with the audience! *(Brian Cooper)*

post-war airshows and displayed a pair using JATO gear from water on at least one occasion. Generally, though, the type was too much of a workhorse during the 1950s and 1960s to endear itself to display organisers. This changed when the popularity of former Second World War aircraft, or 'warbirds' as they have become known, began to increase from the 1970s onward.

In the USA, the Confederate Air Force (CAF) has operated no fewer than five Catalinas over the years, two being PBY-5As and the remainder PBY-6As. They tended to fly at CAF events, and rarely ventured off to other shows, although, for a brief period, the organisation did operate one of the PBY-5As and a PBY-6A together at the same time. Sadly, the CAF's association with the Catalina has been an unhappy and sometimes tragic one, with two PBY-6As being lost in fatal crashes, another PBY-6A being virtually destroyed on the ground by high winds and a PBY-5A being allowed to deteriorate beyond economic repair through neglect and lack of finance. The CAF currently owns a former fire-fighting PBY-6A, N324FA, and at the 1999 Midland CAF *Airsho* even used it to carry out a mock water bombing attack on the airfield.

Elsewhere in the USA and Canada, sporadic air display performances have been given by Catalinas, most notably by the National Warplane Museum's PBY-6A N7057C in the late 1980s and early 1990s and the Canadian Warplane Heritage Canso A C-FPQL toward the end of the 1990s. On one memorable occasion, the Province of Saskatchewan put up all three of its Canso water bombers and performed a low-level water drop to the delight of the spectators, but this was very much an isolated event!

It was in Europe that the Catalina was to establish itself as an airshow 'star', and this was entirely due to one individual aircraft. When Plane Sailing Air Displays purchased a former survey *Super Cat* in South Africa and flew it to England in February 1985, they embarked on what was to be a thirteen-year period of intensive display work throughout Europe. During this time, the aircraft, initially registered G-BLSC but later re-registered in Bermuda as VR/VP-BPS, flew in RAF and then RCAF markings and endeared itself to huge numbers of display-goers. It was supported by its own 'fan club', the Catalina Society, and did a huge amount to rekindle memories and create new interest in the type. Later it was joined by other PBYs that occasionally flew at European shows, but it was Plane Sailing's aircraft that was regarded as THE Cat! It regularly operated from water and represented RAF Coastal Command in the 1995 flypast over Central London and the Royal Family at Buckingham Palace to mark the 50th anniversary of VE Day, an occasion when this writer was privileged to be on board. Sadly, and through no fault of the crew or owners, it was badly damaged in an unfortunate accident on Southampton Water, Hampshire, in July 1998, that, at least temporarily, ended its display days, although the aircraft was later sold to new owners who are currently restoring it to flying condition. Meanwhile, Plane Sailing plan to operate another Catalina at some future date.

This Catalina also appeared in at least two motion pictures, one filmed in Norway in 1985 and the other a few years later, when it was involved in filming on the Thames for the film *Golden Eye*, starring the actor Charles Dance. At various times, other Catalinas have appeared in such films as *Steelyard Blues, Always* and *Tora! Tora! Tora!* In the last film, Catalina N6108 appeared in a flying role, but a number of other redundant PBY airframes were destroyed in a re-creation of the Pearl Harbor bombing.

A number of Catalinas were used in the making of the motion picture *Tora! Tora! Tora!* Most were destroyed in the Pearl Harbor re-enactment, but N6108 had a flying role. Pictured here at Long Beach, California, it wears pseudo-US Navy markings as aircraft 4 of VP-24.
Peter Keating Collection

Notable Long-Distance Flights

The Catalina was noted for its ability to fly long distances, and this was put to good use during the war on long-range reconnaissance flights and, most famously, on the QANTAS *Double Sunrise* flights between Ceylon and Australia. In peacetime, such quasi-military roles were made redundant, but, none the less, Catalinas have continued to make lengthy flights when necessary. There have been many transatlantic flights, and these have continued right up to the present day as surviving aircraft have been delivered to new owners. In the 1960s and 1970s, numerous Atlantic crossings were made by Canadian water bombers on their way to European contracts, mainly in France but occasionally in Scandinavia. Three Chilean aircraft even made the lengthy journey from their home country across the Andes and the South Atlantic to Spain. Similarly, survey PBYs roamed worldwide on geophysical work. The 75th anniversary of US Naval Aviation was celebrated in style by two civil-registered Catalinas in 1986 when they flew from the USA to Plymouth, England, thus re-enacting the similar flight by NC-4 flying boats in 1919.

Perhaps most notable have been the various exotic charters in which surviving Catalinas have been involved. From 1989 to the mid-1990s, the Catalina Safari Company operated a former RCAF Canso A C-FJCV, later Z-CAT, on charters up and down the length of Africa stretching from Cairo to the Victoria Falls and out to Zanzibar. The numerous charters flown were a success, despite the somewhat adverse picture painted by

the well-known BBC TV documentary, *The Last African Flying Boat*, which played up the 'adventurous' side of the undertaking, thus possibly putting off some potential clients! Whilst the idea of emulating the luxury of the old Imperial Airways flying boats was not really possible in a Catalina, the tours were none the less marvellous experiences, and this writer counts himself most fortunate to have accompanied the owners, Pierre and Antoinette Jaunet, on one of the East African charters in the summer of 1992 in Z-CAT.

The former RCAF Canso A Z-CAT was used for a number of years in the 1980s and '90s on charter flights in Africa. Here it is seen by its temporary anchorage on Lake Kivu on the Zaire/Rwanda border in 1992. Owner Pierre Jaunet is in the bow compartment, whilst pilots Bryan McCook and Dave Evans look on.
Dhar Color Bukavu

Plane Sailing's *Super Cat* VR-BPS on the water at Bimini Island in the Bahamas during the 1994 Peter Stuyvesant Travel Odyssey.
Frans Lemmens/Eurotrading

Eventually, the unpredictability of operating in Africa in those times, especially during the Gulf War, led the Jaunets to sell Z-CAT, and it went to new owners in New Zealand. The timing was fortunate as the troubles in Burundi, Zaire and Rwanda during the first half of the 1990s would have made at least the East African charters impossible. Z-CAT did still have one big journey to make before the New Zealand trip, however. The Peter Stuyvesant Travel Company planned to fly what it called a *Travel Odyssey* during the summer of 1993. Its creative promotional team decided that an amphibious Catalina would be the ideal aircraft to transport lucky passengers on a flight from Europe across to South, Central and North America, then on to Europe again. Peter Stuyvesant found the ideal aircraft and operating company in the form of the British-registered Cyclone-powered Catalina G-BLSC owned by Plane Sailing Air Displays of Duxford, England. G-BLSC had passenger seats installed and was decorated in a striking new paint scheme representing Peter Stuyvesant's colours, but at the eleventh hour, the British Civil Aviation Authority placed administrative obstacles in the way that were impossible for Plane Sailing to comply with on cost and time grounds. Faced with the possibility of not having a Catalina to operate on its charter, Peter Stuyvesant turned to Zimbabwe and the Jaunet's Z-CAT.

Z-CAT was made ready and flew the entire planned journey, but with the addition of positioning flights from Zimbabwe to Holland and back to Zimbabwe at either end of the charter, the latter being spoilt somewhat by engine problems. None the less, it was no mean achievement to complete the contract successfully.

Peter Stuyvesant Travel actually planned a series of *Travel Odysseys*, although in the end only two trips came to fruition. The second was carried out in 1994, and this time Plane Sailing was able to carry out the flying using their Catalina, by now registered in Bermuda. Again, the itinerary took in Latin and North America and involved outward and homeward legs across the South and North Atlantic respectively. Apart from some engine trouble in Brazil, the second Odyssey was carried out very successfully, and it was a disappointment to Plane Sailing that commercial factors unconnected with the Catalina led to further flights by Peter Stuyvesant being cancelled.

To date, the most recent two-way trip across the Atlantic has been that flown by the French-operated but Canadian-registered Canso C-FCRR that flew from France to South America to commemorate the pioneering postal flights on that route years before. The return flight was made via the USA and Canada, thus completing yet another epic Catalina journey.

It seems that despite the fact that surviving Catalinas had all reached at least their 55th birthday by the end of the second millennium, some of them were still capable of carrying out very long over-water trips without incident, surely a great tribute to the design and the present-day owner-operators who have kept them flying.

The following chapter describe post-war Catalina usage country by country, grouped within geographical areas, namely Africa, Australia and New Zealand, Canada, Europe including Scandinavia and the Soviet Union, Central and South America, the Near East, South East Asia and the USA.

Four
AFRICA

Very few Catalinas have operated in Africa since the Second World War, although, during that conflict, many aircraft of the Royal Air Force, South African Air Force, USAAF and US Navy operated from bases that covered almost the entire circumference of that vast continent. Since then, only a handful of commercial Catalinas have been registered in African countries, although occasional examples have been used for geophysical survey work, notably in South Africa, and various aircraft have staged through African countries on delivery flights. With the exception of South Africa, no African countries have operated military Catalinas, although Egypt is reported to have had one in its Royal Flight and Ethiopia was supposed to have been involved in the purchase of several ex-Royal Norwegian Air Force examples from the USA. In the case of Egypt, it is almost certain that no such aircraft existed, and the Ethiopian deal never reached fruition.

EGYPT

Alexander Frater, in his book *Beyond the Blue Horizon*, records a conversation with an Egyptian in which they discuss King Farouk and his aircraft. The Egyptian claimed that Farouk had a Catalina flying boat that was sent to England to be rebuilt to the King's own specification as a luxury air yacht, complete with walls covered in polar bear skin! An article on the Egyptian Air Force in *Air Pictorial* for April 1994 also mentions King Farouk's Catalina, claiming that it was not used by the King's personal pilots very much but was instead attached to 4 General Reconnaissance Squadron at Dakhayla near Alexandria, where it was generally flown by the Station Commander, Grp Capt Muhammed Farag. Apparently, this Catalina was listed in the British Air Attaché's report dated 1 January 1950, but was not listed in his later report of 24 January 1952.

No photographic evidence has surfaced to confirm the existence of this mystery Catalina, and it is possible that it could be a mis-identification of the Grumman Mallard, two of which did serve with the Egyptian Air Force. It seems most unlikely that an Egyptian Air Force Catalina ever visited England as claimed by Alexander Frater's companion. The answer may lie in an article in the 24 July 1953 issue of *Flight* magazine, in which mention is made of King Farouk ordering a *Landseaire* PBY-5A conversion from Southern California Aircraft Corporation, an aircraft that was destined not to be delivered because of the King's abdication. To add to the mystery, USAAF records reveal that OA-10A 44-34066 was apparently transferred to Egypt at the end of October 1946

ETHIOPIA

It has been reported that a number of former Royal Norwegian Air Force (RNoAF) PBY-5A Catalinas were to be supplied to the Ethiopian Air Force, although it is certain that delivery did not take place. Having been retired

48332/KK-D of 333 Squadron, Royal Norwegian Air Force, was one of the PBY-5As that were supposedly destined for the Ethiopian Air Force. In the event, none of them were delivered to Africa and they were scrapped at Wiesbaden in West Germany.
Air Britain

VP-KKJ *Namnagani* pictured at Blackbushe, England. It had a chequered history in the USAAF and as a commercial aircraft in the Philippines, Hong Kong, India and Sweden before flying out to East Africa. It ended its days in the USA.
Jennifer M. Gradidge

by the RNoAF, they were returned to the US forces who had originally supplied them and were flown to Wiesbaden in West Germany during mid-1961. There they were subsequently scrapped. The five aircraft involved were serialled 46580, 46588, 46638, 48332 and 48382, these identities being based on the original US Navy BuAer serials.

KENYA

Two Catalinas have appeared on the Kenyan civil aircraft register, although only one of them actually flew in the country, the other remaining in the USA.

The first example was VP-KKJ. This was an ex-USAAF OA-10A amphibian that had seen post-war service with airlines in the Philippines, Burma and Hong Kong before flying briefly with Kalinga Airlines in India. It then went to Sweden prior to being registered in Kenya in 1952. It was flown to England and departed from Blackbushe, Hampshire, to Nairobi in September of that year, still in its Swedish markings. Acquired by East African Airways Corporation (EAAC), it was to be used by a subsidiary company known as Seychelles and Kilimanjaro Air Transport Services Ltd, or SKAT, for exploring the possibility of operating charter flights around various East African lakes, as well as to the Seychelles and Indian Ocean islands. The heavily overloaded PBY routed Blackbushe–Marseilles–Benina–Wadi Halfa–Port Sudan–Nairobi in what turned out to be a somewhat fraught trip, aggravated by a lack of appropriate charts.

Although it was used for proving flights to various locations in mainland East Africa and out into the Indian Ocean and for passenger and freight flights, it proved uneconomic. Clearly, the commercial world was not yet ready for a return to the romance of flying boats in exotic African locations! However, VP-KKJ, or *Namnagani* as it had been christened, was about to make its mark in the

film world. EAAC had been engaged in various charter flights during the making of both *King Solomon's Mines* and *The African Queen* in 1950 and 1951. When, in late 1952, EAAC was approached by MGM to conduct support flights during the making of John Ford's film *Mogambo*, starring Clark Gable, Ava Gardner, Grace Kelly and Donald Sinden, VP-KKJ was used to fly from Nairobi up to Bukoba on Lake Victoria.

After this film work, EAAC had no further use for VP-KKJ, and it was sold in the USA, where it became N1508V, its eventual fate being unknown, although it did make the trip across the Atlantic to America. Prior to its export to the USA, the Dutch-owned Bataafsche Petroleum Mij company had applied for a Certificate of Airworthiness for the aircraft, but the acquisition did not progress any further.

The other Catalina to gain Kenyan marks was the much-registered former RCAF Canso A, serial 9793. It seems likely that the allocation in 1964 to Atlantic General Enterprises Inc. was never formally taken up, even though the registration 5Y-KUD was painted on the aircraft whilst stored at Fort Lauderdale in Florida. It seems most unlikely that it ever journeyed to Kenya, however. This aircraft was subsequently placed on the Honduran register and went on to fly in a number of countries before being lost after ditching in the Pacific Ocean.

In more recent times, Kenyan skies and the waters of Lake Victoria have been graced by the Catalina Safari Company Canso A C-FJCV/Z-CAT, although these flights ceased with its subsequent export to New Zealand.

Kenyan nationality marks had changed from VP-K to 5Y-K by the time that this Boeing of Canada-built Canso A was allocated the identity 5Y-KUD. It is shown on the ramp at Fort Lauderdale, Florida, probably the nearest it actually got to Africa!

Peter Keating Collection

Table 3. Kenyan Catalinas

Registration	C/n	Type	Place of Manufacture	Previous id(s)	Notes
VP-KKJ	CV-593	OA-10A	Canadair (Cartierville)	SE-BUB SE-XAD VT-DEX VR-HDS PI-C258 44-34082 (USAAF) Bu68046 ntu (US Navy)	To USA as N1508V, 1954.
(VP-KUD)/ 5Y-KUD	22022	Canso A	BOE CAN	HP-289 HK-996X OB-LDM-349 YV-P-APE 9793 (RCAF)	To Honduras register as HR-236, 12/1965. Then to N6108, TG-BIV, N5404J, ZK-PBY ntu. Lost in Pacific, 16/1/1994.

SOUTH AFRICA

At the end of the Second World War, a number of former RAF Catalinas that had flown with 262 Squadron and then 35 Squadron, South African Air Force, were located at Durban's Congella flying boat base in various states of airworthiness or overhaul. There they stayed whilst instructions were awaited concerning their disposal. In the end, all of these aircraft were scrapped locally during 1946, including two, FP251 and FP288, for which potential buyers had apparently been found. The fifteen aircraft involved were:

Catalina Mk IB	Catalina Mk IVB
FP174	JX284
FP185	JX319
FP226	JX337
FP251	JX348
FP254	JX353
FP279	JX362
FP288	
FP307	
FP322	

Since the demise of those fifteen Catalinas, no further examples have been registered in South Africa, although geophysical survey work has brought the occasional visitor to the country. During the second part of the 1990s, the American-registered Catalina N9521C was based at Lanseria, but this left for the USA in the summer of 1999, the trip being prematurely terminated in the UK. In October of the same year, the Canadian-registered aircraft C-FPQO arrived from Tanagra in Greece to take up residence at Rand.

ZIMBABWE

In the late 1980s through to 1994, the Harare-based Catalina Safari Company used a former RCAF Canso A on charter flights throughout the eastern side of Africa, from Cairo in the north to its home base in Zimbabwe and out to some of the western Indian Ocean Islands. Initially flown with its Canadian registration C-FJCV, it was later re-registered Z-CAT and continued to operate in and out of exotic land and water locations until exported to New Zealand, where it became ZK-PBY. A more detailed history of this aircraft may be found under the entry for New Zealand in Chapter Fourteen.

During August, 1992, the Catalina Safari Company of Zimbabwe operated its Z-CAT on a ten-day East African charter that routed Nairobi (Wilson)–Rusinga Island, Lake Victoria–Kisumu–Mwanza–Bukavu–Kigoma–Mahale Beach, Lake Tanganyika–Tabora–Zanzibar–Tanga–Nairobi (Wilson). Z-CAT is pictured at Tabora during a mid-day refuelling stop before departing to Zanzibar.
Author

Table 4. Zimbabwean Catalinas

Registration	C/n	Type	Place of Manufacture	Previous id(s)	Notes
Z-CAT	CV-357	Canso A	CAN VIC (Cartierville)	C-FJCV CF-JCV 11054 (RCAF)	To New Zealand as ZK-PBY which see chapter 14.

Two further ex-RCAF Canso As were due to start operating on tourist flights based in Zimbabwe towards the end of 1999. This plan did not come to fruition and the pair remained in Canada, even though a great deal of work had already been carried out on the airframes to de-convert them from water bombers and to prepare them for their new passenger-carrying role. The two aircraft involved were C-FNJB and C-FNJF.

Five
AUSTRALIA AND NEW ZEALAND

The Air Forces of both Australia and New Zealand were flying Catalinas at the close of the Second World War and continued to do so for some time after. In addition, various commercial companies and airlines used the type, although at the present time (late 2000), there is only one airworthy example in the area, that being New Zealand's ZK-PBY.

AUSTRALIA

MILITARY CATALINAS

The Royal Australian Air Force (RAAF) started to operate Catalinas as early as March 1941, and it went on to receive a total of 168 examples of various marks, the last being delivered just after the end of the Second World War. The serial blocks of RAAF Catalinas can be summarised as listed below, although it should be noted that some of the amphibious versions were subject to local conversions to flying boat format through the removal of their undercarriages. These latter aircraft became known as the PBY-5AM:

Model 28-5MA	A24-1 to A24-18
Model 28-5MC	A24-19 to A24-27 (diversions from RCAF Canso/RAF Catalina IIA)
PBY-4	A24-28 to A24-29
PBY-5	A24-30 to A24-68
PBY-5A	A24-69 to A24-114
PB2B-1	A24-200 to A24-206
PB2B-2	A24-300 to A24-309
PB2B-2	A24-350 to A24-386

Note: The spurious RAAF serial A24-387 was used from the 1980s onward by the Confederate Air Force PBY-5A N68756.

By the end of hostilities, many of the earlier RAAF Catalinas had been lost through attrition and enemy action, and a few of the wrecks are still extant. Some others were reduced to spare parts as the war's end approached. As this book is primarily intended to survey peacetime Catalina operations, the valuable wartime contribution made by the RAAF Catalina squadrons is outside its scope, but their exploits have been covered in other published works – see the Bibliography.

Almost as soon as hostilities were over, the Catalina squadrons began to find themselves surplus to requirements. No. 42 Squadron disbanded in November 1945, and whilst both 20 and 43 Squadrons transferred to Rathmines, it was only a few months before they too ceased to exist. No. 11 Squadron was disbanded in February 1946.

This left only the various Catalina-equipped Air Sea Rescue (ASR) flights still operational. These were 111 ASR Flight, initially at Madang, New Guinea, but at Port Moresby in Papua New Guinea from March 1946; 112 ASR Flight at Darwin; 113 ASR Flight which moved from Labuan in Borneo to Rathmines in January 1946; 114 ASR Flight at Cairns and later Townsville, and 115 ASR Flight which was disbanded in March 1946 at Morotai.

No. 113 Flight later served at Iwakuni in Japan, but ceased to exist after returning to Australia in April 1946. No. 111 ASR Flight was the next to go when it halted operations in January 1947. Nos. 112 and 114 were disbanded in October 1947, and the remains of the flights were re-formed as the Search and Rescue Wing based at Rathmines, later to be renamed 11 (General Reconnaissance) Squadron, but still flying Catalinas. By 1950, only two Catalinas were on 11 (GR) Squadron strength, operating out of Darwin, and the unit did not last beyond the end of that year. Thus ended the Catalina's illustrious operational career with the RAAF.

One example did serve with the RAAF's Aircraft Research and Development Unit (ARDU) based at Point Cook. This aircraft was PBY-5A A24-104, and it was used to trial the use of Jet Assisted Take Off, or JATO. Equipped with four JATO units, two on each side of the aft hull, trials had commenced in May 1948. However, the trials were interrupted when the Catalina was required to fly down to the Australian research base at Macquarie Island in the Antarctic in order to transport a new member to the 1948 Macquarie Island Expedition Party. A24-104 flew from Point Cook on 22 July and routed via Hobart, Tasmania. It arrived at its eventual destination on 4 August and anchored in Buckles Bay. The Catalina departed later the same day using its JATO equipment, and returned to Rathmines via Christchurch, New Zealand. After a spell with 11 Squadron, it went back to ARDU until November 1948, and was eventually one of several Catalinas presented to the Netherlands Government for continued military usage.

The retired RAAF Catalinas were assembled at either No. 1 Flying Boat Repair Depot, Lake Boga, or at Rathmines, where they awaited an uncertain future.

Some were scrapped whilst others were offered for sale/tender on the commercial market, many in poor condition. In the end, a few examples acquired civilian registrations, but many were scrapped by their new owners. A number were presented to the Government of the Netherlands for operation in Dutch New Guinea. These latter aircraft were overhauled first by Bristol Aviation at Bankstown.

Table 5 shows the fates of the RAAF Catalinas that were extant after the end of the Second World War. The initials CDC stand for the Commonwealth Disposals Commission. Those aircraft that were sold on the commercial market are also covered in the section on Australian Commercial Catalinas.

Table 5. Australian military Catalinas

Serial	C/n	Type	Place of Manufacture	Previous id(s)	Notes
A24-2	40	Model 28-5MA	CON SD	VH-AFC A24-1 ntu	Sold by CDC to Botterill & Fraser, 12/1947.
A24-4	113	Model 28-5MA	CON SD	VH-AFE	Sold by CDC to Kingsford-Smith Aviation Svs, 10/1946.
A24-10	270	Model 28-5MA	CON SD	VH-AFK	Sold by CDC to Botterill & Fraser, 12/1947. Sold to R. R. Cobley as VH-BEF ntu. Subsequently to Major E. C. Daniels and A. E. S. Taylor. Scrapped at Lake Boga.
A24-14	313	Model 28-5MA	CON SD	VH-AFO	Sold by CDC to Kingsford-Smith Aviation Svs, 10/1946.
A24-19	382	Canso/ Catalina IIA	CON SD	VA734 (RAF) V9734 9734 (RCAF)	As above
A24-21	389	Canso/ Catalina IIA	CON SD	VA736 (RAF) V9736 9736 (RCAF)	Sold by CDC to J. E. Wood, 4/1948.
A24-26	292	Canso/ Catalina IIA	CON SD	VA711 (RAF) V9711 9711 (RCAF)	Sold by CDC to W. or N. R. Carpenter Pty, 10/1946. To Botterill & Fraser then R. R. Cobley as VH-BDP. Crashed on take-off, Djambi, Sumatra, as RI-005, 29/12/1948.
A24-27	316	Canso/ Catalina IIA	CON SD	V9717/ VA717 (RAF) 9717 (RCAF)	Sold by CDC to Kingsford-Smith Aviation Svs, 10/1946.
A24-28	7	PBY-4	CON SD	Bu1219 (US Navy)	As above
A24-29	4	PBY-4	CON SD	Bu1216 (US Navy)	As above. Current as paddle boat conversion on Murray River – see Chapter 14.
A24-30	(Composite airframe)	PBY-5	CON SD	Bu2305(US Navy)/Y-72 (NEIAF)	Sold by CDC to Kingsford-Smith Aviation Svs, 10/1946. This aircraft has often been incorrectly quoted as the former US Navy Bu08114.
A24-31	1047	PBY-5	CON SD	Bu08153 (US Navy)	Sold by CDC to Australair Ltd, 11/1947.
A24-35	1055	PBY-5	CON SD	Bu08161 (US Navy)	Sold by CDC to S. Middlemiss for Barrier Reef Airways, 11/1947.
A24-37	1094	PBY-5	CON SD	Bu08200 (US Navy)	Sold by CDC to Australian National Airways, 10/1946.
A24-40	1095	PBY-5	CON SD	Bu08201 (US Navy)	As above.
A24-44	1101	PBY-5	CON SD	Bu08207 (US Navy)	Sold by CDC to Kingsford-Smith Aviation Svs, 1/1948.
A24-46	1186	PBY-5	CON SD	Bu08272 (US Navy)	Sold by CDC to C. K. Campbell, 11/1947.
A24-47	1198	PBY-5	CON SD	Bu08284 (US Navy)	Sold by CDC to J. E. Wood, 11/1947.
A24-51	1257	PBY-5	CON SD	Bu08333 (US Navy)	Sold by CDC to Australair, Ltd, 11/1947.
A24-55	1260	PBY-5	CON SD	Bu08336 (US Navy)	Sold by CDC to C. K. Campbell, 11/1947.
A24-56	1200	PBY-5	CON SD	Bu08286 (US Navy)	Sold by CDC to Kingsford-Smith Aviation Svs, 1/1948.
A24-57	1264	PBY-5	CON SD	Bu08340 (US Navy)	Sold by CDC to Australair Ltd, 11/1947.
A24-58	1265	PBY-5	CON SD	Bu08341 (US Navy)	Sold by CDC to S. Middlemiss for Barrier Reef Airways, 11/1947.
A24-59	1324	PBY-5	CON SD	Bu08400 (US Navy)	Sold by CDC to John Fairfax & Sons Pty Ltd (Sydney Morning Herald), 3/1947.
A24-60	1328	PBY-5	CON SD	Bu08404 (US Navy)	Sold by CDC to C. K. Campbell, 11/1947.
A24-61	1330	PBY-5	CON SD	Bu08406 (US Navy)	As above.
A24-62	1340	PBY-5/ Catalina IVA	CON SD	JX238 (RAF)	Sold by CDC to Kingsford-Smith Aviation Svs Ltd, 1/1948.
A24-63	1341	PBY-5/ Catalina IVA	CON SD	JX239 (RAF)	Sold by CDC to Australair Ltd, 11/1947.
A24-65	1433	PBY-5	CON SD	Bu08489 (US Navy)	Sold by CDC to C. K. Campbell, 11/1947.
A24-66	1443	PBY-5	CON SD	Bu08499 (US Navy)	Sold by CDC to J. E. Wood, 11/1947.
A24-68	1458	PBY-5	CON SD	Bu08504 (US Navy)	Sold by CDC to Kingsford-Smith Aviation Svs, 1/1948.
A24-69	See note at end of list	PBY-5A	CON SD	See note at end of list	Destroyed by fire whilst moored at East Arm, Darwin, 14/12/1945. Submerged wreck still there.
A24-70	1613	PBY-5A	CON SD	Bu34059 (US Navy)	Damaged beyond repair when blown ashore at Broome, WA 28/10/1945.

N6453C is typical of a US West Coast borate bomber in the early 1970s. A Wright Cyclone-powered Super Cat, it has retained its original PBY-6A rudder. This particular example was operated by Hemet Valley Flying Services.

After being withdrawn from service by the Royal Danish Air Force, PBY-6A L-866 was presented to the RAF and flown to Colerne, where it is seen in full RDAF colours. It is now preserved in the RAF Museum, Cosford.
MAP

When Geoterrex Surveys of Ottawa first operated its
Catalina CF-MIR, it was painted in this magnificent colour
scheme. It flew all over the world on geophysical survey
work before being sold to British owner Plane Sailing Air
Displays in 1984.

Plane Sailing's Catalina was operated throughout Europe,
and, latterly flew in the colours of RCAF 9754/P, as flown
by Flt Lt David Hornell. It is shown here flying over
Zweibrucken in Saarland, Germany, viewed from the co-
pilot's seat of Basler Turbo DC-3 N96BF
Author

A sunset view of Z-CAT of the Catalina Safari Company anchored at Mahale Camp, Lake Tanganyika, Tanzania, in August 1992, during an East African charter.
Author

Robert Franks frequently used his PBY on water, as evidenced by this lovely view of N69RF on Clear Lake, California, in September 1992.
via Adrian Balch

In the 1970s, airborne fire suppression in the Canadian Province of Saskatchewan was carried out by Norcanair. Their fleet included C-FUAW/16, shown here in 1978. It is still a fire fighter with Buffalo Air in the North-West Territories.
MAP

Further west, British Columbia used the fire-fighting services of Victoria-based Flying Fireman Ltd. At the end of a busy season, PBY-5A C-FFFA rests at its home base with a sister aircraft.
Author

After a spell with the Greenpeace organisation, N423RS was stored at Duxford in England awaiting a buyer. It was pictured there in late 1998.
Author

Imported into Canada having originally served with the US forces, CF-DFB flew with a number of operators before being preserved at Botwood, Newfoundland. It was one of several examples used by Austin Airways, in whose livery it is shown here.

Painted to commemorate the crossing of the Atlantic by
US Navy NC-4s in 1919, Wilson Connie Edwards's PBY-6A
N4NC visited RNAS Yeovilton after re-enacting the flight in
the summer of 1986.
MAP

ASPAR's PBY-6A CC-CCS keeps company with the one-
time OA-10A CC-CDT at Salamanca in Spain during
September 1991.
Michael Prophet

Jacques Cousteau used this beautiful PBY-6A N101CS
Calypso to support his marine operations. Sadly, his son
Phillipe was killed in it when it crashed in Portugal.

In 1996, Aerocondor were using SAE.SA's Catalina EC-
FMC on fire-fighting contracts in Spain, one of a number of
the type that had migrated to that country in the late 1980s
and early 1990s.
Roberto Yáñez

Venezuelan-registered YV-O-CFO-4 was one of two
Catalinas used to support dredging operations in and
around the Orinoco.

The large fleet of water bombers used by Ontario's Avalon
Aviation were all painted bright orange, although some had
started out in red and white colours. When the company
ceased trading, its PBY-6A C-FHNH was in Europe, and it
has remained in storage in England since the mid-1980s!
This photo was taken at North Weald.
Author

PBY-5 A24-66/R is known to have served during the war with 43 Squadron and 2 Operational Training Unit before being sold as surplus to J. E. Wood in late 1947. It did not aspire to a civilian identity and was probably broken up for spares. It is seen here landing at Rathmines, NSW.

Serial	C/n	Type	Place of Manufacture	Previous id(s)	Notes
A24-71	1611	PBY-5A	CON SD	Bu34057 (US Navy)	Sold by CDC to Kingsford-Smith Aviation Svs, 1/1948.
A24-72	1612	PBY-5A	CON SD	Bu34058 (US Navy)	Sold to Grant Trading Pty Ltd, 1/1953. Scrapped.
A24-75	1659	PBY-5A	CON SD	Bu48297 (US Navy)	Sold by CDC to Mr Kennedy, 5/1947.
A24-77	1663	PBY-5A	CON SD	Bu48301 (US Navy)	Sold by CDC to C. K. Campbell, 11/1947.
A24-78	1664	PBY-5A	CON SD	Bu48302 (US Navy)	Sold by CDC to S. Middlemiss for Barrier Reef Airways, 11/1947.
A24-79	1706	PBY-5A	CON SD	Bu48344 (US Navy)	Sold by CDC to A. W. Guthrie, 11/1947.
A24-80	1711	PBY-5A	CON SD	Bu48349 (US Navy)	Sold by CDC to Kingsford-Smith Aviation Svs, 1/1948.
A24-81	1712	PBY-5A	CON SD	Bu48350 (US Navy)	As above.
A24-82	See note at end of list	PBY-5A	CON SD	See note at end of list	Sold by CDC to S. Middlemiss for Barrier Reef Airways, 11/1947.
A24-83	1708	PBY-5A	CON SD	Bu48346 (US Navy)	Sold by CDC to Kingsford-Smith Aviation Svs, 1/1948.
A24-84	1707	PBY-5A	CON SD	Bu48345 (US Navy)	As above.
A24-85	1713	PBY-5A	CON SD	Bu48351 (US Navy)	As above.
A24-86	1718	PBY-5A	CON SD	Bu48356 (US Navy)	Sold by CDC to J. E. Wood, 11/1947.
A24-87	1710	PBY-5A	CON SD	Bu48348 (US Navy)	Sold by CDC to John Fairfax & Sons Pty Ltd (Sydney Morning Herald), 3/1947.

Serial	C/n	Type	Place of Manufacture	Previous id(s)	Notes
A24-88	1714	PBY-5A	CON SD	Bu48352 (US Navy)	Sold by CDC to Kingsford-Smith Aviation Svs, 1/1948.
A24-89	1716	PBY-5A	CON SD	Bu48354 (US Navy)	Sold by CDC to S. Middlemiss for Barrier Reef Airways, 1/1947.
A24-92	1855	PBY-5A	CON SD	Bu46491 (US Navy)	To Dutch Government as 16-223, 1953. Used for spares only.
A24-93	1715	PBY-5A	CON SD	Bu48353 (US Navy)	Sold by CDC to Kingsford-Smith Aviation Svs, 1/1948.
A24-95	1854	PBY-5A	CON SD	Bu46490 (US Navy)	Sold by CDC to John Fairfax & Sons Pty Ltd (Sydney Morning Herald), 11/1947.
A24-97	1897	PBY-5A	CON SD	Bu46533 (US Navy)	Sold by CDC to C. K. Campbell, 11/1947.
A24-99	1899	PBY-5A	CON SD	Bu46535 (US Navy)	To Dutch Government as 16-224, 1953. Scrapped at Biak, New Guinea, 7/1957.
A24-102	1942	PBY-5A	CON SD	Bu46578 (US Navy)	Sold by CDC to C. K. Campbell, 11/1947.
A24-103	1943	PBY-5A	CON SD	Bu46579 (US Navy)	Sold by CDC to Australian National Airways, 10/1946.
A24-104	1958	PBY-5A	CON SD	Bu46594 (US Navy)	To Dutch Government as 16-220, 1953. Scrapped, Biak, New Guinea, 11/1956.
A24-105?		PBY-5A	CON NO	?(US Navy)	Lost in crash near Georgetown, Queensland, 7/5/1950.
A24-106	1969	PBY-5A	CON NO	Bu46605 (US Navy)	Damaged beyond repair after colliding with hangar, Darwin, 26/11/1946.
A24-109	1972	PBY-5A	CON NO	Bu46608 (US Navy)	Sold to Airmotive Supply Corpn, USA 1953.
A24-110	1983	PBY-5A	CON NO	Bu46619 (US Navy)	To Dutch Government as 16-221, 1953. Scrapped, Biak, New Guinea, 8/1956.
A24-111	1984	PBY-5A	CON NO	Bu46620 (US Navy)	To Dutch Government as 16-222, 1953. Scrapped, Biak, New Guinea, 4/1958.
A24-112	1985	PBY-5A	CON NO	Bu46621 (US Navy)	To Dutch Government as 16-225, 1953. Scrapped, Biak, New Guinea, 1/1957.
A24-113	1986	PBY-5A	CON NO	Bu46622 (US Navy)	Hull damaged and sank, Champagney Islands, 4/6/1946.

Serial	C/n	Type	Place of Manufacture	Previous id(s)	Notes
A24-114	1987	PBY-5A	CON NO	Bu46623 (US Navy)	Sold to Airmotive Supply Corpn USA, 1953.
A24-200	61133	PB2B-1/ Catalina IVB	BOE CAN	JX617 (RAF) Bu44227 (US Navy)	As above.
A24-201	61124	PB2B-1/ Catalina IVB	BOE CAN	JX612 (RAF) Bu44218 (US Navy)	As above.
A24-202	61132	PB2B-1/ Catalina IVB	BOE CAN	JX616 (RAF) Bu44226 (US Navy)	Sold to Butler Air Transport, 10/1946.
A24-300	61135	PB2B-2/ Catalina VI	BOE CAN	JX619 (RAF) Bu44229 (US Navy)	Sold by CDC to QANTAS, 10/1946 and used for spares.
A24-302	61136	PB2B-2/ Catalina VI	BOE CAN	JX620 (RAF) Bu44230 (US Navy)	Sold to Airmotive Supply Corpn USA, 5/1953.
A24-303	61137	PB2B-2/ Catalina VI	BOE CAN	JX621 (RAF) Bu44231 (US Navy)	Sold by CDC to Asian Airlines Pty Ltd, 1/1948 then to QANTAS, 9/1949 as VH-EBA.
A24-304	61143	PB2B-2/ Catalina VI	BOE CAN	JX627 (RAF) Bu44237 (US Navy)	Sold by CDC to Poulson & Middlemiss for Barrier Reef Airways, 10/1946.
A24-305	61134	PB2B-2/ Catalina VI	BOE CAN	JX618 (RAF) Bu44228 (US Navy)	Sold by CDC to Asian Airlines Pty Ltd 1/1948 then to QANTAS as VH-EBB. Used for spares in 1951.
A24-306	61139	PB2B-2/ Catalina VI	BOE CAN	JX623 (RAF) Bu44233 (US Navy)	Sold by CDC to QANTAS, 12/1946 and used for spares.
A24-307	61138	PB2B-2/ Catalina VI	BOE CAN	JX622 (RAF) Bu44232 (US Navy)	Sold to Airmotive Supply Corpn USA, 5/1953.
A24-309	61142	PB2B-2/ Catalina VI	BOE CAN	JX626 (RAF) Bu44236 (US Navy)	Sold by CDC to QANTAS, 12/1946 and used for spares.
A24-350	61185	PB2B-2/ Catalina VI	BOE CAN	JX661 (RAF) Bu44279 (US Navy)	Sold by CDC to Capt P. G. Taylor, 10/1946. To W. R. Carpenter as VH-ALN. To QANTAS as VH-EBC. Broken up and scrapped in 1958.
A24-351	61192	PB2B-2/ Catalina VI	BOE CAN	JZ833 (RAF) Bu44286 (US Navy)	Sold by CDC to A. C. M. Jackaman, 12/1946. To Netherlands Government as P-208. Scuttled in Surubaya, 1950.
A24-352	61184	PB2B-2/ Catalina VI	BOE CAN	JX660 (RAF) Bu44278 (US Navy)	Sold to Airmotive Supply Corpn USA, 5/1953.
A24-353	61187	PB2B-2/ Catalina VI	BOE CAN	JZ828 (RAF) Bu44281 (US Navy)	Reduced to spares in 1948.
A24-354	61188	PB2B-2/ Catalina VI	BOE CAN	JZ829 (RAF) Bu44282 (US Navy)	Sold by CDC to QANTAS, 12/1946 and used for spares.

This fine study is of JZ841, a Boeing of Canada-built PB2B-2 that was intended for the RAF but went instead to the RAAF as A24-360, arriving just before the war's end. Initially on the strength of 43 Squadron and painted black overall, it soon moved on and flew with both 113 and 115 Air Sea Rescue Flights until it was withdrawn and sold to the Airmotive Supply Corporation. It is shown here with an eyeball turret, forward radome and long exhaust covers that were part of the wing de-icing system. The last PB2B-2 built, it carried the name of the RCAF VC winner David Hornell at a handover ceremony at the Vancouver factory, but this was soon removed. The last two batches of Boeing-built Catalinas totalled 107 airframes, which seems to explain why the number 107 is painted on the port engine cowling.

Serial	C/n	Type	Place of Manufacture	Previous id(s)	Notes
A24-355	61195	PB2B-2/ Catalina VI	BOE CAN	JZ836 (RAF) Bu44289 (US Navy)	As above, 10/1946.
A24-356	61191	PB2B-2/ Catalina VI	BOE CAN	JZ832 (RAF) Bu44285 (US Navy)	Sold by CDC to R. Carr, 10/1946.
A24-357	61157	PB2B-2/ Catalina VI	BOE CAN	JX633 (RAF) Bu44251 (US Navy)	Sold by CDC to QANTAS, 10/1946 and used for spares.
A24-358	61172	PB2B-2/ Catalina VI	BOE CAN	JX648 (RAF) Bu44266 (US Navy)	Sold by CDC to Capt P. G. Taylor, 10/1946. To Netherlands Government as P-207. Scuttled, Surubaya, 7/1950.
A24-359	61188	PB2B-2/ Catalina VI	BOE CAN	JZ831 (RAF) Bu44284 (US Navy)	Sold to Airmotive Supply Corpn USA, 5/1953.
A24-360	61200	PB2B-2/ Catalina VI	BOE CAN	JZ841 (RAF) Bu44294 (US Navy)	As above.
A24-361	61167	PB2B-2/ Catalina VI	BOE CAN	JX643 (RAF) Bu44261 (US Navy)	Sold by CDC to F. H. Bridgewater for Island Airways, 9/1946 as VH-BDQ. To QANTAS, 11/1949 as VH-EBU. Wfu, 1952.
A24-362	61104	PB2B-2/ Catalina VI	BOE CAN	JZ835 (RAF) Bu44288 (US Navy)	Sold by CDC to Butler Air Transport, 10/1946.

Serial	C/n	Type	Place of Manufacture	Previous id(s)	Notes
A24-363	61153	PB2B-2/ Catalina VI	BOE CAN	JX629 (RAF) Bu44247 (US Navy)	Sold to Airmotive Supply Corpn USA, 5/1953.
A24-364	61197	PB2B-2/ Catalina VI	BOE CAN	JZ838 (RAF) Bu44291 (US Navy)	Sold by CDC to Poulson & Middlemiss for Barrier Reef Airways and Ansett Flying Boat Svs Pty Ltd as VH-BRB. Wfu, 1953.
A24-365	61162	PB2B-2/ Catalina VI	BOE CAN	JX638 (RAF) Bu44256 (US Navy)	Crashed into sea south-east of Mindanao, 10/10/1945.
A24-366	61170	PB2B-2/ Catalina VI	BOE CAN	JX646 (RAF) Bu44264 (US Navy)	Sold by CDC to A. C. M. Jackaman, 12/1946. To Netherlands Government as P-210. Scuttled, Surubaya, 7/1950.
A24-367	61198	PB2B-2/ Catalina VI	BOE CAN	JZ839 (RAF) Bu44292 (US Navy)	Sold by CDC to QANTAS, 10/1946 and used for spares.
A24-368	61160	PB2B-2/ Catalina VI	BOE CAN	JX636 (RAF) Bu44254 (US Navy)	Sold to Airmotive Supply Corpn USA, 5/1953.
A24-369	61193	PB2B-2/ Catalina VI	BOE CAN	JZ834 (RAF) Bu44287 (US Navy)	Sold by CDC, 10/1946 to Poulson & Middlemiss for Barrier Reef Airways and Ansett Flying Boat Svs Pty Ltd as VH-BRA. Wfu, 1953.
A24-371	61165	PB2B-2/ Catalina VI	BOE CAN	JX641 (RAF) Bu44259 (US Navy)	Loaned and later sold to QANTAS, 12/1949 as VH-EBD. Scrapped in 1958.

Serial	C/n	Type	Place of Manufacture	Previous id(s)	Notes
A24-372	61186	PB2B-2/ Catalina VI	BOE CAN	JX662 (RAF) Bu44280 (US Navy)	Loaned and later sold to QANTAS, 2/1949 as VH-EAX. Written off at Lord Howe Island, 23/6/1949.
A24-373	61155	PB2B-2/ Catalina VI	BOE CAN	JX631 (RAF) Bu44249 (US Navy)	Sold to Airmotive Supply Corpn USA, 5/1953.
A24-374	61164	PB2B-2/ Catalina VI	BOE CAN	JX640 (RAF) Bu44258 (US Navy)	Sold to Airmotive Supply Corpn USA, 5/1953.
A24-375	61176	PB2B-2/ Catalina VI	BOE CAN	JX652 (RAF) Bu44270 (US Navy)	Sold to Airmotive Supply Corpn USA, 5/1953.
A24-376	61161	PB2B-2/ Catalina VI	BOE CAN	JX637 (RAF) Bu44255 (US Navy)	Sold by CDC to Butler Air Transport, 10/1946.
A24-377	61196	PB2B-2/ Catalina VI	BOE CAN	JZ837 (RAF) Bu44290 (US Navy)	Sold to Airmotive Supply Corpn USA, 5/1953.
A24-378	61159	PB2B-2/ Catalina VI	BOE CAN	JX635 (RAF) Bu44253 (US Navy)	Loaned and later sold to QANTAS, 10/1947 as VH-EAW. Destroyed by bomb explosion at Rose Bay, 27/8/1949.
A24-379	61166	PB2B-2/ Catalina VI	BOE CAN	JX642 (RAF) Bu44260 (US Navy)	Sold by CDC to QANTAS, 10/1946 and used for spares.

PB2B-2 Catalina A24-372 soldiered on with the RAAF's 20 Sqn until passing to QANTAS as VH-EAX in February 1949. This photo was taken at anchor in Rose Bay, Sydney, before it was lost in a crash at Lord Howe Island on 23 June of the same year.
QANTAS via François Prins

A24-385 was given to Capt P. G. Taylor for his pioneering flights from Australia to Chile and back. Registered as VH-ASA, it is shown at RAAF Rathmines before departing on the first stage of its journey. JATO (Jet Assisted Take Off) bottles can be seen aft of the rear wing struts.
Geoff Goodall via Bob Livingstone

Serial	C/n	Type	Place of Manufacture	Previous id(s)	Notes
A24-380	61189	PB2B-2/ Catalina VI	BOE CAN	JZ830 (RAF) Bu44283 (US Navy)	Sold to Airmotive Supply Corpn USA, 5/1953.
A24-381	61163	PB2B-2/ Catalina VI	BOE CAN	JX639 (RAF) Bu44257 (US Navy)	Crashed at Lord Howe Island, 28/9/1948 during night navex whilst with 11 Sqn.
A24-382	61156	PB2B-2/ Catalina VI	BOE CAN	JX632 (RAF) Bu44250 (US Navy)	Sold to Airmotive Supply Corpn USA, 5/1953.
A24-383	61169	PB2B-2/ Catalina VI	BOE CAN	JX645 (RAF) Bu44263 (US Navy)	Sold to Airmotive Supply Corpn USA, 5/1953.
A24-384	61199	PB2B-2 Catalina VI	BOE CAN	JZ840 (RAF) Bu44293 (US Navy)	Sold by CDC to Capt P. G. Taylor, 10/1946. To Netherlands Government as P-209. Scuttled, Surubaya, 1950.
A24-385	61154	PB2B-2/ Catalina VI	BOE CAN	JX630 (RAF) Bu44248 (US Navy)	To Capt P. G. Taylor as VH-ASA *Frigate Bird II*, 8/1950. Current – see Chapter 14.
A24-386	61158	PB2B-2/ Catalina VI	BOE CAN	JX634 (RAF) Bu44252 (US Navy)	Sold to Airmotive Supply Corpn USA, 5/1953.

Note: Various sources have quoted the c/n and previous identity for both A24-69 and A24-82 as 1610 and Bu34056. A24-69 seems the most likely candidate for these identities, leaving those for A24-82 unknown.

COMMERCIAL CATALINAS

The first Catalinas to appear on the Australian civil register were in fact the initial aircraft destined for the Royal Australian Air Force during the early part of the Second World War. These were in effect ferry registrations only,

and are included here for the sake of completeness. All the aircraft were built by Consolidated at San Diego as Model 28-5MAs, equivalent to the PBY-5, and were delivered during 1941.

Table 6. Initial Australian commercial Catalinas

Civil Registration	C/n	Military Serial	Notes/Fate
VH-AFA	27	A24-1(2)	ex-AH534 (RAF). Crashed on take-off, East Arm, Darwin, 30/8/1945. Wreck still extant. See Chapter Twenty-one.
VH-AFB ntu	57	–	Intended for RAAF as A24-2 but not delivered. To RAF as DP202 and later transferred to RCAF in Canada as replacement for W8430. Subsequently to Netherlands Navy as P-200.
VH-AFC	40	A24-2	Ex-A24-1(1) ntu. Sold by CDC to Botterill & Fraser, 12/1947.
VH-AFD	78	A24-3	Destroyed at Port Moresby, PNG by enemy action, 28/2/1942.
VH-AFE	113	A24-4	Sold by CDC to Kingsford-Smith Aviation Svs, 10/1946.
VH-AFF	164	A24-5	Destroyed at Port Moresby, PNG by enemy action, 24/4/1942.
VH-AFG	189	A24-6	Destroyed at Port Moresby, PNG by enemy action, 28/2/1942.
VH-AFH	218	A24-7	Destroyed at Port Moresby, PNG by enemy action, 28/2/1942.
VH-AFI	250	A24-8	Shot down by Japanese fighter, Salamaua, 21/1/1942.
VH-AFJ	259	A24-9	Shot down by Japanese fighter, Salamaua, 21/1/1942.
VH-AFK	270	A24-10	Sold by CDC to Botterill & Fraser, 12/1947. Sold to R. Cobley as VH-BEF but ntu. To Major E. C. Daniels and A. E. S. Taylor. Scrapped at Lake Boga.
VH-AFL	279	A24-11	Sank in heavy sea, Kavieng, 15/1/1942.
VH-AFM	299	A24-12	Destroyed in storm at Rathmines, 15/9/1942.
VH-AFN	307	A24-13	Lost in enemy action, Rabaul, 24/2/1942.
VH-AFO	313	A24-14	Sold by CDC to Kingsford-Smith Aviation Svs, 10/1946.
VH-AFP	322	A24-15	Crashed into hill at Port Moresby, PNG after take-off, 8/12/1941.
VH-AFQ	332	A24-16	Damaged beyond repair after water loop at Rathmines, 10/4/1943.
VH-AFR	342	A24-17	Used as spares, 1945.
VH-AFS	350	A24-18	Shot down by Japanese aircraft, Coral Sea, 4/5/1942.

Immediately post-war, a large number of former RAAF Catalinas were acquired from the surplus stocks at Lake Boga and Rathmines. Not all of the new owners were intending to use their aircraft for flying purposes, and many were reduced to spares or used for non-aviation purposes. The latter included conversion to marine vessels such as pleasure boats and houseboats, some of which still survive. A small number of Catalinas did, however, go on to see commercial use in Australia, and were later joined by other examples of non-Australian origin. Sadly, there are no airworthy Catalinas in Australia now, although a few preserved examples do exist on static display.

The owner-operators of Catalinas in Australia are analysed below in alphabetical order, and Table 7 gives full details of the individual aircraft that were Australian-registered.

VH-AGB came to Australia from Canada to carry out aerial survey work with Adastra Hunting Geophysics, whose titles are painted on the upper hull in this view at Sydney, taken in May 1958. In addition to a MAD tail below the rudder, a wire coil is supported by struts above the rear hull.
Peter Keating Collection

Adastra Hunting Geophysics

In November 1956, the former Canadian survey Catalina CF-GKI was placed on the Australian register as VH-AGB in the name of Adastra. It only remained registered for around six months, after which it languished at Mascot. It was later sold to Trans-Australia Airlines (TAA), which used it for spares for its own VH-SBV at nearby Bankstown.

Airmotive Supply Corporation USA

No fewer than nineteen surplus Catalinas were acquired from RAAF stocks after the war by this American company, and these are all listed toward the end of Table 5 above. It is most likely that all of these aircraft were used for spares recovery only.

Ansett Flying Boat Services

Ansett became the owner of two Catalinas, VH-BRA and

Ansett Flying Boat Services operated three Catalinas at various times, the last being VH-BRI, which was photographed at Rose Bay, Sydney, in November 1960. The name *The Golden Islander* is painted on the 'clipper' bow just ahead of the cockpit.
Peter Keating Collection

VH-BRB, when it took over Barrier Reef Airways in 1953. VH-BRA was flown on a small number of charter flights from Rose Bay, Sydney, out into the Pacific, taking in such destinations as Noumea, Suva, Papeete and Samoa. The Catalinas did not last long with Ansett, however, and the registrations were cancelled during the same year, the airframes being scrapped.

This was not the end of Ansett's Catalina operations, though, as in 1959 they acquired the amphibious PBY-5A VH-BRI and had it flown from the USA. From October 1959, it flew services linking Proserpine and Hayman Island, but in July 1962 it sank after a heavy landing at Hayman Island. It was salvaged but never flew again and was converted into a motor cruiser, in which format it still survives.

Asian Airlines Pty Ltd

Two Catalinas were purchased from the RAAF by Asian Airlines, these being the PB2B-2s A24-303 and A24-305. They both ended up with QANTAS. Asian Airlines also acquired the former A24-75 in December 1947, and it became VH-BDY before being withdrawn in July 1949.

Australair Ltd

Four Catalinas were obtained from RAAF stocks after the war, but they appear to have faded into obscurity thereafter. The aircraft were A24-31, A24-51, A24-57 and A24-63.

Australian National Airways

Another company that acquired surplus military Catalinas that do not appear to have gone on to fly again. The three examples were A24-37, A24-40 and A24-103.

Australian Selection Ltd – *see* Selco Exploration Company

Australasian Petroleum

This company was involved in exploration in New Guinea and used two PBYs to support its operations. They were actually flown by World Wide Air Services. The first was VH-WWB and was acquired in March 1956. The other was VH-WWC, taken on in August 1957. WB sank after hitting a log on the Kikori River in New Guinea on 16 June 1957. Its replacement was VH-WWC, and this continued in operation until sold to Trans-Australia Airlines in 1961.

Barrier Reef Airways

This company was formed by Stewart Middlemiss and Chris Poulsen just after the war. The company purchased eight surplus RAAF Catalinas, five of which (from Lake Boga) were used for spares recovery. Two aircraft were registered in Australia and the final example, A24-304, disappeared into obscurity. The two aircraft that did reach the civil register later went to Ansett Flying Boat Services Pty Ltd.

The five Lake Boga machines used for spares were A24-35, A24-58, A24-78, A24-82 and A24-89. The other three aircraft from Rathmines were A24-304, A24-364/VH-BRB and A24-369/VH-BRA.

Barrier Reef Airlines set up its base on the Brisbane River and started flights in April of 1947 that included regular trips to the Lindeman and Daydream Islands. These were mostly flown using VH-BRA *Beachcomber*, whilst VH-BRB *Buccaneer* remained in reserve. The latter was damaged when it collided with a boat at Daydream Island on the last day of January 1950. Both aircraft went to Ansett Flying Boat services when that company obtained the controlling interest in Barrier Reef Airlines around 1953.

Botterill & Fraser

This partnership had three Catalinas to its name. The first was A24-2, but they seem to have done nothing with it, at least not in terms of operations, and it is presumed that it was used as spares. A24-10 was sold to R. R. Cobley, who applied for the registration VH-BEF. A Certificate of Airworthiness was not issued and the airframe was scrapped at Lake Boga.

A24-26 was obtained from W. R. Carpenter, who had had it registered as VH-BDP. The marks lapsed in December 1947, and it seems that Botterill & Fraser sold the aircraft to R. R. Cobley, who later used it in Indonesia.

Bridgewater, F. H.

This individual obtained one Catalina for a proposed airline that would have linked Lord Howe Island with Sydney. These plans did not come to fruition, and the aircraft – A24-361 – went to Island Airways Ltd as VH-BDQ, and later still to QANTAS.

Butler Air Transport

Three surplus Catalinas were acquired by Butlers, but they do not seem to have been used subsequently and did not proceed to civil registry. Their military serials were A24-202, A24-362 and A24-376.

Campbell, C. K.

The owner of eight ex-RAAF Catalinas that were presumably used as a spares source after the Second World War. The eight were A24-46, A24-55, A24-60, A24-61, A24-65, A24-77, A24-97 and A24-102.

Carpenter, W. R.
(see also Island Airways Ltd)

In addition to the Catalinas acquired by Carpenter for use by Island Airways, he also owned the former A24-26 and had it registered as VH-BDP. It was sold to Botterill & Fraser and later went to Indonesia.

Shown in RAF colours in this official photograph, JX637 went to the RAAF as A24-376 and was acquired by Butler Air Transport in October 1946. No civilian identity was subsequently allocated to it, however.
MAP/Real Photos

Carr, R.

Obtained A24-356 for purposes unknown.

Cobley, R.,
trading as Richard Conway Aviation

Cobley had two Catalinas. The first was the one-time A24-10 that he purchased from Botterill & Fraser. It was scrapped at Lake Boga without flying in its reserved markings VH-BEF.

The other Cat was VH-BDP, ex-A24-26. This was made airworthy and taken to Indonesia, where Cobley flew it for the Republicans during 1948 as RI-005.

Daniels, Major E. C. & Taylor, A. E. S.

These two gentlemen appear to have had some involvement with Catalina A24-10/VH-BEF after R. Cobley's application for a Certificate of Airworthiness did not proceed. The aircraft was scrapped at Lake Boga.

Executive Air Services

This company was the registered owner of a geophysical survey *Super Cat* between August 1972, and November 1979. It then went to H. C. Sleigh Aviation and Western Commander, and is now undergoing restoration with the RAAF Museum. Its Australian identity was VH-EXG.

Grant Trading Pty Ltd

The quoted purchasers of surplus airframe A24-72 of which nothing further is known.

Guthrie, A. W.

A. W. Guthrie purchased A24-79 from the RAAF, but it was probably scrapped or used for spares subsequently.

H. C. Sleigh Aviation

The registered operators of the survey-equipped Catalina VH-EXG from November 1979 to May 1984.

Island Airways Ltd

Island Airways, formed by W. R. Carpenter, owned two Catalinas. The first was the former A24-350 obtained from Marinair in May 1947. It became VH-ALN *Island Chieftain* and was later sold to QANTAS as VH-EBC. The other aircraft was A24-361, originally purchased from the RAAF by F. H. Bridgewater. This too went to QANTAS, becoming VH-EBU. The Island Airways registration VH-BDQ was not used. Whilst owned by Island Airways, VH-ALN was mainly used on transport services around New Guinea, based on Madang, but the company went out of business after little more than a year following the loss of one of their Lockheed Hudson aircraft.

Jackaman, A. C. – *see* Marinair

John Fairfax & Sons Pty Ltd

This company was connected with the Sydney Morning Herald, and, for reasons unknown, purchased three surplus RAAF Catalinas that were not heard of again. They were A24-59, A24-87 and A24-95.

Kennedy, ?

In May 1947, the buyer of A24-75. It was sold on to Asian Airlines and became VH-BDY.

Kingsford Smith Aviation Services

Nineteen ex-RAAF Catalinas are recorded as having been sold to this company after the Second World War. It is assumed that they were acquired for spares recovery, as none of them proceeded to Australian registry. The individual aircraft are listed in Table 5 above.

Marinair

Marinair was a company formed by A. C. M. Jackaman, R. Mueller and the well-known Australian Aviator Capt P. G., later Sir Gordon, Taylor. The intention was to operate passenger flights between Sydney and Lord Howe Island, but these plans were thwarted when the appropriate licences were not forthcoming. The company did, however, acquire five Catalinas from the RAAF for use by Marinair, these being A24-350, A24-351, A24-358, A24-366 and A24-384. A24-350 passed to W. R. Carpenter and his Island Airways Ltd as VH-ALN. The other four aircraft ended up with the Netherlands Government after plans for Marinair folded. Their subsequent Dutch identities were, in order of RAAF serials, P-208, P-207, P-210 and P-209. P. G. Taylor also operated A24-385 as VH-ASA – see separate entry under Taylor.

QANTAS

QANTAS was no stranger to the Catalina, having had some of its pilots involved in the delivery from the USA of early RAAF machines during 1941. It also operated the famous *Double Sunrise* communication flights between Perth and Ceylon from 1943 to 1945, using former RAF machines with British civil registrations.

After the war's end, QANTAS purchased a number of late-mark Catalina flying boats from both the surplus RAAF stocks at Rathmines and other airlines. Whilst some were used as a spares source, seven were put into passenger service operating routes around the Pacific and, eventually in 1949, to New Guinea. The Catalina operations were ultimately concentrated in New Guinea, where they continued until mid-1958.

QANTAS operated post-war flying boat services out to Lord Howe Island using ex-RAAF PB2B-2 Catalinas, including VH-EAW, here disembarking passengers in December 1947. This particular Catalina was blown to pieces by a saboteur in the summer of 1949.
QANTAS via François Prins

The Catalinas used for spares recovery were A24-300, A24-306, A24-309, A24-354, A24-355, A24-357, A24-367 and A24-379.

Those registered were VH-EAW, VH-EAX, VH-EBA, VH-EBB, VH-EBC, VH-EBD and VH-EBU. VH-EBC was acquired from Island Airways and VH-EBA and VH-EBB came from the defunct Asian Airlines. Although registered, the latter two were not used and were reduced to spares.

The QANTAS Catalina operations were not without some drama. VH-EAX was terminally damaged when its moorings broke and it was blown onto rocks at Lord Howe Island on 23 June 1949, whilst VH-EAW was destroyed at its moorings at Rose Bay just over two months later by a saboteur's device that exploded, blowing the airframe apart and sinking it.

Richard Conway Aviation
– see **Cobley, R. R.**

Selco Exploration Company
For a brief period of six months during 1964, Selco had the Wright Cyclone-powered Catalina VH-UMS registered to it, and it was operated on behalf of Australian Selection Ltd in the geophysical survey role. It soon returned to Canada, however.

Sydney Morning Herald
– see **John Fairfax & Sons Pty Ltd**

Taylor, Capt P. G.
Gordon Taylor is well-known for his association with various Catalinas and the long-distance flights that he carried out in them. Before the Second World War, he captained the Model 28-3 NC777 (the second *Guba*) on flights to survey flying boat routes across the Indian Ocean from Australia to East Africa. During the war, he used the 45 Group Catalina JX275 *Frigate Bird* to carry out a pioneering flight linking Mexico with Australia.

After the war, he had a vision to create an air link between South America and Australia. Taylor persuaded the Government to supply him with the former RAAF PB2B-2 A24-385 that was in store at Rathmines. He took it over in August 1950, and had it registered as VH-ASA, with the name *Frigate Bird II*. He and his crew left Sydney's Rose Bay on 13 March 1951, and after many adventures reached Quintero in Chile on 26 March. The flight had taken them from Sydney to Chile via Grafton, Noumea, Suva, Samoa, Aitutaki, Tahiti, Mangareva and Easter Island. The description of this flight and the return journey in Taylor's book *Frigate Bird* is one of the most exciting aviation books ever written. VH-ASA survived long periods of subsequent storage to be exhibited at the Powerhouse Museum in Sydney.

P. G. Taylor was also associated with Marinair – see entry above.

Trans-Australia Airlines
TAA acquired its first Catalina in 1961, when it purchased VH-WWC from the Australasian Petroleum Company. It was used around various points in Papua New Guinea but, at Daru on 26 April 1962, after the port wingtip was submerged by a wave during a cross-wind landing, the hull was holed and the Catalina sank. After

---

Another Australian operator to fly Catalinas on passenger-carrying services was Trans-Australia Airlines (TAA). VH-SBV was purchased from Cathay Pacific in Hong Kong after VH-WWC was lost in an accident. After arrival in Australia, it had its undercarriage removed and became a pure flying boat. It retained its blisters and its bow turret glazing was merely covered over.

Its pioneering work over, Capt P. G. Taylor's *Frigate Bird II* was moved from one storage site to another until eventually preserved in the Powerhouse Museum in Sydney. When seen in January 1964, it was in open store at Rose Bay.
Geoff Goodall via Bob Livingstone

a while, it was replaced by the former Hong Kong-registered PBY-5A amphibian VR-HDH. It was given the Australian identity VH-SBV and was later converted to flying boat configuration. It was finally taken out of service in January 1966, and found its way onto the Port Moresby fire dump. It was later rescued, and can now be found under restoration in the RNZAF Museum at Point Cook. TAA also owned the former Adastra Surveys PBY-5A VH-AGB, but this was used for spares recovery only and was scrapped in 1967.

Western Commander

Western Commander was the final owner of the Cyclone-powered Super Cat VH-EXG before it was withdrawn at Essendon in the late 1980s. It is now with the RAAF Museum.

Wood, J. E.

J.E. Wood acquired four ex-RAAF Catalinas (A24-21, A24-47, A24-66 and A24-86), but nothing further is known.

Table 7. Post-war Australian civil registered Catalinas

Registration	C/n	Type	Place of Manufacture	Previous id(s)	Notes
VH-AGB (1) ntu	61154	PB2B-2/ Catalina VI	BOE CAN	A24-385 (RAAF) JX630 (RAF) Bu44248 (US Navy)	Reservation for Capt P. G. Taylor Re-registered VH-ASA.
VH-AGB (2)	CV-359	Canso A	CAN VIC (Cartierville)	CF-GKI 11055 (RCAF)	Reg'd 11/56 to Adastra Hunting Geophysics. Wfu at Mascot. Sold to TAA and used as spares source at Bankstown. Scrapped at Caringbah, NSW, 5/1967.
VH-ALN	61185	PB2B-2/ Catalina VI	BOE CAN	A24-350 (RAAF) JX661 (RAF) Bu44279 (US Navy)	Reg'd 5/1947 to Island Airways. *Island Chieftain.* To QANTAS 4/1949 as VH-EBC. NB – some sources quote RAAF p/i as A24-354.

Registration	C/n	Type	Place of Manufacture	Previous id(s)	Notes
VH-ASA	61154	PB2B-2/ Catalina VI	BOE CAN	VH-AGB(1) ntu A24-385 (RAAF) JX630 (RAF) Bu44248 (US Navy)	Reg'd 3/1951 to Capt P. G. Taylor. *Frigate Bird II.* Withdrawn 6/1954. Current – see Chapter Fourteen.
VH-BDP	292	Canso/ Catalina IIA	CON SD	A24-26 (RAAF) V9711/VA711 (RAF) 9711 (RCAF)	Reg'd 6/1947 to W. R. Carpenter Pty Ltd. To Botterill & Fraser. Wfu, 19/12/1947. Restored to R. R. Cobley/ Richard Conway Aviation, 1/1948. Sold in Indonesia as RI-005, 1948. Crashed at Djambi, Sumatra, 29/12/1948.
VH-BDQ ntu	61167	PB2B-2/ Catalina VI	BOE CAN	A24-361 (RAAF) JX643 (RAF) Bu44261 (US Navy)	Island Airways *Island Warrior.* Not taken up. To QANTAS as VH-EBU, 11/1949.
VH-BDY	1659	PBY-5A	CON SD	A24-75 (RAAF) Bu48297 (US Navy)	Asian Airlines Ltd. Wfu, 7/1948.
VH-BEF	270	Model 28-5MA	CON SD	A24-10 (RAAF) VH-AFK	R. R. Cobley. CofA not granted. Scrapped at Lake Boga, late 1940s.
VH-BRA	61193	PB2B-2/ Catalina VI	BOE CAN	A24-369 (RAAF) JZ834 (RAF) Bu44287 (US Navy)	Reg'd 9/47 to Barrier Reef Airways. *Beachcomber.* To Ansett Flying Boat Svs. Wfu, 5/1953.
VH-BRB	61197	PB2B-2/ Catalina VI	BOE CAN	A24-364 (RAAF) JZ838 (RAF) Bu44291 (US Navy)	Reg'd 9/1947 to Barrier Reef Airways. *Buccaneer.* To Ansett Flying Boat Svs. Wfu, 4/1953.
VH-BRI	1735	PBY-5A	CON SD	N95R N10018 Bu48373 (US Navy)	Reg'd 10/1959 to Ansett Transport Industries, later Ansett Flying Boat Svs. *The Golden Islander.* Sank at Hayman Island, Queensland, 8/7/1962 after heavy landing. Current as motor launch – see Chapter Fourteen.
VH-EAW	61159	PB2B-2/ Catalina VI	BOE CAN	A24-378 (RAAF) JX635 (RAF) Bu44253 (US Navy)	Reg'd 10/1947 to QANTAS. Exploded and sank due to sabotage, Rose Bay, 27/8/1949.
VH-EAX	61186	PB2B-2/ Catalina VI	BOE CAN	A24-372 (RAAF) JX662 (RAF) Bu44280 (US Navy)	Reg'd 2/1949 to QANTAS. Dbr when blown onto rocks at Lord Howe Island, 23/6/1949.
VH-EBA	61137	PB2B-2/ Catalina VI	BOE CAN	A24-303 (RAAF) JX621 (RAF) Bu44231 (US Navy)	Reg'd 9/1949 to QANTAS ex-Asian Airlines ntu. Wfu and used as spares, 3/1954.
VH-EBB ntu	61134	PB2B-2/ Catalina VI	BOE CAN	A24-305 (RAAF) JX618 (RAF) Bu44228 (US Navy)	Ex-Asian Airlines ntu. Not used and broken up for spares, 2/1951.

By the time this photograph was taken in February 1953, QANTAS had withdrawn its PB2B-2 Catalina VH-EBU, and it was in open storage at Rose Bay, Sydney, awaiting the breakers.
Don MacKay via Jennifer M. Gradidge

Registration	C/n	Type	Place of Manufacture	Previous id(s)	Notes
VH-EBC	61185	PB2B-2/ Catalina VI	BOE CAN	VH-ALN A24-350 (RAAF) JX661 (RAF) Bu44279 (US Navy)	Reg'd 4/1949 to QANTAS. *Island Chieftain*. Wfu 11/1958 and used for spares. NB – some sources quote RAAF pi as A24-354.
VH-EBD	61165	PB2B-2/ Catalina VI	BOE CAN	A24-371 (RAAF) JX641 (RAF) Bu44259 (US Navy)	Reg'd 12/1949 to QANTAS. *Island Patrol*. Wfu 11/1958 and used for spares.
VH-EBU	61167	PB2B-2/ Catalina VI	BOE CAN	VH-BDQ ntu A24-361 (RAAF) JX643 (RAF) Bu44261 (US Navy)	Reg'd 11/1949 to QANTAS. *Island Warrior*. Wfu 11/1952 and used for spares.
VH-EXG	CV-369	Canso A	CAN VIC (Cartierville)	N609FF N609F CF-NJD 11060 (RCAF)	Reg'd 9/1972 to Executive Air Svs. To H. C. Sleigh then Western Commander. Wfu at Essendon. To RAAF Museum and current – see Chapter Fourteen.
VH-SBV	CV-592	OA-10A	CAN VIC (Cartierville)	VR-HDH 44-34081 (USAAF) Bu68045 ntu (US Navy)	Reg'd 10/1962 to Trans-Australia Airlines. Wfu 5/1966. To Port Moresby fire dump and then New Zealand. Current – see Chapter Fourteen.
VH-UMS	1649	PBY-5A	CON SD	CF-JMS N10017 Bu48287 (US Navy)	Reg'd 4/1964 to Selco Exploration Co. Returned to Canada as CF-JMS, 11/1964. Later N16647, C-GGDW, N16647 and N287. Current – see Chapter Nineteen.

Registration	C/n	Type	Place of Manufacture	Previous id(s)	Notes
VH-WWB	1830	PBY-5A	CON SD	N68753 Bu46466 (US Navy)	Reg'd 3/1956 to Australasian Petroleum Co. and flown by World Wide Air Services. Sank in Kikori River, New Guinea after hitting log, 16/6/1957.
VH-WWC	1859	PBY-5A	CON SD	N68766 Bu46495 (US Navy)	Reg'd 8/1957 to Australasian Petroleum Co. and flown by World Wide Air Services. Sold to Trans-Australia Airlines, 7/1961. Sank at Daru, New Guinea after hitting object in water, 26/4/1962.

When Trans-Australia Airlines first acquired its Catalina VH-SBV from Cathay Pacific, it was an amphibian, although its undercarriage was subsequently removed. It is seen here ground-running with Sunbird Services logos and an incomplete port blister assembly.
Peter Keating Collection

For a brief few months during 1964, the Australian register was graced by this Cyclone-powered Super Catalina. Previously operated in Canada as CF-JMS, it became VH-UMS with survey company Selco Exploration. Here on the ramp at Mascot, it displays Super Canso (sic) titles on the lower rudder, cargo hatches in place of blisters, prop spinners and an observation dome in place of the bow turret. This aircraft survives today in the USA as N287.
Jennifer M. Gradidge

NEW ZEALAND

MILITARY AIRCRAFT

The Royal New Zealand Air Force (RNZAF) originally received 56 Catalina flying boats. The first 22, received in 1943, carried RNZAF serials NZ4001 to NZ4022 and were built by Consolidated at San Diego. Thirteen were to PBY-5 standard whilst the other nine were Catalina MkIVAs diverted from the RAF. The remaining 34 aircraft were Boeing of Canada-built PB2B-1s, originally intended for the RAF as MkIVBs. They received RNZAF serials NZ4023 to NZ4056 and were delivered in 1944. A further 14 aircraft, intended to replace losses, were cancelled before delivery. The faithful wartime service given by these Catalinas is outside the scope of this book, but suffice to say they served with distinction with 6 Squadron out of Lauthala Bay, Fiji, from October 1943, later being joined by 5 Squadron. The type also equipped 3 (Flying Boat) Operational Training Unit.

At the war's end, 6 Squadron and 3 (FB) OTU were both disbanded, leaving 5 Squadron as the sole RNZAF Catalina user. Initially, 5 Squadron provided both air-sea-rescue cover from various bases and transportation for the thousands of returning RNZAF personnel scattered around the vast Pacific area, including Australia. Its base was transferred from Segond Channel to Lauthala Bay, Fiji, in November.

As the need for personnel transport diminished, so the air-sea-rescue role came to predominate. The main

base was still Lauthala Bay in Fiji, but with a small detachment at Hobsonville, Auckland. In addition, the Catalinas of 5 Squadron provided relief flights during the aftermath of a hurricane that hit the area in December 1948. By the summer of 1946, the RNZAF still had no fewer than 48 Catalinas on strength, but the majority of these were in reserve or languishing in open storage at Hobsonville, in what was becoming a vast Catalina graveyard. In order to comply with the terms of Lend-Lease, under which the aircraft had been supplied by the USA in the first place, most of the aircraft in the graveyard were allowed gradually to deteriorate, although the USA agreed that a number of aircraft should remain flying to provide essential ASR cover in the Pacific region. Initial plans to scuttle the Cats at sea were abandoned, however.

Typical example of a wartime RNZAF Catalina is NZ4025, a Boeing of Canada-built PB2B-1. Here flying as GF-C of 3 Operational Training Unit, it survived the war and remained on military strength, albeit in storage, until 1951, when it was finally withdrawn and scrapped.

In the summer of 1947, two of the RNZAF Catalinas were loaned to the civil airline TEAL – see *NZ Commercial Catalinas*. This airline was also responsible for major Catalina servicing for the RNZAF from 1950 onwards.

In 1949, 5 Squadron took on a maritime reconnaissance role once more, still operating from Fiji. Surplus Catalinas still gradually found their way to the graveyard at Hobsonville for storage. By late 1952, around six Catalinas were still operational, but they were finally retired in October 1953, thus ending 5 Squadron's association with the type. Meanwhile, in March of 1952, 6 Squadron was issued with a small number of Catalinas, and they continued to serve until April 1954, being scrapped at the end of 1955.

The last of the Hobsonville Catalinas lingered on until 1956 and were sold as scrap to New Zealand Metal Smelters although a good number had been badly damaged in a storm at Hobsonville in 1951 and most had been scrapped in 1952. One solitary aircraft escaped and was sold to a local man, Jack Sellars, of Wellsford, Northland, who intended using it as a pleasure boat on local waters. It was towed to Whangateau, but the plans came to naught, and after the outer wing panels were removed, the hull lingered on until it was finally sold for scrap in the late 1960s.

In post-war service, RNZAF Catalinas carried hull codes according to their allocated squadron. From 1949, 5 Squadron aircraft carried the codes KN-, followed by the individual aircraft letter, e.g. NZ4055/KN-L. Many of the stored airframes that abounded at Hobsonville still carried the PA- codes of 6 Squadron.

The following RNZAF Catalinas had been lost in wartime accidents prior to September 1945:

PBY-5

NZ4001 ex-Bu08280, NZ4002 ex-JX232, NZ4003 ex-JX234, NZ4006 ex-JX236, NZ4013 ex-Bu08468, NZ4020 ex-Bu08435, NZ4022 ex-Bu08516, NZ4040 ex-Bu73057

PB2B-1

NZ4031 ex-Bu73031

Catalinas assembled at Hobsonville and subsequently scrapped during the early 1950s were:

PBY-5

NZ4005 ex-JX233, NZ4007 ex-JX237, NZ4008 ex-JX230, NZ4009 ex-JX231, NZ4010 ex-JX228, NZ4011 ex-JX235, NZ4012 ex-Bu08450, NZ4014 ex-Bu08464, NZ4015 ex-Bu08453, NZ4016 ex-Bu08466, NZ4017 ex-Bu08467, NZ4018 ex-Bu08488, NZ4019 ex-Bu08438 and NZ4021 ex-Bu08487

PB2B-1

NZ4023 ex-Bu72997, NZ4024 ex-Bu72999, NZ4025 ex-Bu73000, NZ4026 ex-Bu73013, NZ4027 ex-Bu72998, NZ4028 ex-Bu73015, NZ4029 ex-Bu73030, NZ4030 ex-Bu73016, NZ4032 ex-Bu73032, NZ4034 ex-Bu73044, NZ4035 ex-Bu73045, NZ4036 ex-Bu73046, NZ4037 ex-Bu73047, NZ4038 ex-Bu73048, NZ4039 ex-Bu73055,

NZ4029/PA-A, a PB2B-1 Catalina of 6 Squadron, lingered on at Hobsonville until 1951, when it was finally scrapped. *MAP/Real Photos*

The RNZAF's penultimate Catalina to be delivered was NZ4055. Here she is at rest in the idyllic surroundings of Lauthala Bay in Fiji, wearing the codes of 5 Squadron. She was destined to be the last RNZAF PBY extant after being sold to a civilian in 1956, only to be scrapped in the late 1960s. *RNZAF via Adrian Balch*

Many of the RNZAF Cats ended their days in storage at Hobsonville including these six engine-less examples.

In reflective mood is this post-war shot of 5 Squadron's NZ4050/KN-G at Hobsonville. It flew on until the summer of 1951, when it was condemned. *MAP*

NZ4041 ex-Bu73058, NZ4042 ex-Bu73029, NZ4043 ex-Bu73014, NZ4044 ex-Bu73059, NZ4047 ex-Bu73095, NZ4049 ex-Bu73113, NZ4050 ex-Bu73096, NZ4052 ex-Bu73115, NZ4053 ex-Bu73116, NZ4054 ex-Bu73114, NZ4056 ex-Bu44203.

NZ4055 ex-Bu44202 was sold to J. Sellars ex-Hobsonville as described above, and was eventually scrapped in the 1960s at Whangateau.

Two RNZAF Catalinas are known to have become ground instructional airframes at the end of their operational lives. The first was PBY-5 NZ4004 ex-Bu08373, and this became INST120 with No. 1 Technical Training School at Hobsonville before being scrapped there. The other was PB2B-1 NZ4045 ex-Bu73060, used briefly for training engineers and gunners, also at Hobsonville, before it too was retired to the scrap yard.

A further Catalina has no official fate recorded, this being PB2B-1 NZ4040. Table 8 records Catalinas lost as the result of post-war accidents:

Table 8. Post-war losses of New Zealand military Catalinas

Serial	Type	Previous id	Squadron and Code	Details
NZ4033	PB2B-1	Bu73043 (US Navy)	5 Sqn	Suffered heavy landing at Mechanics Bay, Auckland, 14/2/1946 and damaged beyond repair. Subsequently broken up.
NZ4046	PB2B-1	Bu73056 (US Navy)	5 Sqn KN-A	Sank following forced landing on sea, south of Suva, Western Fiji caused by engine failure and subsequent fire, 7/10/1952.
NZ4048	PB2B-1	Bu73098 (US Navy)	5 Sqn KN-C	Crashed on take-off Satapuala, Western Samoa, 12/12/1950.
NZ4051	PB2B-1	Bu73097 (US Navy)	5 Sqn KN-H	Crashed on take-off, Evans Bay, Wellington, NZ, 7/2/1950. Remains sold as scrap.

COMMERCIAL AIRCRAFT

As related above, two RNZAF Catalinas were briefly

ZK-AMP was an RNZAF aircraft (NZ4038) that was loaned to Tasman Empire Airways Ltd (TEAL) for surveying airline routes post-war. It bears the TEAL emblem and the name *Marora* on the bow.
Jennifer M. Gradidge

loaned to Tasman Empire Airways Ltd (TEAL). These were NZ4035 and NZ4038. The first was used from October 1947 for crew training purposes as ZK-AMI, and was returned to the RNZAF at Hobsonville shortly after, only to be scrapped there. It flew in a basic RNZAF colour scheme of grey upper surfaces and white hull. The civil registration appeared in large black letters on the aft hull and TEAL's logo was painted on the bow.

NZ4038 saw use as a survey aircraft from April 1949 on what was to become the *Coral Route* around the Pacific area, using various Short flying boats, but it too was scrapped at Hobsonville after being returned to the RNZAF. It used the civil registration ZK-AMP aft of the blisters and was painted white overall. The titles *Tasman Empire Airways Ltd Survey Aircraft* appeared on the hull behind the wing lift struts. The New Zealand flag was painted on the vertical tail surfaces forward of the rudder, and it too had the TEAL logo on the bow. It was given the name *Marora*.

With the return of ZK-AMI and ZK-AMP to the RNZAF, many years were to elapse before another Catalina was to be registered in New Zealand, although occasional visiting examples were seen. The unfortunate Australian Catalina, VH-SBV, that had nearly been destroyed on the fire dump at Port Moresby, Papua New Guinea, was rescued and went to the RNZAF Museum via the Museum of Transport and Technology (MoTaT). This machine is fully described in Chapter Fourteen.

Then, in 1994, a small group of individuals became determined to see an airworthy Catalina flying again in New Zealand. They eventually sourced a Catalina in Mena, Arkansas, and a deal was struck. The appropriate registration ZK-PBY was reserved for it, and it was made fully airworthy and ferried to California prior to its delivery flight to New Zealand. Sadly, an engine problem led to a night-time forced landing in the vicinity of Christmas Island, between Hawaii and Tahiti, following which the damaged airframe sank for ever into the deep Pacific Ocean. The New Zealand Catalina Group got over

The ZK-PBY that never was. Although allocated those marks, N5404J never wore them as it was lost at sea en route to New Zealand in January 1994, as described in the text. This photo was taken eight months before that at Smartt Field, Missouri.
Hank Hancock

The New Zealand Catalina Group's second attempt at ferrying a Catalina to its home country was successful, and the former Z-CAT now flies regularly from both water and land as ZK-PBY.
via Marlene Gray

this huge setback and purchased a second aircraft, the well-known Catalina Safari Company's Zimbabwe-based Z-CAT. This was successfully flown to New Zealand, arriving at New Plymouth on 26 October 1994.

Allocated the previously unused marks ZK-PBY, it has flown safely ever since and is currently painted to represent the RNZAF Catalina NZ4017/XX-T of 6 Squadron. In the late summer of 1999, the New Zealand Catalina Group purchased the unidentified former US Navy Catalina hull that had previously been stored at Ephrata, Washington State, USA, with SLAFCO.

Table 9. New Zealand Commercial Catalinas

Registration	C/n	Type	Place of Manufacture	Previous id(s)	Notes
ZK-AMI	28134	PB2B-1	BOE CAN	NZ4035 Bu73045 (US Navy)	Registered 6/7/1947. Returned to RNZAF 15/11/1948 and scrapped at Hobsonville. Registration cancelled, 26/11/1948.
ZK-AMP	28137	PB2B-1	BOE CAN	NZ4038 Bu73048 (US Navy)	Registered 16/12/1948. *Marora*. Returned to RNZAF and scrapped at Hobsonville, 5/1952. Registration cancelled, 10/6/1952.
ZK-PBY ntu	22022	Canso A	BOE CAN	N5404J TG-BIV N6108 HR-236 5Y-KUD HP-289 HK-996X OB-LDM-349 YV-P-APE 9793 (RCAF)	Reservation for the New Zealand Catalina Group. Lost in Pacific Ocean, 16/1/1994.
ZK-PBY (2)	CV-357	Canso A	CAN VIC (Cartierville)	Z-CAT C-FJCV CF-JCV 11054 (RCAF)	New Zealand Catalina Group. Painted as NZ4017/XX-T. Current – see Chapter Fourteen.

Six

CANADA

During the Second World War, Canada was both a major user of the Catalina/Canso, and also a large-scale producer, many examples being built by Canadian Vickers, later Canadair, at St Hubert and Cartierville, Quebec, and by Boeing of Canada at Sea Island, Vancouver, British Columbia. Canadian-built Catalinas were delivered not only to the Royal Canadian Air Force but also to the Royal Air Force, Royal Australian Air Force, Royal New Zealand Air Force, United States Navy and the United States Army Air Force. The RCAF used the type both at home and from bases in Iceland, and amongst many acts of bravery, one was singled out for recognition by the award of the Victoria Cross, albeit posthumously. The recipient was Flt Lt David Hornell of 162 (BR) Squadron, who was flying Canso A serial number 9754, hull code P on 24 June 1944, when the U-boat U-1225 was successfully sunk, but only at the cost of the aircraft and three of the crew. This was the first RCAF VC of the Second World War to be awarded.

Given Canada's close involvement with operating and building Catalinas, it is perhaps not surprising that the type should continue in use post-war, especially as it had proved to be both rugged and adaptable. In addition, many of the later aircraft to be delivered were still 'low time' airframes when the war finished. Thus, many amphibious examples remained in Canadian military service until the 1960s and dozens more went on to have long commercial careers throughout the country. Indeed,

so useful was the type that many Catalinas of non-Canadian origin were acquired by civilian operators, and to this day some examples are still in use in Canada, although now much reduced in numbers compared with the 'glory days' of the late 1950s and 1960s.

MILITARY CATALINAS/CANSOS

Before looking closely at the Royal Canadian Air Force's post-war use of the Catalina, it is appropriate to explain their use of the terms Catalina and Canso, as this has caused confusion to some in the past. Over the years, the incorrect theory that a Canso is an amphibious Catalina has gained acceptance, although not, it has to be said, in the majority of serious published sources. None the less, there are still many individuals who hold to this erroneous view that probably goes back to wartime. The correct position is as follows. When the RCAF ordered Catalinas, they decided to allocate their own name to the type (a present-day example of this Canadian practice is the name *Aurora* given to Lockheed P-3 Orions of the Canadian Armed Forces).

Initially, the name *Convoy* was to be used for Catalinas ordered for the RCAF, but good sense prevailed when it was realised what confusion was likely to result when the type was used on convoy escort! Another name was hastily substituted and the aircraft was named *Canso* after the Strait of Canso, the stretch of water that separates Nova Scotia and Cape Breton Island. The amphibious examples were given the suffix A to distinguish them from the smaller number of pure flying boat Cansos in RCAF service. Thus, any Catalina ordered on a Canadian contract and flown by the RCAF was a Canso or Canso A, depending on whether it had an undercarriage or not. It does not follow that the name applied to all Canadian-manufactured PBYs nor did it strictly apply to the small number of RAF Catalinas loaned to the RCAF early in the war. Since the war, it has been the Canadian habit to refer to any Catalina as a Canso in pretty much the same way as the British will see a C-47 and call it a Dakota or a T-6 and call it a Harvard!

The following Cansos were ordered for use by the RCAF:

9701 – 9736	Model 28-5MC/ Canso	Consolidated, San Diego (9 to RAAF 20 to RAF)
9737 – 9750	Model 28-5AMC/ Canso A	Consolidated, San Diego
9751 – 9805	Canso A	Boeing Aircraft of Canada – built from Consolidated manufactured parts

A typical wartime scene at Torbay, Newfoundland, showing RCAF Canso As 9793 and 9813 in November 1944. Both were on the strength of 160 Whaler Squadron. 9813 went on to serve with the Argentine Navy after its retirement in 1946, whereas 9793 enjoyed a long and varied existence before being lost in the Pacific Ocean in January 1994. *A. E. Hill*

9806 – 9835	Canos A	Canadian Vickers, St Hubert
9836 – 9844	Canso A	Canadian Vickers, Cartierville
11001 – 11100	Canso A	Canadian Vickers, Cartierville

For the sake of completeness, the following Catalinas were aircraft ordered for the RAF but used by the RCAF in Canada. They were replaced by 29 aircraft within the RCAF order 9701 to 9736, nine of which were then diverted to the RAAF as shown above:

Catalina MkI	W8430, W8431, W8432, Z2134, Z2136, Z2137, Z2138, Z2139, Z2140 and DP202
Catalina MkIIB	FP290, FP291, FP292, FP293, FP294, FP295, FP296 and FP297
Catalina MkIVA	JX206, JX207, JX209, JX211, JX212, JX213, JX217, JX219, JX571, JX572, JX579 and JX580

Many of the RCAF aircraft were struck off charge shortly after the war's end, following periods of storage at various locations around Canada, although in some cases the derelict airframes lingered on for years. About forty to fifty others, presumably those in better condition, went on to serve the RCAF in support roles for many years. Reflecting their changed role, a good number of these were converted to transports, with bow and blister turrets being replaced by clipper bows and cargo doors respectively.

Trials with JATO (Jet Assisted Take Off) led to the first assisted take-off by a Canso in November 1947, and this equipment went on to see regular use. The last active RCAF Canso was withdrawn from service in April 1963, after serial number 11089 flew the last operation on the 8th of that month. Some former RCAF Canso As were sold to overseas air arms, including those of Denmark, Sweden, Brazil and Argentina and to commercial operators, mainly within Canada. In particular, those Canso As retired in the 1960s found a ready market amongst smaller airlines and water bombing companies. A small number became instructional airframes with the RCAF, and those known to have been used in this way are 9761 that became A525 and was finally struck off charge (soc) in April 1954, 9772/A510 (soc February 1953) and 9817/A507 (soc November 1948).

The following RCAF squadrons used Canso As into the post-war period:

13 (PR) Squadron – This squadron was involved in Arctic mapping flights, and used Canso As out of Rockcliffe, Ontario, until, in April 1947, it was redesignated as 413 (PR) Squadron, taking on the famous *Tusker* Squadron name from its wartime predecessor. During 1946, one of 13 Squadron's crews rediscovered the Spicer Islands that had defied location for some fifty years!

Canso A 9831 was an early withdrawal from RCAF service, and is seen here in April 1947, in the hangars of de Havilland Canada awaiting refurbishment for the Royal Danish Air Force, with which it served as FM56, later 82-856. The RCAF roundels and fin flashes have been crossed through, presumably to indicate that the aircraft was no longer on RCAF charge.
Rod Brown via Peter Keating

Post-war, the RCAF was a frequent user of Jet Assisted Take Off (JATO) equipment on its Cansos. Here 408 Squadron's 11056 is helped aloft during 1953. This aircraft went on to become a water bomber in the Province of Quebec with the registration CF-PQI.
MAP

408 (PR) *Goose* **Squadron** – Also based at Rockcliffe, 408 had re-formed there in early 1949 and flew mapping flights in Northern Canada alongside a mixed fleet of Lancasters, Noorduyn Norseman and Dakotas. The Lancasters soon took over from the other types. From 1949 to 1951, squadron hull codes AK were used, but were replaced with MN in 1951.

413 (PR) *Tusker* **Squadron** – This Rockliffe-based squadron carried on the mapping work from 13 Squadron and, like 408 Squadron above, flew Cansos

A fine aerial view of 121 (S&R) Flight's Canso A 11067 showing that unit's QT hull codes as worn just after the war ended. This aircraft also went on to have a career as a commercial fire fighter, this time as CF-NTL.
Robert Tracz

amongst a varied fleet that also included Lancasters, Norseman, Dakotas and B-25 Mitchells. In addition to mapping, it also carried out SAR and transport flights, and its aircraft were the first Cansos in RCAF service to regularly use JATO (Jet Assisted Take Off) equipment. The squadron disbanded at the end of October 1950. It had used the hull code AP.

123 (S&R) Squadron – Canso As were used by this squadron out of Sea Island, Vancouver, on British Columbia's West Coast. It was later renumbered as 121 (S&R) Flight.

102 (S&R) Flight – Rescue duties were flown from Trenton, Ontario, using Canso As.

103 (S&R) Flight – As above but based at Greenwood, Nova Scotia, using the hull code QZ.

111 (S&R) Flight – This Canso A unit was based at Winnipeg, Manitoba.

121 (S&R) Flight – See 123 (S&R) Squadron above. It used the hull code QT.

In looking at the disposal of the RCAF Cansos, it becomes obvious that two distinct periods of operation were involved. The first period ended at the latter part of 1947, by which time a large number had been retired or, in some cases, sold to the commercial sector, both within Canada and further afield. The second period saw examples fly on with the RCAF until as late as the early 1960s, at which point retirement from the military led to a new civilian career in many instances. Tables 10 and 11 reflect these two periods, and show, firstly, those Cansos that survived the Second World War but were retired by the beginning of 1948 and went on to fly with commercial or overseas military users, and secondly, those that continued in use after the 1947 watershed. Table 10 does not show the sixteen Cansos that were supplied to the

Argentine Navy during 1947 as, unfortunately, the RCAF serials for these aircraft are not known.

Table 10. RCAF Canso As retired prior to 1/1948

Serial	C/n	Place of Manufacture	Struck Off Charge	Disposal – for subsequent history/fate see entries under country of registration
9738	395	CON SD	4/1946	To Canadian commercial as CF-FOQ.
9741	403	CON SD	2/1947	To Argentine Navy as 0279.
9740	401	CON SD	2/1946	To Colombia as C-134/HK-134.
9743	409	CON SD	2/1947	To Argentine Navy as 0275.
9747	420	CON SD	2/1946	To France as F-BBCB.
9749	425	CON SD	2/1946	To France as F-BBCC. Later XT-1401 and B-1401.
9750	427	CON SD	3/1946	To Canadian commercial as CF-DIL.
9752	21981	BOE CAN	10/1946	To Brazil as FAB6527. Current – see Chapter Sixteen.
9755	21984	BOE CAN	4/1946	To Canadian commercial as CF-CRV.
9757	21986	BOE CAN	11/1946	To Canadian commercial as CF-SAT.
9759	21988	BOE CAN	2/1947	To Argentine Navy as 0276.
9760	21989	BOE CAN	1/1947	To Indonesia as PK-CTD.
9761	21990	BOE CAN		To G/I airframe as A525. Struck off charge 4/1954.
9763	21992	BOE CAN	2/1947	To Argentine Navy as 0263.
9766	21995	BOE CAN	1/1947	To Indonesia as PK-CTC.
9767	21996	BOE CAN	4/1946	To Canadian commercial as CF-CRR.
9768	21997	BOE CAN	2/1947	To Argentine Navy as 0239.
9769	21998	BOE CAN	4/1946	To Colombia as C-133/HK-133.
9770	21999	BOE CAN	5/1946	To Colombia as C-82.
9772	22001	BOE CAN		To G/I airframe as A510. Struck off charge, 2/1953.
9775	22004	BOE CAN	2/1947	To Argentine Navy as 0261.
9776	22005	BOE CAN	11/1946	To Jamaica as VP-JAO. Later VP-BAN and VP-JAT.
9777	22006	BOE CAN	11/1946	To Brazil as PP-PCY – some sources quote PP-PCX (see RCAF 9806).
9779	22008	BOE CAN	2/1947	To Swedish Flygvapnet as 47003.
9780	22009	BOE CAN	4/1946	To Indonesia as PK-AKC.
9782	22011	BOE CAN	2/1947	To Argentine Navy as 0274.
9783	22012	BOE CAN	2/1947	To Swedish Flygvapnet as 47002.
9791	22020	BOE CAN	2/1946	To France as F-BBCD. Later XT-1402 and B-1402.
9792	22021	BOE CAN	10/1946	To Brazil as PP-PDB.
9793	22022	BOE CAN	4/1946	To Venezuela as YV-P-APE then OB-LDM-349, HK-996X, HP-289, 5Y-KUD, HR-236, N6108, TG-BIV, N5404J and ZK-PBYntu.
9794	22023	BOE CAN	10/1946	To Canadian commercial as CF-FAN.
9796	22025	BOE CAN	8/1946	To Indonesia as PK-CTA.
9797	22026	BOE CAN	4/1946	To Canadian commercial as CF-BSK.
9806	CV-240	CAN VIC St Hubert	11/1946	To Brazil as PP-PCX – but see also RCAF 9777.
9810	CV-244	CAN VIC St Hubert	2/1947	To Swedish Flygvapnet as 47001.
9812	CV-246	CAN VIC St Hubert	1/1947	To Indonesia as PK-CTB.
9813	CV-247	CAN VIC St Hubert	4/1946	To Argentine Navy as 0102.
9814	CV-248	CAN VIC St Hubert	4/1946	To Indonesia as PK-AKS.
9817	CV-251	CAN VIC St Hubert		To G/I airframe as A507. Struck off charge, 11/1948.
9818	CV-252	CAN VIC St Hubert	2/1947	To Argentine Navy as 0280.
9822	CV-256	CAN VIC St Hubert	3/1946	To Canadian commercial as CF-CRQ.
9823	CV-257	CAN VIC St Hubert	9/1945	To Canadian commercial as CF-DTR. Later to HK-1510E.
9828	CV-262	CAN VIC St Hubert	2/1947	To Argentine Navy as 0291.
9831	CV-265	CAN VIC St Hubert	2/1947	To Royal Danish Air Force as FM56 then 82-856.
9835	CV-269	CAN VIC St Hubert	6/1947	To Colombia as HK42X/E.
9836	CV-270	CAN VIC Cartierville	2/1947	To Argentine Navy as 0262.
9837	CV-271	CAN VIC Cartierville	11/1945	To Canadian commercial as CF-CRP.
9838	CV-272	CAN VIC Cartierville	10/1946	To Brazil as FAB6525. Later to N4934H and current – see Chapter Nineteen.
9840	CV-274	CAN VIC Cartierville	4/1946	To Royal Danish Air Force as FM51 then 82-851.
9841	CV-275	CAN VIC Cartierville	6/1947	To Argentine Navy as 0238.
9844	CV-278	CAN VIC Cartierville	4/1946	To Colombia as C-1511.
11002	CV-280	CAN VIC Cartierville	11/1946	To Argentine Navy as 0234.
11004	CV-282	CAN VIC Cartierville	11/1946	To Brazil as PP-PCZ.
11009	CV-287	CAN VIC Cartierville	10/1946	To Brazil as FAB6522.
11016	CV-294	CAN VIC Cartierville	8/1946	To Canadian commercial as CF-IHB, possibly via US civil registration.
11020	CV-298	CAN VIC Cartierville	10/1946	To Brazil as FAB6524.
11027	CV-309	CAN VIC Cartierville	12/1947	Possibly to Hong Kong as VR-HEG.
11028	CV-310	CAN VIC Cartierville	6/1947	To Canadian commercial as CF-FZJ.
11029	CV-311	CAN VIC Cartierville	2/1947	To Canadian commercial as CF-IDS.
11034	CV-316	CAN VIC Cartierville	11/1946	To Royal Danish Air Force as FM53 then 82-853 and L-853.
11039	CV-321	CAN VIC Cartierville	11/1946	To Royal Danish Air Force as FM54 then 82-854.
11049	CV-347	CAN VIC	4/1946	To Royal Danish Air Force as FM52 then 82-852.
11052	CV-353	CAN VIC Cartierville	6/1947	To Canadian commercial as CF-FVE.
11053	CV-355	CAN VIC Cartierville	2/1947	To Argentine Navy as 0292.
11054	CV-357	CAN VIC Cartierville	6/1947	To Canadian commercial as CF-JCV.
11055	CV-359	CAN VIC Cartierville	6/1947	To Canadian commercial as CF-GKI.
11058	CV-365	CAN VIC Cartierville	6/1947	To Canadian commercial as CF-IHA.
11068	CV-385	CAN VIC Cartierville	10/1946	To Brazil as FAB6523.
11072	CV-393	CAN VIC Cartierville	10/1946	To Brazil as FAB6526.
11082	CV-413	CAN VIC Cartierville	5/1946	To Venezuela as YV-AQA then YV-C-AQA.
11083	CV-415	CAN VIC Cartierville	10/1946	To Canadian commercial as CF-FAR.
11090	CV-429	CAN VIC Cartierville	3/1946	To Canadian commercial as CF-OBK.
11096	CV-441	CAN VIC Cartierville	10/1946	To Canadian commercial as CF-IHN.
11097	CV-443	CAN VIC Cartierville	11/1946	To Royal Danish Air Force as FM55 then 82-855.
11098	CV-445	CAN VIC Cartierville	3/1946	To Canadian commercial as CF-DIK.

Table 11. RCAF Canso As retired 1948 onward

Serial	C/n	Place of Manufacture	Struck Off Charge	Disposal – for subsequent history/fate see entries in country of registration
9815	CV-249	CAN VIC St Hubert	5/1961	To Canadian commercial as CF-NJB.
9825	CV-259	CAN VIC St Hubert	8/1950	Current at Campbellford, Ontario – see Chapter Fifteen.
9829	CV-263	CAN VIC St Hubert	8/1950	
9830	CV-264	CAN VIC St Hubert	9/1961	To Canadian commercial as CF-PQK.
9839	CV-273	CAN VIC Cartierville	8/1950	
11003	CV-281	CAN VIC Cartierville	1/1961	To Canadian commercial as CF-UKR.
11005	CV-283	CAN VIC Cartierville	5/1961	To Canadian commercial as CF-NJF.

When photographed at a snowy Montreal-Dorval in February 1964, former 408 (PR) *Goose* Squadron Canso A 11003 did not appear to have much future ahead of it. It is sans rudder, engines and rear wing surfaces, but it was eventually rebuilt and went on to fly as a water bomber in France and South America.
Peter Keating Collection

Serial	C/n	Place of Manufacture	Struck Off Charge	Disposal – for subsequent history/fate see entries in country of registration
11006	CV-284	CAN VIC Cartierville	5/1950	
11008	CV-286	CAN VIC Cartierville	5/1950	
11012	CV-290	CAN VIC Cartierville	5/1950	
11015	CV-293	CAN VIC Cartierville	6/1962	To Canadian commercial as CF-FFX.
11018	CV-296	CAN VIC Cartierville	10/1950	
11024	CV-302	CAN VIC Cartierville	10/1961	To Canadian commercial as CF-NTK.
11030	CV-312	CAN VIC Cartierville	8/1949	
11033	CV-315	CAN VIC Cartierville	4/1962	To Canadian commercial as CF-OFJ.
11035	CV-317	CAN VIC Cartierville	7/1949	
11040	CV-329	CAN VIC Cartierville	11/1961	To USA as N9752Z.
11041	CV-331	CAN VIC Cartierville	7/1959	
11042	CV-333	CAN VIC Cartierville	12/1960	To Canadian commercial as CF-PQF.
11044	CV-337	CAN VIC Cartierville	12/1954	
11045	CV-339	CAN VIC Cartierville	8/1950	
11046	CV-341	CAN VIC Cartierville	10/1952	
11047	CV-343	CAN VIC Cartierville	4/1962	To Canadian commercial as CF-OFI.
11048	CV-345	CAN VIC Cartierville	3/1948	
11051	CV-351	CAN VIC Cartierville	11/1948	Cat B damage in accident at Patricia Bay, Vancouver Island, British Columbia, 14/4/1948.
11056	CV-361	CAN VIC Cartierville	12/1960	To Canadian commercial as CF-PQI.

Serial	C/n	Place of Manufacture	Struck Off Charge	Disposal – for subsequent history/fate see entries in country of registration
11057	CV-363	CAN VIC Cartierville	9/1949	
11060	CV-369	CAN VIC Cartierville	5/1961	To Canadian commercial as CF-NJD.
11067	CV-383	CAN VIC Cartierville	10/1946	To Canadian commercial as CF-NTL.
11069	CV-387	CAN VIC Cartierville	8/1950	
11070	CV-389	CAN VIC Cartierville	10/1952	
11073	CV-395	CAN VIC Cartierville	12/1955	
11074	CV-397	CAN VIC Cartierville	11/1961	To Canadian commercial as CF-OWE.
11075	CV-399	CAN VIC Cartierville	6/1962	To Canadian commercial as CF-OMO.
11079	CV-407	CAN VIC Cartierville	11/1962	To Canadian commercial as CF-PQP.
11081	CV-411	CAN VIC Cartierville	8/1948	
11084	CV-417	CAN VIC Cartierville	9/1961	To Canadian commercial as CF-PQL.
11085	CV-419	CAN VIC Cartierville	7/1946	To USA as N68742.

The QZ hull codes on 11047 identify it as belonging to the post-war 103 (S&R) Flight based at Greenwood, Nova Scotia. Pictured during 1949, it is still flying with Buffalo Airways in the North-West Territories as C-FOFI.
MAP

Serial	C/n	Place of Manufacture	Struck Off Charge	Disposal – for subsequent history/fate see entries in country of registration
11087	CV-423	CAN VIC Cartierville		To National Aeronautical Collection of Canada, Rockcliffe, Ontario, 1965. Current – see Chapter Fifteen.
11088	CV-425	CAN VIC Cartierville	12/1960	To Canadian commercial as CF-GMS.
11089	CV-427	CAN VIC Cartierville	11/1962	To Canadian commercial as CF-PQO. Last Canso A in RCAF service.
11091	CV-431	CAN VIC Cartierville	5/1961	
11093	CV-435	CAN VIC Cartierville	4/1961	To Canadian commercial as CF-NJL.
11094	CV-437	CAN VIC Cartierville	5/1961	To Canadian commercial as CF-NJE.
11095	CV-439	CAN VIC Cartierville	8/1955	Cat A crash damage at Sea Island, Vancouver, British Columbia, 19/7/1955.
11099	CV-447	CAN VIC Cartierville	4/1951	
11100	CV-449	CAN VIC Cartierville	4/1961	To Canadian commercial as CF-NJP then to France as F-ZBAR. Nose survived and current – see Chapter Seventeen.

COMMERCIAL CATALINAS

As already related, the Catalina/Canso found a ready market with Canadian commercial operators, not only after the war's end, but also later in the 1960s when the RCAF finally disposed of the last of their fleet. Unlike the other Commonwealth air forces, including the RAF, RNZAF and, to a lesser extent, the RAAF, the RCAF operated mostly amphibious Catalinas, and the flexibility of this variant meant that the type was well suited to a variety of uses in Canada, on both land and water. Thus, the post-war years saw Cats being flown in the passenger and airfreight role, for aerial survey and photography and, in particular, for fighting forest fires. In the latter role, the type was used by both Provincial Governments and commercial operators, and a small number continue in use in the private sector still. In the main, Canadian-operated PBYs were based on the PBY-5A/Canso A version, although a small number of PBY-6As did appear. Canadian airworthiness rules decreed that several of the PBY-6As were de-converted by the installation of PBY-5A vertical tail surfaces. A small number of Cyclone-powered *Super Cats* also flew with Canadian companies.

The following companies and organisations are known to have operated Catalinas/Cansos on the Canadian civil register. In this list, the registrations are shown in the style used up to the mid-1970s, i.e. CF-***, unless they were only used in the later C-F/G***format. Table 12 following this list gives fuller details of each of the individual aircraft known to have operated under Canadian registry.

Aero Magnetic Surveys: CF-DFB

Aero Trades Western, Winnipeg, Manitoba: CF-JCV

Air Caledonia, Vancouver, BC: C-FJCV
Air Caledonia based their C-FJCV at Vancouver International and used it for charter flights around the western British Columbia coast during the early 1980s, before it was retired and flown into storage in Nevada.

Austin Airways, Timmins, Ontario:
CF-AAD, CF-DFB, CF-FAR, CF-IEE, CF-IHB, CF-JCV. CF-JTL, C-GGDW
Austin Airways first acquired a Catalina when one of its customers, the Canadian Nickel Company, specified its need for one. CF-FAR was obtained and its blisters were removed to be replaced by cargo hatches. The conversion to commercial standards was carried out by Aircraft Industries of Canada at St Jean, Quebec, and it entered service in March 1952. Incredibly, just a few days later, CF-FAR suffered a fuel control problem, and, with both engines stopped, was landed wheels-up on compacted ice near Churchill. The plane was later flown off the ice with its wheels still up! Less fortunate was CF-IHB when, on 2 July 1959, it was lost in a crash just after take-off from the water at Povungnituk, Quebec, after engine failure caused by contaminated fuel.

Austin eventually operated the Catalina/Canso for no less than 25 years, different examples being acquired and disposed of along the way. They were used for passenger and freight carrying to some of the most

When this photograph was taken, probably in the 1960s, CF-JCV was being operated by Austin Airways. It now flies regularly in New Zealand with the Catalina Group as ZK-PBY.
Jennifer M. Gradidge

This shot of Avalon Aviation's CF-HHR was taken at Sudbury in August 1978. Originally a US Navy PBY-5A, it carried out several U-boat attacks. It is now in Holland as PH-PBY and under restoration back to airworthy condition. *Peter Keating Collection*

inhospitable 'airfields' in Northern Canada, and were inevitably involved in various incidents over the years. CF-FAR was involved in at least two accidents in addition to the ice landing mentioned above. On 11 March 1956, it overshot the runway at Timmins, then, on 14 January 1956, it undershot at the same location. Finally, on 27 December 1956, it was wrecked when it crashed into a forested area near Timmins.

Many of Austin's Catalina flights were centred on Moosonee, and ranged far and wide from there. During the 1950s, the Cats were used to support the work on the Mid Canada Line of defences, along with many other aircraft operated by the smaller Canadian charter companies. Austin Airways was also involved in very early trials of water bombing equipment using one of its Catalinas, CF-JTL.

Avalon Aviation, Parry Sound, Ontario:
CF-CRR, CF-GLX, CF-HHR, CF-HNF, CF-HNH, CF-IZO, CF-IZZ, CF-PIU, CF-VIG

Avalon was originally formed in 1971 by Robert *Moose* Murdoch at Red Deer, Alberta, and operated as an independent water bombing company. Murdoch was a pioneer in the field of aerial fire-fighting and carried out his own conversion work on Catalina hulls. However, by 1979, he was advertising Avalon for sale and the company was purchased by Frank and Bruce Powell, who moved the base of operations to Parry Sound, Ontario. Their growing fleet of Catalinas was chartered to users all over Canada, and two of the PBY-6As were even used in Norway. In order to extend the life of the PBY, Avalon seriously considered producing a Rolls Royce Dart turboprop conversion, but this never came to fruition.

Avalon went into liquidation in the mid-1980s when the Canadian Government decided to favour more modern equipment for its contracts, and the entire fleet, bar one PBY-6A (C-FHNH), was assembled at Parry Sound to await disposal. All of them eventually found new homes, some as water bombers and others as display aircraft. C-FHNH remained in Europe, having been in Norway at the time of Avalon's demise. In its heyday, Avalon operated one PBY-6A, CF-VIG, as a crew ferry, but this had already been sold prior to the company winding down.

Awood Air – *see* Flying Fireman Ltd

Buffalo Airways, Red Deer, Alberta:
C-FNJE, C-FNJF, C-FOFI, C-FPQM, C-FUAW

Buffalo Airways became a major operator of Catalinas in the late 1990s, when it acquired various examples that had previously flown with the water bombing fleets of the Provinces of Quebec, Saskatchewan and Newfoundland and Labrador. Thus they formed the last large-scale fleet of water bombing Catalinas in Canada, and, at the time of writing, they are still active.

Can-Air Services, Edmonton, Alberta and Vancouver, BC: CF-DIL, CF-SAT

Can-Air flew charters out of Edmonton and around Western Canada, in particular for the sport fishing fraternity, during part of the 1970s and early 1980s. At least one of the two aircraft operated for one year under the banner of Pacific Airboats Ltd. CF-DIL was named *The Fisherman Special*. CF-SAT was still wearing Can Air livery when it was destroyed in a botched salvage attempt at Honolulu after a forced landing on water in April 1986.

Canadian Aero Services: CF-JJG

An aerial survey company that used CF-JJG, a Catalina that was to serve with a number of other companies in the same role.

Canadian Aircraft Sales: C-FPQF, C-FPQO

This company briefly owned two of the former Province

CF-CRQ of Canadian Pacific Airlines is seen taxiing with both its floats and retractable undercarriage extended. The wheels could be lowered once on the water to provide extra manoeuvrability. This photo must have been taken pre-June 1949, as it was written off in an accident on the 9th of that month. It was originally RCAF 9822.
Jennifer M. Gradidge

of Quebec fire-fighting Canso As after they were sold off in 1994. Both went to Greece for Athenian Airlift. Prior to their export, these aircraft were also registered to Pro Air.

Canadian Pacific Airlines, Vancouver, BC: CF-CRP, CF-CRQ, CF-CRR, CF-CRV
Canadian Pacific acquired four former RCAF Canso As via the Crown Assets disposals process in 1946, and they were converted to passenger and cargo configuration by Aircraft Industries of Canada. They were used on Western Canada services, taking in such destinations as Prince Rupert and Sandspit. One landing at the latter location was a belly landing on grass with one main gear up and a full load of passengers, none of whom was harmed. The four aircraft were given CPA fleet numbers as follows: CF-CRP/231, CF-CRQ/232, CF-CRR/233 and CF-CRV/234. Photos of the last aircraft show that at different times it flew both with and without blisters.

CF-CRQ was written off at Osiska Lake on 9 June 1949. Another crash involved CF-CRV, which was lost in an accident at Prince Rupert on 11 May 1953, when, during a heavy landing, the nose section broke away. One passenger and a stewardess lost their lives. CF-CRP was sold to Trans Labrador Airlines in 1957, and CF-CRR went to Northland Airlines in the summer of 1960.

Catalina Safari Company, The: C-FJCV
C-FJCV remained on the Canadian register for some time after it was acquired by Pierre Jaunet's Zimbabwe-based Catalina Safari Company. After conversion to a more comfortable passenger interior than had previously been the case, it left Victoria, BC, and was used in Africa for tourist charters before being reregistered in Zimbabwe as Z-CAT.

Chiupka Airways: CF-NJE

Conifair/Royal Aviation: C-FPQL, C-FPQM
This company intended using two of the former Quebec Province aircraft for fire fighting in the forestry protection role, but instead they were put up for sale c.1994 and sold on to Buffalo Airways.

Department of Transport: CF-DTR

Dorosh, David: CF-NJL
David Dorosh has owned this former Canso A transport since it was retired by the RCAF in 1961. Intended for aerial survey, these plans fell through, and David Dorosh had it flown to its present home at Gananoque in 1962. It is still there and is kept in good condition, but has not flown for many years. However, it is in a potentially airworthy state.

Dorval Air Transport, Dorval, Montreal, Quebec: CF-IHJ
This company is known to have operated CF-IHJ during support work for the building of the military communications networks in the north of the country in the mid-1950s.

Eastern Canada Stevedoring: CF-JCV

Eastern Provincial Airways Ltd, St Johns, Newfoundland: CF-CRP, CF-HFL, CF-HGE, CF-IHA, CF-NJC, CF-NWY
Eastern Provincial operated a handful of PBYs around Newfoundland during the latter part of the 1950s and early 1960s, and, as was typical for the type, they were

CF-FFW was one of a large number of diverse Catalinas operated by Flying Fireman Ltd, of Victoria, British Columbia, on water bombing duties. It is unusual in having a Super Catalina-type rudder whilst retaining the original P&W R-1830s.
Peter Keating Collection

used for a mixture of passenger and freight carrying and were also used during the construction of the DEW-Line. The latter included the carriage of fuel oil. It was on one such fuel flight that CF-HFL was lost when it crashed near Sona Lake, Goose Bay on 1 October 1957. The wreck remained *in situ* for many years and is a present-day survivor – see Chapter Fifteen.

In the 1960s, Greenlandair leased two of the EPA Catalinas for coastal ice patrols and on supply flights to the Kulusuk DEW-Line radar site on Greenland's east coast. One of these aircraft, CF-IHA, was lost on 12 May 1962, when it crashed at Godthab with the loss of fifteen passengers. The nose-wheel doors had malfunctioned during a water landing, causing the Catalina to decelerate rapidly and nose under.

Field Aviation: CF-HHR, CF-HTN, CF-IZZ, CF-NJP, CF-NWY
Field Aviation was associated with the Catalina/Canso as both an operator and a conversion company engaged in water bomber variants.

Flying Fireman Ltd, Victoria, BC: C-FDIL, CF-FFA, CF-FFW, CF-FFX, CF-FFY, CF-FFZ, CF-IHN, CF-NTL, C-GFFC, C-GFFD, C-GFFH, C-GFFI, C-GFFJ
Flying Fireman Ltd was formed in 1965 at Victoria Airport, Vancouver Island, adjacent to the old RCAF flying boat base at Patricia Bay. The company was taken over from the founder, Bud Rude, by the Wood family in 1977 and later renamed Awood Air. Bud Rude continued to operate a former Flying Fireman PBY-6A in the USA under the name Flying Fireman Inc. Although the large fleet of Flying Fireman Catalinas and Cansos were based at Victoria, they flew throughout Canada on lease to

Provincial authorities who needed fire-fighting capability during times of high risk to their forests. Having been obtained at different times and from various sources, the fleet was an odd mixture of aircraft, some having Pratt & Whitney engines, whilst others had Cyclones. Many had different tails, with standard, horn-balanced, PBY-6A and *Super Cat* examples all being in evidence! Most of them also had registration in the FF series (standing for Flying Fireman).

At one time the largest PBY water bombing fleet in the world, Flying Fireman gradually disposed of its fleet through the early 1980s, by which time the Canadair CL-215 had become the predominant water bomber in Canada. A number of its Cats were lost in accidents, whilst the survivors found their way to various parts of the world, including Spain, where a small number remain in use.

Geoterrex, Cartierville, Toronto, Ontario: C-FMIR, C-GGDW
Also operated N4760C, N609FF and N610FF on the US register. A geophysical survey company that used Cyclone-powered Super Catalinas on exploration flights throughout the world until the mid-1980s.

Great Lakes Paper Co: CF-VIG

Greenlandair
– see Eastern Provincial Airways

Hicks & Lawrence, St Thomas, Ottawa:
C-FNJC, C-FNJE, C-FNJF, C-FOFI
During the mid-1990s, Hicks & Lawrence acquired a number of surplus Cansos from the water bombing fleets of the Province of Saskatchewan and the Province of Newfoundland and Labrador. In the short term, at least one was chartered to Enterprise Air of Oshawa to provide crew training for other Catalina operators, but all four aircraft were eventually sold to other companies, two to Buffalo Airways and two to a Malaysian-backed consortium which flew the pair to Nanaimo on Vancouver Island for conversion to passenger-carrying format.

Now preserved in Newfoundland, CF-DFB was operated as
a geophysical survey aircraft in the 1950s and 1960s by
Kenting, part of the Hunting Group. With blisters gone but
bow turret still in place, it has had various items of survey
gear slung around its airframe.
Jennifer M. Gradidge

Hollinger Ungava Transport, Montreal, Quebec:
CF-DIK

Hunting Surveys – see Kenting

Ilford Riverton Airways, Winnipeg, Manitoba:
CF-CRR, CF-DIL, CF-GLX, CF-NJE, CF-OWE
Ilford Riverton flew a number of Catalinas on passenger
flights around Western Canada, although by 1981 only
CF-OWE remained on the inventory.

Jonathon Seagull Holdings, Victoria, BC: C-FOWE
C-FOWE was acquired from Ilford Riverton Airways and
totally overhauled by Flying Fireman Ltd at Victoria, BC,
for Robert Franks, the work being completed by 1986. It
is believed that the above-named company may have
been his.

Kenting/Kenting Earth Sciences, Toronto, Ontario:
CF-DFB, CF-GKI, CF-IGJ, CF-IKO, CF-IZZ, CF-JJG,
CF-JMS, CF-NJB, CF-NJF, CF-NWY, CF-UAW,
CF-UKR
At various times between the early 1950s and early 1970s,
all the above Catalinas are believed to have been operated by Kentings, part of the Hunting Group, some as
survey aircraft and others as water bombers. In particular, a number were regularly chartered to the French
Protection Civile organisation for fire fighting in the South
of France and Corsica. The survey aircraft roamed far
and wide on contract work and cropped up as far afield
as Australia and the UK.
   Two of the Catalinas, CF-IGJ and CF-IJJ, went to the
Falkland Islands to carry out a mapping contract during
1956, moving on to Antarctica at the end of the year.

Huntings were involved in mapping and survey in the
Falkland Islands and Antarctica, starting in 1956 with
Catalinas CF-IGJ and CF-IJJ. One of them is seen here in
less than ideal conditions!
via Barry Dowsett

   Kenting's final PBY, CF-JJG, remained with the company well into the late 1980s, by which time it was flying
with the amended registration C-FJJG.

Laurentian Air Services, Dorval, Montreal, Quebec:
CF-MIR

Leaseway Ltd: CF-NTL

Leasair: CF-IHC

Maritime Central Airlines: CF-FAN, CF-GBQ
MCA appears to have operated at least two Catalinas,
their use including support of the DEW-Line network.
CF-FAN was lost in May 1952, when it landed on water
with its main undercarriage extended. Inevitably, the aircraft came to a sudden halt and nosed under, with the
loss of its three crew. At the time of the accident, CF-FAN
was   operating   a   freight   charter   from   Gander,

Newfoundland, to Cartwright, Labrador. CF-GBQ was substantially damaged in a DEW site landing on 23 August 1956, but its ultimate fate is not known.

Midwest Airlines, Winnipeg, Manitoba: CF-CRR, CF-GLX, CF-NJE, CF-PIU

Miron & Freres, Cartierville, Quebec: CF-MIR

Miron & Freres acquired this ex-US Navy PBY-5A in 1959/60, and had it converted by Noorduyn Norseman Aircraft Ltd to a Wright Cyclone-powered *Super Cat*, complete with air stair, prop spinners and boats under each wing. It was used for some years as an executive yacht and went on to serve with a number of survey firms before becoming a hugely popular air display aircraft in Europe.

Montreal Air Services, Montreal, Quebec: CF-IZO, CF-IZU. CF-IZZ

National Tankers Ltd: CF-NTL

Newfoundland & Labrador Forestry Service: CF-CRP, CF-DFB, CF-IGJ, CF-IZU, CF-NCJ, CF-NJC, CF-NJE, CF-NWY, CF-OFI, CF-OFJ

The Province of Newfoundland and Labrador Air Services Division operated a large fleet of brightly coloured Catalinas on fire-fighting duties for many years, and still had a small number in reserve at the end of the twentieth century, although, in the main, their place had been taken by custom-made Canadair CL-215s some time previously.

Norancon Exploration Ltd: CF-DIK

This exploration company is known to have operated an ex-RCAF Canso A in the early post-war years.

Norcanair/North Canada Air Ltd, Prince Albert, Saskatchewan: CF-IDS, CF-IZO, CF-NJB, CF-UAW, CF-NJF

Norcanair flew Catalinas in the fire-bombing role in Saskatchewan from 1971 onwards until, in 1980, three of the fleet were taken over by the Province of Saskatchewan for the same purpose. CF-IZO was sold to Avalon Aviation.

Nordair, Montreal, Quebec: CF-DIL, CF-EMW, CF-FKV, CF-NJE

Nordair flew a number of Catalinas during the late 1950s and early 1960s, and usage included flights to Ungava, where a number of minor incidents during water operations caused repairable damage. CF-EMW was not so fortunate, as it was destroyed when it capsized whilst landing on a glassy lake surface 155 miles west of Knob Lake, Quebec, during a freight flight. The crew was lost in this accident.

Northern Wings, Sept Iles, Quebec: CF-FZJ, CF-IHN, CF-IIW

Formed in 1945, Northern Wings started flying non-scheduled services the following year linking various locations in Eastern Canada. The company still had two Catalinas on charge by the end of 1963, but one previous aircraft had been lost on 11 April 1957. This accident involved CF-FZJ, which crashed onto a frozen lake surface at Little Manicouagon Lake in poor visibility. It was carrying a cargo of fuel oil to Jeannine Lake at the time. Two months later, CF-IIW survived substantial damage after a heavy landing on Lac Rapide.

Northland Airlines, Winnipeg, Manitoba: CF-CRR, CF-GLX, CF-IDS, CF-PIU

Northland Outdoors of Canada: CF-OWE

Northward Air Services/Northward Aviation: CF-PIU

Ontario Central Airlines, Kenora, Ontario: CF-OWE

Ontario Department of Lands & Forests: CF-OBK

This government agency used a solitary ex-RCAF Canso A during 1946 and 1947 for spraying infestations of budworm close to the Port Arthur and Fort William areas of Northern Ontario. This was a continuation of work originally trialled using three military amphibious Cansos on the strength of 170 Ferry Squadron Aerial Spraying Detachment.

Pacific Western Airlines, Vancouver, BC: CF-GHU, CF-GLX

This well-known Canadian airline operated a brace of Catalinas on airline services during its early days, having inherited them from Queen Charlotte Airlines.

Pro-Air – see Canadian Aircraft Sales

Quebec, Province of: CF-PQF, CF-PQI, CF-PQK, CF-PQL, CF-PQM, CF-PQO, CF-PQP

A fleet of former RCAF Canso As was acquired surplus by the Province of Quebec in the early 1960s, and they continued in use for thirty years until the survivors were sold by tender. Originally flown in bright yellow livery

Pacific Western Airlines used CF-GLX on passenger and cargo flights in the 1960s. It has a clipper bow and horn-balanced rudder, together with various added access hatches and extra glazing. Originally a USAAF OA-10A, it was lost in a crash as recently as August 1997.
Peter Keating Collection

Two of the Province of Quebec Canso fire-fighting force are illustrated here in between missions at Manawaki in July 1980. The nearest aircraft is C-FPQM.
Peter Keating Collection

with red trim, this was later changed to blue trim. Hull titles were bilingual as befits the French-speaking areas in which the aircraft were employed. All the Quebec Cansos had registrations in the PQ series, denoting Province of Quebec.

Quebecair, Dorval, Quebec: CF-IHA, CF-IHD

Queen Charlotte Airlines, Vancouver, BC: CF-FOQ, CF-GHU, CF-GLX
Based on the Fraser River in Vancouver, QCA had operated a number of different seaplanes and flying boats, including the venerable Supermarine Stranraer, before acquiring three PBYs. The latter were a real mixture, one being an ex-RCAF Canso A, one a US Navy PBY-5A and the third a former USAAF OA-10A! The airline flew a mix of charter and scheduled services around Western British Columbia, using both water and land. Catalina destinations included Port Hardy, Kitimat, Ocean Falls and Kemano, as well as Vancouver. CF-FOQ, the former Canso, was destroyed on 17 October 1951, when it crashed on Mount Benson, near Nanaimo on Vancouver Island. It was flying Kitimat–Vancouver with a load of twenty passengers and four crew, none of whom survived. The aircraft was some miles off course at the time of the crash.

QCA was taken over by Pacific Western Airlines in June 1955, and PWA continued to operate the two surviving Catalinas for some time.

Questor Surveys: CF-JMS
A former US Navy PBY-5A, this aircraft was converted for survey work and later became a Cyclone-powered *Super Cat*. It went out to the South Pacific on contract in 1964 and then briefly flew on the Australian register before being restored to Canadian registry.

Saskatchewan, Province of, La Ronge, Saskatchewan: C-FNJB, C-FNJF, C-FUAW
The Provincial Government of Saskatchewan Air Transportation Service took over three Cansos from Norcanair in 1980 and used them to fight forest fires within the Province until they were retired in the mid-1990s and disposed of.

Spartan Air Services: CF-EPX, CF-GBQ, CF-JJG
Spartan Air Services used a number of war-surplus aircraft types for aerial survey work in both North and South America, and these included the de Havilland Mosquito and Lockheed P-38 Lightning. It also used the Canso and is known to have flown at least two examples during the mid-1950s. CF-EPX was destroyed near Pabbay Island on 22 December 1955, whilst on a long flight from Greenland to Prestwick. This was part of a planned flight to Pakistan, where it had been engaged to carry out survey work. After running out of fuel, the aircraft crash-landed close to the shore.

St Felicien Air Services, St Felicien, Quebec: C-FNJE, C-FPIU
This airline is known to have operated at least two PBYs during the latter part of the 1970s in the Province of Quebec. CF-NJE was repaired after hitting a rock during a water landing and overshoot near Fort Chimo in September 1977.

Survair, Ottawa, Ontario: CF-JJG, CF-MIR, CF-NJE

Tacair Systems: C-FIZO

Trans Labrador Airlines, Mount Joli, Quebec: CF-CRP
Trans Labrador operated at least one PBY. Records show that on 28 March 1957 one example drifted out to sea off Seven Islands Bay, Gulf of St Lawrence, after ditching. It eventually sank. As CF-CRP has survived to the present day, it seems that this must have been a replacement aircraft for that lost.

Transair, Winnipeg, Manitoba: CF-GLX, CF-HHR, CF-HTN, CF-IEE, CF-SAT

Amongst other uses, Transair flew its Catalinas on passenger services out of Lynn Lake and on support flights for the Cold War communications networks in Northern Canada during the early 1950s. It still had Cats on the inventory into the 1960s.

Wheeler Airlines/Wheeler Northland, Montreal, Quebec: CF-DIL, CF-EMW, CF-FKV, CF-FVE, CF-IHC, CF-ILK

World Wide Airways, Montreal, Quebec: CF-IZU, CF-IZZ

Wearing a vivid orange, green and white colour scheme, C-FCRP was operated by the Province of Newfoundland Forest Service as Tanker 6 from 1973 to around 1990. It is still to be found in the North Atlantic Aviation Museum at Gander.
MAP

Table 12. Canadian commercial Catalinas

Registration	C/n	Type	Place of Manufacture	Previous id(s)	Notes
CF-AAD	1658	PBY-5A	CON SD	N68746 Bu48296 (US Navy)	Austin A/W, 1966–72. Crashed, Poste de la Baleire, Great Whale, Quebec, 24/9/1972.
CF-BSK	22026	Canso A	BOE CAN	9797 (RCAF)	Registered c.late 1940s. Cancelled by 1966.
CF-CRP	CV-271	Canso A	CAN VIC (Cartierville)	9837 (RCAF)	Canadian Pacific A/L, 1945–57. Trans Labrador A/L, 1957–70. Eastern Provincial A/W, 1970–3. Govt Newfoundland & Labrador, 1973–90. To North Atlantic Aviation Museum and current – see Chapter Fifteen.
CF-CRQ	CV-256	Canso A	CAN VIC (St Hubert)	9822 (RCAF)	Canadian Pacific A/L 1946 – 6/1949. Written off at Osiska Lake, Quebec, 9/6/1949.
CF-CRR	21996	Canso A	BOE CAN	9767 (RCAF)	Canadian Pacific A/L, 1946–60. Northland A/L, 1960. Midwest A/L, 1970. Ilford Riverton A/W. 1973–7. Avalon Aviation 1977–95. Legend Air, France and current as C-FCRR– see Chapter Seventeen.
CF-CRV	21984	Canso A	BOE CAN	9755 (RCAF)	Canadian Pacific A/L, 1946–53. Crashed at Prince Rupert, BC, 11/5/1953.
CF-DFB	CV-605	OA-10A	Canadair (Cartierville)	TF-RVG NC65715 44-34094	Aero Magnetic Surveys, 1952–6, Kenting

Registration	C/n	Type	Place of Manufacture	Previous id(s)	Notes
				(USAAF) Bu68058 ntu (US Navy)	Avn 1956–9, Hunting Surveys 1960, Kentings 1965–71, Austin A/W 1971–8, PN&L 1978–90. To static display at Botwood and current as C-FDFB– see Chapter Fifteen.
CF-DIK	CV-445	Canso A	CAN VIC (Cartierville)	11098 (RCAF)	Norancon Exploration. Hollinger Ungava Transport, 1951–3. Sank during 1953 and written off.
CF-DIL	427	Canso A	CON SD	9750 (RCAF)	Nordair. Wheeler A/L & Wheeler Northland A/W,

The former RCAF Canso A 11098 is seen wearing small Norancon Exploration titles below the cockpit soon after being declared surplus and becoming CF-DIK. Externally, it is in virtually stock military condition.
MAP

Can-Air operated two former Canso As on fishing charters in and around British Columbia. C-FDIL is seen resting at Vancouver in May 1980.
Peter Keating Collection

Registration	C/n	Type	Place of Manufacture	Previous id(s)	Notes
CF-DRN	?	?	?	?	Ilford Riverton A/W 1972–3, Can Air 1974–81, Flying Fireman/Awood Air 1983–92. To Spain as EC-313/EC-FRG, 1993. To USA as N314CF and current – see Chapter Nineteen. Possible registration allocation – details unknown.
CF-DTR	CV-257	Canso A	CAN VIC (St Hubert)	9823 (RCAF)	Dept of Transport, Ottawa. To Colombia as C-1510, later C-1510E and HK-1510E. Destroyed in mid-air collision with FAC F-47D Thunderbolt, Colombia, 26/9/1953.

Registration	C/n	Type	Place of Manufacture	Previous id(s)	Notes
CF-EMW	1742	PBY-5A	CAN VIC (St Hubert)	N5805N Bu48380 (US Navy)	Wheeler A/L *c.*1956. Nordair. Lost in water landing accident, 155 miles N of Knob Lake, Quebec, 8/7/1961.
CF-EPX	'6'	PBY-5A?	?		Spartan Air Services Ltd. Ditched nr Pabbay Island whilst en route Greenland-Prestwick, 22/12/1955.
CF-EZX	1555	PBY-5A	CON SD	N68165 Bu34001 (US Navy)	Cancelled by 1966.
CF-FAN	22023	Canso A	BOE CAN	9794 (RCAF)	Maritime Central Airlines. Destroyed in water landing accident, Sandwich Bay, Labrador, 18/5/1952.
CF-FAR	CV-415	Canso A	CAN VIC (Cartierville)	11083 (RCAF)	Austin AW, 1952–6. Crashed nr Timmins, Ontario, 27/12/1956.
CF-FFA	1886	PBY-5A	CON SD	N5585V Bu46522 (US Navy)	Flying Fireman/ Awood Air 1972–90. To USA as N2172N and current – see Chapter Nineteen.
CF-FFW	1960	PBY-5A	CON NO	N45998 N6070C Bu46596 (US Navy)	Flying Fireman/ Awood Air 1968–93. To Spain as EC-314, later EC-693. Current as 'DR.1-1/74-21 – see Chapter Seventeen.

Flying Fireman's CF-FFX was originally the RCAF's 11015. In this superb shot, it is seen in post-war RCAF Rescue livery, complete with JATO bottles on the rear hull.

Registration	C/n	Type	Place of Manufacture	Previous id(s)	Notes
CF-FFX	CV-293	Canso A	CAN VIC (Cartierville)	CF-UVD ntu CF-OMU ntu 11015 (RCAF)	Flying Fireman.
CF-FFY	1842	PBY-5A	CON SD	N6069C Bu46478 (US Navy)	Flying Fireman. Crashed whilst fighting fire, Shawnigan Lake, BC, 8/8/1968.
CF-FFZ	1966	PBY-5A	CON NO	N6071C Bu46602 (US Navy)	Flying Fireman. To USA as N4NC ntu then N607CC. Current – see Chapter Nineteen.
CF-FKV	CV-332	OA-10A	CAN VIC (Cartierville)	TF-RVR 44-33880 (USAAF) Bu67844 ntu (US Navy)	Nordair. Wheeler A/L. To France as F-WMKS then 32/F-YCHB, CC-CDT. Current – see Chapter Seventeen.
CF-FOQ	395	Canso A	CON SD	9738 (RCAF)	Queen Charlotte Airlines. Destr on crash on Mt Benson, Vancouver, BC, 17/10/1951.
CF-FVE	CV-353	Canso A	CAN VIC (Cartierville)	11052 (RCAF)	Wheeler A/L/ Wheeler Northland A/W 1965–73. Wfu
CF-FZJ	CV-310	Canso A	CAN VIC (Cartierville)	11028 (RCAF)	Northern Wings. Destroyed after crashing at Little Manicouagon lake, 11/4/1957.
CF-GBQ	456?	?	?	?	Spartan Air Services. Maritime Central Airlines. Substantial damage in Northern Canada landing accident, 23/8/1956.

Registration	C/n	Type	Place of Manufacture	Previous id(s)	Notes
CF-GHU	?	PBY-5A	?	N5609V Bu21232 (US Navy)	QCA, later PWA 1951–7. To N2763A. Current – see Chapter Nineteen.
CF-GKI	CV-359	Canso A	CAN VIC (Cartierville)	11055 (RCAF)	Kenting Avn. To Australia as VH-AGB, 11/1956.
CF-GLX	CV-560	OA-10A	CAN VIC (Cartierville)	44-34049 (USAAF) Bu68013ntu (US Navy)	Queen Charlotte A/L, later PWA 1951–65. Northland A/L 1965–70. Midwest A/L 1970–2. Transair 1972–4. Ilford Riverton A/W 1974–7. Avalon Avn 1979 to 2/1996. To N3000T ntu. To USA as N322FA and destroyed in crash, Ramona, Ca, 1/8/1997.
CF-GMS	CV-425	Canso A	CAN VIC (Cartierville)	11088 (RCAF)	To CF-PQM in 1965, which see.
CF-HFL	'110'/ 520	PBY-5A	CON SD	VP-JAU VP-BAR NC18444 Bu05021	Eastern Provincial A/W 1953–7. Current – see Chapter Fifteen. Alternative p/is NC33301 and Bu08087 also quoted.
CF-HGE	CV-422	OA-10A	CAN VIC (Cartierville)	VP-BAB N95454, HK-43E C-43E, C-43X NC95494 44-33925 (USAAF) Bu67889 ntu (US Navy)	Eastern Provincial A/W, 1956.
CF-HHR	300	PBY-5A	CON SD	N18446 Bu2459 (US Navy)	Transair 1953 to 1969. Field Avn 1969–72. Avalon Avn 1972 to 1995. To Holland as PH-PBY ntu, N27311, PH-PBY and current – see Chapter Seventeen.

CF-GKI travelled widely as a survey aircraft with Kenting Aviation, and ended its days in Australia as VH-AGB.

Registration	C/n	Type	Place of Manufacture	Previous id(s)	Notes
CF-HNF		PBY-6A	CON NO	F-ZBAW N7082C Bu64097 (US Navy)	Avalon Avn. 1975–91. To USA as N7179Y. Current – see Chapter Nineteen.
CF-HNH		PBY-6A	CON NO	F-ZBAV N2846D N5555H Bu64017 (US Navy)	Avalon Avn 1974 to 1988. To UK as G-BPFY then N212DM/ G-BPFY/ N212DM/ G-BPFY/ N285RA. Current – see Chapter Seventeen.
CF-HTN	1637	PBY-5A	CON SD	CF-NTJ N1556M Bu48275 (US Navy)	Transair 1956– 65. Field Avn 1970–1. Crashed whilst firebombing 500 miles N of Edmonton, Alberta, 3/9/1971.
CF-HTO	?	?	?	?	Possible registration allocation – further details not known.
CF-HVV	1593	PBY-5A	CON SD	N68956 Bu34039 (US Navy)	To French Aéronavale as F-WMKS/39, 1965.
CF-IDS	CV-311	Canso A	CAN VIC (Cartierville)	11029 (RCAF)	Northland A/L 1965–70. North Canada Air 1970–3 then Norcanair.
CF-IEE	1566	PBY-5A	CON SD	N1947M Bu34012 (US Navy)	Transair 1953 to 1967. Austin A/W 1967 to 1970. Sank at Sugluk, Quebec during storm, 1970.
CF-IGJ	1791	PBY-5A	CON SD	N1565M Bu48429 (US Navy)	Kenting Avn, 1955–9. Government of Newfoundland & Labrador 1965–80. Damaged beyond repair in forced landing, Sherbrooke, Quebec, 19/12/1980. Wreck to St Jean.
CF-IHA	CV-365	Canso A	CAN VIC (Cartierville)	11058 (RCAF)	Quebecair 1955 to 1962. EP A/W 1962 and lsd to Greelandair. Crashed at Godthab, Greenland, 12/5/1962.
CF-IHB	CV-294	Canso A	CAN VIC (Cartierville)	N? 11016 (RCAF)	Austin A/W 1955–9. Crashed at Povungnituk, Quebec, 2/7/1959.
CF-IHC	CV-520	OA-10A	CAN VIC (Cartierville)	N62043 44-34009 (USAAF) Bu67973 ntu (US Navy)	Wheeler A/L 1955–6. Leasair, 1965. To France as F-WMKR then 20/F-YCHA, CC-CDU, CC-CGY. Current – see Chapter Sixteen.

Registration	C/n	Type	Place of Manufacture	Previous id(s)	Notes
CF-IHD	1810	PBY-5A	CON SD	N31234 Bu48448 (US Navy)	Quebecair 1956 –66. To France as F-WMKT then 48/F-YCHC. Fate not known.
CF-IHJ	1643	PBY-5A	CON SD	N1540M Bu48281 (US Navy)	Dorval A/T 1956. To N68623. Derelict at Long Beach, Ca, by 1967.
CF-IHN	CV-441	Canso A	CAN VIC (Cartierville)	11096 (RCAF)	Northern Wings 1965–70. Flying Fireman 1970-4. To C-GFFD, 1975, which see.
CF-IIW	CV-483	OA-10A	CAN VIC (Cartierville)	N1942M 44-33972 (USAAF) Bu67936 ntu (US Navy)	Northern Wings c.1965. To USA as N3202, 1969. To Canada as C-GFFC, 1975, which see.
CF-IJJ	1684	PBY-5A	CON SD	N1564M Bu48322 (US Navy)	Kenting. To France as F-ZBAQ. Written off at Veine, Bouches-du-Rhone, 8/11/67 after porpoising during practice water ops on lake.
CF-IKO	909	PBY-5A	CON SD	Bu08090 (US Navy)	Kenting Aviation, 1956 to 1957. Used by Hycon Aerial Surveys Co, Ca, USA.
CF-ILK	1797	PBY-5A	CON SD	N31233 Bu48435 (US Navy)	Wheeler Airlines, St Jean, PQ c.1955.
CF-IZO	2009	PBY-6A	CON NO	N10013 Bu46645 (US Navy)	Montreal A/S 1956–64. Saskatchewan Govt 1964. North Canada Air/Norcanair 1965–81. Avalon Avn 1981 to 1989. Tacair Systems. To Holland 1989. Later to Norway. Current – see Chapter Seventeen. PBY-5A tail.
CF-IZU	2019	PBY-6A	CON NO	N10014 Bu46655 (US Navy)	World Wide A/W 1956. Montreal A/Svs 1965–6. PN&L, 1966 onward. Current – see Chapter Fifteen. PBY-5A tail.
CF-IZZ		PBY-6A	CON NO	N10011 Bu64064 (US Navy)	World Wide A/W 1956. Montreal A/Svs 1965–6. Kenting Avn 1966. Field Avn 1968–70. To France as F-ZBAZ. Back to CF-IZZ, 1973. Avalon Avn, 1975–91. To Spain as EC-940, later EC-FMC. Current – see Chapter Seventeen. PBY-5A tail.

Registration	C/n	Type	Place of Manufacture	Previous id(s)	Notes
CF-JCV	CV-357	Canso A	CAN VIC (Cartierville)	11054 (RCAF)	Eastern Canada Stevedoring Co 1956–60. Austin A/W 1960–76. Aero Trades Western 1976–82. Air Caledonia 1982 to 1986. The Catalina Safari Co 1987–90. Re-regd in Zimbabwe as Z-CAT, 7/1990. To New Zealand as ZK-PBY, 10/1994 and current – see Chapter Fourteen.
CF-JJG	1785	PBY-5A	CON SD	N4002A Bu48423 (US Navy)	Survair 1965–6. *Explorer One.* Canadian Aero Service 1968–70. Spartan A/S 1973 to 1974. Kenting Earth Sciences 1976–86. To N423RS, 1986. Current – see Chapter Seventeen.
CF-JMS	1649	PBY-5A	CON SD	N10017 Bu48287 (US Navy)	Questor Surveys 1964. To Australia as VH-UMS, 1964. Restored to Questor Surveys as CF-JMS, 1964. Kenting Aviation. To N16647, 1975. Re-registered in Canada as C-GGDW, 1980, which see.
CF-JTL	1574	PBY-5A	CON SD	N10022 Bu34020 (US Navy)	Austin A/W, 1960. Used for early water bombing trials with external tanks. To French Aéronavale as F-WMKR/20, 1965.

The so-called *Super Canso* S/C1000 CF-MIR is pictured here with Wright R-2600 Cyclones and under-wing dinghies whilst owned by Quebec-based Miron & Freres in the early 1960s. Much later on, it was to become a very well-known aircraft on the European air display circuit. *Peter Keating Collection*

Registration	C/n	Type	Place of Manufacture	Previous id(s)	Notes
CF-MIR	1997	PBY-5A	CON NO	N10023 Bu46633 (US Navy)	Miron & Freres 1957–61. Laurentian A/S 1964–5. Survair 1965. To USA as N608FF, c.1965. Restored to Geoterrex/ Terra Surveys, 1970. To UK as G-BLSC, 1984. Later VR-BPS/ VP-BPS. Current – see Chapter Seventeen.
CF-NCJ	CV-420	OA-10A	CAN VIC (Cartierville)	44-33924 (USAAF) Bu67888 ntu (US Navy)	Government of Newfoundland & Labrador c.1973.
CF-NJB	CV-249	Canso A	CAN VIC (St Hubert)	9815 (RCAF)	Kenting Avn 1965–74. Norcanair 1976–9. Province of Saskatchewan. Current – see Chapter Fifteen.
CF-NJC	CV-430	OA-10A	CAN VIC (Cartierville)	44-33929 (USAAF) Bu67893 ntu (US Navy)	Eastern Provincial A/W, 1965–70. Government of Newfoundland & Labrador, 1970–97. Hicks & Lawrence. Current – see Chapter Fifteen.
CF-NJD	CV-369	Canso A	CAN VIC (Cartierville)	11060 (RCAF)	To USA as N609FF 1966–72. To Australia as VH-EXG, 1972. Current – see Chapter Fourteen.
CF-NJE	CV-437	Canso A	CAN VIC (Cartierville)	11094 (RCAF)	Chiupka A/W 1965. Midwest A/L 1970. Nordair A/A 1971–2. Ilford Riverton A/W 1973. St Felicien A/S and Survair 1973–6. Government of Newfoundland & Labrador, 1978–97. Hicks & Lawrence. Buffalo A/W. Current – see Chapter Fifteen.

CF-IHC was wearing Canadian Marconi titles when seen coming in to land in the 1950s. It is now a Chilean-registered water bomber operating in Spain and Portugal. *Eric Dumigan*

Buffalo Air operated C-FNJE in the North-West Territories of Canada as a fire-fighting tanker until it crashed in July 2001. Minimal changes had been made to its former Province of Newfoundland and Labrador livery.
MAP

Registration	C/n	Type	Place of Manufacture	Previous id(s)	Notes
CF-NJF	CV-283	Canso A	CAN VIC (Cartierville)	11005 (RCAF)	Kenting Aviation 1965–74. Norcanair 1976–79. Province of Saskatchewan, 1960–97. Hicks & Lawrence. Current – see Chapter Fifteen.
CF-NJL	CV-435	Canso A	CAN VIC (Cartierville)	11093 (RCAF)	David T. Dorosh from at least 1970. Current – see Chapter Fifteen.
CF-NJP	CV-449	Canso A	CAN VIC (Cartierville)	11100 (RCAF)	Field Avn. To France as F-ZBAR, 1963. Nose section current – see Chapter Seventeen.
CF-NTJ	1637	PBY-5A	CON SD	N1556M Bu48275 (US Navy)	To CF-HTN, which see.
CF-NTK	CV-302	Canso A	CAN VIC (Cartierville)	11024 (RCAF)	Marks possibly not taken up – to CF-UAW, which see.
CF-NTL	CV-383	Canso A	CAN VIC (Cartierville)	11067 (RCAF)	National Tankers Ltd, 1965. Leaseway Ltd, 1970. Flying Fireman 1971–8. Crashed whilst water bombing, Snow Lake, Manitoba, 21/5/1978.
CF-NWY	1666	PBY-5A	CON SD	N1555M Bu48304 (US Navy)	Field Avn, 1961–65. Also Kenting Aviation. To Eastern Provincial A/L. Government of Newfoundland & Labrador.

Registration	C/n	Type	Place of Manufacture	Previous id(s)	Notes
CF-OBK	CV-429	Canso A	CAN VIC (Cartierville)	11090 (RCAF)	Ontario Dept of Lands & Forests 1946–7. To Brazil as PP-PCW c.1965/1968. Written off in crash, Canutama, Para, Brazil, 17/10/1968.
CF-OFI	CV-343	Canso A	CAN VIC (Cartierville)	. 11047 (RCAF)	Government of Newfoundland & Labrador 1965 to c.1997. Hicks & Lawrence. Buffalo A/W and current – see Chapter Fifteen.
CF-OFJ	CV-315	Canso A	CAN VIC (Cartierville)	11033 (RCAF)	Government of Newfoundland & Labrador 1965 to c.1996.
CF-OMO	CV-399	Canso A	CAN VIC (Cartierville)	11075 (RCAF)	To USA as N610FF, 1966. Crashed on take off, Rhinelander, Wisconsin, 15/10/1970.
CF-OMU (ntu)	CV-293	Canso A	CAN VIC (Cartierville)	11015 (RCAF)	To CF-UVD ntu. To CF-FFX, which see.
CF-OWE	CV-397	Canso A	CAN VIC (Cartierville)	11074 (RCAF)	Ontario Central A/L 1965–70. Ilford Riverton A/A. 1977–83. Northland Outdoors of Canada. To USA as N691RF, 6/1984. Also N923CL? Restored as C-FOWE to Jonathon Seagull Holdings, 9/1985. To USA as N69RF, 3/1989 and current as N222FT– see Chapter Nineteen.

CF-OWE is pictured here during the 1960s when it was on the strength of Ontario Central Airlines.
Aviation Photo News

Registration	C/n	Type	Place of Manufacture	Previous id(s)	Notes	Registration	C/n	Type	Place of Manufacture	Previous id(s)	Notes
CF-PIU		PBY-6A	CON NO	N6681C Bu64092 (US Navy)	Northward A/S 1965. Northward Avn 1966. Northland A/L 1968. Midwest A/L 1969–70. Ilford Riverton A/W 1973. St Felicien A/Svs 1973–6. Avalon Avn 1979–97. To USA as N324FA, 11/1997 and current – see Chapter Nineteen.	CF-PQO	CV-427	Canso A	CAN VIC (Cartierville)	11089 (RCAF)	Province of Quebec 1963–94. Pro Air Avn Intl. To Athenian Airlift Svs of Nicosia. To South Africa, 1999 and current – see Chapter Thirteen.
						CF-PQP	CV-407	Canso A	CAN VIC (Cartierville)	11079 (RCAF)	Province of Quebec 1964–87. Crashed at la Cache, Quebec, 18/7/1987.
CF-PQF	CV-333	Canso A	CAN VIC (Cartierville)	11042 (RCAF)	Province of Quebec 1965–94. Pro Air Avn Intl. To Cyprus as 5B-PBY, 1994 and current – see Chapter Seventeen.	CF-SAT	21986	Canso A	BOE CAN	9757 (RCAF)	Transair 1956–65. W Bernard 1970. Can-Air Svs 1976–86. Sank Maui, Honolulu, 14/4/1986.
CF-PQI	CV-361	Canso A	CAN VIC (Cartierville)	11056 (RCAF)	Province of Quebec 1961–5.	CF-UAW	CV-302	Canso A	CAN VIC (Cartierville)	CF-NTK 11024 (RCAF)	Kenting A/C 1970. Norcanair 1973–80. Province of Saskatchewan 1980 to c.1997. Buffalo A/W and current – see Chapter Fifteen.
CF-PQK	CV-264	Canso A	CAN VIC (St Hubert)	9830 (RCAF)	Province of Quebec 1965–94. Foundation Aerovision Quebec and current – see Chapter Fifteen.	CF-UKR	CV-281	Canso A	CAN VIC (Cartierville)	11003 (RCAF)	Kenting Avn 1966. To France as F-ZBAX, 1966. Later to 81/F-YEIC, CC-CDS. Crashed during water bombing nr Chiguayante, Chile, 8/4/1979.
CF-PQL	CV-417	Canso A	CAN VIC (Cartierville)	11084 (RCAF)	Province of Quebec 1965–94. Conifair/Royal Aviation. To Canadian Warplane Heritage c.1997 and current – see Chapter Fifteen.	CF-UVD (ntu)	CV-293	Canso A	CAN VIC (Cartierville)	CF-OMU (ntu) 11015 (RCAF)	Re-registered CF-FFX which see.
						CF-VIG	2026	PBY-6A	CON NO	N788C N9588C Bu46662 (US Navy)	Great Lakes Paper Co 1967–73. Avalon Avn 1975–9. To USA as N1022G, later N999AR and N4NC. Current – see Chapter Nineteen.
CF-PQM	CV-425	Canso A	CAN VIC (Cartierville)	CF-GMS 11088 (RCAF)	Province of Quebec 1965–94. Conifair/Royal Aviation. To Buffalo A/W c.1997 and current – see Chapter Fifteen.	C-GFFC	CV-483	OA-10A	CAN VIC (Cartierville)	N3202 CF-IIW N1942M 44-33972 (USAAF) Bu67936 ntu (US Navy)	Flying Fireman/ Awood Air 1975–89. To SLAFCO in USA and current – see Chapter Nineteen.

CF-SAT of Can-Air was dead-sticked onto a snow-covered field in Alberta after engine failure in the 1970s. It was safely flown out again by Ray Bernard – with the wheels still retracted!
Alan Macnutt

Registration	C/n	Type	Place of Manufacture	Previous id(s)	Notes	Registration	C/n	Type	Place of Manufacture	Previous id(s)	Notes
C-GFFD	CV-441	Canso A	CAN VIC (Cartierville)	CF-IHN 11096 (RCAF)	Flying Fireman 1975–84. Written off in crash at Thunder Bay, 14/5/1984.	C-GFFJ		PBY-6A	CON NO	N6456C Bu63996 (US Navy)	Flying Fireman 1980. Destroyed in crash during water pick-up, Sioux Lookout/ Jackson Lake, Ontario, 12/7/1981.
C-GFFH	2008	PBY-6A	CON NO	N6458C Bu46644 (US Navy)	Flying Fireman/ Awood Air 1979–89. To Spain as EC-359, later EC-EVK and current – see Chapter Seventeen.	C-GGDW	1649	PBY-5A	CON SD	N16647 CF-JMS VH-UMS CF-JMS N10017 Bu48287	Possibly Austin Airways 1975–7. Geoterrex/ Terra Surveys 1980–5. To USA as N16647 1985. Later N287 and current – see Chapter Nineteen.
C-GFFI		PBY-6A	CON NO	N6453C Bu64041 (US Navy)	Flying Fireman 1979–86. To USA as N85U 1986. Current – see Chapter Nineteen.	C-GVTF ntu	1522	PBY-5A	CON SD	N5582V Bu33968 (US Navy)	Reservation not used. To USA as N84857 and current – see Chapter Nineteen.

Seven
CENTRAL AND SOUTH AMERICA AND THE CARIBBEAN

ARGENTINA

The Aviación Naval Argentina was no stranger to Consolidated flying boats prior to obtaining Catalinas as it had operated six of the earlier P2Y-3 Ranger biplane flying boats with the Escuadrilla de Patrulleros at Puerto Belgrano from the Summer of 1937. Ten years later, they were well and truly obsolete and in urgent need of retirement. The Argentines chose the Catalina as a suitable replacement and, in 1946, acquired their first example.

This initial Catalina is known to have been a Canadian-built, former RCAF example that had been acquired by Captain Stephen A Richards and taken to Argentina in June 1946. It does not seem to have acquired a civilian identity and was sold to the Argentines in the following October. It was given the Argentine serial 0102 and squadron code 2-P-10 and its new owners were so impressed by the improved performance over the P2Y-3s that they set about finding more PBYs. They hoped to acquire a further 24 aircraft.

In the following year, they managed to acquire 14 examples via the US company Babb Co Inc, all from ex-Royal Canadian Air Force stocks although some sources have claimed them to be former US military examples. Before delivery, all were overhauled by Canadian Car

and Foundry of Cartierville, Montreal. Two were used for spares and never saw active service although they did go to Argentina. All the aircraft were delivered in batches between 1947 and 1949, some being flown in formation via the Pacific then over the Andes and the others via the Atlantic route. One was involved in a forced landing on a farm near Cartierville on a pre-delivery test flight following engine failure but was only slightly damaged. These former Canso As equipped the Escuadrilla Aeronaval de Patrulleros and were operated by 3 Escuadra Aeronaval (3rd Fleet Air Wing) from Punta del Indio (BAPI)) and by 2 Escuadra Aeronaval from Commandante Espora air base (BACE).

Each unit had six aircraft and they were used on coastal patrols, SAR missions and transport flights. All the Catalinas were equipped with JATO (Jet Assisted Take Off) bottles to enhance performance when heavily laden. Poor weather conditions at BAPI led to frequent serviceability problems and their aircraft were gradually transferred to 2 FAW at BACE. For a while, a detachment of Catalinas flew out of Ushuaia on patrol flights along the Chilean border in order to reconnoitre disputed territory. As well as the uses listed above, the Catalinas flew as trainers and at times were also fully armed with machine guns, torpedoes and bombs. In addition, they helped to map areas of the Antarctic by carrying out photographic and surveying flights and two of the type made history when, on February 7th, 1952, they landed in Antarctic waters, the first aircraft to do so.

In September, 1955, the PBYs joined other Argentinian aircraft in military operations during the revolution and are known to have used machine guns and dropped bombs in anger, one Catalina (2-P-7) sustaining some 92 strikes from small arms fire in the process! Ironically, when Peron was overthrown, he was flown to exile in Paraguay in another Catalina from that country!

The last notable missions involving Argentine Navy Catalinas were in May 1958 and October 1959 when the type was used to search for submarines that had been detected in Argentine waters. These operations were known as *Golfo Nuevo* and *Comodoro Rivadavia* respectively.

Eventually, the Catalinas were replaced by Martin Mariners and Lockheed Neptunes although two of the Cats continued to fly until the early 1970s with Escuadrilla Aeronaval de Propósitos Generales (General

This photograph shows the first Argentine Navy Catalina 0102/2-P-10 c.1949. Supposedly a former US-built aircraft, it came to Argentina from Canada, but its previous identities are not known. Later, its hull codes were changed to 2-P-304.
via Jorge Félix Núñez Padin

Subsequent Argentine Navy PBYs came from former RCAF stocks, but their Canadian serials are not known. Judging by Canso A 11088 in the background, this photo of 2-P-20 was probably taken in Canada before the delivery flight south.
Jennifer M. Gradidge

Purpose Squadron) as transports and communications aircraft. One of these Catalinas, coded 1-G-1, was the last Catalina in Argentinian service and it was finally retired in 1971 at Punta del Indio. It may have lingered on in storage for a time but did not last long enough to survive as a preserved aircraft. Subsequently, attempts were made in the 1990s to obtain the former Paraguayan PBY-5A used for the Peron flight for preservation in Argentina but the plans did not come to fruition.

Four digit serials were allocated to the Argentine Navy Catalinas and these remained constant but with a variety of squadron hull codes being used. Initially, all the Catalinas carried hull codes in the series 2-P-10 to 2-P-24 (two of the four aircraft that were used for spares did not receive codes). This batch of identities followed on from the earlier Consolidated P2Y-3s that had been allocated serials within the series 2-P-1 to 2-P-9. Shortly after entering service, and after the P2Y-3s had been retired, the remaining airworthy Catalinas were re-numbered 2-P-1 to 2-P-12. A further example became 2-P-13 but did not fly again and was broken up for components recovery. A change in codes came when the 3 FAW aircraft had the prefix changed from 2 to 3. A small number of Catalinas bore the prefix 5 indicating their allocation to the detachment located at the Base Naval de Submarinos. The last of the type to survive carried prefixes 1 and 3 when in use with the Escuadrilla Aronaval de Propósitos Generales. A summary of squadrons and units that operated Catalinas, along with their hull codes, appears below.

The Catalinas were operated in overall silver/grey colours with blue/white/blue rudder stripes. However, the aircraft of the Escuadrilla Aeronaval de Exploración y Grupo Aéreo de la Flota were given liberal amounts of bright red around the bow area, the wingtips and rear hull whilst the upper wing surfaces inboard of the tips were painted bright yellow. These colours were intended to help location in the event of a forced landing on the ice of the Antarctic area. At least one Catalina (0236/2-P-6) of

Serial 0262/2-P-15 is seen here in 1948 during a break from its patrol missions. It later became 2-P-301 with the 3rd Reconnaissance Squadron. It has a small numeral 6 on the fixed vertical tail.
via Jorge Félix Núñez Padin

the Escuadrilla de Patrulleros de la Fuerza Aeronaval de la Zona Naval Marítime was given a black bow and rear hull band with sharks-mouth insignia below the bow turret!

Aircraft 2-P-7 suffered a forced landing at Harden Green airfield near Commandante Espora on 30 January, 1959, and 2-P-12 was badly damaged in an accident at Commandante Espora on 5 December, 1956. A number of other Argentine Catalinas were involved in accidents and mishaps but were subsequently repaired to fly again.

Argentine Navy Catalina Squadrons and Units:

Escuadrilla de Patrulleros/Escuadra Aeronaval No 2, Fuerza Aeronaval de la Zona Naval Marítime (1949-1954). Code 2-P

Escuadrilla de Patrulleros/Escuadra Aeronaval No 3, Fuerza Aeronaval de la Zona Naval del Plata (1949-1954). Code 3-P

1 Escuadrilla de Patrulleros (1955-1956). Code 2-P

Escuadrilla Aeronaval de Exploración y Grupo Aéreo de la Flota (1957-1958). Code 5-P

3 Escuadrilla Aeronaval de Exploración (1959). Code 2-P

Escuadrilla de Propósitos Generales/Escuadra Aeronaval No 3 (1959-1963). Code 3-G

2 Escuadrilla de Propósitos Generales/Escuadra Aeronaval No 2 (1961-1963). Code 2-G

1 Escuadrilla de Propósitos Generales/Escuadra Aeronaval No 1 (1964-1966). Code 1-G

Escuela de Aviación Naval (1967-1971). Code 1-G

Grupo Aerobanal Antártico (1952-1957).

Table 13. Argentine Navy Catalinas

Serial	C/n	Type	Place of Manufacture	Previous id(s)	Squadron Codes/ Fate
0102	CV-247	Canso A	CAN VIC St Hubert	9813 (RCAF)	2-P-10, 2-P-1, 15-P-1, 2-P-304, 2-G-2, 1-G-2. Wfu, Resolución, 12/1967.
0233	CV-477	OA-10A	CAN VIC Cartierville	FT998 (RCAF) 44-33966 (USAAF)	2-P-11. Dismantled and used as instructional airframe, Puerto Belgrano, 9/1947.
0234	CV-280	Canso A	CAN VIC Cartierville	11002 (RCAF)	2-P-12. Wfu, 9/1947.
0238	CV-275	Canso A	CAN VIC Cartierville	9841 (RCAF)	2-P-13, 2-P-11, 2-P-6, 5-P-2, 3-G-2. Wfu, Resolución, 1964.
0239	21997	Canso A	BOE CAN	9768 (RCAF)	2-P-14, 2-P-12. Damaged beyond repair, Ushuaia, 4/1949.
0261	22004	Canso A	BOE CAN	9775 (RCAF)	2-P-15, 2-P-14, 2-P-3, 5-P-6, 2-P-302, 3-G-3, 1-G-1. Wfu, 11/1971.
0262	CV-270	Canso A	CAN VIC Cartierville	9836 (RCAF)	2-P-16, 2-P-15, 2-P-4, 5-P-4, 2-P-301. Wfu, Resolución, late-1959.
0263	21992	Canso A	BOE CAN	9763 (RCAF)	2-P-17, 2-P-16, 2-P-5. Wfu, Resolución, 1960.
0274	22011	Canso A	BOE CAN	9782 (RCAF)	2-P-18, 2-P-13, 2-P-2. Wfu, Resolución, 1958.
0275	409	Canso A	CON SD	9743 (RCAF)	2-P-19, 3-P-1, 2-P-7, 5-P-7, 5-P-3, 2-P-7, 2-P-305, 3-G-1. Wfu, Planilla, 1961.

Serial	C/n	Type	Place of Manufacture	Previous id(s)	Squadron Codes/
0276	21988	Canso A	BOE CAN	9759 (RCAF)	2-P-20, 3-P-2, 2-P-8, 5-P-5, 2-P-303. Wfu, 9/1959.
0279	403	Canso A	CON SD	9741 (RCAF)	2-P-21, 3-P-3, 2-P-9. Wfu, Resolución, 1958.
0280	CV-252	Canso A	CAN VIC St Hubert	9818 (RCAF)	2-P-22, 3-P-4, 2-P-10. Wfu, Resolución, 1960.
0291	CV-262	Canso A	CAN VIC St Hubert	9828 (RCAF)	2-P-23, 3-P-5, 2-P-11. Wfu, 11/1958.
0292	CV-355	Canso A	CAN VIC Cartierville	11053 (RCAF)	2-P-24, 3-P-6, 2-P-12. Wfu, 11/1958.

BAHAMAS

Two local airlines flew Catalinas in the Bahamas after the Second World War. The first was Bahamas Airways Ltd, which operated a single amphibious example from 1947 onwards on charters and on services linking West Palm Beach in Florida and Nassau's Oakes Airport. It is known to have flown from both land and water. Originally purchased for the civilian market by the aircraft brokers Charles E. Babb Co, it was converted for 20-passenger use by Pan American in Miami, the re-work being completed in December 1946. It was registered to Bahamas Airways on 6 January the following year, and although initially named *Sailfish*, became *Eleuthera* in 1951. In August 1953, it was sold in Canada.

In 1957, Bahamas Airways needed to use the passenger-carrying capabilities of a Catalina again, and it leased the American-registered N4936V from Alaska Coastal-Ellis Airlines for 12 months or so, but it did not aspire to a Bahamian registration.

Table 14. Bahamas Airways Ltd Catalinas

Registration	C/n	Type	Place of Manufacture	Previous id(s)	Notes
VP-BAB	CV-422	OA-10A	CAN VIC (Cartierville)	N95494 44-33925 (USAAF) Bu67889 ntu (US Navy) Note 1	Sold in Canada as CF-HGE, 8/1953. Sank after forced landing 3km off Sept Iles, 13/9/1962.
N4936V	1705 Note 2	PBY-5A	CON SD	Bu48343 (US Navy)	Leased. Returned to USA and sank after nosing over on landing at Otter Lake, Chicago Island, Alaska, 2/10/1964.

Note 1: VP-BAB has had the additional previous identities of C-43X, C-43E and HK-43E quoted for it, but these may belong to a different Catalina.

Note 2: Previous identity Bu48362 has been quoted as an alternative, but this does not match c/n 1705. It may possibly be a composite airframe.

Bahamas Airways used two Catalinas, but only one aspired to a Bahamian registration. VP-BAB is seen here, apparently without aileron gust locks in place!
Peter Keating Collection

This rare photo shows the Bermudan-registered Catalina VR-BAB, not to be confused with the Bahamas Airways aircraft VP-BAB. VR-BAB was a former RAF Catalina IIA that had been used by 45 Group in Bermuda.
via Colin Pomeroy

The other airline in the Bahamas to fly Catalinas was Caribbean International Airways, which is known to have had three registered to it in 1949 and through into the early 1950s. Two examples were later re-registered in Jamaica with the same company.

Although these three Catalinas were only registered in the Bahamas for a short period, this time was not without incident. VP-BAN suffered substantial but repairable damage when it collided with two yachts during a water take-off from St Vincent on 2 July 1950. It had to be beached nearby, but there were no injuries to those on board. A more serious accident involved sister aircraft VP-BAO on 9 April. Whilst being ferried from Miami to Kingston via Nassau, both engines stopped and a forced landing was made in a heavy sea south of Kingston. Although accomplished successfully, the Catalina later sank. Subsequent investigation concluded that the main cause of the accident was fuel starvation brought on by various servicing and operating irregularities.

The other, better-known, Bermudan-registered Catalina was Plane Sailing Air Displays' Duxford, England-based VR-BPS. It only carried the registration on its hull on a few occasions, as it usually flew in period military marks. It is seen here performing in a show at Shoreham, Sussex, the day after returning from two hard months of water operations around the coasts of Italy.
Niall Cooper

Table 15. Caribbean International Airways Catalinas

Registration	C/n	Type	Place of Manufacture	Previous id(s)	Notes
VP-BAN	22005	Canso A	BOE CAN	VP-JAO 9776 (RCAF)	Re-registered in Jamaica as VP-JAT, 2/1951. Damaged beyond repair at Palisadoes, Jamaica, 21/8/1951.
VP-BAO	'118'/ 528	PBY-5A	CON SD	NC68713 Bu05029 (US Navy)	Sank in Caribbean Ocean, south of Kingston, Jamaica 9/4/1950.
VP-BAR	'110'/ 520	PBY-5A	CON SD	NC18444 Bu05021 (US Navy)	Re-registered in Jamaica as VP-JAU, 2/1951. Later to CF-HFL and current – see Chapter Fifteen.

Note: VP-BAR has also been quoted as ex-NC33301, Bu08087 (US Navy)

BERMUDA

Two commercial Catalinas have appeared on the Bermudan civil register, one soon after the end of the Second World War and the other in the 1990s. Bermuda itself had been no stranger to the Consolidated Catalina, as, during the war, the island was used as a staging post by the type, and many were delivered to the Royal Air Force via the seaplane base at Darrell's Island. Indeed, it was a former RAF Catalina IIA that became the first of the type to be registered in Bermuda. It had not seen squadron service but had been on the strength of 45 Group based in Bermuda. When the war ended, it was sold to the local Air Adviser, Wing Commander E. M. Ware. He and a partner had intended to use two ex-RAF Catalinas as the basis of a new airline to be called the Bermuda Air Cargo Company. One aircraft, JX293, was found to be heavily corroded and did not enter service, but the other, VA712, was converted to carry freight and flew as VR-BAB for a while until the company was forced out of business by more powerful competitors, such as

This unidentified PBY-5A Catalina of the Força Aérea Brasileira (FAB) is shown after the Second World War with its 'eyeball'-style turret and ordnance under each wing. The anchor stowage hatch in the bow is open. The rudder bears green and yellow vertical bands.
Museu Aéroespacial via Ricardo Bonalume Neto

Toward the end of their flying career with the FAB, the surviving Catalinas of 1ºETA had their vertical tail adorned with this emblem, showing a winged tortoise. The legend reads *De vagar mas chego la*, or I go slow but I get there. The squadron number has been sprayed out in this photo. *L. E. Miller*

PBY-5A 14, formerly US Navy Bu46553, later became serial 6514. This picture was taken in the Rio area just after the war. The aircraft lasted in FAB service until April 1972, when it was lost in an accident.
Museu Aéroespacial via Ricardo Bonalume Neto

BOAC. It was sold in the USA and then found its way to the French Pacific. Whilst in commercial use in Bermuda, VR-BAB carried its registration in huge letters along the mid-hull from aft of the cockpit to just forward of the blisters.

The second Catalina on the Bermudan register was the well-known example based at Duxford, England, operated by Plane Sailing Air Displays. It was registered as VR-BPS in 1994, and later became VP-BPS when changes were forced on the entire Bermudan register in 1997. The Bermudan registration came about because it enabled more flexible operation than was possible on the UK register at the time, but the aircraft was later de-registered after its 1998 accident in England.

Table 16. Bermudan registered Catalinas

Registration	C/n	Type	Place of Manufacture	Previous id(s)	Notes
VR-BAB	296	Canso/ Catalina IIA	CON SD	VA712 (RAF) V9712 (RAF) 9712 (RCAF)	To USA then to F-OAVV, 11/1952. Destroyed in accident, Raiatea, 19/2/1958.
VR-BPS/ VP-BPS	1997	PBY-5A	CON NO	G-BLSC, C-FMIR N608FF, CF-MIR N10023, Bu46633 (US Navy)	De-registered, late-1999. Current – see Chapter Seventeen.

BRAZIL

MILITARY AIRCRAFT

Brazil was the recipient of Catalinas during the Second World War when they were supplied by the USA under the Lend-Lease programme. A total of 7 PBY-5s were delivered to the Força Aérea Brasileira (FAB) in January 1943 from US Navy units already serving in the area, and these equipped 1º Grupo de Patrulha at Belém, 2º Grupo de Patrulha at Rio de Janiero–Galeão and 3º Grupo de Patrulha at Florianopolis. A further 15 amphibious PBY-5As were delivered from the US Navy, the transfer date

being recorded by a contemporary issue of *Aeroplane Spotter* as 8 December 1944. During the war, these Catalinas were kept busy on coastal patrols and were used in anger, one of the early PBY-5s being responsible for the sinking of the German U-boat U-199 on 31 July 1943, in the Atlantic Ocean off Rio de Janeiro.

Post-war, the surviving aircraft were allocated to 1º and 2º Grupo de Aviacao at Belém. The remaining PBY-5s were operated by 1º GAv and the amphibious PBY-5As by 2º GAv. Harsh operating conditions meant that by the end of the 1940s corrosion was taking its toll on the airframes, although some aircraft were reconditioned and replacement aircraft were acquired, including a solitary PBY-6A, two PBY-5As from the Brazilian oil company Petrobás and one from the local airline Cruzeiro.

A total of twelve Catalinas was flown to the USA, where they were converted to transport configuration by Pan Air Corporation of New Orleans. Work included the removal of armament and the bow and blister turrets. Thus configured, the aircraft soldiered on in ever-decreasing numbers, flying freight and passengers into more remote parts of the Amazon Basin. The last examples were on the strength of Belém-based 2º GAv and 1ºETA (Esquadráode Transporte Aéreo). Aircraft of the latter unit carried its winged tortoise emblem and the motto *I go slow but I get there* on the tail. The final destination for the transport flights was Ypiranga, until eventually, in 1982, an airstrip had been hacked out of the jungle there. Thus the need for water operations came to an end, and with it the Catalina era in Brazil.

Five of the FAB PBY-5As were sold in the USA and endured adventurous ferry flights north, whilst another -5A and the solitary PBY-6A were preserved in Brazil.

The initial seven PBY-5s were known by their former US Navy identities, but also carried hull numbers starting at 1. These seven were then renumbered with FAB serials 6500 to 6506, and the serials 6507 to 6527 were given to the later PBY-5As. At least some of these later aircraft also carried hull codes, and photos exist of 10, 14 and 16. Finally, serials 6550 to 6552 were given to two late

This 1970 photograph shows 6526 with CA-10 designation on the fin. Colours are grey and white overall with black lettering and trim. 6526 had originally flown with the Royal Canadian Air Force as a Canso A, serial 11072.
MAP

PBY-5A acquisitions and the solitary PBY-6A. Brazilian records show that the final serial 6553 was allocated to a former civilian aircraft, although in the event it did not enter FAB service and was reduced to spares. The Catalinas were also given type designations that were painted with the serial on the airframe. These designations changed several times, starting as CA-10, then CA-10A and lastly C-10A, where C and A indicated Transport and Amphibian respectively.

Table 17. FAB Catalinas

Serial	C/n	Type	Place of Manufacture	Previous id(s)	Notes
6500	1059	PBY-5	CON SD	Bu08165 (US Navy)	
6501	1079	PBY-5	CON SD	Bu08166 (US Navy)	
6502	1070	PBY-5	CON SD	Bu08185 (US Navy)	*Arara*
6503	1080	PBY-5	CON SD	Bu08186 (US Navy)	
6504	1136	PBY-5	CON SD	Bu08242 (US Navy)	
6505	1137	PBY-5	CON SD	Bu08243 (US Navy)	
6506	1214	PBY-5	CON SD	Bu08300 (US Navy)	(US Navy)
6507	1818	PBY-5A	CON SD	Bu46454 (US Navy)	May also have carried serial P4.
6508	1819	PBY-5A	CON SD	Bu46455 (US Navy)	
6509	1820	PBY-5A	CON SD	Bu46456 (US Navy)	Sold in USA as N4582T and current – see Chapter Nineteen.
6510	1821	PBY-5A	CON SD	Bu46457 (US Navy)	Sold in USA as N4582U and current – see Chapter Nineteen.
6511	1823	PBY-5A	CON SD	Bu46459 (US Navy)	
6512	1860	PBY-5A	CON SD	Bu46496 (US Navy)	

Serial	C/n	Type	Place of Manufacture	Previous id(s)	Notes
6513	1888	PBY-5A	CON SD	Bu46524 (US Navy)	
6514	1917	PBY-5A	CON SD	Bu46553 (US Navy)	Written off in an accident in Amazon area, 13/4/1972.
6515	1918	PBY-5A	CON SD	Bu46554 (US Navy)	
6516	1919	PBY-5A	CON SD	Bu46555 (US Navy)	
6517	1920	PBY-5A	CON SD	Bu46556 (US Navy)	
6518	1922	PBY-5A	CON SD	Bu46558 (US Navy)	
6519	1923	PBY-5A	CON SD	Bu46559 (US Navy)	
6520	1946	PBY-5A	CON NO	Bu46582 (US Navy)	Sold in USA as N4583A and current – see Chapter Nineteen.
6521	1784	PBY-5A	CON SD	Bu48422 (US Navy)	Written off, 8/2/1968.
6522	CV-287	Canso A	CAN VIC (Cartierville)	11009 (RCAF)	
6523	CV-385	Canso A	CAN VIC (Cartierville)	11068 (RCAF)	
6524	CV-298	Canso A	CAN VIC (Cartierville)	11020 (RCAF)	
6525	CV-272	Canso A	CAN VIC (Cartierville)	9838 (RCAF)	Sold in USA as N4934H and current – see Chapter Nineteen.
6526	CV-393	Canso A	CAN VIC (Cartierville)	11072 (RCAF)	
6527	21981 (Note 1)	Canso A	BOE CAN	9752 (RCAF)	Preserved at Campos dos Afonsos, Rio de Janiero – see Chapter Sixteen.
6550	1681	PBY-5A	CON SD	PT-AXL N9504C Bu48319 (US Navy)	Written off in crash landing on river at Santo Antonio do Ica, Brazil, 4/10/1978.
6551	1959	PBY-5A	CON NO	PT-AXM N9501C Bu46595 (US Navy)	Sold in USA as N4583B and current – see Chapter Nineteen.
6552	2007	PBY-6A	CON NO	PP-PEB PT-BBQ N9556C Bu46643 (US Navy)	Preserved in Belém – see Chapter Sixteen.

Serial	C/n	Type	Place of Manufacture	Previous id(s)	Notes
6553ntu	CV-240 (Note 2)	Canso A	CAN VIC (St Hubert)	PP-PCX 9806 (RCAF)	Intended for FAB *c.*1965 but not used and reduced to spares at Belém by 5/1978.

Notes:
1. The construction number for FAB 6527 has been quoted as BP.3075 although the origin of this is not known.
2. Brazilian records quote two c/ns and previous identities for the prospective 6553. Those shown above are generally accepted, but c/n 22006 ex RCAF 9777 is also quoted. The latter should be Brazilian commercial PP-PCY

PT-BGA is shown here in the colours of SAVA, which would date the photo around the early 1960s.

COMMERCIAL AIRCRAFT

It will be seen from Table 17 below that a considerable number of Catalinas were operated commercially in Brazil, as well as by the military. As with many of the PBYs operated in Latin America, information on the exact histories of the aircraft involved is not easy to come by. What is shown below is an amalgamation of data taken from various sources, but there are a number of gaps as far as constructors' numbers and previous identities are concerned.

The main operators were as follows:

Panair do Brasil

This airline flew a number of Catalinas from 1948 onwards, having obtained them from various sources. They were used on services around the Amazon, taking in such far-flung destinations as Belém, Manaus and Iquitos. The airline was declared bankrupt in February 1965. At least one of its Catalinas – PP-PCX – passed to the Air Force, although it was not used and was subsequently scrapped after some years in storage.

VASD (Viação Aérea Santos Dumont)

An airline formed during the Second World War that

This rare picture shows the aircraft that was to become the solitary Força Aérea Brasileira (FAB) PBY-6A, although the tall fin and rudder are obscured. Here, it is registered as a Brazilian commercial aircraft with the identity PT-BBQ, although it went on to become 6552 and is today preserved at Belém.
Jennifer M. Gradidge

acquired two PBY-5s from the Rubber Development Corporation in Belém for use on coastal routes, but their usage was short-lived, lasting only until early 1946. It is thought that these two Catalinas later passed to TABA (Transportes Aéreos Bacia Amazonica).

Aéro Geral

Aéro Geral was originally founded in 1942, but was revamped in 1947, after which it too acquired a number of Catalinas from US stocks in Brazil. They continued to fly the Catalinas until the early 1950s, although one example is known to have crashed in June 1951.

One of the former Aéro Geral Catalinas (PP-AGU) was acquired by Paraense Comercial Ltda, which went on to fly a number of others. Another known Catalina operator was Cruzeiro, which flew three examples – PP-PCW, PP-PEB and PP-PEC.

Table 18. Brazilian commercial Catalinas

Registration	C/n	Type	Place of Manufacture	Previous id(s)	Notes
PP-ABC	1781	PBY-5A	CON SD	Bu48419 (US Navy)	Leased to Panair do Brazil as PP-PDR, 1965–71.
PP-AGA	'87'/883	PBY-5A	CON SD	NC33300 Bu08064 (US Navy)	Aéro-Geral Ltda. To PT-ANU, 8/1952 then PP-BTD and PT-BGB.

Registration	C/n	Type	Place of Manufacture	Previous id(s)	Notes
PP-AGB		PBY-5A			Aéro Geral Ltda.
PP-AGC		PBY-5A			Aéro Geral Ltda. Accident, 2/6/1951.
PP-AGD		PBY-5A			Aéro Geral Ltda.
PP-AGH	1995	PBY-5A	CON NO		Aéro Geral Ltda. To PP-AMR.
PT-AMR	1995	PBY-5A	CON NO	PP-AMR Bu46631 (USNavy)	Paraense Comercial Ltda, Belém. To N74694 by 1966.
PT-ANU	'87'/883	PBY-5A	CON SD	NC33300 PP-AGA Bu08064 (US Navy)	Paraense Comercial Ltda, Belém, 8/1952. To PP-BTD, 7/1957 then PT-BGB.
PT-APK – not taken up – see PT-AXX					
PT-ASN	1792	PBY-5A	CON SD	N1522V Bu48430 (US Navy)	
PT-ASX		PBY-5A?		YV-P-AEP (see note 1)	Paraense Comercial Ltda, Belém. To PT-BTC then PT-BGA, 7/1957.
PT-AXL	1681	PBY-5A	CON SD	N9504C Bu48319 (US Navy)	To FAB as 6550 Written off in crash landing on river at Santo Antonio do Ica, Brazil, 4/10/1978.
PT-AXM	1959	PBY-5A	CON NO	N9501C Bu46595 (US Navy)	To FAB as 6551 Sold in USA as N4583B and current – see Chapter Nineteen.
PT-AXX	1599	PBY-5A	CON SD	Bu34045 (US Navy)	To PT-APK but ntu. Written off, 8/5/1953.
PT-BBD	'91'/887	PBY-5A	CON SD	N6470C Bu08068 (US Navy)	To PP-PEC.
PT-BBP		PBY-6A	CON NO	N7860B Bu64063 (US Navy)	Servicios *Aérotaxi Abast do Vale*, Belém. Accident, 9/8/1963.
PT-BBQ	2007	PBY-6A	CON NO	N9556C Bu46643 (US Navy)	To PP-PEB then FAB as 6552 Preserved in Belém – see Chapter Sixteen.

Panair do Brasil's PBY-5A PP-PEC is seen at an unknown interior airfield c.1961. It later went on to fly with Cruzeiro. The Catalina port wing in the foreground belongs to the military Catalina CA-10 6508.
G. A. Jenks Collection

Registration	C/n	Type	Place of Manufacture	Previous id(s)	Notes
PT-BGA		PBY-5A?		PT-BTC PT-ASX YV-P-AEP (see note 1)	Paraense Transportes Aereos SA, Belém. To SAVA, 1961.
PT-BGB	'87'/883	PBY-5A	CON SD	PP-BTD PT-ANA PP-AGA NC33300 Bu08064 (US Navy)	SAVA, 11/1960.
PP-BLA		PBY-5A		PP-SDA	VASD then TABA.
PP-BLB		PBY-5A		PP-SDB	VASD then TABA, later Cia. De Transportes Aéreos Bandierante. Destroyed after landing accident on water, Iguape, Brazil, 30/9/1949.
PP-BTC		PBY-5A?		PT-ASX YV-P-AEP (see note 1)	Paraense Transportes Aéreos SA, Belém. To PT-BGA.
PP-BTD	'87'/883	PBY-5A	CON SD	PT-ANU PP-AGA NC33300 Bu08064 (US Navy)	Transportes Aéreos SA, Belém, 7/1957. To PT-BGB, 11/1960.
PP-PCW	CV-429	Canso A	CAN VIC (Cartierville)	CF-OBK 11090 (RCAF)	Cruzeiro. *Pedro Teixeira*, Panair do Brasil, São Paulo 1965–8. Written off in crash, Canutama, Para, Brazil, 17/10/1968.
PP-PCX	CV-240 (see Note 2)	Canso A	CAN VIC (St Hubert)	9806 (RCAF) (see Note 2)	*Antonio Pedroso de Alvarenga* Panair do Brasil. To Força Aérea Brasileira, 2/1956 and allocated serial 6553 but not taken up. Scrapped at Belém by 1978.
PP-PCY	22006 (see Note 3)	Canso A	BOE CAN	9777 (RCAF) (see Note 3)	*Antonio Dias Adorno* Panair do Brasil, 1964.

Another SAVA Catalina was PP-BTD, the former US Navy PBY-5A Bu08064. This aircraft had flown in South America during the Second World War in support of the provision of rubber to the USA. By the time it was photographed, the blisters and bow turret had been replaced and wheel trim had been added.
Jennifer M. Gradidge

Registration	C/n	Type	Place of Manufacture	Previous id(s)	Notes
PP-PCZ	CV-282	Canso A	CAN VIC (Cartierville)	11004 (RCAF)	*Jaycomo Raymundo de Noronha* Panair do Brasil.
PP-PDB	22021	Canso A	BOE CAN	9792 (RCAF)	Panair do Brasil. Crashed on Amazon at Parantins after hitting submerged object after flight from Belém, 18/4/1956.
PP-PDR	1781	PBY-5A	CON SD	PP-ABC Bu48419 (US Navy)	*Pedro Vaz de Barros* Panair do Brasil 1965–71.
PP-PEB	2007	PBY-6A	CON NO	PT-BBQ N9556C Bu46643 (US Navy)	Cruzeiro. To FAB as 6552 Preserved in Belém – see Chapter Sixteen.
PP-PEC	'91'/887	PBY-5A	CON SD	PT-BBD N6470C Bu08068 (US Navy)	Panair do Brazil, 1964. Cruzeiro.
PP-PLB					CTAB. Crashed in Brazil, 30/9/1949.
PP-SDA		PBY-5A			VASD. To PP-BLA.
PP-SDB		PBY-5A			VASD. To PP-BLB.

Note 1: The aircraft PT-ASX/PT-BTC/PT-BGA is often quoted as the former RCAF Canso 9746, c/n 417. However, this latter aircraft is known to have become N59D/N5907/N81RD/N5907/N5PY, and this author is not convinced that it saw service in Brazil before appearing on the US register.

Note 2: PP-PCX. Brazilian records show two possible identities for this aircraft. The first, generally accepted, version is as shown in the table above. The other is c/n 22006, ex-RCAF 9777 built by Boeing of Canada – see Note 3 below.

Note 3: PP-PCY. This is normally quoted as c/n 22006 ex-RCAF 9777, but see PP-PCX above. However, the c/n CV-242 ex-RCAF 9808 built by Canadian Vickers at St Hubert has also been suggested.

CHILE

MILITARY AIRCRAFT

The first Catalinas delivered to the Fuerza Aérea Nacional de Chile were supplied by the USA under Lend-Lease arrangements, and consisted of three PBY-5 flying boats delivered from the end of March 1943. They were used for patrol flights along Chile's extensive Pacific coastline by Grupo de Aviación 2 from Quintero,

Valparaiso. In 1948, Grupo 2 became the Escuadrilla de Exploración y Rescate (SAR Squadron). It is thought that Grupo 8 also flew Catalinas for a time, probably alongside Douglas Invaders. The survivors of the three flying boats remained in service long after the end of the Second World War, and were still in use until the mid-1950s. The Catalina fleet was later augmented by amphibious PBY-5A and OA-10A examples supplied by and purchased in the USA.

A total of at least twelve examples were operated in all, although exact details are difficult to ascertain because of changes to the serials that they carried. The first three aircraft were serialled 400 to 402, and later examples followed on in the same numeric sequence, but some were later re-serialled in the 560 range, and tie-ups are not known. In the Chilean Air Force numbering system, serials in the 400 to 499 range denoted communications types, whilst those in the 500 to 599 range indicated miscellaneous aircraft.

One of the amphibious aircraft, 405 *Manutara*, was used to make the first flight between Chile (Coquimbo-La Serena) and Isla de Pascua, or Easter Island, in 1950. However, the aircraft was badly damaged when taking off for the return journey from the rough waters surrounding this Pacific island. It had to be taken ashore, where it was stored for a time before being shipped back to Chile for repairs on board the Chilean Navy vessel *Pinto*. It was later re-serialled as 560 *Manutara II* and flew successfully from Quintero to Easter Island and back to Quintero. The captain for the Easter Island flights was Roberto Parragué, who later operated commercial Catalinas in Chile with his own company ASPAR.

Table 19. Catalinas of the Fuerza Aérea Nacional de Chile

Serial	C/n	Type	Place of Manufacture	Previous id(s)	Notes
400	1215	PBY-5	CON SD	Bu08301 (US Navy)	Withdrawn from use after accident, 10/9/1948.

Seen at anchor off Quintero air base in this rare photo is the Fuerza Aérea Nacional de Chile PBY-5 flying boat, serial 402. On the original photo, the designation PBY-5 is written on the lower rudder, whilst the former US Navy serial appears on the base of the fin as 08433.
via Sergio Barriga Kfret

Coming in over the threshold at Quintero air base is the Chilean military Catalina serial 408. It has yellow and black 'Rescue' bands painted around the rear hull.
via Sergio Barriga Kfret

Serial	C/n	Type	Place of Manufacture	Previous id(s)	Notes
401	1216	PBY-5	CON SD	Bu08302 (US Navy)	Accident 20/5/1953. Withdrawn from use, 3/1960.
402	1367	PBY-5	CON SD	Bu08433 (US Navy)	Accident 5/10/1953. Withdrawn from use, 3/1960.
403					
404	463	PBY-5A	CON SD	Bu7295 (US Navy)	
405 (later 560)	CV-304	OA-10A	CAN VIC (Cartierville)	44-33868 (USAAF) Bu67832 ntu (US Navy)	To 560.
406 (later 561)	CV-604	OA-10A	CAN VIC (Cartierville)	44-34093 (USAAF) Bu68057 ntu (US Navy)	To 561.
407					
408					
409					
560	CV-304	OA-10A	CAN VIC (Cartierville)	405 (FANdeC) 44-33868 (USAAF) Bu67832 ntu (US Navy)	
561	CV-604	OA-10A	CAN VIC (Cartierville)	406 (FANdeC) 44-34093 (USAAF) Bu68057 ntu (US Navy)	
562					Accident. 26/1/1958.
563	1787	PBY-5A	CON SD	N68743 Bu48425 (US Navy)	Withdrawn from use, 5/1961.
564	1627	PBY-5A	CON SD	N68745 Bu48265 (US Navy)	Withdrawn from use, 9/1963.
565	1822	PBY-5A	CON SD	N68769 Bu46458 (US Navy)	Damaged beyond repair in accident, 1/12/1960.
566					
567					
568					
569					

COMMERCIAL AIRCRAFT

Catalinas are known to have been operated by three Chilean companies, and one of these is still very much operational, with no fewer than three of the type active on fire-fighting duties in Spain and Portugal.

AÉRO PESQUERA CATALINA SA

This airline had a PBY-5A registered to it as long ago as April 1951, although little is known about the company, and the registration CC-CAK that had been allocated to the Catalina was subsequently cancelled, date unknown.

ASPAR's PBY-6A CC-CNP is shown in Canada during its conversion to a water bombing fire-fighter.
Peter Keating Collection

Table 20. Aéro Pesquera Catalina SA

Registration	C/n	Type	Place of Manufacture	Previous id(s)	Notes
CC-CAK	1813	PBY-5A	CON SD	N1932M Bu48451 (US Navy)	Registration cancelled sometime after 4/1951.

TRANSA-Chile

The next company to acquire PBYs was TRANSA-Chile, which acquired two of the breed. These were both former US Navy PBY-6As and were purchased in 1957 after spending several years in storage in the USA. They were flown to Chile, and one example – CC-CNF – was converted for commercial use by PANAERO, whilst similar work on the other aircraft – CC-CNG – was halted before completion. TRANSA only flew CC-CNF for a short time before taking it out of service, and it was sold to ASPAR in 1960. ASPAR had already acquired the partially converted CC-CNG the year before.

Table 21. TRANSA-Chile

Registration	C/n	Type	Place of Manufacture	Previous id(s)	Notes
CC-CNF	2043	PBY-6A	CON NO	N9562C Bu46679 (US Navy)	To ASPAR in 1960 as CC-CCS. Current.
CC-CNG	2029	PBY-6A	CON NO	N9555C Bu46665 (US Navy)	To ASPAR in 1959 as CC-CNP. Current.

Aéroservicio Parragué Ltda (ASPAR)

Aéroservicio Parragué Ltda, or ASPAR as it is more commonly known, was formed by General Roberto Parrague, a former Chilean Air Force pilot who had carried out a number of long-distance flights from Chile to Easter Island in a military Catalina. He formed ASPAR in the late 1950s, and initially obtained two PBY-6A Catalinas from the defunct Chilean airline TRANSA-Chile. One aircraft had been only partially converted for civilian use,

Once an OA-10A with the USAAF, CC-CDT later served as a commercial aircraft in Iceland and Canada, and then with the Aéronavale in the Pacific, before going to Chile as a passenger aircraft. After this photo was taken, it became a water bomber.
Jennifer M. Gradidge

and ASPAR completed this work, putting it into service in 1960 when it was joined by the second example. They became CC-CNP and CC-CCS respectively.

Amongst its early operations were flights to Easter Island, a distance of more than 2,000 miles across the Pacific Ocean from Chile, as pioneered a few years before by ASPAR's owner. By the mid-1960s, schedules were also being flown to Tahiti, although low demand led to this route's discontinuation in 1969. New work was necessary to keep the company operating, and attention was focused on aerial forest-fire-fighting. Serious fires in Chile were fought using aircraft leased from Canada and the USA, but after a Canadian example was destroyed in a crash in 1969, ASPAR decided to enter the market, offering lower prices. CC-CNP was ferried to Canada for conversion to a water bomber, and it returned to Chile in November 1969, ready to start work.

General Parrague started to look for additional aircraft. He was aware of the three French Aéronavale Catalinas in Tahiti, where they had remained in storage since 1971 after being withdrawn from supporting the French nuclear testing in the area. He offered to buy one of these aircraft, but in response, the French donated all three aircraft to ASPAR! In August 1973, they were transported as deck cargo from Tahiti to Valparaiso aboard the freighter *Buque Andino* and then taken to Quintero air base, where they were overhauled. They were eventually completed and flown to Santiago between April 1974 and March 1975.

ASPAR continued to fly a mix of passenger/transport and water bombing operations, and gradually more of the fleet were converted to the bombing role, using Chile's plentiful lakes for 'ammunition'. Passenger services to the Isla Juan Fernández were often difficult because of the local geography, weather conditions and lack of navaids, and these flights were eventually abandoned. In addition to passengers, these operations had also been used to transport lobsters to the mainland for sale.

ASPAR had always looked wider than the Chilean borders for work for its aircraft, and when, in the late 1980s, Spain needed additional aircraft to combat forest fires, the Chilean company successfully tendered for the contract. Initially, two of its Catalinas (CC-CDT and CC-CNP) were involved, and they were flown all the

way from Chile to Spain in 1988. The ferry flight commenced on 25 June 1988 at Santiago, and it routed Mendoza, Argentina; Asuncion, Paraguay; Campo Grande, Brazil; Brasilia, Recife and Fernando de Noronha, all in Brazil; Dakar, Senegal; Las Palmas, Madrid, and, finally, Zaragoza. The Catalinas flew together for the entire flight, which ended on 8 July. Later, in June of 1991, the two Cats were joined by PBY-6A CC-CCS following its post-crash rebuild – see below. Although it was originally intended to ship the Catalinas back to Chile at the end of the contract, they were used in Spain longer than intended, and to date they remain there, although utilisation has decreased. They are operated in conjunction with FAASA (Fumigacion Aérea Andaluza SA) on behalf of ICONA (Instituta Para la Conservation de la Naturaleza). One of the aircraft was transferred to the Spanish register for a while but the other two remained Chilean registered. From time to time, they have also been used for fire-fighting work in neighbouring Portugal with Aerocondor.

In ASPAR service, the Catalinas were allocated hull code numbers in common with most water bombing types. These were originally based on either the former Canadian Vickers construction number or, in the case of the ex-US Navy machines, the 'last two' of the BuAer serial. Later, the system was rationalised so that the numbers ran from 31 to 35 respectively.

Aerial fire-fighting, being somewhat more risky than passenger flying, means some accidents were perhaps inevitable. One of the ASPAR Catalinas was written off in a crash in April 1979. CC-CDS was fighting a forest fire near Chiguayante when its port wing hit trees and it hit the ground, killing all three crew members. Another example – CC-CCS – suffered severe damage in January 1986, when it hit a rock whilst alighting on Lake Gutierrez near San Carlos de Bariloche in the Argentine. The captain was killed and the aircraft sank although it was later salvaged, roaded 1,200 km back to Chile, and rebuilt by ASPAR at its Los Cerrillos base in Santiago. This very extensive rebuild was completed at the end of 1988, and CC-CCS was put back into service.

Table 22. Aéroservicio Parragué Ltda (ASPAR)

Registration	C/n	Type	Place of Manufacture	Previous id(s)	Notes
CC-CCS	2043	PBY-6A	CON NO	CC-CNF N9562C Bu46679 (US Navy)	Fleet numbers 79 and 34. Current – see Chapter Seventeen.
CC-CDS	CV-281	Canso A	CAN VIC (Cartierville)	81 (Aéronavale) F-YEIC (callsign) F-ZBAX CF-UKR 11003 (RCAF)	Fleet number 81 and 31. Written off in crash, Chigyuante, 8/4/1979.
CC-CDT	CV-332	OA-10A	CAN VIC (Cartierville)	32 (Aéronavale) F-YCHB (Callsign) F-WMKS CF-FKV TF-RVR 44-33880 (USAAF) Bu67844 ntu (US Navy)	Fleet number 32. Current – see Chapter Seventeen.
CC-CDU	– see CC-CGY below				
CC-CGY	CV-520	OA-10A	CAN VIC (Cartierville)	CC-CDU 20 (Aéronavale) F-YCHA (Callsign) F-WMKR CF-IHC N62043 44-34009 (USAAF) Bu67973 ntu (US Navy)	Code numbers 20 and 33. Used for spares at Los Cerrillos, Santiago and current – see Chapter Sixteen.
CC-CNP	2029	PBY-6A	CON NO	EC-FXN CC-CNP CC-CNG N9555C Bu46665 (US Navy)	Fleet numbers 65 and 35. Current – see Chapter Seventeen.

COLOMBIA

MILITARY AIRCRAFT

The Fuerza Aérea Colombiana (FAC) received up to thirteen Catalinas of various marks from 1947 onwards, having been a beneficiary under the Rio Pact of that year.

The Pact covered the supply of five aircraft, later examples being acquired from other sources. The first examples were operated out of the air base at Cartagena, although aircraft were later based at both Madrid and Tres Esquines and possibly at El Dorado. By 1961 the Catalinas had been augmented in the search-and-rescue role by Kaman Huskie helicopters, although a few of the Catalinas are known to have remained in service at least until the very end of the 1960s. A small number lingered on in the scrap yard at Madrid's Barroblanco air base, and, indeed, one still remains there. At various times, some of the Catalinas operated with the military airline SATENA (Servicio de Aéronavegación a Territorios Nacionales, or Air Navigation Service to the National Territories). These aircraft retained their military serials, however.

The Catalina serials were in the range 601–700, used by the FAC to signify transport category types. Table 22 below shows known serials and details. The serial block for the thirteen aircraft may have run from 611 onward.

Table 23. Fuerza Aérea Colombiana

Serial	C/n	Type	Place of Manufacture	Previous id(s)	Notes
612	CV-523	OA-10A	CAN VIC (Cartierville)	44-34012 (USAAF) Bu67976 ntu (US Navy)	*El Gato.* Known to have flown with SATENA. To HK-2115X and current – see Chapter Sixteen.
620					Disappeared without trace, 13/3/1957.
619	1817	PBY-5A	CON SD	N1518V Bu46453 (US Navy)	Currently derelict at Barroblanco air base, Madrid – see Chapter Sixteen.
621					Known to have flown with SATENA. Destroyed off La Pedrera, Morichal, 26/11/1966.

FAC-620 of the Fuerza Aérea Colombiana, date and location not known. This aircraft went missing in 1957. *via Ron Mak*

Taken at Bogota, this photo proves that 612 had a PBY-6A fin and rudder whilst serving with the FAC, although it is believed to have been built as an OA-10A. *Ron Mak*

Serial	C/n	Type	Place of Manufacture	Previous id(s)	Notes
622					Known to have flown with SATENA. Written off after striking log on landing and sinking, Morichal, 10/7/1965.

Note: The following ex-USAAF aircraft are known to have been supplied to the FAC, although tie-ups with FAC serials are not known.
OA-10A 44-33921 (USAAF) c/n CV-414 ex-Bu67885 ntu (US Navy)
OA-10A 44-33922 (USAAF) c/n CV-416 ex-Bu67886 ntu (US Navy)
OA-10A 44-33996 (USAAF) c/n CV-507 ex-Bu67960 ntu (US Navy)
OA-10A 44-34013 (USAAF) c/n CV-524 ex-Bu67977 ntu (US Navy)
OA-10B 45-57833 (USAAF)

COMMERCIAL AIRCRAFT

A number of Colombian airlines and companies operated Catalinas of various marks and origins, mainly in the early post-war years. Information on some of these aircraft is sparse, but what is known is shown in Table 23 below. Known operators were:

AVIANCA	Aérovias Nacionales de Colombia SA
VIARCO	Vias Aéreas Colombianos
AIDA	Agencia Interamericano de Aviola Ltda
TALA	Transportes Aéreas Latinamericanos
LAICA	Lineas Aéreas Interiors de Catalina
TEXACO	
HANSA	
Aérovias Hoffmann	(possibly same company as HANSA) Aérotarzoo, Ltda
Aéropesca Ltda	(no registration known but Lloyds of London records show a Catalina operated by them was lost in a crash at Puerto Arturo on 4 November 1965)

Table 24. Colombian commercial Catalinas

Registration	C/n	Type	Place of Manufacture	Previous id(s)	Notes
C-43X/C43E	See HK-43E				
C-82	21999	Canso A	BOE CAN	9770 (RCAF)	VIARCO.
C-131	CV-396	OA-10A	CAN VIC (Cartierville)	44-33912 (USAAF) Bu67876 ntu (US Navy)	AVIANCA c.1946. Identity has been quoted as c/n 409/Bu33912 and CV-409/RCAF 11060. The latter is certainly incorrect, whilst the former is based on confusion between USAAF 44-33912 and US Navy Bu33912. Bu33912 was not, in any case, a Catalina serial.
C-133	See HK-133				
C-134	See HK-134				
C-135	1551	PBY-5A	CON SD	N10021 Bu33997 (US Navy)	AVIANCA c.1946.

Registration	C/n	Type	Place of Manufacture	Previous id(s)	Notes
C-406		PBY-5A			VIARCO. Destroyed in water landing accident, Buenaventura, Colombia, 20/12/1946.
C-414	'119'/ 529	PBY-5A	CON SD	Bu05030 (US Navy)	VIARCO. Substantially damaged in crash near Madrid, Bogota, 10/1/1948.
C-1000	See HK-1000E				
C-1001	See HK-1001E				
C-1510/ C-1510E	See HK-1510E				
C-1511	CV-278	Canso A	CAN VIC (Cartierville)	9844 (RCAF)	TEXACO.
HK-42X/ HK-42E	CV-269	Canso A	CAN VIC (St Hubert)	9835 (RCAF)	TEXACO.
HK-43E	CV-422	OA-10A	CAN VIC (Cartierville)	C-43E C-43X NC95494 44-33925 (USAAF) Bu67889 ntu (US Navy)	TEXACO. Usually reported as going to USA as NC95494 then to VP-BAB and CF-HGE. Sank after forced landing 3 km off Sept Iles, 13/9/1962. Registration cancelled.
HK-132		PBY-5A			
HK-133	21998	Canso A	BOE CAN	C-133 9769 (RCAF)	AVIANCA c.1946 To AIDA Crashed into high ground at Quetame Hill, Bojaca, Colombia, 8/12/1956.
HK-134	401	PBY-5A	CON SD	C-134 9740 (RCAF)	AVIANCA c.1946 Destroyed in water landing accident, Buenaventura Bay, Colombia, 5/2/1949.

PBY-6A HK-957X of Aerotarzoo was decidedly non-airworthy by the time this photograph was taken in Colombia in the early 1970s.
MAP

Registration	C/n	Type	Place of Manufacture	Previous id(s)	Notes
HK-368		PBY-5A?		? (US Navy)	H. Gutierrez c.1959 Thought to have passed to Fuerza Aérea Colombiana, serial not known.
HK-427	Not confirmed/ Quoted in Air Britain's *Civil Aircraft Registers of Colombia* but probably a mis-identification of HK-42X				
HK-661X		PBY-6A	CON NO	N7480C Bu64068 (US Navy)	Not converted. Derelict at Bogota in US Navy c/s with hull code 201/B c.1972.
HK-811X/ HK-811		PBY-6A	CON NO	?/hull code 206/R (US Navy)	TALA. Written off c.1958.
HK-916X		PBY-5A			Recorded at Miami, 12/1956.
HK-957X		PBY-6A	CON NO		Aerotarzoo Ltda, Leticia. Withdrawn and stored at Bogota by 9/1972.
HK-963		PBY-6A	CON NO	?(US Navy)	Aérovias Hoffmann, Bogota. Registration cancelled.
HK-970		PBY-6A	CON NO	?(US Navy)	Aérovias Hoffmann, Bogota. Registration cancelled.
HK-996X	22022	Canso A	BOE CAN	OB-LDM-349 YV-P-APE 9793 (RCAF)	To HP-289 then HR-236, 5Y-KUD, N6108, TG-BIV, N5404J and ZK-PBY ntu. Sank after forced landing Hawaii – Tahiti, 16/1/1994.
HK-1000E		PBY-5?	CON SD	C-1000	AIDA c.1953. Destroyed in crash while landing on Caqueta River

Registration	C/n	Type	Place of Manufacture	Previous id(s)	Notes
					near Lapedrera, Colombia, 31/1/1955.
HK-1001E		OA-10A?		C-1001	AIDA. Destroyed in crash following engine failure near El Refugio, Colombia, 15/3/1960.
HK-1020	1750	PBY-5A	CON SD	N1521V Bu48388 (US Navy)	LAICA. Destroyed in water landing at Villavincencio, Colombia, 11/6/1973.
HK-1510E	CV-257	Canso A	CAN VIC (St Hubert)	C-1510E CF-DTR 9823 (RCAF)	TEXACO. Destroyed in mid-air collision with FAC F-47D Thunderbolt, Colombia, 26/9/1953.
HK-2115 HK-2115P/ HK-2115X	CV-523	OA-10A	CAN VIC (Cartierville)	612 (FAC) 44-34012 (USAAF) Bu67976 ntu (US Navy)	Registered c.1983/4 as a Consolidated A-10, c/n '34012' to Ana Zazzu de Borde. To TALA. Current – See Chapter Sixteen. Now has PBY-6A-style rudder.
HK-2116 ntu	1817*	PBY-5A	CON SD	619 (FAC) N1518V Bu46453 (US Navy)	Registered c.1983/4 as a Consolidated A-10 to Ana Zazzu de Borde. Believed unconverted for commercial use and still on dump at Barroblanco/ Madrid AFB.

*Identities shown are not confirmed.

Looking magnificent after being saved from dereliction on the dump at Barroblanco, Madrid is HK-2115 of TALA. There appears to be a radome on the starboard wing leading edge, outboard of the engine.
Steve Kinder

One of the two known PBY-5As to be used by the Cuban Navy in the post-Batista period. It is presumably either serial number 72 or 73, but the numbering on the tail is unfortunately not clear enough to be interpreted.
George Farinas via Ron Mak

CUBA

MILITARY AIRCRAFT

The pre-war Cuban Air Force was known as the Cuerpo de Aviación, Ejército de Cuba, or CAEC. As such, it entered the immediate post-war years short of money and aircraft. Then, in 1947, the US initiative known as the American Republics Project, or ARP, resulted in the supply of two ex-USAAF OA-10A Catalinas. In April 1952, the CAEC was reconstituted as the Fuerzas Aéreas Ejército de Cuba, or FAEC.

Meanwhile, the air arm of the Cuban Navy was also trying to expand, and according to Dan Hagedorn's book, *Central American and Caribbean Air Forces*, it received two venerable PBY-2 flying boats that were seized from the Caribbean Legion at Cayo Confites in August 1947. These veterans lasted until at least 1952, when they were joined by two amphibious Catalinas. The latter aircraft were serialled 72 and 73, so it is possible that the earlier PBY-2s were 70 and 71. Then, in September 1954, the two PBY-5As of the FAEC were transferred to the Navy, apparently on instructions from the President. Two of the amphibious Catalinas survived beyond the Batista years, and they were probably withdrawn and scrapped locally.

Whilst in service, the PBYs were used for coast guard and SAR work and also for fishery protection duties to the south east of the island. In the main, they flew from Mariel air base, although maintenance was carried out at Campo Columbia in Havanna.

Table 25. Cuban military PBYs

Serial	C/n	Type	Place of Manufacture	Previous id(s) Notes
70?		PBY-2	CON SD	(US Navy)
71?		PBY-2	CON SD	(US Navy)
72		PBY-5A		
73		PBY-5A		
190	CV-450	OA-10A	CAN VIC (Cartierville)	44-33939 (USAAF) Bu67835 ntu (US Navy)
191	CV-307	OA-10A	CAN VIC (Cartierville)	44-33871 (USAAF) Bu67903 ntu (US Navy)

COMMERCIAL AIRCRAFT

In addition to the military Catalinas operated in Cuba, there was one solitary civilian example. This was registered as a PBY-5A Catalina and was allocated the registration CU-N616. Nothing more is known of its origins or fate.

DOMINICAN REPUBLIC

MILITARY AIRCRAFT

The Armada de Republica Dominicana (Dominican Navy) obtained four PBY-5A Catalinas from March 1952 onward. They were coded GC-14 to GC-17 and were based at Cuidad Trujillo. The naval air arm ceased to exist in early November 1952, and all of its aircraft were transferred to the Aviación Militart Dominicana (AMD).

Catalina GC-14 of the Dominican Navy was probably photographed at the Ontario, California, factory of Southern California Aircraft Corporation, which specialised in conversion work on former US military PBYs.
via Barry Dowsett

The four PBYs were allocated new air force serials between 2901 and 2905, although aircraft GC-16 crashed before taking up its new identity. Exact tie-ups are not known.

The other numbers in the 2901 series were used by Catalinas obtained directly by the AMD. It had acquired two in early 1952 and one in October 1953. One further aircraft was added to the fleet in March 1954. Allowing for the naval aircraft written off and the fact that one of the air force aircraft was acquired for Presidential use and may not have carried a military identity, that leaves five aircraft that appear to fit neatly into the 2901 to 2905 sequence.

One of the Catalinas lasted at least until mid-1957, when it was to be found serving with the Escuadron de Caza-Bombardero. Some of the previously retired examples were subject to a proposed sale to Ecuador, but that country did not proceed with the deal when they discovered how worn out the Dominican aircraft were!

Table 26. Dominican Republic military Catalinas

Serial	C/n	Type – see Note 1	Place of Manufacture	Previous id(s)	Notes
GC-14					To AMD, 11/1952.
GC-15					To AMD, 11/1952.
GC-16					Crashed at La Romana and damaged beyond repair, 19/11/1952.
GC-17					To AMD, 11/1952, possibly as 2902.
2901					
2902				GC-17? (Dom Navy)	
2903					
2904					
2905					

Note 1: The Dominican Catalinas were a mixture of PBY-5As and OA-10As.
Note 2: One of the aircraft acquired direct by the AMD was PBY-5A c/n 1753 ex-N68763, Bu48391 (US Navy), and it came from Southern California Aircraft Corporation of Ontario, California.
Note 3: The Presidential Catalina is described below.

COMMERCIAL AIRCRAFT

One Catalina appeared on the Dominican Republic civil register, this being the aircraft used by President Trujillo as his personal aircraft. Registered as HI-24, it had been converted to Landseaire configuration by Southern California Aircraft Corporation. It was written off in September 1954.

Table 27. Dominican presidential Catalina

Registration	C/n	Type	Place of Manufacture	Previous id(s)	Notes
HI-24	1802	PBY-5A	CON SD	N54982 N68751 Bu48440 (US Navy)	*San Christobal.* Written off, in crash, 21/9/1954.

ECUADOR

The Fuerza Aérea Ecuatoriana (FAE) was created in 1947 as part of that year's Rio Pact, Ecuador being a signatory. Previously, the military air arm had been known as the Fuerza Aérea del Ejército Ecuatoriano. It is believed that three Catalinas were acquired by the newly formed air force, and these were used for coastal patrols and transport flights around the country and out to the Galapagos Islands. The flights were flown under the auspices of TAME (Transportes Aéreos Militares Ecuatorianos).

Of the three Catalinas that served with the FAE, one, serial 53602, has survived and may be found preserved in the compound of the Museu Aéronautico del Espace at the Mariscal Sucre airfield, Quito. The serials of the other two PBYs are not known. Normally, FAE serials are based on the manufacturer's construction numbers, but in the case of 53602 this is not so, as that number bears no

resemblance to any Catalina c/n, nor, indeed, to any US or Canadian military serial.

Table 28. Ecuadorian Catalina

Registration	C/n	Type	Place of Manufacture	Previous id(s)	Notes
53602	?	PBY-5A?	?	?	

GUATEMALA

Guatemala's sole Catalina was registered to Troya SA as TG-BIV in February 1980, and spent much of its time in that country in external storage at La Aurora Airport before being sold in the USA by its owner, Meldy Fernandez. It was cancelled from the Guatemalan register in June 1988.

Prior to going to Guatemala, TG-BIV had been stored at San Jose in Costa Rica before being overhauled by Coopesa. It had at one time been used by the famous oceanographer Jacques Cousteau, who also owned a PBY-6A, N101CS. Earlier still, TG-BIV had been a participant in the Bay of Pigs operation (see entry under Panama) and had flown in the aerial scenes for the motion picture *Tora! Tora! Tora!*

TG-BIV is the only Catalina to have been registered in Guatemala. It flew little and was exported to the USA, only to ditch in the Pacific Ocean en route to New Zealand in January 1994.
Ron Mak

By 1977, the Fuerza Aérea Ecuatoriana PBY-5A 53602 was looking somewhat worse for wear, with broken blister perspex and sagging floats. It is now in better condition, preserved in Quito.
MAP

HR-236 was another registration carried by the much-travelled former RCAF Canso A 9793. In its varied career, it was operated on the civil registers of Venezuela, Peru, Colombia, Panama, Kenya, Honduras (seen here), the USA and Guatemala.

Table 29. Guatemalan Catalina

Registration	C/n	Type	Place of Manufacture	Previous id(s)	Notes
TG-BIV	22022	Canso A	BOE CAN	N6108 HR-236 5Y-KUD HP-289 HK-996X OB-LDM-349 YV-P-APE 9793 (RCAF)	To N5404J 6/1988, ZK-PBY (ntu). Lost in Pacific, 16/1/1994.

HONDURAS

Only one commercial Catalina was registered in the Honduras, and it seems likely that the marks were never formally taken up, although they are known to have been painted on the airframe. Indeed, it is probable that HR-236 never actually flew in the Honduras at all. The registration was reserved in December 1956, for the Caribbean Seafood Production Corporation, but the aircraft was subsequently re-registered in the USA and was eventually lost after a forced landing in the Pacific Ocean on 16 January 1994.

Table 30. Honduran Catalina

Registration	C/n	Type	Place of Manufacture	Previous id(s)	Notes
HR-236	22022	Canso A	BOE CAN	5Y-KUD HP-289 HK-996X OB-LDM-349 YV-P-APE 9793 (RCAF)	Sold in USA as N6108. To TG-BIV, N5404J, ZK-PBY (ntu). Lost in Pacific, 16/1/1994 .

JAMAICA

The Jamaican civil register boasted two airlines operating Catalinas, both fairly soon after the end of the Second World War. The first company was Cayman Islands Airways Ltd, which flew with a solitary former RCAF Canso A, VP-JAO. This did not stay with the company for very long, and was sold to Caribbean International Airways and registered in the Bahamas in 1949. The latter airline subsequently re-registered its Catalinas on the Jamaican register, and so the former VP-JAO returned as VP-JAT in February 1951.

Whilst wearing the registration VP-JAO, this aircraft sustained substantial damage at Miami after landing with its undercarriage partially retracted. The date of this incident was 2 January 1950, and the owners were quoted as Caribbean International Airways, so it presumably had not been painted with its new Bahamas registration at that time.

Table 31. Cayman Islands Airways Ltd

Registration	C/n	Type	Place of Manufacture	Previous id(s)	Notes
VP-JAO	22005	Canso A	BOE CAN	9776 (RCAF)	To VP-BAN, 1949 then VP-JAT, 2/1951. Damaged beyond repair at Palisadoes, Jamaica, 21/8/1951.

The second Jamaican airline to fly Catalinas was Caribbean International Airways Ltd, whose aircraft had previously been registered to the same company on the Bahamas register. Of the Jamaican-registered craft, VP-JAT and VP-JAU were the ex-Bahamas examples, whilst VP-JAW was a later, albeit short-lived addition. VP-JAT was damaged beyond repair in bad weather at Palisadoes in August 1951. The unfortunate VP-JAW was acquired in November 1951, and force-landed on the sea off Grand Cayman on 2 January 1952. This accident happened soon after departure on a flight to Tampa, Florida, and although salvage was attempted, it proved impossible and was abandoned. There were no casualties amongst those on board.

Table 32. Caribbean International Airways Ltd

Registration	C/n	Type	Place of Manufacture	Previous id(s)	Notes
VP-JAT	22005	Canso A	BOE CAN	VP-BAN VP-JAO 9776 (RCAF)	Damaged beyond repair at Palisadoes, Jamaica, 21/8/1951.
VP-JAU	'110'/ 520	PBY-5A	CON SD	VP-BAR NC18444 Bu05021 (US Navy)	Sold in Canada as CF-HFL, 11/1953 and current – see Chapter Fifteen.
VP-JAW	'187'/ 341	PBY-5A	CON SD	N74692 Bu2475 (US Navy)	Sank after forced landing on sea near Grand Cayman, 2/1/1952.

MEXICO

MILITARY AIRCRAFT

From 1950 onwards, Mexico obtained a number of Catalinas for use by the Escuela de Aviación Naval, and these were flown in both patrol and transport roles, as reflected by their serial prefixes – MP for Marina Petrullero and MT for Marina Transporte. The first example was acquired in 1950 and was converted for use as a Presidential aircraft, although it later went to the Navy.

By 1957, a further four aircraft had been obtained, and they were operated by the Segundo Escuadron Aéronaval, or 2nd Naval Squadron, at Mexico City.

The Catalinas suffered a number of accidents, and the survivors had been retired by 1960, their ultimate fate not being known. The accidents included that involving the former presidential aircraft MT-02. In April 1956, it was involved in rescuing the crew of a vessel that had caught fire at sea 95 miles west of Celestrum. After taking the crew on board, MT-02 nosed in on take-off, causing damage to the bow, port engine and hull. A naval ship rescued both crews, but although the Catalina was the subject of a salvage attempt, it subsequently sank.

In a totally different colour scheme is this Mexican Navy PBY MP-52 at Mexico City. The original caption on the back of the print states that it was a PBY-6A of the 2nd Naval Squadron.
Ing Enrique Velasco via Santiago A. Flores

Table 33. Mexican Navy Catalinas

Serial	C/n	Type	Place of Manufacture	Previous id(s)	Notes
MT-02				XB-LEX	Delfin. Sank after take-off accident, near Celestrum 4/1956.
MT-03					El Marinero.
MP-51		PBY-5A			
MP-52		PBY-6A?			
MP-53		PBY-5A			
MP-54		PBY-5A			

COMMERCIAL AIRCRAFT

In addition to Mexico's military Catalinas, there were also a number of civilian-registered examples, shown in Table 34 below.

Table 34. Mexican commercial Catalinas

Registration	C/n	Type	Place of Manufacture	Previous id(s)	Notes
XB-FAB	'80'/ 876	PBY-5A	CON SD	N18441 Bu08057 (US Navy)	
XB-GET	CV-489	OA-10A	CAN VIC (Cartierville)	N67135 44-33978 (USAAF) Bu67942 ntu (US Navy)	

Mexican Navy Catalina MT-03 showing its air stair and clipper bow.
via Jack Meaden

MT-02 was the former Mexican Presidential Catalina. Its history prior to being registered in Mexico as XB-LEX is not known.
Ing Enrique Velasco via Santiago A. Flores

Registration	C/n	Type	Place of Manufacture	Previous id(s)	Notes
XB-LEX					Presidential aircraft. To Mexican Navy as MT-02. Sank after take-off accident, near Celestrum 4/1956.
XB-NUJ					Mexican Navy?
XB-PIB		PBY-6A	CON NO	Bu64045 (US Navy)	Sold in USA as N6986C. Crashed, Winslow, Arizona, 25/6/1961.
XB-YUP					Mexican Navy?

The FAP Catalina T-29/2002 suffered a number of embarrassing undercarriage problems over the years, one of which is seen here.

PANAMA

Although Panama had no Catalinas within its Air Force, two civilian Catalinas carried Panamanian registrations. The first was HP-289, this being the much-registered Boeing Canada-built Canso A that started life with the Royal Canadian Air Force and then passed through the civil registers of no fewer than six Central and South American countries, as well as those of Kenya and the USA, before being exported to New Zealand, ditching in the Pacific on its delivery flight there in 1994.

The registered owner in Panama was Turismo Aereo, the period of registration being from approximately 1960 through to August 1963. What is particularly interesting about this period is that at some point it was operated by the CIA-backed company Southern Air Transport as a communications aircraft during the Cuban crisis, specifically the Bay of Pigs operation. It is likely that this Catalina was also involved with the CIA-backed Fuerza Aérea de Liberacion. Fitted out with appropriate electronic equipment in Miami in the early part of 1961, it was codenamed *Swan Island*. The intention was to fly the Catalina at altitude around the invasion area of Cuba and transmit radio broadcasts back to the CIA HQ in Virginia.

The other Panamanian Catalina was HP-425. This was registered to Cia Darienitas de Servicios SA in 1966, but did not last long as it was written off in an accident in Belize on 11 July 1967, following a nose gear collapse.

Table 35. Panamanian Catalinas

Registration	C/n	Type	Place of Manufacture	Previous id(s)	Notes
HP-289	22022	Canso A	BOE CAN	HK-996X OB-LDM-349 YV-P-APE 9793 (RCAF)	To 5Y-KUD, HR-236, N6108, TG-BIV, N5404J and ZK-PBY ntu. Lost in Pacific, 16/1/1994.
HP-425	1596	PBY-5A	CON SD	N282X N5803N Bu34042 (US Navy)	*Anayasi.* Written off, Belize, 11/7/1967.

PARAGUAY

Two Catalinas were operated in Paraguay, and they saw service with both a commercial airline and the military. They were originally acquired by Lineas Aéreas de Transporte Nacional, or LATN, in 1954, and once they had been delivered to Paraguay, they had their gun turrets removed and the hulls converted for passenger carrying. The following year, both aircraft, by now registered in Paraguay as ZP-CBA and ZP-CBB, were transferred to the Transporte Aéreo Militar (TAM) of the Fuerza Aérea del Paraguaya (FAP or Paraguayan Air Force), ZP-CBA becoming T-29 and ZP-CBB, T-31.

On 3 October 1955, T-29 was used to fly General Juan Perón, the deposed president of the Argentine, into exile in Paraguay. The Catalina was flown to Argentina, where it landed on the River Plate close to the Paraguayan warship *Paraguay*. Perón was taken aboard the Catalina and flown to Asuncion.

In 1956, both T-29 and T-31 were returned to LATN, and they reverted to their former Paraguayan civil registrations. ZP-CBB was subsequently destroyed when it crashed and sank on the Paraguay River during a post-overhaul test flight. The pilot, Major Leo Nowak, and one other crew member were killed. Subsequently, ZP-CBA lapsed into disuse and it stood in the open at LATN's base at Asuncion until, in the 1970s, it was again transferred to the FAP. It was re-issued with its original serial, T-29, and was used for flying passengers, cargo and mail, as well as for carrying out the occasional search-and-rescue flight. It was withdrawn from use at Asuncion in November 1979, and remained in store there.

In 1988, it was decided to put T-29 back into service, and it was completely overhauled, repainted and reserialled 2002. Flown by the Grupo de Transporte Aéreo (GTA), it was plagued with serviceability problems, particularly relating to its nosewheel system, and it was soon withdrawn again. Although rumours abounded that it was to go to a museum in the Argentine, it was sold in the USA, where it remains.

In the late 1980s, 2002 was refurbished and is seen here at Asuncion undergoing extensive maintenance.
Ron Mak

PERU

MILITARY AIRCRAFT

Known until 1949 as the Cuerpo de Aéronáutica del Peru (Peruvian Air Corps), the Peruvian Air Force received second-hand military equipment as agreed under the 1947 Rio Pact. As a result, at least two, possibly three, PBY-5A-type Catalinas were supplied for operation by the Servicio de Reconocimiento Marítimo y Búsqueda y Rescate (Maritime Reconnaissance and SAR Service). In July 1950, the air arm was renamed the Fuerza Aérea Peruana. Later, three ex-USAAF OA-10As were also acquired, and the surviving Catalinas soldiered on until at least the late 1960s, when they were replaced by the Grumman Albatross. One Catalina is known to have been lost in a crash on 23 December 1967.

The confirmed Peruvian Catalina serials were in the 300 series, denoting a transport type. One of the FAP Cats has survived and is currently to be found on gate guard duties at the Antiguo Aeropuerto air base in Iquitos, athough it bears no trace of its true identity.

Table 36. Paraguayan Catalinas serving with LATN and the FAP

Registration	C/n	Type	Place of Manufacture	Previous id(s)	Notes
ZP-CBA// T-29/ ZP-CBA/ T-29/2002	1737	PBY-5A	CON SD	N4937V Bu48375 (US Navy)	Sold to USA as N96FP, 1993. Later N96UC. Current – see Chapter Nineteen.
ZP-CBB/ T-31/ ZP-CBB	1608	PBY-5A	CON SD	N1557M Bu34054 (US Navy)	Written off after sinking, 21/8/1957.

Note: The construction number and previous identities for ZP-CBB/T-31 are 'best guess' and not confirmed. Both N4937V and N1557M were at one time registered to the same Burbank, California-based company, Fleetways Inc.

During its time in Paraguay, the military Catalina T-29/2002 also flew with LATN as ZP-CBA, as shown here.
Jennifer M. Gradidge

Table 37. Peruvian military Catalinas

Serial	C/n	Type	Place of Manufacture	Previous id(s)	Notes
378	CV-502	OA-10A	CAN VIC (Cartierville)	44-33991 (USAAF) Bu67955 ntu (US Navy)	
379	CV-476	OA-10A	CAN VIC (Cartierville)	44-33965 (USAAF) Bu67929 ntu (US Navy)	
380 381	*	?			* see note below
(either 380 or 381)	CV-531	OA-10A	CAN VIC (Cartierville)	44-34020 (USAAF) Bu67984 ntu (US Navy)	

Note: s/n 380 has been quoted as '11040', and it has been suggested that this is a former RCAF Canso A serial. However, RCAF 11040 remained in service with the RCAF until November 1961, and then went to the USA as N9752Z with B. B. Burson & Associates of Columbia, California, with whom it flew as a fire fighter.

Unfortunately, the under-wing serial on this Fuerza Aérea Peruana Catalina cannot be confirmed, although it appears to be 379. The rear blisters have been replaced with a cargo hatch.

COMMERCIAL AIRCRAFT

During the Second World War, the Peruvian airline Faucett operated two PBY-5 Catalinas on behalf of the US Rubber Development Corporation, ferrying passengers and rubber between Peru and the USA. Two civilian Catalinas appeared on the post-war Peruvian civil register, although they were separated by many years. The first was registered in February 1955, but soon moved on to Colombia. The other flew with the Peruvian airline LORASA (Loretana de Aviacion SA), and although now dismantled and neglected after many years of open storage, still exists at Iquitos Airport.

LORASA's OB-T-251 seen before it lapsed into dereliction at Iquitos.
MAP

VENEZUELA

Although the Venezuelan armed forces were not Catalina operators, a number did appear on the civil register and one remains current.

Early post-war examples were used by oil companies such as Shell and TEXACO as transport aircraft, whilst Transporte Aereo Transandino had two Catalinas on strength in the late 1940s. Later, a small fleet of beautifully kept Catalinas was used by the Orinoco Mining Company, later the Corporacion Ferrominera de Orinoco, at Puerto Ordaz, for ferrying personnel out to the huge ore carriers and the dredgers that keep the Orinoco River navigable. These two Catalinas were purchased in the USA, one in 1960 and the other five years later, and they were both converted for high-density passenger use by Pan Air Corporation of New Orleans. The conversion of the second aircraft, YV-P-DPZ, was complicated when a

Table 38. Peruvian commercial Catalinas

Registration	C/n	Type	Place of Manufacture	Previous id(s)	Notes
OB-LDM-349	22022	Canso A	BOE CAN	YV-P-APE 9793 (RCAF)	To Colombia as HK-996X then HP-289, 5Y-KUD, HR-236, N6108, TG-BIV, N5404J and ZK-PBY. Lost in Pacific, 16/1/1994.
OB-LBA-251/ OB-M-251/ OB-T-251	1868	PBY-5A	CON SD	N1513V Bu46504 (US Navy)	LORASA. Current at Iquitos – see Chapter Sixteen.

hurricane hit the overhaul facility in 1966, causing serious damage to the partially converted airframe. The sister aircraft YV-P-EPZ was unfortunate enough to land in a partially silted channel at San Felix on 27 January 1976, causing substantial damage to the hull and flooding the airframe. The aircraft was towed ashore and repaired, flying again in the following May.

Table 39. Venezuelan commercial Catalinas

Registration	C/n	Type	Place of Manufacture	Previous id(s)	Notes
YV-AQA	CV-413	Canso A	CAN VIC (Cartierville)	11082 (RCAF)	Registered c1947 to Transporte Aéreo Transandino. Re-registered as YV-C-AQA. Written off, 10/1947.
YV-C-AQA	See YV-AQA above				
YV-C-AQB	'122'/ 918	PBY-5A	CON SD	N1818M Bu08099 (US Navy)	Registered c.1947 to Transporte Aéreo Transandino. Cancelled from register and possibly sold via the USA to the Israeli Air Force. See Chapter Nine.
YV-P-AEP				N68741*	Cia. Shell de Venezolana SA. Sold in Brazil 2/1955 as PT-ASX then PP-BTC and PT-BGA. * pi often quoted as RCAF 9746, but this is believed to be another aircraft – see N5PY, Chapter Nineteen.

Registration	C/n	Type	Place of Manufacture	Previous id(s)	Notes
YV-P-APE	22022	Canso A	BOE CAN	9793 (RCAF)	Registered to TEXACO Ltda post-1946. Sold as OB-LDM-349 then HK-996X, HP-289, 5Y-KUD, HR-236, N6108, TG-BIV, N5404J and ZK-PBY ntu. Lost in Pacific, 16/1/1994.
YV-P-APJ		PBY-5A			Destroyed after crashing into sea at Puerto Cabello Harbour, Venezuela, 15/7/1948.
YV-P-DPZ	See YV-584CP				
YV-P-EPX	See YV-485C				
YV-P-EPZ	See YV-485C				
YV-O-CFO-2	See YV-584CP				
YV-C-CFO-4	See YV-485C				
YV-56CPntu	See YV-485C				
YV-63CPntu	See YV-584CP				
YV-209CP	1808	PBY-5A	CON SD	N5591V Bu48446 (US Navy)	Registered 1978 to P Bottome, Caracas. Sold in USA as N285NJ, 8/1985. Destroyed in crash at Turin, Italy, 21/5/1989.
YV-485C	1774	PBY-5A	CON SD	YV-585CP YV-56CP ntu YV-O-CFO-4 YV-P-EPZ YV-P-EPX N96R N10024 Bu48412 (US Navy)	Registered to Orinoco Mining Company, later Corporacion Ferrominera de Orinoco, as YV-P-EPX, 6/1960. To Camaronera del Sur SA, Puerto Ordaz as YV-485C then to SERVES at Caracas-Maiquetia. Sold in USA as N7238Z, 4/1997 and current – see Chapter Nineteen.

The Texas Petroleum Company, better known as TEXACO, operated Catalina YV-P-APE in Venezuela in the early post-war years, before selling it to Peru.
Jennifer M. Gradidge

Caracas-Charallave is the location for this November 1983 photo of YV-209CP owned by Peter Bottome. Later sold in the USA, it subsequently came to a sticky end at Turin, Italy, in 1989.
Ron Mak

Registration	C/n	Type	Place of Manufacture	Previous id(s)	Notes
YV-584CP	1736	PBY-5A	CON SD	YV-63CP ntu YV-O-CFO-2 YV-P-DPZ N9507C Bu48374 (US Navy)	Registered to Orinoco Mining Company, later Corporacion Ferrominera de Orinoco, as YV-P-DPZ, 1965. To Camaronera del Sur SA, Puerto Ordaz as YV-584C then to SERVES. Current at Puerto Ordaz – see Chapter Sixteen.
YV-585CP		See YV-485C			

Still in the beautiful blue and white colours it wore as YV-O-CFO-4 with Ferrominera de Orinoco is YV-585CP, shot in 1985.
MAP

SUNDRY OPERATORS

Central and South American politics being somewhat non-conventional at times, it is hardly surprising that various groups have put together small fleets of aircraft in order to further their aims. Readers interested in such organisations are well advised to read Dan Hagedorn's book, *Central American and Caribbean Air Forces*.

One of these groups was **La Legion Caribe**, or **The Caribbean Legion**, a Costa Rican organisation supported by Guatemala and formed in 1948. The Legion acquired two Catalinas whilst operating out of Aurora in Guatemala, and they were used in mid-June 1949 for a proposed invasion of Dominica, to which the Legion was opposed. The Catalinas were part of a small invasion force, and one landed on the sea near Luperon but was

fired on and sunk by aircraft – believed to be Beaufighters and Mosquitoes – of the Dominican Air Force. The Catalina that was lost had been illegally exported from the USA by Earl Adams and M. R. Finley.

Table 40. La Legion Caribe Catalinas

Registration	C/n	Type	Place of Manufacture	Previous id(s)	Notes
N1096M	'56'/ 652	PBY-5A	CON SD	Bu04480 (US Navy)	Sunk by Dominican forces, Luperon, 19/6/1949.
?	?	PBY-5A	?	?	Identity not known.

Eight
EUROPE

Appropriately registered Canso A 5B-PBY is seen here sharing the Tanagra ramp in April 1997 with its former Quebec water bombing partner C-FPQO. Colours are yellow with blue trim.
Paul Barnfield

CYPRUS

One Catalina has appeared on the Cypriot register, namely 5B-PBY. Owned by Athenian Airlift Services, it is actually based, not in Cyprus at all, but at Tanagra in Greece. For a while, it was joined by the same company's Canadian-registered Catalina C-FPQO, although this was subsequently sold and left for South Africa in the latter half of 1999. Both aircraft are described fully in the entry for Greece in Chapter Seventeen.

Table 41. Cypriot Catalina

Registration	C/n	Type	Place of Manufacture	Previous id(s)	Notes
5B-PBY	CV-333	Canso A	CAN VIC (Cartierville)	C-FPQF CF-PQF 11042 (RCAF)	

DENMARK

MILITARY AIRCRAFT

The Danish Naval Air Arm, later the Royal Danish Air Force (RDAF), had an uninterrupted association with the Catalina from 1947 through to 1970, using both the Canso A/PBY-5A and PBY-6A variants.

The Danes' initial need was for a flexible transport aircraft capable of land and sea operations over long distances that could also carry out the task of surveying and mapping in and around Greenland. Thus it was that in 1946 a party of engineers and pilots was sent to the USA and Canada to evaluate suitable types, although they already had the PBY high on their wants list. The Canadian War Assets Administration was disposing of surplus amphibious Canso As from various locations through Ambrose Aviation Corp of New York. After careful inspection, six aircraft were eventually selected, although, later, three of these were sold elsewhere and so had to be replaced by different examples. The six Cansos finally selected were ferried to de Havilland Canada at Downsview for a thorough overhaul prior to delivery to Denmark. Once airworthy, aircrew training and familiarisation took place in Florida using some of the freshly renovated aircraft.

The first three Danish Catalinas to be delivered were FM51, FM52 and FM56, and they flew Downsview, Toronto–Gander, Newfoundland–Keflavik, Iceland–

This pre-delivery shot, probably taken in Canada, shows the future RDAF FM-53. It was destined to be the last of the original batch of RDAF Cats in service, eventually being destroyed in a nasty crash on water in December 1969. *MAP*

Aalborg, Denmark, then on to Copenhagen, arriving at their final destination on 6 June 1947. The other three Cats were ferried across the North Atlantic in the following June and July.

Initially, the six Cansos were operated by 1 Luftflotille (Air Group) out of Copenhagen, and they supplied the survey and radio sites in Greenland on a rotational basis, operating on both land and water. Other work occasionally came the Catalina's way, and in December 1950, aircraft 852 flew to Angola and back to support the *Galathea Expedition* there. This was not the only flight to Africa, as 851 went to Mombasa for the same purpose in the early part of the following year. In February 1953, several of the Danish Catalinas took part in relief work in Holland during severe flooding. During their RDAF service, the PBY-5As were fitted with a large teardrop-shaped radome above the cockpit.

In February 1951, 1 Luftflotille had been renumbered as Esk721, and in the latter part of 1952 it changed its base from Copenhagen Harbour to Kastrup Airport, moving again, this time to Værløse, on 1 April 1956. Back in 1951, a pair of former US Navy PBY-5As were obtained to supplement the ex-Canadian Canso As, but by 1958 replacements were needed for the surviving examples. After carefully considering various types, the Danes decided on more Catalinas, and the tall-tailed PBY-6A variant was chosen. Eight were taken out of storage at Litchfield Park, Arizona, and taken to the Catalina refurbishment specialists, Pan Air Corp of New Orleans, the city where they had originally been built by Consolidated.

The mixed fleet of Catalinas continued to fly in

both Denmark and Greenland until, in May 1961, the remaining aircraft were transferred to Esk722, which operated in the SAR role as well as supporting the Greenland facilities. Still based at Værløse, the Cats were often detached to both Aalborg and Skrydstrup. Helicopters replaced the Catalinas within Esk722 in February 1966, and the remaining aircraft went back to Esk721. One PBY-5A, L-853, soldiered on as a trainer alongside the PBY-6As, but it was lost in a fatal water landing accident at Gilleleje, north of Zeeland, on 11 December 1969. Finally, the end for the Danish Catalina fleet came on Friday 13 November 1970. The last three airworthy PBY-6As carried out a farewell flypast around various RDAF bases before entering retirement. A number of examples of both PBY-5A and PBY-6A lingered on and some have been lovingly restored, although two of the PBY-6As were later lost in fatal flying accidents in the USA under private ownership; these two

Illustrating the second variation in RDAF Catalina serial presentation is 82-852. The name Papoose can just be seen on the bow behind the turret, whilst the port blister has been modified with a solid section in the middle of the glazed panels.
Royal Danish Air Force Historical Section

accidents are detailed in Chapter Twenty. The PBY-6As in Danish service were distinctive because of the unique shape of their radome above the cockpit and forward of the wing – very different from that carried by the Danish PBY-5As.

Table 41, detailing the individual RDAF Catalinas, shows various serial formats. The first aircraft had serials prefixed with the letters FM for Flying boat Monoplane. Later, the Catalina was give the type number 82 and these numerals became the prefix. In 1960, yet another system was adopted, and the remaining RDAF Cats were given serials prefixed with the letter L. Their colour scheme consisted of light grey overall, with red or dayglo orange applied to bow, tail and wingtips.

Table 42. Catalinas operated by Royal Danish Air Force

Serial	C/n	Type	Place of Manufacture	Previous Identity	Name	Notes
FM51/ 82-851	CV-274	Canso A	CAN VIC (St Hubert)	9840 (RCAF)		Retired, 10/1953. Scrapped, Værløse.
FM52/ 82-852	CV-347	Canso A	CAN VIC (Cartierville)	11049 (RCAF)	Papoose	Retired, 10/1960. To Værløse fire dump, 1971.
FM53/ 82-853/ L-853	CV-316	Canso A	CAN VIC (Cartierville)	11034 (RCAF)	Pluto	Crashed off Gilleleje, 11/12/1969 during water landing. Wreck recovered to Værløse for investigation, 1/1970.
FM54/ 82-854	CV-321	Canso A	CAN VIC (Cartierville)	11039 (RCAF)	Taterat	Retired, 12/1960. Scrapped, Værløse.
FM55/ 82-855	CV-443	Canso A	CAN VIC (Cartierville)	11097 (RCAF)	Mallemuk	Retired, 8/1958. To NCO school and later to Værløse fire dump.
FM56/ 82-856	CV-265	Canso A	CAN VIC (St Hubert)	9831 (RCAF)	Nauja	Retired, 2/1956. Scrapped, Værløse.

Serial	C/n	Type	Place of Manufacture	Previous Identity	Name	Notes
82-857/ L-857	928	PBY-5A	CON SD	Bu08109 (US Navy)	Munin	Retired, 10/1967. Used for spares at Værløse but later preserved at Sola, Norway and current – see Chapter Seventeen.
82-858	1967	PBY-5A	CON NO	Bu46603 (US Navy)	Hugin	Retired, 10/1955. Scrapped, Værløse.
82-861/ L-861		PBY-6A	CON NO	Bu64035 (US Navy)	Sirius	Retired, 11/1970. Preserved at Helsingore and current – see Chapter Seventeen.
82-862/ L-862		PBY-6A	CON NO	Bu64102 (US Navy)		Destroyed in hangar fire at Narssarsuaq, Greenland, 24/10/1963.
82-863/ L-863		PBY-6A	CON NO	Bu63998 (US Navy)	Patron II	Retired, 11/1970. Sold in USA as N16KL. Destroyed in crash, Texas, 13/10/1984 – see Chapter Twenty.
82-864/ L-864		PBY-6A	CON NO	Bu64046 (US Navy)	Talivtak	Destroyed in hangar fire at Narssarsuaq, Greenland, 24/10/1963.
82-865/ L-865		PBY-6A	CON NO	Bu64032 (US Navy)	Rodolph	Crashed after hitting mountain, Cape Desolation, Greenland, 10/8/1963.
82-866/ L-866		PBY-6A	CON NO	Bu63993 (US Navy)		Retired, 1970. To RAF Museum as 8466M – see Chapter Seventeen.
82-867/ L-867		PBY-6A	CON NO	Bu63997 (US Navy)		Lost off Upernavik, 3/5/1964 after engine failure. Hull trapped by advancing ice after forced landing.

The final type of serial presentation is shown on L-853, shortly before it was written off at Gilleleje.
Jennifer M. Gradidge

Seen from the flight engineer's station of PBY-6A L-868 is sister aircraft L-861 overflying some ice floes in King Oscar's Fjord, east Greenland, during July 1970. L-861 has survived and is now to found at Helsingore.
Erik Brøgger via Torben Jensen

Serial	C/n	Type	Place of Manufacture	Previous Identity	Name	Notes
82-868/ L-868		PBY-6A	CON NO	Bu64000 (US Navy)	*Bøve*	Retired, 11/1970. Sold in USA as N15KL. Destroyed in crash in Texas, 18/8/1975 – see Chapter Twenty.

FRANCE

MILITARY OPERATORS

France's first attempt at purchasing Catalinas was frustrated by the outbreak of the Second World War and the subsequent occupation of the country. The PBY-5s (Consolidated Model 28-5MFs) intended for France were instead diverted elsewhere, and it is generally accepted that the 30 aircraft involved were taken on by the Royal Air Force, the serials AH530 to AH569 usually being quoted for the batch. Later in the war, two French units were equipped with former US PBY-5A Catalinas, and after working up to operational standard, they flew under US Navy jurisdiction in Morocco, Corsica and Italy. These units were Flottille 6FE and 8FB. The latter was renumbered Flottille 8F and went to Indo-China in late 1945, retaining its Catalinas until 1950, when Consolidated Privateers replaced them.

At the war's end, France had purchased 20 of the

PBY-6A L-868, later to be lost in a crash in Texas whilst with the Confederate Air Force, is seen here displaying the unique RDAF style of radome above the cockpit.
Peter Keating Collection

original PBY-5As and also acquired some former USAAF OA-10As. By 1958, all had been retired and scrapped, but not before some examples had seen active service, not only in Indo-China as previously mentioned, but also in Algeria. A number of the Catalinas also operated from home bases in France. Known post-war Catalina operators included Flotilles 1S, 4S, 5S, 8S at Saigon-Tan Son Nhut, 12S, 22S at Agadir and 52S at Lartigue.

Serial numbers for the former American aircraft operated by the French Aéronavale have been quoted as shown in the following list.

The French Aéronavale was supplied with a small number of former-USAAF OA-10A Catalinas, including 44-34065, which served as 1.S.5 of l'Escadrille 1S. It is believed that this photo was taken in France.
MAP

PBY-5A Bu46560 was supplied to the Aéronavale and flew on into the 1950s, as evidenced by this shot, taken during Farnborough week at Blackbushe in Hampshire, England, when it was on the strength of l'Escadrille 1S.
Jennifer M. Gradidge

Serials	Quantity
Bu46560 to Bu46574	15
Bu48306 to Bu48313	8
Bu48357 to Bu48363	7
Bu48365	1
Bu48368	1
44-34019	1
44-34059	1
44-34063	1
44-34065	1
Total	36

This close-up of an unidentified Aéronavale Catalina shows the eyeball turret of later marks and the insignia of Flotille 8FE.

These aircraft were not to be the Aéronavale's last association with the Catalina however. In the 1960s, a number of amphibians were acquired by the Section de Liaison du Pacifique (SLPAC) to support the French nuclear testing activities in the Pacific. SLPAC was formed at the beginning of October 1964 and eventually, a total of six Catalinas were used. Three examples (20, 39 and 48) were delivered, via Brisbane, in April 1965 and two more (the second 20 and 32) followed over the next two years. At least the first three aircraft were initially ferried to UTA (Union de Transports Aérien) who prepared the aircraft for military service at Le Bourget before being delivered to the Pacific. One further aircraft, probably an attrition replacement, was delivered via France and Bahrein in April, 1968, this being serial 81. In the main, these Catalinas had come from Canadian operators. Three of the Catalinas were lost in accidents. Aircraft 20 suffered a heavy landing on water at Hikuera on 2nd September 1965. The hull was split open and the aircraft had to be run aground. The next day, serial 39 flew into Hikuera

Another view of a Flotille 8FE aircraft is shown here with the code 8.F.3.

but broke away from its moorings during the night and was badly damaged on a nearby coral reef. Both of these aircraft had to be written off. The third loss involved 48 which was written off in a water landing at Reao after nose gear door failure on 20th April 1966.

After a few years use, the three survivors were withdrawn and stored in Tahiti before being donated by the French Government to the Chilean operator ASPAR. They were shipped as deck cargo to South America and all three have survived, two in airworthy condition. In French military service, the Catalinas were given two-figure hull codes that, in the case of the ex-US Navy aircraft, corresponded with the 'last two' of the BuAer serial and, for the former RCAF examples, equated to the Canadian Vickers construction number. This explains why two separate aircraft carried the code 20 at different times.

Canso A 81/F-YEIC passed through Bahrein during April 1968 en route for Tahiti and the French nuclear testing grounds.
A. W. Steele

F-WMKR served with the French Centre d'Experimentation du Pacifique in Tahiti as serial number 20 before being given to the Chilean operator ASPAR.
MAP

Table 43. Catalinas operated by the Aéronavale from Tahiti post-war

Serial	C/n	Type	Place of Manufacture	P/i(s)	Notes
20/F-YCHA	1574	PBY-5A	CON SD	F-WMKR CF-JTL N10022 Bu34020 (US Navy)	1965. Written off, Hikuera, 2/9/1965.
20 (2)/ F-YCHA	CV-520	OA-10A	CAN VIC (Cartierville)	F-WMKR CF-IHC N62043 44-34009 (USAAF) Bu67973 ntu (US Navy)	1966. To CC-CDU then CC-CGY. Current – see Chile Survivors.
32/F-YCHB	CV-332	OA-10A	CAN VIC (Cartierville)	F-WMKS CF-FKV TF-RVR 44-33880 (USAAF) Bu67844 ntu (US Navy).	1966. To CC-CDT Current - see Spain Survivors.

Serial	C/n	Type	Place of Manufacture	P/i(s)	Notes
39	1593	PBY-5A	CON SD	F-WMKS CF-HVV N68956 Bu34039 (US Navy)	1965. Damaged at Hikuera, 4/9/1965 and believed scrapped at Papeete.
48/F-YCHC	1810	PBY-5A	CON SD	F-WMKT CF-IHD N31234 Bu48448 (US Navy)	1965. Damaged in accident, Reao, 20/4/1966, and believed scrapped at Papeete.

Rarely illustrated in the past, this view shows the Air France Catalina F-BBCC at an unknown location, possibly in the USA. Confirmation of its RCAF past was displayed by the serial 9749 on the fin just above the French civil registration.
Jennifer M. Gradidge

Serial	C/n	Type	Place of Manufacture	P/i(s)	Notes
81/F-YEIC	CV-281	Canso A	CAN VIC (Cartierville)	F-ZBAX CF-UKR 11003 (RCAF)	1968. To CC-CDS. Destroyed in crash, Chiguayante, Chile, 8/4/1979.

Note: The identities of F-BMKR, F-BMKS and F-BMKT have also been quoted in addition to F-WMKR, F-WMKS and F-WMKT. However, the F-BM** marks are known to have been allocated to other, entirely different types and so their use on these three Catalinas is unconfirmed.

COMMERCIAL OPERATORS

In the early post-war years, a number of French airlines flew Catalinas, although none of these were actually operating within mainland France itself, but rather in various far-flung outposts of French influence. This was to remain the case until the 1960s, when the type was used in the South of France on fire-fighting duties. The identities of the Pacific-area commercial Catalinas have suffered somewhat from inaccurate reporting in the past, particularly in an Australian magazine source dating back to 1971. The versions published here are believed to be the correct ones.

Air France

A little-known facet of the French flag carrier's history is that, post-war, it operated three Catalina amphibians. All former Royal Canadian Air Force Canso As, they were registered F-BBCB, F-BBCC and F-BBCD, and were based at Fort de France in Martinique. They were used on flights to Port of Spain, Pointe à Pitre and San Juan in the Caribbean.

Officially sold by the RCAF in February, 1946, all three aircraft were rebuilt by Convair and delivered to Air France in the summer of 1947, although they appear to have been initially registered to SGAC. They were configured to seat between 20 and 22 occupants, but did not remain in service for long, and F-BBCC and F-BBCD were sold in January 1951 to Foshing Air Transport. F-BBCB remained with Air France for a few more months until passing to the subsidiary company TRAPAS.

Although Air France's use of the Catalina was brief and has received very little attention in later years, their livery none the less appeared again on another Catalina during 1998, when the French-owned but Canadian-registered Catalina C-FCRR was painted in their colours. It was shown in a display of vintage aircraft in the Champs Elysées in Paris before flying across the Atlantic to Chile and Brazil to commemorate mail flights flown earlier in the century by French flying boats.

Table 44. Air France Catalinas

Registration	C/n	Type	Place of Manufacture	Previous id(s)	Notes
F-BBCB	420	Canso A	CON SD	9747 (RCAF)	To TRAPAS – see entry below.
F-BBCC	425	Canso A	CON SD	9749 (RCAF)	To Taiwan as XT-1401 then B-1401.
F-BBCD	22020	Canso A	BOE CAN	9791 (RCAF)	To Taiwan as XT-1402 then B-1402.

TRAPAS

Société Française de Transports Aériens du Pacifique Sud, or TRAPAS, was founded on 25 October 1946, and operated out of Noumea in New Caledonia and Tahiti. It is known to have flown four Catalinas, including F-BBCB, a former Air France machine. The first two machines – F-BCJG and F-BCJH – arrived in Noumea during the summer of 1947 after being converted for commercial use in the USA. In the case of F-BCJG, it was the first time that a French-registered aircraft had crossed the Pacific Ocean. They were joined by F-BDRN from Honolulu in July 1948. After Air France had finished with F-BBCB, it too joined TRAPAS. TRAPAS also operated three Republic Seabee 4-seater amphibians, although their use was short-lived.

After the arrival of the first Catalina, a survey flight to the New Hebrides was carried out, followed by a weekly passenger service connecting Noumea with Port Vila and

Shown on the vast expanse of Oakland Airport, California, is the TRAPAS Catalina F-BCJG during its delivery flight to the Pacific in early June 1947. It was destroyed in an accident less than a year later.
William T. Larkins

Espiritu Santo. In addition, flights were made in August 1947 on behalf of the Government to the Wallis and Futuna Islands to provide badly needed medical supplies. Once F-BCJH had arrived, a further survey flight was made to Tahiti via Fiji, Samoa and the Cook Islands. During this flight, the Catalina took part in the search for the schooner *Tahitienne* that was in trouble with faulty engines and damaged sails. The Catalina successfully located the vessel after seven hours' flying. Later, the TRAPAS Catalinas were to be involved in other searches for ships in distress in the Pacific. This second survey flight prefaced regular services linking Papeete with Nadi and scheduled services by international carriers. Some of these flights also took in Tonga. To give some idea of the scale of these services, the distance from Noumea to Papeete is 2,700 nautical miles, and the Catalinas took 20 to 23 hours to complete this at an average speed of 120–125 knots. Once established, the Catalinas would also fly to Bora-Bora and the Raiatea islands during the 'stopover' at Papeete.

In addition to the scheduled services, TRAPAS undertook some charters with their PBYs, including a small number of flights to New Zealand and one to Australia.

On 14 March 1948, Magenta in New Caledonia was hit by a hurricane and F-BCJG was destroyed, although its registration was not cancelled until as late as December 1956. F-BCJH was damaged at Magenta by the same hurricane, but was repaired by Barrier Reef Airways at Brisbane.

TRAPAS flew its Catalinas until August 1951. Eight months before, Air France had taken a majority share holding in TRAPAS, and upon the sale of the Cats, TRAPAS effectively ceased to exist. In common with the national carrier's own Catalinas, the TRAPAS survivors ended up being sold in the Far East.

Unfortunately, no details of the location or date for this view of RAI's F-OAVV are known. The aircraft was unusual inasmuch as it was a pure flying boat Catalina and ex-RAF. *John Evans Collection*

Samoa, Fiji and Noumea.

The two Catalinas flown by RAI were unusual inasmuch as they were both operated as pure flying boats rather than amphibians. Indeed, F-OAVV was an ex-Royal Air Force Catalina IIA and as such is one of very few former RAF Cats to see post-war commercial service. It was originally built by Consolidated as a Canso for the Royal Canadian Air Force, but was one of several diverted to the RAF to replace earlier loaned Catalinas. It became VA712 in the batch of serials allocated years ahead of their time sequentially following the incorrect allocation of V9712, a Westland Lysander serial. Indeed the latter identity was painted on the airframe at first. It never served operationally with the RAF but was allocated to 45 Group in Bermuda. At the war's end, it was sold to Wing Commander E. M. Ware, the Director of Civil Aviation in Bermuda, and became VR-BAB. It was sold in the USA in January 1951, and then went to RAI in November the following year. It was registered as F-OAVV to the Minister of French Colonies.

It flew with RAI until it was lost in a tragic accident on 19 February 1958. On that day, it was approaching to land on a very smooth surface at Raiatea in the Leeward

Table 45. TRAPAS Catalinas

Registration	C/n	Type	Place of Manufacture	Previous id(s)	Notes
F-BBCB	420	Canso A	CON SD	9747 (RCAF)	To Thailand as HS-POF, 8/7/1951.
F-BCJG	'16'/423	PBY-5A	CON SD	Bu7258 (US Navy)	Destroyed 14/3/1948. *Nouvelle-Hébrides.*
F-BCJH	933	PBY-5A	CON SD	Bu08114 (US Navy)	To Republic of China as B-1403 *Nouvelle-Calédonie.*
F-BDRN	'55'/851	PBY-5A	CON SD	NC49692 Bu08032 (US Navy)	To Republic of China as B-819/B-831 *Tahiti.*

RAI (Régie Aérienne Interinsulaire)

RAI operated services on behalf of the French Department of Public Works in French Polynesia. These flights linked the Society, Tuamoto and Austral Island groups with Papeete in Tahiti. RAI had originally flown a Grumman Widgeon and Mallard until taken over by the French Government in 1953. In addition to the routes mentioned above, one-off flights were also operated, and these included trips to the Tuamoto Archipelago, the Gambier Islands and even as far as New Zealand via

The other RAI Catalina was originally a US Navy PBY-5A, but as can be seen in this shot, its amphibious undercarriage was removed during its airline career. Visible in this ground-running shot are the beaching gear and its radome atop the forward hull. Unusual is the shape of the 'clipper' bow which seems to have an overhang on the upper part. *MAP*

Another view of F-OAYD, this time after withdrawal and in storage at Raiatea prior to being scuttled. Its engines and floats have been removed. Clearly visible is the plating that covers the former main undercarriage bay.

Islands when the starboard float hit the water, causing the Catalina to crash with the loss of 15 lives out of the 26 aboard. The dead included RAI's chief pilot, Capt Allais. The Catalina was destroyed in the impact, sinking a few minutes after the crash. Various alternative identities have been quoted for F-OAVV, but those quoted here and in Table 45 are believed to be the correct version.

The other RAI Catalina, F-OAYD, was originally built as a US Navy PBY-5A, but it had its amphibious landing gear removed whilst flying with RAI, although, unusually for a civilian Cat, it carried a large radome above the cockpit section. It was modified to carry a horn-balanced rudder and a 'clipper' bow in place of the turret, the profile of the latter being distinctly different from all other known conversions. It also had its blisters removed. Sadly, this PBY also met its end at Raiatea when it was damaged beyond repair in a heavy water landing there in October 1960. As related in Chapter Twenty-one, it was salvaged, stripped of useful components and then towed out into the lagoon and scuttled. Its abandoned hulk still remains below the surface today, a plaything for the local marine life. Once again, the identities quoted here are believed to be the accurate ones, despite alternatives being published elsewhere in the past.

Table 46. RAI Catalinas

Registration	C/n	Type	Place of Manufacture	Previous id(s)	Notes
F-OAVV	296	Canso / Catalina IIA	CON SD	VR-BAB VA712 (RAF) V9712 (RAF) 9712 (RCAF)	Destroyed in accident, Raiatea, 19/2/1958.
F-OAYD	1689	PBY-5A	CON SD	N1520V Bu48327 (US Navy)	Written off in heavy landing, Raiatea, 10/1960. Scuttled.

Note: F-OAVV has been reported elsewhere as c/n 1296 ex-Bu08372 and as NEIAF serial Y-44 c/n 293, whilst F-OAYD has been linked with c/n 1685, Bu48323 and also with c/n 1687.

Protection Civile

Mainland France saw the return of Catalinas in the 1960s, when the Government-funded Protection Civile took on several examples to combat forest fires in the South of France and Corsica. A specialist operating base was formed in June 1963 at Marseille-Marignane, which, because of its coastal location, could function as both a land and flying boat base. Its first two Catalinas were obtained in Canada, where they had been converted for the water bombing role by Field Aviation. One was a PBY-5A, the other a Canso A, and they were registered F-ZBAQ and F-ZBAR respectively, the F-ZB series of markings being specifically reserved for aircraft and helicopters of the Protection Civile. It is worth noting that from time to time, the same registrations have been used by more than one machine.

In 1964, two PBY-6As were obtained, also from Canada, and they were overhauled by Heli Service and then put into service as F-ZBAV and F-ZBAW. They continued in use until the early 1970s, when they were disposed of. Over the years, the Protection Civile used a number of other Catalinas, leasing them from Canadian operators Kentings and Fields as needed. The last Catalina season was in 1973, after which more modern equipment took over. In addition to their registrations, each of the Catalinas was given a call sign ending in *Pelican*, and that matched the coloured band painted on the rear hull. The individual allocations are shown in Table 46. They also carried the Protection Civile's military-style marking of an orange triangle on a blue roundel background.

Table 47. Catalinas owned and leased by the Protection Civile, 1963–73

Registration	C/n	Type	Place of Manufacture	Previous id(s)	Notes
F-ZBAQ	1684	PBY-5A	CON SD	CF-IJJ N1564M Bu48322 (US Navy)	*White Pelican.* Written off at Veine, Bouches-du-Rhone, 8/11/67 after porpoising during practice water ops on lake.

F-ZBAQ was one of the Catalinas actually owned by the Protection Civile, as opposed to the larger number that were leased during the fire-fighting season from Canadian operators. The operator's insignia can be seen ahead of the forward wing strut, whilst the coloured identification band – in this case, white – is aft of the former blister position. *Peter Keating Collection*

Registration	C/n	Type	Place of Manufacture	Previous id(s)	Notes
F-ZBAR (1)	CV-449	Canso A	CAN VIC (Cartierville)	CF-NJP 11100 (RCAF)	*Red Pelican* Used for spares after damaged in accident on Donzere Canal in July 1964, and later derelict at Marseille. Nose section current – see Chapter Seventeen.
F-ZBAR (2) & F-ZBBC	CV-249	Canso A	CAN VIC (St Hubert)	CF-NJB 9815 (RCAF)	*Red Pelican* (2) Returned to Canada as CF-NJB and current – see Chapter Fifteen.
F-ZBAV		PBY-6A	CON NO	N5555H N2846D Bu64017 (US Navy)	*Green Pelican.* Sold in Canada as CF-HNH. Later became G-BPFY, N212DM and N285RA. Current – see Chapter Seventeen.
F-ZBAW		PBY-6A	CON NO	N7082C Bu64097 (US Navy)	*Yellow Pelican* Sold in Canada as CF-HNF. Later became N7179Y and current – see Chapter Nineteen.
F-ZBAX	CV-281	Canso A	CAN VIC (Cartierville)	CF-UKR 11003 (RCAF)	*Grey Pelican* (1). Stored then to Aéronavale as 81/F-YEIC then to Chile as CC-CDS. Destroyed in crash, Chigyuante, Chile, 8/4/78.
F-ZBAY & F-ZBBD	CV-283	Canso A	CAN VIC (Cartierville)	CF-NJF 11005 (RCAF)	*Blue Pelican* Returned to Canada as CF-NJF and current – see Chapter Fifteen.
F-ZBAZ		PBY-6A	CON NO	CF-IZZ N10011 Bu64064 (US Navy)	*Black Pelican* PBY-5A rudder. Returned to Canada as CF-IZZ and later to Spain as

Registration	C/n	Type	Place of Manufacture	Previous id(s)	Notes
					EC-940 and EC-FMC. Current – see Chapter Seventeen.
F-ZBBC	– see F-ZBAR above				
F-ZBBD	– see F-ZBAY above				
F-ZBBE	1637	PBY-5A	CON SD	CF-HTN CF-NTJ N1556M Bu48275 (US Navy)	*Grey Pelican* (2) Returned to Canada as CF-HTN and destroyed in crash, 500 miles north of Edmonton, 3/9/71.

ICELAND

The Catalina was no stranger to Iceland during the Second World War, as both flying boat and amphibian variants were stationed there with various squadrons of the US Navy, Royal Air Force and Royal Canadian Air Force. Many long and arduous operations were flown from Icelandic bases up into the Arctic and far into the North Atlantic, and some of these resulted in successful attacks on German U-boats. The history of Icelandic Catalina operations in wartime has been well documented in other works and is not therefore repeated here. Less well known is the history of commercial Catalina operations in that part of the world. A number of PBYs were flown by Icelandic airlines and official bodies, and these users are described below.

Although it is now many years since any Catalinas have operated with Icelandic owners, the type has continued to pass through the country on delivery flights or charters with surprising regularity. No doubt these birds of passage bring back fond memories to those who flew them with Iceland's pioneering post-war airlines.

Flugfélag Islands (Iceland Airways)

Flugfélag Islands was originally established in 1937 as Flugfélag Akureyrar (Akureyri Airways), and it operated a WACO YKS-7 floatplane on what are generally considered the first continuous scheduled commercial flights in the country. In 1940, a name change resulted in the airline becoming the third company to bear the name Flugfélag Islands, and it set up operations at Reykjavik. Despite the war raging around it, Iceland maintained a busy commercial aviation sector for the carriage of both passengers and freight, including mail.

In 1944, Flugfélag obtained a Catalina flying boat for 463,217 Icelandic Kronur and had it registered TF-ISP. Later, in 1949, it was named *Sæfaxi*, although locals tended to refer to it as *Pétur*. It had originally been operated in the USA and South America by the United States Rubber Company as NC33304, having been built originally for the US Navy. Delivered to Iceland on 13 October

All the Flugfélag Islands Catalinas were unusual. TF-ISP, seen here at its mooring, was one of the very few pure flying boat Catalinas to see commercial service after the war, although it first carried passengers as early as 1944. It retains its bow turret, although the blisters have gone. The cockpit-roof-mounted pitot tube is non-standard.
via Grétar Felixson

The other two Flugfélag Islands Catalinas were both from the batch of 12 Catalina III amphibians delivered during WWII to the RAF. TF-ISJ was formerly FP530 and is pictured, minus blisters, after it had been re-named *Sólfaxi*. *via Snorri Snorrason*

TF-ISK *Skyfaxi* about to take on passengers through the aft hatch. It was scrapped at Reykjavik after sustaining damage in September 1958. *via Snorri Snorrason*

1944, it had departed from New York La Guardia Airport two days earlier, routeing Botwood, New Foundland–Goose Bay, Labrador–Reykjavik. After arrival, it first underwent modification and servicing before entering service with Flugfélag with the capability of carrying 22 passengers. On 11 July 1945, it made the first passenger and mail flight to the United Kingdom from Iceland, when it operated to Largs in Scotland under the command of the airline's chief pilot, Jóhannes R. Snorrason. This was also the first time that an Icelandic aircraft had flown abroad with such a cargo. Altogether, three flights were made to Largs, two of which continued to Copenhagen and one to Bergen in Norway. Its last flight with Flugfélag was on 5 November 1952, and it was then stored at Reykjavik Airport and used for spares recovery. Its registration was cancelled on 5 March 1955, although the hull was still to be seen at Reykjavik as late as 1959. When flying with Flugfélag, *Sæfaxi* retained its nose turret, less armament, but had fore and aft passenger windows in place of the rear blisters.

In late 1945, Flugfélag acquired two more Catalinas. If TF-ISP was unusual in being a very early commercial PBY, then these two other examples were just as unusual, but for different reasons. The new arrivals were both from the small batch of amphibious Catalina IIIs used by the Royal Air Force. Although the RAF flew several hundred Catalinas, only a dozen MkIIIs were ordered, serialled FP525 to FP536. Two of these – FP530 and FP532 – remained with 45 Group and were used for crew ferry flights in support of the North Atlantic aircraft delivery routes, although, ironically, they do not appear to have visited Iceland in that role. Both were officially returned to the USA at the end of December 1945, and were then sold to Flugfélag, FP530 becoming TF-ISJ *Sólfaxi* and FP532 becoming TF-ISK *Sæfaxi*. TF-ISJ was delivered from Montreal-Dorval on 9 January 1946, but did not arrive at Reykjavik until 2 February as various technical

snags dogged the flight. TF-ISK followed from Dorval on 26 September 1946, but also suffered engine problems, so that it eventually reached Reykjavik on 6 October. Both flights were under the command of Johannes Snorrason, Flugfélag's chief pilot, and were routed via Goose Bay and Narsarssuaq. After interior modification, both were used on passenger flights around Iceland and, on occasions, out to Greenland. The two Cats continued to sport their nose turrets, but, like TF-ISP, they had their blisters removed and replaced by more conventional hull windows and loading hatch.

In 1954, TF-ISJ was re-named *Sæfaxi* after its flying boat predecessor TF-ISP, and it continued in use until its Certificate of Airworthiness expired in April 1961. It was, however, allowed one last flight to Greenland and back in the following August, after which it was stored at Reykjavik for a while, eventually being scrapped around 1962. Lloyds of London records reveal that on 12 May 1952, TF-ISJ lost its port propeller, complete with reduction gear, during a water take-off from Borgarnes, resulting in substantial damage to the hull and cockpit window structure, although without casualties amongst those on board. Photographs of the damage reveal that the captain must have had a miraculous escape!

TF-ISK did not last quite so long, as it was withdrawn from use after an accident at Akureyri on 6 September 1958. Photos exist of this aircraft with a crumpled upper bow area, and it is likely that this was as a result of the accident at Akureyri. The Catalina was making a water landing at Siglufjördur when a nose-wheel door caved in. Suspecting that the hull might be holed, the pilot aborted the landing, took off again and landed at the nearby airfield of Akureyri. However, upon landing, the nose wheel was jammed in the retracted position. The nose hit the runway quite hard and caused considerable damage to the hull. Although it returned to Reykjavik, it was

scrapped and its registration cancelled on 1 October 1961. This ended the airline's involvement with Catalinas, although the company continued to thrive and eventually became Icelandair. It later merged with Loftleidir Icelandic Airlines, another one-time Catalina operator, as related below.

The Flugfélag Catalinas flew in an orange, grey and white scheme, although TF-ISP seems to have been painted in an all-white or light grey livery later in its career.

Another present-day survivor is Loftleidir's former TF-RVR. It was originally a USAAF OA-10A, and later served in the Pacific with the French Aéronavale before ending up as a water bomber with Chilean company ASPAR. It currently lives in Spain and Portugal.
via Grétar Felixson

Loftleidir Icelandic Airlines

Formed in March 1944, Loftleidir started life spotting shoals of herring for the Icelandic fishing fleets, but soon started passenger flights in competition with Flugfélag. Later, it moved into the international flight market, eventually merging with Flugfélag, by then known as Icelandair, to form a new Icelandair. Back in the late 1940s and early 1950s, the two airlines were flying the same equipment – the Catalina!

Loftleidir's first PBY was acquired in March 1949 from the USA, where it had been on the US civil register. Given the marks TF-RVG in the following July and the name *Vestfirdingur*, it was used on domestic flights around Iceland and out to Greenland. It was retired in February 1952. There followed a period of storage at Reykjavik until it was sold in Canada, departing Iceland in February 1953. It later had a new career as a Canadian water bomber, and is still to be found preserved in Newfoundland.

The other Loftleidir Catalina was TF-RVR. This was a later acquisition, coming from the USA in April 1951. After arrival, it received the usual attention to bring it up to airline standard, and was placed on the Icelandic register in the following July. It too was used in Iceland and Greenland until 1952. Like TF-RVG, it went to a Canadian owner when Loftleidir had finished with it, later seeing military service in the Pacific with the French Aéronavale, and then flying as both a passenger airliner and a water bomber with the Chilean operator ASPAR.

Both TF-RVG and TF-RVR kept their nose turrets whilst flying with Loftleidir, but the rear blisters were replaced with a large entry door for passenger and cargo use.

Table 48. Catalinas operated by Flugfélag Islands/Iceland Airways

Registration	C/n	Type	Place of Manufacture	Previous id(s)	Notes
TF-ISJ	'79'/489	PBY-5A/Catalina III	CON SD	FP530 (RAF) Bu04990 (US Navy)	*Sólfaxi*, later *Sæfaxi*. Scrapped at Reykjavik during early 1960s.
TF-ISK	'81'/504 (S/n also quoted as '94')	PBY-5A/Catalina III	CON SD	FP532 (RAF) Bu05005 (US Navy)	*Skyfaxi*. Damaged at Akureyri 6/9/1958 and withdrawn. Scrapped at Reykjavik.
TF-ISP	'92'/1019	PBY-5	CON SD	NC33304 Bu08125 (US Navy)	*Sæfaxi*. Withdrawn late 1952 and stored at Reykjavik. Scrapped there by 1960.

TF-RVG at anchor in Iceland during its time with Loftleidir. It survives today on display at Botwood in Newfoundland.
via Grétar Felixson

Table 49. Catalinas operated by Loftleidir Icelandic Airlines

Registration	C/n	Type	Place of Manufacture	Previous id(s)	Notes
TF-RVG	CV-605	OA-10A	Canadair (Cartierville)	NC65715 44-34094 (USAAF) Bu68058 ntu (US Navy)	*Vestfirdingur*. To CF-DFB, 2/1953. Current at Botwood, Newfoundland as 'E1497' – see Chapter Fifteen.

Registration	C/n	Type	Place of Manufacture	Previous id(s)	Notes
TF-RVR	CV-332	OA-10A	CAN VIC (Cartierville)	44-33880 (USAAF) Bu67844 ntu (US Navy)	*Dynjandi.* To CF-FKV, 7/1952 To F-WMKS, 2/1966 then F-YCHB/32. To CC-CDT, 1973 and current – see Chapter Seventeen.

Flugmálastjórn/Icelandic Directorate of Civil Aviation

The Icelandic Civil Aviation Authority acquired a PBY-6A from the US Navy in 1954. It had previously run aground at πørshöfn, also known as Thorshoefn, on Iceland's north-east coast that summer whilst serving with FASRON 107 at Keflavik. The US Navy did not want to salvage the Catalina and decided to dispose of it locally. A temporary fix was carried out by the DCA at the site where it had been damaged, and it was then flown to Reykjavik, registered TF-FSD in September 1954, and flown on to Copenhagen for more permanent repairs and overhaul by SAS. It returned to Iceland in May 1955, and was subsequently passed to the Coast Guard, becoming TF-RAN – see entry below. Prior to sale to the Coast Guard, TF-FSD flew in its original US Navy dark blue colours.

Table 50. Catalina operated by Icelandic Directorate of Civil Aviation

Registration	C/n	Type	Place of Manufacture	Previous id(s)	Notes
TF-FSD	2015	PBY-6A	CON NO	Bu46651 (US Navy)	To TF-RAN, 12/1955 – see below.

Landhelgisgœslan/Icelandic Coast Guard Division of Air Operations:

The Icelandic Coast Guard acquired PBY-6A TF-FSD from the Directorate of Civil Aviation in December 1955, and in the following April, it was re-registered TF-RAN and named *Ran* after the Norse goddess of the same name.

Photos of PBY-6A TF-FSD when owned by the Icelandic Directorate of Civil Aviation are rare. This picture shows it in stock military condition shortly after repairs to damage sustained when operated by the US Navy in the 1950s.
via Grétar Felixson

The Icelandic Coast Guard acquired TF-FSD and had it re-registered TF-RAN. Shown outside its own hangar at Reykjavik, it still has a radome above the flight deck and displays the name *Ran* below the modified bow turret glazing.
via Grétar Felixson

Ran's first flight with the Coast Guard was on 29 December 1955, when it carried out a fisheries patrol, and during its time with the Coast Guard, it flew no fewer than 350,000 nautical miles. During these flights, it was involved in the arrest of 14 trawlers that were illegally fishing in Icelandic waters. Its most famous success was on 16 December 1956, when it captured the vessel *Cape Cleveland* and escorted it into port at Nordfjördur. It is said that *Ran* was the first aircraft to be used exclusively for fishery protection duties.

TF-RAN's last flight was on 13 December 1962, after which it was withdrawn because of corrosion problems. The Certificate of Airworthiness expired on 12 January 1963. It was placed in open storage at Reykjavik, and during 1967 was blown onto its back during a severe gale. It was later scrapped, and the story goes that the remains were buried at Reykjavik during construction work at the airport!

When with the Coast Guard, TF-RAN flew in an overall colour scheme of gloss medium grey with black lettering. The Icelandic State flag was carried prominently on the tail, and the blue and white Coast Guard pennant was painted below the cockpit. Although externally it was virtually a stock PBY-6A, the nose turret framing was changed so that the glazed panels were optically flat and hubs were added to the main wheels.

Table 51. Catalina operated by Icelandic Coast Guard

Registration	C/n	Type	Place of Manufacture	Previous id(s)	Notes
TF-RAN	2015	PBY-6A	CON NO	TF-FSD Bu46651 (US Navy)	*Ran.* Flew with Coast Guard as TF-FSD initially. Withdrawn from use, 12/1962 and scrapped in 1967 at Reykjavik after gale damage.

NETHERLANDS

The Netherlands' first association with the PBY dates back to before the Second World War. The type had already been built in relatively modest numbers of various marks for the US Navy, and it seems that NV Nederlandsche Vliegtuigenfabriek Fokker, better known as Fokker, were appointed as general representatives for Consolidated in Europe in February 1938. They were already European Sales Representatives for Douglas. Fokker archives contain a sales brochure bearing their name, a photo of a PBY-2, hull number 11-P-12, and the title *Consolidated PBY – The Sentinel of the Pacific*. Whether Fokker actually sold any PBYs is not known, but it seems likely that when the Dutch military first acquired Catalinas, they were ordered direct from Consolidated. Probably, the outbreak of the Second World War scuppered Fokker's plans to market and sell the PBY in Europe. As related below, the Dutch were none the less to have a long association with the type, mainly as a military aircraft, both during and after the Second World War. Post-war, the type was mainly operated in the Netherlands East Indies, later the Indonesian Republic after independence, and then in New Guinea.

MILITARY AIRCRAFT

The Royal Netherlands Naval Air Service (MLD, or Marine Luchtvaart Dienst) ordered 48 PBYs under contract number N-36 in October 1940. These were required to supplement an order for Dornier Do24 flying boats that had only been partly fulfilled when Germany invaded the Netherlands. The first PBY batch, numbered Y-38 to Y-73 and designated Model 28-5MN (M = Military, N = Netherlands), were delivered between August and October 1941. The remainder were given the serials Y-74 to Y-85 and were delivered in August 1942. These latter amphibious aircraft were designated Model 28-5AMN. A further two PBY-5s, serialled Y-86 and Y-87, were obtained from US Navy stocks. All 50 aircraft served with 321 Squadron, and their wartime exploits have been written about in other authors' works. Suffice to say that attrition took its toll, and only 11 of the 50 survived the end of hostilities to continue flying post-war. All of these are listed in Table 52 on page 121 and as will be seen, these and other later Catalinas were subject to various serial amendments over the years as numbering systems were changed.

During the war, six Catalinas IVBs were obtained on loan from the RAF and given serials Y-88 to Y-93, but they were soon returned and this Dutch serial batch was reallocated to a further six aircraft from the same source in July 1946. These stayed with the Dutch, although all were scuttled at Morokrembangan, Surubaya, during 1950 with the exception of one that had been lost in an earlier accident.

The next Catalinas to be acquired were initially numbered P-200 to P-210, although at least some of these had the letter prefix changed to 16- subsequently. They were delivered in 1946 and 1947. The first seven aircraft had all served with the Royal Canadian Air Force, despite their RAF serials, and most of them had flown with West Coast squadrons. Six of these aircraft are known to have been acquired by the Dutch from Aircraft Industries of Canada, St Jean, Quebec, and were overhauled by de Havilland Canada at Toronto Island Airport before delivery. One aircraft – DP202 – was of particular interest as it had originally been intended for the RAAF but was substituted by another aircraft and went to Canada via the RAF instead. The other four in the batch were former Royal Australian Air Force aircraft, although originally intended for both the US Navy and RAF! All four had been acquired at Rathmines via the Commonwealth Disposals Commission by Capt P. G. Taylor and A. C. M. Jackaman. It had been intended to use them on commercial services between Sydney and Lord Howe Island by Island Airways, but this venture failed when the necessary licence was not granted by the Australian authorities, and they were sold to the Dutch. These four Catalinas were the odd ones out in the Dutch fleet because they were the tall-tailed PB2B-2 version.

In 1951, there followed six amphibious PBY-5A Catalinas numbered P/16-211 to P/16-216. All were ex-US Navy aircraft and were given US civil registrations for the flight across the Atlantic before being overhauled by Aviolanda and put into service. One was lost in an accident on delivery and never took up its intended allocation of 16-211, this serial being given to another aircraft instead. Two of these PBY-5As, 16-212 and 16-216, remained in Holland with 8 Squadron on SAR and training duties, but the remainder went out to the East Indies

This view of PBY-5 Y-87 was taken in the Netherlands East Indies prior to July 1946, when it would have been re-serialled P-87. It crashed in New Guinea in October 1946. The Dutch nationality markings are shown aft of the blisters in the form of the tricolour.

Post-war, the Dutch changed earlier styles of nationality marking to the red/white/blue/orange roundel, as seen here on Catalina IVA P-203, formerly JX219 and operated by the RCAF. It was scrapped at Biak, New Guinea, in late 1951.

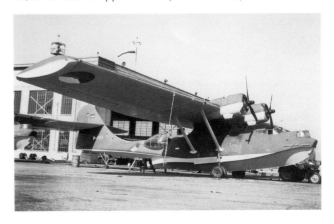

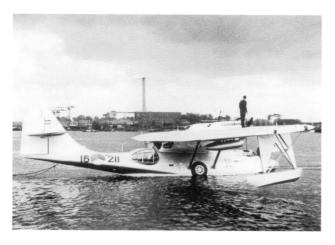

PBY-5A 16-211 is seen with under-wing long-range tanks at Aviolanda's water-side factory at Papendrecht in Holland. It hit a mountain in the Lebanon when returning to Holland from the Far East in December 1952.
via Nico Geldhof

Prior to joining the MLD, PBY-5A 16-224 had served with the RAAF as A24-99, originally being built for the US Navy as Bu46535. It was scrapped at Biak as late as 1957.
Jennifer M. Gradidge

16-215 in the foreground was one of the ex-US Navy batch acquired by the MLD in 1951, whilst 16-218 in the background was a much earlier aircraft, having been ordered as a Model 25-5AMN and originally serialled Y-83. The photo was taken off the New Guinea coast.
via P. P. Staal

and served with 321 Squadron. No. 16-212 has survived to the present day.

The serials 16-217 to 16-219 were given to three aircraft in the original wartime batch, and allocations then continued through to 16-225. These last six aircraft were again amphibians and had come from the Royal Australian Air Force. Unlike the earlier Australian Catalinas, these had not been acquired via the commercial market but had been presented to the Dutch by the RAAF. They were obtained in May 1953, and were initially overhauled by Bristol Aviation at Bankstown, being delivered to the Dutch over the next eighteen months or so.

The following MLD squadrons were equipped with the Catalina post-war.

7 Squadron

This squadron was formed at Biak in Surubaya, Java, on 23 December 1949 with six Catalinas that had previously operated with the OVTS, or Oosterlijk Verkennings en Transport Squadron, at Morokrembangan, also in Surubaya. They were used on maritime patrol duties for just over a year until 7 Squadron disbanded on 1 February 1951. The Catalinas were transferred to 321 Squadron, also resident at Biak.

8 Squadron

During the early 1950s, 8 Squadron re-formed at Valkenburg in Holland, and in 1953, two amphibious PBY-5A Catalinas were taken on strength for search-and-rescue duties in the North Sea. They were replaced by Martin Mariners in 1956. The two Catalinas involved were 16-212 and 16-216.

321 Squadron

Originally formed on 1 June 1940, as a Dutch squadron within the Royal Air Force, and subsequently merged with 320 Squadron, 321 Squadron re-formed in August 1942 at China Bay, Ceylon, equipped with Catalinas. It flew patrols throughout the Indian Ocean theatre and had detachments in South Africa. In July 1945, the Cats moved base to the Cocos Islands and thence to Kemojoran and Tandjong Priok, Java. The squadron passed to Dutch MLD control in December 1945, and in late 1946 was renamed the OVTS, or Oosterlijk Verkennings en Transport Squadron. It operated with both Dakotas and Catalinas until 1 February 1950, the Catalina element then becoming 321 Squadron again.

In 1949, a move to Biak in Dutch New Guinea followed Indonesia's independence, and the squadron took on 7 Squadron's Cats in February 1951. Its roles in New Guinea included patrol flights, maritime exercises, ground support for marines in the dense jungle and cargo flights, some of the latter even including livestock! By 1957, the remaining Catalinas had all been scrapped and replaced by less flexible and less popular Martin PBM-5A Mariners.

Table 52. MLD Catalinas post-WWII

Serial	C/n	Type	Place of Manufacture	Previous id(s)	Notes
Y-45	298	Model 28-5MN	CON SD		321 Sqn code A, AA. Withdrawn from use, 12/1945 approx. Some sources claim this later went to RAAF as A24-28.
Y-57	344	Model 28-5MN	CON SD		321 Sqn code E, EE. Withdrawn from use, 1946 and scrapped, Morokrem-bangan, Surabaya.
Y-62	355	Model 28-5MN	CON SD		321 Sqn code F, FF. Written off in crash landing, Biak, New Guinea 18/10/1945.
Y-69/P-69/ 16-69	376	Model 28-5MN	CON SD		321 Sqn code H,HH. Scrapped at Morokrem-bangan, Surabaya, 1947.
Y-74/P-74	837	Model 28-5AMN	CON SD		321 Sqn code J, JJ. Scrapped at Morokrem-bangan, Surabaya, 1946.
Y-75/P-75 16-75	838	Model 28-5AMN	CON SD		321 Sqn code K, KK. Scrapped at Biak, New Guinea, 12/1952. Used call sign PMPGE.
Y-76/P-76/ 16-76	839	Model 28-5AMN	CON SD		321 Sqn code L, LL. Also served with 7 Squadron. Scrapped at Biak, New Guinea, 2/1952. Used call sign PMPGF.
Y-77/P-77/ 16-77	840	Model 28-5AMN	CON SD		321 Sqn code M, MM. Also served with 7 Squadron. Scrapped at Biak, New Guinea, late 1951.
Y-79/P-79/ 16-79/ 16-217	842	Model 28-5AMN	CON SD		321 Sqn code O, OO. Preserved at Biak, New Guinea, from early 1950s but scrapped there c.1958.
Y-82/P-82/ 16-82	845	Model 28-5AMN	CON SD		321 Sqn code Q, QQ. Written off in crash near Seroei 28/12/1950 whilst with 7 Squadron. Used call sign PMPHB.
Y-83/P-83/ 16-218	846	Model 28-5AMN	CON SD		321 Sqn code S, SS. Scrapped at Biak, New Guinea, 1957.
Y-85/P-85/ 16-85/ 16-219	848	Model 28-5AMN	CON SD		321 Sqn code T, TT. Also served with 7 Squadron. Destroyed by fire at Biak, New Guinea, 30/10/1954 and struck off charge, 11/2/1956.
Y-86/P-86/ 16-86	1320	PBY-5	CON SD	Bu08396 (US Navy)	321 Sqn code U, UU. Scrapped at Biak, New Guinea, 8/1/1949.
Y-87/P-87/ 16-87	1321	PBY-5	CON SD	Bu08397 (US Navy)	Crashed at Woendi Island, New Guinea, 13/10/1946.
Y-88(2)/ p-88		PB2B-1/ Catalina IVB	BOE CAN	JX276 (RAF)	Code C. Scuttled at Morokrembangan, Surabaya, 7/1950.
Y-89(2)/ P-89		PB2B-1/ Catalina IVB	BOE CAN	JX288 (RAF)	Code D. Fate as above.
Y-90(2)/ P-90		PB2B-1/ Catalina IVB	BOE CAN	JX289 (RAF)	Code F. Fate as above.
Y-91(2)/ P-91		PB2B-1/ Catalina IVB	BOE CAN	JX298 (RAF)	Code G. Fate as above.

Serial	C/n	Type	Place of Manufacture	Previous id(s)	Notes
Y-92(2)/ P-92		PB2B-1/ Catalina IVB	BOE CAN	JX354 (RAF) Bu73005 (US Navy)	Code S. Fate as above.
Y-93(2)/ P-93		PB2B-1/ Catalina IVB	BOE CAN	JX359 (RAF) Bu73010 (US Navy)	Code V. Caught fire whilst refuelling at Balikpapan, 5/11/1947.
P-200	57	Catalina I	CON SD	DP202 (RAF/ RCAF) A24-2 ntu (RAAF) VH-AFB ntu	Scrapped at Biak, New Guinea, 2/1952.
P-201	1156	Catalina IVA	CON SD	JX206 (RCAF)	Scuttled at Morokrembangan, Surabaya, 7/1950.
P-202/ 16-202	1106	Catalina IVA	CON SD	JX572 (RCAF) Bu08212 (US Navy)	Known to have been with 7 Squadron. Fate as above.
P-203	1179	Catalina IVA	CON SD	JX219 (RCAF)	Known to have been with 7 Squadron. Scrapped at Biak, New Guinea, 10/1951.
P-204	160	Catalina I	CON SD	Z2137 (RCAF)	Crashed near Gili Manoek, Bali, 26/1/1947.
P-205	1177	Catalina IVA	CON SD	JX217 (RCAF)	Known to have been with 7 Squadron. Scrapped at Biak, New Guinea, 14/11/1951.
P-206/ 16-206	1159	Catalina IVA	CON SD	JX209 (RCAF)	Scrapped at Morokrembangan, Surabaya, 1950.
P-207	61172	PB2B-2/ Catalina VI	BOE CAN	A24-358 (RAAF) JX648 (RAF) Bu44266 (US Navy)	Scuttled at Morokrem-bangan, Surabaya, 7/1950.
P-208	61192	PB2B-2/ Catalina VI	BOE CAN	A24-351 (RAAF) JZ833 (RAF) Bu44286 (US Navy)	Scuttled at Morokrem-bangan, Surubaya, 1950.
P-209	61199	PB2B-2/ Catalina VI	BOE CAN	A24-384 (RAAF) JZ840 (RAF) Bu44293 (US Navy)	As above.
P-210	61170	PB2B-2/ Catalina VI	BOE CAN	A24-366 (RAAF) JX646 (RAF) Bu44264 (US Navy)	As above, 7/1950.
P-211/16-211 ntu	1885	PBY-5A	CON SD	N1493V Bu46521 (US Navy)	Not delivered to MLD as damaged beyond repair in water landing accident near Zwijndrecht, Holland, 23/1/1951.
P-211/ 16-211 (2nd allocation)	1945	PBY-5A	CON NO	N1494V Bu46581 (US Navy)	Hit mountain top, Cedres, Lebanon, 20/12/1952.
P-212/ 16-212	1679	PBY-5A	CON SD	N1495V Bu48317 (US Navy)	8 Squadron, Valkenburg. Current – see Chapter Seventeen.
P-213/ 16-213	1824	PBY-5A	CON SD	N1498V Bu46460 (US Navy)	Crashed at Biak, New Guinea, 28/10/1952.
P-214/ 16-214	1526	PBY-5A	CON SD	N1496V Bu33972 (US Navy)	Scrapped at Biak, New Guinea, 6/1956.
P-215/ 16-215	1947	PBY-5A	CON NO	N1497V Bu46583 (US Navy)	As above.
P-216/ 16-216	1614	PBY-5A	CON SD	N9415H Bu48252 (US Navy)	8 Squadron, Valkenburg. Scrapped at De Kooy, Netherlands 5/1958 and disposed of locally, 1962.
16-217		See Y-79 above			
16-218		See Y-83 above			
16-219		See Y-85 above			
16-220	1958	PBY-5A	CON NO	A24-104 (RAAF) Bu46594 (US Navy)	Scrapped at Biak, New Guinea, 11/1956.

Serial	C/n	Type	Place of Manufacture	Previous id(s)	Notes
16-221	1983	PBY-5A	CON NO	A24-110 (RAAF) Bu46619 (US Navy)	As above, 8/1956.
16-222	1984	PBY-5A	CON NO	A24-111 (RAAF) Bu46620 (US Navy)	As above, 4/1958.
16-223	1855	PBY-5A	CON SD	A24-92 (RAAF) Bu46491 (US Navy)	Used for spares recovery only.
16-224	1899	PBY-5A	CON SD	A24-99 (RAAF) Bu46535 (US Navy)	Scrapped at Biak, New Guinea, 7/1957.
16-225	1985	PBY-5A	CON NO	A24-112 (RAAF) Bu46621 (US Navy)	As above, 1/1957.

COMMERCIAL AIRCRAFT

On 20 March 1953, the Bataafsche Petroleum Mij company made an application for a Certificate of Airworthiness for a Catalina that at that time was on the Kenyan civil register as VP-KKJ. However, this application lapsed and the aircraft eventually found its way to the USA and obscurity. As far as is known, no actual Dutch registration was associated with this application. Also in 1953, the highly appropriate marks PH-PBY were reserved by NV Nederlandsche Nieuw-Guinea Petroleum Maatschappij (NNGPM), but they were not taken up and the aircraft involved became PH-TGP instead. Although the registration PH-TGP is known to have been painted on the airframe, the aircraft itself never visited Holland but went direct to New Guinea from the USA. The unused marks PH-PBY were reserved again, this time in July 1985, when Anne Cor Groenveld of the Dutch Dakota Association applied for them. Again, the application lapsed, and it was not until November 1994 that this registration was finally used by Cat Air and its former Canadian water bombing Catalina. Even then it was

US Navy PBY-5A Bu48383 was the aircraft that briefly became PH-TGP in New Guinea before being re-registered as JZ-POA.
Jennifer M. Gradidge

some time before the aircraft involved actually flew with those marks.

Table 53. Catalinas on the Dutch civil register

Registration	C/n	Type	Place of Manufacture	Previous id(s)	Notes
PH-PBY (1)					Reservation for NV Nederlands Nieuw-Guinea Petroleum Maatschappij, 1953. To PH-TGP – see below.
PH-PBY (2)					Reservation for Anne Cor Groenveld/DDA, 24/7/1985. Not taken up and lapsed.
PH-PBY (3)	Current – see Chapter Seventeen				
PH-TGP	1745	PBY-5A	CON SD	PH-PBY (1) ntu N68768 Bu48383 (US Navy)	Cancelled 15/1/1955 and registered in Netherlands East Indies as JZ-POA.

Still current on the Dutch civil register and under restoration to airworthy condition again is PH-PBY, a former US Navy aircraft with several U-boat attacks to its credit. It is seen here attending an air display at Duxford, England. *Author*

NORWAY

MILITARY AIRCRAFT

The Royal Norwegian Air Force used both flying boat and amphibious Catalinas during World War Two and post-war, and the type equipped two squadrons. 330 (Norwegian) Squadron was formed within the RAF with Norwegian personnel on 25 April 1941, and was unusual in that it was equipped solely with the amphibious Catalina MkIII, very few of these serving with the RAF. However, their use by 330 was brief and the squadron de-activated at Oban in January 1943. When it re-formed it was with Short Sunderlands, and it never flew PBYs again.

No. 333 Squadron had its origins in February 1942, when the Norwegian Detachment, Woodhaven, was formed as a part of 210 Squadron, RAF, at that base near Dundee. It was equipped with a small number of Catalina Mk1s. The detachment later became 1477 (N) Flight, and on 19 May 1943 it achieved full squadron status when it became 333 (Norwegian) Squadron. After three years of active service with many exciting operations behind it, 333 and its Catalinas departed for Norway on 19 June 1945, setting up base at Fornebu. For a time, it carried out transport duties in an almost airline-like manner, ferrying many displaced persons and refugees back to their homes. They also flew as escorts to flights of captured German aircraft being assembled for inspection by the RAF, and in a twist of irony the Catalinas operated alongside two former Luftwaffe Dornier Do24T flying boats for a time, the latter providing ASR cover and being crewed by German personnel under Norwegian commanders.

Control of 333 Squadron passed to the Royal Norwegian Air Force on 21 November 1945. Later, the squadron moved from Oslo-Fornebu to Sola, near Stavanger, and newer Catalinas were acquired to replace

those that were becoming weary from their wartime and immediate post-war activities. Operations settled down to a mixture of transport and SAR flights, although they were occasionally called upon to explode drifting wartime mines and to search for herring shoals! In 1946, detachments to Skattora near Tromso were started, and in June 1950 the squadron moved there, only to return to Sola two years later, although detached flights continued to fly out of Skattora on an occasional basis. As the Cold War developed, 333 Squadron resumed a more military style of operations again, flying regular reconnaissance missions around the Norwegian coast. In 1953–4, the last of the flying boat Catalinas were replaced under the Marshall Plan by a mixture of San Diego and New Orleans-built amphibious PBY-5As from the US Navy, and further detached flights were established at Bodö and Bardufoss. One of these six -5As was lost in a maintenance accident at Horten in June 1960.

By 1961, the Catalinas were deemed to be nearing the end of their useful lives, at least as far as the RNoAF was concerned, and the five remaining examples were replaced by another American amphibian, the Grumman SHU-16B Albatross. The redundant Catalinas were ferried to the 7101st Air Base Wing on the USAF base at Wiesbaden in West Germany, where they were handed back to the Americans. They remained in store there for a time, and rumour has it that they were intended for the Ethiopian Air Force, although this never came about. Ultimately, they were destroyed by a combination of gunnery and fire practice.

During the latter stages of the war, 333 Squadron's Catalinas carried individual aircraft code letters without a prefix. Post-war, the individual letter was prefixed with the squadron code letters KK-, but in August 1946 there was a system change and the prefix K denoting the Catalina type was used, followed by two letters for each individual aircraft. A further change back to the squadron code KK- was subsequently made in January 1951. Many of the 333 Squadron Catalinas carried individual aircraft names, and the known codes and names are shown in Table 53. Wartime grey camouflage was replaced post-war by an overall midnight blue scheme, occasionally with liberal application of dayglo orange to bow, tail and wingtips. The six ex-US Navy PBY-5As had the 'last-three' of the former American serial carried low down on the vertical tail, although paper records refer to these aircraft by the full five-figure number.

The Table 53 lists Catalinas operated by the RNoAF post-war, all of which were with 333 Squadron. Serial numbers W8424, FP121, FP314, FP183, FP222, JX265 and JX224 are not included in the table as they had been struck off charge, lost in action or transferred to other non-Norwegian units prior to the war's end.

The 333 Squadron, RNoAF code KK-D was used on two flying boat Catalinas, JX394 and JX400, both PB2 B-1/Catalina IVBs. This post-war photo does not, unfortunately, identify which of these two aircraft is depicted.
Audun Sjurscike

Table 54. Catalinas operated by RNoAF post-WWII, in order of in-service date

Serial	Type	Place of Manufacture	Known 333 Squadron Code	Name & c/n	Notes – first date shown is initial in-service date
JV933	PBY-5/ Catalina IVA	CON SD	C, K-CC	Jossing II 1501	28/5/1944. ex-Bu08547 (US Navy). Returned to RAF at Wig Bay and struck off charge 3/1947.

Serial	Type	Place of Manufacture	Known 333 Squadron Code	Name & c/n	Notes – first date shown is initial in-service date
JX582	PBY-5/ Catalina IVA	CON SD	KK-A	*Viking II* 1116	22/1/1945. ex-Bu08222 (US Navy). To RNoAF Technical School, Kristiansand as instructional airframe, 1946 – presumed scrapped.
JX573	PBY-5/ Catalina IVA	CON SD	KK-B	*Vingtor V* 1107	6/6/1945. ex-Bu08213 (US Navy). Returned to RAF at Wig Bay and struck off charge 3/1047.
JX382	PB2B-1/ Catalina IVB	BOE CAN	KK-A		25/8/1945. ex-Bu73041 (US Navy). As per JX573 above.
JX356	PB2B-1/ Catalina IVB	BOE CAN	KK-K		21/12/1945. ex-Bu73007 (US Navy). Sank at Alta Fjord, possibly after hitting object on landing, 6/7/1946.
JX394	PB2B-1/ Catalina IVB	BOE CAN	KK-E, K-AD, KK-D		21/12/1945. ex-Bu73065 (US Navy). To RNoAF Technical School, Kristiansand as instructional airframe, 6/1953 – presumed scrapped.
JX412	PB2B-1/ Catalina IVB	BOE CAN	KK-G, K-AK		21/12/1945. ex-Bu73082 (US Navy). Hit mountain top in thick fog, Sotra Island, 6/9/1948.
JX398	PB2B-1/ Catalina IVB	BOE CAN	KK-L, KA-F, KK-F		4/2/1946. ex-Bu73069 (US Navy). Struck off charge, 10/8/1954.
JX410	PB2B-1/ Catalina IVB	BOE CAN	KK-J, K-AH		4/2/1946. ex-Bu73080 (US Navy). Struck off charge, 26/10/1951.
JX400	PB2B-1/ Catalina IVB	BOE CAN	KK-D, K-AG		6/2/1946. ex-Bu73071 (US Navy). Struck off charge 26/10/1951. Possibly used as instructional airframe at Kjevik and later scrapped.
JX411	PB2B-1/ Catalina IVB	BOE CAN	KK-F, K-AI		6/2/1946. ex-Bu73081 (US Navy). Struck off charge, 26/10/1951.
JX395	Catalina	BOE CAN	KK-M, K-AE, KK-E		17/2/1946. ex-Bu73066 (US Navy) Struck off charge, 20/8/1954
JX372	PB2B-1/ Catalina IVB	BOE CAN	KK-H, K-AC, KK-C		27/2/1946. ex-Bu73027 (US Navy). Struck off charge, 5/6/1953.
JX378	PB2B-1/ Catalina IVB	BOE CAN	K-AL, KK-L		24/4/1947. ex-Bu73036 (US Navy). Struck off charge, by 1955.
JX590	PB2B-1/ Catalina IVB	BOE CAN	K-AM		15/5/1947. ex-Bu44192 (US Navy). Found to be corroded and used for spares by 1948.
JX381	PB2B-1/ Catalina IVB	BOE CAN	K-AN, KK-N		29/4/1949. ex-Bu73040 (US Navy). ex-LN-OAP of Vingtor Luftveier. Destroyed in fatal crash at Bjornoya during snow shower after wing hit ground, 28/3/1954.
48382	PBY-5A	CON SD	KK-A	1744	15/10/1953. ex-Bu48382 (US Navy). To USAF at Wiesbaden, 6/1961 and scrapped.
46638	PBY-5A	CON NO	KK-B	2002	12/5/1954. ex-Bu46638 (US Navy). Fate as 48382 above.
46580	PBY-5A	CON NO	KK-C	1944	11/6/1954. ex-Bu46580 (US Navy). Fate as 48382 above.
48332	PBY-5A	CON SD	KK-D	1694	8/7/1954. ex-Bu48332 (US Navy). Fate as 48382 above.
46588	PBY-5A	CON NO	KK-F	1952	3/9/1954. ex-Bu46588 (US Navy). Fate as 48382 above.
46613	PBY-5A	CON NO	KK-G	1977	18/9/1954. ex-Bu46613 (US Navy). Damaged by fire during fuel tank repair at Horten, 9/6/1960. Struck off charge 25/7/1960.

The Norwegians' first PBY-5A was the ex-US Navy Bu48382. It is seen here in full dark blue RNoAF livery and the codes KK-A. In addition to 'eyeball' turret and radar housing, it has long exhausts to feed the wing de-icing equipment.

JX395 K-AE of 333 Squadron during the period that the KK- codes of that squadron had stopped being used. It later became KK-M and was struck off charge in August 1954. The later type of 'eyeball' turret can clearly be seen. *via Morten Andersen*

Of the six RNoAF PBY-5As supplied by the USA, five were scrapped at Wiesbaden in West Germany after the plan to send them to the Ethiopian Air Force fell through. The sixth aircraft, 46613/KK-G, was damaged beyond repair during maintenance in July 1960.

COMMERCIAL AIRCRAFT

Vingtor Luftveier A/S

Vingtor Luftveier A/S was formed in Oslo in 1946 by former Royal Air Force and Royal Norwegian Air Force personnel. Their initial equipment consisted of two ex-RAF Catalina flying boats intended for use on passenger flights down each side of the Oslo Fjord. These services did not commence, partly because of a crash involving one of the Catalinas and the temporary withdrawal of the airline's permit to fly. Eventually, services were flown from early 1948 linking various locations in Northern Norway, but utilisation was low and financial constraints led to the liquidation of Vingtor in April of that year.

The two Catalinas used by Vingtor were registered as LN-OAP and LN-OAR, and at least one was painted in their striking red livery. They were unusual inasmuch as very few RAF Catalinas were released for commercial use once their military career had ended. LN-OAP was a PB2B-1 built by Boeing of Canada and supplied to the RAF as a Catalina IVB. It did not see active service and was sold to Vingtor by the Ministry of Supply in February of 1947. It was delivered from 57MU at Wig Bay to Norway and received its Certificate of Airworthiness on 2 June 1947. Known by Vingtor as *Sky Transport*, it could carry 22 passengers. When Vingtor failed, LN-OAP was sold to the Royal Norwegian Air Force and it flew with 333 Squadron as a passenger and VIP transport from September 1948. Sadly, it was lost in a fatal crash on 28 March 1954, whilst mail dropping. The wreckage can still be found at the crash site to this day.

LN-OAR came from the same stable as LN-OAP, and is known to have been on the strength of 302 Ferry Training Unit, RAF before entering storage at Wig Bay. It was sold to Vingtor on 4 February 1947. Its airline career

Vingtor's LN-OAP Is shown here, still in its basic RAF livery but with civil registration. The military serial JX381 at the foot of the fin has been crudely blanked out.
via Kay Hagby

LN-OAR was the second Vingtor Catalina, and as this air-to-air study shows, it received the airline's full civil livery.
via Kay Hagby

was cut short when, on 5 August 1947, it was operating from Oslo to Tromsö. It crashed on landing in a heavy sea at Svolvaer Harbour in the Lofoten Islands of Northern Norway. The hull was damaged, resulting in water flooding the cabin, although there were no fatalities. LN-OAR never flew again and its registration was cancelled 15 days after the accident.

Table 55. Vingtor Catalinas

Registration	C/n	Type	Place of Manufacture	Previous id(s)	Notes
LN-OAP	29129	PB2B-1/ Catalina IVB	BOE CAN	JX381 (RAF) Bu73040 (US Navy)	To RNoAF as JX381/KA-N, later KK-N. Destroyed in crash at Bjornoya, 28/3/1954 – see Chapter Twenty-one. The previous RAF identity has been incorrectly quoted as JX385 elsewhere.
LN-OAR	?	PB2B-1/ Catalina IVB	BOE CAN	JX419 (RAF) Bu73090 (US Navy)	Damaged beyond repair landing on heavy sea, Svolvaer Harbour, Lofoten Islands, 5/8/1947.

This photo of a Russian PBY almost certainly depicts the single US-built example that was assembled and flown by Consolidated before export. It has a faired-over bow turret and Wright Cyclone R-1820 G-3 engines.

Other Users

Apart from the two Vingtor Catalinas, no other examples of the type have found their way onto the Norwegian civil register. However, two PBY-6A amphibians owned by the Ontario-based Avalon Aviation did operate in Norway with Haydn Air Charter on fire-bombing operations at various times during the late 1970s and early 1980s. They were C-FHNF and C-FHNH; for their subsequent history, see elsewhere in this book. Another former Avalon Catalina – C-FIZO – came to Norway in December 1990 from Holland, and is now preserved on static display at the Royal Norwegian Air Force Museum at Bodö, painted to represent a wartime RNoAF Catalina III of 330 Squadron. The Flyhistorisk Museum at Sola, Stavanger, has a former Royal Danish Air Force PBY-5A in its collection, and this has been restored to represent a post-war PBY-5A of 333 Squadron.

RUSSIA

Early production of the PBY/Consolidated Model 28 flying boat included a Model 28-1 that went to Russia in August 1937 and three further aircraft, all Model 28-2s, that were supplied to the Russians later that year and in 1938. The full story of these aircraft is told earlier in this book in Chapter Two. Once Russia had taken delivery of these aircraft, licence production started at Taganrog of the version known as the GST (Gidro Samolyet Transportnyi, or seaplane transport). It is often stated that around 150 or more examples were built between 1940 and 1941, but it seems more likely that production ceased after fewer than thirty when German forces overran the area. Some sources claim that production later continued, although exactly how many examples were finally built is a mystery. Post-war usage of the type is hard to clarify because of the restrictions on research that abounded in those times, but it is believed that some examples were still in use until 1954. In the 1950s, the ASCC (Air Standards Co-ordinating Committee) allocated the type the name *Mop* in line with its policy of giving Russian aircraft reporting names.

Early versions of the GST were equipped with 840 hp M-62 power-plants and were mainly used in the

N-275 is representative of a Russian-built MP-7, the transport version of the GST. It has the pre-PBY-5 style of rudder, roof-mounted pitot head, streamlined bow turret and Russian engines.
via Marc Commandeur

This head-on view of a Russian GST shows one version of the redesigned bow turret and the engines partially enclosed by their cowlings.
via Marc Commandeur

transport role with Glavsevmorput as the MP7, some of these subsequently seeing use with Aeroflot. Later examples had the more powerful 950 hp M-87 engines, or 1,000 hp Ash-621Rs, and were fitted with armament. Although the GST most closely resembled the early Model 28-1, detail differences included modified bow turrets, different internal equipment and shuttered engine cowlings for improved performance in cold conditions.

During the Second World War, Russia benefited from the supply of aircraft under Lend-Lease, and it was provided with no fewer than 137 Naval Aircraft Factory PBN-1 Nomads, a refined version of the Catalina, with tall tail, modified lower hull and longer bow. Indeed, the supply of Nomads constituted almost all of the production run of 155 aircraft, 17 going to the US Navy and one of the Russian aircraft being lost prior to its delivery. Some PBY-6A amphibians were also set aside for the Soviets, although only 48 were actually delivered before the supply of them was halted by order of the United States Chief of Naval Operations in September 1945. Two aircraft – Bu64084 and Bu64087 – were witheld by the US Navy when further deliveries were stopped. Five examples that were already on their delivery flights were eventually allowed to continue and arrived in Russia

during late October. It is certain, therefore, that at least some of the PBY-6As continued in use after the war's end, particularly in the Arctic area with Glavsevmorput or Arctic Aviation, and one example with the rudder code 18 was seen visiting an air show at Paris Orly in the Summer of 1946. The Russians referred to the PBN-1s as KM-1s. Later, when some of the breed were re-engined with Ash 82FN engines of 1,850 hp, they were designated KM-2s.

It is well known that in the 1990s all manner of the Second World War vintage military aircraft began to surface in the former Soviet Union, and that many of these were later exported to the West. It would seem quite feasible, therefore, that, at some stage, a Soviet GST, PBY-5A or Nomad might come to light!

The following are known identities carried by individual aircraft of Russian PBY variants, some of which may well have flown post-war:

GSTs/MP-7:	N-243, N-244, N-274, N-275, N-308, N-337
PBN-1/KM-1:	L-1467, M-422, N-340, N-341, N-342, N-343, Nose Code 89
PBY-6A:	N-381, Tail code 31
KM-2:	N-481

SPAIN

MILITARY AIRCRAFT

One of the well-kept 'secrets' of Catalina history is the fact that one example was operated by the Ejército del Aire (Spanish Air Force). An amphibious variant, it was originally built by Consolidated at San Diego for the US Navy as a PBY-5A, but was later transferred to the USAAF as an OA-10, serial 42-109020. It was one of at least five to be ferried from the USA to Malta for use as air-sea-rescue aircraft with the 12th Army Air Force under direction from 242 Group, RAF. Three of the aircraft arrived safely at Kalafrana seaplane base on the island of Malta, but two others failed to make it. One only got as far as Puerto Rico before sustaining damage, whilst the inexperienced crew of the fifth aircraft became

A pair of PBN-1 Nomads supplied under Lend-Lease by the USA at rest on a snow-covered slipway somewhere in the Soviet Union. The Russians received 137 Nomads out of a production run of 155.
via Marc Commandeur

The curious style of bow turret glazing peculiar to the variant is shown to advantage in this posed shot of a Nomad and its Soviet crew.
Leonid Ugrjumow via Marc Commandeur

Spain's sole military Catalina, the former USAAF OA-10 serial 42-109020, shown in Ejército del Aire colours.
via P. Whelan

lost and were forced to land at Ifni in the North West Sahara on 7 July 1943. As with all Allied aircraft landing in Spanish territory, the PBY and the crew were interned. Subsequently, the Catalina was reportedly flown by its American captain and a Spanish co-pilot to Casablanca City and then on to Madrid's Barajas airfield on 8 October. One oddity here is that by that time, Casablanca was under Allied control. It was to remain in storage at Madrid until its eventual formal acquisition by the Ejército del Aire on 27 July 1944. On that date, the Catalina was issued with a Spanish logbook and the serial 66-1.

The Cuatro Vientos-based Maestranza Aérea de Madrid (Madrid's Air Repair and Overhaul Workshops) was assigned the task of trying to bring it back to airworthy condition. From September of 1944, until June 1948, it remained on the inventory of the Grupo de Entrenamiento y Transporte del Estado Mayor (High Staff's Transport and Training Group), although no flights appear to have been conducted during this period. From June 1948, the aircraft was a 'hangar queen' at the Cuatro Vientos workshops as no spares were available to get it flying. Then, on 23 July 1951, test flights were conducted from Getafe Air Force Base, and the Catalina was assigned to the Escuela Superior del Vuelo (High Flying School) at Matacán, Salamanca Province, from 31 July actually arriving there on 8 August. It had been reserialled DR.1-1 back in early December 1945, but at Matacán it also acquired the hull code 74-21. The number 74 was the unit code for the school. From this point until the end of December 1953, it recorded flights totalling 158 hours 45 minutes. On 28 December, it flew to the Maestranza Aérea de Léon (Léon's Repair and Overhaul Workshops) for a general overhaul. Once completed, DR.1-1 was transferred to 13 Escuadrón of Grupo Mixto nº 3 (mixed Group 3) based at Mallorca's Son San Juan airfield, where it arrived on 15 July 1954.

On several occasions, the Catalina operated out of Pollensa, a Spanish Air Force seaplane base which was home to the Dornier Do24 flying boats of 51 Escuadrilla de Salvamento (51st SAR Flight) and the Grumman HU-16A Albatross-equipped 50 Escuadrilla de Salvamento.

Finally, on 7 July 1955, the Catalina was flown to Maestranza Aérea de Baleares (Balearic Repair and Overhaul Workshops) for repairs. This work was required following a hydraulic leak that caused an overshoot upon landing and subsequent impact with the stone wall around the airfield's perimeter! Repairs were to prove impossible, as no spares were available locally, a state of affairs that had dogged the aircraft throughout its time with the Ejército del Aire. It was recommended that the aircraft be withdrawn from use, and this was confirmed on 3 September 1956, the official strike-off date being on the 26th. After this, the airframe was scrapped, thus ending the somewhat chequered career of this particular Catalina.

From photographic evidence, 66-1/DR.1-1 seems to have flown in a pale grey, white or silver overall scheme with Spanish national markings. The serial prefix 66 was allocated within the old Nationalist system block 50 to 79 to denote a hidroaviones, or seaplane, type. The solitary Catalina was allocated its own series, hence the serial number 1 after the prefix. In 1946, a new system was instigated and a category for Amfibio de Reconocimiento (Reconnaissance Amphibians) was created with the prefix DR.1 allocated to the Catalina which, of course, was aircraft number 1 in the category.

Although unique and little-known, this Catalina was remembered in the mid-1990s when a Catalina was acquired by the Museo del Aire and displayed in the markings of DR.1-1/74-21 at Cuatro Vientos – see entry under that identity in Chapter Seventeen.

Table 56. Catalina operated by the Spanish Air Force

Serial	C/n	Type	Place of Manufacture	Previous id(s)	Notes
66-1 later DR.1-1	941	PBY-5A	CON SD	42-109020 (USAAF) Bu08122 (US Navy)	Coded 74-21. Withdrawn 26/9/1956 and scrapped.

Representing the various Catalinas that have in recent years migrated to Spain and appeared on that country's civil register is EC-FRG, photographed in September 1994 at San Javier airport. It has since returned to the USA.
Ron Mak

Toward the end of its Spanish service, Catalina 66-1 was re-serialled DR.1.1 and gained the hull code 74-21.
via José Luis Gonzalez Serrano

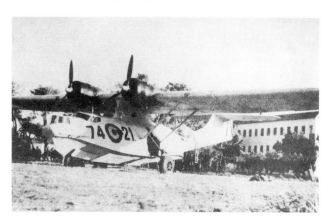

COMMERCIAL AIRCRAFT

In recent years, Catalinas have appeared in Spain on fire-fighting duties, the authorities recognising that the type can still be an efficient and cost-effective alternative to more modern equipment. Whilst three examples were flown across from Chile to operate with ICONA, others were chartered by SAE.SA, and some of these aircraft gained Spanish registrations, whilst one was presented to the Museo del Aire at Cuatro Vientos and painted to represent the sole Ejército del Aire Catalina described above.

All the Catalinas registered in Spain remain current, and Table 56 shows where they are described more fully in this book. The numeric registrations are temporary markings normally issued prior to registration in the alphabetical permanent series.

Table 57. Catalinas on the Spanish Civil Register

Registration	Notes
EC-313	Later became EC-FRG. See N314CF Chapter Nineteen.
EC-314	Later became EC-693. See 'DR.1-1/74-21 See Chapter Seventeen.
EC-359	Later became EC-EVK. See Chapter Seventeen.
EC-593 EC-594 EC-595	These three temporary registrations were allocated to the Chilean Catalinas CC-CCS, CC-CDT and CC-CNP although may not have been taken up, the Chilean identities being retained. The tie-ups between Spanish and Chilean registrations are not known. All three Catalinas are current and are described in Chapter Seventeen.
EC-940	Later became EC-FMC. See Chapter Seventeen.
EC-EVK	Current. See Chapter Seventeen.
EC-FMC	Current. See Chapter Seventeen.
EC-FRG	Current. See N314CF in Chapter Nineteen.
EC-FXN	Current. See Chapter Seventeen.

SWEDEN

MILITARY AIRCRAFT

When the Royal Canadian Air Force began to reduce the size of its amphibious Canso fleet post-war, the Svenska Flygvapnet (Swedish Air Force) was one of the air arms that were happy to receive these second-hand aircraft. In the case of the Swedes, this enabled them to supplement their existing seaplane fleet of Heinkel He 115s and Dornier Do 24s. They acquired three, which were known by the type designation Tp47, the initials Tp indicating the transport role. All of them had originally been taken on charge by the RCAF in March 1943, and had served until February 1947. Their RCAF identities were 9779, 9783 and 9810; the latter two flew with 161 (BR) Squadron, whilst 9779 is known to have been on the strength of 162 (BR) Squadron. The contract to refurbish these Canso As for Swedish military service went to the former Harvard manufacturers Canadian Car & Foundry of St Laurent, Montreal, and the specification involved the removal of the aft blisters, although the nose turrets were retained. Smaller one-piece blister transparencies were installed on the rear hulls of two of the aircraft (47001 and 47002).

The first aircraft was delivered in December 1947, via Keflavik, the other two following shortly after by the Azores route and then on via Manston in Kent. The Catalinas were given the Flygvapnet serials 47001, 47002 and 47003, and initially they were placed on the strength of the Flygraddingsdivisionen (FRAD), part of F2 Wing at Hägernäs, near Stockholm, with whom they flew in

the air-sea-rescue role with the tail codes 01, 02 and 03 respectively. They flew in a natural metal finish with fabric-covered control surfaces in silver and with dayglo orange trim. 47001 and 47003 went on to join F8 Wing at Barkaby, the former aircraft being given the replacement tail code 89, although, later still, this was changed to 79. They continued to operate frequently from Hägernäs because of the water runway there. 47001 at least is known to have operated from water using Jet Assisted Take Off (JATO) bottles.

As already stated, all three Catalinas retained their bow turrets, but they did have detail differences. 47001 and 47002 had AN/APS radar and a parasol antenna within a plexiglas turret, although 47001 later had this position replaced by a fairing of glass fibre covered in black neoprene. 47003 retained the original turret fittings, and this area was used for visual observation.

In addition to ASR flights, the three PBYs were used for ice reconnaissance sorties, transport duties and the carriage of patients to specialist hospitals. During one very harsh winter, at least one of the Catalinas was involved in dropping food supplies to sheep on the Baltic island of Faron.

Sweden's Tp47 47003 is shown at the de Havilland factory airfield at Hatfield in England during a visit with sister aircraft 47002. As the Flygvapnet purchased a number of de Havilland types post-war, the visit may have been connected with those contracts.
Jim Meads

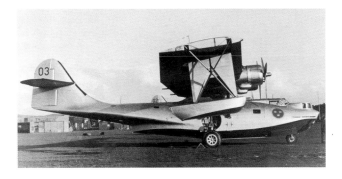

Another view of 47003 and 47002 visiting Hatfield. It was 47002 that was shot down by a Soviet MiG in June 1952.
Jim Meads

47001 was withdrawn from use in mid-1966 with around 6,000 hours on the airframe, and on 1 August that year it was delivered to the Flygvapenmuseum (Swedish Air Force Museum) at Malmslatt, Linkoping, where it remains today on display to the public. It now wears the revised tail code of 79, as allocated to it some years ago in place of 89. 47003 had been withdrawn at the very end of 1960 and was stored at Hägernäs, whilst gradually donating parts to keep 47001 airworthy. It was eventually scrapped by Peterssons of Kolbäck.

47002 gained the rather dubious and unique distinction, for a Catalina, of being shot down by a Russian MiG fighter! On 16 June 1952, this Catalina was being captained by Major Sven Gosta Torngren on an SAR mission to find a missing Flygvapnet C-47, serial 79001. The C-47 was carrying out a flight to check up on a Russian naval exercise and had various radio specialists and their equipment on board. It is thought that the C-47 may well have been shot down. During the Catalina's subsequent search, it was bounced by two MiG 15s, and at 04.20 hours, it was shot down into the sea. The crew were rescued by the German steamer *Munsterland*, and although several were injured, they all survived. The Catalina sank after about twenty minutes, however.

Table 58. Flygvapnet Tp47 Catalinas

Serial	C/n	Type	Place of Manufacture	Previous id(s)	Notes
47001	CV-244	Canso A	CAN VIC (Cartierville)	9810 (RCAF)	To Flygvapen-museum, Malmslatt, 8/1966.
47002	22012	Canso A	BOE CAN	9783 (RCAF)	Sank in Baltic after being shot down by Soviet MiG15, 16/6/1952.
47003	22008	Canso A	BOE CAN	9779 (RCAF)	Reduced to spares at Hagernas and scrapped during 1960s.

TP47 47001 has survived and is preserved at the Flygvapen Museum at Malmslatt, where this photo, showing its modified bow turret, was taken.
Thomas Bergren

Croydon Airport, London was the location for this photo when SE-XAD arrived for maintenance by one of the locally based companies.

COMMERCIAL AIRCRAFT

In addition to the three Flygvapnet Catalinas, one further aircraft had Swedish connections, although this was a civilian-registered machine. Another Canadian-built Catalina, this one served with the USAAF, although it was originally part of a cancelled US Navy order for PBV-1As. After military service, it flew with civilian operators in the Philippines, Hong Kong and India before appearing on the Swedish register as SE-XAD in 1951. Its new owner was Rolf von Barh's Stockholm-based AB Helikopter-Flyg. It was overhauled at Croydon, England, before receiving further work at Stavanger in February 1952. Eventually arriving at Bromma in the following summer, it was re-registered as SE-BUB and was used on charter work around Europe. It was affectionately known as *Be-elSE-BUB* by her crew because of its registration! Between the initial arrival in Europe and subsequent entry into service in Sweden, it lost both its blisters and nose turret.

In late September 1952, SE-BUB was flown out to Nairobi on a 68-hour flight staging London–Marseilles–Malta–El Adem–Wadi Halfa–Port Sudan–Aden–Nairobi–N'dola–Livingstone, and then back to Nairobi again. With the new registration VP-KKJ, the Cat was destined never to return to Sweden, but briefly enjoyed a film career before flying to England and then on to obscurity in the USA. More details of its African period can be found in the relevant part of this book.

Table 59. AB Helikopter-Flyg's Catalina

Registration	C/n	Type	Place of Manufacture	Previous id(s)	Notes
SE-XAD/ SE-BUB	CV-593	OA-10A	Canadair, (Cartierville)	VT-DEX VR-HDS PI-C258 44-34082 (USAAF) Bu68046 ntu (US Navy)	To VP-KKJ then N1508V. Eventual fate not known.

UNITED KINGDOM

After the US forces, the Royal Air Force was the largest single user of the Consolidated Catalina, and during the

Typifying the hard-working Catalinas of the wartime RAF is this well-worn example being hauled up the slipway at Calcutta.
via Geoff Todd

Second World War, the type was used extensively in most theatres of operation. At the war's end, however, the RAF had no further need for its Cats, and, instead, concentrated its flying boat activity on one type, the Short Sunderland, examples of which remained in use well into the 1950s. Most overseas-based Catalinas were disposed of locally, usually by scrapping and/or scuttling, as their squadrons disbanded or returned home to the UK. Home-based aircraft were in the main assembled at various locations such as Wig Bay and Killadeas in Northern Ireland, and then disposed of in the same manner. Thus were the terms of Lend-Lease, under which they had been supplied originally, satisfied.

By the end of 1946, Catalina flying in the RAF had come to an end, and records show that the surviving aircraft were struck off charge in large-scale paperwork exercises by the end of 1947. No RAF examples were saved for posterity, although FP216, a PBY-5B originally intended for the RAF but retained at Pensacola, Florida, for flying training purposes, has survived to the present day after serving as a ground instructional airframe since the mid-1940s.

The first British civil-registered Catalinas were the examples operated by BOAC and Qantas during the war, but these did not go on to fly after the end of hostilities. Post-war, various foreign military and commercial Catalinas passed through UK airports, but it was to be

The first Catalina to grace the post-war British Civil Aircraft Register was G-APZA imported from Rotterdam by T. D. Keegan. It was never put to use and remained in the long grass at Southend until scrapped in 1961.

15 years before, in 1960, another example was to appear on the British register. This was G-APZA, a PBY-5A that was registered to T. D. Keegan and Partners on 14 January 1960. Its new owners had purchased the Cat from storage in Rotterdam, and it was flown into Southend on 17 February. An amphibian, it retained its blisters and bow turret and was, externally at least, in basically stock condition.

Originally a US Navy aircraft taken on charge in October 1943, it had been retired in June 1950 at Philadelphia, and was soon sold to Southern California

Aircraft Corporation of Ontario, California, which had it registered as N68744. Some time after this, it is believed to have been sold to the Israeli Air Force, with which it briefly operated in the SAR role alongside two other PBY-5As. In the book *Balus – The Aeroplane in Papua New Guinea*, reference is made to World Wide Inc, a company that operated Catalinas in Australia and the Pacific, acquiring a surplus PBY-5A from the Israelis in order to fulfil a survey contract in the North Sea. This would have been in the late 1950s, and, registered as N94574, this Catalina flew in World Wide's livery before being retired in somewhat rough condition and being sold to T. D. Keegan to become the aforementioned G-APZA. After its arrival in England, G-APZA remained on the ground at its Essex base and did not fly again. It was broken up in the following November, all trace of it having gone by the middle of the following year. Its British marks were cancelled on 30 July 1960.

With the demise of G-APZA at Southend, the UK was to remain devoid of resident Catalinas for many years, although a number of 'birds of passage' were to pass through, either on 'Northern Route' delivery flights to

Seen outside the Aces High facility at North Weald in Essex is PBY-6A G-BPFY during one of the periods it used that identity. It is now registered in the USA as N285RA, although it still remains at North Weald.
Stephen Dodd

Plane Sailing Air Displays flew its Cyclone-powered Catalina from UK bases between 1985 and 1998, but it rarely carried its British registration G-BLSC on the airframe. One such occasion was in early 1993, when it was due to fly to South America and back on the first Peter Stuyvesant Travel Odyssey. It was photographed at its then home base at Duxford.
Author

new owners on both sides of the Atlantic, or Canadian water bombers on their way to and from fire-fighting contracts in France.

The former Royal Danish Air Force PBY-6A L-866 arrived at Colerne for the RAF Museum Collection in May 1974, and remains at Cosford today, but it was not until December 1984, that another Catalina was to appear on the UK register. This was the Plane Sailing Air Displays *Super Cat* G-BLSC that arrived at Manston in the following February from Johannesburg in South Africa. It went on to become a popular and enduring air display aircraft throughout Europe until its unfortunate sinking in July 1998. Also in the mid-1980s, the former Avalon Aviation PBY-6A C-FHNH arrived from fire-fighting duties in Norway, and has remained a rarely flown UK resident ever since, spending a number of years on the UK register as G-BPFY, although it is currently US-registered.

Table 60. UK civil-registered Catalinas

Registration/ Serial	C/n	Type	Place of Manufacture	Previous id(s)	Notes
G-APZA	1619	PBY-5A	CON SD	N94574 ? (IDFAF) N22B? N68744 Bu48257 (US Navy)	Cancelled 30/7/60 and scrapped at Southend.
G-BLSC	1997	PBY-5A	CON NO	C-FMIR N608FF CF-MIR N10023 Bu46633 (US Navy)	To VR-BPS and current – see Chapter Seventeen.
G-BPFY		PBY-6A	CON NO	N212DM G-BPFY N212DM G-BPFY C-FHNH F-ZBAV N5555H N2846D Bu64017 (US Navy)	To N285RA and current – see Chapter Seventeen.

Nine
THE NEAR EAST

This photo of an IDFAF PBY-5A does not, unfortunately, provide enough clues to identify the individual aircraft, the only visible markings being the Magen David insignia on the forward hull.
Via Shlomo Aloni

ISRAEL

The early history of the Israeli Air Force has been the subject of many books, but none of them have done very much to shed light on its use of the Catalina. Indeed, some of them differ on the number actually operated and the length of time they were used. Although it is known that three PBY-5As were used, some sources only quote two, whilst the date of 1951 has been stated as the initial in-service date even though actual deliveries seem to have been in 1952. What is certain is that by the time the Catalinas had been acquired, the air force, formerly known as the *Chel Ha'avir*, had combined with the army and navy to form the Israel Defence Force, with the airborne element being the Israel Defence Force/Air Force, or IDF/AF. The following notes have been put together from various published sources and private correspondence, and they represent the most likely sequence of events.

The supply of Catalinas to Israel was the result of a change in US policy, and was the first occasion when the export of aircraft to the Israelis was officially sanctioned. It was a condition that the aircraft be unarmed and de-militarised. Although the export permit date has been quoted as 1953, this seems unlikely given the delivery dates shown in Table 60. The American delivery registration N22B was used to ferry at least some and probably all three of the PBYs. This identity had been allocated by the US Federal Aviation Administration (FAA) to

Intercontinental Airways, a company set up by one Al Schwimmer to acquire aircraft for the Israeli forces. N22B was specifically issued for the ferrying of P-51 Mustangs, but it appears from its use on the Catalinas that the Israelis were not too fussy about flouting the rules in order to get badly needed aircraft! It is known for certain that one Catalina carrying the marks N22B passed through London's Heathrow Airport, ex-Iceland, on 30 May 1952, and that during its stay there, it was handled by Israel's national airline, El Al.

All three PBY-5As were former US Navy machines, and they flew with 103 Squadron on coastal patrols and ASR missions from Haifa and Tel Nof, Lod. They were

One of the former IDFAF Catalinas was later sold and registered in the USA to World Wide Inc as N94574. It later turned up at the Paris airfield of Toussus-le-Noble, where it was pictured in June 1959.
Jennifer M. Gradidge

also used to maintain communications with the port of Eilat, at the southern end of the Negev Desert, and often landed on the waters of the Gulf of Aqaba. By late 1954, 103 Squadron had amalgamated with 69 *Paṭishim*, or *Hammers*, Squadron, Wing 4 at Hatzor, and their fleet was a mix of the PBYs, together with B-17s and C-47s. The three Catalinas were withdrawn from use by October 1956, prior to the Sinai Campaign, and they were offered for sale by Bedek Aircraft Ltd during June of that year. One example was subsequently sold to an Australian oil company for operation in Europe's North Sea area.

When initially delivered, the three Catalinas were in a plain dark blue overall colour scheme without military markings, but they soon acquired the Israeli military insignia of a *Magen David* (blue six-pointed star on a white circle background) on the forward hull, upper and lower wing surfaces. The serial number was painted in large white numerals on the base of the vertical tail.

Over the last few years, the IDF/AF Museum has been making determined efforts to obtain a Catalina to display, but to date these have all been frustrated, even though serious interest has been shown in a number of different examples. Indeed, one aircraft is believed to have been acquired, only to suffer a fatal ground accident in Montana prior to delivery – see entry for N84857 in Chapter Nineteen.

Table 61. IDF/AF Catalinas

Serial	C/n	Type	Place of Manufacture	Previous id(s)	Notes
3401	?	PBY-5A		N22B ? (US Navy)	Delivered 2/1952. Struck off charge 1/1955. To Bedek A/C Ltd, Lydda, for storage.
3402	?	PBY-5A		N22B ? (US Navy)	Delivered 4/1952. To Bedek A/C Ltd, Lydda, for storage, 2/1955.
3403	?	PBY-5A		N22B ? (US Navy)	Delivered 2/1952. To Bedek A/C Ltd, Lydda, for storage, 1/1955.

Additional notes:
1. One of the above has been quoted as PBY-5A s/n 122, c/n 918 ex-Bu08099 (US Navy) and N1818M. However, this aircraft has also been quoted as YV-C-AQB of Venezuela's Transporte Aereo Transandino company *c.*late 1940s. Was it acquired in Venezuela and exported to Israel via the USA? The IDF/AF serial tie-up is not known.
2. Another PBY listed above was c/n 1619 ex-N68744 and Bu48257 (US Navy), and it was sold, presumably by Bedek, to World Wide Inc as N94574 in the latter part of the 1950s. It was sold on to the UK as G-APZA. Again, the tie-up to the IDF/AF serial is not known.

Ten
SOUTH-EAST ASIA

One of Amphibian Airways' Catalinas seen stored after withdrawal at Kai Tak Airport, Hong Kong, *c.*1950.
Doug McHard

BURMA

AMPHIBIAN AIRWAYS

Roy Farrell, co-founder of Hong Kong's Cathay Pacific Airways (see entry below), started to look for new business opportunities when he was forced by the British Colonial Government to sell most of his holding in his own creation. So, in 1947, he moved to Manila in the Philippines to set up a new airline, still using the Catalina amphibian that had so impressed him as a type when operating them with Cathay. He went back to the huge aircraft store at Tacloban where he had acquired Cathay's initial aircraft and where there were still surplus USAAF Catalinas to be had. He apparently purchased another four and established his new company, Amphibian Airways. Once the Catalinas had been overhauled, they commenced charter flights and other non-scheduled work, and the airline soon became successful. No evidence has surfaced to confirm that these aircraft were given Philippine registrations, however. Despite Farrell's

efforts not to directly compete with other local airlines, his success soon attracted their attention, and by the end of 1948, he was forced to look elsewhere for work once again.

At that time, there was a need for aircraft to transport Burmese Government troops and equipment around Burma to counteract the Karen revolt that was moving toward a full-blown rebellion. Farrell moved three of his Catalinas to Rangoon, where they were joined by the fourth aircraft a little later. The four Catalinas were registered XY-ABV to XY-ABY inclusive. The fleet of Catalinas made a significant contribution to the Burmese Government, helping to gradually take back control of its airfields, although more than once they came under fire. XY-ABW is known to have suffered substantial damage on 13 April 1949, when its port undercarriage collapsed at Maulmain in Burma, but it was soon made airworthy again.

By mid-1949, there was less work for the four PBYs, although some charter flights did briefly materialise. Maintenance was proving difficult and soon Amphibian Airways was closed down. Whilst XY-ABW remained in Burma, the other three Catalinas flew out to Hong Kong, where XY-ABX joined Macau Air Transport, in which Farrell still had a stake. XY-ABY was sold to Air Hoe, and

XY-ABV languished at Kai Tak until it was scrapped in the early 1950s.

Air Hoe

This obscure airline briefly owned the former Amphibian Airways Catalina XY-ABY. It had been purchased when Amphibian ceased operations in Burma, and it is thought that it was later sold on to China National Aviation Corporation (CNAC), probably as XT-147. Air Hoe was also involved with the one-time Cathay Pacific Catalina VR-HEG.

Jimmy Bo Setyka

This individual acquired one of the former Amphibian Airways Catalinas – XY-ABW – when Roy Farrell transferred his other aircraft to Hong Kong. Setyka used it for Burmese Government work, but its ultimate fate is unknown. It is thought that Setyka never actually paid for the aircraft!

Union of Burma Airways

This company was founded in 1948 and for many years was mainly equipped with C-47s. It did, however, have one Catalina registered to it. This was XY-ADA, but its constructor's number and previous identities are unknown. The registration was cancelled in 1955.

Others

A former USAAF OA-10A was placed on the Burmese register in 1947 as XY-ABH, but its operator is not known.

Although the photo is cropped, the small numerals 147 on the forward hull identify the Catalina in this rare photo as XT-147 of China National Aviation Corporation (CNAC). It was stored at Kai Tak at the time.
P. Trollope

MAINLAND CHINA (*see also* Taiwan/Republic of China)

Photographic evidence exists to confirm that there was a CNAC (China National Aviation Corporation) Catalina registered XT-147 at Kai Tak in the late 1940s. The former Cathay Pacific Catalina VR-HEG is a possible candidate. Another rumoured Chinese Catalina is the former Amphibian Airways XY-ABY that may have gone to CNAC when the former company moved out of Burma in 1949.

DUTCH NEW GUINEA/ NETHERLANDS EAST INDIES

Two Catalinas were placed on the Dutch New Guinea register for the use of the Nederlandsche Nieuw-Guinea Petroleum Maatschapij (NNGPM), a subsidiary of the Anglo-Dutch Shell Company. The registrations allocated were JZ-POA and JZ-POD.

JZ-POA was a former US Navy PBY-5A that had been acquired post-war by the well-known Catalina conversion specialists, Southern California Aircraft Corporation of Ontario, California. It had its blisters and bow turret

Table 62. Catalinas on Burmese civil register

Registration	C/n	Type	Place of Manufacture	Previous id(s)	Notes
XY-ABH	CV-542	OA-10A	CAN VIC (Cartierville)	44-34031 (USAAF) Bu67995 ntu (US Navy)	Registered 1947, owner and fate not known.
XY-ABV	?	OA-10A	CAN VIC (Cartierville)	?	Amphibian Airways. Flown to Kai Tak in 1949 and scrapped there in mid-1950s following hurricane damage on the ground.
XY-ABW	CV-583	OA-10A	Canadair (Cartierville)	44-34072 (USAAF) Bu68036 ntu (US Navy)	Amphibian Airways. To Jimmy Bo Setyka, 1949. Ultimate fate unknown.
XY-ABX	CV-386	OA-10A	CAN VIC (Cartierville)	44-33907 (USAAF) Bu67871 ntu (US Navy)	Amphibian Airways. To Macau Air Transport/ Cathay Pacific Airways as VR-HEV, 9/1949. Impounded in China, 15/12/1950.
XY-ABY	CV-588	OA-10A	Canadair (Cartierville)	44-34077 (USAAF) Bu68041 ntu (US Navy)	Amphibian Airways. To Air Hoe and possibly later to China National Aviation Corpn as XT-147.
XY-ADA	?	?	?	?	Union of Burma Airways. Cancelled, 1955. Scrapped Rangoon, 1954.

JZ-POA is shown picketed out at Kai Tak during what was probably the last days of its existence before being scrapped.
Peter Keating Collection

The other NNGPM Catalina was JZ-POD, and when seen at Kai Tak was still in basic US Coast Guard colours, with PBY-5AG painted on the upper fin.

removed, and cargo doors were installed on both sides of the rear hull. It was sold to Asiatic Petroleum and became PH-TGP, but was delivered straight to New Guinea, although its engines were sent to KLM in Holland for overhaul. Once in New Guinea, it became JZ-POA with NNGPM in early 1955, and served until 1960, when it was withdrawn. It is known to have gone to Kai Tak, Hong Kong, and remained there in somewhat dishevelled condition, probably ending its days there.

The other Catalina, JZ-POD, was a later addition to the NNGPM fleet. It was originally a US Navy and US Coast Guard PBY-5A, and appeared at Kai Tak in the late 1950s, still in full USCG colours, but with the Dutch New Guinea registration painted on the bow beneath the cockpit. Subsequently, it was converted to commercial standard, and, like its sister aircraft, it had blisters and bow turret removed, although the resultant clipper bow was of a slightly different profile from that on JZ-POA. After flying with JZ-POA in New Guinea, it was withdrawn and went back to Kai Tak.

It is worth noting that Air Britain's *South East Asia Civil Aircraft Registers* quotes JZ-POA as a Grumman Mallard and the two Catalinas as JZ-POC and JZ-POD, ex-PK-AKS and PK-AKT respectively. A study of photos of Catalinas JZ-POA and -POD and the two Indonesian machines reveals detail differences to the airframes that suggest that there is no link between them, and it is thought that no Catalina operated as JZ-POC. However, the same publication also suggests that the Shell Catalina PK-AKS became JZ-POC, again without any verification being available elsewhere.

HONG KONG

Cathay Pacific Airways and Macau Air Transport

Now a well-known international airline, Cathay Pacific Airways had its origins in the immediate post-war era of Hong Kong, when two entrepreneurs, Roy C. Farrell and Syd de Kantzow, pooled their resources and formed a small company with two C-47s to fly ad hoc charters out of the colony. They were soon successful, and in addition to passenger and freight work, they soon found a foothold in the lucrative gold-running market between Macau and Hong Kong. They also very soon discovered that the makeshift airfield that they had constructed on the former Macau racecourse was too short for the safe operation of C-47s. When their inaugural flight to Macau ended with a C-47 tearing its undercarriage off on the boundary wall, it was clearly time to look for an alternative! The pair soon decided on purchasing war surplus

Cathay Pacific's first Catalina was VR-HDH, seen at Kai Tak in company with the Amphibian Airways Catalina XY-ABV. By the time this photo was taken, VR-HDH was in the livery of Macau Air Transport Co. It is now to be found in the RNZAF Museum under restoration to static display condition.
Doug McHard

Table 63. Catalinas operated in Dutch New Guinea

Registration	C/n	Type	Place of Manufacture	Previous id(s)	Notes
JZ-POA	1745	PBY-5A	CON SD	PH-TGP PH-PBY ntu N68768 Bu48383 (US Navy)	Probably scrapped at Kai Tak, Hong Kong early-1960s.
JZ-POC					Not thought to have been allocated – see comments above.
JZ-POD	1809	PBY-5A	CON SD	N9510C Bu48447 (US Navy)	As for JZ-POA above.

VR-HDS under armed guard as gold bullion is transferred between the aircraft and an armoured vehicle. Cathay Pacific found these gold charters very lucrative during the heady days of post-war Hong Kong.
via Martin Willing

OA-10A Catalinas that would allow the flexibility of operating from both land at Hong Kong and water at the Macau end. A trip to the Foreign Liquidation Commission dump at Tacloban in the Philippines produced the necessary airframe, and an initial example was chosen, followed by four more.

The first aircraft was registered VR-HDH in November 1946. Of the others, two were in better condition and these became VR-HDS and VR-HDT. VR-HDS was registered in the Philippines before entering Cathay service in Hong Kong. The others later became VR-HEG and VR-HEV, although the latter was to see service with one of Farrell's other companies in Burma first. Eventually, Cathay's success led to its founders having to relinquish control of their airline, as the British Colonial Government did not readily accept the idea of 'outsiders' running a Hong Kong-based business. The pair went on to run other airlines, including Amphibian Airways in Burma and the more local Macau Air Transport Company, or MATCo. Indeed, all of these airlines, including Cathay, had links in terms of both crews and aircraft, and at times it was hard to tell who was operating what. It is known that VR-HDH remained flying with MATCo until as late as 1961 before being sold in Australia.

During the Catalina period, there were two notable incidents that achieved a degree of notoriety. The first involved Catalina VR-HDT. On 16 July 1948, it was operating a charter, and, after taking off from Macau, was taken over at gunpoint by some of the passengers. When

Seen coming ashore with undercarriage down is Cathay's VR-HDT. It was this aircraft that was lost in the infamous hijacking of July 1948.
via Martin Willing

the captain, Dale Kramer, resisted, a fracas developed during which the hijackers fired a number of gun shots, as a result of which Kramer slumped dead over the controls. From a height of some 1,000 ft, the Catalina dived into the sea, killing all on board except one of the Chinese pirates. This first known act of aerial piracy was without legal precedent, and eventually the survivor was released from custody, only to die in suspicious circumstances upon his release to China a few years later. After this incident, Cathay stopped Catalina operations and they were henceforth flown under the Macau Air Transport banner.

The other incident involved VR-HEV, the former Amphibian Airways aircraft. Used by MATCo from September 1949, it was apparently sold back to a Burmese operator in 1950, but on the understanding that it would be flown by a MATCo crew. On a flight from

Another view of VR-HDS, this time anchored on the Irrawaddy River off Magwe in Burma. At the time – November 1948 – it was on charter to Air Burma.
Charles E. Eather via R. G. Labrum/Ken Ellis

Chittagong in the present-day Bangladesh to Hong Kong on 15 December 1950, it was to arrive over Hong Kong and then disappear again, allegedly with radio problems. It later reported that it was on the water and sinking. Subsequently, an RAF Sunderland flying boat observed the PBY under tow in a bay on the island of Wang Kam near Coloane, Macau. The crew were arrested by the Chinese authorities and not released for over eighteen months, and it seems that they must have been involved in smuggling of some sort. The eventual fate of VR-HEV is unknown.

Table 64. Cathay Pacific Airways and Macau Air Transport Catalinas

Registration	C/n	Type	Place of Manufacture	Previous id(s)	Notes
VR-HDH	CV-592	OA-10A	Canadair (Cartierville)	44-34081 (USAAF) Bu68045 ntu (US Navy)	Cathay Pacific. To MATCo, 1/7/1948. To Trans Australia Airlines as VH-SBV, 7/1962. Current – see Chapter Fourteen.
VR-HDS	CV-593	OA-10A	Canadair (Cartierville)	PI-C258 44-34082 (USAAF) Bu68046 ntu (US Navy)	Cathay Pacific, 7/1947. Also flown by MATCo and Air Burma. To Eastern Air Associates, 8/1950. To India as VT-DEX, 12/1950 then to SE-XAD, SE-BUB, VP-KKJ and N1508V. Eventual fate in USA not known.
VR-HDT	?	OA-10A	CAN VIC (Cartierville)	? (USAAF)	Cathay Pacific. *Miss Macau*. To MATCo, 5/1948. Dived into sea off Macau and destroyed, 16/7/1948.
VR-HEG	CV-309 (See note below)	Canso A	CAN VIC (Cartierville)	11027 (RCAF)	Initially used by Cathay for spares, then to Air Hoe. Sold to China National Aviation Corporation, 6/1949. Fate not known.

Registration	C/n	Type	Place of Manufacture	Previous id(s)	Notes
VR-HEV	CV-386	OA-10A	CAN VIC (Cartierville)	XY-ABX 44-33907 (USAAF) Bu67871 ntu (US Navy)	MATCo, 9/1949. Sold to Sun Chiang-liang, late 1950. Impounded in China, 15/12/1950.

Note: c/n CV-309 is generally quoted for VR-HEG. If this is correct, it is the former RCAF Canso A 11027 as shown, but this does not seem to tally with the remaining Cathay fleet that were all acquired from USAAF surplus stocks in the Philippines.

INDIA

Two Catalinas appeared on the Indian civil register during the 1950s. Little is known of either operator, although the aircraft themselves are reasonably well documented. The first to arrive was owned by Kalinga Airlines of Calcutta, a company that also flew C-47s. Their Catalina VT-DEX was registered to them in December 1950, having previously operated in Hong Kong. It cannot have spent very long in India as, by the end of 1951, it was at Croydon Airport in England as SE-XAD, being overhauled for a new owner in Sweden.

The other Indian PBY was VT-DID. This was registered to Airways (India) Ltd in 1955 and stayed with them until August 1961, when it was damaged beyond repair in an accident on the 22nd of that month. It had previously been registered in China and Thailand.

Table 65. Indian commercial Catalinas

Registration	C/n	Type	Place of Manufacture	Previous id(s)	Notes
VT-DEX	CV-593	OA-10A	Canadair (Cartierville)	VR-HDS PI-C258 44-34082 (USAAF) Bu68046 ntu (US Navy)	Kalinga Airlines. To Sweden as SE-XAD, 1951. Later SE-BUB, VP-KKJ and N1508V. Ultimate fate unknown.
VT-DID	CV-519	OA-10A	CAN VIC (Cartierville)	HS-POD HS-PC205 44-34008 (USAAF) Bu67972 ntu (US Navy)	Airways (India) Ltd Damaged beyond repair, 22/8/1961.

INDONESIA

MILITARY CATALINAS

The Angkatan Udara Republik Indonesia (AURI), or Indonesian Air Force, is known to have been equipped with a number of amphibious Catalinas – confirmed serials suggest that there were at least five examples. They served with 5 Squadron at Bugis in Malang until replaced by the Grumman Albatross. One of the PBYs – PB-505 – was still to be found at Bandoeng around 1970, minus its engines. Some sources claim that the AURI received Catalinas from the Dutch MLD, and serials P-208, P-209 and P-210 have been quoted but not substantiated. Another source suggests that the five aircraft came from Garuda Indonesia Airways, but this too seems unlikely as the Garuda aircraft had clipper bows, whereas photographs of the AURI aircraft confirm that they had nose turrets.

The Air Force Museum at Jogyakarta, Jakarta, has a restored PBY-5A on display in the markings of PB-505,

PB-501 was the first of the Indonesian Air Force, or AURI, PBYs, but its pedigree is not known. The crest of 5 Squadron can be seen on the hull below the cockpit.

but it is a former US civil-registered aircraft and does not have an AURI past – see Chapter Eighteen.

Table 66. Indonesian Air Force Catalinas

Serial	C/n	Type	Place of Manufacture	Previous id(s)	Notes
PB-501		PBY-5A			
PB-502		PBY-5A			
PB-503		PBY-5A			
PB-504		PBY-5A			
PB-505		PBY-5A			Extant c.1970

COMMERCIAL CATALINAS

Catalinas were used in Indonesia as airliners and transport aircraft for oil companies, specifically Shell. In addition, two aircraft received early Republic of Indonesia registrations during the struggle for Independence.

Indonesian Airways

During the late 1940s, an Australian pilot named R. Cobley was flying gun-running and supply missions for the Indonesian Republic using his Catalina VH-BDP, a former Royal Australian Air Force flying boat. It became RI-005 in 1948, registered to the quasi-airline, Indonesian Airways, set up by the Republicans, and was used from various lakes and waters in Indonesia and Sumatra. It was lost in a take-off accident on the Batanghari River in the Djambi Province on 29 December 1948. Cobley and his crew lost their lives in this accident. Whilst flying in Indonesia, RI-005 apparently retained its RAAF camouflage.

The second Indonesian Airways Catalina was an amphibious PBY-5A registered RI-006. Of uncertain origin, it may previously have been PI-C274, although confirmation of this would be helpful. On 19 December 1948, it was flying a mission from Maguwo near Djokja to Sumatra and back. Whilst the pilot was away, the airfield at Maguwo was seized by the Dutch, and they captured the Catalina and its surprised crew upon their return! It was damaged by Dutch gunfire during this dramatic return. Later, it was taken to Tjilitjap, and is thought to have been used as a spares source for the Dutch MLD's own Catalinas.

A very rare view of the Catalina RI-006, whose origin is unknown, although it may have come from the Philippines. *via Ron Mak*

Table 67. Indonesian Airways Catalinas

Registration	C/n	Type	Place of Manufacture	Previous id(s)	Notes
RI-005	292	Canso/ Catalina IIA	CON SD	VH-BDP A24-26 (RAAF) VA711/V9711 (RAF) 9711 (RCAF)	R. R. Cobley/ Richard Conway Aviation, 1/1948. Sold in Indonesia as RI-005, 1948. Crashed at Djambi, Sumatra, 29/12/1948.
RI-006				PI-C274?	Used as spares by Dutch MLD post-1948.

Anglo-Dutch Shell Company

The Anglo-Dutch Shell Company had two subsidiary companies operating in Indonesia. These were the NV De Bataafsche Petroleum Maatschappij (BPM) and the NV Nederlansche Nieuw-Guinea Petroleum Maatschappij (NNGPM). BPM had a fleet of aircraft to fly in support of the company's operations in Sumatra, Java and Borneo. Finding its Piper Cubs and Grumman Goose amphibians too restrictive, it decided to obtain Catalinas. Its first was registered PK-AKC, and it was delivered to Kemajoran from Canada, via Oakland, California, arriving in January 1947. It had a standard PBY-5A rudder, clipper bow and hatches in place of the original blisters, this conversion work having been carried out by Canadian Car and Foundry Company. It bore the numeral 3 in black on the vertical tail. PK-AKC was used all around the

The Anglo-Dutch Shell Company acquired its first Catalina from surplus Royal Canadian Air Force stocks. It was delivered to Indonesia in January 1947, and is shown ground-running at Oakland, California, during the trip. *William T. Larkins*

company's area of operations. In September 1949, it embarked on a tour of the area, stretching from Jakarta to the New Guinea borders and covering some 8,361 nautical miles in 14 days. Unfortunately, this aircraft was later lost in a tragic landing accident on a mirror-like water surface at Muntok Bay, Banka Island, that claimed the lives of six people and totally destroyed the airframe. Lloyds of London recorded the operator at the time of the crash as Anglo-Saxon Petroleum.

NNGPM also took delivery of Catalinas in 1947, receiving three that were based at Morotai, New Guinea, but registered on the Indonesian civil register as PK-AKR, PK-AKS and PK-AKT. All are believed to have been former RCAF aircraft, although the previous identity of only one is known. PK-AKR arrived as a basically 'stock' PBY-5A minus armament, but still with blisters and bow turret, though both fittings were later removed by KLM engineers. It was used to fly company personnel from Sorong to Ambon. It suffered a crash landing in Sorong Harbour, during which it struck a coral reef, but was repaired. Later, it crashed in Kowloon Bay near Hong Kong during a post-overhaul test flight on 28 August 1950. The cause was attributed to the unlocked nose-wheel doors breaking away on landing and causing the hull to break when water rushed in through the open space under the flight deck. One crew member lost a leg in the accident.

PK-AKS was also delivered via Oakland, passing

through on Christmas Day, 1946. It had already had its turrets, front and rear, removed. At some stage, it had the number 2 painted on its tail. However, during an overhaul by KLM in August 1949, it was found to have extensive corrosion and it was condemned. Air Britain's *South-East Asia Civil Aircraft Registers* states that this Catalina became JZ-POC in Dutch New Guinea, but no confirmation of this has been found.

Finally, PK-AKT was received, and this too was in commercial format minus turrets. Named *Kaketoe* or Cockatoo, it lasted until February 1953, after which it was stored at Sorong and scrapped in early 1954. It did not become JZ-POD as suggested elsewhere. Its place was taken by another newly acquired Catalina that was initially placed on the Dutch register as PH-TGP and was then transferred to Dutch New Guinea marks as JZ-POA.

Table 68. Shell Petroleum Catalinas

Registration	C/n	Type	Place of Manufacture	Previous id(s)	Notes
PK-AKC	22009	Canso A	BOE CAN	9780 (RCAF)	BPM. Destroyed in landing accident, Muntok Bay, Banka Island, 2/12/1949.
PK-AKR	?			?	NNGPM. Written off, Kowloon, Hong Kong, 28/8/1950.
PK-AKS	CV-248	Canso A	CAN VIC (St Hubert)	9814 (RCAF)	NNGPM. Withdrawn from use after corrosion discovered during maintenance. Air Britain suggests became JZ-POC but this is thought unlikely.
PK-AKT	?			?	NNGPM. *Kaketoe*. Scrapped in 1954.

PK-AKS in typical operating conditions whilst in the ownership of Anglo-Dutch Shell. Its two large cargo doors are clearly visible.
Ray Raynor

KLM-IIB/Garuda Indonesian Airways

After the Second World War ended, civil air operations in the Indonesian islands were re-established. In August 1947, KLM-IIB (KLM Interinsulair Bedrijf, or KLM Interisland Co.) was formed. Although many of the services flown were carried out by C-47s, some areas still did not have suitable landing areas and so flying boats or amphibians were required. As military Catalinas had proved their worth during the war, four former RCAF Canso As were ordered for the new airline and given the registrations PK-CTA to PK-CTD. They were altered inside to carry fourteen passengers, and at first were mainly used on ad hoc charter flights. This conversion work was carried out by Aircraft Industries of Canada Ltd at St Johns near Montreal. Then, five PBY-5As were acquired through the American company Aero Corp of Georgia, becoming PK-CPA to PK-CPE. These were all converted to an 18-passenger layout, and the first was delivered to Indonesia in November 1949. Externally, all nine Cats were minus turrets fore and aft and they had clipper bows. The PK-CP* series could be distinguished from the PK-CT* series as the former had a rounded nose profile, whereas the latter had a more pointed appearance.

When independence was granted to the Dutch East Indies on 29 December 1949, one result was that the aircraft in KLM-IIB's fleet were taken over by the new airline, Garuda Indonesian Airways. The route network was expanded, but by around 1953, the Catalinas had all been retired and it is likely that they were disposed of locally, with the exception of PK-CPC and PK-CTC, both of which had been lost in accidents. PK-CPC had its

Shown with the name Buru and with Garuda insignia on the bow is PK-CPB. Also shown are the additional hull windows and open cowling gills around the engines.
via P. Amos

undercarriage badly damaged, and so the pilot elected to carry out an emergency landing on water nearby. However, the hull had also been damaged and the Catalina sank. PK-CTC crashed at Poso in March 1949.

Table 69. KLM-IIB/Garuda Catalinas

Registration	C/n	Type	Place of Manufacture	Previous id(s)	Notes
PK-CPA	482	PBY-5A	CON SD	NC74693 Bu04983 (US Navy)	KLM-IIB. To Garuda as *Amboina*, 12/1949.
PK-CPB	867	PBY-5A	CON SD	NC? Bu08048 (US Navy)	KLM-IIB. To Garuda as *Bali*, 12/1949. Later *Buru*.
PK-CPC	'86'/882	PBY-5A	CON SD	NC41364 Bu08063 (US Navy)	KLM-IIB. To Garuda as *Ceram*, 12/1949. Crashed and written off, Dabo, Singkep, 29/11/1951.

Registration	C/n	Type	Place of Manufacture	Previous id(s)	Notes
PK-CPD	394	PBY-5A	CON SD	NC1216M NX74632 Bu7243 (US Navy)	KLM-IIB. To Garuda as *Djoronga*, 12/1949.
PK-CPE	'85'/ 495	PBY-5A	CON SD	NC1217M Bu04996 (US Navy)	KLM-IIB. To Garuda as *Ena*, 12/1949.
PK-CTA	22025	Canso A	BOE CAN	9796 (RCAF)	KLM-IIB. To Garuda as *Alor*, 12/1949.
PK-CTB	CV-246	Canso A	CAN VIC (St Hubert)	9812 (RCAF)	KLM-IIB. To Garuda as *Buru*, 12/1949.
PK-CTC	21995	Canso A	BOE CAN	9766 (RCAF)	KLM-IIB. Written off in crash, at Poso, Celebes. 8/3/1949.
PK-CTD	21989	Canso A	BOE CAN	9760 (RCAF)	KLM-IIB. To Garuda as *Oamar*, 12/1949.

PK-CTD was one of the later KLM/Garuda acquisitions. It was formerly the RCAF Canso A serial 9760, and has a different bow shape from the earlier KLM Catalinas. *G. A. Jenks collection*

JAPAN

In one of the ironies of post-war aircraft supply, the Catalina ended up operating, albeit in small numbers, with one of the countries whose armed forces it had previously fought so hard against – Japan!

Two PBY-6As were supplied to the Japanese Maritime Self Defence Force during 1954. They were operated from Omura Air Base, Nagasaki, Kyushu Island, until, on 6 June 1960, one of the aircraft crashed on landing there. The fate of the other aircraft is not known, but it is assumed that it was eventually withdrawn from use and scrapped.

Previously published photos of these two Catalinas would suggest that at first they flew in an overall dark blue colour scheme similar to that of the post-war US Navy PBYs. All lettering was in white. Some time after 1956, at least one of the pair was repainted in a light colour, possibly silver or white, with all lettering in black. The pair were allocated serials in the 4001 to 5999 range of the JMSDF system, indicating that they were twin-engined early warning aircraft.

Table 70. Japanese Maritime Self Defence Force Catalinas

Serial	C/n	Type	Place of Manufacture	Previous id(s)	Notes
5881		PBY-6A	CON NO	Bu64070 (US Navy)	Struck off charge, 16/11/1960.
5882		PBY-6A	CON NO	Bu64095 (US Navy)	Crashed on landing at Omura Air Base, 6/6/1960.

This magnificent photo shows the first KLM Catalina PK-CPA ground-running at Amsterdam-Schipol in November 1949. It later passed on to Garuda. *via Ron Mak*

Both JMSDF PBY-6As are shown in this view. The 'last two' of the serial is carried on the forward hull, which also sports a radome over the cockpit.

A rare air-to-air of JMSDF PBY-6A 5882. It clearly displays the extended exhaust shrouds that fed the wing de-icing equipment. This Catalina was lost in a landing accident at Omura in 1960.
via Jack Meaden

Seen from atop a Catalina wing is an unidentified Philippine Air Force PBY-5A. It appears to be in a dark blue livery, although at least one of its sister aircraft was painted white overall at some stage.
via Bert Anido/Adrian Balch

PHILIPPINES

MILITARY CATALINAS

Three PBY-5A-type Catalinas are known to have served with the Philippine Air Force, and they were given the serials 260, 433 and 833. They were in service from November 1954 onwards, and it seems that 260 and 433 were painted dark blue overall, whilst 833 was white overall, with the serial carried on the bow below the turret. They were equipped with a radome over the cockpit, and two of the aircraft carried names, one being called *The Skipper* and another *Seahawk*, although serial tie-ups are unknown. *Seahawk* also carried an attractive bird motif immediately aft of the bow turret.

During their time with the Philippine Air Force, the Catalinas were used to support F-51D Mustang operations against Muslim separatists in the Sulu Air Task Group in the Sulu Archipelago region of the Southern Philippines. This was in 1955, the Catalinas being needed to escort the Mustangs during long over-water stages. Later, they were used for shoreline surveillance and transport duties. One of the three Cats was lost after a

heavy landing and subsequent sinking in Taal Lake, Luzon. The two survivors were scrapped around 1959 at Nicholls Air Base.

It is believed that a fourth Catalina, serial unknown, was also operated, and that this was destroyed during a take-off from Tacloban when some debris on the water surface was struck – all the crew were lost.

Table 71. Philippine Air Force Catalinas

Serial	C/n	Type	Place of Manufacture	Previous id(s)	Notes
260		PBY-5A		? (US Navy)	
433		PBY-5A		? (US Navy)	
833		PBY-5A		? (US Navy)	
?		PBY-5A		? (US Navy)	

Note: Philippine Air Force serials are usually based on either former US serials or manufacturer's construction numbers. In the case of the three known Catalinas, this has not been confirmed, but would only work if 260 and 433 were ex-US Navy Bu48260 and 48433 respectively. 833 does not have a corresponding Bu number, but could tie up with c/n 1833. The foregoing is conjecture only and not confirmed by any factual data.

COMMERCIAL CATALINAS

A handful of Catalinas were placed on the Philippines register but little is known of their operation. Victor Osias formed Insular Airways (or INACO) and used two PBYs to supply the Indonesian nationalists with arms for use in

Philippine Air Force PBY-5A Seahawk displays its nose art. The personnel in the foreground are a mixture of Catalina and P-51D Mustang aircrew.
via Bert Anido

their struggle against the Dutch. At some point, one of these aircraft was chartered to another local airline, Trans Asiatic Airlines (TAALI). The various aircraft are summarised below:

Table 72. Philippine civil-registered Catalinas

Registration	C/n	Type	Place of Manufacture	Previous id(s)	Notes
PI-C220	?	PBY-5A	?		Insular Airways. Later Trans Asiatic Airlines. Substantial damage in wheels-up landing, Manila, 19/1/1949, but repaired by year-end.
PI-C224	?	PBY-5A	?		Insular Airways. Seized by Dutch authorities whilst operating on behalf of Republicans during Indonesian Independence crisis and impressed by Dutch MLD at Tandjok Priok.

Registration	C/n	Type	Place of Manufacture	Previous id(s)	Notes
PI-C258	CV-593	OA-10A	Canadair (Cartierville)	44-34082 (USAAF) Bu68046 ntu (US Navy)	Amphibian Airways. To Cathay Pacific as VR-HDS, 7/1947 then VT-DEX, SE-XAD, SE-BUB, VP-KKJ and N1508V. Ultimate fate unknown.
PI-C274			Registration not confirmed but believed to have become RI-006 in Indonesia then captured by Dutch, fate unknown		
PI-C747		PBY-6A	CON NO	N7020C Bu64066 (US Navy)	Manila Amphibian Air Services, 1960s. Registration later cancelled.

Clearly displaying its registration and owner's titles is the Trans-Asiatic Airlines PBY-5A PI-C220 at Kai Tak Airport, Hong Kong.
Doug McHard

This semi-derelict PBY-6A pictured at Manila is believed to be PI-C747, formerly of Manila Amphibian Air Services.
Roger Brooks

REPUBLIC OF CHINA / TAIWAN

MILITARY CATALINAS

The Republic of China Air Force (RoCAF) operated a fleet of Catalinas as an interim type between 1954 and 1956 prior to receiving Grumman Albatross amphibians. Their PBYs are believed to have come from surplus US stocks in the Philippines and may have consisted of both PBY-5As and OA-10As. The total acquired was 12, although one aircraft was lost in the Bashi Channel during the ferry flight to Taiwan. They were put into service with the newly formed SAR Squadron at Chiayi Air Base, and are known to have supplied SAR cover for fighter aircraft evacuating Tachen Island in 1955 and for air exercises held over the Taiwan Straits. Sea landing practice was carried out from the seaplane base at Tongkang in Southern Taiwan. From the few photographs that exist of RoCAF PBYs, it seems possible that they were serialled in the range 50000 onward. At least some of the retired RoCAF Cats may have later found their way to China Airlines – see entry below.

The serial below the horizontal stabiliser clearly identifies this Republic of China Air Force Catalina as 50002, although the previous identity of it and the other RoCAF PBYs remains unknown.
The Wings of China

COMMERCIAL CATALINAS

There were several commercial operations using Catalinas in Taiwan during the 1950s and 1960s, some of which had rather shadowy backgrounds linked to the American Intelligence Services. What follows is inevitably not the full picture, but represents as much as it has been possible to ascertain.

China Airlines

In the mid-1950s, the Republic of China Air Force set up an 'airline' to ferry military personnel to and from areas of fighting on the China/Vietnam border, where they were supporting local guerrillas. China Airlines started up in December 1959 with two PBY-5As, B-1501 and B-1503. The need for ferrying these troops soon ceased, but the airline was kept going on a commercial basis, and its Catalinas were hired out to the Defence Ministry and, on occasions, to the US Naval Intelligence unit at Matsu Island. They were operated in a drab dark grey or black overall colour scheme.

Both Catalinas were plagued by corrosion problems, and B-1501 was damaged by a typhoon at Taipei in 1961. B-1503 was written off in January 1967.

Table 73. China Airlines Catalinas

Registration	C/n	Type	Place of Manufacture	Previous id(s)	Notes
B-1501	?	PBY-5A		? (RoCAF) ? (US Military)	Wfu after typhoon damage, Taipei, 1961.
B-1503	?	PBY-5A		? RoCAF ? (US Military)	Written off, 14/1/1967.

Civil Air Transport

Originally founded by Major-General Claire Chennault and Whiting Willauer at the end of the Second World War, Civil Air Transport (CAT) was taken over by the CIA when it was struck by financial problems. CAT flew two anonymous-looking Catalinas, the first being B-819. This arrived in Taiwan in the early 1950s, and was

Believed to have been used for covert operations by Civil Air Transport, a rather plain-looking B-831 sits on the ground at Kai Tak, haven for many PBYs in the late 1940s and 1950s.
Pete Keating Collection

followed later by B-825. The latter aircraft still had its blisters in place, whereas B-819 had had them removed and also had a clipper bow and horn-balanced rudder. Both aircraft were able to utilise JATO (Jet Assisted Take Off) bottles on fittings to the hull either side of the wing lift struts. The two Cats were used for covert purposes over Indonesian waters, and also flew charters, both for US advisers in the area and for civilians. The CIA also ran two other companies in the area – Air Asia and Air America – and it is thought likely that at various times, they also used these Catalinas. A third Catalina was operated during the 1960s, this being B-831 although this aircraft is thought to have actually been B-819 re-registered.

Table 74. Civil Air Transport Catalinas

Registration	C/n	Type	Place of Manufacture	Previous id(s)	Notes
B-819	'55'/851	PBY-5A	CON SD	F-BDRN NC49692 Bu08032 (US Navy)	To B-831 – see below
B-825	933	PBY-5A	CON SD	B-1403 F-BCJH Bu08114 (US Navy)	
B-831	'55'/851	PBY-5A	CON SD	B-819 F-BDRN NC49692 Bu08032 (US Navy)	

Far Eastern Air Transport Corporation

This company was formed in 1957 and flew mainly C-47s. It also had two PBYs in its fleet from 1960 onwards, but it seems likely that these ex-RoCAF machines were not in sufficiently good condition to be used, and they were not flown commercially. However, it is possible that one of them was B-201, as mentioned in the entry for Foshing Air Transport Corporation in the entry below.

Foshing Air Transport's Catalina XT-1402 still shows its former RCAF serial 9791 on the fin above the national flag.

Foshing Air Transport Corporation

Founded in 1951, this airline started with two Catalinas that were obtained in New York, these being former Air France aircraft that had been used in the Caribbean. They were ferried to Taiwan in April/May 1951, by way of New York, Chicago, San Francisco, Honolulu, Guam and Taipei. They entered service in late May as XT-1401 and XT-1402, and were used for charter flights and domestic scheduled services. They were also occasionally used on behalf of the Government for SAR work, and in March 1954 one of the Catalinas was successfully used to rescue alive six crew from a USAF C-119 Packet after they had bailed out following engine failure.

It is believed that another Catalina was later added to the fleet, this being B-201, although it is possible that it was actually owned by Far Eastern Air Transport – see entry for that company above. On 27 June 1955, this aircraft was flying between Kinmen and Matsu, a route known to be more dangerous than others because of its

XT-1402 later became B-1402, and is seen here after suffering a mishap at Taipei on 9 May 1958. This aircraft went missing during October 1958.
via Clarence Fu

Winner Airways operated at least one Catalina around the Far East, and B-303 was a common sight at Kai Tak in the 1960s. The location of this picture is not known.
MAP

proximity to the Chinese mainland. It was attacked by two MiGs but nonetheless returned to its base safely.

XT-1401 and XT-1402 were later re-registered B-1401 and B-1402. A hurricane swept through Taipei on 3 September 1956, and two of Foshing's Catalinas were wrecked as a result, these being B-201 and B-1401. B-1402, known as *Blue Swan*, was also fated to be destroyed, although in more sinister circumstances. On 1 October 1958, it went missing en route Matsu–Taipei. It had been chartered to carry seven passengers to Taipei and departed at 17.45. At 18.10 it made its last transmission to Taipei, the crew stating that it was flying at 1,000 ft some 80 nm away. It did not arrive at its destination, and the reason for its disappearance remains a mystery, although rumours persisted suggesting that it was shot down. Soon afterwards, Foshing ceased to trade, although the name has been resurrected in more modern times by another company.

Table 75. Foshing Air Transport Corpn Catalinas

Registration	C/n	Type	Place of Manufacture	Previous id(s)	Notes
B-201	?			?	Possibly a Foshing aircraft, but may have been Far Eastern Air Transport. Wrecked by typhoon at Taipei, 3/9/1956.
XT-1401/ B-1401	425	Canso A	CON SD	F-BBCC 9749 (RCAF)	Wrecked by typhoon at Taipei, 3/9/1956.
XT-1402/ B-1402	22020	Canso A	BOE CAN	F-BBCD 9791 (RCAF)	Missing between Matsu and Taipei, 1/10/1958.
B-1403	933	PBY-5A	CON SD	F-BCJH (US navy) Bu08114	Believed to CAT as B-825.

Winner Airways

Winner Airways was set up by the National Security Council, but very little is known about its operations. As far as it is possible to tell from available Taiwanese records, the airline had two Catalinas in 1962 and one

from 1963 to 1968. The longer surviving example was B-303. The aircraft were used on charters to Hong Kong, and B-303 was photographed there on a number of occasions.

Table 76. Winner Airways Catalinas

Registration	C/n	Type	Place of Manufacture	Previous id(s)	Notes
B-303	?	PBY-5A		?	
?		PBY-5A		?	Acquisition not confirmed.

THAILAND

The exotically named Pacific Overseas Airways (Siam) Ltd was operating a number of C-47s and a Catalina in the immediate post-war years. The Catalina appears to have come onto the Thai register straight from USAAF surplus stocks in South East Asia, and it was initially registered as HS-PC205 in the first post-war civil sequence. It is known to have suffered some float damage at Macau on 10 July 1949. Lloyds of London records show that the Catalina was landing in Macau Harbour after flying cargo from Bangkok when one wingtip struck a mudbank. The aircraft was beached and later repaired. It was then re-registered on the new Thai civil register as HS-POD. Later, it was sold in India as VT-DID. A second Catalina, registered HS-POF, was also used.

Table 77. Thai civil-registered Catalina

Registration	C/n	Type	Place of Manufacture	Previous id(s)	Notes
HS-PC205/ HS-POD	CV-519	OA-10A	CAN VIC (Cartierville)	44-34008 (USAAF) Bu67972 ntu (US Navy)	To India as VT-DID. Damaged beyond repair, 22/8/1961.
HS-POF	420	Canso A	CON SD	F-BBCB 9747 (RCAF)	Fate not known.

Pacific Overseas Airways (Siam) Ltd Catalina HS-POD overflys Kai Tak during 1951. Once a USAAF OA-10A, it was later exported to India, where it expired during 1961.
Finlay Cunningham/Propliner

Eleven
THE UNITED STATES OF AMERICA

The number of PBY-5As in service with the US Navy after the close of hostilities dwindled rapidly. Bu34039 coded 203/FP is shown running up at Oakland, California, in January 1948, whilst serving with the Naval Air Reserve. It is midnight-blue overall, with white lettering and an orange band around the hull aft of the blisters. The FP on the tail represented F for Oakland and P for Patrol. Bu 34039 eventually went to Canada as CF-HVV, and then ended its days with the Aéronavale in Tahiti.
William T. Larkins

US Navy PBY-6A Bu46683 with vertical rudder markings WHOI. The photo was taken in November 1953, in the Bermuda area.
Peter Keating Collection

MILITARY AIRCRAFT

At the end of the Second World War, the US forces still had fair numbers of Catalinas of various marks on strength, although the days of the pure flying boat versions were over. Post-war usage can be summarised as follows:

United States Navy

The end of hostilities meant the end of any patrol bomber requirement for the US Navy on the scale previously seen during wartime, and the Catalina suddenly found itself staring obsolescence in the face. Most of the operational PBY inventory was retired almost immediately, although a small number soldiered on in the ASR role. VP-73 continued to fly out of Port Lyautey in Morocco and Trinidad in the West Indies using a mix of PBY-5As and -6As, but

in May 1946 the squadron returned to the USA, where it was based for a time at Norfolk NAS, giving air experience flights to naval personnel undergoing training at the US Naval Academy there! VP-32 flew on until mid-1949 with PBY-6As. On the West Coast, VP-62 was still operating PBY-6As in 1946.

By 1948, records show that only five PBYs were retained as operational with the US Navy, although many Navy air stations had based examples in the utility role

An unusual post-war US Navy PBY-6A was Bu64084, seen here at Blackbushe, England. It has had its blisters removed and replaced by what appear to be passenger windows. It is not clear from the original print if the nose turret has been faired over or merely covered with a tarpaulin. At the time this photo was taken, '084 was on the strength of the US Naval Attaché in Greece.
Arthur Pearcy

performing a variety of functions, including transport and air-sea-rescue. The Naval Reserve also continued to fly the type, mostly in the form of PBY-6As, until the start of 1957. The last PBY-6A in use with the US Navy is recorded as being on strength with the Atlanta, Georgia, Reserve Squadron.

Many surplus US Navy Catalinas, both PBY-5A and -6A, were placed in storage and saw later use as commercial machines or with smaller overseas air forces. Litchfield Park storage yard was a gathering place for large numbers of stored PBYs.

Only one solitary complete example of a PBY-5 survived for later preservation, and no attempt was made by the US Navy to save any further Catalinas for posterity. The Naval Aircraft Factory PBN-1 Nomad version of the Catalina, delivered in small numbers to the US Navy, had entered obscurity by the war's end, although two examples later surfaced at the MGM film studio lot in Culver City, California, being scrapped there as late as 1970!

Unusual examples of the Catalina that operated post-war included the one-off PBY-5R *Sea Mare* transport Bu1245 that was struck from charge in 1946, and an unusual PBY-6A Bu64084. The latter was certainly still flying in the early 1950s, when it was on the strength of the US Naval Attaché in Greece, being finally withdrawn in early 1956. It had a rather severely modified bow without a turret and also had its blisters removed and faired over. As such, it resembled many of the later PBY-6A tankers operated by commercial companies on the USA's West Coast in the 1960s.

United States Army Air Force/United States Air Force

The Army had been supplied with substantial quantities of Catalinas during the Second World War, both as diversions from former US Navy stocks and as new-build aircraft. They were in the main used as air-sea-rescue aircraft, and ranged far and wide, being based as far apart as the Pacific Islands and England. Seven Emergency Rescue Squadrons (1st ERS to 7th ERS) were established, and they used a mix of 56 ex-US Navy PBY-5As known as OA-10s, 230 purpose-made OA-10As produced by Canadian Vickers and 75 OA-10Bs equivalent to the US Navy PBY-6A. Boeing of Canada was the source for a further 16 PB2B-2s, but these did not aspire to a USAF designation.

A superb study showing a typical post-war USAF OA-10A-VI, serial 44-33924, in June 1948. Based at Hamilton Field, the photograph was taken in the San Francisco Bay area. The 'buzz' number OB-924 on the bow consists of the 'last three' of the aircraft serial and the letters OB, signifying O for Observation Type and B for Convair under the USAF designation system used between 1945 and 1948.
William T. Larkins

Post-war, the USAAF/USAF continued to fly small numbers of Catalinas. In mid-March 1946, the Headquarters Air Rescue Service under the aegis of Air Transport Command was formed. It consisted of two squadrons and ten detachments located at various land bases around the coasts of the USA, and they operated a total of twelve OA-10A Catalinas in the long-range SAR role, as well as such diverse types as C-47s and B-17s. Later, Catalinas were also operated from Goose Bay in Labrador and, during the Korean War, from Kadena, Okinawa, with the 2nd ERS. The last surviving examples were finally withdrawn in January 1953, replaced by Grumman's Albatross. With the addition of bright yellow and/or orange trim to aid conspicuity, the post-war USAF Catalinas were some of the most attractive military Catalinas ever seen. Quite a number of former Air Force OA-10As survived withdrawal and storage to fly again as commercial aircraft.

United States Coast Guard

In addition to the solitary PBY-5, serial V-189, that was supplied to the USCG in March 1941, many more examples – believed to be in the order of 114 – were taken over from the US Navy during World War Two, and at the end of that conflict a good number were still on charge. Although the fleet started to wind down as soon as the war ended, the USCG's own VP squadron, VP-6, continued to operate out of Bluie West One in Greenland until the start of 1946. By 1950, there were around fifty PBY-5As and six PBY-6As on the Coast Guard roster, and a smaller number continued in service until as late as 1954. In post-war use, they often flew with long-range tanks and lifeboats installed under the wings, and the added thrust from JATO bottles was sometimes employed. Most were silver overall, with broad yellow bands bordered in black around the outer wings and rear hull.

US Coast Guard PBY-6AG Bu64096 shown in July 1952, en route to Hawaii from San Francisco.
William T. Larkins

COMMERCIAL AIRCRAFT

During the war, it is known that a number of commercially registered PBY-5s and PBY-5As were operated by the United States Rubber Company in Brazil in connection with the rubber industry there, presumably because of the importance of this product to the war effort. Photos exist of PBY-5A NC33300 in what appears to be a military livery, but with a large US flag painted on the nose in place of the more normal US military insignia. Although the bow turret clearly remains in place, it is not possible to tell if the blisters are still *in situ*, although indications are that they have been removed and replaced by a further US flag. Known examples of PBYs operated in South America in connection with rubber supplies were registered in the sequence NC33300 to NC33307. These aircraft were delivered as new to the Defense Supplier Corporation and were converted to transport aircraft at Elizabeth City during the early part of 1943 and prior to delivery to Brazil. It is presumed that the aircraft were a mix of flying boats and amphibians because of the absence of land airfields in the Amazon area. At least one of these aircraft went on to fly commercially under Brazilian registry, whilst another ended up in Iceland!

PBY-5A Bu48281 pictured in US Coast Guard livery and markings at San Francisco on 3 April 1947. The blanked-out bow turret and long-range tanks under the wing are noteworthy. The black lettering on the fin and rudder says COAST GUARD V-48281 PBY-5A.
William T. Larkins

Typical of the way many former US Navy Cats looked after withdrawal is this PBY-6A Bu46687. Seen in February 1958 at Casa Grande, Arizona, it is still displaying its Navy livery and ADAK titles on the rudder, but the civilian identity N9581C has been crudely daubed on the hull.
Jennifer M. Gradidge

Once the US forces began to withdraw their stocks of Catalinas from use, it was not entirely surprising that examples would begin to find their way onto the country's civil register. Unlike Canada, however, not many of the type were destined for airline service. Rather, they were snapped up by conversion companies which rebuilt Catalinas to a commercial standard minus their military fittings and then sold them on to overseas airlines, or they were refurbished for onward sale to foreign air forces, mainly in Latin America. As will be seen from the list below, however, a small number of US airlines did fly the type. Later, as PBY-6As became available, a fair number were taken on by forest-fire-fighting and spraying companies, which in many cases had them re-engined with Wright Cyclones. Fire-fighting PBY-5As were very much in the minority. Most of the US Navy Catalinas brought onto the civil market were obtained from the vast aircraft storage yard at Litchfield Park, Arizona, although some came from Philadelphia, with smaller numbers from Seattle, Pensacola and elsewhere. Orange County Airport in Santa Ana, California, became a storage point for ex-military PBY-5As in the 1950s, but it is thought that many of these were broken down for spares use. Some found their way to Steward-Davis of Long Beach, a number subsequently being destroyed during the making of the motion picture *Tora! Tora! Tora!* about the Japanese attack on Pearl Harbor.

Notable companies that either operated Catalinas under US registry or acquired them for sale post-war included the following:

Aero Service Corporation, Philadelphia, Pennsylvania

This company specialised in the refurbishment of surplus military PBYs and is known to have supplied a number to Indonesia in the early 1950s. Known examples registered to Aero Service Corp include N10016, NC1216M, NC1217M, NC41364 and NC74693.

Airborne Fire Attack

Fireman John Wells started this company in the late 1990s in order to compete against other outfits engaged in the forest-fire-fighting industry. He firmly believed that despite the Catalina's age, it could favourably compare on a financial basis with other more modern types. Unfortunately, the agencies involved in hiring aircraft thought otherwise, and the two Catalinas acquired by John Wells were not over-utilised as a result. The first aircraft, PBY-5A N322FA, was destroyed in a crash in August 1997. It was replaced by a PBY-6A, N324FA, but this was soon sold to the Confederate Air Force. Unusually for US-based tankers, they were replenished from lakes rather than from airfield tanks and hoses.

Aircraft Instrument Corporation, Miami, Florida

This company acquired a large number of surplus US military Catalinas during the mid- to late 1950s, and most if not all were placed on the US civil register, as will be seen in the listing that follows. However, in the vast majority of cases, the subsequent history of these aircraft is obscure. Whilst many were most probably broken down for spares recovery, the possibility that some went to foreign, probably Latin American, air forces cannot be discounted.

Alaska Coastal-Ellis Airlines/Alaska Airlines

This company, in its various guises, operated a number of Catalinas, mostly Super Catalinas, on passenger and cargo services around the archipelago of South-East Alaska during the 1960s, serving remote townships that had their own water landing facilities but no hard airstrips. The five known examples to be used were N2763A, N31235, N4760C, N4936V and N5584V.

Antilles Air Boats, St Croix, US Virgin Islands

This company, formed by the famous aviator Charles Blair, operated airline services linking the islands of St Thomas, St Croix and St John in the US Virgin Islands and San Juan and Fajardo in Puerto Rico during the 1960s and early 1970s. Confirmed aircraft were N2763A, N5584V and N5588V.

B. B. Burson Associates, Columbia, California

Operating various PBY-6As, Bursons owned N2886D,

B. B. Burson Associates Inc used this PBY-6A N6453C from its Columbia, California, base. It carries the identifying code 54E in accordance with regulations governing forest fire-fighters, E denoting the State of California. In this photo, it can be seen that the wingtip floats have been removed.
William T. Larkins

This unique four-engined Catalina conversion was operated by the Bird Corporation from Long Beach for a number of years and was known as the *Bird Innovator*. It is pictured at Concord, California, in October 1967.
William T. Larkins

N2887D, N6453C and N9825Z at various times. They were employed in the USA's western states on fire fighting and forestry protection duties until around 1969.

Bird Corporation, Palm Springs, California
The Bird Corporation operated one Catalina, the former RCAF Canso A N5907. It was famously converted into the sole 4-engined *Bird Innovator*, and flew for a while as N81RD before reverting to N5907.

Cal Nat Airways, Grass Valley, California
California National Airways, or Cal Nat, are known to have used at least one Super Catalina, N609FF, as a tanker on fire control duties during the mid-1960s.

California Maritime Airways
California Maritime Airways was a non-scheduled operator based on Burbank, California. Although fairly short-lived, it is known to have flown charters to destinations such as Catalina Island off California's Pacific coast in the early post-war years. It may have operated as many as five Catalinas, known examples being NC18446 and NC95449.

Caribbean Land and Sea Service (CLASS)
This company flew a PBY-5A N10609 named *Caribe Anne* for a while, although the aircraft was very severely damaged, probably by a storm, in the Miami area and was derelict by 1970. The fin bore the legend *Hondo Rico*, although the reasons for this are not known.

Confederate Air Force, Harlingen/Midland, Texas
At various times since the 1970s, regional Wings of the CAF have owned a number of Catalinas, all PBY-6As bar a solitary PBY-5A. They have not been particularly good custodians, as no fewer than four have been destroyed or rendered non-airworthy whilst in their ownership. The PBY-6As lost were N15KL, N16KL and N7179Y, whilst the PBY-5A was N68756. The PBY-6A N324FA remains current.

David Tallichet/Project Catalina/MARC
David Tallichet, a former USAAF B-17 pilot, became well-known for his large-scale acquisitions of 'warbirds' of many types. His company, Military Aircraft Restoration Corporation (MARC), had many dozens of individual aircraft on its books during the 1980s and 1990s. He became particularly interested in Catalinas at the time that the Força Aérea Brasileira disposed of its last remaining examples. Under the banner of *Project Catalina*, he purchased four of the type and ferried them to the USA in rather 'adventurous' flights that were notable for the many snags that cropped up. These four aircraft became N4582T, N4582U, N4583A and N4583B, and all have survived to become exhibits at various US museums, although they are still registered to Project Catalina. It is thought that they were involved in some kind of trade with the US military involving other surplus types that came to Tallichet in return for the Catalinas. A fifth Brazilian PBY – N4934H – was also ferried to the States for what is believed to have been another Tallichet company, Airplane Sales International.

At various times, Tallichet has also been involved with at least two other PBYs, namely N331RS and N4760C, probably on a salvage and spares recovery basis only.

Firefly Inc, Portland, Oregon
Three Catalinas, all Cyclone-equipped Super Catalinas, were owned or leased by Firefly and had the consecutive registrations N608FF, N609FF and N610FF. They are believed to have been used as fire control tankers. However, there is doubt as to whether N608FF was actually converted to a tanker, as it seems to have been used as a survey aircraft only.

Hemet Valley Flying Services of Hemet, California, used a number of fire-fighting PBYs, including this Wright Cyclone-powered PBY-6A N6453C shown at its home base on 4 October 1970. It had previously flown with B. B. Burson, as seen in a previous photo, but comparison of the pictures shows that it now has its floats back in place in addition to the engine conversion. This aircraft is still in use as a fire fighter in the State of Washington, but is now registered N85U.
Norm Taylor Collection

Flying Fireman Inc

An offshoot from the similarly named Canadian water bombing company, Flying Fireman Inc is based at Spanaway, Washington State, and has operated a single example of a Cyclone-powered PBY-6A since 1986. The aircraft, registered N85U, is still in use against fires in the North Western States of the USA, where it has on occasion been joined by one or other of the airworthy SLAFCO examples.

Hemet Valley Flying Services, Santa Rosa, California

Catalinas were included in the varied fleet of fire-fighting aircraft used by Hemet Valley during the 1970s and early 1980s. These included N6453C, N6456C and N6458C.

Leo Demers/Ace Demers, Salem, Oregon

A forestry protection company that flew PBY-5A N4939V and PBY-6A N6453C, and probably operated at least another five examples of the PBY-6A. Flying as Ace Flying Services, it was engaged in forestry spraying using spray bars attached to the wings of its aircraft.

Liston Aircraft, Klamath Falls, Oregon

Operated PBY-6As N6455C and N6458C as either tankers or sprayers.

Monsanto Chemical Co., St Louis, Missouri

Monsanto flew one Catalina, initially as N5804N, and it visited many countries on company business. Later, after

The Monsanto Chemical Company of St Louis operated an executive Catalina for a number of years, firstly as N5804N and then, after conversion to a Super Catalina, as N19Q. The flags of numerous countries that it visited in its line of duty can be seen painted on the pylon behind the wing struts.

conversion to a Super Catalina, it was re-registered N19Q. Now the company is much more well known for its controversial work on genetically modified crops than for its Catalina operation.

Rosenbalm Aviation, Medford, Oregon

Another short-lived Catalina operator, Rosenbalms used N6453C out of Medford as a fire fighter.

Sis-Q Flying Services, Santa Rosa, California

Mainly an operator of smaller types, Sis-Q had one PBY-6A Catalina in its fleet for a time, this being the Cyclone-powered PBY-6A N2886D.

SLAFCO, Moses Lake, Washington

Owned by Robert Schlaefli, this aerial fire-fighting company is now based at Moses Lake in Washington, although it started operations from Port Orchard in the same state. A number of Catalinas of various marks were acquired over the years, although few of them actually flew operationally with SLAFCO, remaining in storage instead. Those that flew regularly were N31235 and N9505C, whilst the others were N2763A, N2886D and N9825Z. In addition, SLAFCO also acquired the Canadian-registered C-GFFC. The entire SLAFCO PBY fleet was put up for auction in August 1999, but whilst the event was in progress, the owner terminated the proceedings, declaring himself unhappy at the size of the bids being made!

Sonora Flying Services, Columbia, California

PBY-6As N6453C, N6454C, N6456C and N6457C were on the inventory of Sonora Flying Services during the early 1960s, when they were used as borate bombers.

Southern California Aircraft Corporation, Ontario, California

This company acquired large numbers of surplus Catalinas for spares use and for conversion to its *Landseaire* standard. Many saw subsequent commercial and private ownership, whilst others went on to serve with foreign air forces, including that of the Dominican Republic.

Steward-Davis Inc, Long Beach, California

Steward-Davis was well known as the company most involved in Super Catalina conversions, and it had a number of Catalinas registered to the company whilst this work was carried out. It is thought that some of these aircraft were reduced to spares and did not go on to fly with new owners.

Thomas Kendall/Catalina Ltd, La Verne, California:

Thomas Kendall purchased a number of PBY-5As from the US Navy, and although most were sold on, two of them remained in his ownership for some time. He used one for a proposed round-the-world flight that was prematurely terminated in Saudi Arabia when the aircraft was attacked by armed horsemen whilst on a rest between flights! The remains of N5593V can still be found there. In the 1980s, another Kendall Catalina, N5595V, was donated by the Kendall family to the San Diego Aerospace Museum, where it is proudly displayed in US Navy colours, not far from where it was originally built. Other Catalinas known to have been in the ownership of Kendall were N5582V, N5584V and N5590V.

Transocean Airlines/Trust Territory Air Service, Guam

In 1950, Transocean Airlines (TALOA) of Oakland, California, successfully tendered for the supply of air services linking the various areas in the Pacific Ocean that made up the Trust Territories, now known as Micronesia. These areas included the Caroline Islands, the Northern Marianas and the Marshall Islands. The services also extended to the island of Guam. TALOA acquired four PBY-5As from the US Navy at a nominal lease costing $1 per annum – a fifth Catalina was never officially taken on. The Catalina was chosen because of its amphibious qualities, there being a lack of suitable airfields in the area to be served. The hulls were modified to carry a mix of cargo and up to ten passengers.

Transocean Airlines named its PBY-5As. N31235 wears the name *Taloa Truk*, as shown on the bow in this air-to-air photograph, although most records suggest that it was N31233 that carried that name.
via Barry Dowsett

The inaugural flight took place in June 1951, and the services continued until around 1958, by which time all the PBYs had been replaced by the Grumman Albatross. The four TALOA Catalinas were registered N31232, '33, '34 and '35.

World Wide Air Services

A number of US-registered Catalinas were operated by this company in Australia, the Pacific and Far East and in Europe during the 1950s and early 1960s in support of the petroleum industry. Known examples were N4938V, N68753, N68766 and N94574.

In Table 77, there are listed as many of the US-registered Catalinas as can be confirmed, although it is quite possible that the list is not totally complete. Because of the sheer number of examples placed on the US civil

Worldwide Air Services used PBY-5A N4938V along with at least three other examples. Still wearing their markings on the nose, it is shown at Toussus le Noble in Paris during June 1959 before flying into obscurity in Libya the following year.
Jennifer M. Gradidge

register, only selected details have been included concerning registered owners and operators. Pre-war civil registrations have been omitted as these are covered in Chapter Two.

Table 78. US-registered Catalinas

Registration	C/n	Type	Place of Manufacture	Previous id(s)	Notes
N101CS		PBY-6A	CON NO	N48129 N6457C NC48129 Bu64071 (US Navy)	The Cousteau Society. Destroyed in crash on River Tagus, Lisbon, Portugal, 28/6/1979. Some parts remained at Museo do Ar, Alverca, Lisbon, and may be current.
N10011		PBY-6A	CON NO	Bu64064 (US Navy)	To Canada as CF-IZZ and PBY-5A tail installed.
N10013	2009	PBY-6A	CON NO	Bu46645 (US Navy)	To Canada 1956 as CF-IZO and PBY-5A tail installed. Current in Norway as 'FP535/X' – see Chapter Seventeen.
N10014	2019	PBY-6A	CON NO	Bu46655 (US Navy)	To Canada 1956 as CF-IZU and PBY-5A tail installed. Current – see Chapter Fifteen.

Registration	C/n	Type	Place of Manufacture	Previous id(s)	Notes
N10016	1624	PBY-5A	CON SD	Bu48262 (US Navy)	Aero Service Corp, Philadelphia. Possibly not converted as semi-derelict by 5/1959.
N10017	1649	PBY-5A	CON SD	Bu48287 (US Navy)	To Canada early-1960s as CF-JMS. Later to Australia as VH-UMS, restored in Canada as CF-JMS, to USA as N16647, Canada as C-GGDW, then USA as N18847 and N287, which see. Converted by Steward-Davis to Super Catalina during 1960s.
N10018	1735	PBY-5A	CON SD	Bu48373 (US Navy)	To N95R, 1959, then Australia as VH-BRI. Current – see Chapter Fourteen.
N10019	1697	PBY-5A	CON SD	Bu48335 (US Navy)	Trade-Ayer c.1956. Destroyed in crash nr Walterboro, N. Carolina caused by fuel contamination, 14/8/1961.
N10021	1551	PBY-5A	CON SD	Bu33997 (US Navy)	To Colombia as C-135.
N10022	1574	PBY-5A	CON SD	Bu34020 (US Navy)	To Canada as CF-JTL, 1960 and to French Aéronavale as F-WMKR/20, 1965.

Extensively stained with dripping oil, former US Coast Guard PBY-5A N10019 is seen at the Linden, New Jersey, base of Trade-Ayer in July 1958, awaiting civilian conversion. It crashed at Walterboro, North Carolina, in August 1961.
Jennifer M. Gradidge

Registration	C/n	Type	Place of Manufacture	Previous id(s)	Notes
N10023	1997	PBY-5A	CON NO	Bu 46633 (US Navy)	Trade Ayer Inc, Linden, NJ. To Canada as CF-MIR, 1957, then USA as N608FF. Back to Canada as CF-MIR, then UK as G-BLSC. To Bermuda as VR-BPS later VP-BPS. Current – see Chapter Seventeen.
N10024	1774	PBY-5A	CON SD	Bu48412 (US Navy)	Trade Ayer Inc, Linden, NJ. To Remmert Werner Inc, St Louis, Mo. as N96R, 1959. To Venezuela 1959 as YV-P-EPX, later YV-P-EPZ, YV-O-CFO-4, YV-56CP, YV-585CP and YV-485C. Current – see Chapter Sixteen.
N1022G	2026	PBY-6A	CON NO	CF-VIG N788C N9588C Bu46662 (US Navy)	To N999AR. Later N4NC. Current – see Chapter Nineteen.
N10609	1758	PBY-5A	CON SD	Bu48396 (US Navy)	Caribbean Land and Sea Service *Caribe Anne/ Hondo Roco.* Derelict in Miami by 1970.
N1096M	'56'/ 652	PBY-5A	CON SD	Bu04480 (US Navy)	La Legion Caribe. Sunk by Dominican forces, Luperon, 19/6/1949.
NC1216M	394	PBY-5A	CON SD	NX74632 Bu7243 (US Navy)	Aero Corp, Atlanta, Ga., 1949. To Indonesia as PK-CPD 1949.
NC1217M	'85'/ 495	PBY-5A	CON SD	Bu04996 (US Navy)	Aero Corp, Atlanta, Ga., 1949. To Indonesia as PK-CPE, 1950.

Registration	C/n	Type	Place of Manufacture	Previous id(s)	Notes
N1275N	1629	PBY-5A	CON SD	Bu48267 (US Navy)	Foreign & Domestic Enterprises, Seattle, Wash., 1966.
N1277N	1793	PBY-5A	CON SD	Bu48431 (US Navy)	Intercoastal Aircraft Inc, Seattle, Wash., 1966.
N1278N	?	?	?	?	No further details known.
N1279N	1743	PBY-5A	CON SD	Bu48381 (US Navy)	Intercoastal Aircraft Inc, Seattle, Wash., 1966.
N1493V	1885	PBY-5A	CON SD	Bu46521 (US Navy)	Intended for Dutch MLD as P-211 but dbr in water landing at Zwijndrecht, Holland, 23/1/1951.
N1494V	1945	PBY-5A	CON NO	Bu46581 (US Navy)	To Dutch MLD 1951 as P-211/ 16-211.
N1495V	1679	PBY-5A	CON SD	Bu48317 (US Navy)	To Dutch MLD as P-212/16-212. Current – see Chapter Seventeen.
N1496V	1526	PBY-5A	CON SD	Bu33972 (US Navy)	To Dutch MLD 1951 as P-214/ 16-214.
N1497V	1947	PBY-5A	CON NO	Bu46583 (US Navy)	To Dutch MLD 1951 as P-215/ 16-215.
N1498V	1824	PBY-5A	CON SD	Bu46460 (US Navy)	To Dutch MLD 1951 as P-213/ 16-213.
N15KL		PBY-6A	CON NO	L-868 (RDAF) 82-868 (RDAF) Bu64000 (US Navy)	Larkin Aircraft Corp, Monterey, Calif., 1972. To J. Church, Monterey, Calif. To Confederate Air Force, Harlingen Tex., 1975. Crashed near Harlingen, Texas, 18/8/1975.
N1508V	CV-593	OA-10A	Canadair (Cartierville)	VP-KKJ SE-BUB SE-XAD VT-DEX VR-HDS PI-C258 44-34082 (USAAF) Bu68046 ntu (US Navy)	Registered c.1954. Fate obscure.
N1513V	1868	PBY-5A	CON SD	Bu46504 (US Navy)	To Peru as OB-LBA-251, OB-M-251 and OB-T-251. Current – see Chapter Sixteen.
N1518V	1817	PBY-5A	CON SD	Bu46453 (US Navy)	
N1519V	1989	PBY-5A	CON NO	Bu46625 (US Navy)	
N1520V	1689	PBY-5A	CON SD	Bu48327 (US Navy)	Babb Co, Linden, NJ, 1953. To French Overseas register mid- to late 1950s as F-OAYD.

Intended for the Netherlands Navy as 16-211, N1493V suffered an accident at Papendrecht in Holland in January 1951, and was damaged beyond repair.
via Ron Mak

Registration	C/n	Type	Place of Manufacture	Previous id(s)	Notes
N1521V	1750	PBY-5A	CON SD	By48388 (US Navy)	To Colombia as HK-1020 by 1973.
N1522V	1792	PBY-5A	CON SD	Bu48430 (US Navy)	Babb Co, Linden, NJ, 1953. To Brazil as PT-ASN.
N1540M	1643	PBY-5A	CON SD	Bu48281 (US Navy)	To Canada as CF-IH J, 1956. Later to N68623, which see.
N1555M	1666	PBY-5A	CON SD	Bu48304 (US Navy)	To Canada as CF-NWY, 1961.
N1556M	1637	PBY-5A	CON SD	Bu48275 (US Navy)	To Canada as CF-NTJ, 1956. Later CF-HTN.
N1557M	1608	PBY-5A	CON SD	Bu34054 (US Navy)	Fleetways Inc, Burbank, Calif., 1960s. Possibly to Paraguay as ZP-CBB and T-31.
N1562M	888	PBY-5A	CON SD	Bu08069 (US Navy)	
N1563M	1903	PBY-5A	CON SD	Bu46539 (US Navy)	Charlotte Aircraft Corp, Charlotte, NC, 1966. Derelict at Elizabeth City. To Gary Larkins, Auburn, Calif., c.1985. To Indonesia as 'PB-505' and current – see Chapter Eighteen.
N1564M	1684	PBY-5A	CON SD	Bu48322 (US Navy)	Charlotte Aircraft Corp, Charlotte, NJ. 1966. To Canada as CF-IJJ, 1965. To France as F-ZBAQ.
N1565M	1791	PBY-5A	CON SD	Bu48429 (US Navy)	To Canada as CF-IGJ, 1965.
N16KL		PBY-6A	CON NO	L-863 (RDAF) 82-863 (RDAF) Bu63998 (US Navy)	Larkin Aircraft Corp, Monterey, Calif., 1972. American Air Museum Society, San Francisco, Calif., 1972. To Confederate Air Force, Harlingen, Tex., 1982. Crashed in sea, Port Isabel, Gulf of Mexico, 13/10/1984.
N1600M	1607	PBY-5A	CON SD	Bu34053 (US Navy)	Export International Corp, New York, 1966.
N16647	1649	PBY-5A	CON SD	CF-JMS VH-UMS CF-JMS N10017 Bu48287 (US Navy)	Questor Surveys, 1973/74. To Canada as C-GGDW, 1975. Rest as N16647. Various owners in Florida. To N287, which see.
N1818M	'122'/ 918	PBY-5A	CON SD	Bu08099 (US Navy)	To Venezuela as YV-C-AQB.
N18426	'71'/ 867	PBY-5A	CON SD	Bu08048 (US Navy)	
N18441	'80'/ 876	PBY-5A	CON SD	Bu08057 (US Navy)	To Mexico as XB-FAB.

Registration	C/n	Type	Place of Manufacture	Previous id(s)	Notes
NC18444	'110'/ 520	PBY-5A	CON SD	Bu05021 (US Navy)	To Bahamas as VP-BAR, 1950, then Jamaica as VP-JAU. To Canada as CF-HFL. Current – see Chapter Fifteen. NB Previous identities also quoted as Bu08067 and NC33301.
NC18446	300	PBY-5A	CON SD	Bu2459 (US Navy)	Various owners including Rio Ten Airways, California, Maritime Airways and Aero Corp. To Canada as CF-HHR, 1965. To Holland as PH-PBY but ntu. Re-registered N27311 then PH-PBY. Current – see Chapter Seventeen.
N19Q	1584	PBY-5A	CON SD	N5804N Bu34030 (US Navy)	Monsanto Chemical Co., St Louis, Mo. *The Pelican.* Super Catalina conversion (by Remmert Werner?). Then various owners including actor James Stewart/ Stewart Enterprises. Written off in water accident off Monte Carlo, 15/8/1972.
N1932M	1813	PBY-5A	CON SD	Bu48451 (US Navy)	To Chile as CC-CAK, 1951.
N1942M	CV-483	OA-10A	CAN VIC (Cartierville)	44-33972 (US Navy) Bu67936 ntu (US Navy)	To Canada as CF-IIW, 1955, then USA as N3202, 1969, then back to Canada as C-GFFC, 1975. Current – see Chapter Nineteen.

Although being operated by Canadian Survey company Geoterrex, N4760C is still wearing the Golden Nugget livery of its former owner Alaska Airlines, in this 1972 photo.

Registration	C/n	Type	Place of Manufacture	Previous id(s)	Notes	Registration	C/n	Type	Place of Manufacture	Previous id(s)	Notes
N1947M	1566	PBY-5A	CON SD	Bu34012 (US Navy)	To Canada as CF-IEE, 1953.	N285NJ	1808	PBY-5A	CON SD	YV-209CP N5591V Bu48446 (US Navy)	Thaddeus Bruno and Enrico Recchi, Fort Lauderdale, Fla., and Turin, Italy, 1985 to 1989. Destroyed in ground accident, Turin, 21/5/1989.
N212DM		PBY-6A	CON NO	G-BPFY N212DM G-BPFY C-FHNH F-ZBAV N5555H N2846D Bu64017 (US Navy)	Consolidated Aviation Enterprises, Burlington, Vt. 10/1988–12/1988 Universal Aviation Corp, Dover, Del., 6/1989 to 3/1/1990. To UK register as G-BPFY again, then N285RA, which see.	N285RA		PBY-6A	CON NO	N212DM G-BPFY N212DM G-BPFY C-FHNH F-ZBAV N5555H N2846D Bu64017 (US Navy).	The Randsburg Corporation, Mesa, Ariz., from 1998 but resident in UK. Current – see Chapter Seventeen.
N22B					This registration is believed to have been used up to three times for delivery flights of Catalinas from the USA to Israel for the Israeli Defence Force Air Force. See Chapter Nine.						
N222FT	CV-397	Canso A	CAN VIC (Cartierville)	N69RF C-FOWE N691RF CF-OWE 11074 (RCAF)	Wilson (Connie) Edwards, Big Springs, Tex., from mid-2000. May have also had N923CL allocated at some point.	N287	1649	PBY-5A	CON SD	N16647 C-GGDW N16647 CF-JMS VH-UMS CF-JMS N10017 Bu48287 (US Navy)	Super Three Inc, Fort Lauderdale, Fla. Steward-Davis Super Cat conversion. Current – see Chapter Nineteen.
N27311	300	PBY-5A	CON SD	PH-PBY ntu CF-HHR NC18446 Bu2459 (US Navy)	Western Aviation Maintenance, Mesa, Ariz., 4/1996 to 2/1997. To Dutch register as PH-PBY. Current – see Chapter Seventeen.	N2886D		PBY-6A	CON NO	Bu64034 (US Navy)	B. B. Burson Associates Inc, Columbia, Calif., 1963 to 1966, then Sis Q Flying Services, Santa Rosa, Calif. from 1969. To SLAFCO from 1978 to 1985 when destroyed in lake accident, Northport, Wash., 29/7/1985. Rear fuselage remains at Ephrata, Wash., Cyclone-powered PBY-6A fire bomber conversion with codes E49, later 49.
N2763A	?	PBY-5A	?	CF-GHU N5609V Bu21232 (US Navy)	Alaska Coastal-Ellis Airlines, later Alaska Airlines, 1957 to 1973. To Antilles Air Boats, St Thomas, US Virgin Islands, 1970 to 1973. Various owners then SLAFCO, Moses lake, Wash., as potential fire bomber from 1982. Current – see Chapter Nineteen. Steward-Davis Super Catalina conversion.	N2887D		PBY-6A	CON NO	Bu64098 (US Navy)	B. B. Burson Associates Inc, Columbia, Calif., 1963. Then Routh Aircraft, Tucson, Ariz., 1963 to 1969. Cyclone-powered PBY-6A fire bomber conversion with code E48 and E93.
N282X	1596	PBY-5A	CON SD	N5803N Bu34042 (US Navy)	Shell Aviation Corp, New York, 1960 to 1963. To Panama as HP-425, 1966.	N3000T ntu	CV-560	OA-10A	CAN VIC (Cartierville)	CF-GLX 44-34049 (USAAF) Bu68013 ntu (US Navy)	Remained as CF-GLX. Later N322FA, which see.
N2846D		PBY-6A	CON NO	Bu64017 (US Navy)	Jaydon Enterprises, Riverside, Calif., 1962 to 1963, then Air Tankers Inc of Seattle, Wash. Operated as fire bomber coded E87. To N5555H, then France in 1964 as F-ZBAV, Canada as C-FHNH, UK as G-BPFY, USA as N212DM then USA as N285RA, which see.	N31232	1682	PBY-5A	CON SD	Bu48320 (US Navy)	Trust Territory Air Svs/ Transocean Airlines, Guam/Oakland, Calif. *Taloa Majuro*. Viking Airlines, Burbank, Calif., 1966 to 1969.

Registration	C/n	Type	Place of Manufacture	Previous id(s)	Notes
N31233	1797	PBY-5A	CON SD	Bu48435 (US Navy)	Trust Territory Air Svs/ Transocean Airlines, Guam/ Oakland. *Taloa Truk*? To Canada as CF-ILK.
N31234	1810	PBY-5A	CON SD	Bu48448 (US Navy)	Trust Territory Air Svs/ Transocean Airlines, Guam/ Oakland. *Taloa Ponape*. To Canada as CF-IHD, then France as F-WMKT and 48/F-YCHC.
N31235	1788	PBY-5A	CON SD	Bu48426 (US Navy)	Trust Territory Air Svs/ Transocean Airlines, Guam/ Oakland. *Taloa Saipan/Taloa Truck*. Then various owners including Pacific Airlines, San Francisco, Calif., and Alaska Coastal-Ellis Airlines/Alaska Airlines Inc to c.1972. Converted to Steward-Davis Super Catalina. To SLAFCO, Moses Lake, Wash., as fire bomber, code 80 and 98. Current – see Chapter Nineteen.
N314CF	427	Canso A	CON SD	EC-FRG EC-313 CF-DIL 9750 (RCAF)	Al Hansen, Mojave, Calif. Current – see Chapter Nineteen.
N3202	CV-483	OA-10A	CAN VIC (Cartierville)	CF-IIW N1942M 44-33972 (US Navy) Bu67936 ntu (US Navy)	To Canada as C-GFFC. Current – see Chapter Nineteen.
N322FA	CV-560	OA-10A	CAN VIC (Cartierville)	CF-GLX N30000T ntu CF-GLX 44-34049 (USAAF) Bu68013 ntu (US Navy)	Airborne Fire Attack. Fire fighter code 115. Destroyed during water pick-up, San Vincente Reservoir, Ramona, California, 1/8/1997.
N324FA		PBY-6A	CON NO	C-FPIU N6681C Bu64092 (US Navy)	Airborne Fire Attack. Fire fighter code 115. To Confederate Air Force. Current – see Chapter Nineteen.
N331RS		PBY-6A	CON NO	N9548C Bu64002 (US Navy)	Rolled Steel Corp, Skokie, Illinois. Canx 19/6/1970 as destroyed. To Victory Air Museum, Mundelein, Ill., c.1976. Remains to David Tallichet and stored at US Air Force Museum, Dayton, Ohio, during mid-1980s. Scrapped by 1990.
NC33300	'87'/883	PBY-5A	CON SD	Bu08064 (US Navy)	US Rubber Co. c.1943. To Brazil post-war as PP-AGU/ PT-ANU, PP-BTD/ PT-BGD.
NC33301	'110'/906	PBY-5A	CON SD	Bu08087 (US Navy)	This aircraft has been quoted as an alternative to NC18444, which see.
NC33302	'111'/907	PBY-5A	CON SD	Bu08088 (US Navy)	
NC33303	'91'/1018	PBY-5	CON SD	Bu08124 (US Navy)	
NC33304	'92'/1019	PBY-5	CON SD	Bu08125 (US Navy)	US Rubber Co. c.1943. To Iceland as TF-ISP
NC33305	'93'/1020	PBY-5	CON SD	Bu08126 (US Navy)	
NC33306	'94'/1021	PBY-5	CON SD	Bu08127 (US Navy)	
NC33307	'163'/1090	PBY-5	CON SD	Bu08196 (US Navy)	
N3784C	1636	PBY-5A	CON SD	Bu48274 (US Navy)	
N3936A	1520	PBY-5A	CON SD	Bu33966 (US Navy)	Stored unconverted at Bradley Field, Windsor Locks, Conn. To Bradley Air Museum, later New England Air Museum. To Kermit Weeks, Tamiami, late 1989 and restored to register. Current – see Chapter Nineteen.
N4NCntu	1966	PBY-5A	CON NO	CF-FFZ Bu46602 (US Navy)	To N607CC, which see.
N4NC (2)	2026	PBY-6A	CON NO	N999AR N1022G CF-VIG N788C N9588C Bu46662 (US Navy)	Wilson 'Connie' Edwards, Big Springs, Tex., 1984. Current – see Chapter Nineteen.
N4002A	1785	PBY-5A	CON SD	Bu48423 (US Navy)	To Canada as CF-JJG, the USA as N423RS, which see.
NC41364	'86'/882	PBY-5A	CON SD	Bu08063 (US Navy)	Aero Corp, Atlanta, Ga. To Indonesia as PK-CPC, 1/50.
N423RS	1785	PBY-5A	CON SD	C-FJJG CF-JJG N4002A Bu48423 (US Navy)	Red Stevenson, Bruce Redding, APEXX Corporation. To Northern Air, Dallas, Tex. Later operated by Greenpeace in Germany. Current – see Chapter Seventeen.

Showing ACE titles under the starboard wing is N4939V in basic stock military configuration. It was formerly US Navy Bu34047.

Registration	C/n	Type	Place of Manufacture	Previous id(s)	Notes
N44BY	CV-465	OA-10A	CAN VIC (Cartierville)	44-33954 (USAAF) Bu67918 ntu (US Navy)	Alaska Historical Aircraft Society, Anchorage, Alaska. To N57875, which see.
N4582T	1820	PBY-5A	CON SD	6509 (FAB) Bu46456 (US Navy)	David Tallichet/ Project Catalina/ Military Aircraft Restoration Corp, Chino, Calif. Current – see Chapter Nineteen.
N4582U	1821	PBY-5A	CON SD	6510 (FAB) Bu46457 (US Navy)	David Tallichet/ Project Catalina/ Military Aircraft Restoration Corp, Chino, Calif. Current – see Chapter Nineteen.
N4583A	1946	PBY-5A	CON NO	6520 (FAB) Bu46582 (US Navy)	David Tallichet/ Project Catalina/ Military Aircraft Restoration Corp, Chino, Calif. Current – see Chapter Nineteen.
N4583B	1959	PBY-5A	CON NO	6551 (FAB) PT-AXM N9501C Bu46595 (US Navy)	David Tallichet/ Project Catalina/ Military Aircraft Restoration Corp, Chino, Calif. Current – see Chapter Nineteen.
N45998	1960	PBY-5A	CON NO	N6070C Bu46596 (US Navy)	To Canada as CF-FFW. To Spain as EC-314 then EC-693. Current – see 'DR.1-1/74-21' in Chapter Seventeen.

Registration	C/n	Type	Place of Manufacture	Previous id(s)	Notes
N4760C	1547	PBY-5A	CON SD	43-43847 (USAAF) Bu33993 (US Navy)	Steward-Davis Super Catalina conversion. Alaska Coastal Airlines/Alaska Airlines. To Maples Aviation and Geoterrex Surveys. Later to David Tallichet and to McChord AFB Museum. Current – see Chapter Nineteen.
NC48129		PBY-6A	CON NO	Bu64071 (US Navy)	To N6457C, N48129, N101CS, which see.
N4855V	1841	PBY-5A	CON SD	Bu46477 (US Navy)	Babb & Co., Linden, NJ.
N4856V	1803	PBY-5A	CON SD	Bu48441 (US Navy)	
N4934H	CV-272	Canso A	CAN VIC (Cartierville)	6525 (FAB) 9838 (RCAF)	Airplane Sales International, Beverley Hills, Calif. Current – see Chapter Nineteen.
N4936V	1705	PBY-5A	CON SD	Bu48343 (US Navy)	Inter Coastal Aircraft Inc, Seattle, Wash. 1953–7. Leased to Bahamas Airways 1957–9. Converted to Steward Davis Super Catalina. To Alaska Coastal – Ellis Airlines, Juneau, Alaska, 8/1959–64. Sank in Otter Lake, Chicago Island, Alaska, 2/10/1964. Possibly a hybrid airframe as pi of Bu48362 has also been quoted.
N4937V	1737	PBY-5A	CON SD	Bu48375 (US Navy)	Trans Alaskan Airlines, 1953. Fleetways Inc, Burbank, Calif.

Registration	C/n	Type	Place of Manufacture	Previous id(s)	Notes
					Sold to Paraguay as ZP-CBA. Later Paraguayan military T-29 and 2002. To USA 1995 as N96FP, which see.
N4938V	1843	PBY-5A	CON SD	Bu46479 (US Navy)	World Wide Air Services, 1956–7 in Australia. Last noted at Idris, Libya c.1960.
N4939V	1601	PBY-5A	CON SD	Bu34047 (US Navy)	Leo Demers, Salem, Oreg., 1966–9.
NC49692	'55'/851	PBY-5A	CON SD	Bu08032 (US Navy)	To France as F-BDRN, 1948, then China as B-819 and B-831.
N49695	926	PBY-5A	CON SD	Bu08107 (US Navy)	
N5PY	417	Canso A	CON SD	N5907, N81RD N5907, N59D NC68741 9746 (RCAF)	Current – see Chapter Nineteen.
N54982	1802	PBY-5A	CON SD	N68751 Bu48440 (US Navy)	Southern California Aircraft Corp, Ontario, Calif. To Dominican Republic as HI-24.
N5555H		PBY-6A	CON NO	N2846D Bu64017 (US Navy)	To France as F-ZBAV, Canada as C-FHNH, UK as G-BPFY, then US register as N212DM and N285RA. Current – see Chapter Seventeen.
N5582V	1522	PBY-5A	CON SD	Bu33968 (US Navy)	Thomas Kendall/Catalina Ltd, 1964. Allocated C-GVTF in Canada but ntu. Re-registered N84857 and current – see Chapter Nineteen.
N5583V	1570	PBY-5A	CON SD	Bu34016 (US Navy)	H&F Flying Club, Carlsbad, Calif., 1962–9. Scuttled in Infernillo Reservoir, Mexico, 19/3/1974.
N5584V	1846	PBY-5A	CON SD	Bu46482 (US Navy)	Thomas Kendall/Catalina Ltd, 1956. To Steward-Davis, Long Beach, Calif., and converted to Super Catalina. To Alaska Coastal-Ellis Airlines, later Alaska Airlines. To Antilles Air Boats, St Thomas, US Virgin Islands, 1970-71. Wfu, St Croix, 7/1971.
N5585V	1886	PBY-5A	CON SD	Bu46522 (US Navy)	To Canada as CF-FFA, 1972. To N2172N, 1990. Current – see Chapter Nineteen.
N5586V	1939	PBY-5A	CON SD	Bu46575 (US Navy)	Steward-Davis Inc, Long Beach, Calif., c.1966.
N5587V	1955	PBY-5A	CON NO	Bu46591 (US Navy)	Steward-Davis Inc, Long Beach, Calif., c.1966. Believed scrapped unconverted – probably destroyed in making of Tora! Tora! Tora! film as derelict at Ford Island, Hawaii, c.1969.
N5588V	'124'/920	PBY-5A	CON SD	Bu08101 (US Navy)	Bird Aircraft, Palm Springs, Calif. To Antilles Air Boats, St Thomas, US Virgin Islands c.1969. Crashed at Wikieup, Arizona, 6/2/1975.
N5589V	1733	PBY-5A	CON SD	Bu48371 (US Navy)	Steward Davis Inc, Long Beach, Calif. Believed scrapped unconverted.
N5590V	1768	PBY-5A	CON SD	Bu48406 (US Navy)	Catalina Enterprise Tiare Tahiti. Thomas Kendall/Catalina Ltd. To San Diego Aerospace Museum, 1986. Current – see Chapter Nineteen.
N5591V	1808	PBY-5A	CON SD	Bu48446 (US Navy)	Magic Carpet. To Venezuela as YV-209CP, 1978. To USA as N285NJ.
N5592V	1764	PBY-5A	CON SD	Bu48402 (US Navy)	Steward Davis Inc, Long Beach, Calif.
N5593V	1759	PBY-5A	CON SD	Bu48397 (US Navy)	Thomas Kendall/Catalina Ltd. Current – see Chapter Thirteen.
N5595V	1993	PBY-5A	CON NO	Bu46629 (US Navy)	Thomas Kendall/Catalina Ltd.
N5609V	?	PBY-5A	?	Bu21232 (US Navy)	Paul Mantz Aviation. To Canada as CF-GHU and USA as N2763A. Current – see Chapter Nineteen.
N57875	CV-465	OA-10	CAN VIC (Cartierville)	N44BY 44-33954 (US Navy) Bu67918 ntu (US Navy)	Alaskan Historical Aircraft Society. Current – see Chapter Nineteen.
N5803N	1596	PBY-5A	CON SD	Bu34042 (US Navy)	To N282X, 1960. To Panama as HP-425, 1966

Registration	C/n	Type	Place of Manufacture	Previous id(s)	Notes
N5804N	1584	PBY-5A	CON SD	Bu34030 (US Navy)	Monsanto Chemical Co., St Louis, Mo., 1955. *The Pelican*. To N19Q, which see.
N5805N	1742	PBY-5A	CON SD	Bu48380 (US Navy)	To Canada as CF-EMW, 1956.
N59D	417	Canso A	CON SD	NC68741 9746 (RCAF)	To N5907, N81RD, N5907 and N5PY, which see.
N5907	417	Canso A	CON SD	N59D NC68741 9746 (RCAF)	Bird Corporation, Palm Springs, Calif. *The Wandering Albatross* Bird Innovator 4-engined conversion. To N81RD and back to N5907. To N5PY, which see.
N6069C	1842	PBY-5A	CON SD	Bu46478 (US Navy)	To Canada as CF-FFY, 1968.
N6070C	1960	PBY-5A	CON NO	Bu46596 (US Navy)	To N45998, which see.
N607CC	1966	PBY-5A	CON NO	N4NC ntu CF-FFZ N6071C Bu46602 (US Navy)	AP Inc, Auburn, Calif., 1986. Current – see Chapter Nineteen.
N6071C	1966	PBY-5A	CON NO	Bu46602 (US Navy)	To Canada as CF-FFZ, then USA as N4NC ntu and N607CC. Current – see Chapter Nineteen.
N608FF	1997	PBY-5A	CON NO	CF-MIR N10023 Bu 46633 (US Navy)	Equitable Leasing Corp, Burbank, Calif. Lsd to Firefly Inc, Aeroservice Corp and Barringer Research. To Canada as CF-MIR, then UK as G-BLSC and Bermuda register as VR-BPS and VP-BPS. Current – see Chapter Seventeen.
N609FF	CV-369	Canso A	CAN VIC (Cartierville)	CF-NJD 11060 (RCAF)	Firefly Inc, Portland, Oreg., 1966–72. Lsd to Cal Nat Airways, Grass Valley, Calif., as water bomber coded E40. To Terra Surveys, Ottawa. To Australia as VH-EXG. Current – see Chapter Fourteen. Super Catalina conversion.
N610FF	CV-399	Canso A	CAN VIC (Cartierville)	CF-OMO 11075 (RCAF)	Firefly Inc, Portland, Oreg., 1964–70. Destroyed in crash, Rhinelander, Wis., 15/10/1970.

Temporarily registered N609FF, this former RCAF Canso A was used by Geoterrex/Terra Surveys for survey work, and it is shown here at Jan Smuts Airport in South Africa in 1967. It is now in the RAAF Museum collection.

Registration	C/n	Type	Place of Manufacture	Previous id(s)	Notes
N6108	22022	Canso A	BOE CAN	HR-236 5Y-KUD HP-289 HK-996X OB-LDM-349 YV-P-APE 9793 (RCAF)	Steward-Davis Inc, Long Beach, Calif. Various subsequent owners then to Guatemala as TG-BIV, then USA as N5404J and ZK-PBY ntu.
N6208H ntu	407	Canso A	CON SD	N68740 9742 (RCAF)	Remained as N68740, which see.
N62043	CV-520	OA-10A	CAN VIC (Cartierville)	44-34009 (USAAF) Bu67973 ntu (US Navy)	To Canada as CF-IHC, 1955. To France as F-WMKR, then 20/F-YCHA. To Chile as CC-CDU then CC-CGY and current – see Chapter Sixteen.
N64T		PBY-6A	CON NO	Bu64031 (US Navy)	California Aircraft and Engine Co., San Lorenzo, Calif., 1963–9. Crashed at Ravina Island nr Ketchtcan, Alaska, 17/12/1959. Wreck not located until 4/7/1961.
N6453C		PBY-6A	CON NO	Bu64041 (US Navy)	Leo Demers, Salem, Oreg. Rosenbalm Aviation, Medford, Oreg. Sonora Flying Service, Columbia, Calif. B. B. Burson Assocs, Columbia, Calif. Hemet Valley Flying Service, Stockton, Calif.

Registration	C/n	Type	Place of Manufacture	Previous id(s)	Notes	Registration	C/n	Type	Place of Manufacture	Previous id(s)	Notes
					Fire-fighting conversion, codes E54 and 54. To Canada as C-GFFI. To USA as N85U, which see. Wright Cyclone-powered PBY-6A.	N6458C	2008	PBY-6A	CON NO	Bu46644 (US Navy)	Farmers Air Services, Klamath Falls, Oreg. To Liston Aircraft, Klamath Falls. (Tanker F46). To Hemet Valley Flying Services, Stockton, Calif. Tanker E83. To Canada as C-GFFH. To Spain as EC-359 and EC-EVK. Current – see Chapter Seventeen.
N6454C		PBY-6A	CON NO	Bu64106 (US Navy)	Sonora Flying Service, Columbia, Calif. See also N9579C/ N7039C/ N7781B.						
N6455C		PBY-6A	CON NO	Bu64069 (US Navy)	Liston Aircraft, Klamath falls, Oreg. Fire-fighting conversion, code F47.	N6459C	2017	PBY-6A	CON NO	Bu46653 (US Navy)	Lost in accident, Columbia, Calif., 18/7/1970.
N6456C		PBY-6A	CON NO	Bu63996 (US Navy)	Sonora Flying Service, Columbia, Calif. Fire-fighting conversion, code E38. To Jack Ulrich, Chiloquin, Oreg. To Hemet Valley Flying Services, Stockton, Calif. To Canada as C-GFFJ, 1980.	N6464C		PBY-6A	CON NO	Bu64088 (US Navy)	
						N6465C		PBY-6A	CON NO	Bu64104 (US Navy)	Aircraft Instrument Corp, Miami, Fla. See also N9571C.
						N6466C	1749	PBY-5A	CON SD	Bu48387 (US Navy)	
						N6468C		PBY-6A	CON NO	N9575C Bu64013 (US Navy)	Aircraft Instrument Corp, Miami, Fla. To N7783B, which see.
N6457C		PBY-6A	CON NO	NC48129 Bu64071 (US Navy)	Sonora Flying Service, Columbia, Calif. Fire-fighting conversion, code E49. To Calypso Air Charters, Miami, Fla. To N48129, later N101CS, which see.	N6469C		PBY-6A	CON NO	Bu64091 (US Navy)	
						N6470C	'91'/ 887	PBY-5A	CON SD	Bu08068 (US Navy)	To Brazil as PT-BBD/PP-PEC.
						N6472C		PBY-6A	CON NO	Bu64014 (US Navy)	
						N6473C	1891	PBY-5A	CON SD	Bu46527 (US Navy)	Derelict, Fort Worth, Tex., c.1968.
						N6474C	1882	PBY-5A	CON SD	Bu46518 (US Navy)	
						NC65715	CV-605	OA-10A	Canadair, (Cartierville)	44-34094 (USAAF) Bu68058 ntu (US Navy)	To Iceland as TF-RVG. To Canada as CF-DFB and current – see Chapter Fifteen. Has been quoted as NC65615 also.

PBY-5A NC68702 *Adventures* keeps company with a P-38 Lightning at Orange County Airport, California, in October 1948. Its fate is not known.

Registration	C/n	Type	Place of Manufacture	Previous id(s)	Notes	Registration	C/n	Type	Place of Manufacture	Previous id(s)	Notes
N66463	1548	PBY-5A	CON SD	Bu33994 (US Navy)		N68746	1658	PBY-5A	CON SD	Bu48296 (US Navy)	Southern California Aircraft Corp, Ontario, Calif. To Canada as CF-AAD,1966.
N66464	1545	PBY-5A	CON SD	Bu33991 (US Navy)							
N6681C		PBY-6A	CON NO	Bu64092 (US Navy)	To Canada as CF-PIU, 1965, then USA as N324FA, which see.	N68747	1747	PBY-5A	CON SD	Bu48385 (US Navy)	Southern California Aircraft Corp, Ontario, Calif.
N67134	CV-305	OA-10A	CAN VIC (Cartierville)	44-33869 (USAAF) Bu67833 ntu (US Navy)		N68748	1770	PBY-5A	CON SD	Bu48408 (US Navy)	Southern California Aircraft Corp, Ontario, Calif.
N67135	CV-489	OA-10A	CAN VIC (Cartierville)	44-33978 (USAAF) Bu67942 ntu (US Navy)	To Mexico as XB-GET	N68749	1776	PBY-5A	CON SD	Bu48414 (US Navy)	Southern California Aircraft Corp, Ontario, Calif.
N67648	456	PBY-5A	CON SD	Bu7288 (US Navy)							
N68165	1555	PBY-5A	CON SD	Bu34001 (US Navy)	To Canada as CF-EZX.	N68750	1800	PBY-5A	CON SD	Bu48438 (US Navy)	Southern California Aircraft Corp, Ontario, Calif.
N68623	1643	PBY-5A	CON SD	CF-IHJ N1540M Bu48281 (US Navy)	Derelict at Long Beach, 6/1968 with Steward-Davis.	N68751	1802	PBY-5A	CON SD	Bu48440 (US Navy)	Southern California Aircraft Corp, Ontario, Calif. To N54982, then Dominican Republic as HI-24.
N68624		PBY-6A	CON NO	Bu64004 (US Navy)							
NC68702	'63'/ 473	PBY-5A	CON SD	Bu04974 (US Navy)	At Orange County, Calif., c.1948. *Adventures.*	N68752	1812	PBY-5A	CON SD	Bu48450 (US Navy)	Southern California Aircraft Corp, Ontario, Calif.
NC68713	'118'/ 528	PBY-5A	CON SD	Bu05029 (US Navy)	To Bahamas as VP-BAO.	N68753	1830	PBY-5A	CON SD	Bu46466 (US Navy)	World Wide Air Services, Port Moresby, PNG. To Australia as VH-WWB, 1956.
N68739	413	Canso A	CON SD	9744 (RCAF)							
N68740	407	Canso A	CON SD	N6208H ntu N68740 9742 (RCAF)	Southern California Aircraft Corp, Ontario, Calif. Various other owners including University of Hawaii and Gary Larkins. To Lone Star Flight Museum, Galveston, Tex. Current – see Chapter Nineteen.	N68754	1916	PBY-5A	CON SD	Bu46552 (US Navy)	Southern California Aircraft Corp, Ontario, Calif.
						N68755	1948	PBY-5A	CON NO	Bu46584 (US Navy)	Southern California Aircraft Corp, Ontario, Calif.
						N68756	1954	PBY-5A	CON NO	Bu46590 (US Navy)	Southern California Aircraft Corp, Ontario, Calif. To various owners including Michael Wansey/Con-federate Air Force. Current – see Chapter Nineteen.
NC68741	417	Canso A	CON SD	9746 (RCAF)	Ruth I Charles Babb Inc, Burbank, Calif. To Southern California Aircraft Corp, Ontario, Calif. To N59D, N5907, N81RD, N5907 and N5PY, which see.						
N68742	CV-419	Canso A	CAN VIC (Cartierville)	11085 (RCAF)	Southern California Aircraft Corp, Ontario, Calif.	N68757	1964	PBY-5A	CON NO	Bu46600 (US Navy)	Southern California Aircraft Corp, Ontario, Calif.
N68743	1787	PBY-5A	CON SD	Bu48425 (US Navy)	Southern California Aircraft Corp, Ontario, Calif. Believed to Israel for IDFAF via N22B.	N68758	2001	PBY-5A	CON NO	Bu46637 (US Navy)	Southern California Aircraft Corp, Ontario, Calif.
N68744	1619	PBY-5A	CON SD	Bu48257 (US Navy)	To Israel's IDFAF, possibly with delivery registration N22B, then N94574 and to UK as G-APZA.	N68762	1652	PBY-5A	CON SD	Bu48290 (US Navy)	Southern California Aircraft Corp, Ontario, Calif.
						N68763	1753	PBY-5A	CON SD	Bu48391 (US Navy)	Southern California Aircraft Corp, Ontario, Calif.
N68745	1627	PBY-5A	CON SD	Bu48265 (US Navy)	Charles Babb Inc, Burbank, Calif. To Southern California Aircraft Corp, Ontario, Calif.	N68764	1772	PBY-5A	CON SD	Bu48410 (US Navy)	Southern California Aircraft Corp, Ontario, Calif.

Photographed at Grand Central Air Terminal, Glendale, California, in March 1957, N68766 later went on to fly with World Wide Air Services based in Papua New Guinea, and became VH-WWC.

Registration	C/n	Type	Place of Manufacture	Previous id(s)	Notes
N68765	1775	PBY-5A	CON SD	Bu48413 (US Navy)	Southern California Aircraft Corp, Ontario, Calif.
N68766	1859	PBY-5A	CON SD	Bu46495 (US Navy)	World Wide Air Services, Port Moresby, PNG . To Australia as VH-WWC.
N68767	1922	PBY-5A	CON SD	Bu46558 (US Navy)	Southern California Aircraft Corp, Ontario, Calif.
N68768	1745	PBY-5A	CON SD	Bu48383 (US Navy)	Southern California Aircraft Corp, Ontario, Calif. To Asiatic Petroleum Corp, NY. To Holland as PH-TGP, 1953. Later JZ-POA in Dutch East Indies.
N68769	1633	PBY-5A	CON SD	Bu48271 (US Navy)	Southern California Aircraft Corp, Ontario, Calif. Has also been quoted as c/n 1822/Bu46458.
N68956	1593	PBY-5A	CON SD	Bu34039 (US Navy)	To Canada as CF-HVV and to French Aéronavale as F-WMKS/39, 1965.
N69RF	CV-397	Canso A CAN VIC (Cartierville)		C-FOWE N691RF CF-OWE 11074 (RCAF)	Robert Franks. To N222FT, 8/2000, which see. May also have been allocated N923CL at some point.
N69043	1599	PBY-5A	CON SD	Bu34045 (US Navy)	To Brazil as PT-AXX and PT-APK ntu.

Registration	C/n	Type	Place of Manufacture	Previous id(s)	Notes
N691RF	CV-397	Canso A	CAN VIC (Cartierville)	CF-OWE 11074 (RCAF)	Robert Franks. To Canada as C-FOWE, then USA as N69RF and N222FT, which see. May also have been allocated N923CL at some point.
N6986C		PBY-6A	CON NO	Bu64045 (US Navy)	James Routh, Long Beach, Calif. Tanker C9. Destroyed in crash, Winslow, Arizona, 25/6/1961.
N7020C		PBY-6A	CON NO	Bu64066 (US Navy)	To Philippines as PI-C747.
N7021C	2037	PBY-6A	CON NO	N9572C Bu46673 (US Navy)	Aircraft Instrument Corp, Miami, Fla. To N7875B, which see.
N7022C	2014	PBY-6A	CON NO	N9561C Bu46650 (US Navy)	Aircraft Instrument Corp, Miami, Fla. To N7878B, which see.
N7023C		PBY-6A	CON NO	Bu64001 (US Navy)	Aircraft Instrument Corp, Miami, Fla. To N7784B, which see.
N7035C	2044	PBY-6A	CON NO	N9573C Bu46680 (US Navy)	Aircraft Instrument Corp, Miami, Fla. To N7787B, which see.
N7037C	2048	PBY-6A	CON NO	Bu46684 (US Navy)	
N7039C		PBY-6A	CON NO	N9579C Bu64106 (US Navy)	To N7781B. See also N6454C.
N7057C		PBY-6A	CON NO	Bu64072 (US Navy)	Various owners. To National Warplane Museum, Geneseo, NY, 1988. Current – see Chapter Nineteen.

Registration	C/n	Type	Place of Manufacture	Previous id(s)	Notes
N7068C	2011	PBY-6A	CON NO	N9576B Bu46647 (US Navy)	To N7879B, which see.
N7082C	'225'	PBY-6A	CON NO	Bu64097 (US Navy)	James Routh, Long Beach, Calif. Tanker E94. To France as F-ZBAW, then Canada as C-FHNF, then USA as N7179Y, which see.
N7179Y	'225'	PBY-6A	CON NO	C-FHNF F-ZBAW N7082C Bu64097 (US Navy)	Current, Confederate Air Force – see Chapter. Nineteen.
N7205Z					Apparently seen at Long Beach, Calif., in an unconverted state c.1960.
N7442C	2046	PBY-6A	CON NO	Bu46682 (US Navy)	
N7443C	2018	PBY-6A	CON NO	Bu46654 (US Navy)	
N7444C	2050	PBY-6A	CON NO	Bu46686 (US Navy)	
N74580	'63'/135	PBY-5	CON SD	Bu2351 (US Navy)	Allocation not confirmed.
N74581	'48'/98	PBY-5	CON SD	Bu2336 (US Navy)	Allocation not confirmed.
N74582	'83'/176	PBY-5	CON SD	Bu2371 (US Navy)	Allocation not confirmed.
N74583	'87'/184	PBY-5	CON SD	Bu2375 (US Navy)	Allocation not confirmed.
NX74632	394	PBY-5A	CON SD	Bu7243 (US Navy)	Maine Air Cargo, c.1946. To N1216M, which see.
N74680	CV-311	Canso A	CAN VIC (Cartierville)	11029 (RCAF)	Northern Consolidated. To Canada as CF-IDS, 1965.
N74692	'187'/341	PBY-5A	CON SD	Bu2475 (US Navy)	To Jamaica as VP-JAW.

Registration	C/n	Type	Place of Manufacture	Previous id(s)	Notes
NC74693	482	PBY-5A	CON SD	Bu04983 (US Navy)	Aero Corp, Atlanta, Ga. To Indonesia as PK-CPA, 12/1949. Possibly ex-PP-AGU and PT-AMR.
N74694	1995	PBY-5A	CON NO	Bu46631 (US Navy)	
N7480C		PBY-6A	CON NO	Bu64068 (US Navy)	To Colombia as HK-661X.
N74821	1696	PBY-5A	CON SD	N9535C Bu48334 (US Navy)	Derelict at Long Beach, c.1963.
N7685C		PBY-6A	CON NO	Bu64083 (US Navy)	Allocation not confirmed.
N7703C		PBY-6A	CON NO	N9584C Bu64087 (US Navy)	Allocation not confirmed.
N7781B		PBY-6A	CON NO	Bu64016 (US Navy)	Aircraft Instrument Corp, Miami, Fla.
N7782B		PBY-6A	CON NO	Bu64010 (US Navy)	Aircraft Instrument Corp, Miami, Fla.
N7783B		PBY-6A	CON NO	N6468C N9575C Bu64013 (US Navy)	Aircraft Instrument Corp, Miami, Fla.
N7784B		PBY-6A	CON NO	N7023C Bu64001 (US Navy)	Aircraft Instrument Corp, Miami, Fla.
N7785B	2051	PBY-6A	CON NO	N9581C Bu46687 (US Navy)	Aircraft Instrument Corp, Miami, Fla.
N7786B	2047	PBY-6A	CON NO	N9580C Bu46683 (US Navy)	Aircraft Instrument Corp, Miami, Fla.
N7787B	2044	PBY-6A	CON NO	N7035C N9573C Bu46680 (US Navy)	Aircraft Instrument Corp, Miami, Fla.
N7858B		PBY-6A	CON NO	Bu64099 (US Navy)	Aircraft Instrument Corp, Miami, Fla.
N7860B		PBY-6A	CON NO	Bu64063 (US Navy)	To Brazil as PT-BBP c.1963.
N7861B		PBY-6A	CON NO	Bu64007 (US Navy)	Aircraft Instrument Corp, Miami, Fla.
N7875B	2037	PBY-6A	CON NO	N7021C N9572C Bu46673 (US Navy)	Aircraft Instrument Corp, Miami, Fla.

Seen soon after being converted to a commercial aircraft by de Havilland of Canada, RCAF Canso A 9794 went to REXCO as NC79997. It is shown in September 1947. *William T. Larkins*

Registration	C/n	Type	Place of Manufacture	Previous id(s)	Notes
N7876B	2027	PBY-6A	CON NO	N95780ntu Bu46663 (US Navy)	Aircraft Instrument Corp, Miami, Fla.
N7877B	2023	PBY-6A	CON NO	N9564C Bu46659 (US Navy)	
N7878B	2014	PBY-6A	CON NO	N7022C N9561C Bu46650 (US Navy)	
N7879B	2011	PBY-6A	CON NO	N7068C N9576C Bu46647 (US Navy)	
N788C	2026	PBY-6A	CON NO	N9588C Bu46662 (US Navy)	To Canada as CF-VIG, then N1022G, N999AR and N4NC. Current – see Chapter Nineteen.
N7880B	2003	PBY-6A	CON NO	N9585C Bu46639 (US Navy)	
N7881B	2031	PBY-6A	CON NO	N9568C Bu46667 (US Navy)	Aircraft Instrument Corp, Miami, Fla.
N7882B		PBY-6A	CON NO	Bu63995 (US Navy)	Aircraft Instrument Corp, Miami, Fla.
N7883B		PBY-6A	CON NO	N9570C Bu64005 (US Navy)	Aircraft Instrument Corp, Miami, Fla.
N7884B		PBY-6A	CON NO	N9969C Bu64033 (US Navy)	Aircraft Instrument Corp, Miami, Fla.
N7885B		PBY-6A	CON NO	N9557C Bu64047 (US Navy)	Aircraft Instrument Corp, Miami, Fla.
N79910	CV-500	OA-10A	CAN VIC (Cartierville)	44-33989 (USAAF) Bu67953 ntu (US Navy)	
NC79997	22023	Canso A	BOE CAN	9794 (RCAF)	Rexco.
N81RD	417	Canso A	CON SD	N5907 N59D NC68741 9746 (RCAF)	Bird Corporation, Long Beach, Calif. Restored as N5907 then to N5PY and current – see Chapter Nineteen.
N84857	1522	PBY-5A	CON SD	N5582V Bu33968 (US Navy)	To C-GVTF ntu. Current as N84857 – see Chapter Nineteen.
N85U		PBY-6A	CON NO	C-GFFI N6453C Bu64041 (US Navy)	Flying Firemen Inc, Spanaway, Wa. Current – see Chapter Nineteen.
N8875G	?	?	?	?	No further details known.

N923CL – may have been allocated to c/n CV-397 – see N222FT/N69RF and N691RF and CF-OWE.

Registration	C/n	Type	Place of Manufacture	Previous id(s)	Notes
N9415H	1614	PBY-5A	CON SD	Bu48252 (US Navy)	To Dutch MLD as P-216/16-216.
N94574	1619	PBY-5A	CON SD	? (IDFAF), N22B? N68744 Bu48257 (US Navy)	World Wide Air Svs, Port Moresby, PNG. To UK as G-APZA.
N95R	1735	PBY-5A	CON SD	N10018 Bu48373 (US Navy)	Remmert Werner, Inc, St Louis, Mo. To Australia as VH-BRI. Current – see Chapter Fourteen.

N95R retains its blisters and bow turret, but has had a horn-balanced rudder installed in this photo. It went to Australia as N95R and survives today as a motor cruiser conversion!

Registration	C/n	Type	Place of Manufacture	Previous id(s)	Notes
N9500C	1950	PBY-5A	CON NO	Bu46586 (US Navy)	
N9501C	1959	PBY-5A	CON NO	Bu46595 (US Navy)	To PT-AXM, FAB6551, N4583B.
N9502C	1988	PBY-5A	CON NO	Bu46624 (US Navy)	Southland Flying Service, Tohula, Miss. To David Tallichet/ Military Aircraft Restoration Co., Chino, Calif.
N9503C	1657	PBY-5A	CON SD	Bu48295 (US Navy)	
N9504C	1681	PBY-5A	CON SD	Bu48319 (US Navy)	To Brazil as PT-AXL then FAB6550.
N9505C	1581	PBY-5A	CON SD	Bu34027 (US Navy)	Alcan Airways, Kingman, Ariz. Later to SLAFCO, Moses Lake, Wash. Tanker 53. Current – see Chapter Nineteen.
N9506C	1857	PBY-5A	CON SD	Bu46493 (US Navy)	
N9507C	1736	PBY-5A	CON SD	Bu48374 (US Navy)	To Venezuela as YV-P-DPZ, 1965, then YV-O-CFO-2, YV-63CP ntu and YV-584CP. Current – see Chapter Sixteen.

Still to be found in Venezuela as YV-584CP, N9507C is seen much earlier in its commercial career, when it still sported a bow turret. The rear ladder provides less than convenient access through the cargo hatch.
Air Britain

Registration	C/n	Type	Place of Manufacture	Previous id(s)	Notes
N9509C	1786	PBY-5A	CON SD	Bu48424 (US Navy)	
N9510C	1809	PBY-5A	CON SD	Bu48447 (US Navy)	To Dutch New Guinea/ Netherlands East Indies as JZ-POD.
N9512C	1695	PBY-5A	CON SD	Bu48333 (US Navy)	
N9520C		PBY-6A	CON NO	Bu64053 (US Navy)	Aircraft Instrument Corp, Miami, Fla. Current – see Chapter Seventeen.
N9521C	1656	PBY-5A	CON SD	Bu48294 (US Navy)	
N9524C	1796	PBY-5A	CON SD	Bu48434 (US Navy)	
N9531C	2049	PBY-6A	CON NO	Bu46685 (US Navy)	Aircraft Instrument Corp, Miami, Fla.
N9532C	2030	PBY-6A	CON NO	Bu46666 (US Navy)	Aircraft Instrument Corp, Miami, Fla.
N9533C		PBY-6A	CON NO	Bu64042 (US Navy)	Aircraft Instrument Corp, Miami, Fla.
N9535C	1696	PBY-5A	CON SD	Bu48334 (US Navy)	Aircraft Instrument Corp, Miami, Fla. To N74821, which see.
N95403	'121'/ 917	PBY-5A	CON SD	Bu08098 (US Navy)	
NC95449	'83'/ 493	PBY-5A	CON SD	Bu04994 (US Navy)	*Miss Chicken of the Seas* California Maritime Airlines c.1948.
N9545C	2053	PBY-6A	CON NO	Bu46689 (US Navy)	Aircraft Instrument Corp, Miami, Fla.
N9546C	2013	PBY-6A	CON NO	Bu46649 (US Navy)	
N9548C		PBY-6A	CON NO	Bu64002 (US Navy)	To N331RS, which see.

Registration	C/n	Type	Place of Manufacture	Previous id(s)	Notes
NC95494	CV-422	OA-10A	CAN VIC (Cartierville)	44-33925 (USAAF) Bu67889 ntu (US Navy)	To C-43X/E and HK-43E then to N95494. To Bahamas as VP-BAB, then Canada as CF-HGE.
N9550C	2016	PBY-6A	CON NO	Bu46652 (US Navy)	
N9551C	2021	PBY-6A	CON NO	Bu46657 (US Navy)	
N9552C	2032	PBY-6A	CON NO	Bu46668 (US Navy)	Aircraft Instrument Corp, Miami, Fla.
N9553C	2006	PBY-6A	CON NO	Bu46642 (US Navy)	
N9554C		PBY-6A	CON NO	Bu64044 (US Navy)	Aircraft Instrument Corp, Miami, Fla. See also N9569C.
N9555C	2029	PBY-6A	CON NO	Bu46665 (US Navy)	To Chile as CC-CNG then CC-CNP. To Spain as EC-FXN, then restored as CC-CNP and current – see Chapter Seventeen.
N9556C	2007	PBY-6A	CON NO	Bu46643 (US Navy)	To Brazil as PT-BBQ and PP-PEB. Later to FAB as 6552 and current – see Chapter Sixteen.
N9557C		PBY-6A	CON NO	Bu64047 (US Navy)	Aircraft Instrument Corp, Miami, Fla. To N7885B, which see.
N9558C		PBY-6A	CON NO	Bu64096 (US navy)	Aircraft Instrument Corp, Miami, Fla.
N9559C		PBY-6A	CON NO	Bu64065 (US Navy)	Aircraft Instrument Corp, Miami, Fla.
N9561C	2014	PBY-6A	CON NO	Bu46650 (US Navy)	Aircraft Instrument Corp, Miami, Fla. To N7022C then N7878B, which see.
N9562C	2043	PBY-6A	CON NO	Bu46679 US Navy)	Aircraft Instrument Corp, Miami, Fla. To Chile as CC-CNF then CC-CCS. Current – see Chapter Seventeen.
N9563C		PBY-6A	CON NO	Bu64008 (US Navy)	Aircraft Instrument Corp, Miami, Fla.
N9564C	2023	PBY-6A	CON NO	Bu46659 (US Navy)	Aircraft Instrument Corp, Miami, Fla. To N7877B.
N9568C	2031	PBY-6A	CON NO	Bu46667 (US Navy)	Aircraft Instrument Corp, Miami, Fla. To N7881B.
N9569C		PBY-6A	CON NO	Bu64044 (US Navy)	Aircraft Instrument Corp, Miami, Fla. To N7884B. See also N9554C.
N9570C		PBY-6A	CON NO	Bu64005 (US Navy)	Aircraft Instrument Corp, Miami, Fla. To N7883B.

This 1954 photo taken at Oakland, California, shows an early US Navy PBY-5A civilianised as N95449 *Miss Chicken of the Seas*. At one time, it was operated by California Maritime Airlines.
Jennifer M. Gradidge

Registration	C/n	Type	Place of Manufacture	Previous id(s)	Notes
N9571C		PBY-6A	CON NO	Bu64104 (US Navy)	See also N6465C.
N9572C	2037	PBY-6A	CON NO	Bu46673 (US Navy)	Aircraft Instrument Corp, Miami, Fla. To N7021C, N7875B.
N9573C	2044	PBY-6A	CON NO	Bu46680 (US Navy)	Aircraft Instrument Corp, Miami, Fla. To N7035C, N7787B.
N9574C		PBY-6A	CON NO	Bu63994 (US Navy)	At Casa Grande, Ariz., un-converted, 3/1957.
N9575C		PBY-6A	CON NO	Bu64013 (US Navy)	To N6468C, N7783B.
N9576C	2011	PBY-6A	CON NO	Bu46647 (US Navy)	Aircraft Instrument Corp, Miami, Fla. To N7068C, N7879B.
N9578C	2027	PBY-6A	CON NO	Bu46663 (US Navy)	Aircraft Instrument Corp, Miami, Fla. To N7876B.
N9579C		PBY-6A	CON NO	Bu64106 (US Navy)	Aircraft Instrument Corp, Miami, Fla. To N7039C then N7781B. See also N6454C.
N9580C	2047	PBY-6A	CON NO	Bu46683 (US Navy)	Aircraft Instrument Corp, Miami, Fla. To N7786B.
N9581C	2051	PBY-6A	CON NO	Bu46687 (US Navy)	Aircraft Instrument Corp, Miami, Fla. To N7785B.
N9582C		PBY-6A	CON NO	Bu64010 (US Navy)	Aircraft Instrument Corp, Miami, Fla. To N7782B.
N9583C		PBY-6A	CON NO	Bu63995 (US Navy)	Aircraft Instrument Corp, Miami, Fla. To N7882B.
N9584C		PBY-6A	CON NO	Bu64087 (US Navy)	Aircraft Instrument Corp, Miami, Fla. Possibly to N7703C.
N9585C	2003	PBY-6A	CON NO	Bu46639 (US Navy)	Aircraft Instrument Corp, Miami, Fla. To N7880B.
N9586C		PBY-6A	CON NO	N9614C Bu64105 (US Navy)	Aircraft Instrument Corp, Miami, Fla.
N9587C		PBY-6A	CON NO	Bu64001 (US Navy)	Aircraft Instrument Corp, Miami, Fla.
N9588C	2026	PBY-6A	CON NO	Bu46662 (US Navy)	To N788C, then Canada as CF-VIG. To USA as N1022G then N999AR and N4NC, which see.
N96FP	1737	PBY-5A	CON SD	2002 FAP T-29 (FAP) ZP-CBA N4937V Bu48375 (US Navy)	Registered 1993. Franks Aircraft, Ft Worth, Tex. Caribbean Air Transport, San Juan. To N96UC, which see.
N96R	1774	PBY-5A	CON SD	N10024 Bu48412 (US Navy)	Remmert Werner Inc, St Louis, Mo. To Venezuela as YV-P-EPX, later YV-P-EPZ, YV-O-CFO-4, YV-56CP, YV-585CP and YV-485C. Current – see Chapter Sixteen.
N96UC	1737	PBY-5A	CON SD	N96FP 2002 (FAP) T-29 (FAP) ZP-CBA N4937V Bu48375 (US Navy)	Universal Associates. Current – see Chapter Nineteen.
N9614C		PBY-6A	CON NO	Bu64105 (US Navy)	To N9586C.
N9752Z	CV-329	Canso A	CAN VIC (Cartierville)	11040 (RCAF)	B. B. Burson & Assocs, Columbia, Calif. Tanker E48.
N9825Z	'235'	PBY-6A	CON NO	Bu64107 (US Navy)	National Air & Space Museum, Washington, DC. To Florida Forestry Board. To SLAFCO, Moses Lake, Wash. Tanker 158. Current – see Chapter Nineteen.
N9969C		PBY-6A	CON NO	Bu64033 (US Navy)	Aircraft Instrument Corp, Miami, Fla. To N7884B, which see.
N999AR	2026	PBY-6A	CON NO	N1022G CF-VIG N788C N9588C Bu46662 (US Navy)	Anchor & Cattle Corp, Grundy, Va. Red Stevenson, Leonard, Okla. *The Searcher*. To N4NC, which see.

Twelve
SURVIVING CATALINAS

From this point, the book is intended as a guide to all Catalinas that have survived to the present day. Each entry gives a brief history of the individual aircraft, highlighting particularly noteworthy events and features and describing its present circumstances. Where relevant data are available, a table gives details of the current markings/registration/serial carried by the aircraft, its construction number, type designation, place of manufacture and all known previous identities. It should be noted that in all cases the type designation refers to that which was given to the aircraft at the time that it was built/delivered, and not necessarily that which is now used by the country of registration or the owner.

One of the problems in drawing up a list of any surviving type of aircraft is exactly where to draw the line as to what constitutes a survivor and what does not. The more obvious candidates are those that are structurally complete and either airworthy or maintained in static display condition by individuals or museum collections. However, I have also included some wrecks and abandoned airframes where they are either basically complete or consist of at least a substantially intact airframe. There then follows a list of some incomplete wrecks that remain scattered around the globe, but where the term 'Survivor' would be an exaggeration.

The Survivors list is by country of residence and not necessarily, therefore, by country of registration. Within each country section, the individual aircraft appear numerically/alphabetically by serial/registration. The vast majority of surviving airframes were originally US Navy, USAAF or Royal Canadian Air Force machines, and so, for ease of reference, the following table shows the 86 survivors whose provenance is known by their original serial, together with details of the country in which that individual aircraft is now domiciled and its present-day serial or registration. The aircraft will be found described in greater detail under that country and identity in Chapters Thirteen to Nineteen.

Table 79. Survivors with original serial numbers shown

Royal Canadian Air Force Cansos:

Serial	Current Identity	Country of Residence
9718	VA718	Diego Garcia
9742	N68740	USA
9746	N5PY	USA
9750	N314CF	USA
9752	6527	Brazil
9767	C-FCRR	France
9810	Fv47001	Sweden
9815	C-FNJB	Canada
9825	9825	Canada
9830	C-FPQK	Canada
9837	C-FCRP	Canada
9838	N4934H	USA
11005	C-FNJF	Canada

Serial	Current Identity	Country of Residence
11007	11007	Canada
11024	C-FUAW	Canada
11042	5B-PBY	Greece
11047	C-FOFI	Canada
11054	ZK-PBY	New Zealand
11060	VH-EXG	Australia
11074	N222FT	USA
11084	C-FPQL	Canada
11087	11087	Canada
11088	C-FPQM	Canada
11089	C-FPQO	South Africa
11093	CF-NJL	Canada
11094	C-FNJE	Canada
11100	F-ZBAR	France

USAAF OA-10As

Serial	Current Identity	Country of Residence
43-43847	N4760C	USA
44-33880	CC-CDT	Spain
44-33929	C-FNJC	Canada
44-33954	N57875	USA
44-33972	C-GFFC	USA
44-34009	CC-CGY	Chile
44-34012	HK-2115P	Colombia
44-34081	VH-SBV	New Zealand
44-34094	C-FDFB	Canada

US Navy PBY-5s, -5As and -6As

Serial	Current Identity	Country of Residence
Bu2459	PH-PBY	Netherlands
Bu05021	CF-HFL	Canada
Bu08109	L-857	Norway
Bu08272	A24-30	Australia
Bu08317	Bu08317	USA
Bu21232	N2763A	USA
Bu33966	N3936A	USA
Bu33968	N84857	USA
Bu34027	N9505C	USA
Bu44248	VH-ASA	Australia
Bu46453	619	Colombia
Bu46456	N4582T	USA
Bu46457	N4582U	USA
Bu46504	OB-T-251	Peru
Bu46522	NX2172N	USA
Bu46527	N6473C	USA
Bu46539	PB-505	Indonesia
Bu46582	N4583A	USA
Bu46590	N68756	USA
Bu46595	N4583B	USA
Bu46596	DR.1-1	Spain
Bu46602	N607CC	USA
Bu46624	N9502C	USA
Bu46633	VP-BPS	UK
Bu46643	6552	Brazil
Bu46644	EC-EVK	Spain
Bu46645	FP535	Norway
Bu46655	C-FIZU	Canada
Bu46662	N4NC	USA
Bu46665	CC-CNP	Spain
Bu46679	CC-CCS	Spain
Bu48287	N287	USA
Bu48294	N9521C	UK
Bu48317	16-212	Netherlands
Bu48368	Bu48368	Australia

Bu48373	VH-BRI	Australia		Bu64017	N285RA	UK
Bu48374	YV-584CP	Venezuela		Bu64035	L-861	Denmark
Bu48375	N96UC	USA		Bu64041	N85U	USA
Bu48397	N5593V	Saudi Arabia		Bu64064	EC-FMC	Spain
Bu48406	N5590V	USA		Bu64072	N7057C	USA
Bu48412	N7238Z	USA		Bu64097	N7179Y	USA
Bu48423	N423RS	UK		Bu64107	N9825Z	USA
Bu63993	L-866/8466M	UK				

Thirteen
SURVIVORS IN THE MIDDLE EAST AND AFRICA

N5593V spent some time at Croydon Airport near London during 1959 before continuing a world tour. This photo was taken on the Croydon tarmac on 31 May of that year.
R. Heron

SAUDI ARABIA

N5593V – Abandoned, Ras Ash Shaykh Humayd, Aqaba, Red Sea

N5593V was just a standard US Navy PBY-5A built at San Diego. What was to make it different from its many brethren was its rather unusual demise. It was acquired by Thomas Kendall from surplus stocks at Litchfield Park after being struck off by the US Navy in August 1956. It was one of a number purchased by him, another being the PBY-5A currently preserved at the San Diego Aerospace Museum in California.

Registered N5593V, the Catalina was refurbished by Kendall as a luxury air yacht, and in 1959 he set off with his family on a round-the-world flight. During this trip, some time was spent at Croydon Airport, where Air Couriers carried out repairs to damage sustained to the bow area. On 30 September 1959, N5593V made the short flight across to Gatwick, thus becoming one of the very

Although this photo was taken in the mid-1980s, N5593V still looks essentially the same as this today at the site where it was abandoned in March 1960.
Douglas Neve

last aircraft to leave Croydon on its official day of closure.

By March 1960, the Kendalls and their Catalina had reached Saudi Arabia, by which time a camera crew from *Life* magazine had joined the crew. On 22 March the

Catalina touched down at Ras Ash Shaykh Humayd on the headland dividing the Red Sea and the Gulf of Aqaba facing Tyran Island. The aircraft was anchored close to the shore and the crew slept on board that night. The following day, the family group were attacked from the headland by gun-toting Saudi Arabian Bedouins. Although the family and camera crew made it back to the Catalina, the aircraft sustained damage from several hundred bullets and had to be abandoned. The Kendalls and party were arrested and held for a few days on suspicion of being Israelis. N5593V was too badly damaged to be salvaged and remained at the site, where it is still a graffiti-covered desert landmark.

Table 80.

Registration/Serial	C/n	Type	Place of Manufacture	Previous id(s)
N5593V	1759	PBY-5A	CON SD	Bu48397 (US Navy)

SOUTH AFRICA

C-FPQO – Antares Air Services, Rand

Canso A 11089 is known to have served with 162 (BR) Squadron, RCAF, during the Second World War and then, post-war, with 102 Search and Rescue Flight at Trenton, Ontario, before being struck off charge in November 1962. It had the distinction of being the very last Canso in RCAF service. It was subsequently taken on strength by the Department of Transport of Quebec for conversion to water bomber configuration. A nominal change of ownership occurred in the 1970s when the firefighting force came under the umbrella of the Government of Quebec, and 'PQO continued in use until 1993, when all the Quebec fleet were retired. It had flown with the codes '15' and '715' during its long service.

Pro Air Aviation International of Bromont, Quebec, purchased the Canso, probably via Canadian Aircraft Sales, and in 1995 it was flown out to Greece, where it joined one of its former colleagues, C-FPQF, which by this time had become 5B-PBY on the Cypriot register. C-FPQO retained its Canadian identity, however, although it was owned by the same operator, Athenian Airlift Services Ltd of Nicosia. For some time, the two Cansos shared tarmac space at Tanagra, but C-FPQO was subsequently advertised for sale. During its sojourn in Greece, C-FPQO had its fire-fighting equipment removed and blisters were put back in place.

In September 1999, it departed for South Africa, arriving at Rand on 7 September for its new owner, Antares Air Services. The delivery flight to Rand was routed via Athens, Luxor, Khartoum, Entebbe, Lilongwe in Malawi

C-FPQO spent some time at Tanagra in Greece where this picture was taken in April 1997, before flying out to South Africa two years later. Its blisters were put back in place prior to that flight.
Paul Barnfield

and Vilanculos in Mozambique. In Vilanculos, C-FPQO was engaged in some film work to support an advertising campaign for the German deodorant company Henkel and their *FA* brand of aftershave. The film company Movie Makers removed the attractive yellow and blue colour scheme in which 'PQO had flown during its time in Quebec, and replaced it with a light blue overall livery, complete with bogus *FA* registration, the latter authorised by the Mozambique Government. Nose art and the name *Caribbean Dream* were also added. Most of the filming took place off the Indian Ocean island of

Margarude, 10 miles offshore of Vilanculos, and after a week, the delivery flight to Rand continued.

By the end of 1999, C-FPQO had acquired a new blue and white colour scheme and awaited its new life in southern climes.

Table 81.

Registration/Serial	C/n	Type	Place of Manufacture	Previous id(s)
C-FPQO	CV-427	Canso A	CAN VIC (Cartierville)	CF-PQO
				11089 (RCAF)

The New Zealand Catalina Group briefly flew its former RCAF Canso A ZK-PBY in Soviet markings before re-painting it as a Royal New Zealand Air Force example. Operating from a picturesque New Zealand lake in 1998, it is shown wearing red stars.
Lawrence Acket via Marlene Gray

The same aircraft subsequently visited South America on the first Peter Stuyvesant Travel Odyssey in 1993. One of the landing places was on the River Manaus in Brazil.
via Michael Prophet

The Government of Quebec used a number of former-RCAF Canso As in the fire-fighting role, all registered in the CF-PQ sequence. CF-PQF is shown here in its yellow and red livery, wearing the Tanker 11 fleet number.

CF-PQF later became C-FPQF and appeared in a revised Quebec Government colour scheme coded 711. This photo was taken in 1986, a few years before it was withdrawn. *MAP*

The Bird Innovator N5907 displays its unique four-engined layout and under-wing dinghies. It flew in this guise for many years, until it returned to the more conventional twin Pratt & Whitney format at the end of the 1990s.

Now the sole fire-fighting company using Catalinas in Canada, Buffalo Air has a varied fleet based at Yellowknife. C-FOFI came from the Province of Newfoundland and Labrador fleet, and still wears the livery of that operator, but with Buffalo titles.
MAP

One of the current Buffalo aircraft – CF-UAW – came from the Province of Saskatchewan forestry protection fleet. It wears the fleet code 708.
MAP

Before moving to the Lone Star Flight Museum in Galveston, Texas, N68740 was stored for a time at Pensacola in Florida, and it is seen there in this 1986 photograph. During restoration to military configuration, a bow turret was put back in place of the clipper bow that it had flown with in civilian ownership.
MAP

Avalon Aviation flew this PBY-6A CF-VIG as a crew transport in addition to its large fleet of fire-bombing Catalinas. It now flies in the USA as N4NC. *MAP*

PBY-5A N68756 is shown in the colour scheme it wore when it was first acquired by the Confederate Air Force. It was later painted in a Royal Australian Air Force scheme. Sadly, it is no longer airworthy.

The Confederate Air Force has operated no fewer than four PBY-6As, three of which have been destroyed or seriously damaged in their ownership. N7179Y flew successfully with them for a year or so, but was badly bent after being blown over by high winds.
Ron Gaffney

Some post-war Catalina conversions involved the removal of the two Pratt & Whitney R-1830s and replacement with Wright Cyclone R-2600s and a larger rudder. One such conversion involved N9505C, now part of the SLAFCO fleet based at Moses Lake in Washington State. This photo was taken during a period of storage in Nevada.
via Eddy Gual

The well-known Super Catalina operated in Europe by Plane Sailing Air Displays shows off its larger engines and rudder, together with perfectly aligned prop blades. At the time, it was operating from Lake Windermere in the English Lake District.
Alan Cox

Now in the USA as N222FT, C-FOWE belonged to Ilford Riverton Airways when seen in 1981. It appears to have received a replacement rudder. The horn balance used on many post-war commercial conversions is evident.
MAP

Pictured in happier times at Vancouver in 1982, C-FSAT was destroyed during recovery operations following a precautionary water landing in Hawaii. Parts were later used in a number of Catalina restoration projects. *Glen Etchells*

Fairly typical of the 'office' in a post-war commercial Catalina water bomber, actually a Buffalo Air example. The linked control wheels are held in place by the red gust lock on the left, whilst the roof-mounted throttle, pitch and trim controls are visible in the centre of the photo. *Michael Prophet*

Fourteen
SURVIVORS IN AUSTRALIA AND NEW ZEALAND

VH-ASA *Frigate Bird II* 'flies' inside the Powerhouse Museum in Sydney. The flags of Chile and Australia can be seen aft of the bow turret in recognition of this aircraft's pioneering flights in 1951.
Stephen Dodd

AUSTRALIA

VH-ASA – New South Wales Museum of Applied Arts and Sciences, The Powerhouse, Sydney, New South Wales.

VH-ASA is something of a rarity amongst surviving Catalinas, firstly because it is one of the few remaining that were originally built by Boeing, and secondly and more importantly, because it is one of only three complete pure flying boat survivors, the others being at the

Museum of Naval Aviation at Pensacola, Florida, and Whaleworld, Albany, Western Australia. All the other complete and original examples are amphibians. It also flew into the history books as the first aircraft to fly from Australia to South America across the South Pacific, and its preservation is therefore highly appropriate.

Completed in November 1944 as a tall-tailed model PB2B-2, it was one of a batch of 67 to be constructed by Boeing at its Sea Island, Vancouver plant under contract NOa-782 for the US Navy. Serialled within the block Bu44228 to 44294, its own identity was Bu44248, but it was diverted to the RAAF when the planned transfer from the US Navy to the RAF as a Catalina Mk VI was cancelled. It eventually flew to the Naval Air Station at Terminal Island, San Pedro, California, and the Royal Australian Air Force detachment there. It was subsequently delivered to Australia, arriving in September

1945, and was taken on charge on the 3rd of that month. It was the second-to-last Catalina to be delivered to the RAAF and was allocated the serial A24-385. Destined not to see any active wartime service, it was switched between various squadrons and periods of inactivity with maintenance units before going into storage at Rathmines, NSW. It was now about to find fame.

In 1950, Captain P. G. Taylor, a highly regarded pilot and navigator with various exploratory flights to his credit, was planning a survey flight to Chile from Australia as a first stage in establishing regular air links along the route. He was allocated a Catalina for the venture, and after visiting Rathmines on Lake Macquarie in New South Wales to inspect those stored there, he chose A24-385. It was formally issued to Captain Taylor on 22 August 1950, and was granted the 'fixed' registration VH-ASA (Australia–South America). The earlier allocation of registration VH-AGB was not taken up, although it was subsequently used by another, unconnected, Catalina. Before leaving Australia, VH-ASA was christened *Frigate Bird II*, the original *Frigate Bird* being the RAF Catalina JX275 that Captain Taylor had flown from Mexico to Australia in 1944.

The subsequent successful crossing to Chile and back was a true adventure, arguably one of the last epic flights of exploration of the propeller age. It is described in Captain, later Sir, Gordon Taylor's book *Frigate Bird*.

After the flight, VH-ASA was gifted to Taylor by the Commonwealth Government. Taylor initially proposed using his aircraft to fly route-proving trips on behalf of South Pacific Airways, which was planning to set up services between Honolulu and Tahiti. Prohibitive costs meant that the Catalina was not converted. VH-ASA was flown to Rathmines for its second period of storage there, being withdrawn from use on 28 June 1954. Whilst there, it suffered at the hands of vandals and souvenir hunters, and upon the closure of the base, it was barged in dismantled state to the old flying boat base at Rose Bay, Sydney, where it arrived on 7 July 1959. It fared little better there, and two years later it was presented to the New South Wales Museum of Applied Arts and Sciences. Unfortunately, the storage resources of the museum were inadequate and *Frigate Bird* was moved around between various locations in the Sydney area, including the old tram depot at Ultimo, where it was towed on its beaching gear on 2 November 1969.

In 1974, arrangements were made with Harold Thomas of the Camden Museum of Aviation for *Frigate Bird* to be displayed at their Camden Airport site, but shortly afterwards, the museum was evicted, so, on 6 April 1974, VH-ASA was taken to the Museum of Applied Arts and Sciences storage facility at Castle Hill. There it remained until a further move to Bankstown Airport in June 1986, where it was restored by Hawker Pacific for permanent display at the museum's new site at the Powerhouse Museum in Ultimo. Because of its size, the Catalina had to be assembled in the museum building before it was completed and opened to the public. Thus, on 30 May 1987, in the small hours, *Frigate Bird* made its last journey, courtesy of a large low-loader, through the streets of Sydney. Once at the Powerhouse, it was reassembled by Hawker Pacific manpower, and on 23 June it was raised up to its final position suspended

from the roof, where it now shares airspace with an Avro 504K replica, de Havilland Moth and Bell 206 helicopter amongst other aircraft. It is the largest exhibit in the museum by a substantial margin!

In the colours it wore when it arrived back in Australia on 21 April 1951, after its epic flight, it now makes a fitting tribute to the courage and pioneering spirit of its crew.

Table 82.

Registration/Serial	C/n	Type	Place of Manufacture	Previous id(s)
VH-ASA	61154	PB2B-2	BOE CAN	VH-AGB ntu A24-385 (RAAF) JX630 ntu (RAF) Bu44248 (US Navy)

(ex-VH-BRI) – Vic O'Hara, Shute Harbour, Queensland

Following its military service with the United States Navy, this PBY-5A was taken out of storage at Litchfield Park, Arizona, and registered as N10018, one of a large batch of consecutive registrations allocated to surplus Catalinas. Its first owner was the St Louis company Remmert Werner, which specialised in civilian Catalina conversions.

By 1958, it had been re-registered as N95R and fully converted for civilian use whilst retaining its blisters and nose turret. Later, the nose turret was replaced with a 'clipper' bow, and an air stair was added to the rear hull. For two years, it was registered to a Missouri-based company before being sold in Australia, where it was delivered in October 1959. The Australian registration VH-BRI was allocated on 28 January the following year.

Christened *Golden Islander* by its new owners, Ansett Flying Boat Services, it was used on services between Proserpine, Queensland, and Hayman Island. It was at

On close inspection, this rather stylish motor cruiser turns out to be a former Catalina! The characteristic hull shape and amphibious undercarriage can be seen in this view, as can the name *Henrietta Hoh* on the upper cabin. It was once VH-BRI of Ansett Flying Boat Services.

the latter location on 8 July 1962 that VH-BRI's flying career came to an end when it suffered a heavy landing that popped a number of rivets in the hull, causing the Cat to sink overnight. Some sources have quoted the sinking as being caused by submerged logs, and even by a whale, but the more mundane reason stated above seems to be the accurate one!

The sunken wreck was acquired for £5 by Vic O'Hara, a cane farmer from Proserpine, who had the wreck refloated using 44-gallon fuel drums, after which it was towed to Shute Harbour by barge. Vic then transported the dismantled aircraft to Cannonville, complete with police escort, and then on to his home town for the start of a lengthy conversion to a motor cruiser. The project was completed in 1975. The lower Catalina hull was retained, complete with main and nose undercarriages and air stair, whilst the upper hull was removed and replaced with a cruiser superstructure.

Two General Motors 120 hp engines power the former flying boat both on water and up onto the shore. The boats' overall length is 55 feet and the interior comfortably sleeps 12 people whilst offering the luxury of a shower, toilet and freezer. When on the water, cruising speed is 10 knots at a fuel consumption of three gallons per hour. This unique conversion, named *Henrietta-Hoh*, became a well-known sight in the area, both on and off the water, and is still to be found around Shute Harbour.

that served with the RAAF both during and after the Second World War. However, its own military career was spent, not with the RAAF, but another Commonwealth air arm – the Royal Canadian Air Force.

Rolling off the Canadian Vickers production line at Cartierville in the Spring of 1944, the RCAF took this particular Canso A on charge on 5 April 1944. It remained in military service for no less than seventeen years, finally being struck off on 25 May 1961. By this time, it had had its blisters removed and replaced by cargo hatches, and its nose turret had been faired over.

After being released by the military, it was initially placed on the Canadian civil regsiter as CF-NJD with Canspec Air Transport Ltd. In 1962, it became N609FF with Cal Nat Airways of Grass Valley, California, and Firefly Inc, based at Portland, Oregon, with whom it flew as a fire fighter. For at least some of this time it carried the United States Forest Service tail code 40E relating to its area of operations, i.e. Region 5, California. By this time, N609FF had been converted to a Wright Cyclone-powered Super Catalina by Fairey Canada Ltd, and this modification included the installation of a much larger rudder to compensate for the combined extra 1,000 hp from the two R-2600s.

By 1967, this Catalina had been acquired by the Canadian aerial survey company Terra Surveys/Geoterrex, and in common with other Catalinas operated by this company, it roamed far and wide on geophysical survey contracts in search of mineral deposits. After spending some time in South Africa, it flew out to Australia via Indonesia, and in August 1972 the US registration was cancelled in favour of Australian marks VH-EXG. For the next few years, it was operated in

Table 83.

Registration/Serial	C/n	Type	Place of Manufacture	Previous id(s)
	1735	PBY-5A	CON SD	VH-BRI N95R N10018 Bu48373 (US Navy)

VH-EXG – Royal Australian Air Force Museum, RAAF Base Amberley, Queensland

Currently located in the Essendon area of Victoria, VH-EXG will eventually become a star exhibit in the Royal Australian Air Force Museum at Point Cook. As such, it will honour the 168 Catalinas of various models

Executive Air Services was using the survey-equipped Super Catalina VH-EXG out of Essendon when this photo was taken there in November 1977. The paraphernalia of geophysical surveying can be seen around the airframe, as can the Geoterrex titles below the cockpit.
Jennifer M. Gradidge

Australia by Executive Air Services, H. C. Sleigh Aviation and Western Commander, all the while retaining its Geoterrex livery.

After several years based in the Essendon area, VH-EXG was retired and replaced by a CASA 212. Placed in open storage at Essendon Airport in 1988, VH-EXG was put up for sale and attracted interest from various parties, including local preservation groups. In due course, the aircraft was purchased by the RAAF Museum, and by June 1993 work was well under way on dismantling the airframe. The wings were taken to the RAAF base at East Sale and the hull to RAAF Laverton. In mid-1996, the dismantled aircraft was roaded to the RAAF airfield at Amberley, where the restoration was continued by the team previously involved in restoring a pair of Douglas Bostons to a superb standard.

At the time of writing, work is under way to restore VH-EXG as an RAAF Catalina, and although the project will be carried out to airworthy standard, it is likely to remain a static exhibit. Modifications have been carried out to the hull that have enabled hull blisters and a nose turret to be re-installed, although the museum is still trying to source guns to place in the latter postion. The tail has also been rebuilt so that a standard PBY-5A rudder can replace the *Super Cat* unit carried in recent years. Some components are being scratch built, whilst others, including the internal gun platforms, have been recovered from wreckage on the Palm Island Reserve off the Queensland coast. The museum is currently on the lookout for two Pratt & Whitney R-1830s to be mounted instead of the Wright Cyclones that powered VH-EXG in the last phase of its flying career. Once completed, the restored aircraft will go to the main RAAF Museum collection at RAAF Base, Point Cook, and current plans are for it to be painted as PBY-5A A24-104, an aircraft that

was used by the RAAF for JATO trials after the war and was eventually supplied to the Dutch government

Table 84.

Registration/Serial	C/n	Type	Place of Manufacture	Previous id(s)
VH-EXG	CV-369	Canso A	CAN VIC (Cartierville)	N609FF CF-NJD 11060 (RCAF)

'A24-30' – Catalina Memorial Park, Lake Boga, Northern Victoria

Lake Boga, Northern Victoria, was home to 1 Flying Boat Repair Depot from June 1942, and remained an important flying boat base until the end of 1947. Although used by a variety of flying boats and seaplanes, it is primarily associated with the Catalina, and it is entirely fitting that the town should have its own example on display.

The efforts of the Lake Boga Lions Club have seen the idea of a memorial grow into reality. Starting in 1978 with the aim of finding a PBY, the volunteers scoured the surrounding area for Catalina remains and spares, and by 1990 a more or less complete Catalina had been mounted on a steel tube cradle in what is now known as the Catalina Memorial Park. Although painted as A24-30, the restoration is an amalgamation of many parts and is a tribute to the hard work of its rebuild team.

The rear hull was painted as '02' when acquired, and may therefore have come from the RAAF Instructional Airframe No.2 which is known to have been used at Lake

Lake Boga's composite Catalina restoration seen in its compound within the town and close to the original RAAF Base. The hull carries the serial A24-30.
Air Britain

Boga and was originally RAAF A24-38/US Navy Bu08203. The cockpit section is said to have originated from a Royal Netherlands East Indies Air Force machine, and serials Y-72 and Y-76 have been suggested, but neither of these is confirmed and should be treated with caution! The wing centre section apparently comes from an unidentified PBY-4 and the engine cowlings are pure DC-3!

The original A24-30 was a PBY-5 sold by the Commonwealth Disposals Commission to Kingsford Smith Aviation Services in October 1946, which had previously seen service with 20 Squadron and 3 OTU.

Table 85. Registration/Serial	C/n	Type	Place of Manufacture	Previous id(s)
'A24-30' (RAAF)		PBY-5	CON SD	(Composite)

A24-46 – Whaleworld Museum, Albany, Western Australia

Frenchman's Bay, Albany, Western Australia, was home to Australia's last whaling station, and the area is now a museum devoted to that trade. Sadly, the proprietor of the museum, John Bell, a qualified seaplane pilot and flying boat enthusiast, died in a plane crash a few years back. In addition to the whaling aspect of his museum, John had also assembled a small collection of aircraft and artefacts devoted to Australia's links with marine aircraft. The largest exhibit is a Catalina, but he also owned a very rare Vought Sikorsky Kingfisher, one of 18 flown by the RAAF. This is painted up as JE-B of 107 Squadron and is virtually complete.

The Catalina was a long-term project and is a credit to its late owner. John Bell acquired quantities of Catalina components from the team constructing the composite Catalina at Lake Boga, Northern Victoria, as described above, and these formed the original basis for the project. The parts had to be transported right across Australia using various trucks and trailers, and a total of six journeys were made! In order to protect the project from the unfriendly elements of the west coast climate, John also had to construct a hangar on site to house his aircraft. The cockpit section and rearmost portion of the hull both came from the Warbirds Aviation Museum at Mildura, Victoria, and the aircraft from which they originally came provided the identity for the rebuild, namely RAAF serial A24-46. This was built by Consolidated at San Diego as a PBY-5 for the US Navy, and was allocated the serial Bu08262. It was delivered to the RAAF in March 1943, and flew with 43 Squadron.

During January 1944, A24-46 was engaged in a minelaying operation on Kau Bay in the Halmahera Islands, north-west of Dutch New Guinea. On the way back home, bad weather prevented a return to 43 Squadron's temporary base at Darwin, so a precautionary landing was made at Melville Bay. During the subsequent refuelling at a naval fuel dump, an electrical spark jumped from the unearthed bilge pump to fuel on the wing, resulting in the trailing edge and ailerons being destroyed. As a result, A24-46 had to be towed 200 miles back to Darwin behind the vessel HMAS *Mercedes* so that repairs could be carried out. At the end of the war, A24-46 was disposed of to a Mr C. K. Campbell for spares recovery, this occurring in November 1947.

Now essentially complete, the Catalina only requires a few components to finish it off. Painted in black overall, the original US Navy star emblem had been clearly visible on the nose prior to its respray because of the effects of years of weathering on the RAAF colours.

Table 86. Registration/Serial	C/n	Type	Place of Manufacture	Previous id(s)
A24-46 (RAAF)	1166	PBY-5	CON SD	Bu08262 (US Navy)

Prior to being painted in an overall black colour scheme, the Whaleworld PBY-5 project was clearly showing its US Navy ancestry inside its purpose-built hangar at Albany. *John Chapman*

Bu48368 – Clyde North Aeronautical Preservation Group, Wagga Wagga, New South Wales

The forward section of this former United States Navy PBY-5A was acquired by the Clyde North Aeronautical Preservation Group (CNAPG) of Wagga Wagga, NSW, during 1997. Previously owned by one Glenis McGowen, the relic had spent many years in use as accomodation for farm workers, and, later, as a storage shed on her farm near Colleambally, NSW. The CNAPG arranged to visit the site after learning of the Catalina's existence whilst visiting nearby Griffith Airport, where they were told it was a 'bomber cockpit'. Subsequently, Glenis McGowan donated the relic to the CNAPG so that it could be restored for static display. Its first public outing was in November 1997, when it was shown off at the Wagga Wagga Airshow.

According to local residents, Bu48368 was one of two Catalinas involved in a mid-air collision during the Second World War. One of the Cats exploded on impact with the ground, but the other crash-landed and later had its hull aft of the forward lift strut removed. It is this aircraft that now survives with the CNAPG.

Table 87.

Registration/Serial	C/n	Type	Place of Manufacture	Previous id(s)
Bu48368 (US Navy)	1730	PBY-5A	CON SD	

NEW ZEALAND

VH-SBV – RNZAF Base Wigram, Christchurch, South Island

The RNZAF Museum Catalina project may be some way

Before going to Australia, Canadian Vickers-built CV-592 flew with Cathay Pacific and Macau Air Transport as VR-HDH. It is seen in the latter company's colours at Hong Kong. At this stage, it did not have blisters, although they were later replaced.
Peter Keating Collection

from completion but it is fortunate that it exists at all. The derelict hulk came very close to extinction on an airport fire dump – indeed a major part of the hull had already been torched when it was removed for preservation.

Ordered as a PBV-1A for the US Navy, this Catalina was diverted, along with many others from the Canadair (formerly Canadian Vickers) production line, to the USAAF, with which it was operated as 44-34081. After its military service, it was put up for disposal by the Foreign Liquidation Commission in Manila and purchased by Roy Farrell and Syd de Kantzow in November 1946. It was flown from Tacloban to Hong Kong for use by the their newly formed Cathay Pacific Airlines, and was registered as VR-HDH on the Hong Kong register in November 1946. It was put into use straight away on Cathay services, including gold charters to Macau. Whilst owned by Cathay Pacific, it was also leased to Macau Air Transport and Air Burma. On 28 October 1947, VR-HDH suffered substantial damage when it had a nose gear collapse on landing at Makati. In July 1948, Macau Air Transport (MATCO) became the registered owners and continued to operate gold charters between Macau and Hong Kong. These flights ceased after the loss of sister Catalina VR-HDT in a fatal hijacking, the world's first such aerial incident, on 16 July 1948.

MATCO continued to use VR-HDH until 1961, mainly on passenger services between Hong Kong, Saigon and Macau. Then, in May 1962, it was sold to Trans Australia Airlines (TAA), which had previously operated another Catalina – registered VH-WWC – that had come to grief in a landing accident at Daru Island, Papua New Guinea (PNG), on 26 April that year. The loss of this aircraft had left TAA without the flying boat capability that it needed to operate services around the PNG area. VR-HDH was overhauled in Hong Kong and painted in full TAA livery whilst retaining its former MATCO registration for the ferry flight to Australia. It was subsequently flown to Bankstown Airport, Sydney, via Manila, Davo, Palau, Wewak, Port Moresby, Cairns, Mackay and Brisbane! After arrival in Sydney it was registered as VH-SBV on 6 July and then underwent a modification programme in the hands of the Bristol Aircraft Company.

It was decided that as the Catalina was to be used solely on water-based operations, it would be converted to pure flying boat configuration by removing the undercarriage and using the empty wheel wells as baggage lockers. This was not done immediately as VH-SBV was due to land at several airfields on its delivery out to PNG. The flight engineer's position in the pylon was removed and necessary instrumentation relocated on the flight deck. The nose turret had at some stage been plated over, although not removed, and this modification remained. The blisters had already been taken off whilst in use in Hong Kong and TAA wanted these replaced. A redundant Catalina was found at neighbouring Mascot airfield, and this aircraft – VH-AGB – was made airworthy and flown across the city to Bankstown, where it not only donated its blisters to VH-SBV but then continued to act as a spares source for some years until finally scrapped in 1967.

By the early autumn of 1962, VH-SBV had been flown to Port Moresby, where its undercarriage was finally removed by TAA staff, and it entered revenue-earning service on 5 November 1962. By 1965, the number of airports and airstrips that had sprung up in the PNG area meant that it was no longer so important for TAA to use a flying boat on its services, and the decision was made to withdraw it. Its final flight to Port Moresby was on 5 January 1966, after which it remained there, suffering from the bane of all water borne aircraft – corrosion! Indeed, legend has it that during a take-off from Port Moresby, the captain's seat dropped through the flooring as a result of corrosion in the legs, causing a sudden nose-up pitch which no doubt caused the co-pilot some concern!

In the following March, it was purchased by a company named Australian Aircraft Sales and underwent an overhaul for new owners, Trans Oceanic Investments. However, VH-SBV continued to languish at Port Moresby until May 1966, when it was acquired by the local airline Patair. The Australian registration was formally cancelled on the 12th. Patair removed the engines, and ownership of the increasingly decrepit airframe was passed to the Territory War Memorial Trust. Later, the wings were hacked off and the hull was taken by road to Port Moresby's Jackson airfield, where it gradually fell apart from the combined effects of the weather and vandalism.

By 1968, VH-SBV had been removed to the airport fire dump, and there it stood on jacks and oil drums, minus outer wing panels and with most of its interior gutted. And there the story would have ended had it not been for the timely intervention of Auckland's Museum of Transport and Technology (MoTaT). They had the intention of acquiring and restoring a Catalina to honour the 56 operated by the Royal New Zealand Air Force. It is said, perhaps apocryphally, that on hearing that the local fire service were to lose their prized possession, the fire chief set fire to it! Whatever the truth, it is a fact that the centre section of the aircraft was very badly damaged by fire prior to its removal to New Zealand.

Upon arrival in New Zealand, the remains of the Catalina were stored at MoTaT's facility at the Sir Keith Park Memorial Airfield at Western Springs, Auckland. Unfortunately, the resources of MoTaT were fully

VH-SBV early on in its restoration by the RNZAF Museum at Wigram. The forward hull is looking good, but the damaged centre section still requires much work. *RNZAF*

stretched, and the Catalina lay in the open, gradually deteriorating further until it was donated, in 1983, to the RNZAF Museum.

Initial component gathering and restoration was carried out at the RNZAF base at Whenuapai, Auckland, and work carried on spasmodically as resources allowed. The centre hull which had been ravaged by fire damage at Port Moresby was meticulously rebuilt, and other valuable components were obtained from the wreck of another Catalina, C-FSAT, which had met an untimely end in Honolulu. In late 1985, the project was moved to Wigram Air Base, Christchurch, and although the rebuild is far from complete, the hull and tail section with restored blisters is on show there inside one of the hangars. A replacement centre-section is still required, as the original was virtually destroyed during the Port Moresby sojourn.

In late 1984, a British aviation magazine reported that Wigram had within its collection of vintage aircraft some components from a PBY-5A Catalina, serial number '44-25158'. These components may have been incorporated into the rebuild of VH-SBV, but it is worth pointing out that serial 44-25158 did not belong to a USAAF Catalina but was in fact allocated to a Lockheed P-38L-LO Lightning!

Hopefully, one day, VH-SBV will take her place in the RNZAF Museum, proudly displaying RNZAF markings.

Table 88.

Registration/Serial	C/n	Type	Place of Manufacture	Previous id(s)
VH-SBV	CV-592	OA-10A	CAN VIC (Cartierville)	VR-HDH 44-34081 (USAAF) Bu68045 ntu (US Navy)

ZK-PBY – The New Zealand Catalina Group, Ardmore, Auckland

Currently the only airworthy Catalina in the Antipodes, ZK-PBY has come a long way from its origins as a Royal Canadian Air Force Canso A. For a time, it could justly claim to be 'the last African flying boat', and, as such, became something of a TV personality through the eponymous BBC TV documentary. It has also had two books devoted to it and its own video! That it ended up in New Zealand at all was the result of misfortune befalling another of the breed.

As aircraft 11054 of the Royal Canadian Air Force, this Canso A is known to have served with 5 (BR) Squadron, having originally been taken on charge in March 1944. It remained with the RCAF until June 1947. Thereafter, its history seems to be unrecorded until it was converted for passenger carrying in Costa Rica during the mid-1950s. It did not aspire to South American registry, as far as can be told, but it did appear on the Canadian register in 1956 when it was allocated the marks CF-JCV with the Eastern Canada Stevedoring Co. of Montreal. After being leased to Notre Dame Airways, it was sold in 1960 to Austin Airways, which operated it for the next sixteen years.

After a time with Aero Trades Western of Winnipeg, it passed to Air Caledonia and was operated out of Vancouver, BC. Eventually, it was flown down to Reno, Nevada, for storage in 1986.

At around this time, a French couple, Antoinette and Pierre Jaunet, were looking for a suitable flying boat to operate on safari-type charters in Africa. The idea of recreating some of the old Empire Airways air routes began to germinate, and this led them to Reno to survey C-FJCV. A purchase was negotiated and the Cat was flown to Victoria, British Columbia, for the necessary work to prepare it for 16-passenger operation in Africa. After work was completed, the interior boasted a small aviation and travel library and bar, a food preparation area and storage space for cooking and eating utensils. There was also a refrigerator, washing facilitiies and a toilet. It left Victoria again on 21 October 1988, bound for Cairo via Medicine Hat, Regina, Fargo, Winnipeg, Ottawa, Stephenville, Gander, Lajes, Lisbon and Montpellier.

Antoinette and Pierre used their enormous experience in operating ground-based safaris to good effect, and a series of successful flights were operated over the next few years, starting with some Trans-Africa trips along the Nile from Cairo southward. It was these early trips that were filmed for the BBC documentary 'The Last African Flying Boat'. Although C-FJCV became synonymous with the lengthy Nile flights because of the film, it was also used for many other shorter trips, including ten-day safaris around East Africa, for example. At the time of purchase by the Jaunets, C-FJCV had been registered to the Catalina Safari Company, and the same owner was quoted when it was re-registered in Zimbabwe as Z-CAT in July 1990.

By the early 1990s, the Jaunets were proposing to establish a more permanent safari operation in Zimbabwe, and Z-CAT did not feature in these plans. The aircraft was put up for sale, but continued to fly charters whilst a buyer was sought. In 1993, it also flew the first Peter Stuyvesant Travel Odyssey from Holland to South America and back when the scheduled aircraft, Plane Sailing's Duxford-based G-BLSC, was unable to make the trip because of official bureaucracy imposed by the British CAA. Meanwhile, thousands of miles away in New Zealand, plans were being made to acquire and operate a Catalina there. In due course, the group, initially known as the Catalina Company, obtained an American-registered PBY-5A in Arkansas, and this was prepared for the long ferry flight to New Zealand. Sadly, N5404C never reached Auckland as engine failure caused a ditching in the Pacific en route Hawaii–Tahiti on 16 January 1994, following which the unfortunate aircraft sank.

With insurance claims settled, the New Zealanders set about finding a replacement PBY, and settled on Z-CAT in Harare. This time, the ferry flight was accomplished safely. Commencing on 13 October 1994, Z-CAT routed Harare–Nampula–Seychelles–Male–Colombo–Medan– Seletar–Den Passar–Darwin– Cairns–Brisbane–Norfolk

Still in its Peter Stuyvesant Travel Odyssey livery, ZK-PBY flies low over the New Zealand countryside with its floats down for the photographer.
via Marlene Gray

Island–New Plymouth. The trip was completed at New Plymouth on 26 October. The longest leg in terms of distance was that between the Seychelles and Male in the Maldives, a total of 1,210 nautical miles, although adverse wind conditions led to the slightly shorter trip between Colombo and Medan in Indonesia taking the longest time – 11.5 hours.

Since arriving in New Zealand, the Catalina has flown frequently during the air show and tourist season under the banner of the Catalina Group. Soon after arrival in New Zealand, Z-CAT was appropriately re-registered ZK-PBY, marks that had provisionally been reserved for N5404C.

Until the end of 1997, ZK-PBY had continued to fly in the livery it had worn when, as Z-CAT, it had flown the first Peter Stuyvesant Travel Odyssey, although with some minor alterations. However, for the 1998 *Warbirds Over Wanaka* airshow, it was repainted to represent a Soviet Catalina, complete with red stars insignia. This was in line with the general theme of that show, which prominently featured warbirds of Russian origin and service. A few months after the show, the red stars were removed and replaced by RNZAF insignia, the serial NZ4017 and squadron code XX-T. It thus represents a 6 Squadron aircraft, the former US Navy Bu08467, that operated out of Segond Channel, New Hebrides, during 1944 and rescued the crew of a downed USAAF B-24 Liberator south of Nauru Island during one of its 'Dumbo' rescue missions.

The unidentified, former-US Navy PBY hulk acquired in 1999 by the New Zealand Catalina Group. This photo was taken at Ephrata in Washington State before the sale.
Heijo Kuil

in the hands of Hemet Valley Flying Services, which, as Catalina operators themselves, presumably used it for spares recovery. It was structurally complete apart from the rear hull and tail, but still had both a bow turret and blister frames. Wearing the remains of its US Navy colour scheme, it appeared to be a surplus airframe unconverted for commercial use and presumably used by SLAFCO for spares. The only identifying marks on the hull were the side-codes '204', although faint traces of a crudely applied and illegible US civil registration were reportedly visible.

The new owners turned out to be the New Zealand Catalina Group, well known for their operations with the airworthy ZK-PBY described in the entry above. The group took delivery of their new acquisition in February 2000, when it arrived at Ardmore.

Since arriving in New Zealand, the new owners have carried out some research and, based on the hull side-code 204, they believe that the original US Navy serial was Bu33979. This aircraft had its final assignment with the Naval Air Reserve Training unit (NARTU) at Sand Point NAS, Seattle, Washington State, during 1949, and at this time is known to have flown in an overall dark blue colour scheme with orange rear hull band, the hull code 204 and tail code 7T. It does not appear to have been allocated a subsequent US civil registration, however. As side-codes were not limited to specific airframes and could be repeated on different examples, this author believes it prudent to continue to categorise this particular Catalina as 'unidentified' until more positive proof of its pedigree is uncovered.

Table 89.

Registration/Serial	C/n	Type	Place of Manufacture	Previous id(s)
ZK-PBY/'NZ4017' (RNZAF)	CV-357	Canso A	CAN VIC (Cartierville)	Z-CAT C-FJCV, CF-JCV 11054 (RCAF)

Unidentified – The New Zealand Catalina Group, Ardmore, Auckland

Robert Schlaefli, owner/operator of the water bombing company SLAFCO Inc of Moses Lake airfield in Washington State, owns a huge Catalina spares holding, most of which is located on premises in Ephrata. On 30 August 1999, the entire spares cache and his five complete Catalinas were put up for auction. This event was the Catalina sale of the century that never was! Half-way through the proceedings, Schlaefli declared himself dissatisfied with the sale prices being achieved and withdrew the various lots. However, some of the items already hammered down did find their way to their new owners. Amongst these was an unidentified former US Navy PBY amphibian, either a PBY-5A or -6A, that had stood on its undercarriage in the spares compound at Ephrata for some years. Prior to being taken to Ephrata, this Catalina had spent some time at Hemet in California

Table 90.

Registration/Serial	C/n	Type	Place of Manufacture	Previous id(s)
N?	?	?	?	Bu? (US Navy)

Fifteen
SURVIVORS IN CANADA

Before being converted to a fire fighter, CF-CRP flew as a commercial aircraft with Eastern Provincial Airways, in whose livery it is seen on a snowy dispersal.
MAP

C-FCRP – North Atlantic Aviation Museum, Gander, Newfoundland

Appropriately, C-FCRP is preserved at that great gateway to the wartime North Atlantic air routes – Gander – not only as a memorial to the water bombing fleet of the Province of Newfoundland and Labrador, but also as a reminder of the Catalinas/Cansos and their crews that flew from there and out over the grey Atlantic waters during the Second World War.

Initially flown by 162 (BR) Squadron, Royal Canadian Air Force as a Canso A, serial 9837, it was acquired by Canadian Pacific Airlines of Vancouver, British Columbia, very shortly after being struck off RCAF charge in 1945, and it stayed with them until 1957. During this time with CPA, it carried the fleet number 231. After Canadian Pacific, it flew with Trans Labrador Airlines and Eastern Provincial Airways of Gander.

Around the early 1970s, it was converted from a passenger-carrying aircraft to a water bomber and flew in Eastern Canada as Tanker 6 in the vivid orange, green and white striped colours of the Province of Newfoundland and Labrador Firefighting Division, whose main operating base was St Johns,

Newfoundland. Later, in line with changing policy, the hull code was extended to 706.

Whilst operating as a water bomber, C-FCRP is known to have suffered at least two accidents. The first occurred on 28 August 1984, when the nose wheel collapsed upon landing at Deer Lake airfield, Newfoundland. The cause of the accident was attributed to hydraulic pressure loss and a faulty nose-wheel lowering ratchet handle. A contributory factor was the deterioration of hydraulic lines through long service. The second incident was on 6 May 1987. On this occasion, the Catalina suffered a brake failure that resulted in it veering off the runway at Gander and ending up in a somewhat undignified pose outside its hangar, minus its nose wheel and with a collapsed starboard main leg.

Cancelled from the Canadian Civil Aircraft Register in June 1996, C-FCRP passed into the care of the Gander-based North Atlantic Aviation Museum, where it is now on external display in the summer months, still proudly wearing its former owner's high-visibility colour scheme. Along with the other complete airframe exhibits belonging to the museum, it is stored internally during the winter months to protect the airframe.

Table 91.

Registration/ Serial	C/n	Type	Place of Manufacture	Previous id(s)
C-FCRP	CV-271	Canso A	CAN VIC (Cartierville)	CF-CRP 9837 (RCAF)

After a varied career, the one-time OA-10A C-FDFB was retired to a beautiful waterside position at Botwood, Newfoundland, where it now resides with the curious markings E1497.
John Line

C-FDFB/'E1497' – Botwood, Newfoundland

Of all the Catalinas of various marks built in Canada by Canadian Vickers, CV-605 is the youngest survivor, being the fourth from last to leave the production line at Cartierville in Quebec. Indeed, by that time, Canadian Vickers had become Canadair Ltd, which referred to its production Catalinas as the Canadair CL-1. Part of a batch of 57 PBV-1A model Catalinas for the US Navy, it was instead diverted to the USAAF as an OA-10A, along with all the others in that batch. However, its military service was to be of only brief duration.

For a short period from December 1946, it appeared on the US Civil Aircraft Register as NC65715, but it was then sold to Loftleidir Icelandic Airlines in March 1949, and became TF-RVG *Vestfirdingur* in the following July. It was used on domestic flights around Iceland and to Greenland. From February 1952 to 1953, it was stored out of use at Reykjavik before being sold to Eric Cradoc.

In 1953, it returned to Canada, this time as CF-DFB, and commenced a long and varied commercial career in that country, serving as a passenger airliner, survey aircraft and, ultimately, as a fire-fighting water bomber. Its first operators were Aero Magnetic Surveys, Kenting Aviation and Hunting Survey Corporation, all based in Toronto. Then, in 1965, it began a passenger-carrying period with Wheeler Airlines of St Jovite Station, Quebec. It then went to Wheeler Northland Airways of St Jean and, in 1971, to Austin Airways of Timmins, Ontario, before returning to its previous operator in 1976. On 15 April 1974, CF-DFB sustained substantial damage at Hamilton, Ontario, when, on a test flight, debris was struck during a water landing. Damage was caused to the bow section which prevented full nose-wheel extension upon landing back at Hamilton. Larry Milberry's excellent book on Austin Airways shows a photo of CF-DFB at Moosonee following another accident on an unknown date, apparently as a result of leaving the runway. Incidentally, the same book quotes the aircraft's constructor's number as 605 and the company of manufacture as Consolidated, although the correct version is shown in the data below.

In 1978, it was acquired by the Province of Newfoundland and Labrador for conversion by Fields Aircraft Services to a fire-fighting machine, and it remained in use until August 1990, when it was withdrawn and replaced by more modern equipment. During its fire-fighting period, C-FDFB flew with the hull code '1', later changed to '701'. Its registration earned it the affectionate nickname **D**estroy **F**robisher **B**ay!

Now preserved at Botwood Air Force Base, Newfoundland, where it has been since mid-1990, its water bombing livery has been replaced by a rather inaccurate WWII RCAF military camouflage scheme of grey and white. The vertical tail sports the 'serial' E1497, although the reason for this is obscure as it has no obvious relevance to any of the aircraft's true identities, nor does it correspond with any other Catalina or Canso serial.

Table 92.

Registration/Serial	C/n	Type	Place of Manufacture	Previous id(s)
C-FDFB/'E1497'	CV-605	OA-10A	CAN (Cartierville)	CF-DFB TF-RVG NC65715 44-34094 (USAAF) Bu68058 ntu (US Navy)

CF-HFL – Atlantic Canada Aviation Museum, Halifax, Nova Scotia

Although there is a long way to go before CF-HFL becomes a fully restored airframe, it is none the less remarkable that it should be on public display at all, given that it crashed over forty years ago! Unfortunately, it also happens to be one of several surviving Catalinas whose history is open to some doubt, with more than one original identity being attributed to it, depending upon which source of information is relied upon.

The 'favoured' version of this Catalina's pedigree is that it started life at San Diego, California, as constructor's number 110, and was delivered to the US Navy as Bu05021 on 27 February 1942. It served at first with the Transition Training Squadron Pacific at San Diego, but went on to serve with various other units, including an assignment to the Atlantic Fleet at Norfolk, Virginia, from September 1943. By late November 1944, Bu05021 was with HEDRON 2/FAW-5, but in the following January it was transferred to the US Coast Guard at Miami. This

posting was a brief one, and in July the Catalina was flown to Seattle and retirement from active military service, finally being struck off on 31 January 1946. It then became NC18444 and was owned at some stage by California Maritime Airlines of Long Beach. Upon the liquidation of that company, it was acquired by the aircraft broker Aero Corp, which sold it on to Caribbean International for operations in the Bahamas, where she was registered VP-BAR in August 1950. Remaining with this airline, it was transferred to the Jamaican register as VP-JAU in February 1951.

Two years later, it was sold to Dominion of Canada Aircraft Brokers, which in turn disposed of it to its final operator, Eastern Provincial Airlines, in November 1953. By now carrying the Canadian registration CF-HFL, it was one of several Catalinas used by this company. On 1 October 1957, 'HFL flew from Goose Bay, Labrador, to Sona Lake with a load of fuel oil. On the return journey, and about fifty miles out from Goose, engine power was lost and the pilot in command was forced to land the Catalina amongst tree tops. It ended up battered and bruised in a marsh, with substantial damage to hull and wings. Although some removable parts were salvaged, the main hulk stayed in place, abandoned and more-or-less forgotten.

Eventually, the wreck was acquired by Lionel Clark, who donated it to the Atlantic Canada Aviation Museum of Halifax, Nova Scotia. Of course, recovery was to be the main challenge, and this was achieved with the aid of a 450 Squadron RCAF CH-147 Chinook helicopter that hauled the old bird aloft as an underslung load. This milestone event occurred on 30 October 1986. The initial destination was Goose Bay although the dismantled airframe was later roaded to Halifax for storage and eventual rebuild. Despite some forty years in the open, the Catalina still bore its faded EPA livery when it was recovered, although a vandal had hacked away the section of hull bearing the airline's motif! In recent times, the museum has had hangarage built, and the Catalina has been taken under cover for restoration. One British publication has listed this Catalina as being on display at the Western Canada Aviation Museum in Winnipeg, Manitoba – this is not the case!

As mentioned earlier, alternative identities have been quoted for this aircraft, namely Bu08087/N33301.

The battered but substantially intact airframe of the former Eastern Provincial Airways CF-HFL after being deposited on the airfield at Goose Bay in October 1986.
Mike Whitehead

Table 93.

Registration/Serial	C/n	Type	Place of Manufacture	Previous id(s)
CF-HFL	'110'/520	PBY-5A	CON SD	VP-JAU VP-BAR NC18444 Bu05021 (US Navy)

C-FIZU – Province of Newfoundland and Labrador Air Services Division, St Johns, Newfoundland

Several non-Canadian-manufactured Catalinas that were constructed as tall-tailed PBY-6A variants later saw service in Canada and were re-equipped with standard PBY-5A rudders to satisfy Canadian airworthiness regulations. C-FIZU is one such Catalina.

Operated for many years as a forest fire fighter with

Although built as a tall-tailed PBY-6A, CF-IZU was clearly displaying its PBY-5-style rudder when working out of Gander with the Newfoundland Forest Service in July 1975.
Adrian Balch

Seen not long after being converted to a fire fighter, CF-NJB of Kenting displays its drop doors in the hull. The blisters have been replaced by an observation dome, and wheel hub covers have been added.
Aviation Photo News

the Province of Newfoundland and Labrador, it was first civilianised as N10014 before being re-registered CF-IZU with World Wide Airways in 1956. It subsequently flew briefly with Montreal Air Services and, for ten years or so, with Eastern Provincial Airways, before being acquired by the Province of Newfoundland and Labrador in 1966. It flew as a water bomber with the tail code '4', which was later lengthened to '704' worn on the forward hull. By the late 1990s, C-FIZU was rarely in use and was being held in reserve at Gander in case of need.

Table 94.

Registration/Serial	C/n	Type	Place of Manufacture	Previous id(s)
C-FIZU	2019	PBY-6A	CON NO	CF-IZU N10014 Bu46655 (US Navy)

C-FNJB – Nanaimo, Vancouver Island, British Columbia

Until the mid-1990s, C-FNJB flew in the distinctive green and bright yellow livery of the Province of Saskatchewan Air Transportation Service forest-fire-fighting division with whom it flew as a water bomber. Latterly, it flew alongside Canadair CL-215 and Grumman Tracker bombers, ultimately being deposed by these more up-to-date aircraft.

Unlike the other two Cansos (C-FNJF and C-FUAW) used by the Province, C-FNJB was built on the original Canadian Vickers production line at St Hubert prior to construction being switched to its new facility at Cartierville. It was built for the Royal Canadian Air Force and served between mid-1943 and 1961, being converted to a military transport aircraft in 1945, sans blisters and nose turret. Shortly after retirement in 1961, it was taken on by Kenting Aviation in Toronto, became CF-NJB and then started its long commercial career as a fire fighter. The conversion work and installation of internal tankage was carried out by local specialists Field Aviation.

Kenting frequently leased its Cats to other operators,

and CF-NJB is known to have served for at least three summer seasons in the South of France with the Protection Civile based at Marseille. It was first registered to them as F-ZBAR for the summer of 1966, and was then flown as F-ZBBC during 1968 and 1969. It is possible that it also served in France in 1967. It was the second Protection Civile Catalina to fly as F-ZBAR, the first having been written off in a crash in July 1964. This latter aircraft was construction number CV-449, ex-RCAF 11000. Both F-ZBARs flew with red identification stripes and were known as *Pelican Rouge*.

In October 1969, CF-NJB returned to Canada from France via Dublin, and Kenting eventually disposed of it to Norcanair of Prince Albert, Saskatchewan, which at that time was responsible for fire-fighting operations in the Province. It flew with that company as Tanker 10. The Province itself became the new owner in 1980, and it was renumbered as Tanker 9.

Maintained in superb condition, C-FNJB attracted the attention of potential new owners when it was put up for disposal, and it was initially purchased by Hicks and Lawrence Ltd and flown to St Thomas, Ontario, in company with C-FNJF. By mid-1997, both Cansos were to be found there out on the tarmac. They were then put up for sale again and were acquired by a Malaysian consortium which was intending using both these former fire fighters on tourist flights in Southern Africa, based in Zimbabwe. The long journey westward was accomplished, only this time way beyond Saskatchewan, to Nanaimo on beautiful Vancouver Island. Here, Ray Williams of Catalina Air Services set about de-converting both Cansos from their former water bombing configuration. Modifications included the removal of the water bombing equipment, the installation of a rear air stair and the fitting of bulged windows and clear, frame-free blisters. C-FNJF was in fact the first to be so converted, whilst C-FNJB was initially placed in store. It too was modified like C-FNJF, in due course. Unfortunately, it seems that the exciting plans for these two aircraft have been abandoned, and both were put up for sale, still located in British Columbia, in the second half of 1999.

Table 95.

Registration/Serial	C/n	Type	Place of Manufacture	Previous id(s)
C-FNJB	CV-249	Canso A	CAN VIC (St Hubert)	CF-NJB F-ZBBC CF-NJB F-ZBAR(2) CF-NJB 9815 (RCAF)

C-FNJC – Province of Newfoundland and Labrador Air Services Division, St Johns, Newfoundland

In its long life, this Catalina has flown as a military aircraft, passenger-carrying transport and forest fire fighter, in that order. It was one of many Catalinas delivered to the USAAF after the original order for US Navy PBV-1As, of which it was one, was cancelled. Photos exist of a USAAF OA-10A with the nose code 929 whilst serving with the 2nd ERS (Emergency Rescue Squadron), 13th Air Force, in the South Pacific during 1944/5, and this code may well tie in with C-FNJC's former identity of 44-33929. Wherever it served, it must have spent some considerable time in storage after being 'demobbed' as it appears to have been first registered as a civil aircraft to Eastern Provincial Airways of Gander, Newfoundland, as late as 1965. EPA used it as a commercial transport until the late 1960s, when it was acquired by the Province of Newfoundland and Labrador for use as a fire fighter, and it has remained in their ownership ever since, although by the late 1990s it was rarely in use, remaining in storage at Gander much of the time.

Initially flown in relatively sober civilian colours, it was later repainted in the fleet's stunning orange, white and green livery for high visibility in fire zones. It is known to have carried two fleet numbers, namely '5' and '701', the latter being allocated after the withdrawal of

In hangared storage at Gander during the summer of 1999, C-FNJC displays its orange, green and white colours with hull code 701 and Province of Newfoundland titles. It saw wartime service with the USAAF as 44-33929.
John Line

sister aircraft C-FDFB that had previously been the holder of that number .

At least one accident has been suffered by this Catalina, and it is believed that this occurred at the end of its ownership by Eastern Provincial; indeed, the event may have precipitated its change of ownership. This incident happened on 28 April 1967, at the start of a training flight with two crew on board. Because of a misunderstanding, the take-off from Gander was attempted with rudder gust locks still in place. The aircraft veered off the runway when swing could not be corrected with rudder input, and substantial damage was caused upon impact with a snow bank.

Table 96.

Registration/Serial	C/n	Type	Place of Manufacture	Previous id(s)
C-FNJC	CV-430	OA-10A	CAN VIC (Cartierville)	CF-NJC 44-33929 (USAAF) Bu67893 ntu (US Navy)

C-FNJE – Buffalo Airways, Yellowknife, North West Territories

C-FNJE spent much of the last twenty years or so of its post-war commercial career flying with the Province of Newfoundland and Labrador water bombing fleet. However, the fact that it has only ever had one civil registration identity belies the number of operators that it has flown with, albeit that in some cases these have been the same basic companies but trading under different names!

A Cartierville-built Canso A, it was originally serialled 11094 and flew with 162 (BR) Squadron in Iceland during the Second World War. It continued to serve the RCAF until 1961, when it was officially struck off charge, and it was then entered onto the Canadian Civil Aircraft Register as CF-NJE. The only subsequent change to this registration was in the mid-1970s when the Canadian authorities changed the presentation of all registration marks by moving the dash from after the 'F' to after the 'C', CF-NJE thus becoming C-FNJE.

Its many operators included Chiupka Airways, Northland Airlines, Midwest Airlines, Nordair and Ilford Riverton Airways, all of which were based in Manitoba. This string of owners took CF-NJE up to the early 1970s, and then, from 1973 to 1976, it flew with St Felicien Air Service of Roberval, Quebec. During this time, it also flew with Survair titles. Finally, around 1978, it became a fire fighter in Newfoundland, operating with the fleet number '7', later '702'.

Like many Catalinas that have survived to the present day, its career has not been accident free, and C-FNJE is known to have survived substantial damage sustained in an accident on 2 September 1977, at Helen's Falls near Fort Chimo, Quebec. At the time of this incident, it was flying a charter with two crew and nine passengers, all of whom were uninjured. The co-pilot elected to land with a 10 kt tailwind but touched down long. The captain took control in order to effect an overshoot, but shortly after becoming airborne again, the port wing and float struck the rocky shoreline alongside the water landing strip being used. Despite the impact, the crew were able to

Nordair's CF-NJE shows the configuration it last flew with in RCAF service – 'clipper' bow and cargo hatch with observation dome. At the time this photo was taken, the airframe had had its nose-wheel doors removed.
MAP

remain in controlled flight, and a safe landing was subsequently accomplished at a nearby airfield.

Having managed to get through almost twenty years' service fighting forest fires in Eastern Canada, it was sold off to Hicks and Lawrence of Ontario, which, by the late 1990s, was buying up surplus Catalinas as they became available from the Provincial fire-fighting fleets. C-FNJE was made available for sale or lease, and an early lessee was Enterprise Air, which used it at Oshawa to train pilots for the Canadian Air Legend Catalina C-FCRR prior to it departing for Africa for film work. C-FNJE was then one of several PBYs acquired by Buffalo Airways for fire-fighting duties in the North West Territories of Canada. Although it retained its Newfoundland colours, the NWT coat of arms was emblazoned on the vertical tail surfaces and it continues to fly with the hull code '702'. Sadly, C-FNJE was involved in a water pick-up accident at Inuvik, NWT on 24 July 2001, as a result of which it sank. At the time of writing it was not known whether salvage was likely.

Table 97.

Registration/ Serial	C/n	Type	Place of Manufacture	Previous id(s)
C-FNJE	CV-437	Canso A	CAN VIC (Cartierville)	CF-NJE 11094 (RCAF)

C-FNJF – Nanaimo, Vancouver Island, British Columbia

Yet another surviving Catalina that owes its continued existence to the need for aerial fire-fighting aircraft, C-FNJF flew in this role for many years, not only in various Canadian Provinces but also in the South of France.

Its military career as a Royal Canadian Air Force

CF-NJF is currently to be found at Nanaimo on Vancouver Island, where it waits to see if it will be flying to Zimbabwe for tourist flights. This shot was taken when being used by Kenting as a water bomber.
MAP

Canso A, serial 11005, included a post-war spell with the famous 413 *Tusker* Squadron which had operated Catalina flying boats with distinction within the Royal Air Force in Scotland and the Indian Ocean Theatre during the Second World War. When 11005 was with 413 Squadron, it was engaged in more peaceful aerial mapping and photographic reconnaissance out of Rockliffe, Ontario, work that mostly took it northward and up into Arctic regions.

In 1963, it renounced its military identity and took up ownership with Kenting Aviation of Toronto, which had it converted to a water bomber by Field Aviation. It spent several seasons in France, as Kenting hired its water bombing fleet out on a regular basis. In France, it was operated by the French Government body, Protection Civile, based at Marseille. In common with all the Protection Civile Catalinas, it bore a coloured identification stripe, in this case blue, on the rear hull, and was known by the call sign *Pelican Bleu*. It is known to have flown in France during the 1966, '67 and '68 seasons, and carried two different French Government registrations, F-ZBAY and F-ZBBD.

In 1974, it parted company with Kenting as it disposed of its fleet, and it then flew for a while with Prince Albert-based Norcanair on fire-fighting duties in Saskatchewan. It was painted in a vivid white, grey and dayglo orange livery with the hull code '14'. Around 1980, it was taken over by the Province of Saskatchewan fire-fighting service at La Ronge, and was eventually repainted bright yellow with green and red trim, coded '7'.

As one of a fleet of three Catalinas flown by the Province, it soldiered on for many years, maintained in superb condition and operated alongside more modern equipment in the fleet, namely Grumman Trackers and Canadair CL-215s. On one memorable occasion, it flew in a local air display with its two sister aircraft, and a formation water drop was carried out at low level!

All good things come to an end and the Province decided to dispose of its Catalinas. C-FNJF flew to St Thomas, Ontario, with C-FNJB, where it was placed on the market by Hicks and Lawrence. Whilst there, both Catalinas were surveyed by representatives of a Zimbabwe-based concern owned by Malaysian businessmen. At that time, they were in the early stages of setting up a tourist charter operation based in Harare in which the two Catalinas were to feature strongly.

In due course, both C-FNJF and C-FNJB were purchased and flown across the Rockies to Nanaimo on Vancouver Island. Once there, C-FNJF was immediately hangared, and work started on stripping out the water tanks from within the hull and replacing them with internal fittings suitable for passenger carrying, including an air stair and panoramic view blisters. The work was carried out by Ray Williams and his local company Catalina Aero Services. C-FNJF remained at Nanaimo and was put up for sale in late 1999 without the operation in Zimbabwe getting off the ground.

Table 98.

Registration/ Serial	C/n	Type	Place of Manufacture	Previous id(s)
C-FNJF	CV-283	Canso A	CAN VIC (Cartierville)	CF-NJF
				F-ZBBD
				CF-NJF
				F-ZBAY
				CF-NJF
				11005 (RCAF)

CF-NJL – David Dorosh, Gananoque, Ontario

CF-NJL is a kind of legend amongst surviving Catalinas, not because of any particularly heroic action or long-distance flights it may have been involved in, but because of its amazing inactivity over a period of many years! Due to its preference for terra firma and the fact that it has been kept hangared and well maintained for so long, it would make an attractive purchase for any prospective Catalina owner, that is always assuming that its present owner can be persuaded to sell!

Following its construction by Canadian Vickers at Cartierville, Quebec, it was delivered to the Royal Canadian Air Force as Canso A, serial number 11093, and it remained on military charge from then until as late as

When on the inventory of 408 Squadron, RCAF, Canso A 11093 carried the hull codes MN-093. The sliding hatches on either side of the hull are clearly visible in the open position. It is now stored at Gananoque, Ontario, by owner David Dorosh.
Air Britain

1961. Post-war, it had been on the strength of 413 (PR) *Tusker* Squadron as a survey aircraft and 408 (PR) *Goose* Squadron, both based at Rockliffe, Ontario. Whilst with the latter squadron, it carried the hull code MN-093.

By the time that it was 'demobbed', 11093 had been relieved of its surplus wartime equipment, so both nose turret and blisters had been removed. In all other respects, however, it was pretty much a stock Canso. It was quickly acquired by David Dorosh, of Edmonton, Alberta, once it was advertised for sale, and it has remained in his ownership ever since, a continuous run of more than 35 years! And so the legend gradually got around – that out in the middle of nowhere in an old wooden RCAF hangar, there was an almost original Canso sitting gathering dust whilst its owner steadfastly held on to it!

In fact, CF-NJL, as it had become, is well looked after and is occasionally hauled out of its equally antique home and has its engines turned. The aircraft is still in its 1960s RCAF colours, although all nationality markings have been removed. The civil registration is still carried as CF-NJL, rather than the later C-FNJL version, which adds to the old fashioned air in the hangar. Perhaps one day, Catalina enthusiast David Dorosh will part with his prized possession – whoever acquires it will certainly be the beneficiary of a very-low-hours airframe. In the meantime, it is still lovingly looked after by its owner.

Table 99.

Registration/ Serial	C/n	Type	Place of Manufacture	Previous id(s)
CF-NJL	CV-435	Canso A	CAN VIC (Cartierville)	11093 (RCAF)

C-FOFI – Buffalo Airways, Yellowknife, North West Territories

In well over fifty years, and until its more recent disposal, Canso A construction number CV-343 had flown with only two operators – the Royal Canadian Air Force and the Provincial Government of Newfoundland and Labrador. Although details of its wartime service are obscure, it is on record that, post-war, it was assigned to 103 Search and Rescue Flight based at Greenwood, Nova

One of the last Catalina water bombers still in active service, C-FOFI currently flies with Buffalo Airways in the North-West Territories. When this photo was taken, probably at Goose Bay, it was still with the Province of Newfoundland fire-fighting fleet as Ianker 3. In the background is an RAF Short Belfast.
via Pavel Vincenc

C-FPQK is now stored for future display at its original birthplace, St Hubert, Quebec. In 1991, it was still working hard as a fire fighter with the Quebec Government fleet.
MAP

Scotia, with whom it carried the Squadron hull code QZ-047.

Its military service came to an end in April of 1962, and it was snapped up by the Newfoundland authorities. Converted to a water bomber, it worked subsequently in many areas of Eastern Canada as a fire-fighting aircraft, and has flown with the fleet codes 3 and 703. Sadly, the Canso was eventually deemed too long in the tooth to compete with more-up-to-date equipment, and the Newfoundland fire-fighting service pensioned off most of its fleet. C-FOFI was sold to Hicks and Lawrence, and by 1998, that company had passed it on to Buffalo Airways, with which it continued to be used against forest fires in the North West Territories. Like its sister aircraft, C-FNJE, it has continued to sport its former owner's vivid orange, white and green livery and hull code 703.

Table 100.

Registration/ Serial	C/n	Type	Place of Manufacture	Previous id(s)
C-FOFI	CV-343	Canso A	CAN VIC (Cartierville)	CF-OFI 11047 (RCAF)

C-FPQK – Foundation Aerovision, St Hubert, Quebec

For many years, the Provincial Government of Quebec, in common with several other similar bodies in Canadian Provinces, maintained a fleet of Canso or Catalina water bombers for use against forest fires. Again, like several others, it has gradually introduced more modern equipment, such as the Canadair CL-215, in order to replace the venerable PBY, although it has to be said that the piston-powered Canadairs are themselves getting a

little long in the tooth and are being superseded by turbine-powered CL-415s. The Quebec Cansos all carried sequential Canadian registrations in the CF- PQ* range, and it is only in the last few years that they have been retired and dispersed.

Unlike its sister aircraft in the Quebec fire-fighting fleet that served into the 1990s, C-FPQK was built at St Hubert by Canadian Vickers rather than at its Cartierville factory to which later production was switched. It flew with the Royal Canadian Air Force as serial number 9830 and remained on military charge until it was struck from the inventory in 1961 after eighteen years' service.

In 1965, it became a water bomber with the Quebec Department of Transport and flew with them as fleet number '12', later being re-numbered '712'. Its colour scheme in the early days consisted of bright yellow with red trim and bi-lingual titles in English and French. Later, the red trim was changed to blue, which looked equally smart, the Quebec Catalina fleet always being maintained in immaculate condition.

Offered for sale along with the others in the fleet in early 1993, it was subsequently gifted to the Foundation Aerovision Quebec, St Hubert, in June 1994, most appropriately as St Hubert was its birthplace. At present, C-FPQK and the numerous other aircraft acquired by the Foundation Aerovision are stored whilst the museum is prepared for opening.

Table 101.

Registration/ Serial	C/n	Type	Place of Manufacture	Previous id(s)
C-FPQK	CV-264	Canso A	CAN VIC (St Hubert)	CF-PQK 9830 (RCAF)

The Canadian Warplane Heritage acquired a Canso A amphibian in the mid-1990s. In 2000, it was painted to represent the RCAF aircraft 9754 as flown by Flt Lt David Hornell. This study was taken on its first public appearance after the hull blisters had been put back in place, *Eric Dumigan*

'9754'/C-FPQL, Canadian Warplane Heritage, Hamilton Airport, Mount Hope, Ontario

'Lucky 13' seems to apply to this particular Canso as, wearing this hull number, later amended to '713', it survived use from 1963 through to 1994 as a water bomber in action against forest fires in Eastern Canada, firstly with the Quebec Department of Transportation and then with the Government of Quebec when its registered owner was renamed. It had previously seen use with the Royal Canadian Air Force, at least part of its wartime service being spent at Patricia Bay, Vancouver Island, with 3 (BR) Operational Training Unit. It has proved to be lucky as it remains in flying condition on the North American air display scene.

After being offered for tender by the Quebec authorities in March 1993, it was one of two Cansos obtained in the following year by Conifair/Royal Aviation, of Mount Joli, Quebec, which planned to continue using both Cansos as fire fighters, the other aircraft being C-FPQM. However, shortly after acquisition, both were placed back on the market. Fortunately, C-FPQL found a ready buyer in the form of the Canadian Warplane Heritage (CWH) of Hamilton, Ontario.

The CWH maintains a large collection of airworthy and ground-based aircraft that commemorate the Canadian's contribution to the Second World War, and it was entirely appropriate that it should acquire a Catalina. At one time, the CWH had been hoping to buy one of the former Avalon Aviation fleet because of its wartime success against a German U-boat, but that was not to be, and C-FCRR, the example involved, eventually

went to France, much to the disappointment of more than a few Canadian enthusiasts. C-FPQL put matters right, however, and its place in the collection meant that for a time at least the CWH had an example of each of the types that led to Second World War Victoria Crosses for RCAF airmen – Canso, Lancaster and Chance Vought Corsair. Sadly, financial considerations led to the disposal of the Corsair in 1998.

Once with the CWH, C-FPQL embarked on a busy schedule of air display appearances in Eastern Canada and the USA, perhaps partly benefiting from the fact that, around that time, the National Warplane Museum of Geneseo, New York, grounded its own Catalina N7057C through shortage of cash. Initially, C-FPQL retained its Quebec Government colours of yellow overall with blue trim, but in the early summer of 2000, it was repainted to represent the RCAF Canso A, serial 9754, that Flt Lt David Hornell flew when he gained his posthumous Victoria Cross. Then, in late June, it had blisters placed back on the rear hull and made its first public appearance with them at the Canada Day airshow at the National Aviation Museum in Ottawa.

Table 102.

Registration/ Serial	C/n	Type	Place of Manufacture	Previous id(s)
C-FPQL	CV-417	Canso A	CAN VIC (Cartierville)	CF-PQL 11084 (RCAF)

C-FPQM – Buffalo Airways, Yellowknife, North West Territories

This Canso served with the RCAF from the time it rolled off the Cartierville factory floor until it was declared surplus to their requirements in 1960. During this time it flew with the serial 11088. Its first identity as a civilian aircraft was CF-GMS, but it was subsequently acquired by the Quebec authorities and converted to take the large

Immaculate Canso water bomber C-FPQM of Buffalo Airways taxies past the photographer at Yellowknife, NWT, in June 1998. Colours are yellow overall, with red trim and black lettering, with the exception of the Buffalo Air titles and emblem, which are green. The letter M appears in yellow in the bombardier's panel.
Michael Prophet

Although now flying with Buffalo Airways in the North-West Territories, this view of C-FUAW was taken at La Ronge in April 1991, when it was still Tanker 8 of the Province of Saskatchewan forestry protection fleet.
Ron Mak

water tanks necessary for the aerial fire-fighting role, becoming CF-PQM, coded '14', later '714' in the process. It stayed in Quebec until retired in early 1993, when it was taken out of service and offered for tender.

After the sales process, C-FPQM, along with sister aircraft C-FPQL, was purchased by Conifair/Royal Aviation of Mount Joli, Quebec, in June 1994. It later passed on to Buffalo Airways for use in the North West Territories, still as a fire fighter. Although remaining in basic yellow overall, Buffalo replaced the blue Quebec trim with red, a finish that harked back to the early days in Quebec when its Cansos wore a similar livery. Its fire-fighting hull code is still 714.

Table 103.

Registration/ Serial	C/n	Type	Place of Manufacture	Previous id(s)
C-FPQM	CV-425	Canso A	CAN VIC (Cartierville)	CF-PQM CF-GMS 11088 (RCAF)

C-FUAW – Buffalo Airways, Yellowknife, North West Territories

Until mid-1997, C-FUAW was one of the three Canso As still in use in the forest-fire-fighting industry in the Province of Saskatchewan, based at La Ronge. Painted in the distinctive green and yellow livery of the Province of Saskatchewan water bombing fleet, it carried the hull code '8'.

Canadian Vickers built C-FUAW for the Royal Canadian Air Force as 11024 and it remained a military aircraft until 1961 when it was withdrawn and the Government sought a new owner on the commercial market. Initially, it was allocated the civilian identity CF-NTK, but this registration was not used and, instead, it became CF-UAW with Kenting of Toronto. It stayed with that company as a fire fighter until 1971, although, unlike many of Kenting's Cats, it does not seem to have

flown out to France for use in the summer season there by the Protection Civile. In 1971, it went to Norcanair in Saskatchewan, and they kept it until 1980, when it was sold to the Province.

When the Saskatchewan fleet was sold off, the other two aircraft went to the same new owner, who intended using them on tourist flights in Africa. C-FUAW, however, stayed relatively local by going to Buffalo Airways in the North West Territories, Again, unlike its two sister aircraft, it retained its tankage for use as a water bomber and now continues to fly as Tanker 708.

It is worth noting that the Canadian authorities list the construction number for C-FUAW as CV-201. This seems unlikely as Canadian Vickers Canso production started at CV-240. CV-302 is the generally accepted version.

Table 104.

Registration/ Serial	C/n	Type	Place of Manufacture	Previous id(s)
C-FUAW	CV-302	Canso A	CAN VIC (Cartierville)	CF-UAW CF-NTK ntu 11024 (RCAF)

RCAF 9825 – Memorial Military Museum, Campbellford, Ontario

In the small Southern Ontario town of Campbellford can be found Harold Carlaw's Memorial Military Museum. For many years now, retired local businessman Harold Carlaw has been accumulating former Royal Canadian Air Force aircraft and artefacts, and the back lot of the premises on which the Museum stands is full of airframes that have been transported to Campbellford from all over Canada. Looming large over all these relics is a Canso!

To be precise, it is a Canso hull sans wings and tail feathers, but a genuine ex-RCAF Canso none the less. It was struck off RCAF charge in August 1950, and

Harold Carlaw's Canso hulk at Campbellford, Ontario, in 1996. The hull is more or less complete, but it lacks wings.
Harold Carlaw

An official RCAF photo dated 12 February 1945, showing Canso A 11007 at its Tofino crash site. The accident happened five days before. The aircraft looks essentially the same still.
via Larry Niven/P. Evans

temporarily stored at Fort Erie before being trucked to Brighton, Ontario. The Canadian Crown Assets Corporation had sold it to George Ventress, and it was one of at least three, possibly four, Cansos to be found there at Brighton in his ownership. One of these others was converted into a motor cruiser for use on the neighbouring lake. This second airframe has also survived and is with Ray Cox in the Seattle area as a spares source. Yet another Brighton airframe is now at Geneseo in New York State.

Once Harold Carlaw had transported his Canso to Campbellford, he set about establishing the identity of his prize. Told to look for the serial plate behind the instrument panel, he found it to reveal the RCAF serial 9825. Although still lying dismantled in the storage compound, it was decided to paint the serial and squadron codes on the hull. Unfortunately, the painter got things wrong, and the finished article ended up as serial 9528, coded Z-BD. Subsequently, it was corrected to 9825/ ZD-B, thus representing a Canso of 116 (BR) Squadron, RCAF, when based at Dartmouth, Nova Scotia, during the period August 1943, to June 1945.

Table 105.

Registration/ Serial	C/n	Type	Place of Manufacture	Previous id(s)
9825 (RCAF)	CV-259	Canso A	CAN VIC (St Hubert)	–

RCAF 11007 – ex-Royal Canadian Air Force, Radar Hill, Tofino, Vancouver Island, British Columbia

Although PBY wrecks are generally outside the scope of this section of the book, 11007 is included because the wreck is virtually complete! Not only that but it is still to be found at its original crash site!

At the time of its accident on 8 February 1945, Canso A 11007/A was officially on the strength of 6 (BR) Squadron, Royal Canadian Air Force, although it had been loaned to 4 (BR) Squadron based at Tofino on Vancouver Island. It had been detailed to fly an anti-submarine mission out of Coal Harbour, but was forced down by engine trouble shortly after departing Tofino

airfield for the return flight. 11007 had taken off at 23.00 hours and was not far clear of the end of the runway when the port engine quit. The pilot, Ronnie Scholes, attempted to make it back to Tofino but was too low to turn and unable to sustain sufficient height, so elected to carry out a straight-ahead forced landing in a forested area on Radar Hill, fortunately without any serious injury to the crew members. Having been assessed as beyond salvage, some moveable parts were taken away from the wreck, which was left at the spot. It was officially struck off RCAF charge on 13 April 1945, some eighteen months after being delivered.

Because of the remoteness of the site within the Pacific Rim Park in which it lies, 11007 has survived intact and without any significant vandalism. The Canadian Museum of Flight and Transportation at Langley, British Columbia, is interested in recovering 11007 for display at its site, and in 1997 was negotiating with the property owner for authorisation to remove the airframe to Langley for restoration. Some years ago, the wreck was apparently in the ownership of the Commonwealth Military Aviation Museum, now known as the British Columbia Aviation Museum. For the time being though, the Canso remains on its lonely crash site surrounded by pine forest.

Table 106.

Registration/ Serial	C/n	Type	Place of Manufacture	Previous id(s)
11007 (RCAF)	CV-285	Canso A	CAN VIC (Cartierville)	--

RCAF 11087 – National Aviation Museum, Rockcliffe, Ontario

11087 is one of a very small number of PBYs that have survived without having had a post-war commercial career – indeed, it remained on the strength of the Royal Canadian Air Force from its delivery in June 1944 until its preservation.

It was constructed by Canadair at Cartierville and flew with 121 (S&R) Flight out of Sea Island, Vancouver, post-war. It would have carried the hull codes QT-087

The National Aviation Museum collection at Rockcliffe, Ontario, includes a Canso A, serial 11087. Unfortunately, it is held in storage and is not normally on public view, a great pity for an aircraft with such a distinguished RCAF service.

with that unit. Other users included Eastern Air Command, North West Air Command, 102 (S&R) Flight at Trenton, Ontario and 103 (S&R) Flight at Greenwood, Nova Scotia. Once it had been retired from service in the early 1960s, it was flown to the National Aeronautical Collection of Canada at Rockcliffe, Ontario, where it has remained ever since, although the name of the collection

changed to the National Aviation Museum in 1982. Sadly, no particular prominence has been given to this exhibit, at least in recent times, and it currently languishes in hangared storage. It wears a somewhat worn camouflage scheme and really looks as if it could do with some attention. Certainly the type's reputation during the Second World War and its lengthy post-war RCAF service qualify it for a more public position within the museum.

Table 107.

Registration/Serial	C/n	Type	Place of Manufacture	Previous id(s)
11087 (RCAF)	CV-423	Canso A	CAN VIC (Cartierville)	--

Sixteen
SURVIVORS IN CENTRAL AND SOUTH AMERICA

Taxiing out at Tabatinga airfield in Brazil during November 1977 is CA-10 6527. At this time, the remaining FAB Catalinas were still in use on supply flights in the interior, using both land and water to alight on.
Ron Mak

BRAZIL

6527 – Museu Aeroespacial da Força Aérea Brasileira, Campo dos Afonsos Air Base, Rio de Janiero

Brazil operated Catalinas of various marks both during and after the Second World War. Although mainly originating from United States Navy stocks, a few came from the Royal Canadian Air Force, and the example in the Brazilian Air Force Museum is one of these.

6527 was a product of the Sea Island, Vancouver, factory of Boeing Aircraft of Canada. In fact, it was the second Catalina to be built there and, as such, was one of a batch for the RCAF that was constructed from parts supplied by Consolidated in San Diego. First flown in the summer of 1942, it was taken on charge as an RCAF

Canso A on 3 December that year and remained on strength until the beginning of October 1946. It is known to have spent at least part of its Canadian career with 3 (BR) Training Unit at Patricia Bay, Vancouver Island, British Columbia.

Along with five other ex-RCAF Cansos, it was sold to the Força Aérea Brasileira (FAB) and flew with them until July 1980, after which it was delivered to Campo dos Afonsos for preservation. Prior to this, it had been used on supply missions deep into the Amazon region of Brazil in the days before airstrips were carved out of the jungle. It was therefore regularly operated from the mighty Amazon river by its unit, 1° ETA (Esquadrao de Transporte Aéreo). Its normal base was Belém. The Brazilian serial 6527 was at various times prefixed by the letters CA (C = transport, A = Amphibian). In addition, the Catalinas were allocated the FAB type number 10. Thus, the serial was presented as CA-10 6527, CA-10A 6527 and C-10A 6527 at different periods in the aircraft's service. One unexplained detail to be found in the aircraft's documentation is the 'constructor's number' BP.3075. The origin of this is not known.

This venerable Catalina still sports the attractive grey and white FAB colour scheme that it wore for many years,

Showing one of the several styles of serial presentation used by the FAB, C-10A 6552 was the sole PBY-6A on the inventory. In this June, 1988 photo, it is seen on gate guardian duties at Belém air base.
Ron Mak

and in addition, carries the badge of 1 ETA on its tail, namely a winged tortoise and the motto '*I go slow but I get there*'.

Table 108.

Registration/ Serial	C/n	Type	Place of Manufacture	Previous id(s)
6527 (FAB)	21981/ 'BP.3075'	Canso A	BOE CAN	9752 (RCAF)

6552 – Forca Aérea Brasiliera, Belém Air Force Base, Belém

6552 was the odd Catalina in the Força Aérea Brasiliera inventory, it being the only PBY-6A model to be operated by them. The seventh PBY-6A to be built, it rolled off the New Orleans production line as Bu46643, destined for the US Navy. It was accepted on charge on 20 February 1945, and was struck off in August 1956. After storage at Litchfield Park in Arizona, it became N9556C on the US Civil Aircraft Register, and eventually passed to the FAB, possibly as an attrition replacement. Later, it was operated by Panair do Brazil and Cruzeiro do Sul, and was registered intitially as PT-BBQ, then PP-PEB, before returning to the FAB. Eventually, it was withdrawn again, and after a period of storage at Manaus, it was flown to Belém for further storage and eventual preservation. It is now to be found in 1° ETA markings in the

centre of the air base, although there are plans to have it restored further and moved to a new museum in Belém's city centre.

Table 109.

Registration/ Serial	C/n	Type	Place of Manufacture	Previous id(s)
6552 (FAB)	2007	PBY-6A	CON NO	PP-PEB PT-BBQ 6552 (FAB) N9556C Bu46643 (US Navy)

CHILE

CC-CGY – Museo Nacional de Aéronautico Chile, Los Cerrillos Airport, Santiago, Chile

Unlike its three fellow ASPAR Catalinas, CC-CGY has not enjoyed a flying role for many years, and has in fact suffered the indignity of acting as a spares source for its colleagues in order to keep them flying. It is now most unlikely that it will ever fly again, as for many years it has occupied a position in the aircraft graveyard at Santiago's airport, a sorry shadow of its former self. Now it is in the hands of the National Aeronautical Museum of Chile and hopefully will be restored to static display standard in due course.

Intended for the United States Navy as a PBV-1A, it was instead diverted to the USAAF as a model OA-10A, and was delivered from Canadian Vickers as 44-34009. Nothing is known of its subsequent post-war time with the US civil markings N62043, but it became CF-IHC in Canada in the mid-1950s. Sometime after this, it had its

Still in full Aéronavale livery, aircraft 20 is loaded as deck cargo on the *Buque Andino* in the port at Papeete before being shipped to South America in August 1983.
Peter Keating Collection

blister turrets removed and flew with the Canadian Marconi Company as an airborne test and development laboratory. It was later flown by Quebec-based Wheeler Airlines and, briefly, by Leasair of Ottawa until, in 1964, it was one of three Catalinas acquired by Union de Transports Aériens to which it was initially registered F-WMKR. It is known to have passed through UK airspace in 1964, presumably on delivery from Canada to France. It was converted for military use by UTA at Le Bourget, Paris, and was then used in the Pacific by the Aéronavale during one of the periods of French nuclear testing in that area. With the tests over, this Catalina was stored in Tahiti until, in 1973, it was donated by the French authorities to ASPAR. In French military service it had carried the serial '20' and used the radio call sign F-YCHA.

ASPAR (Aéroservicio Parragué Ltda) was formed in the late 1950s and has operated various Catalinas ever since, both in the passenger/freight and aerial fire suppression roles. General Parragué, the company founder, offered to buy one of the French military Catalinas that had been stored on Tahiti since 1971, and to his surprise was offered all three as a gift! They were shipped to Chile during August 1973, and after thorough overhaul were flown on to Santiago. By now registered CC-CDU, this aircraft arrived in October 1974, and was subsequently allocated the ASPAR fleet numbers 32 and 33. Later re-registered CC-CGY, it lay idle at Los Cerrillos, still in Aéronavale colours, for many years, donating parts to ASPAR's other airworthy Catalinas, thus enabling them to stay active as water bombers, latterly in Spain and Portugal.

By 1997, CC-CGY had been donated to the Museo Nacional de Aéronautico Chile (Chilean National Aeronautical Museum), and it was moved across Los Cerrillos airfield to join its collection. Although currently derelict, it will no doubt be restored in due course to represent one of the Fuerza Aérea de Chile Catalinas

operated in the 1950s and 1960s, although by the end of 2000, no progress toward this goal was noticeable!

Table 110.

Registration/ Serial	C/n	Type	Place of Manufacture	Previous id(s)
CC-CGY	CV-520	OA-10A	CAN VIC (Cartierville)	CC-CDU
				20 (Aéronavale)
				F-YCHA
				F-WMKR
				CF-IHC
				N62043
				44-34009 (USAAF)
				Bu67973 ntu (US Navy)

COLOMBIA

HK-2115P – TAC, Villavicencio

A number of Catalinas were operated by the Fuerza Aérea Colombiana (FAC) from the late 1940s onwards, the last being used well into the 1980s. Typically for Latin American Catalinas, their previous identities are rather obscure. By the early 1990s, two examples, a PBY-5A and what appeared to be a PBY-6A, were still to be found in deteriorating condition on the dump at Barroblanco Air Base, Madrid, Bogota. The FAC serials were 619 and 612 respectively. In 1993, work had begun on returning FAC 612 to airworthy condition, a seemingly impossible task! However, the rebuild crew worked wonders, and the aircraft, resplendent in red/white/blue/grey colours and with the registration HK-2115, was rolled out and subsequently flown. It was initially operated in Transportes Aéreas Latinamericanos (TALA) titles, although these were later changed to TAC. The company was owned by the Catalina's captain, Giovanni Borde.

The previous identity of FAC612 is not known for certain, although if it is a genuine PBY-6A, it must have been a former US Navy aircraft. It is possible that parts of FAC 619 may have been used in the rebuild, and, indeed, the

In immaculate external condition at Madrid Air Force Base, Bogota, TALA's HK-2115 was awaiting a flight test when seen in late 1994. Its exact previous identity is still subject to some doubt. Note the small radome on the outer starboard wing leading edge.
Steve Kinder

current aircraft could be something of a hybrid. The marks HK-2115 had previously been allocated to a Catalina in 1983, this aircraft being identified as '34012', with the type designation Consolidated A-10 (sic). The registered owner was none other than Ana Zazzu du Borde! It seems that the marks were not used at the time, although, interestingly, the previous identity of 34012 is sometimes quoted in connection with FAC 612, even though 34012 was not a PBY-6A but a USAAF OA-10A (44-34012). Could it be, therefore, that the present HK-2115P is indeed that same aircraft but with a PBY-6A tail substituted for the original unit? Prior to its rebuild, and when resident on the dump at Madrid in FAC colours, it was known to have had a PBY-6A tail unit in place, so it is not a very recent addition. The book *Warbirds Directory* prefers an alternative version, which would have this aircraft as the former US Navy PBY-5A Bu34012 as opposed to USAAF 44-34012. This PBY-5A became CF-IEE in Canada post-war, and whilst with Austin Airways, was lost in a sinking at Sugluk, Quebec, in 1970. Is it possible that it was salvaged, rebuilt and modified as a PBY-6A? It seems unlikely, as Larry Milberry's book on Austin Airways states that after the crash, the wreck was refloated using oil drums, after which it was stripped of useful components and then scuttled. The 44-34012 version of FAC612's history is the one shown below, and confirmation of its accuracy would be welcomed.

During its time with the Colombian forces, FAC612 was converted to a transport and used by SATENA (Servicio de Aéronavigacion a Territorios Nacionales), the military airline of Colombia, and it carried the name *El Gato*. It continued to fly in military markings before being consigned to Barroblanco's dump.

Sadly, during 1997, this Catalina was impounded at Villavicencio by the Policia Nacional in connection with alleged drug-running flights. Consequently, open storage has begun to take its toll on the neglected airframe once more, although its engines have been kept serviceable through occasional run-ups.

Although faded, the markings of the Fuerza Aerea Columbiana can still be seen just aft of the original blister position, whilst the serial FAC619 appears on the vertical fin. This photo was taken at the Barroblanco dump, Madrid, Bogota, on 8 September 1997.
Steve Kinder

remained on the dump at Barroblanco, and it was still there in the late 1990s in faded FAC colours.

It is possible that this Catalina was the example registered as a Consolidated A-10 to Ana Zazzu de Borde around 1983/4 as HK-2116. This theory is supported by the fact that FAC612 was registered to the same owner as HK-2115P (described above) and at the same time. If so, it clearly has not been restored to airworthy condition like its partner. Table 106 shows the possible identity, assuming this theory is correct.

Toward the end of its flying career, FAC619 appeared in a film entitled *All the Way Boys*, in which some civilian flyers planning an insurance scam arrange a fake crash, only to end up suffering mechanical problems and a real accident! In fact the film crash is a spoof, with the Catalina actually landing on an airfield behind trees so that it appears to be crashing in a forest! In the film, 612 retains its full FAC colour scheme.

Table 111.

Registration/ Serial	C/n	Type	Place of Manufacture	Previous id(s)
HK-2115P	CV-523	OA-10A	CAN VIC (Cartierville)	HK-2115 HK-2115X FAC 612 44-34012 (USAAF) Bu67976 ntu (US Navy)

Table 112.

Registration/ Serial	C/n	Type	Place of Manufacture	Previous id(s)
619	1817	PBY-5A	CON SD	N1518V Bu46453 (US Navy)

FAC 619 – Fuerza Aérea Colombiana, Barroblanco Air Base, Madrid, Bogota

Unfortunately, nothing is known of the origins of this aircraft, but it served with the Fuerza Aérea Colombiana (FAC) until apparently 'preserved' at Cundinamaica, Barroblanco Air Force Base. In 1993 it was noted there minus engines, and was reportedly scrapped by late 1994. It may be that parts were used in the rebuild to flying condition of the Catalina FAC612/HK-2115P described in the previous entry.

Although thought to have succumbed completely, it later transpired that the substantial remains of FAC619

ECUADOR

53602 – Museo Aéronautico de la Fuerza Aérea Ecuatoriana, Mariscal Sucre, Quito

As is often the case with Latin American Catalinas, the identities of those operated by the Fuerza Aérea Ecuatoriana (FAE) are shrouded in mystery. It is known that three PBY-5As were used by the Grupo de Transportes Aéreos Militares (Military Air Transport Group). The Catalinas formed a patrol Escuadrilla which amongst other things was also responsible for certain transport operations to and from the Galapagos Islands.

The Museo Aéronautico de la Fuerza Ecuatoriana Catalina is kept in the open, along with many of their larger exhibits. The airframe is light grey overall, with red float tips and hull lightning flash.
Steve Kinder

This is how the unidentified FAP Catalina looked on the gate at Antiguo Aeropuerto, Iquitos, in November 1996. It is believed to have subsequently moved to Lima.
Peter R. Foster

It is known that they were also flown under the auspices of the quasi-airline Transportes Aéreos Militares Ecuatorianos (TAME), based at Quito's Mariscal Sucre Airport.

53602 appears to be the only survivor of the trio, and now forms part of the Ecuadorian Air Force Museum at Mariscal Sucre. It was repainted in the mid-1990s in an overall grey scheme with dayglo orange lightning flashes. FAE serials are sometimes, but not always, derived from the airframe construction numbers or former identities such as US military serial numbers. In the case of 53602, neither explanation seems plausible, however.

PERU

OB-T-251 – ex-LORASA, Iquitos

This Catalina is one of a small number known to have been operated by Peruvian commercial airlines. In this case the airline was LORASA (Loretana de Aviacion SA) of Berglere, Iquitos.

The United States Navy had taken delivery of this San Diego-built Catalina on 12 February 1944, and it remained on strength until struck off whilst in storage at Litchfield Park, Arizona, in June 1950. Quite when the Catalina went to Peru is not known, but it served with LORASA until that company folded during the latter half of the 1970s. It spent some time in store at Iquitos in company with another Catalina, this second aircraft being reported as an ex-Fuerza Aérea del Peru example, identity unknown. This second Catalina was probably the example now preserved at Lima and described below.

OB-T-251 remained at Iquitos, and over the years its condition has gradually deteriorated. By 1998, the hull was basically intact although much faded, whilst its wings were lying in the long grass nearby. The engines have long since been removed, as has the tailplane, and these items were apparently sold to an American. Although the airframe could make the basis for a restoration project, it seems likely that for the time being at least it will remain at the back of the Faucett Cargo hangar at Francisco Sereda Vigneta airport, gradually rotting away.

Table 113.

Registration/ Serial	C/n	Type	Place of Manufacture	Previous id(s)
53602 (FAE)	?	PBY-5A	?	?

As can be seen, OB-T-251 is deteriorating and may soon be beyond saving. It is pictured at Iquitos in October 1996.
Peter R. Foster

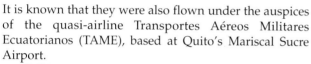

Table 114.

Registration/ Serial	C/n	Type	Place of Manufacture	Previous id(s)
OB-T-251	1868	PBY-5A	CON SD	OB-M-251 OB-LBA-251 N1513V Bu46504 (US Navy)

Unidentified – Museo de la Fuerza Aérea del Peru, Las Palmas Air Force Base, Lima

The Fuerza Aérea del Peru (FAP) operated a number of Catalinas of various types during the 1960s, and the example that spent some time on external display at

With substantial holes in the rudder fabric and flat tyres, YV-584CP is seen at Puerto Ordaz in 1993. It is still there!
Ron Mak

the military airfield of Antiguo Aéropuerto was probably one of these. Although it carried full FAP livery, there were no external markings that give a clue as to the actual identity of this particular aircraft.

Although an amphibian, the Catalina had been mounted a few inches above the grass with its undercarriage retracted. Its bow turret and blisters had been removed during its Peruvian military service, or possibly before, the latter being replaced, at least on the port side, by a hatch and smaller perspex 'bubble'.

It is believed that this Catalina is the one that has now appeared at the recently formed Peruvian Air Force Museum in Lima.

Table 115.

Registration/ Serial	C/n	Type	Place of Manufacture	Previous id(s)
?	?	PBY-5A?	?	? (FAP)

VENEZUELA

YV-584CP – Caribbean Airline Services Inc, Puerto Ordaz

Venezuela's sole surviving Catalina saw many years service as an aerial taxi for the Orinoco mining companies. It was built at San Diego and flew with the US Navy, being struck off charge in August 1956, after storage at Litchfield Park, Arizona. Its first commercial owner was George B. Alder of Chatanooga, followed by the Carolina Aircraft Corporation of Miami, and it was registered as N9507C. Later, it was further converted for passenger-carrying use by Pan Air in New Orleans, and became YV-P-DPZ, first with the Orinoco Mining Company then, as YV-O-CFO-2, with Corporacion Ferrominera de Orinoco CA.

After years of hard work in the Orinoco area, it was acquired by Camaronera del Sur and then Italo Compagna/SERVES, but it remained in storage at Puerto Ordaz whilst its Orinoco companion, YV-485C (now in the USA as N7238Z) was restored to full airworthy condition. In June 2000, both aircraft were sold to Anthony Tirri of Caribbean Airline Services Inc at San Juan, Puerto Rico. YV-584CP has not flown since 1979, although it remains in potentially airworthy condition and so will, presumably, be ferried to San Juan in due course.

Table 116.

Registration/ Serial	C/n	Type	Place of Manufacture	Previous id(s)
YV-584CP	1736	PBY-5A	CON SD	YV-63CP ntu YV-O-CFO-2 YV-P-DPZ N9507C Bu48374 (US Navy)

Seventeen
SURVIVORS IN EUROPE

PBY-6A 82-861 pictured before it was re-serialled L-861.
Noteworthy is the earlier form of radome above the
cockpit. It was later replaced with a larger unit peculiar to
the RDAF Catalinas.
Royal Danish Air Force Historical Section

DENMARK

L-861 – Danmarks Tekniske Museum, Helsingör/Elsinore

Post-war, the Royal Danish Air Force flew a mixture of
Catalinas – eight Canso As/PBY-5As and, later on, eight
PBY-6As. They were used in particular to support survey
operations in Greenland and subsequently to maintain
links with Danish outposts there.

Denmark's sole surviving Catalina is one of the
second batch to be delivered, and is a PBY-6A model,
serialled L-861. It started life in New Orleans, and once
completed there in June 1945, was delivered to the US
Navy as Bu64035. Between then and its retirement to the
storage yard at Litchfield Park, Arizona, it flew with various units, including FAW- 8, FAW-2 and VU-4, and was
based at such locations as Terminal Island and Alameda,
California; Pearl Harbor, Hawaii; Norfolk Island,
Virginia; and Seattle, Washington.

It went into storage at Litchfield Park in July 1953,
after its final posting in Atlanta, but flew out again to

Part-way through its restoration to display standard and
awaiting its engines and outer wing panels, L-861 is seen
at Værloese in May 1994.
Torben Jensen

New Orleans in December 1956. Here, it was refurbished
by Catalina specialists Pan Air Corporation for supply to
the Royal Danish Air Force, and was delivered to them at
Værløse in April 1957. It served until 1970, being allocated at different times to Esk 721 and Esk 722. Its final flight
was on 13 November 1970, by which time it had amassed
5,770 hours in the air.

At Værløse, it was stored by Air Material Command

until October 1977, when it was transferred to the Danish Aviation Museum (Danmarks Flyvemuseum). It remained at Værløse, however, and was worked on by personnel from the Flyvevabnets Samling (RDAF Historical Section). For a time, it was stored at nearby Malov, but was returned to the main base in June 1981, with work continuing to bring L-861 up to static exhibition standard.

By 1994, the hull, centre section and engines were complete, and in this condition it was displayed at that year's Værløse open day. It looked superb in its red and grey RDAF colours. On the night of 21–22 November 1996, the hull and tail section were moved by road from Værløse to the Danmarks Tekniske Museum (Danish Technical Museum) at Helsingör/Elsinore in Northern Sjælland. At that time, the wings were still being worked on at Værløse, but were due to follow on to Helsingör in due course.

Table 117.

Registration/ Serial	C/n	Type	Place of Manufacture	Previous id(s)
L-861 (RDAF)		PBY-6A	CON NO	82-861 (RDAF) Bu64035 (US Navy)

FRANCE

C-FCRR – Canadian Air Legend, St. Etienne

The term 'warbird' has become an overused expression in recent years, and now seems to cover virtually any ex-military type. In Catalina terms, C-FCRR is a true warbird as it can claim not only active wartime service but a U-boat destruction to its credit.

Shortly after being delivered to the Royal Canadian Air Force, Canso A, serial 9767, was being operated by

162 (BR) Squadron as aircraft 'S'. On 17 April 1944, whilst it was under the command of F/O T. C. Cooke, the U-boat U-342 was attacked on the surface, south-west of Iceland. The attack was sufficiently accurate to cause the U-boat to explode and sink. U-342 was on her maiden voyage, having sailed out of Bergen some two weeks previously.

Eventually struck off charge in April 1946, 9767 was soon acquired by Canadian Pacific Airlines and registered CF-CRR. During its fourteen-year tour of duty with CPAL, it flew as a passenger and freight aircraft with the fleet numbers 233 and 933. Early on, it had its blisters and nose turret removed. Just before being disposed of by CPAL, on 23 April 1959, CF-CRR suffered substantial damage in a cross-wind water landing at Terrace, BC, and as a result, the Canso had to divert to the nearby land airport and make a nose-wheel-up landing.

There followed a succession of Canadian airline owners, including Northland Airlines, Midwest Airlines and Ilford Riverton Airways, before acquisition by Avalon Aviation for use as a water bomber. Initially based at Red Deer, Alberta, from 1977, it was later to call Parry Sound, Ontario, its home, and it was there that it entered long-term storage when Avalon ceased operations during the late 1980s.

As a water bomber, C-FCRR carried the hull code '1' and, later, '791'. In the rough and tumble of fire-fighting operations, accidents will happen and C-FCRR was involved in two of note. The first was at Sylvan Lake, Alberta, on 27 May 1978, when serious damage was sustained after stalling onto the water whilst carrying out water pick-up training. The aircraft was hurriedly beached before it sank. The outer section of the starboard wing was destroyed in this incident and was replaced with an unused wartime component complete with original RCAF roundels! The second accident was on 30 May 1981, when the left-hand nose-wheel door tore off during a water pick-up on Complex Lake, NWT. The aircraft nosed down and sank but was salvaged to fly again! Other scrapes included an overrun on take-off from an airfield in Saskatchewan that resulted in the damaged airframe having to be airlifted out by helicopter, and a nose-wheel collapse on landing in the mid-1980s. All in all, an eventful period!

During its time in storage at Parry Sound, it was the subject of several purchase attempts by groups keen to preserve it, particularly because of its wartime history. However, all failed, and in 1994 it was acquired by Franklin Deveaux of Dijon-based Canadian Air Legend. He had blisters replaced on the aft hull and other overhaul work carried out by Tom Reilly of Kissimmee, Florida, and then, in the spring of 1995, C-FCRR left Canada for France. Upon arrival, it was initially overhauled at Dinard by Société Cooperative Aéronautique before flying to Toulouse, where it was resprayed by Aérospatiale in a striking grey and blue scheme.

In October 1995, it departed for Africa equipped as a flying TV studio for use in a French TV natural history series called *Operation Okavango*. Its initial destination was Djibouti, followed by the Comoro Islands, then Kenya and Ethiopia. The operations in Ethiopia were not without incident – whilst being filmed taxiing out of the water after a lake landing, the bow became stuck fast in

In 1998, C-FCRR had been painted up in an Air France colour scheme, although the hull was liberally covered with sponsor's insignia, including those of TAM, La Poste and Breitling.
MAP

Following its accident in 1964, the remains of F-ZBAR languished at Marseille for some time, as shown here.

mud and the Catalina had to be ignominiously lifted out of its predicament by the Mil-8 support helicopter that was accompanying it on the trip. Even this was not straightforward, as the downdraught damaged the Cat's port aileron in the process!

After a period at Harare in Zimbabwe, C-FCRR returned to France, and by mid-1997 was at Arrachon/La Teste de Buch minus its *Okavango* titles but named *Capt Tom Cooke,* after its illustrious wartime captain. It was later repainted in an Air France colour scheme with the name *Princesse des Etoiles* and flown to Le Bourget, Paris, on 23 August 1998, where it was dismantled by the British firm Edwards Brothers Aviation, previously involved in the African filming, and trucked to the Place de la Concorde on the Champs Elysées. There, it was placed on public display during September, along with a great number of other vintage aeroplanes, to celebrate 100 years of aviation.

With its Parisian appearance over, it was taken back to Le Bourget and flown south again ready for its next adventure – a transatlantic flight to Chile and Brazil via East and West Africa! The main reason for this epic flight was to commemorate the Aéropostal mail flights flown by Jean Mermoz between France and Dakar, Senegal, instigated in 1930. The Catalina left Toulouse on 14 October, and by 28 November 1998, C-FCRR had arrived in Santiago, a follow-on flight to Brazil being made on the 3rd of that month. For these flights, many sponsorship logos adorned the Catalina's hull and tail, including that of the Brazilian airline TAM, which was taking delivery of new airbus aircraft, the PBY being involved in the handover ceremony. At the completion of the ceremonies, C-FCRR flew north and spent some time at Oshawa, Ontario, where maintenance was carried out before leaving on 8 June 1999, crossing the Northern Atlantic via Reykjavik and Shannon, before arriving at Dinard in Brittany. A few weeks later, it was being kept busy as an aerial camera platform for the 11 August total eclipse of the sun.

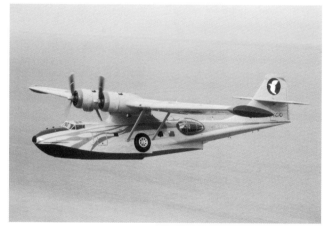

Before C-FCRR departed for filming work in Africa, it was painted in a grey and blue *Okavango* livery. This photo was taken on an air test in the vicinity of Mont St Michel in October 1995.
Xavier Meal

Table 118.

Registration/ Serial	C/n	Type	Place of Manufacture	Previous id(s)
C-FCRR	21996	Canso A	BOE CAN	CF-CRR 9767 (RCAF)

F-ZBAR – Musée de Tradition de l'Aéronautique Navale, Rochefort-Soubise

The naval aircraft collection at Rochefort-Soubise includes the nose section of F-ZBAR, a former Protection Civile water bomber. Acquired in 1991 from the Escadrille Pegase at Aix-les-Milles, the complete airframe had previously lain derelict at the Protection Civile base at Marseille following an accident on the Donzère Canal in July 1964. It had formerly been registered in Canada with Field Aviation, which carried out the conversion to water bomber status, and before that had served in the Royal Canadian Air Force as 11100, the last of their Cansos to be built.

Table 119.

Registration/ Serial	C/n	Type	Place of Manufacture	Previous id(s)
F-ZBAR	CV-449	Canso A	CAN VIC (Cartierville)	CF-NJP 11100 (RCAF)

GREECE

5B-PBY – Athenian Airlift Services, Tanagra

For many years, the Provincial Government of Quebec operated a sizeable fleet of former Royal Canadian Air Force Canso As in the water bombing role. These immaculate veterans worked hard, and inevitably some were lost in accidents. By the early 1990s, five remained in use alongside other more modern types such as the Canadair CL-215. In 1993, all five, including C-FPQF, later to become 5B-PBY, were retired and offered for tender.

Originally delivered to the RCAF from Canadian Vickers in February 1944, this aircraft remained in service until as late as December 1960, when it was struck off charge. During its RCAF career, it is known to have served, post-war, with 408 (PR) Goose Squadron in the photographic reconnaissance role. This squadron was formed at Rockcliffe, Ontario, in January 1949, in order to map the Canadian northlands.

After retirement, a new lease of life followed with the Quebec Government, and although the name of the operating department was subject to change over the years, the Canso's role of forest protection remained constant. Each season, CF-PQF and its companions flew wherever they were needed throughout Quebec. Initially painted bright yellow with red trim, the red was later replaced by blue, whilst the hull identity code of 11 was subsequently amended to 711.

In the early 1990s, the Quebec Department of Supply and Services sold C-FPQF to an aircraft broker known as Canadian Aircraft Sales, which later advertised it for sale at US$315,000. At some point it was also registered to Pro Air International of St Hubert.

The Canadian registration was cancelled in August 1994, being replaced by the appropriate Cypriot markings 5B-PBY. Having been stored at Bromont, Quebec, it was ferried to Athens in September that same year via Sydney, Nova Scotia; St Johns, Newfoundland; the Azores; and Palma. It arrived in Athens on 12 September.

Prior to departing Canada, 5B-PBY had its yellow and blue colour scheme modified slightly, and the emblem of the Greek TV company, *ANT 1*, was added to the forward hull and under the wings. It was named *Villa Franca*. At the time of its registration in Cyprus, the owners were Athenian Airlift Services Ltd of Nicosia.

By early 1997, it was to be seen on the apron at Tanagra in the company of a second former Quebec water bombing Canso, C-FPQO, an unusual sight for that part of the world! By this time, it had also had its rear hull blisters installed in their rightful place. C-FPQO subsequently flew off to new owners in South Africa in 1999, but 5B-PBY has remained in Greece.

Table 120.

Registration/ Serial	C/n	Type	Place of Manufacture	Previous id(s)
5B-PBY	CV-333	Canso A	CAN VIC (Cartierville)	C-FPQF CF-PQF 11042 (RCAF)

5B-PBY comes in over the Athens Airport threshold at the conclusion of its delivery flight from Canada in September 1994.
John Reynolds

THE NETHERLANDS

16-212 – Militaire Luchtvaart Museum, Valkenburg

Although 16-212 cannot lay claim to be the longest-standing European Catalina survivor – that title belongs to L-857, the former Danish PBY-5A now in Norway – it does none the less have the distinction of being in continuous preservation for longer than any other PBY in Europe, having been on display to the public since mid-1957! After serving in the US Navy as Bu48317, it became one of a batch of six former US Navy PBY-5As to be purchased for use by the MLD (Marine Luchtvaart Dienst, or Royal Dutch Naval Air Service), and it was delivered to Valkenburg in early 1952 for overhaul. Prior to delivery, it had been placed on the US Civil Aircraft Register as N1495V. In MLD service, it became 16-212, although it is often referred to as P-212. Both the serial sequences commencing P- and 16- denoted aircraft types used in the Patrol role, the prefix 16- replacing the earlier use of P-. As far as is known, 16-212 never actually wore the earlier style of serial presentation.

Unlike most of the batch of six that it belonged to, 16-212 did not go out to Dutch New Guinea with 321 Squadron but, instead, remained in Holland with 8 Squadron as a training and search-and-rescue aircraft. The type was replaced by Martin Mariners in late 1956, and 16-212 was withdrawn from service in July 1957.

After being struck off charge, it was placed on display in the Bosbad recreation ground at Hoeven, close to the Bosschenhoofd road in Northern Brabant. Eventually, in October 1982, it was removed, and restoration commenced, firstly at Gilze-Rijen and then at Valkenburg. Its place at Hoeven was taken by a Grumman Tracker. Then, in April 1984, and with its restoration work completed, it was placed on display at the Militaire Luchtvaart Museum at Kamp Zeist, Soesterberg, where it remained until early 1996. By this time, its external condition had again deteriorated through being housed out of doors for so many years, and it was therefore moved again, this

time back to Valkenburg by road in April 1996, for more restorative work. The work is ongoing at the present time, the project being in the care of the Neptune Association. Once complete, the restored airframe will once more become a static exhibit at Soesterberg/Kamp Zeist. Toward the end of 1998, it was estimated that completion of the restoration work would take another two years.

Over the years, 16-212 has suffered from innacurate reporting of its identity and its type designation in several written works. Table 115 is the correct version.

Table 121.

Registration/ Serial	C/n	Type	Place of Manufacture	Previous id(s)
16-212 (MLD)	1679	PBY-5A	CON SD	N1495V Bu48317 (US Navy)

PH-PBY/'Y-74' – Stichting Neptune Association, Valkenburg

This particular Catalina's claim to fame is that of being the oldest example of the type in airworthy condition anywhere in the world. Added to that, it had an exciting war record! It was built at the Consolidated San Diego factory in the autumn of 1941 and delivered to the US Navy as Bu2459 on 15 November. It served with both 7 and 8 Patrol Wings and is known to have been assigned to VP-73 and VP-84 based at Reykjavik, Iceland. On 20 August the following year, Bu2459, bearing the individual aircraft code 'R', was flying from Reykjavik to provide airborne cover for Convoy SN-73, which was sailing south-east of Iceland. U-boat U-464, on its maiden voyage and captained by Kapitanleutnant Otto Harms, was spotted by 2459's crew and depth-charged, the resultant explosion causing mortal damage to the boat and leading to its sinking, although not before it had returned fire. Then, on 5 October 1942, it was again involved in an attack when Type VIIC submarine U-582 was spotted shadowing convoy HX-209 some 400 miles south of

16-212 was a Blackbushe, Hampshire, visitor during the Farnborough air show week in September 1955. The lettering on the fin beneath the tailplane reads KON MARINE.
Jennifer M. Gradidge

During its 1995 delivery flight from Canada to Holland, C-FHHR visited the Fighter Meet air display at North Weald, England, and it is seen here rolling down the runway on arrival. It had already been painted as RNEIAF Y-74.
Stephen Dodd

Before being grounded, Cat Air's Catalina flew to the seaplane meeting on the Wannsee in Berlin held in August 1998. By this time, it was carrying its Dutch civil registration and modified RNEIAF livery, the rudder being all orange, with a black border.
Ron Mak

Iceland. Again, depth-charges were dropped, causing the U-boat to disappear underwater, leaving oil on the surface. In his book *Search, Find and Kill*, Norman Franks quotes the Catalina involved in this attack as being coded 'I', so presumably Bu2459's earlier 'R' code had been changed in the interim period. At the end of 1942, Bu2459 was transferred from VP-73 to VP-84, still in Iceland.

The next attack came on 14 April 1943, whilst serving as aircraft 'G' and under the command of Lt W. A. Shelvin when Bu 2459 was blooded again. The German submarine U-528 was attacked and damaged after being straddled by depth-charges. U-528, a type-IXC/40 submarine commanded by Kapitanleutnant Georg von Rabenau, was on her maiden patrol and had to limp back towards her French port, only to be sunk prior to arrival by a Halifax II, HR942, of 58 Squadron, RAF.

At the beginning of 1944, Bu2459 returned to the USA and a posting to the US Coast Guard at Elizabeth City, North Carolina. Being an early US Catalina, it did not see military service beyond the war and was struck off charge at the end of October 1945. Within twelve months, a new commercial owner had been found in the form of Ric-Ter Airways, which registered it NC18446, later N18446. A whole string of subsequent owners followed before it passed from the US Register in November 1953.

The previous month, N18446 had been acquired by the Canadian airline Transair of Winnipeg and it became CF-HHR. It was used in Northern Canada and also flew under the name of Central Northern, an associated company of Transair. After long and hard use, CF-HHR was disposed of to Field Aviation, which carried out the necessary work for a water-bomber conversion.

Once the conversion had been completed, CF-HHR was sold to Avalon Aviation, which used it on fire-fighting contracts all over Canada. One season, it was flown all the way to Chile for similar work in that country. The hull codes 3, later 793, were used in Avalon service.

Following Avalon's collapse in the mid-1980s, this Catalina, along with the rest of its fleet, went into an extended period of open storage at Parry Sound, Ontario.

After some nine years, C-FHHR was acquired by the Dutch group, Cat Air, with the intention of operating it on the European air show scene and to carry out tourist charters. After extensive overhaul and a repaint to represent the former Dutch military PBY-5A Catalina, Y-74, C-FHHR flew again on 1 April 1995, and it was subsequently flown across the Atlantic via Moncton, Stephenville, Goose Bay, Keflavik, Glasgow and North Weald, to arrive at Rotterdam on 14 May. Although not part of the flying display, it briefly shared ramp space at North Weald's Fighter Meet Air Show with Plane Sailing's British-based PBY-5A when it passed through en route to Holland.

Since its arrival in Europe, 'Y-74' has performed in the air and on water at a number of locations and displays both within and outside Holland. During the winter of 1995/6, blister turrets from the ex-MLD PBY-5A 16-212 at Valkenburg were borrowed and then apparently traded for another set in the USA, which were installed on the rear hull. Although the Dutch markings PH-PBY had been reserved in the name of M. A. P. van Schie in November 1994, they were not used initially and were cancelled in November 1995. Incidentally, this was the third occasion on which the registration PH-PBY had been reserved; two earlier applications for other owners and other Catalinas were not taken up. It continued to fly as C-FHHR until, on 19 April 1996, it was registered in the USA as N27311 to Western Aviation Maintenance of Mesa, Arizona. Its colour scheme was then modified so that the rudder bore the overall orange associated with the Netherlands East Indies Air Force. On 6 February

1997, it finally took up the Dutch marks PH- PBY when it was registered to Marien van Schie. Later, on 13 October, the registered owner was amended to Cat Air NV of Lelystad.

Since being imported into Holland, PH-PBY has had a number of operating bases, including Eindhoven, Valkenburg and then Lelystad. In the spring of 1998, it was announced that Cat Air and its Catalina would be involved in a proposed venture for an aviation theme park at Lelystad to be called Airworld Lelystad. Sadly, many of the plans announced for this aircraft by Cat Air have not come to fruition. It flew fewer air shows than anticipated and never carried out any long-distance charters such as those to Africa which had been envisaged in the early days. One of PH- PBY's last public appearances was on Berlin's Wannsee at the seaplane meeting held there to commemorate the 50th anniversary of the Berlin Airlift. Ultimately, Cat Air failed financially, and PH-PBY was grounded at Schipol, entering a period of storage during which its condition deteriorated whilst it was advertised for sale. Its blisters were reclaimed by the Stichting Neptune Association, which were restoring PBY-5A 16-212 at Valkenberg. Then, in 1999, it was announced that the SNA would take-over custody of PH-PBY and be responsible for its complete overhaul and return to fully airworthy condition. Accordingly, it was ferried by air from Schipol to Valkenburg on 11 May 1999. Its return to the air is eagerly anticipated by European Catalina enthusiasts.

PH-PBY has been quoted by some sources as an ex-RCAF Canso, serial 11022, and also as ex-RAF VA719. Neither of these theories is correct.

Freshly repainted as a 330 (Norwegian) Squadron Catalina III FP535/X, C-FIZO makes a fine sight.
Terje Kristiansen

Table 122.

Registration/ Serial	C/n	Type	Place of Manufacture	Previous id(s)
PH-PBY/'Y-74' (RNEIAF)	300	PBY-5A	CON SD	N27311 C-FHHR PH-PBY ntu C-FHHR CF-HHR N(C)18446 Bu2459 (US Navy)

NORWAY

'FP535'/X – Royal Norwegian Air Force Museum, Bodö

When production of the amphibious PBY-5A Catalina ceased, the later, tall-tailed, PBY-6A variant continued to be produced by Consolidated at its New Orleans plant sited on Lake Ponchartrain. The Royal Norwegian Air Force Museum Catalina was the seventh aircraft in a batch of fifity-nine PBY-6As, and it was delivered to the United States Navy with the serial Bu46645. It was taken on charge on 21 February 1945, and is known to have served with the patrol squadron VPB-62 before being declared surplus in May 1956, by which time it had been placed in storage at Litchfield Park, Arizona. It was subsequently purchased by the second-hand aircraft dealer Trade Ayer and became N10013.

It was not long before N10013 had been sold in

Canada, where it became CF-IZO. Between 1956 and 1981, it served with a succession of Canadian operators, including Montreal Air Service, the Saskatchewan Government and North Canada Air Ltd/Norcanair. Fairly early in its commercial career, it was converted to the forest-fire-fighting role, and it continued to be used as such when it was acquired by Avalon Aviation, with which it flew as tanker 8, later 798. At some point, its tall PBY-6A tail and rudder was replaced by a stock PBY-5A unit, which has been retained to the present time.

A period of open storage at Parry Sound, Ontario, followed Avalon's demise, but in September 1989 it was flown across the Atlantic over a two-day period, routing Oshawa–Gander– Shannon–Eindhoven. It touched down in Holland on 27 September. C-FIZO's new owners were B. Johnson, the President of Tech Air Systems, and Jan

Former Royal Danish Air Force PBY-5A L-857 rotting away on the dump at Værloese in 1977.

An amazing transformation had occurred to L-857 by the mid-1990s. Now painted as 48382/KK-A of 333 Squadron RNoAF, it was out for a breather on the concrete at Sola when seen here. It is painted midnight blue overall.
Pål Forus

Verhoeven, General Manager of Flight Support Europe. Although plans were released suggesting that the Catalina would be refurbished and operated on the European air display scene, this came to naught, as did possible sales to both the Israeli Air Force Museum and the Foynes Flying Boat Museum. On 26 July 1990, C-FIZO departed Eindhoven bound for Oslo and the Forsvarsmuseet (Norwegian Armed Forces Museum). Initially based at the military airfield of Gardermoen, C-FIZO remained in its orange Avalon colours whilst work proceeded on its restoration to display condition. This work, to airworthy standard, included the fitment of blisters on the rear hull and a nose turret, some of this work being carried out by the Norwegian company Fred Olsen. The Canadian registration C-FIZO was cancelled in March 1993.

As restoration neared completion, the Catalina was repainted to represent a 330 (Norwegian) Squadron Catalina III amphibian, serial FP535, hull code 'X', as operated during World War Two. The original FP535 was lost in action when it failed to return from a patrol out of Reykjavik, Iceland on 5 November 1942.

The first flight after restoration occurred in June 1994, and was followed by a small number of air show and special event appearances before a ferry flight to the newly relocated museum at Bodö in the Arctic Circle on 30 July. These flights appear to have been made without

a registration being allocated and using the old US Navy serial as a call sign! Although in airworthy condition, it seems unlikely that 'FP535' will fly regularly, if at all, in the future, and its location up in the north of Norway means it will only be seen by the more intrepid enthusiast!

Table 123.

Registration/ Serial	C/n	Type	Place of Manufacture	Previous id(s)
'FP535' (RAF)	2009	PBY-6A	CON NO	C-FIZO CF-IZO N10013 Bu46645 (US Navy)

L-857 – Flyhistorisk Sola Museum, Sola, Stavanger

Norway's second preserved Catalina was rescued from an uncertain fate in neighbouring Denmark, and, once complete, will make a superb representation of a post-war Royal Norwegian Air Force PBY-5A.

This Catalina is a relatively old example, having left the San Diego production line in the summer of 1942. It was taken on charge by the United States Navy as Bu08109 on 22 September and remained in service until summer 1951. During its initial military career, it served at such diverse locations as NAS Alameda, California; Whidbey Island, Washington; and Kodiak, Alaska. Post-war, it was supplied to the Royal Danish Air Force (RDAF), with whom, along with another ex-US Navy PBY-5A, it joined six ex-RCAF Canso As that had been acquired a few years before.

Serialled 82-857, it initially flew with Esk 721 out of Kastrup, Copenhagen, and was named *Munin* after

Odin's raven. In 1960, in line with the new Danish military aircraft numbering system, it was re-serialled L-857, and it remained in active service as such until 1967. Although most of its time was spent with Esk 721, it did spend a brief time during 1961–2 with Esk 722. Its last flight was on 14 October 1967, after which it was withdrawn from service and transferred to Air Material Command for storage at Værløse. It had accumulated 6,083 airframe hours.

After a period of neglect and deterioration, L-857 was disposed of to a local farmer, Jens Larsen, and in late 1982 it was transported to his farm at Plejerup on condition that it was not sold or transferred to any other party without the prior consent of the RDAF.

The Catalina remained at Plejerup in ever worsening condition until November 1989. It was then acquired by the Flyhistorisk Museum of Sola and moved by low-loader to their premises, arriving on 17 November. With the benefit of hangarage, the restoration project moved on steadily in the hands of hard-working volunteers. By 1995, much work had been completed on the hull, inner wing sections and engines, and the aircraft had received a striking Royal Norwegian Air Force dark blue livery. It thus represents the PBY-5A serial 48382 operated by 333 Squadron during the period 1953–61.

CC-CCS sits in the sun at Palma del Rio, Spain, in June 1991. The long-range under-wing tanks used on its ferry flight from Chile can be seen outboard of each engine. The port side cargo hatch is in the up position.
Ron Mak

Table 124.

Registration/ Serial	C/n	Type	Place of Manufacture	Previous id(s)
L-857 (RDAF)	928	PBY-5A	CON SD	82-857 (RDAF) Bu08109 (US Navy)

SPAIN

CC-CCS – ASPAR, Palma del Rio, Cordoba

This particular Catalina has been registered in Chile since 1957, but has spent the last few years based in Spain and Portugal on forest-fire-fighting duties.

A New Orleans-built US Navy aircraft, it was issued with the serial Bu46679 and served as a military aircraft between April 1945, and August 1956, the last portion of that time being spent in storage at Litchfield Park. Sometime after being declared surplus, it was sold to the Miami-based Aircraft Instrument Corporation, to which it was registered N9562C. Later it turned up in Chile as CC-CNF with the airline TRANSA, and after civilian conversion by FANAERO, it flew with them until 1959 when it was acquired by Roberto Parragué, a well-known Chilean military Catalina pilot, who ran the airline Aeroservicios Parrague Ltda, or ASPAR.

CC-CNF remained in storage with ASPAR for many years, but was put into service in 1980 with the new registration CC-CCS and the fleet number 79. It was converted to a water bomber around 1979, and as Tanker 34, flew in this role until it sank on landing upon Lago Gutierrez near San Carlos de Bariloche in Argentina on 27 January 1986. During the landing run, the hull struck a rock, as a result of which the captain was killed. At the time, it was engaged in fighting a forest fire in one of Argentina's national parks. It was salvaged a few weeks later and dismantled ready for the 1,200 km road journey

back to Santiago, where it was rebuilt by ASPAR's engineers. The work was completed at the end of 1988 and it was subsequently put back into service.

In June 1991, it was ferried across the South Atlantic to Spain for operation there with ICONA (Instituta Para la Conservacion de la Naturaleza, or the Spanish Ministry of Land and Forest Management).

ICONA continued to operate CC-CCS each summer season in various parts of Spain, although as the 1990s progressed, its usage lessened, partly for mechanical reasons but also because of competition from more modern equipment. None the less, it was to be found operating in Portugal at the end of the decade, still in the ownership of ASPAR but on charter to Pinhancos-based Aerocondor. In addition to both ASPAR and Aerocondor titles, it carries the fleet number A1 in place of the earlier tanker number 34, and the legend Bombieros on the upper hull just aft of the wing pylon.

Table 125.

Registration/ Serial	C/n	Type	Place of Manufacture	Previous id(s)
CC-CCS	2043	PBY-6A	CON SD	CC-CNF N9562C Bu46679 (US Navy)

CC-CDT – ASPAR, Palma del Rio, Cordoba

This Catalina was one of 230 originally ordered for the US Navy as PBV-1As but instead delivered to the USAAF as OA-10As. All were built at Cartierville, Montreal, by Canadian Vickers, later Canadair. Construction number CV-332 was serialled 44-33880. In April 1951, it went to Iceland and flew with Loftleidir/Icelandic Airlines as TF-RVR until, in July 1952, it returned to Canada, the land of its birth, where it became CF-FKV with Maritime Central Airlines. Whilst in Iceland, TF-RVR had been used mainly on domestic flights around the country, although it had also flown trips to Greenland. Based at Reykjavik, it was named *Dynjandi*.

For a short period, CF-FKV flew with Wheeler

Before being used as a fire fighter, ASPAR's CC-CDT was used for passenger and cargo flights in Chile. It is seen here moored on Lake Vichuquen, 100 miles south-west of Santiago in late November 1980.
Stephen Simms/Propliner

Table 126.

Registration/ Serial	C/n	Type	Place of Manufacture	Previous id(s)
CC-CDT	CV-332	OA-10A	CAN VIC (Cartierville)	32 (Aéronavale) F-YCHB (Aéronavale call sign) F-WMKS CF-FKV TF-RVR 44-33880 (USAAF) Bu67844 ntu (US Navy)

Airlines, based at St Jovite Station, Quebec. In February 1966, the Catalina was acquired by the French airline Union de Transports Aériens, or UTA, for operation out of Tahiti in the Pacific Ocean. When the French Government needed transport aircraft to support the nuclear trials activity in the Pacific, F-WMKS became 32/F-YCHB with the French Navy and flew with them until the early 1970s, when it was retired and stored at Papeete.

In 1973, aircraft 32 and two other Catalinas also in store at Papeete were gifted to Roberto Parragué for use by his airline ASPAR, and were shipped to Chile as deck cargo aboard the freighter *Buque Andino*. Operated by ASPAR as CC-CDT/Tanker 32 (a reflection of its former Aéronavale serial), it flew across to Spain for charter work in the fire-fighting role in July 1988, along with its sister aircraft, PBY-6A CC-CNP.

CC-CDT has continued to be based in southern Spain since 1988, although ASPAR offered it for sale, ex-Spain, during early 1996. The three ASPAR PBYs operating in Iberian skies (CC-CCS, CC-CDT and CC-CNP) were allocated temporary Spanish registrations in the summer of 1995, these being EC-593, -594 and -595. The tie-ups with the Chilean registrations are not known. At the end of the 1990s, CC-CDT was being used with the other two ASPAR Catalinas by Aerocondor of Pinhancos in Portugal.

CC-CNP – ASPAR, Palma del Rio, Cordoba

Like the Chilean operator ASPAR's other Spanish-based PBY-6A CC-CCS, CC-CNP started life on the New Orleans production line as part of an order for the US Navy. It flew with that air arm as Bu46665, and briefly became N9555C when finally declared surplus to requirements in August 1956. It had previously been in storage since the early 1950s.

The American registration was brief, as by 1957 it had been transferred to the Chilean civil register as CC-CNG. The registered owner was TRANSA, which also owned the future CC-CCS mentioned above. However, TRANSA did not use CC-CNG and it remained in storage until 1959, when it too was bought by Roberto Parragué's ASPAR, becoming CC-CNP in the process.

Some years previously, Roberto Parragué had attempted a South Pacific crossing in a Chilean military Catalina which he had named *Manutara* after the bird of the same name. In honour of that aircraft, Snr Parragué named CC-CNP *Manutara II*. In 1970, CC-CNP was ferried to Canada for conversion to a water bomber so that

PBY-6A CC-CNP undergoes maintenance at its Santiago base some years before the three airworthy ASPAR Catalinas departed for Spain. The hull is supported by a set of Catalina beaching legs whilst the main wheels have been removed.
Jennifer M. Gradidge

ASPAR could diversfy into the forest-fire-fighting business. In this new role, CC-CNP was first given the tanker number '65', but later became '35'. Along with the PBY-5A CC-CDT, CC-CNP flew to Spain in July 1988, and has remained there since, flying under charter to ICONA.

In the summer of 1995, the Spanish markings EC-FXN were taken up, but a projected contract in Sweden fell through. Prior to this re-registration, temporary Spanish marks were allocated, although it is not known if they were worn – see comments under CC-CDT above.

By the end of the decade, the Chilean registration CC-CNP had been restored and it was operating in Portugal, still owned by ASPAR but flying with Aérocondor.

PBY-5A c/n 1960 masquerades as the Ejercito del Aire's sole Catalina DR.1-1/74-21 in the museum collection at Cuatro Vientos, Madrid, in 1996.
Roberto Yáñez

Table 127.

Registration/ Serial	C/n	Type	Place of Manufacture	Previous id(s)
CC-CNP	2029	PBY-6A	CON NO	EC-FXN CC-CNP CC-CNG N9555C Bu46665 (US Navy)

'DR.1-1/74-21' – Museo del Aire, Cuatro Vientos

The Ejercito del Aire (Spanish Air Force) possessed one solitary Catalina for a period during the latter part of the Second World War and until the late 1950s. This aircraft was in fact a USAAF OA-10A, serial 42-109020, that had landed at Ifini in the Spanish Sahara on 7 July 1943, after the crew had become lost whilst en route from the USA to Malta. It was subsequently flown to Casablanca and then on to Barajas, and was acquired by the Ejercito del

Aire in early 1944. It later became DR.1-1 in Spanish service, but throughout its time in Spain suffered from shortages of spares. It was scrapped in 1956 or 1957. Despite this PBY's relative obscurity, the Museo del Aire at Cuatro Vientos wished to acquire a Catalina for its collection in order to commemorate it. The influx of water bombing Catalinas to Spain in the late 1980s was to provide the museum with just such an opportunity.

PBY-5A construction number 1960 saw service with the US Navy and then went into American commercial ownership in the mid-1950s, first as N6070C and then as N45998. Its activities in this period are obscure, but in 1968 it was acquired by Flying Fireman Ltd, of Victoria, British Columbia, for forest-fire-fighting duties. It was re-registered CF-FFW, later C-FFFW, and at some point its stock fin and rudder were replaced by the much larger 'Super Cat' or Davis-style unit. Curiously, the original

Pratt & Whitney R-1830 power-plants were retained, making C-FFFW something of an oddity. During its days with Flying Fireman, it carried the hull code 4, later changed to 774.

By its nature, aerial fire fighting is full of incident, and C-FFFW saw its share. Whilst on charter in Ontario on 15 May 1984, it sank on Silver Lake but was subsequently salvaged and returned to service. The accident happened whilst engaged on a water pick-up when the port engine lost power and the take-off was abandoned. The crew observed an abnormally low cylinder head temperature on the engine but attempted another take-off. This too was abandoned as the aircraft failed to rise up onto the 'step'. The crew then realised that the Catalina had adopted a pronounced tail-down attitude and that water from the lake was entering the aircraft from the former gunner's hatch in the aft lower hull. They abandoned the aircraft, which sank up to its lower wing level.

Investigation showed that the engine problem was due to a valve failure in the number one cylinder of the port engine. The gunnery hatch was found to be open, the hatch structure having failed in overload whilst operating on the lake. Subsequently, it was proved that the hatch had been locked using the aligning pin only, and not the six-point lever-action slide mechanism that normally gives the hatch its structural integrity. The pre-flight check failed to reveal that the hatch had not been closed correctly. The flight was the first operation on water since the aircraft had been ferried to Ontario from its British Columbia base, so it was presumed that the hatch had been poorly secured at some unknown time prior to that flight.

Sadly, Flying Fireman, by now known as Awood Air Ltd, decided to dispose of its fleet of Catalinas at the close of the 1980s. The fleet was dispersed, with the salvaged C-FFFW going to Spain, where Chilean operator ASPAR had already established the effectiveness of using Cats there. Another operator, SAE.SA (Servicios Aereos Espanoles SA), began to assemble a fleet of Catalinas, and one of these was C-FFFW. It flew across the Atlantic in 1993 and was delivered to Cuatro Vientos. However,

SAE.SA did not use this particular PBY for water bombing and it remained in store, still in Flying Fireman livery, complete with its *Bubbles* nose-art. In February 1996, it was donated by SAE.SA to the Museo del Aire, and has since been painted to represent its Spanish Air Force predecessor, although the livery details are not quite authentic. It was formally accepted by the museum on 12 February 1996.

Table 128.

Registration/ Serial	C/n	Type	Place of Manufacture	Previous id(s)
'DR.1-1/74-21' (Ejercito del Aire)	1960	PBY-5A	CON NO	EC-693 EC-314 C-FFFW CF-FFW N45998 N6070C Bu46596 (US Navy)

EC-EVK – SAE.SA, Cuatro Vientos

An early PBY-6A, construction number 2008 became Bu 46644 after delivery from New Orleans, and it served until the 1950s, whereupon it was placed in store with many others of the breed at Litchfield Park. Reprieved from the scrapman, it was sold onto the commercial market to Leo J. Demers and became N6458C. Later, it flew with Farmers Air Service of Klamath Falls, Oregon, and Liston Aircraft at the same location, and it operated throughout the West Coast as tanker E46 and, later, E83. Its last American owner was Hemet Valley Flying Services of Hemet, California, with which it flew between 1968 and 1978. In 1978, N6458C became C-GFFH with Flying Fireman at Victoria, BC, and it continued to fight forest fires until its retirement in 1989. It was known as *Die Tolle*, or *The Madman*!

With the Spanish authorities wanting to increase the capacity of their fire-fighting fleets, C-GFFH crossed the Atlantic to join its new owner, SAE.SA, which chartered the Cat to ICONA. Its ferry flight took it from Vancouver to Tenerife via Thunder Bay, Ontario; St John, Newfoundland; and Santa Maria, Azores. The flight took just under 39 hours. Initially allocated the Spanish temporary registration EC-359, it became EC-EVK in July 1990, and was repainted in a vivid yellow and red high-visibility colour scheme. It soon acquired the hull code 71.

In July 1996, it went to Portugal for a fire-fighting contract there as insufficient work was available for it in Spain that year. It was leased by the Portugese company Aérocondor and was operated on behalf of the Lisboa and Vale do Tejo fire brigades in Aérocondor/ATA titles. By 1999, EC-EVK was back at Cuatro Vientos awaiting its next call to battle.

Bright yellow and red PBY-6A EC-EVK on the ramp at Cuatro Vientos during June 1991. It wears the titles of ICONA for whom it was operating under charter from its owner, SAE.SA.
Ron Mak

Table 129.

Registration/ Serial	C/n	Type	Place of Manufacture	Previous id(s)
EC-EVK	2008	PBY-6A	CON NO	EC-359 C-GFFH N6458C Bu46644 (US Navy)

EC-FMC – SAE.SA, Cuatro Vientos

EC-FMC is the odd-man-out amongst SAE.SA's fleet of four Catalinas, it being the only one not to come from the retired fleet of Flying Fireman of Victoria, British Columbia. Instead, it was once part of the large Catalina fleet operated by Avalon Aviation of Parry Sound, Ontario. Its water bombing role goes further back than that, however.

Built as a PBY-6A, it had been delivered to the US Navy and served until the 1950s before being sold via the US Civil register to World Wide Airways in Canada as CF-IZZ in 1956. At some point in its civilian life, the PBY-6A fin and rudder were replaced with a standard PBY-5A unit, retained to this day.

Having served with World Wide, CF-IZZ was acquired by Montreal Air Service in 1965, but a year later, ownership passed to Kenting Aviation Ltd of Toronto, which at that time was carrying out water bomber conversion work on Catalinas. CF-IZZ was fitted with the standard two-door drop system and was then chartered to the French Government fire-fighting organisation Protection Civile at Marseille. It served in France for several season as F-ZBAZ and was known to them by the call-sign *Black Pelican*, an appropriate black band being painted around the rear hull.

In 1973, ownership passed to Field Aviation Co Ltd of Toronto, which remained the owner until 1977, when CF-IZZ was sold to Avalon Aviation, based initially at Red Deer, Alberta, and then at Parry Sound, Ontario. It flew with the tanker code '5', later modified to '795'.

Prior to being painted yellow overall, SAE.SA's EC-FMC was still flying in the orange livery of its former Canadian owner, Avalon Aviation. The underside of the hull was light blue. Photo taken at San Javier in September 1994. *Ron Mak*

Following Avalon's demise, C-FIZZ remained in storage at Parry Sound until sold to SAE.SA and delivered to Spain in July 1991. There it carried on work as a water bomber on contract to ICONA, subsequently being registered EC-940 on the Spanish temporary register. In June 1992, it became EC-FMC. By 1995, its Avalon colours of bright orange had been replaced by overall yellow with ICONA titles.

In 1996, it flew on fire-fighting duties with Aérocondor/ATA in Portugal with its sister aircraft EC-EVK. By the end of the 1998 season, it was to be found looking rather work-worn at Ocana, wearing ATA titles and with the tanker number 72 on the nose, but by late summer 1999, it was back in store at Cuatro Vientos.

Table 130.

Registration/ Serial	C/n	Type	Place of Manufacture	Previous id(s)
EC-FMC		PBY-6A	CON NO	EC-940 C-FIZZ CF-IZZ F-ZBAZ CF-IZZ N10011 Bu64064 (US Navy)

SWEDEN

Fv.47001/79 – Flygvapenmuseum, Malmslatt, Linköping

Fv.47001 is the sole survivor of three ex-Royal Canadian Air Force Canso As acquired by the Flygvapnet (Swedish Air Force) in 1947. It was the odd one out of the three as it had been built by Canadian Vickers rather than Boeing of Canada, the constructors of Fv.47002 and 47003. Unusually for surviving Canadian Vickers Cansos, it had

Fv.47001 is seen at a show at Malmslatt during May 1972. Its modified bow turret area and teardrop blister on the cargo door aft of the wing can be seen to advantage. *Norm Taylor Collection*

Table 131.

Registration/ Serial	C/n	Type	Place of Manufacture	Previous id(s)
Fv.47001/79 (Flygvapnet)	CV-244	Canso A	CAN VIC (St Hubert)	9810 (RCAF)

originated on the company's St Hubert production line, whereas almost all of the other surviving PBYs from Canadian Vickers were built at Cartierville. Serialled 9810, it had been taken on charge by the RCAF on 30 March 1943, and served with 161 (BR) Squadron until struck off charge on 20 February 1947. Whilst with that unit, it would have operated out of Dartmouth, Nova Scotia; Gaspe; and Yarmouth. No. 161 Squadron disbanded on 31 May 1945, and 9810's subsequent movements are not known.

Sweden was an early recipient of surplus Allied aircraft, and the three Catalinas were delivered in 1948 for search-and-rescue use. Whilst the first two were delivered in April of that year, it was not until June 1949 that 47001 arrived in Sweden. In Flygvapnet service, the three Cansos were designated Tp47, Tp being the designation for Transport Aircraft. However, the Swedes always referred to them colloquially as Catalinas. The first unit to use them was Flotilj 2 at Hägernäs, just to the north of Stockholm, and during this time, 47001 flew with the tail code '01'. From 1960, 47001 transferred to Flotilj 8 at nearby Barkaby, with which it was coded '89'. Its last flight occurred on 1 August 1966, when it was delivered to Malmslatt for the Flygvapenmuseum. By that time, it had flown in the region of 6,000 hours in a variety of tasks, including transport and search-and-rescue. For its Swedish service, it had been modified with a blanked-over bow turret and a cargo door incorporating a small fixed blister that replaced the original, larger, unit.

Since being resident at Malmslatt, 47001 has had to remain out of doors in the elements, and it has been difficult to maintain it in first-class condition. During its time at the museum, it has had its tail code changed to '79'.

UNITED KINGDOM

N285RA – The Randsburg Corporation, North Weald, Essex

When the Canadian water bombing company Avalon Aviation folded in the 1980s, this Catalina was the only member of its fleet located outside Canada. Thus it was destined not to return to its home base at Parry Sound, Ontario, and join its brethren, but instead ended up in long-term storage at various locations in England, interspersed by very occasional engine runs and ferry flights.

But, to start at the beginning, Consolidated produced the aircraft at New Orleans and it served with the US Navy as Bu64017. It is known to have operated out of Niagara Falls Naval Air Station at some point, as the name of this base was still to be found emblazoned on the side of the hull after it had been pensioned off from military service. Following the inevitable period of post-Navy storage, it was placed on the US register as N2846D, and initially it went to Seattle in Washington State, where it sat, still in crudely obliterated US Navy markings. It passed through several owners, including Foreign and Domestic Enterprises Inc and Jaydon Enterprises of Riverside, California, and it then went on to fly with various West Coast operators as 'Tanker E87' after being converted to a water bomber. By 1964, it had been re-registered as N5555H and had flown out to France, where it was overhauled by Heliservice before joining the fleet of the French Government Protection Civile organisation based at Marseille Marignane, with which it was registered as F-ZBAV, using the radio

Soon after being demobbed from the US Navy, PBY-6A
Bu64017 was to be seen in Seattle, still in its military
colours with serial on the fin and NIAGARA FALLS painted
in the hull aft of the blisters. The civil registration N2846D
has been crudely scrawled on the hull. It can now be found
at North Weald as N285RA.
Jennifer M. Gradidge

call-sign *Pelican Vert*, or *Green Pelican*. Soon afterwards, it
suffered a forced landing in the countryside during a
fire-fighting mission when it was hit by a fuel transfer
problem. It was repaired *in situ* and flown out shortly
afterwards. It spent several years operating in the South
of France before being acquired in 1974 by Avalon
Aviation, which registered it as C-FHNH. It flew out to
Canada via the UK and then entered a time of storage at
St Jean, minus engines, before being overhauled and
placed into service with its new owners. At this time, its
blisters were removed, and these were eventually purchased by Plane Sailing Air Displays, which used them
on its own British-registered Catalina G-BLSC based at
Duxford.

Avalon chartered its Catalinas out to other operators
from time to time, and C-FHNH was flown across the
Atlantic again in May 1978, this time to Norway. There, it
was operated in the summer months by Fornebu-based
Haydn Air Charter, whose titles were emblazoned on the
forward hull. In time, it also acquired a set of F-16-style
Royal Norwegian Air Force fin flashes, and it carried the
Avalon fleet number 6 on the rudder. Most winters, it
was stored when not in use at Notodden airfield near
Oslo, although at the end of the 1982 season it was flown
to Alverca in Portugal for maintenance and repainting. It
returned to Oslo in April of the following year, loaded
with spares recovered from the ill-fated Cousteau
PBY-6A N101CS which had crashed in Portugal during
1979.

During September 1985, C-FHNH was flown from
Norway to East Midlands Airport at Castle Donington

for short-term storage and maintenance, but in the following summer it was transferred to Exeter for further
storage. Whilst there, it suffered damage to its wing leading edge and hull when, on the night of 27 March 1987, it
was struck by DC-3 G-AMHJ which had 'weather-
cocked' in a strong gust of wind. The damage was soon
repaired, and on 2 November 1988 it was flown up to
North Weald with the US civil registration N212DM that
had been allocated on 25 October (the British registration
G-BPFY had also been granted to Aces High and cancelled on the same day). Although the American owners
were Consolidated Aviation Enterprises of Burlington,
Vermont, the Catalina was still very much associated
with Aces High, and the British and American marks
were 'switched' a number of times over the following
years, as can be seen from Table 131.

The ferry flight to North Weald from Exeter did not
go entirely smoothly, with undercarriage retraction problems being experienced. The main undercarriage was
manually extended over North Weald, but upon touch-
down, the starboard unit collapsed because the down
lock had not engaged fully. The Catalina was skilfully
handled to a smooth halt on the grass beside the runway
by Captain 'Dizzy' Addicott, with minimal damage to
the keel and starboard float. Aces High retained the
Catalina at North Weald and although plans to fly it on
the airshow circuit as a US Navy Catalina were reported,
this came to naught. It remained stored at North Weald,
until March 1990, when it was taken on by Doug
Arnold's Warbirds of Great Britain organisation, and it
was subsequently flown to their base at Biggin Hill in
Kent on the 5th of that month. There then followed yet
another period of inactivity, for the most part incarcerat-
ed in Arnold's hangar under tight security, as was typical
of that outfit's policy. Occasionally pushed outside to
make room for other aircraft and for engine runs, it was
still at Biggin when Doug Arnold died, and it was to be
the only (and largest) member of his substantial fleet of
warbirds to remain there for any length of time after his

death, the rest being rapidly dispersed to different locations.

Eventually, on 21 August 1996, Dizzy Addicott and Keith Sissons flew it back to North Weald and into the care of Aces High once more, although this time they were only caretakers. On 10 October, it was registered to Bitteswell Ltd of Bournemouth, believed to be another Arnold company.

Since arriving in the UK in 1985, this Cat has hardly flown, and it just cries out for a new operator. At various times, there have been potential buyers for it, but all have fallen through. These have included the Israeli Air Force Museum, which wanted it for its collection at Hatzerim, and the PBY Catalina Foundation, which intended taking it to its base at Santa Rosa, California, and keeping it in an airworthy condition in US Navy markings. Biggin Hill-based Shipping and Airlines Ltd expressed an interest in obtaining it for use by an Italian company which wished to operate it on services between Naples and Ischia, whilst another party was intending to ferry scuba divers around in the Arabian Gulf. An interesting project which also failed to come off would have involved this PBY in a television travel programme with former Catalina pilot and TV personality Hughie Green.

On 19 August 1998, the British markings G-BPFY were cancelled from the CAA register and the aircraft entered another long period of external storage, still at North Weald, but this time in the care of another Arnold family company, Flying 'A' Services. That September, it was placed on the US civil register as N285RA, the new owner being the Randsburg Corporation of Mesa, Arizona. Despite this, it has remained firmly ground-bound at North Weald.

Greenpeace used PBY-5A N423RS in the North Sea area and in the Mediterranean during 1997–8. When seen at Duxford in 2000, the rainbow insignia of its operator could still be seen on the pylon, upper hull and vertical tail. *Author*

Table 132.

Registration/ Serial	C/n	Type	Place of Manufacture	Previous id(s)
N285RA		PBY-6A	CON NO	G-BPFY
				N212DM
				G-BPFY
				N212DM
				G-BPFY
				C-FHNH
				F-ZBAV
				N5555H
				N2846D
				Bu64017 (US Navy)

N423RS/'JV928/Y' – Super Catalina Restoration, Lee-on-Solent, Hampshire

The first US Navy squadron to operate Bu48423 was VP-73, based at Floyd Bennet Field, New York, and they took the aircraft on charge in January 1944. Later, it flew rescue missions from San Juan in Puerto Rico but came back to the mainland USA at the start of 1946. Thereafter, its military career is somewhat obscure, although it is known to have been struck off in July 1956, before being allocated the US civil registration N4002A. The mid-1960s onwards have seen this Catalina better documented, however. Survair of Ottawa, Canada, had the aircraft registered as CF-JJG, and it then flew with a number of Canadian survey companies, including Canadian Aero Service Ltd, which named it *Explorer One*, Spartan Air Services and, latterly, Kenting Earth Sciences, also of

Ottawa. Indeed, CF-JJG was the last of a number of different Catalinas and Cansos flown by this company, and it spent no fewer than 22 years with them. At different times, it flew with various types of survey equipment slung around its airframe, and these included a huge circular aerial array on a frame ahead of the bow, as well as a very large boom at the rear of the hull housing an electromagnetic receiver coil and magnetometer sensing head. Whilst quite a few survey Cats were similarly equipped, CF-JJG seemed to carry the largest and ugliest types of gear, particularly when it was with Kenting! Needless to say, with all this equipment cluttering up the airframe, the overall length of it was substantially increased and water operations were out of the question!

Ultimately, C-FJJG was to be one of the longest-lived survey Catalinas, indeed probably the last in service, remaining with Kenting until 1986, by which time rival firm Geoterrex had disposed of its own Catalina fleet. In 1986, it became N423RS on the US register, the registration reflecting the 'last three' of its US Navy serial and the initials of its new owner, Red Stevenson. Stevenson was no stranger to Catalinas, having briefly owned the PBY-6A now with Wilson 'Connie' Edwards as N4NC. N423RS was flown down to Reno in June of 1986 for storage in the sympathetic climate there. Ownership then passed first to Bruce Redding and then to APEXX Co Inc, before Dr Reginald Slade of Northern Air Inc, Dallas, Texas, became the proud owner in November 1987. He continued to operate it in the two-tone blue colour scheme worn toward the end of its Kenting days, but with the addition of nose art and the name *Polar Cat*.

Dr Slade based his PBY at Clebourne in Texas, but regularly used it to fly parties of sport fishermen up into Northern Canada for fishing trips, sometimes in the company of his other aircraft, a Grumman Turbo Goose amphibian. Usually based at Yellowknife, the Cat would range far and wide during these trips before returning to the warmer climes of Texas.

In 1997, N423RS was acquired by the interestingly named company Catalina Angels Ltd of Galesburg, Illinois, to which it was registered in that October. It had previously flown across the Northern Atlantic during August, staging through Kulusuk, Reykjavik and Sumburgh before arriving at Hamburg in Germany on the 26th. During the crossing, it was forced to stay at Narsassuaq, Greenland, for a few days with technical problems. By the end of the year it had been repainted in an overall white and dark blue scheme complete with the rainbow insignia and titles of its new user, the environmental organisation Greenpeace. They used the Catalina on reconnaissance flights over the North Sea and up as far as Norway, searching for vessels and rigs causing pollution there. It also ventured out to the Mediterranean, and was briefly based at Palma in the summer of 1998 whilst searching for fishing vessels using the dragnet method of catching fish.

In September 1998, N423RS flew to Duxford, England, where it was to be prepared for its return journey to the USA. In the event, it was decided to retain the Catalina at Duxford under the care and maintenance of the local Catalina operator Plane Sailing Air Displays whilst various options for its future use were considered. The registered owner was changed to Southern Aircraft Consultancy Inc of Cornwall on 9 November 1998.

Then, in the late summer of 2000, it was announced that N423RS and its associated spares package had been acquired by Super Catalina Restoration of Lasham, Hants, which had previously acquired the damaged airframe VP-BPS (described below) from its insurers after its accident on Southampton Water in July 1998. N423RS remained at Duxford until the following summer when it was repainted as RAF Catalina IVA JV928, just as its sister aircraft VP-BPS had flown some years previously when on the British register. Now based at Lee-on-Solent, it is available for air display work.

Table 133.

Registration/ Serial	C/n	Type	Place of Manufacture	Previous id(s)
N423RS	1785	PBY-5A	CON SD	C-FJJG CF-JJG N4002A Bu48423 (US Navy)

N9521C – Weavair Inc, North Weald, Essex

Since it was manufactured in 1943, this Catalina has flown as a military sub-hunter, private transport, fuel hauler and air display star! It also got mixed up with drugs! At the time of writing, it is half way into a ferry flight between South Africa, where it has spent the last few years in private ownership, and the USA, where it is intended to be based in future. However, it remains to be seen if and when this ferry flight is completed.

As Bu48294, it was built at San Diego in a batch of 200 PBY-5As serialled Bu48252 to 48451, being part of the large contract number NOa(s)-464 of August 1943. It was accepted onto military charge in November 1943, and is known to have spent some of its service life with VP-92, whose duties included anti-submarine missions out over the Atlantic from its bases in Casablanca and Port Lyautey, Morocco. It is claimed that it was involved in one attack against a U-boat, although further details are not known. Included in the various naval air bases that

Bu48294 flew from are San Diego, Norfolk, Seattle, Philadelphia, New York and Memphis. Later, it flew with the US Coast Guard and was retired in 1953 to the great Catalina bone-yard at Litchfield Park, Arizona, where it was formally deleted from the military inventory on 27 August 1956. Fortunately, it did not meet its appointment with the smelter but eventually embarked on a commercial career instead.

Registered as N9521C, it was owned by a succession of individuals and companies throughout the late 1960s, including use in South America, before ending up with Buddy Woods in Palmer, Alaska, around 1978. Here, it was used to transport passengers around to fishing sites, but a subsequent change of use saw it hauling fuel to various locations in that huge state. Internally, it was equipped with 1,500 US gallon flexible bag-tanks. Ownership passed to Catalina Flying Inc of Anchorage in 1983, and it remained with the company until some time in 1987. By this time, it was sporting a vivid colour scheme of white overall with large blue diagonal stripes on the hull. Its blisters and bow turret had long since been removed, and its rudder had been converted to the horn-balanced variety.

Around the mid- to late 1980s, N9521C fell into bad company! A Colombian outfit acquired the old warbird and it was put to the use that so many other aircraft have been involved in with that country's less law-abiding entrepreneurs. In the end, it was caught 'in the act' off the Florida coast and impounded, whilst its crew were taken into custody by the DEA (Drug Enforcement Agency)! Upon disposal, the Cat was acquired by Gus Vincent, who had it flown to Santa Rosa in California, where it was slowly renovated and repainted in a late Second World War US Navy colour scheme. Blisters and a bow turret were found for it, the latter coming from the unfortunate N84857 that had been badly damaged in a taxiing accident at Lewistown, Montana. Much of this work was carried out by the local firm Aerocrafters, but in the end, Vincent sold the aircraft on, this time to new owners in Europe.

The work to re-install the bow turret on N9521C is plain to see in this photo taken at Santa Rosa in California before the aircraft left for Italy.
Stuart Daglish

After a few years in Europe, N9521C moved on to South Africa, and is seen with engine cowlings removed at Lanseria in November 1997.
Ian Burnett

Aided and operated by Simpson Wallace Enterprises, N9521C was acquired by Joe Tosolini and Guido Bonfiglio for operation in Switzerland and Italy, and Aerocrafters was able to complete its rebuild for the new owners. Prior to flying out across the North Atlantic, N9521C lost its US star and bar insignia and acquired large International Red Cross emblems on the forward hull instead. The delivery flight was made by Tosolini and co-pilot Marco Pellegrini, together with Aerocrafters' Lynn Hunt, and commenced from Santa Rosa routeing via Idaho, Michigan, Maine, Gander in Newfoundland, Greenland, Reykjavik, Gothenburg in Sweden and Germany. The trip lasted a total of 62 hours and eventually terminated at its new base at Malpensa in Milan, Italy, on 21 May 1995. N9521C thus became only the second Catalina to be based in Italy in modern times, the first – N285NJ – having been briefly resident at Turin before being written off in a landing accident there in September 1987.

It was not very long before N9521C was appearing at air displays, its debut being the show at Padova on 17 June. The next day, it went on to become the largest seaplane ever to operate from Milan's Idroscalo, the original 1930s seaplane base, and later in the year it also flew from the Canal Grande in Venice as part of the Ciel e Acqua (Sky and Water) seaplane gathering . Whilst based in Europe, it flew at a fair number of airshows, although these were mainly confined to Switzerland and Italy. It was christened *Cat the Legend*.

Sadly for European seaplane enthusiasts, N9521C was to spend only two seasons in Italy before being sold by Guido Bonfiglio to new owner G. Macpherson. Italy's loss was South Africa's gain, and N9521C resided at Lanseria for a time, arriving there on 30 August 1997. Although still retaining the accurate-looking US Navy blue/grey colours, the US Navy and Red Cross insignia had all been removed, although the fin still wore the numerals 48294 in recognition of its original identity.

It did not aspire to a South African registration, and during the autumn of 1999 it left South Africa for the USA under the command of Chuck Ellsworth. The ferry flight became somewhat protracted when engine problems hit the aircraft and an enforced stay in Jeddah, Saudi

Arabia, ensued. It finally arrived at North Weald in England on 4 March 2000, bearing the rather appropriate name Phoenix on the port bow! The last stages of its journey to the UK had taken in Alexandria, Iraklion, Reggio di Calabria, Ajaccio and Lyon. In the autumn of 2000, N9521C was being advertised for sale with zero-time engines and total airframe hours of 4,500. However, it stayed at North Weald and, in July 2001, was temporarily repainted as Catalina I AH545/WQ-Z of 209 Squadron, RAF for some aerial film work off the Essex coast, complete with dummy depth charges.

Table 134.

Registration/ Serial	C/n	Type	Place of Manufacture	Previous id(s)
N9521C	1656	PBY-5A	CON SD	Bu48294 (US Navy)

(Unregistered ex-VP-BPS) – Super Catalina Restoration, Lee-on-Solent, Hampshire

If there is a single Catalina that has done more than any other example to revive and promote interest in the type, then it must be the one operated for several years by Plane Sailing Air Displays. Active on the European air show circuit from May 1985, it was displayed in front of hundreds of thousands of spectators, including the British Royal Family, made dozens of water landings and take-offs and crossed the Atlantic Ocean on charter work, once in each direction. Becoming one of the most popular British-based display aircraft, it exhibited consistently reliable performance and was probably the most frequently flown Catalina in the world until it was involved in an unfortunate accident in 1998. It was keenly supported by the membership of the Catalina Society, the first 'fan club' devoted to the type.

Unlike many of the remaining airworthy Cats, *Killer Cat* owed its post-war survival, not to the water bombing industry, but to the aerial photography and surveying business. However, its beginnings can be traced back to the end of 1944 at Consolidated's Lake Ponchartrain plant in New Orleans. It was there that PBY-5A construction number 1997 rolled down the line to become the US Navy's Bu46633. They took it on charge on 5 January 1945. It was one of the last PBY-5A models to be built in New Orleans, as, shortly thereafter, production switched to the taller-tailed PBY-6A variant.

Its military service was to last until January 1953, and during the intervening years, it was operated by FAW-14, VPB-100, VPB-53, NARTU San Diego, NARTU Los Amitos and NARTU Memphis. It is known to have been based at various locations, including Pearl Harbor; Alameda, California; Chincoteague; and Seattle. Once retired, Bu46633 joined others of its breed in the desert at the US Navy storage facility at Litchfield Park, Arizona. It remained there in the open, being struck off military charge in May 1956.

In that same year, it was purchased from the US military by the aircraft broker Trade Ayer Inc of Linden, New Jersey, and was registered to that company as N10023. It had several other Catalinas on charge, at least some of which were flown to Linden, so N10023 may well have ended up there. Subsequently it was sold in Canada as CF-MIR and delivered to its new owners Miron and

Immediately prior to being acquired by Plane Sailing Air Displays in 1984, C-FMIR was in use on geophysical survey work in South Africa. Here, it is parked up in between flights. Colours were silver overall, with red cheat line and black trim.
Jennifer M. Gradidge

Freres of Cartierville, Quebec, home of large-scale Catalina and Canso production a few years beforehand. The local firm of Noorduyn Norseman Aircraft was engaged to convert the Catalina for commercial operation and to modify it to a Super Cat in line with other conversions carried out in the USA by Steward-Davis. In the process, CF-MIR was equipped with Wright R-2600 Cyclone engines of 1,700 hp each, a 'clipper' bow in place of the nose turret, a taller and broader rudder and other refinements, such as an air stair, prop spinners and wheel 'hub caps'. The blister turrets were removed and replaced by a two-piece cargo door on the port side and a smaller emergency exit door on the starboard side. Most of the internal partitions were opened up, allowing more room between bulkheads for executive use. The conversion was completed by Noorduyn in December 1960, and on an early test flight, it suffered a minor accident when one main undercarriage leg folded up on landing at Cartierville.

According to a small plaque on the flight deck, the conversion was named a *Super Canso S/C 1000*, even though the term Canso is not appropriate for this former US Navy aircraft. As far as I have been able to ascertain, this is the only Super Catalina conversion carried out by Noorduyn.

Miron and Freres flew CF-MIR in the executive role, complete with under-wing dinghies, until some time in 1964. In September of that year, it was taken on by Laurentian Air Services of Ottawa, but ownership changed again some twelve months later when it was acquired by another local firm, Survair. In mid-1967, the US registration N608FF was allocated to the aircraft for Equitable Leasing of Burbank, which leased it on to several firms in turn, including Firefly Inc of Portland, Oregon; Aeroservice Corp of Philadelphia; and Barringer Research, another survey company. Firefly Inc is known to have operated Catalinas in the fire-fighting role, but it

is doubtful that N608FF was so converted. Indeed, I have not come across any photographic evidence as yet that proves that it was ever painted up with this registration.

Later, it went back to Canada again as CF-MIR and flew with Questor Surveys before being purchased by Geoterrex Surveys of Ottawa. Geoterrex operated it as one of a fleet of Super Cats on geophysical survey work the world over, both under its own name and that of Terra Surveys. Latterly, CF-MIR found its way to South Africa, where it carried out mineral survey flights equipped with a cable looped from bow to tail and back again via each wingtip, a stinger magnetometer tailboom and a trailing 'bomb' containing further surveying equipment which could be paid out on a long cable and winch from the rear of the airframe when in flight. Incidentally, an earlier photograph of CF-MIR when with Survair shows it with large wingtip end-plates, which presumably contained survey equipment but must have been removed after a short period of use.

Eventually, Geoterrex disposed of its Catalinas, and in 1984 CF-MIR was offered for sale 'as is' in South Africa. At this time, two Royal Air Force fast jet pilots, Paul Warren Wilson and John Watts, wanted to acquire a Catalina to display as a unique 'warbird' on the burgeoning European air display scene. It was also envisaged that it would be used for film, promotional and charter work as such opportunities arose. Having looked at, and rejected, two ex-Brazilian Air Force PBYs, a visit to South Africa was arranged and CF-MIR was purchased. Joined by the aviation photographer Arthur Gibson, the two pilots formed Plane Sailing Air Displays, to which the Catalina was registered as G-BLSC on 17 December 1984.

The aircraft was flown to the UK from South Africa over a seven-day period, routeing Johannesburg–Lusaka–Nairobi–Khartoum–Alexandria–Palermo–Cagliari–Marseille–RAF Manston, where it arrived on 20 February 1985. It later flew to RAF Barkston Heath in Lincolnshire, its base for the next two years, before moving on to Duxford in Cambridgeshire, its home until the summer of 1998. Whilst at Barkston Heath, it was lovingly overhauled by the newly formed volunteer support team – the *'Cat Pack'* – and painted in RAF Coastal Command colours to represent aircraft JV928/Y of 210 Squadron in which Flt Lt John Cruickshank won his

Victoria Cross. It received *Killer Cat* nose art on the bow – a cartoon cat clutching a submarine in its claws.

During 1990, a pair of fully operating blisters were placed back in position on the rear hull, a project aided by apprentices from the now defunct airline Dan Air and carried out at Manchester Airport. A change of colour scheme came in 1993 when the aircraft was repainted to represent the other Victoria Cross Catalina, 9754/P of 162 (BR) Squadron, Royal Canadian Air Force, in which Flt Lt David Hornell was mortally wounded in the action that was to see him posthumosuly awarded the highest honour for gallantry. This all-white scheme enabled rapid repainting on those occasions when charter and contract work dictated that additional trim be worn. Thus the airframe has carried the corporate colours of Peter Stuyvesant Travel and the Nastro Azzuro brand of Italian Beer. In 1997, it also wore the logo of S Orsola Asti whilst advertising Italian wine!

In 1994, the Catalina was removed from the British Civil Aircraft Register and re-registered in Bermuda as VR-BPS in order to allow less-restricted passenger-carrying capability. Later, in 1997, the Bermudan markings had to be changed to VP-BPS when China claimed the VR-B series as part of the handover of Hong Kong.

Prior to the accident in 1998, this Catalina's biggest adventure was undoubtedly to cross the Atlantic to South America to take part in the 1994 Peter Stuyvesant Travel Odyssey. This charter was spread over more than two months, and the stages were Duxford–Oporto–Lanzarote–Sal–Praia–Natal, then to Rio and La Paz and on through Central America to Miami, and back across the Northern Atlantic route via St Johns to Shannon and Duxford. The following year, VR-BPS was a priviledged participant in the commemorative flypast over Central London and Buckingham Palace on the 50th Anniversary of VE Day, when it represented RAF maritime aviation. Additionally, it was operated from water, both inland and coastal, on numerous occasions.

All this came to an end during a promotional flight involving water landings and take-offs from Southampton Water in Hampshire on 27 July 1998. Whilst accelerating to take-off speed during a touch-and-go landing, VP-BPS went out of control, swung violently to port and took on water after coming to a standstill. All but two of the 18 occupants safely evacuated the aircraft before it sank up to its wings. Sadly, two passengers lost their lives, having been unable to leave the forward section of the aircraft before it filled with water. In the circumstances, it was some comfort to the pilots and owners when the Air Accident Investigation Branch (AAIB) investigated the accident and attached no blame to the operator or crew. It transpired, according to the AAIB report, that first one, then the other, nose-wheel door had detached from the hull after one of the torque tubes had failed because of internal corrosion. The sudden deceleration that this failure caused had led to an inrush of water that tore open the cockpit flooring, allowing water to enter the inner hull. The area of corrosion was found in a part of the structure not included in normal maintenance schedules.

The damaged airframe was recovered and moved to Hamble, where it was stored until purchased from the insurers by a new group who planned to repair and fly the Catalina. Soon after work had started on the rebuild, the project was moved to Lasham, also in Hampshire, during May 1999. Work has continued to bring the airframe up to airworthiness since then. At the time that this book was going to press, plans were afoot for a further move to the former HMS *Daedalus* airfield at Lee-on-Solent.

From May 1985 until the tragic accident on Southampton Water on 27 July 1998, this Catalina could

For its first few years on the UK air show circuit, Plane Sailing's Catalina G-BLSC flew in 210 Squadron markings as JV928/Y. After its blisters had been put back in place, it also wore the titles of the now-defunct British airline Dan-Air, whose engineering division had carried out the work. Photo taken at North Weald, 1990.
Author

justly claim to be the most consistently active example of its type in the world, although, at the time of the accident, its airframe age was only 13,000 hours young!

Table 135.

Registration/ Serial	C/n	Type	Place of Manufacture	Previous id(s)
–	1997	PBY-5A	CON NO	VP-BPS VR-BPS G-BLSC C-FMIR N608FF CF-MIR N10023 Bu46633 (US Navy)

8466M/L-866 (RDAF) – RAF Cosford, Shropshire

Although hardly representative of an RAF example, Cosford's preserved Catalina is none the less a valuable part of the museum collection there. It has been maintained in superb external condition over the last few years since it was brought indoors from external display and repainted. In deference to its former operators, it has retained Royal Danish Air Force colours.

The first operator of this PBY-6A, however, was the United States Navy, which took delivery of it from Consolidated, New Orleans, in May 1945, its first flight having taken place on 28 April that year. Between that

time and its retirement in 1953, it flew with a host of units, including FAW-14, FAW-8, FAW-2 and VPB-71, operating from such diverse locations as Terminal Island, California, and the Naval Air Stations at Alameda, Pearl Harbor, Philadelphia, Mustin, Willow Grove, Seattle and Norfolk. It was delivered into storage at Litchfield Park, Arizona, on 13 October 1953. It remained there until refurbished for the flight to Pan Air's facility at New Orleans on 18 March 1957. Pan Air was a commercial company that was specialising in bringing former American military Catalinas up to serviceable condition again so that they could be supplied to other air forces. Bu64017 was destined to join the Royal Danish Air Force, which was already flying Canso A and PBY-5A models and was now taking delivery of PBY-6As. The work was completed by Pan Air the following December, and with its new Danish serial 82-866 it was delivered to Værløse, arriving there on the 18th. It then received further modifications from the Danish Air Force Air Material Command to prepare it for air force service . These modifications included the large radar fairing atop the cockpit with its shape unique to the RDAF 'Milcats'.

From 1958 onwards it flew with Esk 72 at Værløse, and is known to have used the radio call-sign OVJBF at some point. It was transferred to Esk 722 in May 1961, having been re-serialled L-866 the year before. In February 1966, it returned to Esk 721 and it continued serving the RDAF until early 1970, by which time it had amassed around 3,700 hours' flying time with them. At this point, a major overhaul was needed, but as the remaining Catalina fleet was due to be withdrawn later that year, L-866 was grounded and it stayed in storage at Værløse until 30 May 1974, when it was gifted to the RAF Museum and flown to Colerne in Wiltshire, where it

Shiny L-866 at the RAF Museum, Cosford, where it is displayed in full RDAF livery, complete with liberal amounts of dayglo orange on the bow and tail.

joined the RAF Museum Reserve Collection. This was to be its last flight, which brought total airframe hours since first flight to 5,343. In its time with the RDAF, it was used on search-and-rescue missions, maritime patrols and transport flights. It was frequently flown on the 4,000-mile round trip to Greenland, where it resupplied weather and radio stations as well as monitoring the movement of ice floes. During one such sortie in 1968, it struck an iceberg whilst taxiing on Greenland's east coast, and because of extensive damage to the bow, it was beached at Danesborg and temporarily repaired before a more permanent job could be carried out at Mestersuig.

Soon after its delivery to Colerne, that RAF base was closed down and the aircraft stored there had to be dispersed. L-866 was dismantled by personnel from 71 Maintenance Unit and taken by road to RAF Cosford, where it became part of the growing collection of aircraft there. This collection beame known as the Cosford Aerospace Museum and then, in 1998, the Royal Air Force Museum, Cosford. The RAF Maintenance Serial 8466M is allocated to this Catalina.

Table 136.

Registration/ Serial	C/n	Type	Place of Manufacture	Previous id(s)
L-866/8466M (RAF g/i)		PBY-6A	CON NO	L-866 (RDAF) 82-866 (RDAF) Bu63993 (US Navy)

Eighteen
SURVIVORS IN ASIA

DIEGO GARCIA, INDIAN OCEAN

VA718/K – ex-Royal Air Force, Diego Garcia Island

VA718 just about qualifies as a survivor in this section because, although it has lain derelict on Diego Garcia since 1944, it is basically still a fairly complete airframe, albeit well beyond restoration to flying condition, or indeed static display for that matter.

It was originally built by Consolidated at San Diego on Contract C-78 as part of an order for 36 Model 28-5MC (MC = Military Canada) aircraft serialled 9701 to 9736 for the Royal Canadian Air Force. Had these Catalinas stayed with the RCAF, they would have been known as Cansos (pure flying boats as opposed to Canso A amphibians), but a number of them went straight to the Royal Air Force as replacements for aircraft 'borrowed' earlier, and were given Catalina IIA designations. They were initially allotted RAF serials in the V series, but these duplicated a batch of Westland Lysanders. The solution was found by renumbering the aircraft with serials commencing VA, even though they were sequentially several years ahead of their logical issue date. Thus RCAF 9718 was at first given the serial V9718, but became VA718. It was formally taken on charge by the RCAF on 21 October 1941, and struck off as supplied to the RAF on 15 November.

It was ferried across the Atlantic, still painted as 9718, on delivery to the RAF, and arrived at Saunders Roe, Beaumaris, Anglesey, on 18 March 1942, under the command of Captain Hearsum. It stayed until 2 April, when

On the beach – VA718 seen at its resting-place after the storm of 16 September 1944. Since this picture was taken a few years ago, the hulk has deteriorated further.

it flew to Scottish Aviation at Greenock, returning to Beaumaris on the 24th. On 15 June 1942, it departed for Lough Erne in Northern Ireland, its conversion to RAF standards completed.

At Lough Erne, it joined 240 Squadron, which was preparing to fly out to the Far East. In due course, VA718 went with the Squadron to its new base at Redhills Lake although it may well have operated subsequently from any of 240's detached bases at Coconada, Cochin, Koggala, Addu Atoll, Kelai, Diego Garcia or China Bay! In 240 Squadron service, it was coded 'K'.

Diego Garcia was at that time designated as 29 Advanced Flying Boat Base, and in the early hours of 16 September 1944, it was hit by a hurricane. At that time, VA718 was moored off the shore, having flown there to shadow a Japanese submarine It had left Kelai in the Maldives, where it had been unable to refuel because the petrol bowser had been sunk. On arrival at Diego Garcia, the Catalina's tanks were almost dry and so the airframe was very light. The storm was so severe that the plane guards were unable to save the aircraft by starting up its engines, and the hapless Catalina ended up beached some distance away. Two other Catalinas were swept away by the same storm but were successfully recovered. Incredibly, VA718 has remained on the beach at Diego Garcia ever since, gradually falling to bits, no doubt aided by local souvenir hunters or those who can use sections of old aluminium! By 1998, the rear hull aft of the blisters had disappeared, as had the starboard outer wing.

It should be noted that some sources have in the past quoted the place of manufacture for the batch of Catalinas including 9718/VA718 as Canadian Vickers at Cartierville, Quebec. This is not the case. In addition, the storm location has been described as Diego Suarez (Madagascar), which, although a Catalina base, was not the location of the incident described. The wreck is most certainly at Diego Garcia, hundreds of miles from Diego Suarez!

Table 137.

Registration/ Serial	C/n	Type	Place of Manufacture	Previous id(s)
VA718 (RAF)	318	Canso/ Catalina IIA	CON SD	V9718 (RAF) 9718 (RCAF)

INDONESIA

'PB-505' – TNI-AU Museum, Jogyakarta, Jakarta

This late-1943-vintage PBY-5A served its country with

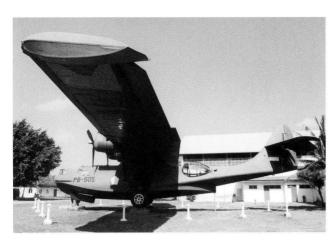

At some point after this 1990s photograph was taken, a covered shelter was built over some of the TNI-AU museum exhibits, including the Catalina.
via Martin Willing

the US Navy as Bu46539, being taken on charge on 2 March 1944. It flew with Fleet Air Wing 14 and VPB-53 before passing to the US Coast Guard at Elizabeth City, North Carlolina. Declared obsolete in July 1946, it was disposed of to the Charlotte Aircraft Corporation of Charlotte, North Carolina. Sadly, it was destined to remain in the open, unconverted, until 1985, by which time it had become derelict in California. It has been said that it was used as a duck hatchery at some stage!

The hulk was acquired by Gary Larkins and taken to Auburn, California for restoration. During the rebuild, the name Ol' #9 was found on the hull under several layers of paint. The original intention of the rebuild was to produce an airworthy restoration. However, it was instead sold to the famous air-speed record holder, Darryl Greenamyer, who then traded it to Indonesia, in exchange for other aircraft, for display in a museum there.

During the 1950s, the Indonesian Air Force (Angakan Udara Republik Indonesia, or AURI, and later to become the TNI-AU) operated several PBY-5A amphibians which were acquired from an unknown source, and they were keen to obtain one to preserve in honour of these aircraft. Darryl Greenamyer's Catalina was initially imported into Indonesia for the Amerta Dirgantara Museum at Kalijati military airfield, West Java, where an air force officer was assembling a collection of historic aircraft. After his untimely death in an air crash, N1563M remained stored at Kalijati. By mid-1993, it had been placed on outdoor display at Jogyakarta Air Force Base, painted to represent an original AURI aircraft, serial PB-505, of 5 Squadron. Subsequently, an open-sided shelter was erected to protect the Catalina from the elements. 'PB-505' is in the care of the TNI-AU (Tentara Nasional Indonesia – Angkatan Udara, or Indonesia Armed Forces Air Force) Museum of Dirgantala Mandala on Jakarta's Adisutijiptu Airport.

Table 138.

Registration/ Serial	C/n	Type	Place of Manufacture	Previous id(s)
'PB-505' (AURI)	1903	PBY-5A	CON SD	N1563M Bu46539 (US Navy)

Nineteen
SURVIVORS IN THE UNITED STATES OF AMERICA

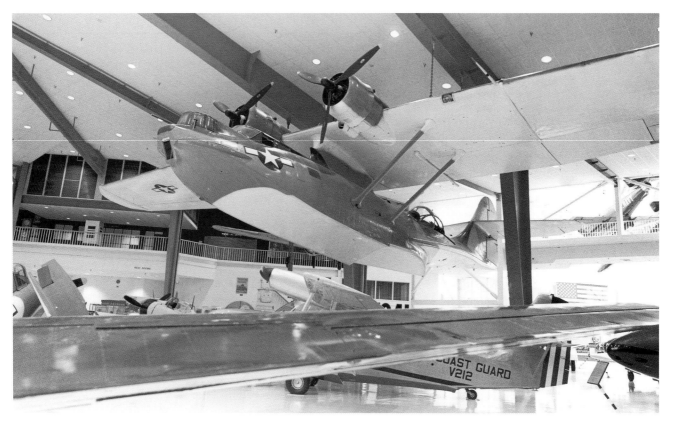

PBY-5 Bu08317 flies from the roof of the US Naval Aviation Museum, Pensacola, Florida. It is the only complete and restored PBY-5 in existence.
via James D. Mooney

Bu08317 – United States Naval Aviation Museum, Pensacola, Florida

Bu08317 has the distinction of being the only complete surviving PBY-5 in the world – indeed, it is one of only two intact pure flying boat Catalinas remaining, all the others being amphibians (the other boat is the PB2B-2 VH-ASA at the Powerhouse Museum, Sydney, Australia, although Albany's PBY-5 at the Whaleworld Museum in the same country is close to complete, lacking only the outer wings). How appropriate, therefore, that it should be preserved for visitors to see at the Museum of Naval Aviation at Pensacola in Florida. There, it is kept in good condition inside the museum buildings, suspended above the other exhibits by cables attached to the roof.

It was built at San Diego for the US Navy as part of the batch of 426 PBY-5s serialled Bu08124 to 08549, ordered on contract number NOs 91876 of April 1942.

After its military service was over, it eventually entered into storage at the Norfolk Naval Air Station in Virginia, and it is known to have been there between roughly 1965 and 1973, kept on behalf of the National Air and Space Museum. Although still the owner, the NASM decided to loan this unique aircraft to the Museum of Naval Aviation, and it has been at Pensacola since 1973. As will be seen from the next entry, although it is the only complete PBY-5 flying boat, it none the less shares the large base at Pensacola with another incomplete example!

Table 139.

Registration/ Serial	C/n	Type	Place of Manufacture	Previous id(s)
Bu08317 (US Navy)	1231	PBY-5	CON SD	

FP216 – Pensacola, Florida

Although not complete, FP216 is a truly unusual Catalina relic that deserves its place in any list of survivors. Unfortunately, it is not on public view at the present time, although there are hopes that it will one day go on display at the Museum of Naval Aviation at Pensacola.

FP216 was built at San Diego, and a plate on the instrument panel shows the manufacture date as 14 July 1942, and an MFG number 117, possibly a construction number, but more likely a 'set number' used on the production line to identify the individual aircraft within its contract. Although ordered for the Royal Air Force, hence its serial, it was one of a number of Catalinas held back in the USA and used for training purposes. As such, it would have worn US markings whilst retaining its RAF identification. It is known to have served with VN8D8A, a Pensacola-based seaplane advanced training squadron, and was struck off charge after a water loop in East Bay on 28 May 1944. The hull was badly wrinkled around Bulkhead Six, but the basically intact airframe was saved from scrapping so that it could carry out ground-based duties.

The wings were removed and the entire hull was built into the side of a building on the base at Pensacola. There, it was used by the Land Survival Training Center. The 'outer wall' was left in its original condition, but on the inside of the building, the hull was cut away to show the interior fittings. Thus, virtually all of its original equipment has remained in place and the whole exhibit gives a very good idea of the construction methods used on the PBY.

FP216 was built into the wall of the Land Survival Center on the air base at Pensacola. The hull was full length and was complete with starboard wing and engine.
Torben Jensen

This is how FP216 looked inside the Pensacola building where it resided for so many years. The cutaway format revealed the inside structure and equipment. The airframe is now in storage on the base, awaiting a decision on its future.
Norm Stutzer

Over the years, the 'Cutaway PBY' remained in use until, around 1997, it was decided that the Land Survival Center itself would be demolished. Fortunately, various interested parties are determined to see that FP216 is not demolished with it, and there are plans afoot to save this important exhibit. Spearheaded by members of the PBY Catalina International Association, a fund has been set up to have the Catalina moved, restored and then placed on display beneath the PBY-5 Bu08317 which is suspended from the roof of the Museum of Naval Aviation elsewhere on the base at Pensacola. The two Catalinas together would make a very unusual dual exhibit, and it is to be hoped that this project is successful. In the meantime, the hull has now been separated from the building and is undergoing restoration at Pensacola before going on display.

Table 140.

Registration/ Serial	C/n	Type	Place of Manufacture	Previous id(s)
FP216 (RAF)	'117'/ 803	Catalina I/PBY-5B	CON SD	

C-GFFC – SLAFCO Inc, Moses Lake, Washington

Despite its Canadian civil registration, C-GFFC has spent the last few years across the border in Washington State, where it is currently held in storage as part of the fleet of Robert Schlaefli's SLAFCO Inc at Moses Lake. Schlaefli owns the largest single fleet of Catalinas in the world, although only two of these aircraft – both Wright Cyclone-powered *Super Cats* – are currently in flying condition. The others, including C-GFFC, are retained in readiness for possible future use, although, as years go by, it has to be wondered if they will ever see water bombing service again in the face of competition from more modern equipment. Indeed, the whole SLAFCO

Still Canadian registered, but part of the SLAFCO fleet for some years, C-GFFC is seen at its Moses Lake base in early 2000. Colours are grey uppers with red hull and trim. *A. E. Hawkins*

fleet was put up for auction in 1999, although the sale did not in the end proceed, at least as far as the complete aircraft were concerned.

After seeing service with the USAAF as an OA-10A, it was sold on the American market as N1942M before being re-registered as CF-IIW in Canada. It is known to have flown with Pacific Western Airlines and with Northern Wings out of Seven Islands, Quebec, during the 1950s. Whilst with Northern Wings, it sustained serious damage when it crashed on landing at Lac Rapide on 6 June 1957. There were no injuries to the occupants and the aircraft was soon repaired.

In 1969, it was once more registered in the USA, this time as N3202, the new owner being Universal Air Leasing of Grand Blanc, Michigan. That ownership was brief, and the following year it was acquired by Richard L. Rude, who at that time was the owner of the fire-fighting company Flying Fireman Ltd, of Victoria, British Columbia. With them, it took on its second Canadian registration when it was allocated its present marks C-GFFC. Whilst with Flying Fireman, it had to be salvaged when, in 1981, it was threatened by encroaching ice during a spell on the water! Flown as Tanker 6, later 776, it remained with Flying Fireman when the company was taken over by Alexander Wood, and it stayed with the company until around 1988, when it was withdrawn. Sometime after this, it flew south to Moses Lake, where it remained, still in Flying Fireman's grey and red livery but part of SLAFCO's fleet.

For reasons unknown, the construction number quoted on the Canadian Civil Aircraft Register for this Catalina is '013'.

Table 141.

Registration/ Serial	C/n	Type	Place of Manufacture	Previous id(s)
C-GFFC	CV-483 (register quotes 013)	OA-10A	CAN VIC (Cartierville)	N3202 CF-IIW N1942M 44-33972 (USAAF) Bu67936 ntu (US Navy)

N2172N – Erickson Group Ltd, Tillamook Naval Air Station Museum, Tillamook, Oregon

When Flying Fireman wound down its once extensive fleet of Catalinas and disposed of them, none were destined to remain in Canada. Of those that found their way across the border into the USA, Catalina constructor's number 1886 did not move too far away and is today preserved in a museum in nearby Oregon State.

One of no fewer than 330 Catalinas built under Contract NOa(s)-464 at San Diego, California, it fell within the serial batch Bu46450–46579, the remaining 200 aircraft being numbered Bu48252–48451. Accepted by the US Navy on 22 February 1944, it became Bu46522 and eventually ended its service days at the US Navy's storage facility at Litchfield Park, Arizona, being officially struck from the Navy inventory on 27 August 1956.

It was saved from an ignominious end and placed on the US civil register as N5585V, and by 1963 it was registered to the Summer Institute of Linguistics, Glendale, California. The Institute owned it until 1966, when it passed on to Jungle Aviation and Radio Service of Waxhaw, North Carolina. In 1970, it went to Flying Fireman of Victoria, BC, and was converted to a forest fire fighter. With the new identity CF-FFA, it was to remain with that organisation until 1990, by which time the owner's title had been changed to the somewhat less colourful Awood Air Ltd. During its long period of service as a water bomber, it operated with the hull code 7, later changed to 777.

In January 1990, Jack Erickson of Erickson Air Crane Company, Central Point, Oregon, purchased C-FFFA, as it had become, and it flew south to be based at Medford in the same State. It was registered as N2172N the following month and was subsequently painted in a US Navy colour scheme bearing its genuine US Navy serial Bu46522. Sadly, on 8 July 1994, it was badly damaged during a water take-off from Devil's Lake near Lincoln

N2172N enjoying the fresh air at Tillamook. It has a somewhat 'mixed' colour scheme, and carries the serial 46522 on the vertical tail in yellow. *Heijo Kuil*

City, Oregon, when it hit a boat dock. At the time of the accident, the wind was gusting to 30 kt. The two crew on board were carrying out training flights but escaped unharmed. The NTSB accident report attributed the cause of the accident to the pilot's failure to maintain clearance from the boat dock during the aborted take-off. Contributory causes included the pilot's poor in-flight decision to land on the narrow lake under unfavourable wind conditions and to then attempt a take-off in a strong cross-wind.

Repairs to hull damage were carried out, and the Catalina was later flown off the lake, although it sustained further damage to one wingtip during the landing roll when it arrived back at Tillamook. Subsequently, N2172N was placed on display as a static exhibit at Jack Erickson's museum at Tillamook on Oregon's northern coast. Here, it is housed within the largest timber-framed building in the USA, formerly used to hangar airships during the Second World War. Later, it was returned to airworthy condition once more, and from time to time its owners display it at West Coast airshows, an example being the display at the Naval Air Station at Whidbey Island in neighbouring Washington State in July 1998.

This particular PBY is unusual amongst latter-day fire-fighting Catalinas because both its nose turret and blisters were retained. So, apart from its horn-balanced rudder, it remains in almost stock external condition.

Table 142.

Registration/ Serial	C/n	Type	Place of Manufacture	Previous id(s)
N2172N	1886	PBY-5A	CON SD	C-FFFA CF-FFA N5585V Bu46522 (US Navy)

N222FT – Wilson 'Connie' Edwards, Big Springs, Texas

Thanks to the investment of a large amount of dollars, this particular Catalina appears in the Survivors section of this book rather than in the list of recent losses! However, it could have been a different story following an unfortunate landing accident back in 1986.

Forty-two years previously, construction number CV-397 was completed at Cartierville, Quebec, home of Canadian Vickers, and it was taken on strength by the Royal Canadian Air Force as serial 11074. Between then and November 1961, when it was finally struck off charge, it is known to have served with 413 (PR) Squadron, the post-war successor to the famous Canadian Tusker Squadron within the RAF. The post-war 413 was formed from an earlier unit – 13 (PR) Squadron – and it is possible that 11074 flew with that squadron also. No. 13 Squadron was based at Rockcliffe, Ontario, and flew mapping flights up into the Arctic – indeed, it 'rediscovered' the Spicer Islands, which had previously been lost for almost fifty years! It was redesignated 413 Squadron on 1 April 1947, the original RAF Squadron having been disbanded in February 1945. The 'new' 413 carried on with the aerial mapping role using a mixture of Cansos, Lancasters, Dakotas, Norseman and B-25 Mitchells. They also flew humanitarian missions during

particularly bad floods in the Winnipeg area in 1950. It was an early user of JATO (Jet Assisted Take Off) equipment on Cansos. The unit was disbanded in October 1950, and 11074 must have gone on to another unit until its eventual withdrawal, by which time it had lost its blisters and nose turret.

By 1965, it had been registered as CF-OWE to Ontario Central Airlines, which was based at both Kenora, Ontario, and Gimli, Manitoba, and the company held on to it until the 1970s, although towards the end of its ownership it was in a pretty poor state. Photos taken at the time show it in open storage minus engines and with the nose weighted down by concrete blocks to prevent it falling back onto its tail. However, Catalinas have shown powers of regeneration throughout their history, and CF-OWE was refurbished for further passenger service, this time with Winnipeg-based Ilford Riverton Airways, which had it painted up in a colourful yellow and green livery. 1983 saw it briefly registered to Northland Outdoors of Canada before it was sold to Robert J. Franks of Los Angeles and re-registered as N691RF in June 1984.

Franks had the aircraft virtually rebuilt by engineers from Flying Fireman Ltd, of Victoria, BC, which at that time was drastically slimming down its own Catalina operation. The rebuild included the replacement of blisters, the port unit being a tinted one-piece blown perspex unit which hinged upwards for easy passenger access. It was again re-registered, this time as C-FOWE, in 1985 before being cancelled once more in March 1989, in favour of the slightly modified US marks N69RF. Although it continued to be owned by Franks, the registered owners changed a few times, including periods with Jonathon Seagull Holdings and Flying Catalina Corporation.

Soon after Robert Franks acquired his Catalina, he decided to fly it across the Atlantic in company with Wilson 'Connie' Edwards's PBY-6A N4NC to commemorate 75 years of US Naval Aviation. Details of that trip can be found under the entry for N4NC. For the journey, C-FOWE, as she was then still registered, was painted in an attractive colour scheme with commemorative 75th anniversary insignia, although the finished effect was somewhat less outrageous than that applied to N4NC! Sadly, C-FOWE managed to attract more attention than intended when, at the end of the outward journey to Plymouth, England, it spectacularly water-looped during its landing. The following details are taken from the official accident report.

The accident occurred at 10.50 hours on 31 May 1986, when the aircraft landed at Plymouth Harbour with seven on board, four crew and three passengers, of whom one crew member and one passenger sustained minor injuries. C-FOWE approached to land off Plymouth Hoe on a water landing strip 1,220 × 122 metres marked out in the harbour by Royal Navy patrol craft which had previously searched the area for floating debris and kept it clear of other craft. Visibility was good beneath a 1,500 ft cloudbase, and the wind was from the north-west at 5 knots, giving a cross-wind for landing of about 3 knots from the right.

The Catalina touched down some 460 metres after the start of the landing strip after an extended flare, during which it flew in a level attitude over the water for some

Now in the USA as N222FT, this superb photo shows it as
C-FOWE on the day it left Plymouth, England, after being
repaired following the unfortunate accident in May 1986.
The one-piece tinted perspex blister on the starboard side
is of note.
Western Morning News, Plymouth

200 metres. Touchdown was gentle and in a normal attitude, but some three seconds after initial water contact
and about one second after the bow settled on the water,
the aircraft yawed sharply to starboard, and at the same
time, a surge of engine power was heard. The rudder was
seen to move fully to the left as yaw developed, but the
aircraft turned through approximately 40 degrees before
the yaw was checked. Throughout this time, both
wingtip floats were clear of the water, but as the Catalina
straightened up, the starboard float knocked over an
inflatable buoy without any apparent damage to the aircraft. Immediately afterwards. the left wing struck a solid
channel marker buoy which tore off a substantial part of
the port wing and float, causing the Catalina to pivot violently to the left, the hull momentarily leaving the water
before dropping hard on the left side of the nose and
coming to rest with the hull slowly filling with water. The
passengers were safely taken off and the Catalina was
quickly towed to a beaching area, where it partially sank
in shallow water in a level attitude .

Subsequent inspection of the airframe showed that
the nosewheel doors were both missing, and they
were not recovered. It was evident that they had been
violently ripped off during the landing and that high
hydrodynamic forces had been experienced in the
nose-wheel bay. Available evidence indicated that
the nose-wheel doors were fully closed at touchdown.
The pilot later stated that he considered his approach and
landing had been normal with touchdown at 75 knots.
He could not account for the undemanded yaw and had
no recollection of having applied power at any time after
touchdown.

C-FOWE was brought ashore and hangared at the old
RAF base of Mount Batten, minus 19 ft of its port wing.

A later view of Canso CV-397 shows it in the USA
registered as N69RF. Although the bow turret has been
removed, the bomb-aimer's window has been retained.
The neat forward entry hatch and collapsible ladder can be
seen ahead of the undercarriage.
Ray Williams/Catalina Aero Services

Over the next few weeks, spare parts, including a spare
wing from British Columbia, were brought across the
Atlantic, and it was repaired by the owner's staff and
personnel from the Royal Navy and Plymouth Executive
Aviation Ltd ready for its test flight on 8 October. The
next day, it departed for Canada, initially flying to Exeter
before flying on to Lisbon and the Azores, then St Johns,
Newfoundland, and Thunder Bay, Ontario. Once back in
Canada, further refurbishment was carried out on
Vancouver Island by Catalina operators Flying Fireman
Ltd. The wrecked outer wing and float found their way
to Duxford for Plane Sailing Air Displays, to be used for
spares recovery. In March 1999, N69RF was re-registered
to Omni Enterprises of Sandpoint, Idaho. In the spring of
2000, the Catalina was offered for sale at US$875,000, and
it was subsequently purchased by none other than the

afore-mentioned Wilson 'Connie' Edwards. By the end of the summer, it had acquired rather flamboyant nose art with the name *Flyin' Turtle*, and in August 2000 a new registration – N222FT.

Table 143.

Registration/ Serial	C/n	Type	Place of Manufacture	Previous id(s)
N222FT	CV-397	Canso A	CAN VIC (Cartierville)	N69RF C-FOWE N691RF CF-OWE 11074 (RCAF)

N2763A – SLAFCO Inc, Moses Lake, Washington

The largest fleet of PBYs extant in the USA, indeed the only fleet now remaining there, is that owned by Robert Schlaefli's company SLAFCO Inc, based at the former USAF bomber base of Moses Lake, Washington. Of the five complete examples that he owns, two have been kept fully airworthy and in regular use whilst the others wait in the wings in case of need. N2763A is one of the complete airframes, but has not flown in recent times, although it could no doubt be turned into a 'flyer' in a short space of time, especially in view of SLAFCO's large Catalina spares holding.

N2763A's United States Navy history is unfortunately obscure, but it is known to have carried the military serial Bu21232. This serial was a solitary allocation in the middle of a large batch of Curtiss Helldivers of various marks – indeed, serial 21232 was allocated to a Helldiver, but this original reservation was not taken up. For reasons I have not been able to ascertain, this Catalina's construction number appears to be unknown and is not quoted at all in the US Civil Aircraft Register. Other sources have tended to use the US Navy serial as the c/n. It is therefore not possible to ascertain its exact pedigree, although it may possibly have been a rebuild that was allocated a brand-new serial or a transfer from the USAAF.

Its first commercial owner was Paul Mantz Aviation, which used it with the registration N5609V between 1947 and 1949. It seems likely that its acquisition may have had something to do with the movie industry, as Paul Mantz was very much involved with aviation-related films and filming, and later went on to found Tallmantz Aviation with like-minded Frank Tallman. The next owner was International Aviation Corporation of Glendale, California, but this company quickly sold it on to Queen Charlotte Airlines of Vancouver, BC, in 1951, and it remained with that company until 1957, operating with the Canadian identity CF-GHU and named *Kitimat Queen*. It was mainly used on services linking Vancouver, Ocean Falls, Kemano, Port Hardy and Kitimat, where the Alcan company ran a smelter. Whilst retaining the blister turrets, the nose turret was replaced with a clipper bow.

Queen Charlotte Airlines was absorbed into another well-known Canadian carrier, Pacific Western, which took on CF-GHU, but by the end of 1957, the new registration N2763A had been allocated to it and it was flying with Alaska Coastal-Ellis Airlines of Juneau, Alaska. This airline used a number of Catalinas, and in addition to N2763A, two others have survived, namely N31235 (also with SLAFCO) and N4760C, now at McChord Air Force Base. It was to stay in Alaska whilst the owner metamorphosed into Alaska Coastal Airlines, and then Alaska Airlines. Then, in the early 1970s, came a new operator in warmer climes – Antilles Air Boats, owned by the famous aviator Charles Blair and based at St Thomas in the US Virgin Islands.

By the end of the decade, N2763A was to be found withdrawn from use at Watsonville in California, and although it was to be briefly owned by a gentleman from Santa Cruz, California, it was sold on to Robert Schlaefli in 1982 and it has been at Moses Lake ever since. At the time of purchase, the wings were wearing military

In March 1970, N2763A could be seen at Litchfield Park in Arizona in the colours of former operator Alaska Airlines. *Jennifer M. Gradidge*

colours that had been painted on for film use, and these have remained.

In common with the other three Catalinas operated by Alaska Coastal-Ellis Airlines, N2763A was converted to a *Super Cat* by Steward-Davis – indeed, contemporary editions of *Jane's All the World's Aircraft* used a photo of N2763A to illustrate the relevant entry in the book. N2763A remains in this *Super Cat* format today with its 'Davis' tail and Wright R-2600 engines.

N2763A was unsold after the auction of SLAFCO's assets in 1999.

Table 144.

Registration/ Serial	C/n	Type	Place of Manufacture	Previous id(s)
N2763A	?	PBY-5A	?	CF-GHU N5609V Bu21232 (US Navy)

This is how Super Cat N287 looked at Fort Lauderdale in October 1991. It is gloss black overall, and lacks rudder and nose-gear doors. Both props are feathered in this view. *Erik Derogee*

N287 – Super Three Inc, Weeks Air Museum, Kendall – Tamiami Airport, Tamiami, Florida

N287 can attribute its survival into the late 1990s, not to the fire-fighting industry, but to the other area of activity that found the PBY so useful – the aerial surveying business. The ability to fly low and slow for long periods, and at the same time offer an airframe large enough to sling around it the paraphernalia that goes with the job, meant that a good number of Catalinas saw use throughout the world on mapping projects and in search of minerals and oil.

But, before N287 was converted for its geophysical survey role, it served the US Navy as PBY-5A, Bu48287, having been built at San Diego, California. It was used as a military aircraft from November 1943, to July 1956, when it was finally struck off charge and consigned to mothballing at Litchfield Park, Arizona.

Its first civil identity was N10017, one of a batch of consecutively registered ex-US Navy PBY-5As. By the end of the 1950s, it was flying with Toronto-based Questor Surveys Ltd as CF-JMS, and at some point after joining the company it was converted to a Wright R-2600-powered *Super Cat* by Timmins Aviation. Prior to this, it had had its blisters removed and replaced by hinged hatches, whilst still retaining the bow turret. In 1964 there was a change of operator when it briefly joined the Australian civil register as VH-UMS, flying as such with Selco Exploration and Australia Selection Pty. By the end of the year, however, it was back on the Canadian register as CF-JMS again, this time with Barringer Surveys Ltd, which is known to have flown several Catalinas in the survey role. Prior to this, it was seen at Nandi Airport, Fiji, in full Selco titles but with its Canadian registration. It may also have operated with Kenting at around this time, after returning to Canada. Questor Surveys re-acquired CF-JMS c.1970 and continued to fly it until 1974, latterly on the US register as N16647. There reportedly followed a period of activity with Austin Airways of Timmins, Ontario, presumably as a passenger aircraft, and it was around this time that it became C-GGDW. It is worth pointing out that Larry Milberry's book on the history of Austin Airways does not confirm C-GGDW as being operated by that airline, however.

Another survey company was the next operator when Geoterrex Surveys, also known as Terra Surveys, took delivery and flew it out of Ottawa. It flew three other *Super Cats* but it is not known if C-GGDW roamed as widely around the world as they did.

It was retired in 1985 along with the rest of the Geoterrex PBY fleet, and flew south to Opa Locka in Florida, where it joined its new owner, Jack Leavis, who had it returned to the US register as N16647. It spent several years in storage at Opa Locka, during which ownership briefly transferred to Jim Dent's Air Adventures, after which it was flown to Fort Lauderdale in February 1990. It was later transferred to Charlie Clements, a former partner of Dent, and Tracy Clark of Super Three Inc, Coral Gables, Florida, in the following July, but the airframe remained at Fort Lauderdale. By this time its survey gear had been removed and there were plans to replace the previously removed bow turret and waist blisters, although, to date, these additions have still not been made! Re-registered N287 in July 1991, it was slowly restored to an airworthy state and received a gloss black overall colour scheme to represent a US Navy 'Black Cat' whilst retaining its Cyclones and 'Davis' tail. During its protracted restoration, the seaplane operators Chalks of Miami assisted with the work.

The intention was that, once airworthy again, N287 would go to Kendall – Tamiami Executive Airport. Eventually, in 1998, this came to pass and the *Super Cat* was placed on display at Kermit Weeks's Weeks Air Museum whilst still maintained in airworthy condition. However, by the summer of 2000, N287 was on the market and awaiting a new owner.

Table 145.

Registration/ Serial	C/n	Type	Place of Manufacture	Previous id(s)
N287	1649	PBY-5A	CON SD	N16647 C-GGDW N16647 CF-JMS VH-UMS CF-JMS N10017 Bu48287 (US Navy)

N31235 – SLAFCO Inc, Moses Lake, Washington

Amongst surviving PBYs, N31235 is unusual inasmuch as it served the US authorities both as a military aeroplane and then, later, as a civilian-registered machine.

Its initial operator was the United States Navy, which took delivery of it from San Diego in January 1944. Its last operational base was NAS Seattle, where it was struck from military charge in October 1951. Then, instead of entering a long period of storage in the desert, like most of its sister aircraft, it was one of four PBY-5As acquired for operation with Transocean Airlines, to which it was allocated the markings N31235, the same registration that it has carried for the intervening 48 years or so! It also bore the name *Taloa Saipan*. Transocean had successfully bid for the contract to operate air services around what has become known as Micronesia, consisting of the Pacific Ocean islands of the Marshalls, Carolines and Marianas. The services, known as the Trust Territory Air Services, were flown by Transocean on behalf of the US Department of the Interior, which had accepted responsibility for the area's administration from the US Navy. The services included routes taking in Agana on Guam (the main operating base), Truk, Ponape, Majuro, Saipan, Yap and Koror, all of which were spread over a huge expanse of ocean. The operations were carried out on a mixture of water and hard runways, depending on what was available at the various destinations. At this stage in its career, N31235 still retained its hull blisters, but had a clipper bow in place of the forward turret and a horn-balanced rudder.

In 1955, N31235 was declared to be somewhat over the hill – ironic in view of its continued airworthy state in the twenty-first century! – and it was sold to Thorne Engineering of Los Angeles. However, on 30 September 1955, whilst on its delivery flight back to Los Angeles from Guam, it suffered an engine failure between Honolulu and Oakland. This happened too late in the journey to enable a return to Honolulu, and with the fuel state becoming serious, Captain Clark Dixon elected to put the Catalina down on the sea after a US Coast Guard vessel had guided the crew toward a passing freighter, the *Harry Culbreath Victory*. The ship's crew took the four occupants of the PBY aboard safely and then did the same with the amphibian by using the ship's derrick, although some damage was inevitably caused during the winching.

Following its successful recovery, N31235 was rebuilt by Long Beach Aeromotive Inc, and passed through two more owners before being taken on by Pacific Airlines of San Francisco in 1958. The airline held onto it until 1961, and it is interesting to note that it was not until around this time that some former US military Catalinas were coming into commercial ownership for the first time, whereas N31235 had already been earning its keep for some ten years! As with many Cats of this era, it underwent the Steward-Davis treatment and became a *Super Cat* with Wright Cyclone engines.

The next operator was to be Alaska Coastal-Ellis Airlines of Juneau, Alaska, which flew it along with three other *Super Cats* and through several name changes until 1970. Two years later, Robert Schlaefli purchased it and it has remained in regular use since, being converted to a

In 1992, N31235 appeared in a green livery with red undersurfaces and Vivident chewing gum titles for a commercial. *Eddy Gual via Michael Prophet*

fire-fighting aircraft for his SLAFCO fleet. It has carried the hull codes 80 and 98 over the years, and currently wears an overall green colour scheme that it acquired some years back when operating in the Bahamas for a Vivident chewing gum commercial!

Table 146.

Registration/ Serial	C/n	Type	Place of Manufacture	Previous id(s)
N31235	1788	PBY-5A	CON SD	Bu48426 (US Navy)

N314CF – Al Hansen, Mojave, California

N314CF is one of the few remaining ex-RCAF Canso As built by Consolidated rather than Canadian Vickers/Canadair. It was the last of a batch of 14 aircraft from Contract C-78, serialled 9737 to 9750. It was delivered to the Royal Canadian Air Force on 13 January 1942, and served until February 1946, when it was struck off charge. This also makes it one of the oldest surviving PBYs. RCAF records show that it flew with 116 (BR) Squadron, which, between its formation in June 1941 and disbandment in June 1945, operated out of Dartmouth, Nova Scotia; Botwood; Shelbourne; Gander; and Sydney.

After its wartime service, 9750 became CF-DIL on the Canadian civil register, and although its early commercial career is unclear, it later flew as an airliner with Wheeler Airlines, Wheeler Northland Airlines and Ilford Riverton Airways. It is known that during the latter part of the 1950s, it flew with Nordair as, whilst with that company, it suffered substantial damage in a landing accident at Ungava, Province of Quebec. This happened on 17 July 1958, there being no injuries to the occupants.

In 1974, it changed ownership again and flew with Vancouver-based Can Air, which operated at least two Catalinas on fishing charters up into the north of British Columbia, the other known example being CF-SAT. CF-DIL became known as the *Fisherman's Special*. In 1983, it joined others of the breed as a rather late addition to the water bombing fleet of Flying Fireman of Victoria, British Columbia, possibly as an attrition replacement. It became Tanker '5', later '775'. Flying Fireman became Awood Air in 1988.

Al Hansen's N314CF spent many years in Canada as CF-DIL before going to Spain as a water bomber and then on to the USA. Here, it shows the later style of Canadian marking C-FDIL.
MAP

After retirement by Awood, tanker 775 made its way across the Atlantic to join the growing fleet of Catalina variants at work in Spain on contract to ICONA. In C-FDIL's case, the new owner was SAE.SA, and in April 1993 it became EC-FRG after a brief period with the temporary markings EC-313. Mainly based at Cuatro Vientos and still in the red and white colours it had worn in Canada with Flying Fireman, it spent most of 1995 idle there. Later, its lower hull was painted dark blue. Then, in October 1996, EC-FRG was sold by SAE.SA – its Spanish marks were eventually cancelled by the late summer of 1997. By the time of its sale, its hull code had changed again, this time to 73. Its new owner was Al Hansen, and he had it flown to Mojave in November 1996. It had been registered as N314CF in the previous October. Hansen subsequently had it painted in an early US Navy colour scheme with pre-war 'meatball' insignia and red and white striped rudder. His plans at the time of purchase included installation of a replacement set of hull blisters, the originals having long since been removed.

In mid-1999, there was talk of N314CF being operated by John Wells's Airborne Fire Attack company, but this plan did not come to fruition. Another venture that it was linked to was a search for the crash site of Sigismund Levanevski's Russian N-209 aircraft, believed to be in the vicinity of Camden Bay, west of Kaktovik in Alaska. When the Russian aircraft originally disappeared on a flight from Moscow to Fairbanks in August 1937, the famous Consolidated Model 28 flying boat *Guba* was subsequently used in the search. N314CF duly left California for Alaska in August 1999, but in the event, weather conditions prevented a repetition of the original search. This Catalina is still equipped with fire-fighting gear should it be needed in that role again.

In the summer of 2001, it was reported that Hansen had sold N314CF to the Australian group Historic Aircraft Restoration Society (HARS) of Sydney and that it was to be ferried to Australia and then maintained in airworthy condition.

Table 147.

Registration/ Serial	C/n	Type	Place of Manufacture	Previous id(s)
N314CF	427	Canso A	CON SD	EC-FRG EC-313 C-FDIL CF-DIL 9750 (RCAF)

N324FA – American Air Power Heritage Flying Museum, Southern Minnesota Wing, Confederate Air Force, Fleming Field, Minneapolis/St Paul, Minnesota

When preliminary work on this book first started, N324FA was still registered in Canada as C-FPIU, and was one of a large number of Catalinas of various types and shapes that were held in storage at Parry Sound in Ontario. They were there because their owner, Avalon Aviation, had ceased trading and was being wound up. In the end, C-FPIU was destined to be the last of its once proud fleet to remain in Ontario, as all the others were gradually dispersed around various parts of the globe.

One of only a few PBY-6A models to retain its taller rudder in Canadian service, it had first seen use with the US Navy as Bu64092. After completing its service to the nation, it was first taken out of storage for use by the Carstedt Sales Corporation of Long Beach, California, and it then went to Canada as CF-PIU for a succession of owners, firstly as a transport and then, latterly, as a water bomber. Its airline owners included Northward Air Service, Northland Airlines, Midwest Airlines, Ilford Riverton Airways and St Felicien Air Service. Then, having plied its trade around mid-Canada with these companies for so long, it was acquired by Avalon in 1979 and became its Tanker 7, later re-coded 797.

In common with its Avalon brethren, it was

In its blood-red fire-fighting colours, N324FA/115 is seen on the tarmac at Midland, Texas, during the Confederate Air Force Airsho in 1999.
Daniel J. March

withdrawn in 1988 and stored, although it was well maintained and regularly serviced by local engineer Ross McEwen. Its sale in the USA in late 1997 was, unfortunately, the result of an accident that befell another former Avalon aircraft, C-FGLX. This latter aircraft had become N322FA with Wells Aviation Inc, a company owned by John Wells, but was written off in a nasty accident in August 1997. However, John Wells and his co-pilot survived the crash, albeit with serious injuries, and he was sufficiently convinced of the Catalina's continued viability as a water-based fire-fighting machine that he went back to Parry Sound in October of the same year and snapped up C-FPIU. Prior to this, it had been rumoured that C-FPIU was destined for an owner in Germany, possibly for operation by Greenpeace, but this must have fallen through, and the environmental pressure group eventually operated another Catalina – N423RS – instead.

In November 1997, the markings C-FPIU were cancelled from the Canadian Civil Aircraft Register and the new registration N324FA was allocated. It had been flown down from Canada to Ryan-Hemet Field in California, itself a former Catalina fire-fighting base, and it was painted in the same blood-red colours as the ill-fated N322FA. Once repainted, it was moved on to Carson City for the necessary work to bring it up to FAA registration standards. By the spring of 1998, it had commenced water bombing in California, upholding the long tradition of Catalina fire fighting in the USA. In order to promote the effectiveness of aerial fire fighting in Southern California, N324FA moved south, along with C-FLYL *Hawaii Mars,* one of the two huge Martin JRM-3 Mars flying boats normally based with Forest Industries Flying Tankers (FIFT) on Vancouver Island, to Long Beach for a series of promotional demonstrations to the Los Angeles County Fire Department. It seems, however, that those responsible for chartering fire-fighting aircraft felt that the Catalina and Mars were too long in the tooth and opted for more modern equipment instead. Both aircraft returned to their bases, although, in the year 2000 when terrible fires ravaged the western USA, a Martin Mars did fly south again to do battle. N324FA was subsequently put up for sale at $395,000. Around this time, it

was used in the Hollywood motion picture *Magnolia,* starring Tom Cruise. Whatever the final price paid, new owners appeared in the form of the Confederate Air Force, which wanted to replace its N7179Y, yet another former Avalon PBY-6A that had been critically damaged by strong winds at its Minnesota base in May 1998.

The CAF took N324FA on in mid-May 1999, and initially, it went to its Inland Empire Squadron at Riverside in California, supposedly for a repaint in US Navy colours and for the removal of its fire-fighting equipment. However, when it appeared at the CAF's 1999 air display at Midland, Texas, it was still in civil colours and had its tanks in place.

Table 148.

Registration/ Serial	C/n	Type	Place of Manufacture	Previous id(s)
N324FA		PBY-6A	CON NO	C-FPIU CF-PIU N6681C Bu64092 (US Navy)

N3936A – Kermit Weeks, Fantasy of Flight Aviation Theme Park, Polk City, Florida

That this Catalina has survived so long is perhaps somewhat surprising, considering that it has not flown for well over forty years and that it fell victim to the notorious tornado that struck its resting place at Bradley Locks, Connecticut, on 3 October 1979. But, survive it has, and its future seems assured, as in more recent times it has been acquired by millionaire aircraft collector and museum owner Kermit Weeks, a man with a reputation for superbly restored warbirds and other antique aeroplanes. When it will fly again, or indeed be fully restored, is anybody's guess, as there is an enormous amount of work in progress on the Weeks collection, some of which was caused in 1992 by Hurricane *Andrew* when it hit the Tamiami part of Florida, but the Catalina's long-term future now must be considered to be safe.

Used by the United States Coast Guard after delivery from San Diego's Catalina production line, Bu33966 was an early PBY-5A, construction number 1520. During its military service, it was also used by various US Navy units, including VP-AM-5 and VP-AM-2 and FASRON 110. Its first post-military use was with a US-based contractor involved in construction of the DEW-Line project in Northern Canada and Alaska in the early 1950s. Although it had by this time been registered as a civilian aircraft with the marks N3936A, its commercial conversion was minimal, and it still retained all of its external military fittings, including bow turret, blisters and colour scheme. It also still retained its basic US Navy dark blue colours, and the fin bore traces of the word Philadelphia upon it, signifying one of the USN bases it had been attached to.

By 1955, it was to be found withdrawn from use and semi-derelict at Bradley Field, Windsor Locks, Connecticut, and although it was registered to a number of owners in the intervening period, it was to stay at Windsor Locks for the next 34 years or so. Back in 1964, however, it had become part of the Connecticut Aeronautical Historical Association's Bradley Air

Before being acquired by Kermit Weeks, PBY-5A N3936A had lain derelict for years. This photo was taken as long ago as 1965, when it was already showing clear signs of deterioration. The lettering on the tail under the registration reads PHILA.PA, whilst the original BuAer number 33966 is just visible above.
Peter Keating Collection

Museum, and in 1981 ownership passed to what had by then become the New England Air Museum. Little work was done on the airframe, and it remained stored and dismantled in the open, gradually deteriorating. In May 1988, the US Civil Aircraft Register recorded a restoration of ownership back to the Connecticut Aeronautical Historical Society.

Salvation came in the form of Kermit Weeks in 1989, and the Catalina was registered to him that November and taken to the Tamiami area to join what was to become the Weeks Air Museum. Initially stored in the locality, the aircraft had been moved to Kermit's Fantasy of Flight aviation theme park at Polk City, Florida, by the start of 1996, and there the substantially complete airframe will be rebuilt.

Table 149.

Registration/ Serial	C/n	Type	Place of Manufacture	Previous id(s)
N3936A	1520	PBY-5A	CON SD	Bu33966 (US Navy)

N4NC – Wilson 'Connie' Edwards, Big Springs, Texas

If you happen to be a millionaire and a flying boat fan to boot, then a Catalina is the obvious plaything! Of course, life is not that simple and PBYs take some looking after. Fortunately, Wilson 'Connie' Edwards, an oilman from Big Springs in Texas, has done just that for a number of years, and has regularly flown his PBY-6A on land and water, even venturing as far as Europe back in 1986. More recently, he has also acquired the former Canso A N222FT!

In common with all other PBY-6As, Bu46662 was built in New Orleans by Consolidated, and it served its native country's Navy well before being left in the Arizona desert at Litchfield Park, if not to rot then certainly to

fade! Luckily, it was to re-emerge and embark on a commercial career. Little is known of its early commercial use in the United States, but in 1967, it was re-registered in Canada as CF-VIG, and between then and 1973 its owner was the Great Lakes Paper Company of Fort Williams, Ontario, with which it presumably flew as a passenger aircraft, although PBY-6As were not usually used in that role in Canada. Avalon Aviation, then based at Red Deer, Alberta, became its owner in 1974, and it was used as a crew ferry in support of that company's large fleet of water bombing Catalinas. CF-VIG was not converted to a bomber itself, however.

Briefly placed on the US Civil Aircraft Register as N1022G in 1979, it later became N999AR in June 1980, when ownership was vested in the interestingly named Anchor & Cattle Corporation of Grundy, Virginia. This ownership most likely explains why a large anchor was later painted on the Catalina's fin, although, coincidentally, the Great Lakes Paper Company also used an anchor in its corporate logo. In 1984, it acquired the name *The Searcher* whilst being owned by Red Stevenson, who based it in Leonard, Oklahoma. Very shortly thereafter it became the property of Connie Edwards, who has operated it ever since, initially retaining its registration N999AR, but later changed to its current marks N4NC. The reason for this latter registration becomes clear when it is realised that Connie's PBY was one of two that flew across the Atlantic Ocean to Plymouth, England, in 1986 to commemorate the 75th anniversary of US Naval Aviation and the 67th anniversary of the flight of the Curtiss NC4 flying boat across that same expanse of water in 1919. Indeed, the NC-4 is represented by an appropriate silhouette worn on the rudder of the Catalina, as well as in the US registration. The two Cats departed New York on 8 May and flew to Plymouth, Devon, via Chatham; Maine; Halifax, Nova Scotia; St John's, Newfoundland; Ponta Delgada; Lisbon; and La Coruna, Spain. Unfortunately, the triumphal arrival on water by N4NC at Plymouth on 31 May was somewhat marred when, some fifty minutes later, the accompanying PBY-5A Catalina C-FOWE, now N222FT, water-looped and partially sank. N4NC subsequently flew out of Plymouth harbour to the Royal Naval Air Station at

Wilson 'Connie' Edwards overflies RNAS Yeovilton, Somerset, in PBY-6A N4NC during its brief UK visit in 1986.

Yeovilton in Somerset, and thereafter back to the USA. It departed via the Azores on 5 June. For its two-way trans-Atlantic voyage, N4NC was equipped with under-wing long-range fuel tanks.

Since then N4NC has made regular air display appearances in the USA and still wears the vivid colour scheme in which it flew to the UK. It has a luxury interior fit as befits the somewhat flamboyant owner, often to be seen flying in a U-boat commander's cap and patch-bedecked leather jacket! The Catalina is sometimes flown in company with the owner's Grumman Albatross.

In early 1999, Wilson Edwards placed a substantial part of his warbird collection up for disposal, including many fighters last seen in the *Battle of Britain* motion picture back in the late 1960s. However, he must enjoy his Catalina too much as it was not included in the inventory for sale.

N4582T, now at Floyd Bennett Field, is seen at Springfield, Ohio, at the end of the delivery flight from Brazil in July 1984. It retains part of its original FAB livery.
Norm Taylor Collection

Table 150.

Registration/ Serial	C/n	Type	Place of Manufacture	Previous id(s)
N4NC	2026	PBY-6A	CON NO	N999AR N1022G CF-VIG N788C N9588C Bu46662 (US Navy)

N4582T – Project Catalina, National Air Park Museum, Floyd Bennett Field, Brooklyn, New York

This Catalina is the first of five described in this chapter which owe their survival into the 1990s to the Brazilian Air Force and the subsequent acquisition by the well-known American aircraft collector/trader and former wartime B-17 pilot, David Tallichet.

Following service with the US Navy, PBY-5A construction number 1820 was eventually supplied to the Força Aérea Brasileira (FAB), with which it flew as 6509. The FAB used a substantial fleet of Catalinas both during the Second World War and then post-war. Some of its PBY-5As and a solitary PBY-6A soldiered on into the early 1980s, flying supply trips into remote locations on the Amazon until forest clearance allowed air strips for landplanes to be built. Once finally retired, the survivors were offered for sale, and they were surveyed by various interested parties, including the British-based pilots John Watts and Paul Warren Wilson, who eventually purchased the Canadian C-FMIR in South Africa instead, having been put off by the generally rough condition that the Brazilian aircraft had lapsed into following their withdrawal. It is only fair to point out, however, that when in service, the FAB Cats had been kept in very good order.

Notwithstanding their state, David Tallichet of the Military Aircraft Restoration Corporation (MARC) was sufficiently interested in obtaining several examples of the withdrawn PBYs from Brazil, and he eventually arranged for no fewer than five of them to be flown to the USA. Once there, he concluded a deal which resulted in the Catalinas being preserved in non-airworthy condition at various US military air bases, while he received examples of recently retired transport aircraft in exchange. Thus, the FAB's 6509 became N4582T, and, still

in its basic FAB colours, it was flown north in company with sister aircraft 6520/N4583A and 6551/N4583B on what was to prove to be a ferry flight full of technical faults and drama! The route flown was Belém–San Juan–Orlando, where the three Catalinas were rested awhile. N4582T was then flown on to Ohio, where it was intended to go on display at Dayton, home of the USAF Museum, although, in the end, its place there was taken by another example. However, during the flight, a substantial part of elevator fabric tore away and it was decided that a landing would be made at Springfield Airport, near Dayton. The problems were not over for David Tallichet and his co-pilot Roy Degan, as on landing the nose wheel collapsed! Damage to the nose was minimal, however.

For some time, N4582T remained registered to Tallichet's company, Project Catalina, of Long Beach, California, and it was temporarily stored at Pensacola, but was destined to go on display at the United States Marine Corps Museum at Cherry Point, North Carolina. Later, the decision was taken to loan the PBY out for renovation, and so it was dismantled and roaded to Brooklyn, New York. Here, it can now be found at Floyd Bennett Field in the Blue Nose Hangar, being restored by the resident Historic Aircraft Restoration Project (HARP) as part of a wider project to preserve the area's aviation heritage.

Table 151.

Registration/ Serial	C/n	Type	Place of Manufacture	Previous id(s)
N4582T	1820	PBY-5A	CON SD	6509 (FAB) Bu46456 (US Navy)

N4582U/'44-34077' – Project Catalina, Rescue Memorial Museum, Kirtland Air Force Base, Albuquerque, New Mexico

As can be seen from Table 152, N4582U was the production line neighbour of N4582T described above, so it is something of a coincidence that they should both have served with the Força Aérea Brasileira after the US Navy, and gone on to be saved for subsequent preservation. In fact, not only did the two aircraft have

Home for the former Força Aérea Brasileira Catalina
N4582U is now Kirtland Air Force Base. Albuquerque, New
Mexico, where it is on display as OA-10A 44-34077.
Andy Robbins

consecutive constructor's numbers and US Navy
Bu numbers, but also FAB serials and commercial registration suffixes!

Flown by the FAB as 6510, it enjoyed a long career in
Brazil before being acquired by David Tallichet's Project
Catalina in 1983. Because of various technical problems,
6510 did not make the ferry flight to the USA with the
other three ex-FAB PBY-5As described above but had to
be brought on later. It suffered a fuel leak whilst on the
first leg of its journey between Belém and Trinidad, but
landed with enough fuel in hand for a safe arrival.
However, the landing itself was nearly a disaster, as,
upon touch-down, the pilots sensed that the starboard
main gear was collapsing. Responding rapidly, they
applied power and lifted off again. The gear was hand-
cranked back down and locked, and second time around,
the leg held. An enforced stay in Trinidad then followed
whilst the fuel leak was solved. Subsequently, it flew on
to Orlando, then Memphis, Montgomery, and, finally,
Albuquerque in New Mexico.

At Kirtland Air Force Base in Albuquerque, it was put
on display at the museum there and painted up as a

United States Coast Guard OA-10A, USAF serial
44-34077. Since then, it has been kept in good condition,
even though permanently kept in the open, and has had
at least one full repaint. It is nominally still the property
of Project Catalina of Long Beach, California, and is still
registered to that company on the United States Civil
Aircraft Register.

Table 152.

Registration/ Serial	C/n	Type	Place of Manufacture	Previous id(s)
N4582U/'44-34077' (USAF)	1821	PBY-5A	CON SD	6510 (FAB) Bu46457 (US Navy)

N4583A – Project Catalina, US Naval Air Museum, Jacksonville Naval Air Station, Florida

Given the amount of Catalina activity that took place at
Jacksonville during the Second World War, it is most
appropriate that one of the PBY-5As 'rescued' from Brazil
in 1983 by David Tallichet should end up on display
there. Kept out in the open, it forms a wonderful back-
drop for ex-servicemen visiting their old base!

FAB 6520 was one of three ex-FAB Cats to fly up to the
USA from Brazil, and after arrival at Orlando, it spent
some time at Pensacola in the same State before going on
to Jacksonville, where it has been on display since 1986.
It has been painted in a US Navy two-tone blue colour

Jacksonville, Florida, is an appropriate final resting place for the former US Navy PBY-5A Bu46582, although, sadly, its blisters and bow turret are no longer in place.
Dr Tom Garrett

Although originally a US Navy PBY-5A, Bu46595 has ended up preserved in the USAF Museum in Ohio masquerading as a USAAF OA-10A, 44-33879 *Snafu Snatchers*.
USAFM

scheme, with pre-war 'meatball'-style roundels on the forward hull. The rudder carries the serial 6582, a shortened version of its former US Navy BuAer number and the hull code J1-P-17 after a Jacksonville, or 'Jax', unit. The United States Civil Aircraft Register, which often quotes Bu numbers as construction numbers, misquotes Bu46582 as Bu46852.

Table 153.

Registration/ Serial	C/n	Type	Place of Manufacture	Previous id(s)
N4583A/'6582'	1946	PBY-5A	CON NO	6520 (FAB) Bu46582 (US Navy)

N4583B – Project Catalina, United States Air Force Museum, Wright Patterson Air Force Base, Dayton, Ohio

It is good that the United States Air Force Museum at Wright Patterson Air Force Base, Dayton, Ohio, should have an example of a Catalina on display within its superb collection, considering the sterling service given by the Catalina to the USAAF both during and after the Second World War. Perhaps the surprising thing is that it took so long for the USAF to obtain one, and that, when it did, it came from a private collector!

Yet another David Tallichet acquisition from Brazil, N4583B is unusual in that it had both a commercial and military career in that country. Registered as PT-AXM, it flew with Panair to Brasil in the early 1960s on services linking Belém, Manaus and Iquitos in Peru before becoming C-10A serial 6551 with the Força Aérea Brasileira. Prior to all of this, its early history saw it flying with the United States Navy as Bu46595, as well as a brief period on the US Civil Aircraft Register as N9501C.

After its long service with the FAB, it was retired and offered for sale before eventually coming into the hands of David Tallichet's Project Catalina. It was flown on an adventurous delivery flight to the USA, routeing Belém–San Juan–Orlando, where it was temporarily stored.

Once 'home' in the USA, N4583B was traded with the USAF, and it went to Dayton in July 1984, where it was promptly stripped down and resprayed to represent a USAAF OA-10A Catalina, serial number 44-33879, with the nose art and name Snafu Snatchers. It thus represents an aircraft that served in the Pacific with 2 ERS, 13th Air Force. It is still officially registered to Tallichet's Project Catalina of Long Beach, California. During the restoration to museum condition, some parts from the wrecked PBY-6A N331RS were used. This latter aircraft, or parts of it, had been parked at Dayton by its owner, Aero Nostalgia of Stockton, California, but once N4583B's restoration was complete, the remains of the PBY-6A were removed.

Table 154.

Registration/ Serial	C/n	Type	Place of Manufacture	Previous id(s)
N4583B/'44-33879' (USAAF)	1959	PBY-5A	CON NO	6551 (FAB) PT-AXM N9501C Bu46595 (US Navy)

N4760C – McChord Air Force Base Museum, Washington State

Amongst the Catalinas described in this chapter, N4760C is unusual in that it was an early example of a diversion from a US Navy order to the USAAF. Originally built by Consolidated at San Diego as construction number 1547, it had been intended for delivery to the US Navy as Bu33993 under contract number NXa 13595 of October 1942. As such, it was one of a batch of 100 PBY-5As serialled Bu33960 to 34059, of which some 31 were transferred to the USAAF with serials 43-43839 to 43-43863 and 43-47956 to 43-47961. Thus, the prospective Bu33993 became 43-43847 and was taken on charge in August 1943.

In civvy street it became N4760C, and from the late 1940s through to the early 1970s it flew in Alaska, being part of the fleet of Alaska Coastal Airlines of Juneau, then

Alaska Airlines of Seattle. Early on during this period it was converted by Steward-Davis to a Wright Cyclone-powered *Super Cat*.

Around 1972, it was briefly owned by Stan Burnstein of Continental Aviation Company, Tulsa, before passing through several different registered owners who appear to be parts of the same organisation, namely Geoterrex/Terra Surveys of Ottawa, Ontario. Geoterrex was well known in the 1970s and 1980s for operating a fleet of *Super Cats* in the aerial surveying role, and although its association with the Catalina ended some years ago, the company still exists and flies throughout the world. It flew N4760C widely, initially still in the magnificent white, black, red and gold *Golden Nugget* livery of Alaska Airlines which had remained in place on the airframe, but then later in a rather more anonymous natural metal finish. At various times, it was to be seen working in Iceland, Ireland, the United Kingdom, France and the Channel Islands, amongst other places.

Whilst back flying in the USA, it suffered port engine failure on 22 March 1983, and force-landed, wheels up, in a field at Lynn, south-east of Granton, Wisconsin, resulting in a badly crumpled starboard wing, broken port wingtip and battered hull. The engine fault had occurred whilst the PBY was flying at only 500 ft, and, despite application of full power on the good engine by the Geoterrex captain, Roger Mott, altitude could not be maintained. The accident report quotes the Catalina as being 1,800 kg under its maximum gross weight at the time. The five crew who were aboard escaped unharmed but damage to the aircraft was classified as substantial.

After all removable items had been salvaged, the hulk was initially left with the local farmer on whose land the Catalina had landed, but in due course the remains were acquired by warbird collector and trader David Tallichet, who around that time was busy gathering whole and incomplete PBYs from all over North and South America. It came under the umbrella of his Military Aircraft Restoration Co (MARC) of Chino, California, although it is most unlikely that the hulk actually went there, as it is

known to have been stored in Kansas for a time. Later, it was trucked to McChord Air Force Base in Washington State for rebuild and eventual display at the base air museum there. By the end of December 1987, the dismantled airframe was laid out at McChord like a giant construction kit and work commenced on piecing it back together again. The intention was to create a Catalina representing an OA-10A of the USAAF, serial 44-34033, as based at McChord at the start of the 1950s when C Flight of the 4th Air Rescue Squadron was based there.

The rebuild involved replacing the Cyclone engines with Pratt and Whitneys and the tall *Super Cat* tail with a regular PBY-5A one. In fact, a tail from a former RCAF Canso was found, still with its Canadian military insignia in place! In the course of restoration, the team responsible have also put blisters back onto the rear hull. By 1998, the restoration was nearing completion.

Table 155.

Registration/ Serial	C/n	Type	Place of Manufacture	Previous id(s)
N4760C	1547	OA-10	CON SD	43-43847 (USAAF) Bu33993 ntu (US Navy)

N4934H – Airplane Sales International, USS Lexington Museum, Corpus Christie, Texas

Unlike the four other Catalinas that were imported into the USA from ex-Força Aérea Brasileira (FAB) stocks, N4934H had originally seen military service with the Royal Canadian Air Force as a Canso A, serial 9838. As such, it was the third Canso to roll off the Cartierville, Quebec, production line, earlier Canadian Vickers aircraft having been built at its St Hubert factory. For at least part of the time that it flew with the RCAF, it was on the strength of 3 (BR) Operational Training Unit at Patricia Bay, Vancouver Island, British Columbia. Retired at the end of the war, it was very soon acquired by the FAB and allocated the serial 6525.

With others of its type, it was used in the Amazon

N4760C during restoration at McChord Air Force Base in Washington State. When seen in June 1996, the airframe had been converted back to PBY-5A standard from Super Catalina format, and both blisters and bow turret had been grafted back on.
Heijo Kuil

N4934H served post-war with the Força Aérea Brasileira as 6525. This photo, taken shortly after the war, shows it still with bow turret and blisters, keeping company with a P-47 Thunderbolt.
Museu Aéroespacial via Ricardo Bonalume Neto

area for over 25 years, and during this time, it was sunk twice, the second occasion being in 1976 when it struck a submerged log. It spent 16 days semi-submerged before being refloated with the aid of inflated Catalina tyre tubes. After essential maintenance, it was flown off the water to Tapurucura near the Colombian border, where it was destined to be parked out in the open until 1984. Its wings were then removed from the hull and it was barged down the Amazon to Belém, a journey of 28 days! It was then cosmetically restored with the intention of displaying it at Belém air base. However, the powers that be decided that as there was already a superbly restored PBY-5A in the air force museum in Rio, 6525 would be disposed of. Thus, in 1985, it was registered to Beverley Hills-based Airplane Sales International as N4934H, having been ferried from Belém to Albuquerque, New Mexico, in July 1984. In 1988, it went on display at the United States Naval Aircraft Museum at Corpus Christie, Texas, where it was given a US Navy colour scheme and the spurious serial USN 6525, obviously based on its former Brazilian military identity. Later, its custodian became the USS Lexington Museum, and it is planned that, in due course, the airframe will be moved to the museum's site aboard the USS *Lexington* itself, which is docked at Corpus Christie.

The aircraft still sits on the US Civil Aircraft Register as N4934H, the address of the owner being the same as that for Project Catalina, which owned the four other former FAB Catalinas imported in the 1980s.

Table 156. Registration/ Serial	C/n	Type	Place of Manufacture	Previous id(s)
N4934H	CV-272	Canso A	CAN VIC (Cartierville)	6525 (FAB) 9838 (RCAF)

N5PY – Ron Ruble, Aurora, Portland, Oregon

For many years, this particular Catalina turned heads because of its truly unique configuration – it had four engines! To those in the know, it is famous for its appearance – those who are not familiar with it are most likely to dispute that any four-engined Cat ever existed! Well, exist it most certainly did, and it has enjoyed an interesting and varied career, although it has now returned to a more conventional twin-engined layout.

The Bird Corporation of Palm Springs, California, was, in the 1960s, the world's leading manufacturer of medical respirators. Early in the decade, the company acquired a PBY-5A Catalina with the intention of using it as a flying classroom, office, hotel and transport for medical teaching teams. Christened *The Wandering Albatross*, it was originally built by Consolidated in San Diego for the RCAF as a Canso A, serial 9746. It was one of 14 Model 28- 5AMCs ordered under Contract C-78 and delivered in late 1941, and thus preceded the larger batches of Cansos built for the RCAF by Boeing of Canada and Canadian Vickers. Officially taken on charge by the RCAF on 13 January 1942, it is known to have served with 162 (BR) Squadron out of Yarmouth, Nova Scotia, before being retired in September 1946. It suffered Category B damage in early 1943, although nothing more is known of the circumstances.

Immediately after being declared surplus and sold by the War Assets Corporation, it was purchased by the firm of aircraft brokers Charles H. Babb Inc of Burbank, which had it registered as NC68741. Later, it was converted to a full commercial standard by Southern California Aircraft Corporation of Ontario, California, and two years later, in 1956, it was registered as N59D. By this time, it had passed through a number of owners and been converted to *Landseaire* standard with rear air stair, horn-balanced rudder, clipper bow, wheel hub covers, passenger windows, mounting steps beneath the blisters and a one-piece, blown perspex blister on the starboard side. It was again re-registered, this time as N5907, around the end of 1958.

N5907 was sold to Bird Oxygen Breathing Equipment Inc in late 1962, ownership later changing to the Bird Corporation. It was initially flown in its *Landseaire* configuration, having had its colour scheme of white with blue and yellow trim replaced with an overall white and black livery with red crosses and Bird emblems.

Within a year, Bird had the horn-balanced rudder replaced with a larger unit more normally seen on the so-called *Super Cat* conversions, although, unlike these souped-up variants, N5907 retained its Pratt & Whitney engines rather than having them replaced with the Wright R-2600s more normally associated with the large 'barn door' rudder. Later, Bird converted its Catalina to a four-engined aircraft, and the conversion is fully described in Chapter Three. Bird even tried to market the design, known as the *Bird Innovator*, to other operators, but no further conversions were carried out.

Undeterred by the absence of orders, the Bird Corporation began to operate its highly unusual aircraft all over the United States in the role for which it had been intended – supporting the company's range of medical products. In the time that it spent in Bird's ownership, it was kept in immaculate condition. The company maintained a superb hangarage facility at Palm Springs Airport which featured sophisticated fire protection systems, including automatic doors and a winch which would tow the aircraft from the hangar in the event of a fire.

All the distinctive features of the one-off Bird Innovator can be seen in this shot taken at Concord, California, in October 1967.
William T. Larkins

Around April 1969, the Bird Corporation reserved a set of registrations for its fleet of aircraft, and these included the marks N81RD for the Innovator. The significance of this registration became apparent when it was painted on the aircraft, the numeral 8 being painted more like the letter B so that the finished result looked like NB1RD, a crafty form of advertising. A similar trick was used on the company's Lockheed 18 N381RD.

In July 1976, the Innovator was sold by the Bird Corporation, and it reverted to its former registration N5907 when it passed on to Madden Aircraft Sales, and then Atlas Aircraft Corporation of Long Beach, before being purchased by Pyramid Aviation of Cotati, California, in late 1978. Pyramid was awarded a major contract by the United States Government through the office of the National Oceanic and Atmospheric Administration (NOAA) under the Department of Commerce. The purpose of the contract was to conduct a porpoise and dolphin count covering an area from San Diego, California, in the north to Lima, Peru, in the south.

The NOAA's final report was published in January 1980, and gave several reasons for choosing Pyramid's Innovator for the contract. The normal flying speed of 115–120 knots enabled tight turns to be pulled in order to monitor sightings of porpoise and dolphin schools. The fuselage benefited from the large tear-drop-shaped blisters fitted toward the rear and known as one of the wartime Catalina's most distinctive recognition features.

On the Innovator, the starboard blister was moulded from one piece of solid plexiglass, and the absence of framework gave unobstructed viewing. This and the

more conventional blister on the port side resulted in a full 180-degree field of view on each side of the aircraft, together with downward views as close as one tenth of a mile from the aircraft's track when flying straight and level. In addition, the nose was modified by Pyramid to house an 18 in x 24 in plexiglass bubble window (since removed) which was used for forward observation by a crew member in a prone position. This allowed 180-degree vision in both horizontal and vertical planes. NOAA used the aircraft on missions of over twelve hours' duration covering 1,500 nautical miles, although the potential endurance was even greater at up to 1,900 nm or sixteen hours at 120 kt.

For the NOAA contract, six observers and their equipment, together with three pilots, were required, and the Innovator easily carried their weight together with a full fuel load, all at a contract rate that allowed a sufficient number of flights to achieve the project objectives within budget. Following this unusual project, for which the Innovator seems to have been ideally suited, Pyramid Aviation Inc offered it to potential clients as a unique land-sea-air machine for both marine and land-based operations and projects, varying from recreational safaris to geological surveys. It is known to have been involved on film work of some sort between May and July 1980, when it was based at Yolo County Airport for operations in the Bay Area of San Francisco, but by September 1981, it had been sold again, this time to Research Data Inc, to which it remained registered until sometime in 1990.

It is interesting to note that when it was offered for sale by Pyramid, it was advertised as having no corrosion history as it had never been in salt water, and also that it had no history of damage. This latter point seems to overlook the two accidents that it had had up to that point! The first was on 6 December 1963, not long after it had been acquired by Bird. Upon landing at Memphis,

For a time, Bird flew its Innovator with the 'fixed' registration N81RD painted in such a way that it spelled the owner's name.
MAP

Tennessee, after a local sightseeing flight and with a total of 11 souls on board, the pilot reported that he felt quite certain he had extended the landing gear and received a safe-for-landing light indication. None the less, the aircraft touched down and slid to a halt on its hull. Witness and passenger statements and the physical evidence surrounding the accident showed that at touchdown, the left main and nose gears were fully retracted. Also, as near as can be determined, the right main gear was retracted until the aircraft stopped, and the pilot, noting the gear position selector was in the neutral position, moved it to the extended down position. Examination of the landing gear system revealed the springs which assist in actuating the gear control were out of the assembly. These components would not, however, prevent extension of the landing gears under normal procedures. The accident enquiry concluded that the pilot had failed to extend the gear prior to landing. There were no injuries to those on board.

The second accident occurred on 17 May 1980 whilst under Pyramid's ownership. A crew of two plus two passengers were on a training flight out of Davis, California. Upon take-off, at about 400 ft and during initial power reduction, the fire warning actuated and the pilot reported smoke and fire in the two main engines. The pilot returned to Davis Airport and landed, but the nose gear had failed to extend and the Innovator received damage to the hull and the right-hand underwing float, the latter suggesting that the landing was a somewhat bumpy one to say the least!

By 1985, N5907 was to be found in open storage at Tico Airport in Florida, and this was to remain its home for some time whilst its owner advertised it for sale. This process became quite protracted, and the Innovator rapidly became part of Tico's scenery, although the aircraft was kept in generally good condition. Eventually, the Innovator was sold to Dick Durand of Albuquerque, New Mexico and in the summer of 1991, he had it registered as N5PY to his company Westernair Inc. Dick had the aircraft put through a major ten-month refurbishment both inside and out that saw it put back into the air in a smart new colour scheme of white with blue and maroon trim. The year 1991 also saw it placed as a lot in the aircraft auction held at the Museum of Flying at Santa Monica to which it was flown, but it was not sold. Around that time, it was described by one aviation magazine in the 'States as being equipped internally with 6 rooms, a stainless steel galley with microwave, refrigerator, 3-burner range, bath and shower with 80 gallon hot water tank, custom AM-FM 8-track stereo with 6 speakers, telephone and dual TV inputs. It also offered sleeping for 7 or 'more if friendly', four engines with 2,500 gallon fuel capacity, 6 bilge pumps, anchor with 175 ft chain, two 14 ft outboard skiffs, Loran, GPS, weather radar, dual heaters and full radio deck. The article summed up by describing N5PY as 'luxuriously appointed throughout – it also flies'!

After the Santa Monica auction, it remained in the hands of Westernair and the Durand family. Rumours from time to time surfaced suggesting that it had gone down to South America to operate, and more drastically, that it had been de-converted back to twin-engine configuration. The South American rumour seems to have

been incorrect, and in early 1998 it was being advertised as an attraction at a North West Coast air show giving joy rides as the world's only four- engined PBY. However, some time around mid-1998, it was indeed turned back into a twin-engined Cat after its Lycomings and their associated equipment were removed by the Vintage Aircraft Restoration Company of Aurora, Oregon. N5PY is now based at that location with Ron Ruble, who acquired it during 1997. Opinions are probably divided as to whether removing the two engines was a good thing aesthetically, but one thing is for sure, it was a unique Catalina!

This Cat has frequently been quoted as having an early post-war history on the Venezuelan and Brazilian registers as YV-P-AEP and PT-ASX/PT-BGA respectively before returning to the USA as N59D. This writer does not believe this version of its history to be correct, and photographs of PT-BGA would seem to bear this out, as the positioning of passenger windows is different to those on N59D.

Table 157.

Registration/ Serial	C/n	Type	Place of Manufacture	Previous id(s)
N5PY	417	Canso A	CON SD	N5907
				N81RD
				N5907
				N59D
				NC68741
				9746 (RCAF)

N5590V – San Diego Aerospace Museum, Balboa Park, San Diego, California

The San Diego Aerospace Museum's PBY-5A last took to the air in the summer of 1988, but this was no powered flight! It was suspended beneath a large crane as it was hoisted into the confines of the Museum courtyard for permanent external, pylon-mounted display.

Built in the same city of San Diego by Consolidated in 1943 as construction number 1768, it was delivered to the US Navy on the last day of 1943 as Bu48406. It served in the Pacific, patrolling the Marshall and Gilbert Islands before ending up with the United States Coast Guard. After being struck off charge in the summer of 1956, and having spent some time at Litchfield Park, Arizona, in storage, it was acquired by Thomas M. Kendall and his company, Catalina Ltd, of La Verne, California, and registered as N5590V. It is known that Kendall purchased some other Catalinas at this time, including N5593V, now derelict in Saudi Arabia.

The Kendall family used N5590V not only for their own travels but also for film work that included an appearance in the movie The Devil at Four O'Clock. It also participated in the NCAR Line Island Experiments of 1966–7. At some stage, an emblem with the words TIARE TAHITI was painted on the bow, and this appears to have been during a period when it was leased to Catalina Enterprise. The Kendall family finally retired their Catalina in 1977, and from then on it languished at Van Nuys Airport in California with its white and blue colour scheme fading fast and with massive oil stains accumulating on the forward hull beneath the Pratt & Whitneys. With its flat tyres almost hidden in the grass, it was looking really forlorn by the mid-1980s. The United States Civil Aircraft Register shows that in 1984, N5590V was registered to the International Centre for Environmental Research of Wilmington, Delaware, but it was back with the Kendalls after a year or so.

Fortunately, a reprieve came in 1986 when the Kendalls donated the aircraft to the San Diego Aerospace Museum, which had just been revived in its new location at the old California Pacific International Exposition Building in Balboa Park. The original museum had opened in the early 1960s, and by 1965 was housed in the San Diego Hall of Science building. This was almost totally destroyed by an arsonist in 1977, taking much of the Consolidated archive with it.

It was natural that, given San Diego's historical link with Consolidated, the new museum should want to have an example of its most famous aircraft on display. So, after four months of hard work at Van Nuys, the aircraft was flown by Robert Kendall to North Island Air Station at San Diego. Here, the PBY was treated to considerable care and attention by a volunteer force made up of many individuals, including Catalina enthusiasts from the US Navy, Convair (formerly Consolidated-Vultee) and the Museum itself. All-important financial assistance came from Convair's successor, General Dynamics, and from the N. Paul Whittier Confidence Foundation and the Reuben H. Fleet Foundation Fund of the San Diego Community Foundation.

After restoration, N5590V was resprayed in a smart US Navy colour scheme of dark blue, grey and white and with its original BuAer number on the tail. This was done by the Navy as part of its contribution toward celebrating 75 years of US Naval Aviation. It was rolled out from the Naval Aviation Depot hangar at NAS North Island in October 1986, and it was subsequently barged across San Diego Bay to the General Dynamics Convair factory at Harbor Drive, adjacent to Lindbergh Field, San Diego International Airport. There, another team made up of retired Consolidated/Convair men continued with the restoration. This team of workers consisted of many who were renewing their acquaintance with the PBY, having either flown them or worked on them in the past. Their work included the replacement of the clipper bow, a post-war modification, with a restored 'eye-ball' type turret.

The Catalina's second roll-out occurred on 3 August 1988. The outer wings were then removed and, on the 6th, the hull was towed through the streets of San Diego on its undercarriage, this all taking place during the early hours of the morning and with a police escort. The wings followed on flat-bed trailers.

After arrival at the Balboa Park site, the Catalina was placed in the car park whilst the outer wings were put back on. Then, at 04.00 hours on Monday 8 August, the big lift commenced! A large crane from the Owl Crane Company hoisted the Catalina aloft and gently lowered it again onto its resting place atop metal pedestals. Here, perched in the air in flying attitude with undercarriage up, it looks somewhat hemmed in, but it was none the

PBY-5A N5590V was dismantled and re-assembled in the grounds of the San Diego Aerospace Museum, where it dominates the grounds outside the museum building. *San Diego Aerospace Museum*

less the star of the party two days later when no fewer than 157 members, staff and volunteers attended to admire the exhibit's inauguration at the Museum. The Catalina is item 49-30-A in the Aerospace Museum inventory.

Table 158. Registration/ Serial	C/n	Type	Place of Manufacture	Previous id(s)
N5590V/Bu48406 (US Navy)	1768	PBY-5A	CON SD	Bu48406 (US Navy)

N57875 – Alaskan Historical Aircraft Society, Anchorage, Alaska

As with N5590V described in the previous entry, this Catalina's last foray into the air was not under its own power, although in the case of N57875 the 'flight' was at a higher altitude and over a greater distance. In fact, it was suspended underneath a heavy-lift helicopter! But let us start at the beginning and then learn more of its last conventional flight.

Towards the end of the Second World War, many Catalinas originally ordered for the US Navy were transferred prior to delivery to the USAAF, which operated its own air-sea-rescue service. Canadian Vickers-built PBV-1A serial Bu67918 was one of these transfers, and it saw service with the USAAF instead, with the alternative serial 44-33954 and the type designation OA-10A. It saw service with various units until in April 1947, it was allocated to the 10th Air Rescue Squadron based at Elmendorf Air Force Base in Alaska, where it was operated alongside such diverse types as the Sikorsky H-5 helicopter, Grumman Duck amphibians and SB-17 Flying Fortresses. Five months after arrival, the Catalina was flying some distance away from its base when the starboard engine threw a rod and the plane was forced to land on shallow water at Dago Lake on the Alaskan Peninsula, many miles from civilisation. This happened on 30 September 1947. According to contemporary reports, the crew were flying low and chasing bears over the tundra at the time!

Various attempts were made to recover the Catalina, but these were not successful, and after the accidental loss of a replacement engine in the surrounding water, along with damage sustained to several Noorduyn Norseman aircraft used as crew ferries, official interest in retrieving the aircraft waned. The guards who had been posted to watch over the wreck were instructed to sever the control cables and hydraulic lines, and the previously lightly damaged airframe was abandoned to the severe Alaskan elements.

Soon after the incident, the wreck was put up for tender, but all bids were below the minimum reserve price and were therefore rejected by the authorities. Alaskan law of the time dictated that the best offer made at any subsequent auction had to be accepted, and when an Anchorage contractor later offered the handsome sum of US$58 for it, he and his sons became the proud owners of one surplus OA-10A Catalina! The Richards family found that their initial enthusiasm was dampened when they discovered that flying their aircraft off the lake was impossible owing to the USAAF's efforts at demobilising

it. They therefore exchanged some of the components from the Catalina with a local airline in a trade for a Piper Cub floatplane, thus once more leaving the big amphibian to its fate. Thereafter, the combined forces of vandals and climate ensured that over the ensuing years, the *Queen of Dago Lake* became a weather-beaten shadow of its former self. Local pilots who used it as a navigational aid came to know the area of water around it as *PBY Lake*.

There the story might have ended, and Dago Lake would have become the location at the head of this entry, were it not for the determined intervention of the Alaskan Historical Aviation Society (AHAS). The AHAS was formed in 1977 with the aim of promoting, preserving and protecting all aspects of Alaska's aviation history. The main driving force behind the organisation, Ted Spencer, and his colleagues convinced the Federal Government that the many old aircraft wrecks in the State were potentially historic objects. In 1981, the AHAS donated a derelict B-25 Mitchell bomber to Clear Air Force Base, and this was airlifted out by Sikorsky CH-54 helicopter, an experience which was to prove invaluable to the AHAS at a later date in connection with the Dago Lake Catalina.

Fired by this early success, the AHAS turned its attention to the Cat. After a while, the owner of the wreck, Fred Richards, agreed to donate the airframe to the Society, and after a long and frustrating period of negotiation with the Bureau of Land Management and the State of Alaska, the way became clear for the AHAS to take over responsibility for the wreck. In the meantime, this

On 22 August 1987, OA-10A 44-33954 flew again, courtesy of an Alaskan ANG CH-54 Skycrane helicopter. It is seen en route from King Salmon to Anchorage.
Ted Spencer/AAHM

did not prevent an enterprising individual succeeding in removing the centre-section fuel tanks with an axe, although surprisingly without too much damage being inflicted on the aircraft.

Once in possession of the wreck, the AHAS now faced the massive problem of recovering it. It managed to obtain the co-operation of the 207th Aviation Section of the local Air National Guard unit, and a plan was formulated to move the derelict airframe by CH-54 helicopter. On 28 September 1984, the CH-54, plus other support helicopters and fixed-wing aircraft, set out to King Salmon Air Force Base, which was to become the base of the retrieval operation. The next day's first task was to get the Catalina hulk into an upright position, which was achieved using airbags. Once quantities of silt had been removed from the hull's interior, an attempt was made to lift the Catalina from its long-term resting place. The first try proved that the helicopter was too heavy, and the PBY refused to budge, but after the CH-54 had burned off some of its fuel load, a second attempt proved more fruitful. However, an altitude of only some 10 ft was achieved, but at least this enabled the Catalina to be moved to a more convenient position. The *Queen of Dago Lake* had flown again!

On 30 September 37 years ago to the day since its unscheduled arrival at Dago Lake, and now somewhat lighter after the removal of more silt and equipment, the CH-54 managed to 'fly' the Catalina to within 22 miles of King Salmon. Following various trials and tribulations, the AHAS 'prize' was eventually deposited at King Salmon a week later. It was to be a further three years before another CH-54 transported 44-33954 to its final destination at Anchorage, where it was gently lowered to the ground on 22 August 22 1987. Even this was achieved only after a heart-stopping moment when a lifting strap gave way whilst in flight and the precious cargo had to be put down and re-secured. Once at Anchorage, it was to pass into the care of the Alaska Aviation Heritage Museum.

Work continues to restore this former USAAF OA-10A to museum standard, but it has to be carried out in the open so progress is slow. By 1999, the Catalina was standing on its own undercarriage and the outer wing panels had been put back in place. The project is located on the south shore of Lake Hood alongside Anchorage International Airport. At the time of its original 'flight' from Dago Lake, the US civil registration N44BY was apparently allocated, and later this was changed to N57875, although prospects of it flying under its own power again would seem to be unlikely.

Florida. It had begun to look a little sorry for itself with its US Navy colour scheme fading away, but it has recently been renovated thanks to the efforts of the PATRON 45 Association. Its hull proudly displays the Association's Squadron code 45-P-3.

Having been on military charge with the US Navy during the Second World War as Bu46602 and ending its military career in storage at Litchfield Park, Arizona, it briefly became N6071C with an unidentified owner before moving to Canada as CF-FFZ in the late 1960s. Its commercial career up to that point is unfortunately obscure, although there is a theory that it was operated in Brazil as both a commercial and a military aircraft. Although this is unconfirmed at present, it is known that the aircraft did serve with VP-45 during the Second World War, and that unit did fly in Brazil. The VP-45 Association says that the logbooks covering the post-war period are incomplete, although they seem to indicate that Bu46602 had returned to the USA by November 1946, being located at the NAS, Philadelphia. Did it go back to Brazil?

In Canada, it was part of the large fleet of water bombing Catalinas and Cansos operated out of Victoria, British Columbia, by Flying Fireman Ltd. With that company, it was identified by the hull code 3, later lengthened to 773. At some point, it acquired a Davis tail, more normally associated with the Cyclone-powered *Super Cats*, although it retained its standard R-1830s. This fairly unorthodox, although not unique, configuration, remained until quite recently.

In 1986 when Flying Fireman called it a day as far as PBYs were concerned, interest in CF-FFZ, as it had become, was shown by Wilson 'Connie' Edwards of Big Springs in Texas, and he got as far as reserving the registration N4NC for it. In the event, these were not taken up and he purchased another Catalina instead – the PBY-6A N999AR which in due course took up the unused marks N4NC. Later in the same year, CF-FFZ was purchased by AP Inc of Auburn, California, and in 1990, it went to Pensacola. The 1995 United States Civil Aircraft Register quotes the registered owner as the Museum of Naval

---

Until its recent restoration and repaint, N607CC looked like this, with faded US Navy blue and grey colours and *Super Cat*-style rudder.
MAP

Table 159.

Registration/ Serial	C/n	Type	Place of Manufacture	Previous id(s)
N57875	CV-465	OA-10A	CAN VIC (Cartierville)	N44BY ntu 44-33954 (USAAF) Bu67918 ntu (US Navy)

N607CC – United States Naval Aviation Museum, Pensacola, Florida

For some time now, N607CC has been resident at the United States Naval Aviation Museum at Pensacola,

Aviation, the former owner being the Florida Aircraft Leasing Corporation from November 1991 onward. The registration N607CC was cancelled in August 1999.

By the early part of 2000, Bu46602 had acquired a conventional PBY-5A rudder in place of its earlier *Super Cat* type, and an 'eyeball' turret. It had also received a new colour scheme to more accurately portray a US Navy PBY-5A.

Table 160. Registration/ Serial	C/n	Type	Place of Manufacture	Previous id(s)
N607CC	1966	PBY-5A	CON NO	N4NC ntu C-FFFZ CF-FFZ N6071C Bu46602 (US Navy)

N6473C – Possibly in Fort Worth area, Texas

Something of a mystery ship, N6473C is rumoured to exist still, although its current status is not entirely certain. It is, however, still listed on the United States Civil Aircraft Register. What is beyond doubt is that it was built in San Diego by Consolidated with construction number 1891 and the allocated military identity of Bu46527. It flew with the US Navy from February 1944, and after its retirement was stored in Arizona at the Litchfield Park US Navy storage facility before being struck from the inventory in August 1956.

It seems likely that it was released onto the commercial market but remained unconverted from its stock military configuration. It was reported to be in the Fort Worth, Texas, area in 1968. The Confederate Air Force were interested in acquiring a derelict PBY that they had discovered at Meacham Field, Fort Worth in the early 1970s. and there must be a good chance that this was N6473C, which was, apparently, owned by Tandy Industries of Oklahoma City. Although Tandy was willing to donate the Catalina to the CAF, the Confederates did not accept it after restoration costs were deemed to be too high for their available resources. Quite what happened to the airframe after this is not known, and it may

be that it was scrapped.

Table 161. Registration/Serial	C/n	Type	Place of Manufacture	Previous id(s)
N6473C	1891	PBY-5A	CON SD	Bu46527 (US Navy)

N68740 – Lone Star Flight Museum, Galveston, Texas

In November 1940, Contract C-78 was placed with Consolidated for the construction of 14 amphibious PBY-5As for the Royal Canadian Air Force. To be known as Canso As , they were serialled 9737–9750, and followed an earlier order for pure flying boat Cansos with serials 9701–9736. The Canso A batch was built at San Diego between November and December 1941, and included aircraft 9742, construction number 407. It was taken on charge by the RCAF on 2 January 1942, and served until September 1946, when it was struck off charge. During its active service, some of its time, if not all, was spent with 5 (BR) Squadron which was based at various times at Dartmouth in Nova Scotia, Gander, Torbay, Yarmouth and Gaspe in Quebec, until the Squadron's disbandment in June 1945.

After a period of post-war storage, it was purchased by Southern California Aircraft Corporation of Ontario, California, a company known to have converted a number of ex-military Catalinas and Cansos for commercial operators and foreign air arms. One of that company's specialities was the conversion known as the *Landseaire*, which involved removing the nose turret, installing an air stair, luxury interior and horn-balanced rudder, and modifying the blisters to make entrance easy for passengers. 9742 underwent such a conversion and was registered as N68740 in 1951. It has retained this registration ever since, despite passing through the ownership of a long line of companies, including Flying Bonefish Inc of Carson City, Nevada, and Freeport Indonesia Inc of New York. It was with the latter mining company that it flew communications services between Darwin in Australia, New Guinea and West Irian.

A ragged N6473C at Fort Worth in 1968. Its ultimate fate is uncertain.
MAP

Now preserved at Galveston in the Lone Star Flight Museum, N68740 flew extensively as a civil aircraft during the 1970s. It is shown visiting Oakland, California.
Arthur Pearcy

Its next owners were Lee Otterson and Bill Farinon, and, whilst nominally based in California, it was used for a 'world' tour which, in the event, seems to have taken in mainly Far Eastern and Antipodean destinations – it was certainly not seen in Europe. At around this time, it was used in a movie entitled *Mysterious Island of Beautiful Women*, and this involved it in some air-to-air work and also some filming on a beach, although the location for this is not known. By 1981, it was owned by the University of Hawaii and based at Honolulu, but later went into storage with Aero Nostalgia of Stockton, California.

In 1990, Gary Larkins, well known for his involvement with a number of Catalinas, acquired N68740 and it then went to the Naval Air Station at Pensacola in Florida. It remained there for some time before moving to Texas and the Lone Star Museum of Flight. It had a nose turret grafted back on and was sprayed up in a US Navy colour scheme.

In December 1992, the US registration N6208H was reserved for it in the name of H. Wells, but this transfer does not seem to have taken place.

Table 162.

Registration/ Serial	C/n	Type	Place of Manufacture	Previous id(s)
N68740	407	Canso A	CON SD	N6208H ntu N68740 9742 (RCAF)

N68756 – American Air Power Heritage Flying Museum, Rio Grande Valley Wing, Confederate Air Force, Brownsville, Texas

With its origins going back as far as the early 1960s, the Confederate Air Force has, over the years, amassed a very large collection of predominantly Second World War combat aircraft. It is hardly surprising, therefore, that during its expansion, the CAF should want to add a PBY to its 'battle order'. In fact, over the years, the CAF has operated no fewer than five Catalinas – three PBY-6As and two PBY-5As, one of which is the subject of this particular profile. Sadly, the CAF's association with the type has been far from happy, and two of its three survivors are non-airworthy at present.

N68756 is one of a batch of 59 PBY-5A Catalinas built at New Orleans that were ordered for the US Navy, and it flew with them as Bu46590 from 31 August 1944, onward. Whilst in military service, it is known to have flown patrols in the Atlantic theatre with VPB-84 out of Quonset Point, Rhode Island, and training missions on the Pacific Coast whilst with HEDRON 8 based at NAS Alameda, San Francisco. Its next assignment was with the US Coast Guard based in Miami. Thereafter, '590 had a series of postings that saw it flying with VP-AM-5 at Whidby Island, Washington, and later at Nome in Alaska. It then briefly appeared on the inventory of FASRON 110 but was consigned to the NAMC at Philadelphia around July 1948, being formally struck off charge in June 1950.

It was acquired by Catalina specialists Southern California Aircraft Corporation of Ontario, California, and converted by them for civilian use with a luxury interior. The first owner was the Fullerton Oil Company

of Pasadena in 1952, which used it extensively as a VIP transport before selling it to the American TV personality Herb Schriner in mid-1960. During his ownership, the Catalina's interior was further modified to resemble the Jules Verne submarine *Nautilus*!

Schriner owned N68756 for most of the 1960s, but it was sold after his death in a car crash to Endicot P. Davison, who flew it in Canada and in the Caribbean, holding on to it until 1977, when it passed to the Quebec Labrador Mission Foundation of Ipswich, Massachusetts. The Foundation used it for ferrying supplies to those in need in remote regions of Northern Canada.

Then, in August 1979, it was delivered to Harlingen in Texas to become part of the Confederate Air Force collection under the sponsorship of 'Colonel' Michael Wansey, who at that time was owner of Australian DC-3 operator Rebel Air, as well as the Douglas DC-2 VH-CDZ and Fairey Firefly WD828. The original intention had been to have the PBY as the flagship of an Australian Wing of the Confederate Air Force, although it was to remain based in the USA.

When N68756 first arrived in Texas, it was resplendent in an attractive colour scheme of white overall with red and blue trim, but this did not last for long. The Catalina was soon inside the CAF hangars undergoing an extensive inspection and overhaul, not just for subsequent local use but for a proposed trip to Australia and back – 9,700 miles and 55 hours' flying time each way! The purpose of this trip was twofold. Firstly, the CAF wished to spread goodwill among its supporters throughout the Pacific area, and secondly, the trip would coincide with the 60th anniversary of the formation of the Royal Australian Air Force, which was, of course, a major operator of the type during and after the Second World War. As work progressed, the civilian livery was replaced with a RAAF livery of silver-grey overall with light blue hull undersurfaces, later to be replaced by yellow. The standard blue and white RAAF roundels were applied to the rear hull, together with the bogus serial A24-387, the highest originally allocated to genuine RAAF Cats being A24-386. It was also given the somewhat uncomplimentary name *Sea Bitch*. Theoretically, the aircraft was intended to represent an aircraft of the 113th Air Sea Rescue Squadron, although liberties were taken with the squadron codes that appeared as NB-N, the initials of Wansey's Australian TV station! The correct codes for that Squadron were NR-. NBN was a major sponsor of the flight, finance also coming from Colonel Wansey himself, the CAF and the RSL Building Society of Newcastle, NSW.

Prior to the trip, the Catalina had a fit of truculence during a test flight when the port engine blew before the CAF's 1980 air show at Harlingen. Not satisfied with this, another engine was written off after the Cat had been taken to Dallas for radio equipment installation, and a precautionary landing had to be made at Grayson County Airport, Sherman, where the aircraft stayed until yet another unit was installed.

In fact, the flight to Australia technically started off from Sherman and routed Tulsa, Tucson, Phoenix and San Francisco, where N68756 temporarily lodged at NAS Alameda on the Eastern Bay before the journey proper. Crew for the flight were Ed Vasser, Bill Hawkins, Les

N68756 was painted to represent a RAAF PBY, and received the spurious serial A24-387. This picture was taken during the Australian visit in the early 1980s.
Peter Keating Collection

Risley, Pete Peterson, Ron Himmelberg, Cam Bailey and Trevor Fuller. Mike Wansey joined the crew in Hawaii.

On 24 January 1981, N68756 left Alameda for Monterey, where the tanks were topped up before setting off for Hilo, Hawaii, 2,500 miles away. From there, a short transit was made to Honolulu for servicing before moving on to Majuro Atoll in the Marshall Islands, which was only reached after some problems with the starboard engine. Honiara in the Solomons was reached on the 30th after a violent rain storm, and then, on 1 February it was on to Brisbane and Australian soil if not water! There then followed guest appearances all over the country, which did include landings on water from Lake Macquarie near the old RAAF base at Rathmines in New South Wales.

After attracting huge interest in Australia, 'A24-387' returned to the USA in time to make its US display debut at the CAF's Airsho 81, and it subsequently appeared at various air shows, sometimes in company with the CAF PBY-6A N16KL, which at that time was still airworthy, although destined to be lost in a needless crash. It subsequently spent some of its time based with the Pacific Wing of the Confederate Air Force at Oakland, California. However, engine trouble struck again in 1986 when another engine blew whilst attending Harlingen for the annual CAF *Airsho*. A replacement was also blown, and ongoing repair proved just too much financially for the Pacific Wing. This, coupled with various paperwork problems with the FAA, meant that in the end the Cat was virtually abandoned at Harlingen, and by 1994 it was standing on the ramp, engineless and minus control surfaces and tail, awaiting a very uncertain future.

As a result of being left out in the open at Harlingen for such a long time, the condition of N68756 began to deteriorate, and this neglect continued. In 1992, the CAF had reportedly put the aircraft up for disposal, together with a number of other aircraft, in order to raise finance for the organisation's move of base to Midland, Texas. In the end, the decaying and vandalised PBY did not go to Midland but, instead, joined the select band of Catalinas that have been airlifted by helicopter! Some time in 1996,

it was hauled aloft by a Texas Air National Guard CH-47 Chinook and taken from Harlingen to Brownsville, where a long-term restoration was to be undertaken by the Rio Grande Valley Wing of the CAF. At Brownsville, it was hangared at last, albeit in a dismantled state within the Airpower Heritage Flying Museum.

In 1998, following the bad storm damage sustained to the fourth CAF PBY, N7179Y, it is said that the CAF surveyed N68756 at Brownsville with a view to using its wing to replace the written-off unit, but found that it was too badly corroded to be of any use in a rebuild to airworthy condition. It is hoped, therefore, that in the future, work will continue on N68756 to bring it up to museum standard. But even this is a rather sad end for an airframe that has only accumulated some 3,570 flying hours. A possible brighter note was sounded in early 2000, when a sale to Bob Schneider was reported.

Table 163.

Registration/ Serial	C/n	Type	Place of Manufacture	Previous id(s)
N68756	1954	PBY-5A	CON NO	Bu46590 (US Navy)

N7057C – National Warplane Museum, Elmira-Corning, New York

For some time, N7057C kept company with various down-at-heel propliners in one of the less salubrious corners of Fort Lauderdale Airport in Florida, and it seemed as if it might never fly out again. Fortunately, it did and for sometime thereafter it flew regularly with the National Warplane Museum collection at air shows and fly-ins in the Eastern United States. Sadly, it has been ground-bound again more recently, as the NWM's limited financial resources have been concentrated on keeping its B-17 Flying Fortress airworthy.

N7057C was originally laid down as a US Navy PBY-6A as part of contract NOa-259. The batch of 114 aircraft within which it appeared were mostly delivered either to the Soviet Union or to the USAAF as OA-10Bs, but Bu64072 went to the Navy, and after acceptance on 6 August 1945, went on to serve FAW-14, VP-AM-2, VP-62 and FASRON 112 at such diverse bases as Philadelphia, San Diego, New York and Pensacola, before retiring to Litchfield Park, where it was struck from the inventory of the US Navy in October 1956. Its first civilian owner seems to have been Sidney Hendricks, who had it registered as N7057C, although it is known that Bill Le Grand was involved in its conversion to civilian status; as such, it became the first PBY-6A to be certificated for passenger carrying, although plans to use if for this purpose up into Canada did not come to fruition. It subsequently had a number of owners, including the Dorr family.

After purchase by John Dorr, and on its first flight under his ownership, it suffered an accident on 16 December 1964. When the pilot actuated the landing gear to the extended position for a night landing at Phoenix, Arizona, after a flight from Albuquerque, New Mexico, the hydraulic pressure fell to zero and the gear position indicators failed to show a safe-for-landing condition. The pilot executed the emergency gear extension procedure and landed, but in the landing roll the right

Sadly, the National Warplane Museum's PBY-6A N7057C
has not flown for a number of years and remains in store
at Elmira. This fine view could almost be a manufacturer's
pre-delivery photo!
Richard E. Bagg via Dr Tom Garrett

main gear collapsed. Investigation revealed that a
hydraulic leak had developed at the gland nut at the
lower end of the left main gear actuating cylinder and the
hydraulic system was out of fluid. The leak occurred
because the 'O' ring seals had hardened from ageing and
very limited use of the aircraft over the previous eight-
year period. The pilot reported that in his emergency
gear extension procedure, the right gear arm was apparently not fully latched. The probable cause of the accident
was attributed to landing gear extension failure caused
by material failure of the 'O' ring actuating cylinder seals.
Failure of the pilot to ensure that the landing gear was
extended and safe during emergency extension procedures was also a factor. Damage was categorised as
substantial, but neither of the two occupants was injured.
The damage was repaired.

Unfortunately, the owner was not so fortunate, when,
on a subsequent flight, he suffered a fatal heart attack at
the controls. On 6 August 1969, John Dorr took off from
Lake Trembleur, 120 miles north of Prince George, British
Columbia, with his twenty-year-old son John Jr as 'co-
pilot' and a party of twelve fishermen in the passenger
seats. They were bound for home in California. Very
shortly after take-off, John Dorr Sr collapsed and died
from a massive heart attack, leaving his unqualified son
at the controls. With the help of local aircraft, a Catalina

fire-bomber pilot who was on duty at Prince George, and
air traffic controllers there, he was talked down to a safe
landing.

After the Dorr family had sold N7057C, it was owned
by a succession of operators, including Mediterranean
East Ltd, Cims Associates, Aeroborne Enterprises, Bush
Aviation, P & P Charters and Hill Air Corporation. All of
these organisations hailed from Florida, and by the mid-
1980s, the Catalina was to be found languishing at Fort
Lauderdale, as mentioned at the start of this profile. After
military service, it had been painted white with yellow
trim, and this was later changed to light green with dark-
er green trim. During its period of inactivity at Fort
Lauderdale, it was re-painted white overall with black
lettering, whilst yellow trim was added to the engine
cowls. The large numerals 69 were painted on both sides
of the hull forward of the wing. Briefly, N7057C shared
the Fort Lauderdale ramp space with another Catalina,
PBY-5A N285NJ, that had arrived from Venezuela, but
this soon departed for Italy and an unfortunate demise
following brake failure at Turin. Even though N7057C
was getting pretty shabby by this time, things were
beginning to look brighter, and a new owner was on the
horizon.

In 1985, negotiations had begun for the National
Warplane Museum in New York State to purchase the
PBY, and the deal was finally concluded in October 1987,
when ownership was transferred. After a long overhaul,
it was flown to the NWM's home at Geneseo, where further maintenance was carried out. It flew again in July
1989, just in time for the annual NWM *Wings of Eagles* air
display. It was painted up in a US Navy colour scheme of
two-tone blue with white undersurfaces and the hull

code 70-P. The 'meatball'-style nationality marking carried on the nose was colourful but inappropriate for a PBY-6A! Because very little in the way of post-war modification had taken place, the Catalina was in close to stock condition. The blisters and the nose turret were still in place, although the latter had been partially plated over. The turret area was later fully restored and by 1991 it was sporting a late-war 'eyeball'-style turret, apparently after being found in its original packing crate! Various individuals flew the aircraft, and they included Bill Le Grand, whose company was one of the early owners post-war! N7057C was kept busy flying at various US shows, although, in common with many old aircraft, it suffered its share of mechanical problems.

For the 1992 season, N7057C's early-style national insignia had been replaced by the more appropriate blue and white 'star and bar', and the nose code was changed to 62-P. Sadly, funding restrictions have led to the PBY taking a back-seat role to other NWM types, and it has spent some time grounded whilst its airworthy future is decided. It did fly on Christmas Eve, 1997, when it was ferried from Geneseo to the NWM's new base at Elmira-Corning Regional Airport, Horseheads, New York. It is hoped that N7057C will fly again soon when funds permit. In the meantime, the museum is actively seeking a radome to install over the cockpit, as seen on the original military aircraft.

Table 164.

Registration/ Serial	C/n	Type	Place of Manufacture	Previous id(s)
N7057C		PBY-6A	CON NO	Bu64072 (US Navy)

N7179Y – American Air Power Heritage Flying Museum, Southern Minnesota Wing, Confederate Air Force, Fleming Field, Minneapolis/St Paul, Minnesota

As N7082C, this PBY-6A was an early post-war conversion to the fire-bombing role, and this dramatic change of

use from the military aircraft that it was designed as ensured that it survived in airworthy condition until mid-1998. Unfortunately, Mother Nature intervened, and at present it is grounded awaiting possible repairs to massive damage caused by high winds.

In US Navy use, it was serialled Bu64097, and after leaving the New Orleans production line, it served its country from the summer of 1945 until it was retired to the desert of Litchfield Park, where it remained for ten years or so. It was allocated at various times to FAW-8, NARTU New York and NARTU, Atlanta. In 1957, it was registered as N7082C to the Babb Company of Phoenix, which sold it on to Routh Aircraft of Long Beach, with which it became a tanker with the State of California with the fire-fighting code E94. A change of owner occurred again in 1964 before flying out to the South of France, where it joined the varied Catalina fleet of the Protection Civile at Marseille. The Protection Civile used both PBY-5A and -6A Catalinas, and whilst some were chartered from Canadian operators on an annual basis, others, including N7082C, were owned by the organisation. Flying as F-ZBAW, it was prepared for use with the Protection Civile by Heli-Service de France before going on to operate in France and Corsica for nine years, using the call sign *Yellow Pelican*.

In 1974 the decision was taken to dispose of it, and it was registered in Canada as C-FHNF for Avalon Aviation, with which it flew for some years as tanker 4, later 794. During the 1976/7 season, it operated on charter in Norway with Haydn Air Charter, although this contract was later taken on by its sister aircraft C-FHNH.

When Avalon ceased operations in the 1980s, C-FHNF was stored along with most of the company's Catalina

Another PBY-6A no longer flying is the Confederate Air Force aircraft N7179Y. As described in the text, it was badly damaged by high winds in May 1998. This air-to-air photograph was taken during one of the CAF's annual displays.
Peter R. March

fleet at Parry Sound Airport, Ontario, whilst a buyer was found. In March, 1991, it was registered as N7179Y to a partnership trading as Aircraft Marketing Inc of Albuquerque, which had it flown down to Fort Lauderdale in Florida for further storage. It acquired a smart US Navy colour scheme which turned it into one of the more realistic-looking pseudo-military PBYs around. It was put up for sale at the Santa Monica Museum of Flying auction held in October 1991, but it failed to sell. Then, in 1994, it was sold to the Confederate Air Force of Midland, Texas, which displayed it widely over the next three years or so. The Confederates had a rather unfortunate operating record with three previous Catalinas, but it did look as if they had turned the corner with N7179Y, and it was carefully flown and well maintained by the Southern Minnesota Wing of the CAF after it had successfully bid to operate the plane on the CAF's behalf.

Sadly, things turned sour on the night of 30/31 May 1998, when very strong winds hit Fleming Field, Minneapolis/St Paul. N7179Y was picketed out on the ramp and took the full force of the gale. The Catalina was blown up onto one wingtip before crashing down on its bow and landing upside down with a smashed wing and damaged bow and tail. The wing was so badly damaged that it was beyond repair. The CAF set about acquiring a replacement wing in order to carry out a restoration to airworthy condition, but ultimately this proved impossible. In the end, they purchased another Catalina instead, the former Airborne Fire Attack PBY-6A N324FA. Later, however, a wing centre section was acquired at the infamous SLAFCO auction in August 1999, so a rebuild may still be on the cards.

Shorn of the attractive blue and white livery from its Venezuelan days, N7238Z looks rather neglected at San Juan, Puerto Rico, in June 2000.
Michael Prophet

Table 165.

Registration/ Serial	C/n	Type	Place of Manufacture	Previous id(s)
N7179Y	'225'	PBY-6A	CON NO	C-FHNF F-ZBAW N7082C Bu64097 (USA Navy)

N7238Z – Caribbean Airline Services Inc, San Juan, Puerto Rico

In common with a number of ex-United States military Catalinas, N7238Z first saw commercial registry under the ownership of Trade-Ayer of Linden, New Jersey, to which it was registered as N10024 in September 1956. Prior to this, it had left the San Diego factory of Consolidated to serve with the US Navy as Bu48412 until 1953, when it entered storage in Seattle, Washington State. Shortly after aquisition by Trade-Ayer, title passed to Cole Brock Inc and then to Remmert Werner Inc of St Louis, with which it became N96R in 1959. Later that year, it was sold to a Venezuelan operator and was fully converted for civilian use by Pan Air of New Orleans.

The initial operator in South America was the Orinoco Mining Company of Puerto Ordaz, later changing to the Corporacion Ferrominera de Orinoco SA. It wore several different registrations as can be seen in the accompanying list. Fully equipped as a passenger aircraft, it ferried shipping pilots and engineers out to the Orinoco River area where ore carriers picked up their cargoes. This

work was later taken over by Canadair CL-215s. During the period that this particular aircraft was thus employed, and whilst registered YV-P-EPZ , it needed extensive rebuilding after landing in a silted-up channel at San Felix on 27 January 1976.

In 1983, it was acquired by new owners Camaronera del Sur CA, and later, in 1989, by Italo Campagna, trading as SERVES and based at Caracas-Maiquetia Airport. At the time that Campagna purchased the Catalina, it was in good condition, but anti-corrosion work was required after it was left in external storage for a further period at Caracas. By 1993, it was intended that it should be used for flying tourists in its twenty seats on flights to Isla Margarita and Los Rosques, and possibly even out to the Galapagos Islands.

Then, in April 1997, it was allocated a new registration in the USA under the ownership of Caribbean Air Transport Inc, of Carolina, Puerto Rico. In November of the same year, ownership and registry were passed to Serves Import Inc of Miami, a company owned by the same individual, with which it latterly operated in Venezuela. By the middle of 2000, N7238Z was looking pretty sorry for itself, with its formerly immaculate blue and white colour scheme very faded and worn and the cowlings off the engines. However, in June of that year, the aircraft was reportedly sold to Caribbean Airline Services Inc, or CAS, and the new owner was planning to return N7238Z to airworthiness, along with the other ex-SERVES aircraft YV-584CP, at that time still located in Venezuela.

Table 166.

Registration/ Serial	C/n	Type	Place of Manufacture	Previous id(s)
N7238Z	1774	PBY-5A	CON SD	YV-485C YV-585CP YV-56CP YV-O-CFO-4 YV-P-EPZ YV-P-EPX N96R N10024 Bu48412 (US Navy)

N84857 – Ben Kalka, Burlington Washington

But for a tragic ground accident, this particular Catalina would almost certainly be on museum display in Israel by now, filling a gap in that country's collection of preserved military aircraft. Sadly, it was not to be, and the damaged airframe is now on long-term rebuild in Washington State, having recently moved there from remote Montana.

Contract NXa13595 of 11 October 1942 called for the construction of 100 PBY-5A Catalinas, and these were produced from the summer of 1943 through to that autumn. They were allocated the US Navy serials Bu33960 to 34059, and the ninth aircraft, Bu33968, is the subject of this profile. Its wartime and post-war military service over, it was one of a number of former military Catalinas to be saved from scrapping by Thomas Kendall, who had formed Catalina Ltd at La Verne in California. Registered to his company as N5582V in 1964, it later went to Troy Hawkins at Wichita Falls in Texas. Its exact movements during the late 1960s and 1970s are obscure, although it appears to have been allocated the Canadian civil registration C-GVTF at one point. These markings were not taken up, however, and, instead, it was taken on by the Diversified Drilling Muds company, of Cheyenne, Wyoming presumably as a communications aircraft. That company owned it from 1980 until 1985, but it was stored at Lewiston in Montana from at least the spring of 1984. By this stage in its history, it had had its blister turrets removed but still retained a more or less stock flat-topped nose turret. The rudder was of the post-war commercial horn-balanced type.

In 1985, it was earmarked as an exhibit at the Israeli Air Force Museum at Hatzerim. The plan was to fly N84857 to Reno, Nevada, for crew training and then on to Miami for the installation of radio gear before crossing the Atlantic to Tel Aviv. But the delivery flight to Israel never took place as, on 9 May 1985, it rolled off the runway at Lewistown following brake failure whilst taxiing for take-off. Although the pilot attempted a deliberate ground loop, the unfortunate aircraft ended up in a ditch at the bottom of a slope beyond the overrun. No attempt was made to use the hydraulic emergency hand pump to activate the brakes. The impact with the bottom of the gully caused the hull to break, and the nose section folded upwards and back into the cockpit, killing the pilot and injuring the two other crew on board. The damaged airframe was recovered and is still on site with the bow area protected by a temporary cover to enable rebuild work to progress. Its damaged turret area was removed and used to restore the PBY-5A N9521C, currently to be found in the UK. Unfortunately, the restoration process suffered something of a setback when a tornado hit the Lewiston area in August 1999.

After the accident, the Israelis pulled out of the purchase, and N84857 remained with Ben Kalka of Oakland, California. Kalka had apparently put the Israeli deal together and was on board at the time of the accident. It is believed that somewhere along the line, Catalina restorer Ray Cox of Washington State may have been involved in the project to repair this unfortunate Catalina. Connected or not, the damaged airframe was dismantled and trucked to Sound Aircraft, Burlington, Washington State, at the end of 2000 for further repairs and re-assembly. This may involve using the nose section from the unidentified Canso *Sad Sack* which is located at Whidbey Island.

Table 167. Registration/ Serial	C/n	Type	Place of Manufacture	Previous id(s)
N84857	1522	PBY-5A	CON SD	C-GVTF ntu N5582V Bu33968 (US Navy)

N85U – Flying Fireman Inc, Spanaway, Washington State

Although the water bombing company Flying Fireman Ltd, of Victoria, Vancouver Island also known as Awood Air, ceased using Catalinas in Canada by the early 1990s, its American subsidiary company, Flying Fireman Inc, has continued to use a Wright Cyclone-powered PBY-6A in neighbouring Washington State.

N85U has been a water bomber for many years, having started in this trade in California, then migrated to the west coast of Canada before returning Stateside again. It was originally laid down as a US Navy PBY-6A, Bureau of Aeronautics number Bu64041.

Following retirement from military duties, '041 was acquired by Leo Demers of Salem in Oregon and was soon put into use protecting forests. From then and for the next twenty years or so, it operated with a number of companies involved in forestry protection and aerial fire fighting along the length of the United States' West Coast, including such names as Ace Demers; Rosenbalm Aviation of Medford, Oregon; B. B. Burson of Columbia, California; Sonora Flying Service; and the better-known Hemet Valley Flying Services of Hemet, also in California, with whom it flew for ten years. During its time in the USA, it flew with the United States Forest

Following the move from Lewistown, Montana, to Skagit County Airport, Washington, the dismantled airframe of PBY-5A N84857 was stored in the open. The rear hull is shown here, whilst the wings were stored nearby. A new forward section will be grafted on in due course.
Heijo Kuil

Although this photo was taken as long ago as 1987, N85U still works hard as a fire fighter, and looks just as good now as it did then.
Gerald White

N9502C during the late 1980s at Hawkins, Texas.
Heijo Kuil

Service codes E54 and 54. It was also whilst in the USA that its nose turret was removed and its P&Ws were changed for R-2600s, although it retained its PBY-6A tail and blisters.

In May 1979, this Catalina travelled north to Canada to join Flying Fireman, whose fleet of Catalinas had become depleted through attrition. It was re-registered as C-GFFI and given the fleet number 10, later changed to 9 and 779. By 1986, it had returned to the USA for operation in Washington State. Its red and white colour scheme had by this time been replaced by a silver-grey overall scheme with yellow-orange undersides, float tips and engine cowlings, and with the code 85 painted in large numerals across the fin and rudder. During the fire-fighting season, it is variously operated from Tacoma and Deer Park, north of Spokane, on contract to the United States Forest Service.

One interesting point regarding this aircraft is that early photographs taken when demonstrating water drops in California as N6453C show that the wing-tip floats had been removed and the wing tips faired over. The floats were put back in place subsequently when it became a water-based bomber rather than being loaded with borate at ground bases from hoses.

Table 168.

Registration/ Serial	C/n	Type	Place of Manufacture	Previous id(s)
N85U		PBY-6A	CON NO	C-GFFI N6453C Bu64041 (US Navy)

N9502C – Robert R. Schneider, The Australian-American Catalina Memorial Foundation Inc, Hawkins, Texas/Perth, Western Australia

N9502C was built at New Orleans on Contract NOa-464 in late 1944, and flew with the US Navy as Bu46624, having been accepted onto charge on 23 November 1944. It ended its Navy days, like so many other PBYs, in storage at Litchfield Park in Arizona, and was struck off charge in August 1956. During the 1960s, it was owned by Southland Flying Service of Tohula, Mississippi, but it seems possible that it may not have been converted for commercial use. Later, at the end of the 1970s, it became the property of collector David Tallichet and his Military Aircraft Restoration Company (MARC) of Chino, California. It is believed that N9502C is the anonymous Catalina that was displayed for a time in the early 1980s outside the 94th Aero Squadron Restaurant at Clearwater/St Petersburg, Florida.

For some time, N9502C appeared on the US Civil Aircraft Register with the comments 'Sale Reported', but without a current owner listed. The registered address quoted was known to be also that of Project Catalina, the David Tallichet organisation that brought a number of former Força Aérea Brasileira PBY-5As back from Brazil to the USA, which are now on static display at various locations around the country. However, N9502C is not one of the former FAB aircraft nor is it a former Royal Danish Air Force PBY-6A, as was suggested by a contributor to a UK aviation magazine some years ago.

It is almost certain that the dismantled Catalina that subsequently appeared at Hawkins in Texas is N9502C, although the PBY-6A N7885B has also been mentioned and may have been used in this project. Whatever its true identity, this aircraft has been the subject of a restoration project by Robert Schneider since then, and during 1999 plans were announced that were to see the aircraft transported to Australia. There it would form the centrepiece of the Australian-American Catalina Memorial Foundation on the Swan River near Perth, Western Australia. In due course, a purpose-designed museum building will be constructed to hold the Catalina. A formal handover ceremony was held at Hawkins on 25 March 2000, although a subsequent electrical fire in the Catalina's hangar caused some minor heat damage to the vertical tail surfaces. This was repaired and N9502C was taken to San Diego in the summer of 2001 for loading aboard the USS *Comstock* and transportation to Australia, where it will in due course be displayed in Perth.

Table 169.

Registration/ Serial	C/n	Type	Place of Manufacture	Previous id(s)
N9502C	1988	PBY-5A	CON NO	Bu46624 (US Navy)

N9505C – SLAFCO Inc, Moses Lake, Washington State

Of the several surviving Catalinas owned by Robert Schlaefli's SLAFCO Inc and based at the former Strategic Air Command bomber base at Moses Lake in Washington, only two are currently airworthy, and N9505C is one of them, the other being N31235. Unlike N31235, however, N9505C appears to have been converted to an aerial fire-fighting aircraft much earlier in its commercial career, and did not see airline service first.

Following military service with the US Navy, to which it was delivered in the latter half of 1943, it was sold from storage to a firm known as Alcan Airways of Kingman, Arizona. It operated as a forest-fire-fighting company and flew N9505C in a commercial configuration as tanker 9, with blisters still in place but a clipper bow substituted for the original turreted nose. It also had a horn-balanced rudder, but at some later point the tail unit was replaced with the Davis tail configuration and the Wright R-2600 Cyclone power-plants of the Super Catalina variant.

After Alcan's ownership came a very brief period in 1969 with Intercapital Inc of Las Vegas before a sale to its present owners, SLAFCO. It has been based up in northwest USA ever since, although it has spent occasional periods of storage in the sympathetic climate of Tucson, Arizona. In SLAFCO's service, N9505C has carried the fleet number 53.

During the late fall of 1988, N9505C commenced work on a typical fire-fighting contract involving water bombing tracts of forest near Redding in Northern California, work that was carried out alongside the Douglas A-26 Invaders of Lynch Air Tankers, from Billings, Montana. What was different on this occasion was that the action was being filmed for the Steven Spielberg movie *Always*,

a re-make of the earlier film *A Guy Named Joe* that had starred Spencer Tracey. Spielberg's film was to star Richard Dreyfuss, John Goodman and Holly Hunter. A dummy fire-fighting land base was built at the small airfield of Libby in Montana, and N9505C flew there for more filming in June 1989. It is seen at various times during the screenplay, but nowhere more spectacularly than in the opening sequence of the film, where it is shown performing a head-on water pickup, much to the dismay of an initially unsuspecting pair of fishermen in a dinghy, who find themselves right in the PBY's path! For the film, N9505C retained its white, orange and black SLAFCO livery, but with the addition of nose art in the form of a shapely fire-eating lady and the legend *Fire Eaters* alongside, still proudly carried today.

At the end of the 1990s, N9505C was still on standby at its Moses Lake base, supported by SLAFCO's huge spares holding, awaiting the call to action. Two items of non-standard equipment to be found on its bow are a chromium-plated leaping trout ornament and two klaxons, one either side, used to warn of the imminent approach of the Cat, water scoop probe extended, to take on more 'ammunition'!

Like most of SLAFCO's Catalinas, it failed to sell at the August 1999 auction when the owner withdrew them from the sale.

Table 170.

Registration/ Serial	C/n	Type	Place of Manufacture	Previous id(s)
N9505C	1581	PBY-5A	CON SD	Bu34027 (US Navy)

N96UC – Universal Associates Inc, Kendall-Tamiami Executive Airport, Tamiami, Florida

A number of surviving Catalinas can lay claim to wartime action, even successful attacks on U-Boats, whilst others have been used in roles that are far removed from that originally in the mind of the designers. Only one Catalina can claim that it was involved in flying a former President into exile! PBY-5A constructor's number 1737 did just that in 1955!

But to start at the beginning, the records show that 1737 was handed over to the US Navy with the serial Bu48375 on 15 December 1943. It was initially allocated to the Naval Air Reserve Training Unit at Akron, Miami, and then passed on to another unit in Seattle before flying with VPB-6 and the US Coast Guard. 1946 saw it being reconditioned at Seattle before going to the Naval Aircraft Factory in Philadelphia for more work prior to moving to FASRON 102, then VP-AM4. In 1951, it was placed in storage at Sand Point, Seattle, and was struck of charge two years later.

In 1953, it was offered for tender, and Trans Alaskan Airlines became the new owner, the registration N4937V being allocated to it for use on its new machine. It seems that the company did not hold on to its new acquisition for very long, as in 1954 it was sold to a new owner. During that year, it progressed through no fewer than three further owners before being sold to Fleetway Inc of Burbank in November. Fleetway negotiated a sale to the Government of Paraguay, and it was registered in that country as ZP-CBA for use by Lineas Aéreas de

Now a Wright Cyclone-equipped Super Catalina, N9505C is seen here at Long Beach, California, in September 1968, before its conversion.
Peter Keating Collection

Transportes Nacional (LATN). It was converted from military to commercial configuration by the removal of bow turret and blisters and the installation of passenger seats.

After arrival in Paraguay, ZP-CBA was transferred to the military 'airline' TAM (Transporte Aéreo Militar) which was operated under the auspices of the Fuerza Aérea Paraguaya (FAP). It was given the military serial T-29. Then, on 5 October 1955, came its moment of fame when it flew to Buenos Aires in Argentina and landed on the River Plate alongside the Paraguayan warship *Paraguay*, which was undergoing repairs there. After what was apparently a 'hairy' landing in poor weather conditions, T-29 drew close to the warship, and the former Argentine President Juan Domingo Peron was taken on board and flown to Asuncion. Peron had previously been deposed after a coup and had sought political asylum on the ship.

In 1956, T-29 went back to LATN as ZP-CBA and operated alongside another PBY-5A, ZP-CBB, although the latter aircraft was to crash in 1957. A major part of the 1960s saw ZP-CBA in storage at Asuncion, but during the following decade it was made airworthy and flew with the military as T-29 on SAR, passenger, mail and cargo flights. It was retired again in 1979 and put out to grass once more at Asuncion.

In 1988, it was overhauled, repainted and allocated the new serial 2002 for use by the Grupo de Transporte Aérea (GTA), but its return to service was plagued by unreliability problems particularly connected with the engines and nose undercarriage, which was prone to collapsing. When it was airworthy, it was used to fly no less a personage than the Paraguayan President, acting as his number two aircraft. Meanwhile, rumours abounded that 2002 was destined for a museum, either in Paraguay itself or in Argentina. Indeed, an Argentine museum had

reportedly successfully bid for the Catalina, and preparations were supposed to be under way for its delivery flight to the Espora Naval Base at Puerto Belgrano. None of this came about, and by 1993, 2002 was still at Asuncion, although it had been sold in January of that year and placed on the US civil register as N96FP, the registered owner being Franks Aircraft Inc of Fort Worth, Texas. It was some time later that this PBY finally left Asuncion, when it flew Asuncion–Santa Cruz, Bolivia–Manaus, Brazil–Maiquetia, Venezuela–San Juan, Puerto Rico–Fort Lauderdale. The flight was far more protracted than intended, and the plane spent some time at San Juan before moving on to its final destination.

Once in Florida, the smart red and white FAP livery was removed and N96FP was repainted in a military scheme to represent an early US Navy PBY-5. It was sold to Caribbean Air Transport of San Juan on 3 April 1994, and on 9 January the following year to Charles Largay of Universal Associates Inc, to whom it was granted an FAA Standard Airworthiness Certificate in the Transport Category for the carriage of up to 22 passengers. August 1996 saw a change of registration to N96UC, and in February 1997, the Cat was ferried to Miami, where it took up residence at Kendall-Tamiami Executive Airport. At the 1998 Sun'n Fun Fly-in at Lakeland, Florida, it was awarded the Judge's Choice Navy Amphibian award.

Table 171.

Registration/ Serial	C/n	Type	Place of Manufacture	Previous id(s)
N96UC	1737	PBY-5A	CON SD	N96FP 2002 (FAP) T-29 (FAP) ZP-CBA N4937V Bu48375 (US Navy)

N9825Z – Rick Petersen, Moses Lake, Washington State

N9825Z holds the distinction of being the last PBY to be built, the final aircraft in a long and illustrious line that can be traced back to the Consolidated XP3Y-1, serial

Following its protracted delivery from Paraguay to the USA, N96UC is seen performing before the crowd at the Sun'n Fun fly-in at Lakeland, Florida, in April 1998. *Geoffrey P. Jones*

The last Catalina built, N9825Z shares ramp space with two other Catalinas at Moses Lake, Washington, in April 1991.
Ron Mak

9459, that first flew on 2 March 1935. In between then and the final Catalina rolling off the production line, the design had undergone some fundamental changes, the most obvious outward ones being the addition of an undercarriage and rear hull blisters, and the modified fin and rudder. Basically, though, the aircraft was still unmistakably a PBY! The other main change had been the site of construction – the prototype had been built at Buffalo, with production switching to San Diego thereafter. N9825Z was built at New Orleans where production had commenced in 1944. So it was that the final PBY, US Navy serial Bu64107, was completed and delivered to its new owner in September 1945. Thereafter, further planned Catalina production was cancelled because of the war's end.

By the early 1960s, this Catalina was in storage for the National Air and Space Museum, Washington DC, but it was later released onto the commercial market and converted to a water bomber for operation by the Florida Forestry Board of Tallahassee, with which it apparently flew as Tanker 158. Presumably, the museum authorities decided that although Bu64107 was the last of its line, it was not necessarily representative of the earlier PBYs that flew with the US military. Ultimately, the museum's PBY-5, Bu08317, was retained instead, and is currently on loan to the Museum of Naval Aviation at Pensacola in Florida. Bu64107 became N9825Z, and it seems that after a period of protracted inactivity, it was acquired by Washington State-based Catalina operator Robert P. Schlaefli, for use by his company SLAFCO Inc. Since at least the late 1970s, it was held in storage by SLAFCO at Moses Lake, and it was the only one of the company's Catalina fleet to be sold at the 1999 auction of SLAFCO's

assets. The new owner was Rick Petersen, who plans to fly his acquisition to the west coast sometime in 2001. He reports that the airframe has only 2,800 flying hours on it. One interesting feature on this aircarft is that the 'clipper' bow is made of fibreglass, and the original nose profile, complete with bomb aimer's position and turret ring, is still intact underneath!

Table 172. Registration/ Serial	C/n	Type	Place of Manufacture	Previous id(s)
N9825Z	'235'	PBY-6A	CON NO	Bu64107 (US Navy)

Unidentified – Derrick Arnold, Geneseo, New York State

An unidentified but complete Canso hull lies inside a barn at the rural airfield of Geneseo in New York State.

A Cat in its lair. The unidentified Canso hull in its barn at Geneseo, New York, during the early 1990s.
Eric Dumigan

Geneseo was formerly the home of the National Warplane Museum, which did operate its own Catalina whilst based there, but this was PBY-6A N7057C, a completely different aircraft. Owner of the dismantled ex-RCAF relic is Derrick Arnold, who acquired the almost complete hull from a location at Brighton, Ontario, in Canada, also home to the *Sad Sack* airframe described in the entry below. Unlike *Sad Sack*, however, Derrick Arnold's hull is less radically altered and may not have been used as a motor cruiser in the same way. Over the years, Arnold has proposed various schemes for his aircraft, including painting it in RAF markings and mounting it on a school bus chassis to make it taxiable. In the early 1990s, he also placed it on the market for sale, but so far as is known, it remains in the barn at Geneseo in a grey and red colour scheme. Sadly, its original military serial is not known.

Sad Sack loaded on the trailer that transported it across Canada and the USA. It has been used to support various other PBY rebuild projects.
Bill Mackintosh

Table 173.

Registration/ Serial	C/n	Type	Place of Manufacture	Previous id(s)
? (RCAF)	?	Canso	?	–

Unidentified – Ray Cox?, Whidbey Island NAS, Washington State

Although unidentified, this particular Catalina survivor is almost certainly a former Royal Canadian Air Force Canso A amphibian. Ray Cox of Seattle, acquired the virtually complete hull from Brighton, 830 miles south of Ontario, around 1991, and trucked it on a flat-bed trailer across Canada and into the USA, no doubt turning a few heads on the way!

Nicknamed *Sad Sack*, this Canso was one of a number acquired after the Second World War by George Ventress, an entrepreneur and inventor, who also purchased several other aircraft from the Crown Assets Corporation, including examples of such former RCAF types as the Anson, Ventura and, possibly, a Lancaster. Ventress apparently purchased at least three Cansos from a military base near Lake Erie, possibly Dunnsville, and another from Trenton RCAF base, only 20 miles from Brighton. Ventress was awarded the Romeo Vachon Award for outstanding ingenuity in solving aeronautical problems and aircraft retrieval work.

At his Brighton base, he converted the PBY from potential scrap to a 52 ft pleasure cruiser powered by a pair of Ford V-8 engines, and it subsequently became a common sight on Lake Ontario's Bay of Quinte, 60-odd miles north of Rochester, New York. Ventress continued the name *Sad Sack*, as this was apparently its original wartime name.

Eventually, *Sad Sack* was put up for disposal by the Ventress family, and Ray Cox travelled hundreds of miles

to view it, eventually returning with his prize after protracted negotiation. Cox established a reputation for re-engining de Havilland Canada Otter aircraft to turbine power, but has also been involved in the rebuild of the PBY-5A Catalina N84857 in Lewiston, Montana. He was acquiring various Catalina/Canso parts in order to complete this project, hence his interest in *Sad Sack*. Although its blisters and engines were missing, the nose section was basically intact and usable on N84857, whose own unit had been removed and is now to be found on N9521C. Cox also acquired some of the remains of Catalina C-FSAT which came to grief in Honolulu. Using only the forward area of this latter Cat, the tail went to the Royal New Zealand Air Force and the rest went to Alaska for use by the team rebuilding the OA-10A *Queen of Dago Lake* at Anchorage.

It seems unlikely that *Sad Sack* will live to become a fully restored Catalina, but hopefully it will be used to ensure that at least one other PBY will fly again. Meanwhile, the remains are stored in the open at Misty Lane, Whidbey Island.

Two of the other Ventress Cansos have also survived; one can be found at Harold Carlaw's Memorial Military Museum in Campbellford, Ontario, Canada (see Chapter Fifteen), and the other is at Geneseo, New York and is described in the entry immediately preceding this one.

Table 174.

Registration/ Serial	C/n	Type	Place of Manufacture	Previous id(s)
? (RCAF)	?	Canso	?	–

Twenty

TOTAL LOSSES SINCE 1970

This chapter lists Catalinas that have been destroyed in accidents or incidents since January 1970, that date being chosen as a starting point so as to include the majority of Catalinas that readers are likely to recall from recent times but which have not survived through to the present day. No losses prior to that date have been included, although brief details will be found under the individual country headings in the earlier chapters of this book. Also excluded are those Catalinas that have suffered accidents but have survived either relatively intact, or have been, or are in the process of being, rebuilt – these will be found in the main *Survivors* chapters.

Of the 22 total losses since 1970, the countries of registry were as follows:

USA	12
Canada	8
Chile	1
Colombia	1

This split is a fair reflection of the worldwide distribution of Catalinas, especially in the 1970s and 1980s, although the latter part of that decade began to see Catalinas operating in a larger number of non-North American countries, as water bombing and survey companies began to dispose of their fleets.

The countries in which the accidents occurred can be summarised thus:

Canada	7
USA	7
Pacific Area	2
Chile	1
Colombia	1
Portugal	1
Italy	1
Mexico	1
France	1

Eight of the accidents involved Catalinas being operated by water bombing companies, although not all the aircraft were involved in fighting fires at the time of their demise, some being engaged on test flights. Eight losses occurred during operations on water, several involving the loss of nose-wheel doors. Only one of the accidents claimed a Catalina engaged on a fare-paying passenger flight.

CHILE

CC-CDS – ASPAR – Crashed, Chiguayante, Chile, 8/4/1979

CC-CDS was lost on 8 April 1979, whilst it was engaged on forest-fire-fighting duties. It was flying in the

In what appears to be a retouched publicity photo, the former Canso A CC-CDS makes a water drop prior to its demise in 1979.
via Ron Mak

Chiguayante area of Chile when its port wing struck tree-tops with such force that the wing was broken at Station 17, some 18 ft inboard of the wingtip. As a result of this, control was lost and the Catalina crashed and was destroyed on impact. The three crew on board were killed.

This Catalina had been gifted to ASPAR by the French after it had seen use in the Pacific in support of nuclear testing there. It had been shipped from Tahiti to Valparaiso on board a freighter, together with two other former Aéronavale PBYs in 1973. Once overhauled, it entered passenger service with ASPAR as fleet number 31, and in 1975 it had second-hand water bombing equipment installed for the forest-fire-fighting role.

It had originally flown with the Royal Canadian Air Force and then been sold in the 1960s to Kenting Aircraft, which converted it to a fire-bomber. It later saw service with Field Aviation and subsequently spent some time during 1966 and 1967 flying in France on lease to the Protection Civile, with which it flew with the registration F-ZBAX and radio call-sign *Pelican Gris*, or *Grey Pelican*. Whilst in Canada, it flew as CF-UKR. It is known to have been delivered out to the Pacific from France via Bahrein and Karachi during April 1968. Presumably, the water-carrying equipment was stripped out prior to its use by the Aéronavale.

Table 175.

Registration/ Serial	C/n	Type	Place of Manufacture	Previous id(s)
CC-CDS	CV-281	Canso A	CAN VIC (Cartierville)	81 (Aeronavale) F-YEIC (callsign) F-ZBAX CF-UKR 11003 (RCAF)

CANADA

CF-AAD – Austin Airways – Crashed, Poste de la Baleire, Quebec 24/9/1972

Al Seaward and Morley McArthur, captain and co-pilot respectively of Austin Airways Catalina CF-AAD, experienced engine problems which resulted in one prop over-speeding and then refusing to feather. Upon the landing approach at Great Whale, Quebec, it was not possible for the crew to ascertain if the landing gear was locked down, and so they elected to overshoot. The combination of a windmilling prop and low overall power meant that height could not be maintained, and a decision to land straight ahead had to be taken. The options were rock or trees and the crew went for the trees, landing in amongst them, with the result that the aircraft broke up on impact but without serious injury to the pilots, supernumerary crew member or the 13 passengers aboard. The location of the crash was Poste de la Baleire.

Taken on charge by the US Navy in November 1943, it had ended its military service at NAS Philadelphia, where it was struck off charge in June 1950. It was then registered as N68746 to Southern California Aircraft Corporation of Ontario, California, which converted it for commercial use. It went through several other owners

CF-AAD is seen in the livery of Austin Airways, its owner when it crashed in Quebec in September 1972. The nose-wheel doors have been removed.
Jennifer M. Gradidge

before being acquired by Austin Airways of Toronto in 1966, becoming CF-AAD in the process.

Larry Milberry's book on Austin Airways quotes a former company pilot as saying that CF-AAD was a former PBY-6A that had had its tall tail removed and replaced with a PBY-5A unit, although this theory does not tally with the generally accepted constructor's number, which is most certainly that of a PBY-5A.

Table 176.

Registration/ Serial	C/n	Type	Place of Manufacture	Previous id(s)
CF-AAD	1658	PBY-5A	CON SD	N68746 Bu48296 (US Navy)

CF-HTN – Field Aviation – Crashed, 500 miles north of Edmonton, Alberta, 3/9/1971

Having flown with the US Navy as Bu48275, this Catalina was registered in the States as N1556M with Air

Just over a year before its accident in Alberta, CF-HTN is shown here in bare metal, clearly displaying sheeting over the former blister area.
Peter Keating Collection

Corporation of Miami in 1954. It then appeared on the Canadian register as CF-NTJ, although its ownership details are not known. It was later re-registered as CF-HTN to Transair Ltd of St James, Manitoba, with which it flew as a passenger carrier between 1956 and 1966. It was then sold to Field Aviation of Toronto and stayed with that company for three years or so before being lost in a crash north of Edmonton in September 1971. Whilst with Field, it was leased to the French water bombing agency Protection Civile of Marseille, and flew with the call-sign *Grey Pelican*, the second Catalina to do so.

Table 177.

Registration/ Serial	C/n	Type	Place of Manufacture	Previous id(s)
CF-HTN	1637	PBY-5A	CON SD	F-ZBBE CF-NTJ N1556M Bu48275 (US Navy)

CF-NTL – The Flying Fireman Ltd – Crashed west of Snow Lake, Manitoba, 21/5/1978

Prior to operating as a water bomber with Flying Fireman out of Victoria, British Columbia, CF-NTL had flown with Leaseway Ltd of Toronto and National Air Tankers of Calgary. Before that, it had flown with the Royal Canadian Air Force as Canso A, serial 11067.

Taken on by Flying Fireman in 1971, it was numbered Tanker 1 and flew on fire-suppression missions until it was lost in a fatal crash on 21 May 1978.

The accident report cites the Catalina as crashing in a virtually vertical nose-down attitude into tree-covered hills 23 miles west of Snow Lake in Manitoba after carrying out a water drop. Upon impact, it caught fire and was destroyed. It had taken on fuel before the mission, and the accident, in which the two crew were killed, was attributed to momentary fuel starvation in the starboard engine caused by an asymmetric fuel load and crew confusion as to how much fuel was remaining on board.

Crew fatigue was thought to be a contributory factor.

Table 178.

Registration/ Serial	C/n	Type	Place of Manufacture	Previous id(s)
CF-NTL	CV-383	Canso A	CAN VIC (Cartierville)	11067 (RCAF)

C-FIGJ – Province of Newfoundland and Labrador – Crashed, Sherbrooke, Quebec, 19/12/1980

The first commercial owner of this Catalina after it was declared surplus by the US Navy was the Charlotte Aircraft Corporation, which acquired it in 1954 and had it registered as N1565M. In 1965, it was acquired by the Province of Newfoundland and Labrador for fire-fighting duties, and they numbered it with the call sign 2.

Whilst on a flight on 19 December 1980, problems developed with the port engine, which showed signs of low oil pressure and prop revolutions. The engine stopped after a few minutes, and so it was shut down and a decision to divert was taken by the crew. The engine was subsequently re-started but then quit again shortly after. Whilst on finals to Sherbrooke, the starboard engine also stopped and the Catalina was landed some 650 ft short of the runway threshold.

The cause of the crash was found to be fuel starvation, apparently caused by an inaccurate measure of fuel on board prior to the flight. The wreckage was taken to St Jean, Quebec, and was still there in 1992.

Table 179.

Registration/ Serial	C/n	Type	Place of Manufacture	Previous id(s)
C-FIGJ	1791	PBY-5A	CON SD	CF-IGJ N1565M Bu48429 (US Navy)

C-FPQP – Government of Quebec – Crashed Lac Cache, Quebec, 18/7/1987

C-FPQP saw post-war military service with the Royal Canadian Air Force and is known to have been on the

The Flying Fireman Company operated CF-NTL for a few years during the 1970s, and it was number 1 in their fleet. It is seen here at its Victoria, British Columbia, base in 1975.
MAP

This side-view shows former US Navy PBY-5A CF-IGJ in the orange, green and white colours of the Province of Newfoundland and Labrador Forest Service in 1973.
Peter Keating Collection

In the 1970s, the Canso water bombers of the Province of Quebec were flying in a yellow livery with red trim. C-FPQP is seen at Quebec City in 1979 in company with two Canadair CL-215s. It carries the nose code 16 and Gouvernement du Quebec Ministrie des Transports titles on the hull.
Peter Keating Collection

This is what C-FSAT looked like following the botched recovery operation after its landing on water in Hawaii. The hull has been broken in two places.
Ted M. Spencer

strength of 413 (PR) Squadron at Rockcliffe, Ontario, before being sold by the military in 1962. The buyer was the Government of Quebec, which added it to its sizeable fleet of water bombing Cansos.

On 17 July 1987, it was carrying out a touch-and-go landing on Lac Cache in the Province of Quebec when it bounced heavily and nosed in, with one fatality. It was damaged beyond repair and its registration was cancelled in the following October.

Table 180.

Registration/ Serial	C/n	Type	Place of Manufacture	Previous id(s)
C-FPQP	CV-407	Canso A	CAN VIC (Cartierville)	CF-PQP 11079 (RCAF)

C-FSAT – Can-Air Services Ltd – Crashed at Maui, Hawaii, 14/4/1986

Unfortunately, the majority of the damage that effectively destroyed Canso A C-FSAT was caused, not by the initial crash and subsequent sinking, but by the botched attempt at recovery.

This Boeing of Canada-built aircraft was being used for passenger flights by Can-Air on contract to the local government of Truk Island in Micronesia. When the Truk authorities ran out of funding for the services, C-FSAT was flown to Maui, Hawaii, for storage and possible sale. During a subsequent test flight from Kahului Airport, undercarriage problems were encountered and the decision was taken to carry out a water landing 500 yards off the shore of Launiupoko National Park. Contact with a partially submerged reef caused the Cat to sink, but the *coup de grâce* was delivered by the recovery team and their crane, which destroyed the wing and broke the hull.

The wreck of C-FSAT was taken to the local airport and was later dispersed via Seattle-based Catalina rebuilder Ray Cox. He kept some of it for use in his rebuild of N84857 in Montana, whilst some components went to Anchorage, Alaska, to help restore the OA-10A

Queen of Dago Lake. The rear end went out to the Royal New Zealand Air Force Museum to aid restoration of their VH-SBV.

After its military service with the RCAF, 9757 had been disposed of to the Saskatchewan Government, which used it as a transport. It subsequently continued to fly as a passenger aircraft with Central Northern Airlines, Transair and Northland Airlines, before being sold to the Bernard family and Can-Air in Edmonton. In the 1980s, it was operated by Vancouver-based company Pacific Airboats Ltd for operation alongside its other PBY, C-FDIL, but it was returned to Can-Air after a year and then went out to the Pacific.

C-FSAT demonstrated the durability of the Catalina design when, in the 1970s, it was landed, wheels up, in a snow-covered field near Edmonton after fuel problems were encountered. It was successfully flown out of the field, still wheels up and without damage, the following day by veteran Catalina pilot Ray Bernard!

Table 181.

Registration/ Serial	C/n	Type	Place of Manufacture	Previous id(s)
C-FSAT	21986	Canso A	BOE CAN	CF-SAT 9757 (RCAF)

C-GFFD – The Flying Fireman Ltd – Crashed, Thunder Bay, Ontario, 14/5/1984

C-GFFD was totally destroyed, thankfully without loss of life, when it came down in the vicinity of Thunder Bay Airport after its port engine failed shortly after take-off on a training mission. The crew were attempting to make it back to the airport for an emergency landing, but altitude could not be maintained and the wing struck power lines before the Cat hit the ground and slid to a halt. During the landing, the cockpit section was severed from the hull, the starboard engine was ripped from its mounts and the wing was badly broken. The hull from aft of the cockpit position to the pylon was totally smashed.

An aerial cameraman's view of Flying Fireman's C-GFFD crash site at Thunder Bay just after its accident. The detached cockpit section is on the extreme right, whilst the starboard engine is on the ground partly hidden by the movie camera lens. The port propeller is feathered.
Thunder Bay Fire Department

Post-accident, it was determined that the aircraft had not been flown during the previous 14 days and that during that period, it had rained several times. The Catalina had been parked on a sloping area with the port wing low. These conditions allowed an accumulation of water in the left fuel tank through water vapour condensation. Although the crew had checked for water in the tanks as part of their pre-flight routine, the angle of the wing prevented them from being alerted to the large quantity of water that had collected. Subsequently, the water entered the fuel lines when the Catalina was moved, and this caused the port engine to stop after take-off. Recovery from the situation was not possible because of the low altitude and airspeed at the point when the engine quit. As part of the accident investigation, officials discovered an extension lead and fluorescent work lamp within the starboard wing structure, although this lapse in engineering procedure was not a contributory factor in the accident!

At the time of the crash, C-GFFD was one of several PBYs owned by Flying Fireman that were on contract to the Ontario Ministry of Natural Resources in order to fight forest fires in that Province. Flying Fireman had operated it since around 1970, prior to which it had flown with Northern Wings Ltd as a passenger carrier in Quebec from the mid-1960s. Originally, it had been with the RCAF as 11096, and is known to have been with 162 (BR) Squadron at the tail end of the Second World War, when it would have been operated out of Reykjavik, Iceland.

C-GFFJ – The Flying Fireman Ltd – Crashed, Jackson Lake, Sioux Lookout, Ontario, 12/7/1981

Water bombing forest fires has never been the most danger-free type of flying, and Flying Fireman Ltd of Victoria, British Columbia, suffered its share of accidents during the 1970s and 1980s, as evidenced by this chapter.

C-GFFJ was destroyed in July 1981, while on contract work hundreds of miles from its winter base. After completing two successful water pick-ups from the lake at Sioux Lookout, the crew returned for a third. Having alighted on the water surface, the pick-up probe was extended and the Catalina immediately pitched nose down and sank. One of the two crew members suffered serious injuries, but both escaped with their lives. A survey of the wreck revealed that the starboard bomb door had opened during the pick-up run, with the inevitable drag causing a catastrophic slow-down of the airframe. This sudden deceleration wrenched the wings and engines from the mounting pylon.

It was later established that C-GFFJ had a history of hydraulic problems, and that repairs undertaken in the past had not successfully resolved occasional movement of the bomb doors during probe extension. Damage to the Catalina was sufficient for it to be categorised as 'destroyed'.

Prior to its service with Flying Fireman, this aircraft had had a long career as a fire fighter, having started with Sonora Flying Services in California in 1962 as Tanker E38, registration N6456C, then passing on to Jack Urich of Oregon in 1969 before going back to California in 1972 for several years' service with Hemet Valley Flying Services as Tanker E84 and 84. During 1977, it suffered damage from a ground fire at Stockton, California. Flying Fireman acquired it in 1980 and gave it the fleet number 9.

Table 183. Registration/ Serial	C/n	Type	Place of Manufacture	Previous id(s)
C-GFFJ		PBY-6A	CON NO	N6456C Bu63996 (US Navy)

Sharing the Stockton, California, ramp with two other PBY-6As in January 1973 is N6456C/84E of Hemet Valley Flying Services. Later sold as C-GFFJ, it was lost in a water pick-up accident in July 1981.
William T. Larkins

Table 182. Registration/ Serial	C/n	Type	Place of Manufacture	Previous id(s)
C-GFFD	CV-441	Canso A	CAN VIC (Cartierville)	CF-IHN 11096 (RCAF)

COLOMBIA

HK-1020 – LAICA – Crashed Villavicencio, 11/6/1973

Details of the accident that destroyed this Catalina are sparse: what is known is that it crashed whilst carrying out a water landing at Villavicencio in Colombia on 11 June 1973. One crew member was fatally injured. The Catalina was owned by Lineas Aereas Interiores de Catalina (LAICA). Following the accident, the registration marks were cancelled in December 1975.

Built as a US Navy PBY-5A, it had flown as Bu48388 and then spent some time on the US Civil Aircraft Register as N1521V before going to Colombia.

Table 184. Registration/ Serial	C/n	Type	Place of Manufacture	Previous id(s)
HK-1020	1750	PBY-5A	CON SD	N1521V Bu48388 (US Navy)

UNITED STATES OF AMERICA

N15KL – Confederate Air Force, Patrol Wing – Crashed near Harlingen, Texas, 18/8/1975

N15KL was the world-famous Confederate Air Force's first Catalina, a type that it had wanted to operate as part of its inventory for some time, and with which over the years it was to experience bad luck and tragedy.

Acquired by the CAF in late 1972, N15KL was the first aircraft to be flown by its newly-formed Patrol Wing. It was painted up in US Navy colours with the large numerals '18' on the forward hull and the legend *Ghost Squadron* on the base of its fin. Sadly, its time with the CAF was to be short, as, on 18 August 1975, it was totally destroyed when it crashed and caught fire in the vicinity of its base at Harlingen in Texas after departing

The former Royal Danish Air Force PBY-6A L-868 was operated by the Confederate Air Force in the USA, but was destroyed in a crash shortly after take-off from Harlingen in August 1975. It is shown in happier times with the RDAF.

for a proposed trip to Houston. Apparently, power was lost on the starboard engine soon after take-off and at around 200 ft altitude. The crew were unable to land straight ahead because of an inconveniently placed drainage ditch but before an alternative could be considered, the Cat lost airspeed and nosed in, killing three of those on board instantly.

Originally, this PBY-6A had been delivered to the US Navy after its first flight in May 1945, although its logbook entries would seem to suggest that it may have been delivered straight into storage at Litchfield Park in Arizona. In 1957, it was flown out to Pan Air in New Orleans, which overhauled it for service with the Royal Danish Air Force. It served in Denmark and Greenland as 82-868, later L-868, and it was christened *Bruno*. Finally retired in 1970, it was subsequently sold to Larkin Aircraft Corporation of Auburn, California, and was delivered across the North Atlantic, staging through Prestwick in barely disguised RDAF colours on 9 June 1972.

It was later sold to John Church, a CAF 'Colonel', who then sold it on to the CAF when he discovered that they were looking for a PBY.

Table 185. Registration/ Serial	C/n	Type	Place of Manufacture	Previous id(s)
N15KL		PBY-6A	CON NO	L-868 (RDAF) 82-868 (RDAF) Bu64000 (US Navy)

N16KL – Confederate Air Force, Lone Star Wing – Crashed near Port Isabel, Gulf of Mexico, 13/10/1984

Another ex-Royal Danish Air Force PBY-6A, N16KL had been imported into the USA by Larkin Aircraft Corporation at roughly the same time as N15KL described above, and it was ultimately to have a similarly tragic end with the Confederate Air Force. After its arrival in the USA in July 1972, it went to the American Air Museum Society based in San Francisco and seems to have spent some while in store before being acquired by the CAF in October 1982, for its Lone Star Wing at Tyler, Texas. Prior to this, it had been used in the filming of the movie *Midway*, and when taken on by the CAF, had been parked at Lakeland, Florida, for some time.

Once with its new owner, it was refurbished and initially flew in bare metal with US military insignia, often in the company of the CAF's PBY-5A N68756. For the 1984 season, it was completely repainted in an authentic US Navy PBY-6A scheme, making its début at the build-up to the CAF's *Airsho 1984*.

In the event, the Catalina did not take part in the show itself as it was lost just before the start during an air-to-air photographic sortie. With ten souls on board, the Catalina left Harlingen and flew out over the Gulf of Mexico in company with the photographic aircraft. The intention was to carry out a simulated water landing without putting the hull on the water but flying at sufficiently low altitude that a wake would be created by the prop-wash. The NTSB accident report describes what happened next.

With the co-pilot in command, the Catalina was flown

The other CAF PBY-6A to be lost was N16KL. It was destroyed in a fatal crash through pilot error, according to the official accident report.

During the time that it was owned by the actor James Stewart, Super Cat N19Q was lost after it sank in the Mediterranean on 15 August 1972.
Norm Taylor Collection

down to about 6 ft above the water, and then the clearance was gradually reduced to around 6–12 inches above water with an airspeed of 105 mph. The co-pilot inadvertently allowed the aircraft to touch the water surface, and the aircraft decelerated violently and broke up, ejecting several of the occupants and coming to rest inverted. Seven of those on board were killed. Examination of aerial photos shows that at the point of touch-down, the hull was slightly nose-down compared with a normal landing attitude, contact being made at the location of the nose landing-gear doors. Other photos show outward rupturing of the forward hull structure, nose-gear doors missing and various penetrations to the hull surface. The report states that that part of the shallow lagoon was known to have scattered debris from earlier petroleum exploration on it, although no positive determination of contact by the Catalina with submerged objects could be made. The NTSB report closes with the probable causes of the accident quoted as clearance misjudged by the co-pilot, inadequate supervision of the co-pilot by the captain and landing-gear door overload and subsequent separation from the hull. It is worth pointing out that at the time of the accident, the Catalina was said to have flown into fishing nets literally inches above the water surface, and that the tears in the hull were inflicted by the metal stakes holding the nets in place.

The wreck of N16KL was eventually brought ashore some months after the crash and scrapped. The insurance and financial repercussions for the CAF continued to reverberate for some time after, however, not least because there were apparently more people on board at the time of the crash than there were seats available for them to strap into.

N19Q – Stewart Enterprises – Crashed in Mediterranean near Monte Carlo, 15/8/1972

After its military service, this Catalina was modified for commercial use by specialist company Remmert Werner of St Louis. It was flown as N5804N by the Monsanto Chemical Company all over the world on commercial trips, and its hull bore the national flags of numerous countries visited. Monsanto christened its Catalina *The Pelican*. Later, the company had it modified further into a Wright Cyclone-powered *Super Cat* and continued to use it, but registered as N19Q in place of the older marks. After Monsanto sold it, it went through a number of owners until acquired by the famous Hollywood actor James Stewart, who used it as a luxury air yacht.

On 14 August 1972, N19Q was to be seen on the tarmac at Marseille Airport in the South of France. It night-stopped there but was due to fly on to Malaga. The following day, it left Marseille, but upon landing 1,000 metres off Monte Carlo, it hit either a large wave or some surface debris and the hull was holed, whereupon the Catalina took on water and sank. Some personal effects were subsequently recovered, but it is believed the wreck is still underwater.

Table 187.

Registration/ Serial	C/n	Type	Place of Manufacture	Previous id(s)
N19Q	1584	PBY-5A	CON SD	N5804N Bu34030 (US Navy)

N101CS Cousteau Society Inc – Crashed River Tagus, Lisbon, Portugal, 28/6/1979

N101CS was operated by the famous marine explorer Jacques Cousteau and the Cousteau Society at the time of its demise, and sadly, Jacques' son Phillipe was killed in the accident. It had come into the ownership of this well-known organisation in the mid-1970s, having previously flown with a number of other companies and even flying as a fire-fighting machine in the late 1950s and 1960s.

Table 186.

Registration/ Serial	C/n	Type	Place of Manufacture	Previous id(s)
N16KL		PBY-6A	CON NO	L-863 (RDAF) 82-863 (RDAF) Bu63998 (US Navy)

This beautiful PBY-6A Catalina was operated by the famous marine biologist Jacques Cousteau, whose son Philippe was killed when the aircraft crashed during water operations in Portugal. It is seen here in the sun at Long Beach, California, during April 1975.
Peter Keating Collection

Magnificent PBY-5A N285NJ ran off the runway at Turin, Italy, after brake failure, and was destroyed. Its nose art is captioned *Next Objective*.

Whilst owned by the Cousteaus, it flew in a striking white, yellow and black colour scheme and, in common with their vessels, the name *Calypso* on the bow. In 1979, it was given an extensive refit in Portugal and was lost in a crash during the post-overhaul test programme. After flying for some 15 minutes, N101CS made a high-speed run on the River Tagus so that the hull could be checked for leaks. Prior to this, the up-locks on the port main undercarriage had been giving some trouble, but had been locked normally before alighting on the water. Four seconds after touch-down, the Catalina nosed over and turned upside down. The wing separated from its mounts on the pylon and the port engine tore loose, entering the severed cockpit section and crushing Phillipe Cousteau. The other seven occupants survived the crash. It is thought that the crash occurred when the hull hit a submerged sand bar, causing rapid deceleration.

Some wreckage from N101CS is said to survive at the Museu do Ar, Alverca.

Table 188.

Registration/ Serial	C/n	Type	Place of Manufacture	Previous id(s)
N101CS		PBY-6A	CON NO	N48129 N6475C NC48129 Bu64071 (US Navy)

N285NJ – Enrico Recchi – Crashed Turin-Aeritalia Airport, 21/5/1989

Briefly a 'star' visitor to seaplane fly-ins in Italy and the South of France in the late 1980s, N285NJ was destroyed in a landing accident at its home base of Turin. Following brake failure, the Catalina continued to roll at some speed and left the runway, only coming to a halt after hitting a house. The two pilots, including owner Enrico Recchi, were killed, although three passengers escaped.

After retirement by the US Navy, constructor's number 1808 enjoyed a long commercial career, initially with Thomas Kendall and his Catalina Ltd in the mid-1950s. During 1978, its marks N5591V were cancelled from the US register and it went to Venezuela as YV-209CP for Peter Bottome, a TV station owner. In 1985, it returned to Fort Lauderdale in Florida and was re-registered as N285NJ and given a striking pseudo-US Navy colour scheme, the hull code '306' and the name *Next Objective*, complete with Vargas-style pin-up astride a torpedo!

It was delivered to Italy during September 1987, staging through Watertown, New York; Montreal-Dorval; Reykjavik, Iceland; Southend, England; and Le Bourget, Paris, where it stayed for a while before proceeding to Turin.

Table 189.

Registration/ Serial	C/n	Type	Place of Manufacture	Previous id(s)
N285NJ	1808	PBY-5A	CON SD	YV-209CP N5591V Bu48446 (US Navy)

N2886D – SLAFCO Inc, Ephrata, Washington, crashed Northport, Washington, 29/7/1985

After serving with the US Navy, this PBY-6A spent its entire commercial career flying as a fire-fighting water and borate bomber based on the USA's West Coast. Its first owner/operator was Burson Associates Inc of Columbia, California, which flew it between 1963 and 1966. It then spent a number of years through to 1972 with the well-known operator Sis-Q Flying Service Inc of Santa Rosa, which also flew a fleet of Grumman F7F Tigercats in the same fire-bombing role. It carried the tail code E49 at this time. In 1978, it was taken on by Robert Schlaefli's SLAFCO Inc and went up the West Coast, initially to Port Orchard, Washington, where it continued to fly as E49, later 49.

Long before it was converted to a Super Cat, joined the
SLAFCO fleet and crashed in July 1985, N2886D belonged
to B. B. Burson, in whose titles it was seen at Columbia,
California, in October 1963. The very angular 'clipper' bow
on this particular Catalina is evident.
William T. Larkins

Shortly after joining SLAFCO, N2886D suffered substantial damage in a somewhat bizarre incident. On
13 August 1979, N2886D was returning from a water
bombing sortie when a fire developed in the starboard
engine. The pilot in command made a safe landing on
Sproat Lake, Vancouver Island (well known as the base
for FIFT's two Martin Mars flying boats), and the engine
fire was subsequently extinguished by a fire-fighting helicopter using a suspended water bucket!

At some point in its commercial career, it was re-
engined with Wright R-2600 Cyclone power-plants as per
the well-known *Super Cat* conversion, but without the
'Davis' tail normally associated with this marque,
the standard PBY-6A unit being retained instead.

Sadly, on 29 July 1985, N2886D suffered a second,
more serious, accident when it sank on a lake at
Northport, Washington, this time with the loss of the two
crew on board, these being James E. Dunlap and Timothy
J. Trudell. The Catalina was again engaged in a fire-fighting mission and was landing on Franklin D. Roosevelt
Lake to carry out a water pick-up prior to returning to the
fire site on a 70-acre area five miles south of the lake.
About six seconds after touch-down, the bow went down
and the aircraft momentarily disappeared in a cloud of
spray. One witness said that the aircraft went over onto
its back before settling. The wings and engines were torn
from the hull and part of the bow and flight deck
detached from the main airframe. The wreckage drifted
down-stream for four or five minutes and then sank. At
the time of the accident, the Catalina was being rented to

the State of Washington by a firm called Aries Aire Ltd,
whose Chairman was Robert Schlaefli of the same
address as SLAFCO. The NTSB accident investigation
concluded that the water bomber landed on the lake with
the water dump doors partially open during the landing
phase of the water pick-up run. This state of affairs was
caused by the mechanically operated dump door locks
being applied before the dump doors were fully closed
after the previous water drop. The findings of the inves-
tigator were that the pilot in command did not follow the
appropriate checklists and that he was suffering from
chronic fatigue and pressure at the time the accident
occurred.

The wreck of N2886D was recovered from the lake for
the accident investigation, and was subsequently taken
to SLAFCO's premises at Ephrata in Washington. There,
the hull, minus forward section and wings, still sits on its
main undercarriage, a grim reminder of how dangerous
the business of forest fire fighting can be.

Table 190.				
Registration/ Serial	C/n	Type	Place of Manufacture	Previous id(s)
N2886D		PBY-6A	CON NO	Bu64074 (US Navy)

N322FA – Wells Aviation Inc/Airborne Fire Attack, Hood River, Oregon – Crashed, San Vincente Reservoir, San Diego County, California 1/8/1997

One of the large cache of water bombers that remained in
storage for some time after the demise of their operator,
Avalon Aviation of Parry Sound, Ontario, C-FGLX was
one of the last to be disposed of and the first to continue
in use as a fire fighter. Sadly, it was not long in the job.

Prior to its accident, it was operated by Airborne Fire
Attack, the trading name of Wells Aviation Inc, set up
by fireman John Wells. Wells believed that he could
effectively take on his competitors' more modern

Wells Aviation/Airborne Fire Attack acquired the ill-fated N322FA from Avalon Aviation in Canada. It is pictured on the ramp at Thunder Bay, Ontario, in the latter company's orange colours in August 1978.
Peter Keating Collection

equipment at a competitive rate, and so he acquired the Cat in February 1996, and had it painted in a blood-red livery with the white tail code 115 and US registration N322FA. Working for various county and fire authorities on a contract basis, it flew against some 75 fires before its terminal accident in August 1997.

Whilst engaged in combating a forest fire near Ramona, California, John Wells and his co-pilot were putting N322FA down on the San Vincente Reservoir for water pick-ups. On one such approach, they experienced a sudden downdraught at low level which forced the PBY down hard onto the water surface. The nose-wheel doors came away after the impact, and the sudden deceleration flipped the Catalina over onto its back, the cockpit and hull forward of the wing coming away in the process. Although the crew were injured, they survived.

Sadly, N322FA was damaged beyond repair and the registration was cancelled from the USCAR in January 1999. The Confederate Air Force expressed interest at some point in using the wing to repair its own PBY-6A N7179Y, which sustained damage in high winds whilst parked during 1998.

N322FA had seen post-war service as a passenger-carrying aircraft with a list of airlines that reads like a history of internal air services in Canada! These operators included Queen Charlotte Airlines, Pacific Western Airlines, Northland Airlines, Midwest Airlines, Transair Ltd and Ilford Riverton Airways. Avalon acquired it around 1977.

N5404J – The New Zealand Catalina Group – Crashed in Pacific Ocean nr Christmas Island, 16/1/1994

Canso A, serial 9793, can fairly claim to have had more identities than any other PBY, having been allocated commercial registrations in Venezuela, Peru, Colombia, Panama, Kenya, Honduras, the USA and Guatemala. In addition, it had New Zealand markings allocated to it, but these were destined not to be used for reasons outlined below. In a varied life, it flew on wartime operations with 160 (BR) Squadron, Royal Canadian Air Force; with the Texaco petroleum company as an executive aircraft; with the CIA as an airborne communications aircraft during the Bay of Pigs operation in Cuba; and as a film star in the Hollywood movie *Tora! Tora! Tora!*.

In 1993, it was acquired by the New Zealand Catalina Group and flown from Wyoming to California for preparation for the ferry flight across the Pacific Ocean to the Antipodes. Although it was allocated the appropriate New Zealand registration ZK-PBY, it continued to fly as N5404J. Sadly, engine problems occurred on the leg of the journey between Hawaii and Tahiti, and the crew were forced to ditch in darkness in the Pacific in the vicinity of Christmas Island. In the ensuing landing, the Catalina's hull was damaged, and it eventually sank some hours after the crew and passengers had disembarked. Now resting deep under the ocean, N5404J will stay where it is, but the owners went on to overcome this setback and acquired a replacement aircraft that is still being successfully operated today using the previously unused marks ZK-PBY.

Table 192.

Registration/ Serial	C/n	Type	Place of Manufacture	Previous id(s)
N5404J	22022	Canso A	BOE CAN	TG-BIV N6108 HR-236 5Y-KUD HP-289 HK-996X PB-LDM-349 YV-P-APE 9793 (RCAF)

One of the last photos taken of N5404J before she sank in the Pacific Ocean. The picture was taken after the crew had taken to a life-raft, and prior to their rescue.
Ross Ewing

Table 191.

Registration/ Serial	C/n	Type	Place of Manufacture	Previous id(s)
N322FA	CV-560	OA-10A	CAN VIC (Cartierville)	C-FGLX CF-GLX N3000T ntu CF-GLX 44-34049 (USAAF) Bu68013 ntu (US Navy)

N5583V before it fell into bad company. It was a sad loss, not least because it had retained its bow turret and blisters.
MAP

Resplendent in Antilles Air Boats titles and insignia, N5588V sits at Long Beach in November 1968.
Peter Keating Collection

N5583V – Jack Leaf – Scuttled, Infernillo Reservoir, Mexico, 19/3/1974

N5583V was lost, not as the result of an accident, but from deliberate sinking, reminiscent of the way in which many military Catalinas were disposed of immediately after the end of the Second World War, even though the circumstances were somewhat different!

Owned by Jack Leaf and Marvin Gunnufson, N5583V was up for sale when, in 1974, they were approached by an individual who claimed to be representing a well-known American rock band who were considering its purchase. The owners were persuaded to lease it for a trip to Mexico so that the agent could assess its suitability for his clients. The Catalina was flown down to Mexico, where it remained for a few days before being flown back to the USA. The pilot, Morris Bean, had become suspicious of the motives of the possible new owner and had reported his fears to the Drug Enforcement Agency (DEA), who asked Bean to carry out the flight and report back to them.

On the return journey, Bean had a gun pulled on him and was told to land on the Infernillo Reservoir. Despite his suspicions, this still came as something of a shock to Bean, who had thought that this flight was merely a dummy run for a subsequent narcotics smuggling trip. Once on the reservoir, local 'helpers' loaded the PBY with packages, but so many were taken on that it was impossible to take off from the water surface. At this point, the smugglers panicked and ordered the Catalina to be scuttled by the removal of the hull plugs. N5583V settled to the bottom of the reservoir, where it can still be found if anyone wishes to try retrieving it!

Table 193.

Registration/ Serial	C/n	Type	Place of Manufacture	Previous id(s)
N5583V	1570	PBY-5A	CON SD	Bu34016 (US Navy)

N5588V – Victor W Newman – Crashed, Wikieup, Arizona, 6/2/1975

An early PBY5A, N5588V was another Catalina to be

purchased from military surplus by Thomas W Kendall's Catalina Ltd of La Verne, California. However, he sold it on, and amongst its subsequent owners are two interesting names. One is Bird Aircraft of Palm Springs, which is presumably the same company that later acquired another Catalina and converted it to the well-known four-engined *Bird Innovator*. Bird seem to have owned N5588V for a short period only, and it was later acquired and operated by the famous seaplane pilot Charles Blair's company, Antilles Air Boats, of St Thomas in the US Virgin Islands. They held on to it until the early 1970s, but unfortunately it was not to last too much longer after they sold it to Victor W. Newman.

Whilst flying over Wikieup in Arizona, both engines lost power for reasons that could not be ascertained. A forced landing was attempted, but the aircraft was destroyed and the three crew were killed. The official report into the accident states that the pilot in command failed to follow approved procedures.

Table 194.

Registration/ Serial	C/n	Type	Place of Manufacture	Previous id(s)
N5588V	920	PBY-5A	CON SD	Bu08101 (US Navy)

N610FF – Barringer Research Co – Crashed, Rhinelander, Wisconsin, 15/10/1970

The accident involving N610FF was one of the few that occurred to PBYs involved in the survey role. Sadly, the incident was catastrophic and three of the four-man crew were killed.

During its Canadian military service, this Canso A is known to have flown with 162 Squadron in Iceland during the later part of the war as aircraft 'L', and subsequently with the reformed 413 Squadron as AP-K. It went on to serve the RCAF until 1967, after which it briefly became CF-OMO with Fairey Aviation but was almost immediately re-registered N610FF on the US Civil Aircraft Register. It flew as a survey aircraft with Firefly Inc and Barringer Research, and ranged far and wide in this role, being noted as far afield as Bahrein and London-Heathrow during the 1960s. During a survey

Victim of a particularly nasty take-off crash was the Geoterrex survey Catalina N610FF. When on a visit to the UK some time before, it was displaying Barringer Research titles on the forward hull.

contract in Wisconsin, N610FF took off from Oneida County Airport, but accumulated frost on the wing surfaces prevented it from getting properly airborne and it stalled, crashing within the airport boundary.

N6459C – Hemet Valley Flying Services – Crashed, Columbia, California, 18/7/1970

A veteran water and borate tanker, N6459C flew with such well-known fire-fighting operators as Farmers Air Service, Liston Aircraft and Hemet Valley Flying Services, and at various times it carried the tail codes F11 and 77.

Although full details are not known, it was lost in a crash at Columbia, California, on 18 July 1970.

Table 195.

Registration/Serial	C/n	Type	Place of Manufacture	Previous id(s)
N610FF	CV-399	Canso A	CAN VIC (Cartierville)	CF-OMO 11075 (RCAF)

Table 196.

Registration/ Serial	C/n	Type	Place of Manufacture	Previous id(s)
N6459C	2017	PBY-6A	CON NO	Bu46653 (US Navy)

Twenty-one
SCATTERED CATALINA REMAINS – A WORLDWIDE SELECTION

Whilst earlier sections of this book have covered complete surviving Catalina airframes and recent losses through accidents and crashes, there are a considerable number of other Catalina wrecks, artefacts and other remains that can be found throughout the world. The following analysis is not intended to be a complete listing of such items but rather a selection of the known Catalina wrecks and remains sites.

Because the PBY was built as a flying boat for water operation, it was inevitable that, at the end of its useful life, it would suffer the ignominious fate of being scuttled as an easy option for disposal. Thus, large numbers of Royal Air Force Catalinas were deliberately sunk at the war's end, both at home and in foreign waters, in order to satisfy the requirements of Lend-Lease. In the main, these went to 'unmarked graves' in various lakes, lochs and coastal locations, and the exact whereabouts are no longer known, although, from time to time, amateur divers discover airframes and optimistic recovery plans are put in place, only to founder through lack of funds or technical difficulties. RAF Catalinas are known to have been sunk in Lake Victoria near to the flying boat base of Kisumu in Kenya, whilst nearer home other Cats were sent to the bottom of Lough Erne in Northern Ireland. Similarly, Catalina losses from enemy action and technical failure led to a number of examples being consigned to the deep.

Rather than list all known losses, what follows is a list of remains sites, listed alphabetically by country of location, with brief details of the circumstances behind the original loss and where the continued existence of the remains has been recently confirmed or where the location is known for sure. If any readers can add to this list, they are urged to contact the author.

AUSTRALIA

There are known to be various Catalina relics throughout Australia, ranging from small artefacts, through crash sites, to houseboat conversions.

A24-1 – East Arm, Darwin, Northern Territories

Probably the most historically significant crash site in Australia is that of the RAAF Catalina A24-1. Sadly only a wreck and deteriorating rapidly, it is nonetheless rather remarkable that the Royal Australian Air Force's very first military Catalina should have survived the war at all, given the arduous use that their early PBYs were put to. Built with the Consolidated Model Number 28-5MA (MA = Military Australia), the first batch of Catalinas for the RAAF, serialled A24-1 to A24-18, were ordered on a contract signed on 5 August 1940. Delivery was by air from San Diego to Australia, with RAAF crews taking over from Consolidated personnel in Honolulu. The RAAF crews were in fact made up of QANTAS men flying in their capacity as members of the RAAF Reserve.

A24-1 had originally been intended for the RAF as AH534, but was diverted to the RAAF when the intended A24-1 was not ready for delivery on time. Registered temporarily with the civilian registration VH-AFA, this replacement aircraft set off on its delivery flight on 25 January 1941, with a crew including Capt P. G. Taylor as navigator, an airman later to become famous for pioneering long-distance post-war Catalina flights. The flight, which lasted 60 hours and 16 minutes was only the third ever air crossing of the Pacific Ocean.

After delivery to Sydney, A24-1 served with the Seaplane Training Flight at Rathmines, 11 Squadron and 20 Squadron, with which it suffered a grounding on a reef near Port Moresby, Papua, on 31 January 1942. Back with 11 Squadron, A24-1 gained the distinction of sinking a Japanese ship when, on 6 January 1942, after attacking Gasmata airstrip and damaging Zero fighters on the ground, Flt Lt Dave Vernon initiated an attack on the 5,447 ton *Nichiryu Maru* with four 250 lb bombs. Shortly after this, A24-1 was taken off operational flying, and after overhaul, was allocated to 3 Operational Training Unit in April 1943.

At the cessation of hostilities, A24-1 was one of the Catalinas selected to ferry supplies and repatriated personnel to and from Australia. Coded 'K', this venerable Catalina was tasked to fly from Rathmines to Singapore via Cairns, Darwin and Labuan. Darwin was reached on 29 August 1945, under the captaincy of 3 OTU's CFI, Wg Cdr Keith Bolitho, DFC, USDFC. The next day, after an aborted take-off attempt because of leaking engine oil, a second take-off was started, but the aircraft began to bounce uncontrollably once on the step, and the hull was ripped open in the ensuing heavy landing after the throttles had been closed. The back of A24-1 was broken, and

Just recognisable as a Catalina, A24-1 rests in the mud at Darwin's East Arm. The barnacle-encrusted bow turret is in the foreground.
Bill McWhizter

after removing supplies and salvageable spares, the remains were abandoned at the accident site on the eastern shore of Blayden Point and for many years remained substantially intact. However, it suffered badly during the catastrophic Hurricane *Tracy* that struck the Darwin area on Christmas Day, 1974, and has since been the target for spares and souvenir hunters. The present-day wreck is still just recognisable as a Catalina where it rests in its muddy grave, but realistically it cannot be long before all trace of it moulders away.

Table 197.

Registration/ Serial	C/n	Type	Place of Manufacture	Previous id(s)
A24-1 (RAAF)	27	PBY-5	CON SD	VH-AFA AH534 (RAF)

A24-19 – Wallan, Victoria

This ex-Royal Australian Air Force Catalina was known to be under restoration at Wallan in Victoria during the 1980s. However, it was apparently badly damaged during a storm there in 1988, and its present status is unconfirmed. Originally built for the Royal Canadian Air Force as a Canso by Consolidated at San Diego, this aircraft was allocated the RCAF serial 9734, but was diverted to the RAF as a Catalina IIA, serial V9734/VA734, to replace an earlier loaned aircraft. However, it did not see RAF service either, and was instead diverted to the RAAF. As with many Catalinas, there are conflicting theories about its identity. J. A. Griffin in his book *Canadian Military Aircraft Serials and Photographs* quotes the constructor's number as 315, but then incorrectly refers to the airframe as a Canso A (i.e. an amphibian). Other sources quote constructor's number 315 as a Catalina operated by the Netherlands East Indies Air Force as Y-51. The alternative identity of c/n 382 has been offered for A24-19. It was certainly not a PBY-4, as one source would have it. This author prefers the 315/RCAF theory.

Received by the RAAF on 19 March 1942, it was delivered to 20 Squadron the following month, and on 30 April, received damage when its base at Tulagi, British Solomon Islands, was attacked by Japanese bombers. The damage was repaired by using spares from the more seriously damaged A24-23, which was then scuttled. A24-19 was flown out to Rathmines, NSW. Later, it served with 3 Operational Training Unit, and in October 1946 was sold by the Commonwealth Disposal Commission to Kingsford Smith Aviation Services for spares recovery. What happened to it after that until its arrival at Wallan remains something of a mystery.

Table 198.

Registration/ Serial	C/n	Type	Place of Manufacture	Previous id(s)
A24-19 (RAAF)	382	PBY-5	CON SD	VA734 (RAF) V9734 (RAF) 9734 (RCAF)

A24-29 – Murray River, Victoria

One of the more elaborate PBY motor cruiser conversions is also one of the least recognisable. Now sporting single-storey accommodation and paddle wheels, this Catalina is still used for pleasure cruising on the Murray River bordering New South Wales and Victoria, and is owned by Jim Vale. It was originally a PBY-4 with the US Navy serial Bu1216, and it served with a number of US Navy patrol squadrons before ending up in Darwin at the very end of 1941. Later, it became A24-29 with the Royal Australian Air Force, with which it served in a training role. At the end of the war, it was sold to Kingsford Smith Aviation Services and went on to serve as a houseboat, floating gambling den, fishing boat and, ultimately, a diesel-engined, fibre-glass-coated paddle cruiser!

Table 199.

Registration/Serial	C/n	Type	Place of Manufacture	Previous id(s)
A24-29 (RAAF)	4	PBY-4	CON SD	Bu1216 (US Navy)

A24-69 – East Arm, Darwin, Northern Territories

This PBY-5A wreck is in danger of being destroyed through the proposed development of a bulk storage area in the harbour. The local authorities have in fact raised various components from this wreck, including one engine and prop and some smaller components, but it seems unlikely that the rest will be saved if the development goes ahead, despite the efforts of local enthusiasts.

A24-69 had originally been lost when it caught fire whilst moored at Darwin's East Arm.

Table 200.

Registration/ Serial	C/n	Type	Place of Manufacture	Previous id(s)
A24-69	1610	PBY-5A	CON SD	Bu34056 (US Navy)

A24-88 – Location not known

As late as 1988, the hull of this ex-RAAF PBY-5A was known to be in use as a houseboat, its wheel wells faired over and blisters replaced by sliding hatches similar to those seen on early US Navy PBYs. It was originally delivered to the US Navy, but later transferred to the RAAF and was taken on charge by it in March 1944. Initially allocated to 3 Operational Training Unit, it subsequently served with 42 and 11 Squadrons. After the war's end, it was one of many Catalinas sold for spares recovery to Kingsford Smith Aviation Services, which acquired title in January 1948. Its subsequent history is obscure, and confirmation that it continues to exist, and where, would be welcomed.

Table 201.

Registration/ Serial	C/n	Type	Place of Manufacture	Previous id(s)
A24-88 (RAAF)	1714	PBY-5A	CON SD	Bu48352 (US Navy)

A24-206 – East Arm, Darwin, Northern Territories

This Catalina wreck has been pinpointed in the Darwin vicinity, having been destroyed when its depth charges exploded on 20 June 1945. It is another Darwin area wreck that is threatened by the possible future development of a bulk storage area there. Also located in roughly the same position are two further Catalina wrecks, one a US Navy PBY-4 and the other a PatWing 10

aircraft formerly of the Netherlands Navy. A24-206 was a PB2B-1 flying boat.

Table 202.

Registration/ Serial	C/n	Type	Place of Manufacture	Previous id(s)
A24-206 (RAAF)	61123	PB2B-1	BOE CAN	JX611 ntu RAF) Bu44217 (US Navy)

A24-381 – Lord Howe Island, off New South Wales coast

Wreckage of this Catalina, which crashed into high ground on 28 September 1948, still remains on site and consists of fairly substantial chunks of mangled but recognisable components. At the time of the crash, which claimed a number of lives, A24-381 was on the strength of 11 Squadron, RAAF.

Table 203.

Registration/ Serial	C/n	Type	Place of Manufacture	Previous id(s)
A24-381 (RAAF)	61163	PB2B-2	BOE CAN	JX639 ntu (RAF) Bu44257 (US Navy)

Murray River, Echuca, Victoria

In addition to A24-88 and Bu1216 quoted above, a number of other Catalinas were converted for use as houseboats in Australia, and it may be that some of these still exist. At least one was keeping company with a similarly converted Dornier Do24 on the Murray River at Echuca in Victoria some years ago.

Calliope Channel, Palm Island Aboriginal Reserve, off Townsville, Queensland

There are known to be at least two unidentified Catalina wrecks on this reserve, but the local inhabitants are not, apparently, sympathetic to the possibility of their removal. The area was a Second World War US Navy base and, at the end of the war, a number of Catalinas were either bulldozed into the ground or left in various states of decay there, although the two known wrecks sank at their moorings after being fired on by enemy forces. Recently, some components have been recovered for use in the restoration of VH-EXG, currently with an RAAF restoration team at Amberley.

A further wreck in the vicinity of Townsville is A24-52, which is submerged at the entrance to the bay. This aircraft was lost in a landing accident on 7 September 1943.

G-AGFL, G-AGFM, G-AGID and G-AGIE – Off Rottnest Island, Fremantle, Western Australia

These four Catalinas were used by QANTAS on the famous *Double Sunrise* route between Perth, WA and Ceylon during the Second World War. Once they had been replaced by long-haul land-planes, they were no longer required and were handed over to 300 Wing, RAF Transport Command, which had them beached at Nedlands Bay, Perth. Subsequently, they were flown to a position off Rottnest Island during early 1946 and deliberately blown up and sunk in order to comply with

Lend-Lease conditions. The dates of destruction are shown in parenthesis after the registrations in Table 204. In recent times, they have been the subject of various location attempts with a view to raising at least one for salvage and restoration, but to date these have not seen fruition, and, indeed, the exact whereabouts of the airframes seems to be in some doubt although the general location is known.

Table 204. Disposals off Rottnest Island, Fremantle

Registration/Serial Disposal Date	C/n	Type	Place of M'facture	Previous id(s)
G-AGFL (14/2/1946)	'122'/ 808	Catalina I	CON SD	FP221 (RAF)
G-AGFM (24/2/1946)	'145'/ 831	Catalina I	CON SD	FP244 (RAF)
G-AGID (30/1/1946)	1109	PBY-5	CON SD	JX575 (RAF) Bu08215 (US Navy)
G-AGIE (17/1/1946)	1111	PBY-5	CON SD	JX577 (RAF) Bu08217 (US Navy)

G-AGKS – Sydney Heads off Rose Bay, Sydney

G-AGKS was the fifth of the QANTAS aircraft to be deliberately sunk when its useful life was over, but because it was located at Rose Bay at the time, it was scuttled there instead of at Rottnest Island with the others. G–AGKS had suffered from persistent fuel leaks and it was undergoing remedial work at Rose Bay when the decision to withdraw it was made. It was consigned to the deep in March 1946.

Table 205.

Registration/ Serial	C/n	Type	Place of Manufacture	Previous id(s)
G-AGKS	28022	PB2B-1	BOE CAN	JX287 ntu (RAF)

Seen at the boarding jetty at Perth in 1944 is G-AGKS, about to depart for another Double Sunrise flight to Ceylon. It has the fleet number 5 on the fin and SEAC two-tone blue roundels and fin flash. Unlike the rest of the QANTAS war-time fleet, G-AGKS was scuttled at Sydney Heads. *QANTAS via François Prins*

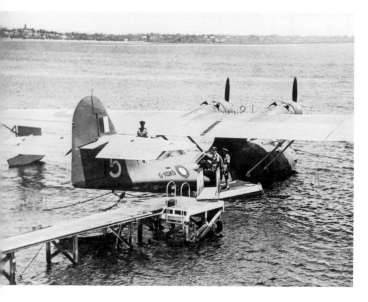

BRAZIL

Some remains of a US Navy PBY-5A Catalina can be found forming part of a memorial in a park in Natal, Brazil. The relics consist of a propeller and hub assembly, and a main undercarriage wheel and leg. These items are apparently from a Catalina bearing the hull side number 83-P-12, i.e. aircraft 12 of Patrol Squadron VP-83. Six Catalinas of VP-83 were based at Natal from April 1942, and aircraft 12 was one of these. It was lost when it crashed into the sea at night.

CANADA

W8432 – near Bella Bella, British Columbia

This early Catalina MkI suffered an accident upon landing at Bella Bella at the conclusion of an anti-submarine patrol over the Pacific Ocean off Canada's west coast. Whilst attempting a blind landing exercise, the pilot failed to round-out early enough, and the Catalina struck the water surface nose down. The hull was broken aft of the blisters, and although it was later salvaged, damage was too severe for repair and it was towed out from the coast and scuttled. This accident occurred on 16 June 1944, whilst being operated by 9 (BR) Squadron, RCAF. There is some interest in raising this wreck, which has been located in about a hundred feet of water, the intention being to incorporate it in a future museum, but these plans must at this stage be considered long term.

Although ordered for the Royal Air Force, W8432 was diverted to the RCAF straight from the production line and never saw RAF service.

Table 206.

Registration/ Serial	C/n	Type	Place of Manufacture	Previous id(s)
W8432 (RCAF)	148	Catalina I	CON SD	–

9789 – Alarm Cove, Llama Passage, Bella Bella, British Columbia

RCAF Canso A 9789 was lost in a crash at Alarm Cove on 30 July 1943, whilst serving with Bella Bella-based 9(BR) Squadron. Of the nine crew on board, one was lost. It is understood that the burned-out wreckage, or part of it, is still on site.

Table 207.

Registration/ Serial	C/n	Type	Place of Manufacture	Previous id(s)
9789 (RCAF)	22018	Canso A	BOE CAN	–

11086 – near Ucluelet, Vancouver Island, British Columbia

Canso A, serial 11086, was operating with 3 Operational Training Unit out of Patricia Bay, Vancouver Island, when, on the night of 2 December 1944, it crashed a few miles north of Kennedy Lake near Ucluelet during a night navigation exercise. The crash site is on a mountain 4,000 ft up, and consequently the wreckage was not located until 1 July the following year. All nine crew on board perished in the crash and subsequent fire, and they are commemorated by a cross-marked burial site close to the wreck.

Table 208.

Registration/ Serial	C/n	Type	Place of Manufacture	Previous id(s)
11086 (RCAF)	CV-421	Canso A	CAN VIC (Cartierville)	–

COCOS (KEELING) ISLANDS, INDIAN OCEAN

JX435 – near Horsbugh Island, Cocos

The remains of Catalina JX435 are still to be found in the clear waters of the Cocos, where it sank after hitting a coral reef on landing on 27 June 1945, with the loss of nine men. At the time of the accident, JX435 was flying with 240 Squadron, and it was flying to the Cocos from Koggala, Ceylon (now Sri Lanka). Recent dives on the wreck show the engines to be intact, along with other scattered wreckage.

Table 209.

Registration/ Serial	C/n	Type	Place of Manufacture	Previous id(s)
JX435 (RAF)		Catalina IVB	BOE CAN	Bu73110 (US Navy)

This extraordinary photo shows F-OAYD in 60 ft of water off Papeete, Tahiti, in 1997, a plaything for inquisitive fish. *Peter Farmer*

FRENCH POLYNESIA

F-OAYD, Raiatea, Papeete, Tahiti

In the late 1950s, F-OAYV was being flown as a pure flying boat in the Pacific with RAI of Papeete, having previously had its amphibious undercarriage removed. It originally flew with the US Navy as Bu48327. It was damaged in a heavy landing at Raiatea in October 1960, and was never flown again. Stripped of useful components, the airframe was towed out into the lagoon there and sunk during November 1962. Its substantially complete remains can still be found in the clear waters there.

Table 210.

Registration/Serial	C/n	Type	Place of Manufacture	Previous id(s)
F-OAYD	1689	PBY-5A	CON SD	N1520V Bu48327 (US Navy)

INDONESIA

A24-45 – Baru Bay, Java

Royal Australian Air Force PBY-5 A24-45 was lost on active service on 20 July 1944. Whilst being flown by 43 Squadron on a shipping search to Namlea Harbour, A24-45 encountered bad weather and failed to return to base. Fifty-one years later, in 1994, woodcutters discovered the wrecked Catalina in mountainous terrain near Baru Bay. Subsequently, an RAAF work party removed the crew's remains and unexploded ammunition from the site, but the wreckage was left where it had crashed all those years previously. The discovery of the wreckage finally refuted claims, made in 1946 by locals, that the Catalina had crashed into the sea in Namlea Bay. It was

subsequently assumed that this must have been an entirely different aircraft.

Table 211.

Registration/Serial	C/n	Type	Place of Manufacture	Previous id(s)
A24-45 (RAAF)	1183	PBY-5	CON SD	Bu08269 (US Navy)

KIRIBATI/GILBERT ISLAND

In 1994, it was reported that a PBY wreck was to be found close to the Catholic Mission on one of the local islands . No further details are known as to the Catalina's identity, although it is assumed to be a US military example.

NEW GUINEA

An unidentified USAAF OA-10A was discovered by locals in thick jungle near Oro Bay, New Guinea, during 1994. Sadly, the deceased crew were still aboard. The wreck remains on site.

NORWAY

JX381, Bjornoya (Bear) Island, Arctic Circle

Whilst involved in dropping mail to a manned radio station at Bjornoya, Royal Norwegian Air Force Catalina JX381 hit the ground and disintegrated, with the loss of eight crew members. Scattered wreckage may still be found at this remote site, the Norwegian squadron codes of KK-N denoting 333 Squadron still being visible on the faded paintwork. The flight had originated at Skattora, Tromsö, and took place on 28 March 1954. The RAF's previous identity for this aircraft has been incorrectly quoted as JX385 in the past.

Catalina IVB JX381 is prepared for what turned out to be its final and tragic last flight at Skattora, Tromsø on 28th March 1954.
via Morten Andersen

Table 212.

Registration/Serial	C/n	Type	Place of Manufacture	Previous id(s)
JX381 (RNoAF)	28129	Catalina IVB/ PB2B-1	BOE CAN	LN-OAP JX381 (RAF) Bu73040 ntu (US Navy)

JX412, Fordesviken, Sotra Island

This Catalina was lost when it just failed to clear the top of a mountain on Sotra Island whilst flying in thick fog on 6 September 1948. One engine from the wreck was later incorporated into a memorial on the spot where the Catalina crashed. At the time of this tragic accident, JX412 was flying as K-KK of 333 Squadron.

Table 213.

Registration/Serial	C/n	Type	Place of Manufacture	Previous id(s)
JX412 (RNoAF)	28172	Catalina IVB/ PB2B-1	BOE CAN	Bu73083 (US Navy)

SOLOMON ISLANDS

Unidentified, Vilu Cultural Village & War Museum, Honiara

Major components from an American PBY-5A Catalina are to be found at this museum site in the Solomon Islands. There are also some remains from at least two US Navy PBYs that were sunk by Japanese aircraft whilst moored at their base at Lake Te'Nggano, Rennell Island, 202 km south of Guadalcanal. A guidebook to the local area states that they are easily snorkelled. These are the survivors from no fewer than eight aircraft that were caught out in the attack.

South West Pacific Area

Known wrecks still to be found extant in this vast area include the following, although no details on their condition are available:

A24-8 (RAAF) off Kavieng harbour – shot down, 21/1/1942
A24-9 (RAAF) lies off Salamaua near Papua New Guinea (PNG) – shot down 21/1/1942.
A24-11 (RAAF) in Kavieng Harbour after take-off accident, 15/1/1942
A24-13 (RAAF) missing off Rabaul 24/2/1942
A24-15 (RAAF) in scrub near Port Moresby, PNG after take-off accident, 8/12/1941
A24-18 (RAAF) south of Rabaul – shot down 4/5/1942
A24-20 (RAAF) off Misima Island 6/5/1942 – enemy action.
A24-22 (RAAF) off Gasmata 8/3/1943 – missing in action.
A24-34 (RAAF) on reef near New Britain, west of Rabaul, after fire and crash-landing, 7/2/1944.
A24-43 (RAAF) Bougainville, PNG, shot down 26/4/1943.

A24-49 (RAAF) East Manokwari, Vogel Kop, Irian Jaya, shot down 29/4/1944
Bu08428 (US Navy) New Ireland, north-east PNG
Bu08436 (US Navy) Nacols, PNG
44-33889 (USAAF) Helen Island, North Moluccas near Biak, Indonesia
(unidentified) on Malendok Island, north-east PNG

UNITED KINGDOM

Z2148 – Near Arisdale, South Yell, Shetland

Z2148 of 240 Squadron flew into high ground at Yell in the Shetlands on 19 January 1942, whilst on approach to land on the water at Sullom Voe. At the time of the accident, it was serving with Lough Erne-based 240 Squadron. It had been engaged on a mission to Northern Norway to search for the *Tirpitz*, but on the way home, the Catalina suffered engine failure. A decision to divert to Sullom Voe was taken, but a flare path was not laid down, and after circling for a while, the Catalina crashed into high ground in the dark. Of the nine crew on board, two survived.

Table 214.

Registration/ Serial	C/n	Type	Place of Manufacture	Previous id(s)
Z2148 (RAF)	183	Catalina I	CON SD	

AH533 – Jura, Hebrides

This 210 Squadron Catalina flew into high ground in bad weather, and the scattered wreckage can still be found at the crash site, close to the property known as *Barnhill*, home to the author George Orwell toward the end of his life. The accident occurred on 15 July 1941.

Table 215.

Registration/ Serial	C/n	Type	Place of Manufacture	Previous id(s)
AH533 (RAF)	21	Catalina I	CON SD	

JX273 – Vatersay, Argyll, Outer Hebrides

JX273 was another night-time casualty. Whilst serving with 302 Ferry Training Unit, Oban, it flew into a hillside at Vatersay on 12 May 1944. A considerable amount of wreckage may still be found there.

Table 216.

Registration/ Serial	C/n	Type	Place of Manufacture	Previous id(s)
JX273 (RAF)		Catalina IVB	BOE CAN	

Additionally, various RAF Catalinas are reported to be submerged beneath the surface at locations in the Scottish Isles and mainland Scotland and in Northern Ireland. These include at least one known example in Lough Erne, Northern Ireland, another just off Cumbrae near Largs and one aircraft close to the Nigg Oil Terminal, Cromarty Firth.

UNITED STATES

Bu7255 – near Fredericksburg, Virginia

The wreck of this PBY-5A is to be found near Fredericksburg, following its crash there in early 1942. It is reported to be a former Norfolk, Virginia-based VP-83 machine.

Table 217.

Registration/ Serial	C/n	Type	Place of Manufacture	Previous id(s)
Bu7255 (US Navy)	418	PBY-5A	CON SD	–

Unidentified – Panamint Springs, Death Valley, South Eastern California

A message posted on the Internet in June 1998 referred to a Catalina that hit a ridge and crashed within sight of Panamint Springs in 1952. The crew, who apparently bailed out prior to the crash, were allegedly connected with the CIA. The remains are supposed to be fairly intact.

Unidentified – Sand Point, Lake Washington, Washington State

There are, apparently, at least three former US Navy Catalinas in the lake here.

There may well be various Catalina remains still to be found in the lots of the various Hollywood film companies, as the type has featured in several motion pictures over the years. An unidentified PBY was reported to be still extant at Universal Film Studios in Hollywood during 1994. Sadly, two surviving PBN-1 Nomads were scrapped at MGM's studios in 1970.

VANUATU (NEW HEBRIDES), SOUTH PACIFIC OCEAN

Bu2389 – Espirito Santu, Vanuatu

The burnt and scattered wreckage of Bu2389, a former US Navy PBY-5, was discovered in January 1994, on a remote ridge on the island of Espirito Santu, one of 83 islands that make up Vanuatu . It bears the hull side-codes 23-P-15 of Patrol Squadron VP-23.

Table 218.

Registration/ Serial	C/n	Type	Place of Manufacture	Previous id(s)
Bu2389 (US Navy)	204	PBY-5	CON SD	–

Appendix 1
DESIGNATIONS APPLIED TO THE PBY/CATALINA FAMILY

A large number of type numbers and designations were allocated to the PBY/Catalina family, and many of these appear throughout this book. The following table gives brief details of each of the designations given and should be used in conjunction with the production table in Appendix 2.

XP3Y-1	Prototype, serial Bu9459
XPBY-1	Rebuild of prototype Bu9459
PBY-1	60 aircraft for the US Navy
PBY-2	50 aircraft for the US Navy
PBY-3	66 aircraft for the US Navy
PBY-4	32 aircraft for the US Navy
PBY-5	Production flying boats for the US Navy
PBY-5R	Used on Bu1245 after conversion from XPBY-5A to transport flying boat *Sea Mare*
SPBY-5	Rumoured to have been used on small number of post-war US Navy PBY-5 flying boats
XPBY-5A	Final PBY-4, Bu1245, rebuilt as prototype amphibian
PBY-5A	Production amphibians for the US Navy
APBY-5A	Usage not confirmed but possibly used post-war
PBY-5AG	US Navy amphibians transferred to US Coast Guard
PBY-5A(M)	Used on some RAAF amphibians when undercarriages removed
PBY-5B	Applied to some production RAF aircraft
PBY-6A	Basically PBY-5A but with horizontal and vertical tail surfaces of PBN-1 Nomad
PBY-6AG	PBY-6As supplied to US Coast Guard
NPBY-6A	Supposedly allocated to US Navy reserved PBY-6As post-war
PB2B-1	Boeing-built PBY-5 equivalent
PB2B-2	As above but with PBN-1 Nomad-style tails
PB2B-2R	As above but transport version for RAAF
PBN-1 Nomad	US Naval Aircraft Factory redesign of PBY-5 flying boat
PBV-1A	Proposed designation for Canadian Vickers-built PBY-5As
Model 28-1	Designation given to first commercial PBY, NC777 *Guba*
Model 28-2	Three aircraft supplied to Russia as pattern aircraft for subsequent licence production
Model 28-3	The second NC777 *Guba*
Model 28-4	Commercial transport NC18997 for American Export Airlines
Model 28-5	Allocated to commercial PBY P9630 supplied to British Air Ministry
Model 28-5ACF	Designation given to some post-war commercial PBY-5A/Canso A conversions
Model 28-5MA	Early RAAF aircraft
Model 28-5MC	Early Consolidated-built aircraft for RCAF – became Cansos in service
Model 28-5AMC	As above but amphibious aircraft – became Canso As in service
Model 28-5ME	Early production aircraft for RAF
Model 28-5MF	Allocated to order for French military but cancelled before delivery
Model 28-5MN	Early aircraft for Dutch Navy
Model 28-5AMN	As above but amphibious aircraft
Canso	Name given to flying boat Catalinas operated by RCAF
Canso A	As above but amphibious versions
Catalina	Type name given to PBY-5 by British and subsequently used by all PBY operators
Catalina I, IA, IB, II, IIA, III, IVA, IVB, V and VI	Designations given to various RAF Catalinas. Catalina III was equivalent to PBY-5A, IVB to PB2B-1 and VI to PB2B-2. The Catalina V was to have been equivalent to PBN-I Nomad but none were built
Convoy	Proposed name for RCAF PBYs but abandoned in favour of Canso/CansoA
CL-1	Canadair (previously Canadian Vickers) designation for late production OA-10As
CV-14	Designation given to PBY types for use in airborne communications from *c.*1980 onward
OA-10	USAAF PBY-5

OA-10A	USAAF PBY-5A equivalent
OA-10B	USAAF PBY-6A equivalent
A-10	Later designation for USAAF OA-10 series
GST	Designation given to some Russian-built PBYs
MP-7	As above for unarmed transport version
Tp-47	Designation given to 3 Catalinas operated by Sweden's Flygvapnet
Bird Innovator	4-engined commercial variant produced by the Bird Respirator Company
Landseaire	Post-war commercial and military conversion produced by Southern California Aircraft of Ontario, California
Mop	NATO reporting name for Soviet PBYs issued by the Air Standards Co-ordinating Committee
Super Catalina	Post-war commercial conversion utilising Wright R-2600 engines of 1,700 hp and, usually, a larger squared-off rudder. Most conversions carried out by Steward-Davis
Super Canso S/C 1000	Solitary Super Catalina conversion by Noorduyn-Norseman Aircraft of Cartierville, Quebec (CF-MIR)
Skybarge	Name given to proposed freighter conversion by Steward-Davis
Turbo Catalina	Proposal for twin-RR Dart turbo-prop water bomber

Appendix 2
SUMMARY OF CONSOLIDATED MODEL 28/PBY/CATALINA/CANSO PRODUCTION

The following table details production broken down by the builder and location. It shows pre-war and wartime contracts together with details of those aircraft diverted 'as new' to air arms other than that originally intended. Construction numbers (c/ns) are shown where known although it should be noted that in some cases during early production, Consolidated used manufacturing or 'mfg' numbers in addition to c/ns and it is known that some of the former were repeated for different batches of aircraft on separate contracts.

Consolidated records show that the New Orleans-built Catalinas were also allocated 'mfg' numbers commencing at 1 and ending at 235 as an alternative to the sequential construction numbers that follow on from San Diego production. Although it is by no means certain that the four-figure numbers were actually carried over, most sources agree that they were certainly used up to and including 2063 and one Consolidated document, albeit emanating from the San Diego office, confirms their use up to 2177 for the final PBY, Bu64107. In order to avoid 'creating history' I have chosen not to quote c/ns in this book beyond the 2063 point but would welcome comment on this. It is noteworthy that some surviving PBY-6As have been quoted on the US Civil Aircraft Register as having c/ns in the 1 to 235 'mfg' sequence, examples being c/n 225 Bu64097/N7179Y and c/n 235 Bu64107/N9825Z.

The table does not include the solitary US Navy PBY-5A Bu21232 as the origin of this aircraft is not known. It

is possible that it may have been a rebuild of an earlier aircraft or, more likely, a transfer from the USAAF but this is not confirmed. It survives today in the USA as N2763A.

CONSOLIDATED AIRCRAFT CORPORATION, BUFFALO, NEW YORK

C/n	Type	Serial Number	Contract No
	XP3Y-1	Bu9459	31792

Later rebuilt as prototype XPBY-1 with same serial and to US Navy under contract 48710.

Consolidated Aircraft Corporation, San Diego, California

C/n	Type	Serial Number	Contract No
1 to 60	PBY-1	Bu0102 to Bu0161	43087

60 aircraft for US Navy originally ordered as P3Y-1s.

C/n	Type	Serial Number	Contract No
1 to 50	PBY-2	Bu0454 to Bu0503	49653

50 aircraft for US Navy.

C/n	Type	Serial Number	Contract No
C-1	Model 28-1	NC777	

Dr Richard Archbold *Guba*. To Soviet Union as URSS-L2.

C/n	Type	Serial Number	Contract No
C-2	Model 28-2	?	

Pattern aircraft for Soviet Union.

C/n	Type	Serial Number	Contract No
	Model 28-2	?	

2 pattern aircraft assembled in Soviet Union.

C/n	Type	Serial Number	Contract No
C-3	Model 28-3	NC777(2)	

Dr Richard Archbold *Guba* (2). Later RAF AM258, British civil G-AGBJ, RAF SM706.

C/n	Type	Serial Number	Contract No
1 to 66	PBY-3	Bu0842 to Bu0907	51701

66 aircraft for US Navy.

C/n	Type	Serial Number	Contract No
1 to 32	PBY-4	Bu1213 to Bu1244	58101

32 aircraft for US Navy.
Bu1219 to RAAF as A24-28. Bu1216 to RAAF as A24-29.

C/n	Type	Serial Number	Contract No
C-4	Model 28-4	NC18997	

American Export Airlines *Transatlantic*. To US Navy as Bu99080.

C/n	Type	Serial Number	Contract No
C-5	Model 28-5	X21732/(N)P9630	

British Air Ministry for evaluation under contract B988730/39.

C/n	Type	Serial Number	Contract No
33	XPBY-5A	Bu1245	58101

1 aircraft for US Navy. Prototype amphibious PBY. Later rebuilt as PBY-5R *Sea Mare*.

C/n	Type	Serial Number	Contract No
Between 1 and 291 – see note below	PBY-5	Bu2289 to Bu2455	NOs-70496

167 aircraft for US Navy.
Bu2290 to USCG as V189.
Note: C/ns allocated as follows: Bu2289 to Bu2293 = c/ns 1 to 5, Bu2294 to Bu2295/50 to 51, Bu2296 to Bu2299/62 to 66, Bu2300/68, Bu2301 to Bu2304/17 to 20, Bu2305 to Bu2309/22 to 26, Bu2310 to Bu2313/28 to 31, Bu2314 to Bu2318/33 to 37, Bu2319 to Bu2324/41 to 46, Bu2325/49, Bu2326 to Bu2327/68 to 70, Bu2328 to Bu2331/772 to 75, Bu2332 to Bu2333/90 to 91, Bu2334 to Bu2335/95 to 96, Bu2336/98, Bu2337/102, Bu2338/104, Bu2339/108, Bu2340 to Bu2341/110 to 111, Bu2342/116, Bu2343 to Bu2344/120 to 121, Bu2345/123, Bu2346/125, Bu2347/128, Bu2348 to Bu2349/130 to 131, Bu2350/133, Bu2351 to Bu2352/135 to 136, Bu2353 to Bu2357/even numbers only from138 to 146, Bu2358 to Bu2365/odd numbers only from 149 to 163, Bu2366 to 2377/even numbers only from 166 to 188, Bu2378/191, Bu2379/193, Bu2380 to Bu2402/195 to 217, Bu2403 to Bu2415/219 to 231, Bu2416 to Bu2421/234 to 239, Bu2422 to Bu2427/243 to 248, Bu2428 to Bu2433/252 to 257, Bu2434 to Bu2435/261/262, Bu2436 to Bu2437/264 to 265, Bu2438 to Bu2439/268 to 269, Bu2440 to Bu2441/271 to 272, Bu2442 to Bu 2443/274 to 275, Bu2444 to Bu2445/277 to 278, Bu2446 to Bu2449/281 to 284 and Bu2450 to Bu2455/286 to 291.

C/n	Type	Serial Number	Contract No
Between 7 and 194 – see note below	Model 28-5ME	W8405 to W8434 Z2134 to Z2153	A-37

50 aircraft for RAF as Catalina I
W8430 to W8432, Z2134 and Z2136 to Z2140 to RCAF retaining RAF serials
Note: C/ns allocated as follows:
W8405 to W8434/ = c/ns 7,39,48,53,56,60,67,77,80,84,86,89,93,99,103, 105, 107, 109, 114, 118, 119, 124, 127, 134, 139, 143, 145, 148, 150 and 152 respectively.
Z2134 to Z2153/ = c/ns 154, 156, 158, 160, 162, 165, 167, 169, 171, 173, 175, 177, 179, 181, 183, 185, 187, 190, 192 and 194 repectively.

C/n	Type	Serial Number	Contract No
6,8,10, 11, 12,14 and 15	PBY-5	AM264 to AM270	A-2587

7 aircraft taken from US Navy production and delivered to RAF as Catalina II. Intended US Navy serials were Bu2294 to Bu2300, these being allocated to replacement aircraft.

C/n	Type	Serial Number	Contract No
Between 9 and 147 – see note below	Model 28-5ME	AH530 to AH569	F-210

40 aircraft for RAF as Catalina I diverted from cancelled French order.
AH534 to RAAF as A24-1 (second allocation).
AH563 to BOAC as G-AGDA.
Note : C/ns allocated as follows:
AH530 to AH569 = c/ns 9, 13, 16, 21, 27, 32, 38, 47, 52, 54, 55, 58, 59, 61, 66, 71, 76, 79, 81, 82, 83, 85, 87, 88, 92, 94, 97, 100, 101, 106, 112, 115, 117, 122, 126, 129, 132, 137, 141 and 147 respectively.

C/n	Type	Serial Number	Contract No
Between 40 and 350 – see note below	Model 28-5MA	A24-1 to A24-18	A-58

18 aircraft for RAAF
The original A24-1 (c/n 40) was re-serialled A24-2, its place being taken by RAF AH534. The original A24-2 (c/n 57) was, in turn, supplied to the RAF as DP202 and later saw service with the RCAF.
Note: C/ns allocated as follows:
A24-1 to A24-18 = c/ns 40, 57, 78, 113, 164, 189, 218, 250, 259, 270, 279, 299, 307, 313, 322, 332, 342 and 350 respectively.

C/n	Type	Serial Number	Contract No
Between 232 and 388 – see note below	Model 28-5MN	Y-38 to Y-73	N-36

36 aircraft for NEIAF
Note: C/ns allocated as follows:
Y-38 to Y-73 = c/ns 232, 241, 249, 260, 266, 276, 293, 298, 301, 303, 306, 308, 311, 315, 320, 326, 330, 336, 340, 344, 348, 351, 352, 353, 355, 358, 361, 363, 367, 369, 372, 376, 378, 381, 385 and 388 respectively.

C/n	Type	Serial Number	Contract No
Between 233 and 389 – see note below	Model 28-5MC	9701 to 9736	CAN-78

36 aircraft for RCAF as Canso.
20 aircraft to RAF as Catalina IIA with serials between VA701 to VA736 and 9 aircraft supplied to RAAF: 9708/A24-25, 9710/A24-22, 9711/A24-26, 9717/A24-27, 9730/A24-23, 9733/A24-24, 9734/A24-19, 9735/A24-20 and 9736/A24-21. Remaining aircraft (9701, 9702, 9704 to 9707 and 9709) stayed with RCAF. Note that the RAF aircraft were initially given serials in the range V9701 to V9736, the last four digits equating to the RCAF serial. However, these RAF identities had already been allocated to a batch of Westland Lysanders. The serials were therefore amended to VA701 to VA736 but only after at least some of the aircraft had been painted in the incorrect format.
Note: C/ns allocated as follows:
9701 to 9736 = c/ns 233, 240, 242, 251, 258, 263, 267, 273, 280, 285, 292, 296, 302, 304, 309, 312, 316, 318, 324, 328, 334, 338, 346, 349, 354, 356, 359, 364, 368, 371, 373, 377, 380, 382, 386 and 389 respectively.

C/n	Type	Serial Number	Contract No
360, 365, 374, 384, 391, 397, 405, 411 and 419 respectively.	Model 28-5ME	AJ154 to AJ162	A-37

9 aircraft for RAF as Catalina I

Bu08384 typifies a US Navy PBY-5. It is equipped with ASV aerials under the wings and an 'eyeball' type bow turret.
via Barry Dowsett

C/n	Type	Serial Number	Contract No
Between 294 and 392 – see note below	PBY-5A	Bu2456 to Bu2488	Nos-70496

33 aircraft for US Navy.
Note: C/ns allocated as follows:
Bu2456 to Bu2488 = c/ns 294, 295, 297, 300, 305, 310, 314, 317, 319, 321, 323, 325, 327, 329, 331, 333, 335, 337, 339, 341, 343, 345, 347, 357, 362, 366, 370, 375, 379, 383, 387, 390 and 392 respectively.

C/n	Type	Serial Number	Contract No
Between 393 and 427 – see note below	Model 28-5 AMC	9737 to 9750	CAN-78

14 aircraft for RCAF as Canso A.
Note: C/ns allocated as follows:
9737 to 9750 = 393, 395, 399, 401, 403, 407, 409, 413, 415, 417, 420, 422, 425 and 427 respectively.

C/n	Type	Serial Number	Contract No
Between 394 and 469 for Bu7243 and Bu7302 and 471 to 544 for Bu04972 to Bu05045 – see note 2 below	PBY-5A	Bu7243 to Bu7302 Bu04972 to Bu05045	Nos-77713

134 aircraft for US Navy of which:
12 to RAF as Catalina III as follows: Bu04985 to Bu04990/FP525 to FP530, Bu05004 to Bu05007/FP531 to FP534, Bu05010/FP535 and Bu05012/FP536.
Note: Bu04972 to Bu05045 were originally ordered for the USAAF with serials 41-18700 to 41-18773 but were diverted to the US Navy.
Note 2: C/ns allocated as follows:
Bu7243 to Bu7302 = c/ns 394, 396, 400, 398, 402, 404, 406, 408, 410, 412, 414, 416, 418, 421, 423, 424, 426, 428, 429, 430, 431, 432, 433, 434, 435, 436, 437, 438, 439, 440, 441, 442, 443, 444, 445, 446, 447, 448, 449, 450, 451, 452, 453, 454, 455, 456, 447, 458, 459, 460, 461, 462, 463, 464, 465, 466, 467, 468, 469 and 470 respectively.
Bu04972 to Bu05045 = c/ns 471 to 544 respectively.

FP536 was one of just 12 amphibious Catalina IIIs ordered by the Royal Air Force. The position of the hull roundel was unusual for RAF Cats as was the repetition of the aircraft serial on the bow above the bomb aimer's position.
MAP/Real Photos

C/n	Type	Serial Number	Contract No
545 to 574 for Bu02948 to Bu02977 and between 575 and 596 for Bu04399 to Bu04420 – see note below	PBY-5A	Bu02948 to Bu02977 Bu04399 to Bu04420	Nos-88476LL

52 aircraft for US Navy of which:
2 aircraft to USAAF as follows: Bu02967 as 41-18772 and Bu02969 as 41-18773.
Note: C/ns allocated as follows:
Bu02948 to Bu02977 = c/ns 545 to 574 respectively.
Bu04399 to Bu04420 = c/ns 576, 575, 578, 577, 580, 579, 582, 581, 584, 583, 586, 585, 588, 587, 590, 589, 592, 591, 594, 593, 595 and 596 respectively.

C/n	Type	Serial Number	Contract No
597 to 686	PBY-5	Bu04425 to Bu04514	NOs-91876

90 aircraft for US Navy.

C/n	Type	Serial Number	Contract No
687 to 836	PBY-5	FP100 to FP249	NOs-88477LL

150 aircraft for RAF as Catalina I.
47 of these aircraft remained in the USA for training with the US Navy but retained their RAF serials.
FP221 and FP244 to BOAC as G-AGFL and G-AGFM respectively.

C/n	Type	Serial Number	Contract No
837 to 848	Model 28-5A MN	Y-74 to Y-85	N-36

12 aircraft to NEIAF.

C/n	Type	Serial Number	Contract No
849 to 942	PBY-5A	Bu08030 to Bu08123	NOs-88476LL

91 aircraft to US Navy of which:
12 to USAAF as OA-10 as follows: Bu08031, Bu08046, Bu08079 to Bu08086 and Bu08090 to Bu08091 became 43-3259 to 43-3270.
3 supplied direct to Defense Supplier Corp for operation in Brazil by US Rubber – Bu08064 to NC33300, Bu08087 to NC33301 and Bu08088 to NC33302.

C/n	Type	Serial Number	Contract No
943 to 1017	PBY-5B	FP250 to FP324	NOs-88477

75 aircraft for RAF as Catalina IB.
FP290 to FP297 to RCAF with RAF serials.

C/n	Type	Serial Number	Contract No
Between 1018 and 1503 – see note below	PBY-5	Bu08124 to Bu08549	NOs-91876

426 aircraft for US Navy of which:
27 to RAF as Catalina IVA as follows: Bu08117, Bu08211 to Bu08225, Bu08532 to Bu08534 and Bu08542 to Bu08549 became JX570 to JX585 and JV925 to JV935 respectively. JX575 and JX577 to BOAC as G-AGID and G-AGIE respectively.
13 to RNZAF as follows: Bu08280/NZ4001, Bu08373/NZ4004, Bu08435/NZ4020, Bu08438/NZ4019, Bu08450/NZ4012, Bu08453/NZ4015, Bu08464/NZ4014, Bu08466/NZ4016, Bu08467/NZ4017, Bu08468/NZ4013, Bu08487/NZ4021, Bu08488/NZ4018 and Bu08516/NZ4022.
36 to RAAF as follows: Bu08150/A24-34, Bu08153/A24-31, Bu08156/A24-32, Bu08159/A24-33, Bu08161/A24-35, Bu08190/A24-36, Bu08200/A24-37, Bu08201/A24-40, Bu08202/A24-43, Bu08203/A24-38, Bu08205/A24-41, Bu08206/A24-39, Bu08207/A24-44, Bu08208/A24-42, Bu08264/A24-50, Bu08268/A24-48, Bu08269/A24-45, Bu08272/A24-46, Bu08284/A24-47, Bu08285/A24-49, Bu08286/A24-56, Bu08332/A24-53, Bu08333/A24-51, Bu08334/A24-54, Bu08335/A24-52, Bu08336/A25-55, Bu08340/A24-57, Bu08341/A24-58, Bu08400/A24-59, Bu08404/A24-60, Bu08405/A24-64, Bu08406/A24-61, Bu08489/A24-65, Bu08499/A24-66, Bu08500/A24-67 and Bu08504/A24-68.
5 to USAAF as OA-10 (*sic*)as follows: Bu08315/42-107401, Bu08318/42-107402, Bu08320/42-107403, Bu08322/42-107404, Bu08330/42-107405.
7 to Força Aérea Brasileira as follows: Bu08165/6500, Bu08166/6501, Bu08185/6502, Bu08186/6503, Bu08242/6504, Bu08243/6505 and Bu08300/6506.
3 to Fuerza Aérea Nacional de Chile as follows: Bu08301/400, Bu0830/401 and Bu08433/402.
5 to Defense Supplier Corp for operation in Brazil by US Rubber as follows: Bu08124 to Bu08127 as NC33303 to NC33306 respectively and Bu08196 to NC33307.
2 to Netherlands East Indies Air Force as follows: Bu08396 to Y-86 and Bu08397 to Y-87.
Note re c/ns: These were allocated as follows – 1018 to 1149/Bu08124 to Bu08255, 1160 to 1169/Bu08256 to Bu08265, 1180 to 1242/Bu08266 to Bu08328, 1253 to 1331/Bu08329 to Bu08407, 1342 to 1406/Bu08408 to Bu08472, 1417 to 1444/Bu08473 to Bu08500 and 1455 to 1503/Bu08501to Bu08549.

C/n	Type	Serial Number	Contract No
Between 1150 and 1513 – see note below	PBY-5B	JX200 to JX269	NOs-91876

70 aircraft for RAF as Catalina IVA of which:
9 to RNZAF as follows: JX228/NZ4010, JX230/NZ4008, JX231/NZ4009,

JX232/NZ4002, JX233/NZ4005, JX234/NZ4003, JX235/NZ4011, JX236/NZ4006 and JX237/NZ4007.

2 to RAAF as follows: JX238/A24-62 and JX239/A24-63.

Note re c/ns.: These were allocated as follows – 1150 to 1159/JX200 to JX209, 1170 to 1179/JX210 to JX219, 1243 to 1252/JX220 to JX229, 1332 to 1341/JX230 to JX239, 1407 to 1416/JX240 to JX249, 1445 to 1454/JX250 to JX259 and 1504 to 1513/JX260 to JX269.

C/n	Type	Serial Number	Contract No
1514 to 1613	PBY-5A	Bu33960 to Bu34059	NXa13595

100 aircraft for US Navy of which:

25 to USAAF as OA-10 serials as follows: Bu33962 as 43-43839, Bu33986 to Bu33998 as 43-43840 to 43-43852, Bu34000 to Bu34001 as 43-43853 to 43-43854, Bu34040 to Bu34041 as 43-43855 to 43-43856, Bu34044 as 43-43857 and Bu34048 to Bu34053 as 43-43858 to 43-43863.

5 to RAAF as follows: Bu34055/A24-69, Bu34056/A24-82, Bu34057/A24-71, Bu34058/A24-72 and Bu34059/A24-70.

C/n	Type	Serial Number	Contract No
1814 to 1943	PBY-5A	Bu46450 to Bu46579	NOa(s)-464

130 aircraft for US Navy of which:

12 to RAAF as follows: Bu 46488/A24-91, Bu46489 to Bu46490/A24-94 to A24-95, Bu46491/A24-92, Bu46532 to Bu46535/A24-96 to A24-99 and Bu46576 to Bu46579/A24-100 to A24-103.

15 (Bu46560 to Bu46574) to French Aéronavale

C/n	Type	Serial Number	Contract No
1614 to 1813	PBY-5A	Bu48252 to Bu48451	NOa(s)-464

200 aircraft for US Navy of which:

6 to USAAF as OA-10A as follows: Bu48364 to Bu48369/43-47956 to 43-47961 (not confirmed).

18 to RAAF as follows: Bu48297/A24-75, Bu48298/A24-74, Bu48299/A24-76, Bu48300/A24-73, Bu48301/A24-77, Bu48302/A24-78, Bu48344/A24-79, Bu48345/A24-84, Bu48346/A24-83, Bu48348/A24-87, Bu48349/A24-80, Bu48350/A24-81, Bu48351/A24-85, Bu48352/A24-88, Bu48353/A24-93, Bu48354/A24-89, Bu48355/A24-90 and Bu48356/A24-86. Bu48347 appears to have been intended for the RAAF but was lost on its delivery flight in 2/1944.

15 (Bu48306 to Bu48313, Bu48357 to Bu48363) to French Aéronavale

CONSOLIDATED AIRCRAFT CORPORATION, NEW ORLEANS, LOUISIANA

C/n	Type	Serial Number	Contract No
? – see note	PBY-5	Bu63992	NOa-259

1 aircraft for US Navy.

Note: No '4-figure' c/n following on from San Diego production appears to have been allocated although it was given the Manufacturing (Mfg) number 1 in the New Orleans sequence.

C/n	Type	Serial Number	Contract No
1944 to 2002 – see note	PBY-5A	Bu46580 to Bu46638	NOa-464

59 aircraft for US Navy of which:

11 to RAAF as follows: ?/A24-105, Bu46594/A24-104, Bu46605 to Bu46608/A24-106 to A24-109 and Bu46619 to Bu46623/A24-110 to A24-114.

Note: also allocated Mfg numbers 2 to 60 in the New Orleans sequence.

PBY-6A Bu64063 was built at New Orleans. It is shown in the dark blue colours of a post-war US Navy unit based in New York. It later served in Brazil as a commercial aircraft.

C/n	Type	Serial Number	Contract No
2003 to 2062	PBY-6A	Bu46639 to Bu46698	NOa-464
2063	PBY-6A	Bu46724	NOa-464
2064 to 2170?	PBY-6A	Bu63993 to Bu64099	NOa-259
2171 to 2177?	PBY-6A	Bu64101 to Bu64107	NOa-259

175 aircraft for US Navy of which:

48 delivered to Soviet Union – Bu46656, Bu46658, Bu46669 to Bu46671, Bu46674 to Bu46678, Bu46690 to Bu46698, Bu46724, Bu64018 to Bu64027, Bu64048 to Bu64052, Bu64073 to Bu64083 and Bu64085 to Bu64086.

75 to USAAF as OA-10B with serials 45-57833 to 45-57907.

Orders for a further 735 aircraft for the US Navy, serials Bu64100, Bu64108 to Bu64441, Bu111149 to 111348 and Bu119779 to Bu119978 were cancelled.

1 aircraft (Bu64096) to USCG as PBY-6AG.

Note: also allocated Mfg numbers 61 to 235 in the New Orleans sequence. Use of c/ns 2064 to 2177 not confirmed.

Naval Aircraft Factory, Philadelphia, Pennsylvania

C/n	Type	Serial Number	Contract No
	PBN-1 Nomad	Bu02791 to Bu02945 Bu02946 (Bu02802 rebuilt after fire damage)	P.O.3-42

155 aircraft built of which:

17 to US Navy.

138 to Soviet Union – Bu02826 and Bu02915 both lost in transit.

Orders for a further 124 aircraft for the US Navy, serials Bu35798 to Bu35921, were cancelled, the serials being reassigned to 123 North American PBJ-1J Mitchells and a solitary Grumman JRF-4 Goose respectively.

This frontal shot very clearly shows the changes made by the Naval Aircraft Factory when creating the PBN-1 Nomad. The bow, float and tail profiles have been redesigned and the mid-hull step has also been modified.

Boeing Aircraft of Canada, Sea Island, Vancouver, BC, Canada

C/n	Type	Serial Number	Contract No
21980 to 22034	PBY-5A	9751 to 9805	

55 aircraft built from Consolidated-manufactured parts for RCAF as Canso As.

C/n	Type	Serial Number	Contract No
	PB2B-1	JX270 to JX344	NOa-1735

75 aircraft for RAF as Catalina IVB.

JX287 to BOAC as G-AGKS.

C/n	Type	Serial Number	Contract No
	PB2B-1	Bu72992 to Bu73116	NOa-1735

125 aircraft allocated US Navy serials for bookkeeping purposes but distributed as follows:

Bu72992 to Bu72996 to RAF as Catalina IVB JX345 to JX349.

Bu72997 to Bu73000 to RNZAF as NZ4023, NZ4027, NZ4024 and NZ4025 – see note at bottom of table.

Bu73001 to Bu73012 to RAF as Catalina IVB JX350 to JX361.

Bu73013 to Bu73016 to RNZAF as NZ4026, NZ4043, NZ4028 and NZ4030 – see note at bottom of table.

Bu73017 to Bu73028 to RAF as Catalina IVB JX362 to JX373.

Bu73029 to Bu73032 to RNZAF as NZ4042, NZ4029, NZ4031 and NZ4032 – see note at bottom of table.

Bu73033 to Bu73042 to RAF as Catalina IVB JX374 to JX383.

Bu73043 to Bu73048 to RNZAF as NZ4033, NZ4035, NZ4036, NZ4037 and NZ4038.
Bu73049 to Bu73054 to RAF as Catalina IVB JX384 to JX389.
Bu73055 to Bu73060 to RNZAF NZ4039, NZ4046, NZ4040, NZ4041, NZ4044 and NZ4045.
Bu73061 to Bu73094 to RAF as Catalina IVB JX390 to JX423.
Bu73095 to Bu73098 to RNZAF as NZ4047, NZ4050, NZ4051 and NZ4048.
Bu73099 to Bu73112 to RAF as Catalina IVB JX424 to JX437.
Bu73113 to Bu73116 to RNZAF as NZ4049, NZ4054, NZ4052 and NZ4053.
NB: Some non-New Zealand sources have quoted the alternative RNZAF serials. NZ4027, NZ4028 and NZ4029 for Bu73015, Bu73030 and Bu72998 respectively.

C/n	Type	Serial Number	Contract No
61094 to 61133	PB2B-1	Bu44188 to Bu44227	NOa-1735

40 aircraft for US Navy of which:
Bu44188 to Bu44201 to RAF as Catalina IVB JX586 to JX599.
Bu44202 to Bu44203 to RNZAF as NZ4055 to NZ4056.
Bu44206 to Bu44219 to RAF as Catalina IVB JX600 to JX613 of which JX611, JX612 and JX613 to RAAF as A24-206, A24-201 and A24-204.
Bu44224 to Bu44227 to RAF as Catalina IVB JX614 to JX617 and supplied to RAAF as A24-205, A24-203, A24-202 and A24-200.

C/n	Type	Serial Number	Contract No
61134 to 61200	PB2B-2	Bu44228 to Bu44294	NOa-782

67 aircraft for US Navy of which:
Bu44228 to Bu44237 to RAF as Catalina VI JX618 to JX627 but supplied to RAAF as follows: JX618/A24-305, JX619/A24-300, JX620/A24-302, JX621/A24-303, JX622/A24-307, JX623/A24-306, JX624/A24-301, JX625/A24-308, JX626/A24-309 and JX627/A24-304.
Bu44246 to Bu44261 to RAF as Catalina VI JX628 to JX662 but supplied to RAAF as follows: JX628/A24-370, JX629/A24-363, JX630/A24-385, JX631/A24-373, JX632/A24-382, JX633/A24-357, JX634/A24-386, JX635/A24-378, JX636/A24-368, JX637/A24-376, JX638/A24-365, JX639/A24-381, JX640/A24-374, JX641/A24-371, JX642/A24-379, JX643/A24-361.
Bu44262 to USAAF (RAF JX644 ntu).
Bu44263 and Bu44264 to RAF as Catalina VI JX645 and JX646 but supplied to RAAF as A24-383 and A24-366.
Bu44265 to USAAF (RAF JX647 ntu)
Bu44266 to RAF as Catalina VI JX648 but supplied to RAAF as A24-358.
Bu44267 and Bu44268 to USAAF (RAF JX649 and JX650 ntu).
Bu44269 remained with US Navy (RAF JX651 ntu).
Bu44270 to RAF as Catalina VI JX652 but supplied to RAAF as A24-375.
Bu44271 remained with US Navy (RAF JX653 ntu).
Bu44272 to USAAF (RAF JX654 ntu).
Bu44273 to Bu44275 remained with US Navy (RAF JX655 to JX657 ntu).
Bu44276 to USAAF (RAF JX658 ntu).
Bu44277 remained with US Navy (RAF JX659 ntu).
Bu44278 to Bu44280 to RAF as Catalina VI JX660 to JX662 but supplied to RAAF as A24-352, A24-350 and A24-372.
Bu44281 to Bu44294 to RAF as Catalina VI JZ828 to JZ841 but supplied to RAAF as follows: JZ828/A24-353, JZ829/A24-354, JZ830/A24-380, JZ831/A24-359, JZ832/A24-356, JZ833/A24-351, JZ834/A24-369, JZ835/A24-362, JZ836/A24-355, JZ837/A24-377, JZ838/A240364, JZ839/A24-367, JZ840/A24-384 and JZ841/A24-360.

A further 18 aircraft c/ns 61201 to 61218 were cancelled but were allocated US Navy serials Bu44295 to Bu44312 and RAF serials JZ842 to JZ859

CANADIAN VICKERS LTD, ST HUBERT, QUEBEC, CANADA

C/n	Type	Serial Number	Contract No
	PBV-1A	Bu03563 to Bu03712	

150 aircraft intended for the US Navy but contract cancelled.

C/n	Type	Serial Number	Contract No
CV-240 to CV-269	Canso A	9806 to 9835	

30 aircraft for RCAF.

CANADIAN VICKERS LTD, CARTIERVILLE, QUEBEC

C/n	Type	Serial Number	Contract No
CV-270 to CV-278	Canso A	9836 to 9844	
CV-279 to CV-303		11001 to 11025	
CV-308 to CV-321		11026 to 11039	
CV-329 to CV-449		11040 to 11100	
(odd numbers only)			

109 aircraft for RCAF.

OA-10As for the USAAF lined up outside the Canadian Vickers production facility at Cartierville, Montreal.

C/n	Type	Serial Number	Contract No
CV-304 to CV-307	OA-10A	44-33868 to 44-33871	NOa(a)-296
CV-322 to CV-328		44-33872 to 44-33878	
CV-330 to CV-448		44-33879 to 44-33938	
(even numbers only)			
CV-450 to CV-551		44-33939 to 44-34040	

173 aircraft for USAAF. Original order was for US Navy as PBV-1A serials Bu67832 to Bu68004 but order cancelled.
44-33965 to 44-33967 given RAF serials FT997 to FT999

CANADAIR LTD, CARTIERVILLE, QUEBEC, CANADA

C/n	Type	Serial Number	Contract No
CV-552 to CV-608	OA-10A	44-34041 to 44-34097	NOa(a)-296

57 aircraft for USAAF. Original order was for US Navy as PBV-1A serials Bu68005 to Bu68061 but order cancelled.

RUSSIAN PRODUCTION, TAGANROG, SOVIET UNION

C/n	Type	Serial Number	Contract No
	GST/MP-7	?	

Total production run, although unknown, estimated by some sources as c150. One aircraft impressed by RAF and became serial HK850.

TOTAL PRODUCTION RUN = 3281 airframes (excluding unknown Soviet production)

San Francisco-based OA-10A 44-33924 powers aloft with JATO assistance in this post-war photograph.
via William Kelly

Appendix 3
SUMMARY OF USAAF
CATALINA SERIALS

Model	Number	Serials	Notes
OA-10-CO	74	41-18700 to 41-18773	Order for USAAF for delivery 12/1941 to 3/1942 but diverted to US Navy as Bu04972 to Bu05045.
OA-10-CO	2	41-18772 to 41-18773	Unused serials from above batch applied to ex-US Navy PBY-5A Bu02967 and Bu02969 respectively.
OA-10-CO	5	42-107401 to 42-107405	ex-US Navy PBY-5s Bu08315, 08318, 08320, 08322 and 08330 respectively. Note: These aircraft were flying boats whereas the OA-10-CO designation gives the incorrect impression that they were amphibians.
OA-10-CO	6	42-109020 to 42-109025	ex-US Navy PBY-5As – original Bu numbers were Bu08122, 05009, 05036, 2456, 2480 and 7246 respectively. 42-109020 was interned by the Spanish and later served with the Spanish Air Force.
OA-10-CO	12	43-3259 to 43-3270	ex-US Navy PBY-5A Bu08031, 08046, 08079, 08080, 08081, 08082, 08083, 08084, 08085, 08086, 08090 and 08091.

Model	Number	Serials	Notes
OA-10-CO	25	43-43839 to 43-43863	ex-US Navy PBY-5A – original Bu numbers were as follows: 43-43839/ Bu33962, 43-43840 to 43-43852/Bu33986 to 33998. 43-43853 to 43-43854/Bu34000 to 34001. 43-43855 to 43-43856/Bu34040 to 34041. 43-43857/Bu34044. 43-43858 to 43-43863/Bu34048 to 34053.
OA-10-CO	6	43-47956 to 43-47961	Possibly ex-US Navy PBY-5A Bu48364 to Bu48369 but not confirmed.
OA-10A-VI	230	44-33868 to 44-34097	Canadian Vickers production for USAAF.
OA-10B-CN	75	45-57833 to 45-57907	Consolidated New Orleans production.
OA-10-CO	2	47-638 to 47-639	ex-US Navy PBY-5A transferred during 1947.
A-10A-CO	3	49-2894 to 49-2896	Ex-US Navy PBY-5A transferred during 1949.

SELECT BIBLIOGRAPHY

The following lists are split into two sections. The first covers those books and significant articles that have a direct relevance to the contents of this publication on peacetime Catalinas, even if their overall coverage is broader. For the sake of completeness, I have also included a second list that details recommended books and articles about the Catalina, but where the subject matter is not specifically related to the type's peacetime role. Many of the publications in these lists have been consulted during the research for this book, and I would like to acknowledge the work done by their authors. It should be noted that these lists are not exhaustive.

List 1:

—— *A Brief History of MOTAT's Catalina*, pamphlet issued by MOTAT

—— Aero Corporation Converts PBYs to Luxury Liners, *Aviation Operations*, March 1950

—— Canadian Catalinas/Cansos (various articles), *BC Aviator Magazine*, May/June 1992

—— *Canadian Pacific Airlines* (History of)

—— *Consolidated PBY – The Sentinel of the Pacific*, Sales Brochure, NV Fokker, Amsterdam, July 1938

—— *History of Beriev*, Vol. 1, 1932–1945

—— *Katalinha*, Russian language booklet, 1995, ISBN 5 858 75036 2

—— Last of the Cats, (reprinted from *QANTAS News*), *AAHS Journal*, Spring 1962

—— Les Debuts D'Une Saga les PBY Catalina (Protection Civile), *Le Trait D'Union*, No. 174 July–August 1997

—— *Les Insignes des Formations de L'Aéronautique Navale 1917–1996*, ARDHAN

—— *New Stamps 3/1993 – Postal Flights in Iceland*, pamphlet published by Frimerkjasalan Postphil

—— *QANTAS at War* (Chapter 23: Across the Indian Ocean)

—— Rebuilding Aircraft for Peacetime Flying, *Canadian Aviation*, 2/1947

—— *Temahœfte nr.1 – Catalina PBY-5A/PBY-6A*, Dansk Flyvehistorisk Forening, ISSN 0109-8292

—— *The Accidental Airline* (Queen Charlotte Airlines)

—— The Magnificat – In Praise of the Consolidated PBY, *Air Enthusiast*, Vols 38, 39

—— The Miss Macau Affair, *Fragrant Harbour*, June 1991

—— Tp47 Catalina, *Kontakt 100*, February 1991 (Swedish Aviation Historical Research Group)

Allen, Eric. *Airliners in Australian Service, Volume 2*, Aerospace Publications Pty Ltd

Allward, Maurice F. Airborne Yachts – Luxury Conversions of Wartime Catalinas, *Flight*, 24 July 1953

Aloni, Shlomo. Israeli Maritime Aviation, *Air International*, January 1996

Ancker, Paul E. *Narsarsuaq Air Base (BW-1) 1941–1958*, Det Grølandske Selskab, ISBN 8 789 20520 0

Andrade, John M. *Latin-American Military Aviation*, Midland Counties Publications, ISBN 0 904 59731 8

Anido, Alberto A. and Austria-Tomkins, Brian. *Pictorial History of the Philippine Air Force*, Anglo-Philippine Aviation

Archbold, Richard. Unknown New Guinea – Circumnavigating the World in a Flying Boat (Guba), *National Geographic Magazine*, March 1941

Bovelt, Allan. Catalinas in the South Pacific, *AAHS Journal*, Winter 1971

Bowers, Peter M. *Boeing Aircraft Since 1916*, Putnam
Long Range Patrol, Airpower, September and November 1994

Brass, L. J. *Indische-Amerikaanscghe Expeditie (Guba)*, unpublished manuscript

Burnett, Ted. Danish Military Catalina Amphibians, *Small Air Forces Observer*, July 1999

Bushell, Bill and Sue. Consolidated PBY Catalina – Aircraft in Detail, *Scale Aircraft Modelling*, May 1983

Byre, David C. Captain P. G. Taylor – Frigate Bird I & II, *Aviation Historical Society of Australia Journal*, June 1974

Cassagnares, Everett. *The Consolidated PBY Catalina*, Profile Publications No. 183

Chapman, John, Goodall, Geoff and Coggan, Paul. *Warbirds Directory*, Warbirds Media Co. Ltd, ISBN 1 870 60146 7

Chorley, Desmond M. Recast Cansos, *Canadian Aviation*, 10/1982

Creed, Roscoe. *PBY – The Catalina Flying Boat*, Airlife Publishing Ltd
Consolidated PBY Catalina, *Fine Scale Modeller*, July 1996

Cull, Brian, Nicolle, David and Aloni, Shlomo. *Wings Over Suez*, Grub Street

Danby, Peter A. *United States Air Force Serials 1946–1977*, Merseyside Aviation Society, ISBN 0 902 42022 4
United States Navy Serials 1941–1972, Merseyside Aviation Society, ISBN 0 950 07808 5

Davies, R. E. G. *Airlines of Latin America*, Putnam
Airlines of Asia Since 1920, Putnam

Davis, Peter J. *East African – An Airline Story*

Delaunay, Pierre *La Trapas 1946–1951* ICARE Magazine No 175, 4/2000

Devins, Bill. Icelandic Goddess – Coast Guard Catalina, *Chine Lines* No. 13 (also article from *Small Air Forces Observer*, April 1982, author not known)

Dyer, John C. The Norwegian Air Force 1945–1978, *Military Aviation Review*, February and March 1979

Eather, Charles (Chic) E. *Syd's Pirates – A Story of an Airline (Cathay Pacific)*, Durnmount-Sydney, ISBN 0 949 75605 9

Ely, Greg, and Veronico, Nicholas. Consolidated PBY Catalina, *CAF Dispatch Magazine*, May and June 1986 (and also various other articles in previous issues)

Ewing, Ross. *Catalina Dreaming*, David Ling Publishing, ISBN 0 908 99039 1

Flug Sagan No. 3 (Journal of Icelandic Aviation Historical Society), various articles on Icelandic Catalinas

Fortner, Alberto P. Catalinas in Chile, *Air Pictorial*, July 1983

Gamble, Peter. The Era of the Pacific Flying Boats, *Australian Aviation*, August 1990

Gavin-Robinson, G. V. and Banks, David. Wings Over the Antarctic, *Esso Air World*, Vol. 9, No. 3

Geldhof, Nico. *Nederlandse Militaire Luchtvaart III – Consolidated PBY-5A Catalina*
Olie-Catalinas in Oost-Indi, *Maanblad Luchtvaart*, April 1990

Gerrits, John. Diego Garcia Catalina, *Warbirds International*

Gilliland, Bob. Catalinas in Service with TAA, *Model Expo 96 Magazine*

Grant, Robert S. Water Bomber, *Aviation News*, 3–16 May 1985
Cansos Over Canada, *Air Classics*, May 1986
Attacking a New Enemy (budworm spraying), *International Air Review*, Spring 1991
Sad Sack, *Warbirds International*, March–April 1991

Green, William and Fricker, John. *The Air Forces of the World*, Macdonald

Gulli, Steim, Hafsten, Björn, and Arheim, Tom. Catalina I Norsk Tjeneste 1942–1961, *Norsk Flyhistorisk Tidsskrift* Nr 3–4/1989

Hagedorn, Daniel P. *Central American and Caribbean Air Forces*, Air Britain, ISBN 0 85130 210 6
Lend-Lease to Latin America, Part II: Navy Aircraft, *AAHS Journal*, Fall 1989

Hall, Alan W. Danish Cats, *Air Pictorial*, December 1962

Hannah, Donald. Warplanes in Civvies No. 6 – The Consolidated Catalina Flying Boat, *FlyPast*, July 1982

Harrison, Kirby. Epic Journey – Two Consolidated Catalinas Recreate Historic Naval Aviation Milestone, *Warbirds International*, Spring 1987

Harrison, Paul, Lockstone, Brian and Anderson, Andy. *The Golden Age of New Zealand Flying Boats*, Random House NZ Ltd, ISBN 1 869 41299 0

Hendrie, Andrew. *Flying Cats – the Catalina Aircraft In Action in World War II*, Airlife Publishing Ltd, ISBN 1 853 10028 5

Hotson, Fred W. *de Havilland in Canada*, CANAV Books, ISBN 0 921 02210 7

Jackson, Paul A. *Dutch Military Aviation 1945–1978*, Midland Counties Publications, ISBN 0 904 59710 5

Jackson, Paul. East Indies Catalinas, *Aviation News*, 13–26 June 1975

Jenks, C. F. L. *New Zealand Military Aircraft and Serial Numbers*, Aviation Historical Society of New Zealand

Jeudy, Jean-Gabriel. *Les Pompiers du Ciel*, Ouest France, ISBN 2 858 82726 5

Karlström, Björn. *Svenska Flygvapnets Transportflygplan 1926–1989*, Flygplans Ritningar 5 Allt Om Hobby, ISBN 9 185 49630 8

Labrum, Dick. Pirates! (Cathay Pacific Catalina gold running), *FlyPast*

le Nobel, Anton. MLD is 60, *Air Britain Digest*, September–October 1977

Leebold, Arthur. Lost at Sea (QANTAS PBYs), *Flightpath*

Legg, David. A Spanish Catalina, *Small Air Forces Observer*, December 1997
England's Big Cats, *Warbirds International*, January/February 1999
Cutaway Catalina, *FlyPast*, November 1999
ASPAR Cats, *FlyPast*
Catalina Type Report, *FlyPast* (various issues)

Linkewich, —. Air Attack on Forest Fires (article – source unknown)

Mak, Ron. Forgotten Canso (RCAF 11007), *Warbirds International*, Winter 1987
FAP Cat, *Warbirds International*, March–April 1991
Saskatchewan Cats, *Warbirds International*, November–December 1991
Saskatchewan's Aerial Fire-Fighters, *Propliner*
Where Empire Boats Once Flew, *Propliner*

Meaden, Jack. The Two Gubas, *Air Britain Digest*, Spring 1991
Gubas and Civil Registered PBYs, *Air Britain Digest*, Summer 1991

Milberry, Larry. *Austin Airways*, CANAV Books
Austin Airways, *Propliner*, Issue 19 (reprinted from Canadian Aviation)

Morawietz, Karl-Heinz. Civilian Catalinas – Airline Liveries, *Scale Aircraft Modelling*, August 2000

Mott, Peter. *Wings Over Ice – The Falkland Islands and Dependencies Aerial Survey Expedition*, published privately, ISBN 0 951 16990 4

Muikoff, Dave. Cousteau's Catalina, *IPMS Canada Magazine*

Muir, David and Hutchinson, Dick. Australian Commercial Cats (various articles), *Australian Plastic Modellers Association Magazine*, 1999

Murray, Robert. Rev. Bob's PBY (N68756), *Seaplane Pilots' Association Magazine*

Musiałkowski, Lechosław. *Lódz latajaca Catalina*, Wydawnictwo Bellona, ISBN 8 311 08355 X

Nemecek, Václav and Smékal, Vykres Stanislav. *GST*

Neal, E. H. Order of the Double Sunrise Parts 1 and 2, *Shell Aviation News*, Nos 413, 414, 1972

Netto, F. C. Pereira. *Aviacao Militar Brasiliera 1916–1984*

Núñez, Jorge Félix. Argentine Navy PBY Cansos, *Propliner*, July–September 1980

Serie Aéronaval No13 – Consolidated PBY-5A Catalina, Museo de Aviacion Naval (Argentina)

Paumier, Leon W. TRAPAS, *Pacific Islands Aviation Society Magazine*, 8/1970

Pearcy, Arthur. *US Coast Guard Aircraft Since 1916*, Airlife Publications, ISBN 1 853 10118 4

Pickier, Ron and Milberry, Larry. *Canadair – The First 50 Years*, CANAV Books

Piercey, Stephen. Up the Orinoco, *Propliner*, No. 2
Queen Charlotte – the no frills airline, *Propliner*, No. 11

Potts, Bruce. New Guinea Cats, *Airways*, July/August 1994

Prophet, Michael. Cat Air, *Warbirds International*, November 1995

Ragnarsson, Ragnar. Catalina Bu2459, *Flying Legends air show programme*, July 1997

Ragnarrson, Ragnar and Sveinsson, Baldur. The Third Cod War (TF-RAN), *Aviation News*, Vol. 4/17

Reynolds, Mike and Rolfe, Mark. The PBV Catalina, *Scale Models International*, February 1996

Saksvik, Torstein. *Siste tur for Catalina K-AK*

Salo, Mauno A. Fate of Guba I, *AAHS Journal*, date unknown

Sapienza, Antonio Luis. PBY-5A in Paraguay, *Small Air Forces Observer*, September 1993

Scanlan, H. *Winged Shell*

Scarborough, Capt William. *PBY Catalina in Action*, Squadron Signal Publications, ISBN 0 897 47149 0
Walk Around PBY Catalina, Squadron Signal Publications, ISBN 0 897 47357 4
The Consolidated PBY – Catalina to Canso, *AAHS Journal*, Spring, Summer and Fall, 1971

Shirley-Beavan, Mike. *The African Catalina*, CBC Publishing, ISBN 0 951 52094 6

Simpson, Andrew. Consolidated PBY-6A L-86618466M, *Small Air Forces Observer*, July 1997

Sinclair, James. Balus – *The Aeroplane in Papua New Guinea, Vol. 1 – The Early Years*, Robert Brown and Associates (Aust) Pty Ltd

Sloat, Chuck. The Ghost of Gananoque (CF-NJL), *Warbirds International*, 4/1994

Smith, Gene. Cat Tales – Cats from Brazil to USA, *Air Classics*, August 1985
Adventure of the Amazon Cats, *Air Progress*
Flying the Last Military Cats, *Seaplanes At War* (Challenge Publications)

Snelson, Chris. Catalina Z-CAT . . . ZK-PBY – The Ferry Flight Zimbabwe to New Zealand, *Scramble Magazine*

Soumille, Jean Claude. *Aviation Française en Indochine 1946–1954*, Association Airdoc

Spencer, Ted M. Queen of Dago Lake, *Warbirds International*, Winter 1986

Cat From Dago Lake, *FlyPast*, February 1988

The Amazing Recovery of the Queen of Dago Lake, *Ghostly Warriors*, Vol. 1, 1989

Spring, Ivan. *Flying Boat: The History of 262 Squadron RAF and the Origins of 35 Squadron SAAF*, Spring Air, ISBN 0 958 39772 4

Stemp, R. W. Flying Boat Turned Mine-Finder, *Western Miner*, February 1976

Steven, Frank. Aerial Fire Suppression, *Shell Aviation News* No. 442

Stewart, John P. US Air Tanker Operations 1968–1978, *Air Britain Digest*, September/October 1978

Taylor, Captain P. G. *Trans-Indian Ocean Survey Flight, June 1939*, Report for Commonwealth Government (copy of original report)

Taylor, P. G. *Frigate Bird – The Dramatic Story of the First Air Crossing of the South Atlantic*, Eden Paperbacks, ISBN 0 207 15571 2

Taylor, Sir Gordon. *The Sky Beyond*, Bantam Air and Space Series, ISBN 0 553 23949 X

The Catalina News, Catalina Society, Issue 1 onwards

van der Klaauw, B. The History of Dutch Naval Aviation, *Air Pictorial*, March 1962

van der Kop, Hans. Dutch Squadron's 50th Anniversary, *Aviation News*, 25 May–7 June 1990

Vercken, Vice-Admiral R. *Histoire Succinte de L'Aéronautique 1910–1998*, ARDHAN

Veronico, Nick. Cat in a Barn (N1563M), *Warbirds International*

Vincent, David. *Catalina Chronicle – A History of RAAF Operations*, Catalina National Committee, ISBN 0 959 60520 7

Wagner, Ray. *The Story of the PBY Catalina*, Flight Classics Aero Biographies

Wegg, John. *General Dynamics Aircraft and Their Predecessors*, Putnam, ISBN 0 851 77833 X

Whitehead, Mike. Cat Lift (CF-HFL recovery), *FlyPast*, March 1987

Another PBY Recovered (CF-HFL), *Warbirds International*

Wikene, Ingwald. The Canso & Catalina in the RCAF, *Canadian Aviation Historical Society Journal*, Vol. 11, No. 1, Spring 1973

Wilkins, Sir Hubert. Our Search for the Lost Aviators (Guba), *National Geographic Magazine*, August 1938

Willing, Martin J. *From Betsy to Boeing – The Aircraft of Cathay Pacific Airways 1946–1988*, Arden Publishing, ISBN 9 622 65002 3

Cathay Pacific Airways 1946–1986 – An Illustrated History, CPAL

The Operations of Amphibian Airways, *The Flyleaf*, Summer 1992

The Gold Run To Macau (Cathay Pacific Catalinas), *The Flyleaf Magazine*, Autumn 1992

Wilson, John. *The Guba Story – A Tribute to an Elderly Lady* (privately published)

Wilson, Stewart. *Catalina, Neptune & Orion in Australian Service*, Aerospace Publications Pty Ltd, ISBN 0 958 79787 0

List 2:

—— Consolidated Catalina in Royal Air Force Service, *Aeromilitaria*, Issue 3/1977 (Air Britain)

—— *Pilots' & Flight Engineers' Notes – Catalina Mks I, IB, II, IV, IVA and IVB* (2nd Edition), The Air Council (Reproduction by Air Data Publications)

—— The Incomparable Catalina (Chapter 9 from *The American Flying Boat*)

Ambrose, Capt L. R. QANTAS Cat Ops, Parts 1–3, *Aeroplane Monthly*, November 1986–January 1987

Baker, Ian K. *Catalina Collection – A Sampling of Camouflage and Markings of Catalinas with the RNZAF, RAAF, RCAF, RAF, USN and VVS*, ISSN 1322-0217

US Navy Aircraft Camouflage and Insignia 1941–1947, ISSN 1322-0217

Banks, Dr Arthur. *Wings of the Dawning – the Battle for the Indian Ocean 1939–1945*, Images Publishing, ISBN 1 897 81770 3

Bayly, G. H. U. 'Terk' 'Bill'. *Cats – Memoirs of 413 Squadron*, Graphic Image

Belcher, Mike. The Strait Goods – A Brief History of the Canso, *IPMS Canada Magazine*, Vol. 25, No. 1

Binning, Arthur J. *Survivors – the Story of the U-188 and Her Sinking*, Norman Gibson

Bunbury, Bill. Cats on the Swan (from the book *Rag Sticks and Wire – Australians Taking to the Air*), ABC Books, ISBN 0 733 30273 4

Carlisle, Lt Robert L., USNR (retd). *P-Boat Pilot – With a Patrol Squadron in the Battle of the Atlantic*, Fifthian Press, ISBN 1 56474 046 3

Christie, Carl A. *Ocean Bridge – The History of RAF Ferry Command*, Midland Counties Publications, ISBN 1 857 80029 X

Crocker, Mel. *Black Cats and Dumbos – WWII's Fighting PBYs*, TAB Books Inc

Franks, Norman. *Search, Find and Kill – The RAF's U-boat Successes in World War Two*, Grub Street, ISBN 1 898 69735 3

Freeman, Brett. *Lake Boga At War – The Inside Story of the secret RAAF Inland Flying Boat Unit – WWII*, Catalina Publications, ISBN 0 646 24705 0

Freeman, Elmer. *Those Navy Guys and Their PBYs – The Aleutian Solution*, Kedging Publishing Co., ISBN 0 963 24630 5

Gallacher, Ian. Long Haul Catalinas (QANTAS), *FlyPast*, July 1986

Garfield, Brian. *The Thousand Mile War – World War II in Alaska and the Aleutians*, Bantam Books, ISBN 0 553 20308 8

Green, William. *Warplanes of the Second World War, Vol. 5: Flying Boats*, Macdonald, ISBN 1 356 01449 5

Gwynn-Jones, Terry. The Black Cats – Australia's Slow Heroes, *Flightpath*, Vol. 11, No. 3

Hancock, Dennis. *Secret Order of the Double Sunrise*

Hayes, Lt (JG) Robert W., USNR (retd). *Bless 'Em All – The Adventures of a Navy 'Black cat' Squadron in World War II*, Willow Creek Publishers

Hilliker, Ivor J. *A Solent Flight*, Kingfisher Publications, ISBN 0 946 18458 5

Hopp, George G. Canadian Convoy Covering Cansos, *Chine Lines*, No. 8

Hughes, Jim. *Airfield Focus 31 – Invergordon*, GMS Enterprises, ISBN 1 870 38461 X

Kinsey, Gordon. *Seaplanes – Felixstowe*, Terence Dalton, ISBN 0 861 38039 8

Knott, Richard C. *The Black Cats*, PSL

Koskela, Col Paul and Wilson, Col Randy. PBY Catalina – By Land or Sea, *CAF Dispatch Magazine*, Summer 1994

Leebold, Arthur. *Silent Victory – Breaking the Japanese Air Blockade Between Australia and Europe*, Banner Books, ISBN 1 875593 11 X

London, Peter. *Saunders and Saro Aircraft Since 1917*, Putnam, ISBN 0 851 77814 3

MacLeod, H. M. Action Stations – For Valour – David Hornell,VC, *Maritime Patrol Aviation*, 3/1991

McCusker, Breege. *Castle Archdale and Fermanagh in World War II*, Necarne Press, ISBN 0 952 15450 1

McVicar, Don. *North Atlantic Cat*, Airlife Publishing Ltd, ISBN 0 906 39325 6

Messimer, Dwight. *In the Hands of Fate – The Story of Patrol Wing Ten 8 December 1941–11 May 1942*, Naval Institute Press

Mills, James C. *Blue Catalinas of World War II*, Sunflower University Press, ISBN 0 897 45190 2

Molson, K. M. and Taylor, H.A. *Canadian Aircraft Since 1909*, Putnam, ISBN 0 370 30095 5

Moss, Peter W. BOAC at War, Parts 3 and 4, *Aeroplane Monthly*, September and October 1975

Mueller, Lt A. J., USNR (retd) and personnel of VP/VPB-33. *Black Cats With Wings of Gold*, Smith-Edwards-Dunlap Co.

Neto, Ricardo Bonalume. Brazil – 1, U-199 – 0, Brazil's Anti-Submarine War, *Air Enthusiast*, No. 56

Nyznik, Paul. The Saviours of Ceylon, *Airforce*, Summer 1998

Owen, Neil and Jones, Phil. *Airfield Focus 25 – Oban and Connel Ferry*, GMS Enterprises, ISBN 1 870 38448 2

Pattison, Barry and Goodall, Geoff. *QANTAS Empire Airways (Western Operations Division) Indian Ocean Service 1943–1946*, Aviation Historical Society of Australia, ISBN 0 95999336 5 4

Pearcy, Arthur. *Lend-Lease Aircraft in World War II*, Airlife Publications Ltd, ISBN 1 853 10443 4

Pomeroy, Colin A. *The Flying Boats of Bermuda*, ISBN 0 969 83324 5

Riddell, Jack. *RAAF Catalina Squadrons First and Furthest – Recounting the Operations of RAAF Catalinas May 1941 to March 1943*, ISBN 0 646 09146 8

Roberts, Fred. Hard Luck Cat (MLD Y-81), *Air Classics*, February 1998

Robertson, Bruce. *British Military Aircraft Serials 1878–1987*, Midland Counties Publications, ISBN 0 904 59761 X

Scarborough, Capt William E., USN (retd). Consolidated-Vultee PBY-5/-5A Catalina, from the book *Historical Aviation Album*, publisher unknown

Schofield, Ernest and Nesbit, Roy Conyers. *Arctic Airmen – The RAF in Spitzbergen and North Russia 1942*, Airlife Publishing Ltd, ISBN 0 718 30660 0

Seymour, Mike and Balderson, Bill. *To the Ends of the Earth – 210 Squadron's Catalina Years*, Paterchurch Publications, ISBN 1 870 74508 6

Sloan, Roy. *Wings of War Over Gwynedd – Aviation in Gwynedd During World War II*, Gwasg Carreg Gwalch, ISBN 0 863 81189 2

Tagg, A. E. and Wheeler, R. L. *From Sea to Air – the Heritage of Sam Saunders*, Crossprint, ISBN 0 950 97393 9

Thurman, Lois and Don. *No Tumult, No Shouting – The Story of the PBY*, Henry Holt & Co., NY

Vincent, Carl. Canso Colour Schemes and Markings, *IPMS Canada Magazine*, Vol. 25, No. 1
    Prelude to Glory – the Story of 162 (BR) Squadron RCAF 1942–May 1944, *High Flight*, Vol. 1, 6 and 7

Ward, Peter. *Airfield Focus 13 – Sullom Voe and Scatsta*, GMS Enterprises, ISBN 1 870 38423 7

Weicht, Chris. *Jericho Beach and the West Coast Flying Boat Stations*, ISBN 0 968 11580 2

Wyatt, Bob. *Black Cats Fly*, Floreat Press, ISBN 0 958 69777 9

In addition to the above books and publications, various smaller articles and items of data have been gleaned over the years from the following sources:

Aeroplane Monthly
Aeroplane Spotter, The
Aeroplane, The
Air Britain *Aeromilitaria*
Air Britain *Archive*
Air Britain *Digest*
Air Britain *News*
Air Britain *RAF Serials* – various
Air Britain *Registers* – various
Air Classics
Air Enthusiast
Air Pictorial
Aircraft Illustrated
Aviation Letter
Catalina Flyer, The
Catalina News, The
Catwalk
Chine Lines
Classic Wings Downunder
Flight
FlyPast
Indian Ocean Flying Boat Association Newsletter
Jane's All the World's Aircraft
Lloyds of London – *Air Accident Records*
PBY Catalina International Association Newsletter
Pilot
Planes
Propliner
Scale Aircraft Modelling
Scale Aviation Modeller International
Small Air Forces Observer
Tropic Tusker Tales
Warbirds International
Warbirds Worldwide
Wings of Fame
Wingspan

Index

Page numbers in *italics* refer to illustrations